Dear Nigel & Gill,

Many thanks for your help in the production of my "mastersworth"

I forgot to mention you in the credits but that does not mean you don't deserve credit!

Best wishes

Neil Baish   22/3/2001

PENAL ASPECTS OF THE UN DRUG CONVENTIONS

PENAL ASPECTS
OF THE
UN DRUG CONVENTIONS

by

Neil Boister

Lecturer,
School of Law,
University of Nottingham,
United Kingdom

KLUWER LAW INTERNATIONAL
THE HAGUE / LONDON / BOSTON

A C.I.P. Catalogue record for this book is available from the Library of Congress

ISBN 90-411-1546-3

Published by Kluwer Law International,
P.O. Box 85889, 2508 CN The Hague, The Netherlands.

Sold and distributed in North, Central and South America
by Kluwer Law International,
675 Massachusetts Avenue, Cambridge, MA 02139, U.S.A.

In all other countries, sold and distributed
by Kluwer Law International, Distribution Centre,
P.O. Box 322, 3300 AH Dordrecht, The Netherlands.

Printed on acid-free paper

Printed in the Netherlands.

For Wendy

TABLE OF CONTENTS

ACKNOWLEDGEMENTS

The following deserve my thanks: David Harris, Hilaire McCoubrey, Alan Rycroft, Ronald Louw, Stephen Girvin, Richard Burchill, Howard Varney and Donald Schnell. Without their support, this study would neither have been undertaken nor continued. Without the support of my wife Wendy, it would not have been completed. My thanks also to the staff at Kluwer Law International.

The financial assistance of the National Research Foundation, South Africa, is also acknowledged. However, the opinions expressed and conclusions arrived at are those of the author alone.

LIST OF ABBREVIATIONS

1961 Commentary	*Commentary on the Single Convention on Narcotic Drugs,* 1961 (New York, 1973) UN Publication Sales No. E.73.XI.1.
1961 Records vol.I	*United Nations Conference for the Adoption of a Single Convention on Narcotic Drugs Official Records Volume I* (New York, 1964) UN Doc. E/CONF.34/24; UN Publication Sales No. 63.XI.4.
1961 Records vol.II	*United Nations Conference for the Adoption of a Single Convention on Narcotic Drugs Official Records Volume II* (New York, 1964) UN Doc. E/CONF.34/24/ Add.1; UN Publication Sales No. 63.XI.5.
1971 Commentary	*Commentary on the Convention on Psychotropic Substances, 1971* (New York, 1976) UN Doc. E/CN.7/589; UN Publication Sales No.E.76.XI.5.
1971 Records vol.I.	*United Nations Conference for the Adoption of a Protocol on Psychotropic Substances Official Records Volume I* (New York, 1973) UN Doc. E/CONF.58/7; UN Publication Sales No.E.73.XI.3.
1971 Records vol.II.	*United Nations Conference for the Adoption of a Protocol on Psychotropic Substances Official Records Volume II* (New York, 1973) UN Doc. E/CONF.58/7/Add.1; UN Publication Sales No.E.73.XI.4.

1972 Commentary   *Commentary on the 1972 Protocol Amending the*
                           Single Convention on Narcotic Drugs, 1961 (New
                           York, 1976) UN Doc. E/CN.7/588; UN Publication
                           Sales No.E.76.XI.6.

1972 Records vol.I   *United Nations Conference to consider*
                           amendments to the Single Convention on Narcotic
                           Drugs Official Records Volume I (New York,
                           1974) UN Doc. E/CONF.63/10; UN Publication
                           Sales No.E.73.XI.7.

1972 Records vol.II.   *United Nations Conference to consider*
                           amendments to the Single Convention on Narcotic
                           Drugs Official Records Volume II (New York,
                           1973) UN Doc. E/CONF.63/10/ Add.1; UN
                           Publication Sales No. E.73.XI.8.

1988 Commentary   *Commentary on the United Nations Convention*
                           Against Illicit Traffic in Narcotic Drugs and
                           Psychotropic Substances, 1988 (New York, 1998)
                           UN Doc. E/CN.7/590; UN Publication Sales
                           No.E.98.XI.5.

1988 Records vol.I   *United Nations Conference for the Adoption of a*
                           Convention against Illicit Traffic in Narcotic
                           Drugs and Psychotropic Substances Official
                           Records Volume I (New York, 1994) UN Doc.
                           E/CONF.82/16, UN Publication Sales No.
                           E.94.XI.5.

1988 Records vol.II   *United Nations Conference for the Adoption of a*
                           Convention against Illicit Traffic in Narcotic
                           Drugs and Psychotropic Substances Official
                           Records Volume II (New York, 1991) UN Doc.
                           E/CONF.82/16/Add.1, UN Publication Sales
                           No.E.91.XI.1.

Multilateral Treaties   *Multilateral Treaties Deposited with the Secretary*
Deposited   *General: Status as at 31 December 1996 (New*
                             York, 1997) UN Doc. St/Leg/Ser.E/15.

TABLE OF DRUG CONVENTIONS

1912 Hague Convention – International Opium Convention, done at the Hague, 23 January 1912, 8 LNTS 187; in force only generally at the end of World War One.

1925 Closed Agreement – Agreement Concerning the Suppression of the Manufacture of, Internal Trade in, and Use of, Prepared Opium, done at Geneva on 11 February, 1925, 51 LNTS 337.

1925 Geneva Convention – International Opium Convention, done at Geneva, 19 February 1925, 81 LNTS 317; in force September 1923.

1931 Closed Agreement – Agreement Concerning the Suppression of Opium Smoking, done at Bangkok, 27 November 1931, 177 LNTS 373.

1931 Geneva Convention – Convention for Limiting the Manufacture and Regulating the Distribution of Narcotic Drugs, done at Geneva, 13 July 1931, 139 LNTS 301; in force 9 July 1933.

1936 Geneva Convention – Convention for the Suppression of the Illicit Traffic in Dangerous Drugs, done at Geneva, 26 June 1936, 198 LNTS 300; in force 26 October 1939.

1946 Lake Success Protocol – Protocol amending the Agreements, Conventions and Protocols on Narcotic Drugs concluded at the Hague on 23 January 1912, at Geneva on 11 February 1925 and 19 February 1925, and 13 July 1931, at Bangkok on 27 November 1931 and at Geneva on 26 June 1936, done at Lake Success, New York, 11 December 1946, 12 UNTS 179; in force 1948.

1948 Paris Protocol – Protocol Bringing under International Control Drugs Outside the Scope of the Convention of 13 July 1931 for Limiting the Manufacture and Regulating the Distribution of Narcotic Drugs, as Amended by the Protocol signed at Lake Success, New York, on 11 December, 1946, done at Paris, 19 November 1948, 44 UNTS 277; in force 1 December 1949.

1953 New York Opium Protocol – Protocol for Limiting and Regulating the Cultivation of the Poppy Plant, the Production of, International and Wholesale Trade in, and Use of, Opium, done at New York, 23 June 1953, 456 UNTS 3; in force 8 March 1963.

1961 Single Convention – Single Convention on Narcotic Drugs, done at New York, 30 March 1961, 520 UNTS 151; in force 13 December 1964.

1971 Psychotropic Convention – Convention on Psychotropic Substances, done at Vienna, 21 February 1971, 1019 UNTS 175; in force 16 August 1976.

1972 Protocol – Protocol Amending the 1961 Convention on Narcotic Drugs, 1961, done at Geneva, 25 March 1972, 976 UNTS 3; in force 8 August 1975.

1988 UN Drug Trafficking Convention – 1988 United Nations Convention Against Illicit Traffic in Narcotic Drugs and Psychotropic Substances, done at Vienna, 20 December 1988, UN Doc. E/CONF.82.15; UKTS 26 (1993); in force late 11 November 1990.

TABLE OF INTERNATIONAL DOCUMENTS

UN Secretariat   *United Nations Conference for the Adoption of a*
                          Protocol on Psychotropic Substances, Official
                          Records, Volume II (New York, 1973) UN Doc.
                          E/CONF.58/7/Add.1; UN Publication Sales
                          No.E.73.XI.4.

UN Secretariat   *Commentary on the Convention on Psychotropic*
                          Substances, 1971 (New York, 1976) UN Doc.
                          E/CN.7/589; UN Publication Sales No.E.76.XI.5.

1972 Protocol Documents:

UN Secretariat   *United Nations Conference to consider*
                          amendments to the Single Convention on Narcotic
                          Drugs, Official Records, Volume I (New York,
                          1974) UN Doc. E/CONF.63/10; UN Publication
                          Sales No.E.73.XI.7.

UN Secretariat   *United Nations Conference to consider*
                          amendments to the Single Convention on Narcotic
                          Drugs, Official Records, Volume II (New York,
                          1973) UN Doc. E/CONF.63/10/Add.1; UN
                          Publication Sales No. E.73.XI.8.

UN Secretariat   *Commentary on the 1972 Protocol Amending the*
                          Single Convention on Narcotic Drugs, 1961 (New
                          York, 1976) UN Doc. E/CN.7/588; UN Publication
                          Sales No.E.76.XI.6.

1988 Convention Documents:

UN Secretariat   *United Nations Conference for the Adoption of a*
                          Convention against Illicit Traffic in Narcotic
                          Drugs and Psychotropic Substances, Official
                          Records, Volume I (New York, 1994) UN Doc.
                          E/CONF.82/16, UN Publication Sales No.
                          E.94.XI.5.

INCB   *Effectiveness of the International Drug Control
                               Treaties: Supplement to the Report of the
                               International Narcotics Control Board for 1994*
                               UN Doc. E/INCB/1994/1/Supp.1, New York,
                               1995.

INCB   *Report of the International Narcotics Control
                               Board for 1995* UN Doc. E/INCB/1995/1, New
                               York, 1996.

INCB   *Precursors and Chemicals Frequently Used in the
                               Illicit Manufacture of Narcotic Drugs and
                               Psychotropic Substances: Report of the
                               International Narcotics Control Board for 1995 on
                               the Implementation of Article 12 of the United
                               Nations Convention Against Illicit Traffic in
                               Narcotic Drugs and Psychotropic Substances of
                               1988* UN Doc. E/INCB/1995/4, New York, 1996.

INCB   *Report of the International Narcotics Control
                               Board for 1996* UN Doc. E/INCB/1996/1, New
                               York, 1997.

UN Secretariat   *Report of the International Conference on Drug
                               Abuse and Illicit Trafficking, Vienna 17-26 June
                               1987* UN Publication A/Conf.133/12, UN Sales
                               No. E.87.I.18, New York, 1987.

UN Secretariat   *Declaration of the International Conference on
                               Drug Abuse and Illicit Trafficking and
                               Comprehensive Multidisciplinary Outline of Future
                               Activities in Drug Abuse Control* UN Publication
                               St/Nar/14, UN Sales No. E.88.XI.1, New York,
                               1988.

UN Secretariat   *Competent National Authorities under the
                               International Drug Control Treaties* UN Doc
                               ST/NAR.3/1993/1.

UN Secretariat

Multilateral Treaties Deposited with the Secretary General: Status as at 31 December 1996 (New York, 1997) UN Doc. St/Leg/Ser.E/15.

UNDCP

World Drug Report (OUP, Oxford, 1998).

UN ODCCP

Financial Havens, Banking Secrecy and Money Laundering (Issue 8 of the UNDCP Technical Series, New York, 1998).

Other international documents:

Council of Europe

Council of Europe Agreement on Illicit Traffic by Sea Implementing Article 17 of the United Nations Convention Against Illicit Traffic in Narcotic Drugs and Psychotropic Substances, *ETS* 156 (1995).

Schengen States

Convention Applying the Schengen Agreement of 14 June 1985 between the Governments of the States of the Benelux Economic Union, the Federal Republic of Germany and the French Republic, on the Gradual Abolition of Checks at Their Common Borders, in force 19 June 1990.

Southern African Development Community (SADC)

Protocol on Combating Illicit Drug Trafficking of 1996, SA Foreign Affairs File NV101517/96.

UK

13 November 1981 Exchange of Notes concerning Co-operation in the Suppression of the Unlawful Importation of Narcotic Drugs into the United States (Cmnd. 8470, 1981).

TABLE OF NATIONAL LAWS,
REGULATIONS AND REPORTS

Australia:
Commonwealth   Australian Crimes (Traffic in Narcotic Drugs
Parliament   and Psychotropic Substances) Act, 1990.
New South Wales   Drug Trafficking (Civil Proceedings) Act, 1990.
South Australia   Controlled Substances Act, 1984.

Afghanistan:
Legislature   Law on Combating Drugs, 1991.

Antigua:
Parliament   Misuse of Drugs Act, 1973.

Austria:
Legislature   Narcotic Drugs Amendment Act, 1977,
                    Bundesgesetzblatt No.1978/532.

Bermuda:
Parliament   Misuse of Drugs Act, 1972.

Canada:
Law Reform   *Extraterritorial Jurisdiction* (Working Paper
Commission   37, LRC Canada, Ottawa, 1984).
Parliament   Narcotics Control Act, RSC, 1970.
                    Narcotics Control Act, RSC, 1985.

Cayman Islands:
Parliament   Confidential Relationship (Preservation) Act 16 of
                    1976.

France:
Parliament   *Loi.No.90-1010 du Novembre 14, 1990.*

India:
Parliament   Narcotic Drugs and Psychotropic Substances Act,
                              1985.

Italy:
Parliament   Decree No.309 of 9 October 1990.

Malaysia:
Parliament   Dangerous Drugs Act 234 of 1952.
                              Dangerous Drugs Amendment Act 293 of 1975.
                              Dangerous Drugs Amendment Act 390 of 1977.
                              Drugs Dependants (Treatment and Rehabilitation)
                              Act 83 of 1983.
                              Dangerous Drugs Amendment Act 553 of 1983.
                              Dangerous Drugs (Special Preventive Measures) Act
                              316 of 1985.
                              Dangerous Drugs Forfeiture of Property, 1988.
                              Dangerous Drugs (Special Preventive Measures)
                              Amendment Act, 1985.

New Zealand: House of Representatives Justice and Law Reform
                              Committee, *Report on International Treaty*
                              Examination of the United Nations Convention
                              Against Illicit Traffic in Narcotic Drugs and
                              Psychotropic Substances 1988, 3 September 1998.

Pakistan:
Legislature   Prohibition (Enforcement of Hadd) Order no.4 of
                              1979.

Singapore:
Legislature   Misuse of Drugs Act, 1973.

South Africa:
Parliament   Abuse of Dependence Producing Substances and
                    Rehabilitation Centres Act 41 of 1971.
                    Drugs and Drug Trafficking Act 140 of 1992.
                    International Co-operation in Criminal Matters Act
                    75 of 1996.
                    Proceeds of Crime Act 76 of 1996.

Switzerland:
Federal legislature   Federal Law on Judicial Assistance in Criminal
                       Matters, 1981.

United Kingdom:
Home Affairs   *Report: Drug Trafficking and Related Serious*
Committee   *Crime* (HC Paper 370 I and 370 II, HMSO, London,
                    1989).
                    Misuse of Drug Act, 1971.
                    Controlled Drugs (Penalties) Act, 1985.
                    Drug Trafficking Offences Act, 1986.
Parliament   Criminal Justice (International Co-operation) Act,
                    1990.

House of Lords   *Report: Money Laundering* (HL Paper 6, HMSO,
Select Committee   London, 1990).
on the European
Communities

Home Office   *Report on the Drug Trafficking Offences Act 1986*
Working Group   (1991).
on Confiscation

United States: 'Report of the US Acting Secretary of State on the
Acting Secretary   Single Convention' (1967) 6 *AJIL* 803-5.
of State

Congress   Harrison Act, 1914, 26 USC sections 4701-4736.
                    Foreign Assistance Act, 1961, 22 USC sections 481-
                    2291(c).

	Comprehensive Drug Abuse Prevention and Control Act, 1970, 21 USC section 881.
	Currency and Foreign Transactions Reporting Act, 1970, 31 USC section 5324.
	Marijuana on the High Seas Act, 1980, 21 USC section 955(b).
	Money Laundering Control Act 1986, 18 USC sections 1956-1957.
	Racketeer Influenced Corrupt Organisations Act 1970, 18 USC section 1961-1968.
	Continuing Criminal Enterprise Act, 1970, 21 USC section 848.
	Drug Abuse Protection Acts of 1986 and 1988, codified at 12/18/31 USC.
	Maritime Drug Law Enforcement Act, 1986, 46 USC section 1903.
	Maritime Drug Law Enforcement Act, 1988, 46 USC section 1907.
	Chemical Diversion and Trafficking Act, 1988, 21 USC section 960(d) and section 801.
Senate	'Report of the United States Delegation to the United Nations Conference for the adoption of a Convention Against Illicit Traffic in Narcotic Drugs and Psychotropic Substances' from *United Nations Convention Against Illicit Traffic in Narcotic Drugs and Psychotropic Substances* Senate Executive Report 101-15, 101st Congress, 1st Session.
National Narcotics Intelligence Committee (NNIC)	*The NNICC Report 1994: The Supply of Illicit Drugs to the United States* DEA-95051 (DEA, Washington, 1995).
DEA	*Nigeria Country Report* (DEA, Lagos, 1995).

Vietnam:

| Legislature | Decree 008-TT/SLU. |

TABLE OF CASES

PCIJ:
The Lotus Case - France v Turkey (1927) PCIJ Reports Series A No.10.

ICJ:
North Sea Continental Shelf Case ICJ Reports, 1969, p. 3.

ECHR:
Air Canada v United Kingdom (1995) 20 ECHR 150.
Salabiaku Case ECHR Series A vol.141-A (1988).
Soering v The United Kingdom ECHR Series A vol.161 (1989).
Welch v United Kingdom (1995) 20 ECHR 247

Australia:
R v Ridgeway (1993) 60 SASR 207.
Ridgeway v Queen (1995) 129 ALR 41.

Austria:
Drug Offences Jurisdiction Case (1991) 86 ILR 550.
Public Prosecutor v Gunther B and Manfred E (1976) 71 ILR 247.

Canada:
Pushpanathan v Minister of Citizenship and Immigration and others [1998]
     4 LRC 365 (SCC).
R v Kerr (1986) 75 NSJ (2d) 305 (CA).
R v Oakes (1986) 50 CR (3d) 1, 24 CCC (3d) 321 (SCC).
R v Sunila and Solayman (1986) 28 DLR 4ᵗʰ 450.
United States v Jamieson 93 CCC 3d 265 (Que. CA. 1994).
United States v Jamieson [1996] 1 SCR 465.

Colombia:

Colombian Constitutional Court, Sentence No. C-221/94, Constitutional Court Gazette 1994 Special Edition.

Denmark:

Thailand Drug Offences (Jurisdiction) Case (1991) 86 ILR 587.

France:

Batkoun (1988) 73 ILR 248.

Germany:

Cannabis Decision, BverfG NJW 1994, 1577.
Public Prosecutor v Gunther B and Manfred A (1976) 71 ILR 247.
Universal Jurisdiction over Drug Offences Case (1979) 74 ILR 166.

Guam:

People of Guam v Guerrero, Criminal Case No. 00001-91, August 1999.

Italy:

Re Pulos 77 ILR 587.

Jamaica:

Forsythe v DPP, The Gleaner, Kingston, 17 May 1997.
R v Dakin [1978] 15 JLR 302 (Jamaica).

South Africa:

Prince v President of the Law Society, Cape of Good Hope and Others, 1998 (8) BCLR 976 (CPD).
S v Bhulwana 1995 (2) SACR 748 (CC).
S v Williams 1988 (4) SA 49 (WLD).
S v Solomon 1986 (3) SA 705 (A).

United Kingdom:

DPP v Doot 1973 AC 807.
Customs and Excise Commissioners v Air Canada [1991] All ER 570 (CA).
Pianka v R [1977] 3 WLR 870.
R v Aramah 1983 CLR 271 (CA).

1

INTRODUCTION

1.1   THE INTERNATIONAL DRUG CONVENTIONS

A Zulu woman arrested for selling cannabis on the streets of Johannesburg, a British tourist returning from the Far-East discovered carrying heroin by customs at Heathrow airport, a Mexican drug dealer facing extradition to the United States, a Bolivian peasant whose crop of coca bushes is being burned by Bolivian authorities, are all being subject to criminal procedures that appear to be national in origin. Yet behind all of these national processes, lies an elaborate international structure of which they, and almost all others subject to it, are unaware. During the course of the twentieth century fourteen international multilateral conventions were established by the international community with the aim of preventing the non-scientific and non-medical production, supply and use of drugs[1] while at the same time assuring their continued availability for medical and scientific purposes.[2] Today the most important of these conventions are:

---

[1]   For the sake of brevity this book will, following UN practice, unless the context demands a different meaning, use the term 'drug' to denote generally: (a) any of the substances, whether natural or synthetic, included in Schedules I and II of the Single Convention on Narcotic Drugs, 1961, and that Convention as amended by the 1972 Protocol (the substances defined as 'drugs' in article 1(j) of the 1961 Convention and as 'narcotic drugs' in article 1(n) of the 1988 Convention); (b) any substance natural or synthetic, or any natural material included in Schedules I, II, III or IV of the 1971 Convention on Psychotropic Substances (the substances defined as 'psychotropic substances' in article 1(e) of the 1971 Convention and in article 1(r) of the 1988 Convention). Although technically plants containing narcotic or psychotropic substances, viz. the 'opium poppy', 'coca bush' and 'cannabis plant', are defined separately in the conventions, for the purposes of this book general remarks about drugs apply to these plants as well. The expressions 'drug abuse', 'drug trafficking' and the like should be construed accordingly.

[2]   B. Renborg, 'International Control' (1957) 22 *Law and Contemporary Problems* 86 at 88. These aims or goals are partially reflected in the preambles of the drug conventions.

·   the Single Convention on Narcotic Drugs, 1961 (hereinafter the 1961 Convention);[3]
·   the Convention on Psychotropic Substances, 1971 (hereinafter the 1971 Convention);[4]
·   the Protocol of 1972 Amending the Single Convention on Narcotic Drugs, 1961 (hereinafter the 1972 Protocol);[5] and the
·   1988 United Nations Convention Against Illicit Traffic in Narcotic Drugs and Psychotropic Substances (hereinafter the 1988 Convention).[6]

Although the substance of these drug conventions is complex, their function is simple. They provide the legal structure for an international system of drug control by defining control measures to be maintained within each state party to these conventions and by prescribing rules to be obeyed by these Parties in their relations with each other. These rules can be categorised according to the two principal methods of achieving drug control, viz.: a) commodity control – the definition and regulation of the licit production, supply and consumption of drugs; and b) penal control – the suppression through criminal law of illicit production, supply and consumption. It is this latter category of rules, the system of rules dedicated by the international community to the penal suppression of illicit drugs, which is the subject of this book.[7] These penal rules create an

---

3   520 UNTS 151; in force 13 December 1964; 143 parties (30/4/1999).
4   1019 UNTS 175; in force 16 August 1976; 159 parties (30/4/1999).
5   975 UNTS 3; in force 8 August 1975, 108 parties (30/4/1999).
6   UN Doc. E/CONF.82.15, UKTS 26 (1993); in force 11 November 1990, 153 parties (30/4/1999).
7   Little has been written about the penal aspects of these conventions. The pre-1988 drug conventions have been subject to a general examination by S.K. Chatterjee in *Legal Aspects of International Drug Control* (Nijhoff, Dordrecht, 1981). W.C. Gilmore's *Combating International Drug Trafficking: The 1988 United Nations Convention Against Illicit Traffic in Narcotic Drugs and Psychotropic Substances* (Commonwealth Secretariat, London, 1991) is a short study of the 1988 Convention for use by Commonwealth nations. A useful official document on the 1988 Convention is the 'Report of the United States Delegation to the United Nations Conference for the adoption of a Convention Against Illicit Traffic in Narcotic Drugs and Psychotropic Substances' from *United Nations Convention Against Illicit Traffic in Narcotic Drugs and Psychotropic Substances* Senate Executive Report 101-15, 101st Congress, 1st Session. Each convention is also the subject of an exhaustive Official Commentary by the UN: *Commentary on the Single Convention on Narcotic Drugs, 1961* (New York, 1973) UN Publication Sales No. E.73.XI.1; *Commentary on the Convention on Psychotropic Substances, 1971* (New York, 1976) UN Doc. E/CN.7/589, UN Publication Sales No.E.76.XI.5; *Commentary on the 1972 Protocol Amending the Single Convention on Narcotic Drugs, 1961*

international illicit drug prohibition system or regime,[8] one of many such systems in international law created by so-called "suppression conventions".[9] It is a system constructed through a smattering of isolated articles in the 1961, 1971 and 1972 instruments but mainly through the complex provisions of the specialist penal instrument, the 1988 Convention. Examination of these technical provisions is the main task of this book, but attention to the technical fluency of the drug conventions must not distract us from the recognition that these provisions have been formulated to control a social and medical problem, the problem of illicit drug supply and use. To understand these provisions, it is crucial first to understand the way in which non-medical and non-scientific drug supply and use has been constructed as a problem in international public morality because these provisions play a critical role in the resolution of this "international drug problem".

The first step towards accepting that there is an "international drug problem" is easy. Although one might dispute the accuracy of the evidence it appears that today the international supply and use of drugs takes place on an enormous scale. The illicit drug business is immense, and steady increases in amounts of drugs seized, reductions in the retail price of drugs, expansions of the diversity of drugs available, together with increases in the amounts of profits laundered, suggest its continued growth.[10] According to the United Nations Drug Control Programme (UNDCP), annual drug sales are now worth billions of dollars and drugs are considered to be the world's second biggest trading

---

(New York, 1976) UN Doc. E/CN.7/588, UN Publication Sales No.E.76.XI.6; *Commentary on the United Nations Convention Against Illicit Traffic in Narcotic Drugs and Psychotropic Substances, 1988* (New York, 1998) UN Doc. E/CN.7/590, UN Publication Sales No.E.98.XI.5.

8   E.A. Nadelmann, 'Global prohibition regimes: the evolution of norms in international society' (1990) 44 *International Organization* 479 uses the label 'global prohibition regime' to describe the various regimes that have been developed to prohibit certain activities globally.

9   International society attempts to suppress a wide range of activities though a large number of treaties. These treaties include the Slavery Convention, 266 UNTS 42; the Hague Convention for the Suppression of Unlawful Seizure of Aircraft, 860 UNTS 105; the Montreal Convention for the Suppression of Unlawful Acts against the Safety of Civil Aviation, 974 UNTS 177; the Convention on the Prevention and Punishment of Crimes against Internationally protected Persons, including Diplomatic Agents, 28 UNTS 1975; the Hostage-Taking Convention, 18 ILM 1456; and the Convention against Torture and Other Cruel, Inhuman or Degrading Treatment or Punishment, 1465 UNTS 85.

10   M. Anderson, *Policing the World* (Clarendon, Oxford, 1989), p.105.

commodity next to armaments.[11] Astronomical profits have been used to create alternative economies and to undermine legislative and political systems.[12] There are millions of users,[13] millions of suppliers[14] and millions of acres of land growing drug-producing plants.[15] It is probably true to say that all countries are affected by both drug use and supply today.[16] International society has responded to this market for drugs by resorting to prohibition.

1.2   PROHIBITION IN NATIONAL AND INTERNATIONAL DRUG POLICY

Official drug policy, whether at the national or international level, depends upon an appreciation of the true causes and consequences of drug use and supply. Chapter Two of this book, concerned with placing the existing international drug control system in historical context, pays particular attention to the inter-relationship between the development of national and international regulation of drugs. As we shall see, during the course of the twentieth century, policy makers in key states, such as the United States, developed the conception that drug use harmed both society and individuals and the shared belief that legal prohibition was its solution. Drug prohibition became official domestic policy and law. The determination that drug-caused harm affects all states provided the moral case for international regulation, the more prosaic difficulty of sup-pressing external sources of drug supply cemented this case, and international law was used to globalise drug prohibition.[17] This international system was developed to suppress supply. Given that supply follows demand, it would seem logical for the international system to address the reasons why people take

---

11   UN Doc. E/CONF.82/SR.1 at p.3.

12   1993 estimates quantified drug money laundering activities at about $500 billion per annum – *Report of the UN Secretary General on control of the proceeds of crime to the Commission on Crime Prevention and Criminal Justice*, UN Doc. E/C.15/1993/4.

13   In 1994 it was estimated that there were five million hard drug users in the European Union and between twenty and thirty million cannabis users – *Newsweek*, 4 July 1994.

14   An estimated 10% of working Bolivians are involved in the illicit coca trade – UNDCP, *Drugs and Development* Technical Report No.1 (1994), p.2.

15   In 1992 the total amount of land under coca and poppy cultivation was estimated at 480 000 hectares – UNDCP, *Drugs and Development* Technical Report No.1 (1994), p.1. In 1995 it was estimated that between twenty and forty thousand hectares of Colom-bian soil were devoted to coca plantations – *The Economist*, 14 January 1995.

16   A point made strongly by the UNDCP's *World Drug Report* (OUP, Oxford, 1998), p.9.

17   M.C. Bassiouni, 'The International Narcotics Control Scheme' in M.C. Bassiouni (ed.), *International Criminal Law Volume 1: Crimes* (Transnational, Dobbs Ferry, 1986), p.507.

drugs. The difficulty is that, other than the rather blunt step of criminalising use and possession, using the criminal law against drugs offers few effective options for dealing with demand. The construction of the drug problem as a legal problem inevitably requires official subscription to the belief that penalisation of supply can solve the drug problem (if only there was more law, and a stronger political will and more money to enforce that law). Ultimately, questions must be asked about the continued appropriateness of the legal solution to the drug problem.

The debate about drug policy is a debate about morality and utility.[18] Arguments that morality must be protected against the evil of drugs are countered by questioning of the general acceptance that there is a human morality worth protecting. Arguments for individual freedom relate to a range of human rights such as privacy, protecting use, and free economic activity, protecting supply. They are countered by pointing out that humans are often not free when they choose to use drugs, either because of an incapacity to make an informed decision or because of addiction. The resulting moral maze means that policy makers tend to rely on materialist arguments. Medical and social pathology arguments provide the orthodox justification for prohibition.

The most immediate consequence of drug use is that it frequently causes medical harm to the consumer, to children in utero and to others through the injuries users inflict, intentionally or negligently, when intoxicated. Advocates of prohibition argue that the physical and mental damage caused to users is irreversible and that addiction is neither effectively treatable nor curable.[19] Doubters dispute the evidence that drugs cause physiological damage, that drug usage is always harmful, that all drugs have the same effects and that rehabilitation is unsuccessful.[20] Some argue that drug use can in fact benefit users through relief, recreation, reinforcement and replenishment.[21]

The secondary consequence of drug use is social harm. Society pays for medical harm, it pays for welfare assistance for users and their families, it pays

---

18 A good overview is provided by W. Morrison, 'Modernity, knowledge and the criminalisation of drug usage' in I. Loveland (ed.), *Frontiers of Criminality* (Sweet and Maxwell, London, 1995), p. 195 at p.199.

19 G. Nahas, 'Drugs, the brain and the law' (1991) 5 *Notre Dame Journal of Law, Ethics and Public Policy* 729 at 736-738.

20 W.B. Eldridge, *Narcotics and the law* (2nd edn, The University of Chicago Press, Chicago and London, 1967) pp.13-34.

21 N. Gilmore, 'Drug use and human rights: privacy, vulnerability, disability, and human rights infringements' (1996) 12 *The Journal of Contemporary Health Law and Policy* 355 at 371.

for lost productivity and it pays through a crime rate driven upwards by drug users desperate for money to finance their habits. But blaming drug use for endemic human ills such as violence, joblessness and child abuse, which like use may also be caused by the user's personality or by social conditions, is to assume a causal link to use that may not exist. Anti-prohibitionists dispute the received wisdom that drug users become weak ineffective members of society, that addicts are criminals, and that addiction is contagious.[22] They point out that studies show that drug users' psychiatric difficulties lead to use, that the law criminalises their conduct, and that it is not drug use but the mores of the societal sub-group they belong to which are anti-social and which encourage use.[23]

Anti-prohibitionists struggle, however, to shift public attention to the failures and costs of prohibition. They point to the massive areas of land under drug cultivation, the push-down-pop-up nature of illicit production, the reliance of many developing states on drug income, the failure of immense interdiction efforts to thwart all but a small percentage of illicit drug imports, and the low impact of street level policing, and argue that these failures indicate that using the criminal law is ineffective in controlling drugs.[24] They argue that using the criminal law against drugs costs society in a number of ways. It increases crime rates by criminalising use and supply, by forcing drug users into property crime to feed habits, and because the limitation of supply drives up profits thus encouraging the growth of crime.[25] Other costs include the dedication of criminal justice resources to drug law enforcement and the punishment of drug offenders, the personal costs to the users of being labelled criminals and of being forced to deal with criminals to get drugs, the costs of the corruption of government officials and the creation of an informant based society, and the medical costs resulting from adulterated drugs and infected needles.[26]

The response of prohibitionists to such arguments is not to deny that prohibition costs society, but to deny that law enforcement policies have failed and to claim that in fact these policies have helped to eliminate suppliers and

---

22 Eldridge supra note 20.
23 Eldridge supra note 20.
24 E.A. Nadelmann, 'Drug prohibition in the United States: costs, consequences and alternatives' (1991) 5 *Notre Dame Journal of Law, Ethics and Public Policy* 783-808.
25 Nadelmann supra note 24.
26 Nadelmann supra note 24.

users while deterring or delaying potential suppliers and users.[27] Although these claims are difficult to substantiate, the medical and social harm prevented by prohibition – harm that the illegality of drugs presently prevents users doing to themselves or others through use – has been identified as the central argument for maintaining prohibition.[28] Uncertainty about the quantity of such prevented harm favours prohibitionists because the future impact of drugs if legalised is unknowable.[29]

Anti-prohibitionists can only speculate on the benefits of legalisation. Comparisons with two legal drugs, tobacco and alcohol, are often made. Anti-prohibitionists point out that the social and financial costs of smoking and drinking alcohol are much greater than the costs of illicit drugs, and argue that illicit drugs should be placed in the same category as tobacco and alcohol, opening them to the same kind of social control processes through education and regulation paid for by the re-routing of law enforcement funding and by taxation.[30] They argue that the licensed sale of drugs for non-medical use would destroy the wealth and corruptive power of drug traffickers because supply would become so much cheaper due to a considerable growth in the efficiency of production and distribution.[31] They note that the resulting cuts in spending and tax benefits could be used to fund treatment programmes and they point to other benefits such as the refocusing of the foreign policy of consumer states on non-drug issues and the rehabilitation of governmental authority in supply states.[32]

Prohibitionists counter speculation about the benefits of legalisation by speculating about its costs. They attack the effectiveness of proposed alternative regulatory measures such as consumption taxes, advertising bans, restrictions on time and place of sale and public anti-drugs education. They argue that society may not be able to withstand the impact of additional massive legal drug

---

27 At a recent press conference General Barry McCaffrey, the incumbent US Drug Czar, when asked whether it was a better idea to invest in health and treatment rather than in 'hopeless suppression', replied that the drug abuse problem had been reduced by fifty per cent in the US since 1979, that the numbers of drug related crimes were dropping, and concluded that the situation was 'hardly hopeless' – US Federal Information Service, 1 November 1999.

28 J. Ostrowski, 'Answering the critics of drug legalization' (1991) 5 *Notre Dame Journal of Law, Ethics and Public Policy* 823 at 824.

29 Ostrowski supra note 28.

30 See J.C. Burnham, 'Comments on Nadelmann' and E.A. Nadelmann, 'Nadelmann's response' (1991) 5 *Notre Dame Journal of Law, Ethics and Public Policy* 810 and 817.

31 Nadelmann supra note 24.

32 Nadelmann supra note 24 at 798.

use and that historical precedent shows that the social costs of legalisation will be greater than prohibition, that drug abuse and crime will increase and medical and social costs will sky-rocket.[33] It is also claimed that while crime to finance use might decrease, crimes committed under the influence would increase. Prohibitionists submit that it is naive to believe that legalisation will kill the illicit market, arguing that illicit production and supply costs will also drop and traffickers will still be able to undercut the licit market.[34] One of the most potent anti-legalisation arguments is that it sends a message of approval of use to those least able to resist, especially children.[35] Prohibitionists question the effectiveness of educating children and point out the difficulties of enforcing purchasing age-limits. Anti-prohibitionists counter by arguing that all users, even children, would be sold better quality drugs under healthier conditions and that profit margins would be much lower and the illicit market less violent. Legalisation would, however, have other less obvious negative effects. Commercial cultivation would probably spell disaster for the rural peasants in producer states who are reliant on drug cultivation as a form of income.[36] Legalisation would also condemn and pacify the marginalised of consumer societies.[37]

It is plain that the debate between the advocates of legalisation and prohibition is polarised; each side addresses the other's weaknesses, neither side appears to have a complete answer. Public attitudes to drugs are confused.[38] There is support for prohibition by a range of people including moral extremists, political opportunists and the genuinely concerned.[39] Although there is also opposition to prohibition, the political appeal of legalisation is low, due to the

---

33 Nahas supra note 19 at 746. See also L.F. Lowenstein, 'Legalizing or not legalizing drugs' (1993) 66 *The Police Journal* 296 at 301.

34 Commentary, 'Combating the drugs menace' (1989) 13 *The Criminologist* 65 at 65. See also J.B. Jacobs, 'Imagining drug legalization' (1990) 101 *The Public Interest* 28-42.

35 D.E. Strebel, 'Comments on Nadelmann' (1991) 5 *Notre Dame Journal of Law, Ethics and Public Policy* 814.

36 N. Dorn, K. Murji, and N. South, *Traffickers: Drug Markets and Law Enforcement* (Routledge, London, 1992), p. XVI.

37 Morrison supra note 18 at 214.

38 See, for example, the studies cited by Lowenstein supra note 33 who examines the empirical research on attitudes to drug usage.

39 P. O'Malley and S. Mugford, 'The demand for intoxicating commodities: implications for the war on drugs' in N. South (ed.), *Drugs, Crime, and Criminal Justice* (Dartmouth, Aldershot, 1995), p. 441 at p.457.

uncertainty of its future effects,[40] and is not likely to grow unless the situation seriously deteriorates.[41] The national practice of states since the 1970s indicates a general reluctance to move away from prohibition. Some states, such as the Netherlands, have adopted more permissive policies in respect of "soft" drugs, but these steps do not present a serious departure from prohibition.[42] Calls for acceptance of the fact of drug usage in the modern consumer society and a shift in focus to the reduction of the harm caused by drug usage and drug law are growing but seem to have had little impact on official policy thus far.[43] Significantly, this political opposition to prohibition has grown almost entirely at the national level and ironically often in the very states that gave birth to prohibition in the first place. Dorn et al argue that legalisation is improbable, 'given the momentum required to reverse the tide of international agreements'.[44] Although its basis may be questionable social policy, drug prohibition through national and international law has taken on an inertia and logic of its own.[45] The dispute about the appropriateness of prohibition should, however, alert us to the difficulties of applying prohibition internationally.

---

40   P. Reuter and R. MacCoun, 'Assessing the legalisation debate' in G. Estievenart (ed.), *Policies and Strategies to Combat Drugs in Europe* (Nijhoff, Dordrecht, 1995) p. 39 at pp. 48-49.

41   Reuter and MacCoun supra note 40 at 45-46, 49.

42   Dutch drug policy distinguishes between "soft" and "hard" drugs, and waives prosecution of possession of small amounts of soft drugs. Consequently there is little risk to traffickers, prices have dropped and the police have been able to identify the areas where drugs are sold so they can police them easily – Anderson supra note 10 at 109; see also on decriminalisation E. Crowther, 'Will three wrongs make a right' (1992) 156 *Justice of the Peace* 654.

43   See O'Malley and Mugford supra note 39 for an interesting analysis of harm reduction as a viable alternative to both prohibition and legalisation.

44   N. Dorn, K. Murji, and N. South, *Traffickers: Drug Markets and Law Enforcement* (Routledge, London, 1992), p. X.

45   See Morrison supra note 18 at 217 who argues that once transformed into issues of crime, penalty, procedure, and law enforcement, prohibition serves to legitimate itself.

1.3   THE CONTOURS OF THE INTERNATIONAL "CONSENSUS" ON THE AP-
           PLICATION OF DRUG PROHIBITION THROUGH INTERNATIONAL LAW

It has been argued that the development of the international drug control system
was largely apolitical.[46] This argument implies that during the early development of the system most states recognised the problem and agreed upon the
method for dealing with it. However, in the early stages of development, many
states in Asia, Africa and South America, where drugs had traditional cultural
or religious uses, did not consider drug use a social problem.[47] Individuals
from North America and Europe assumed the role of moral guardians of international society and after establishing the policy of prohibition in their own
powerful states, became the agents of the international expansion of prohibition.
How they used international law to achieve this expansion is explored in
Chapter Two, but it is enough to state here that in a profoundly political process
the resulting international control system was externally imposed on the majority.[48]

    Although prohibition is the official national and international policy in
respect of drugs today, against this background it seems inevitable that not all
states should currently share a common conception of the drug problem or its
solution. While it is fairly crude to term some states "consumer" states and
others "producer" states given that there are drug consumers and producers in
every state, this dichotomy serves as a useful way of explaining the political
conflict over international drug prohibition. Many wealthy developed states
where there are large consumer markets have governments expressly hostile
to illicit drugs, prepared to open the public purse to suppress them. The United
States, for example, has declared "war on drugs". The position in drug producer
states such as Colombia is more ambivalent. On the whole the governments
of such states subscribe to prohibition, are party to the drug conventions and
have legislation outlawing the production and trafficking in illicit drugs.
However, many of these governments apply this law rather less than enthusiastically. The political and economic elites within these states identify with
the concerns of consumer states. They too have to deal with drug users, their
economies are vulnerable to money laundering and they need to protect civil

---

46   H.L. May, 'Narcotic Drug Control – Development of International Action and the
     Establishment of Supervision under the United Nations' (1948) 441 *International
     Conciliation* 303.
47   Chatterjee supra note 7 at 7-11.
48   Chatterjee supra note 7 at 530-531.

society from lawlessness and corruption. But they are subject to many counter-vailing pressures, ranging from the relatively benign established historical use of a particular substance, such as the chewing of coca leaves in Bolivia, to the more malign interests of established criminal networks. Perhaps the most important variable affecting governmental attitudes to prohibition in these states is the economic role of drug production, because for many agricultural producers of organic narcotic substances licit crops do not provide even remotely the same kind of return on investment. Wealthy drug suppliers also influence the leadership of the states from which they operate, either directly through compulsion or bribery, or indirectly through their massive investment which makes them central to the economic and political stability of these states. In a climate of adverse public opinion and terror, it is difficult to expend revenue on law enforcement while simultaneously cutting off revenue generated by drugs. Many of these central authorities are in any event structurally too weak to enforce an unpopular policy.[49]

It follows that producer and consumer states adopt different attitudes to international drug control and different ideas about who is responsible for the international drug problem. Anderson comments that 'producer countries in the third world ... often naturally take the view that the root cause is the insatiable market for drugs in the rich countries.'[50] Developed consumer states, on the other hand, tend to blame producer states for the drug problem. Unable themselves to stop usage, they externalise responsibility.[51] The way that the international system has developed reflects the balance of power between these two groups of states. Consumer states have used the political and economic pressure at their disposal to get producer states to agree to a system that serves as a vehicle for international co-operation in reducing international supply. Producer states, aware that drug supply and use has negative effects upon their own societies, have complied. However, pressure from consumer states com-

---

49   Dorn et al supra note 36 at X.
50   Supra note 10 at 29.
51   D.F. Musto, *The American Disease: Origins of Narcotics Control* (expanded edition, OUP, New York, 1987), p.206 notes that after World War I the drug problem in the United States was blamed on foreigners. He argues that placing the blame on others both internally (ethnic minorities) and externally (foreigners) allowed drugs to be dismissed as un-American, avoiding the painful and awkward realisation that drug use may be an integral part of American society. At p. 248 he points out that putting the blame on others also permits more punitive measures to be taken against certain of the culprits. The "war on drugs" carries over into a foreign policy that anticipates the policing of the illicit drug traffickers in other states, not by the authorities in those states, nor by international control, but directly by the United States authorities.

bined with the self-interest of the producer state elites is a weak basis for an international consensus on the international resolution of the drug problem. The international system therefore remains a terrain of contest where developing states attempt to shift responsibility for control back on to developed states, both legally, by criminalisation of use, and also financially, by making developed states pay for international enforcement of drug prohibition. However, because the political strength of consumer states enabled them to impose their solution to the drug problem on the international community, the drug conventions are designed chiefly to implement a supply reduction scheme that sees the source of drugs as the problem to be eliminated.[52]

Broadly speaking this scheme involves the criminalisation of conduct involved in different stages in the production and supply of drugs, and measures for the taking of concerted law-enforcement action against each stage of this process. It thus involves measures against the production of drugs. If the source is drug bearing crops, it provides for their eradication through burning, clearing, or poisoning. It encourages crop substitution to attempt to convince farmers to grow legal crops instead. An approach that is similar in concept attacks the supply of chemicals used in drug manufacturing or refinement by either preventing supply or by using these chemicals to identify and eliminate drug manufacturers. Once drugs have been produced, supply interdiction measures are used to prevent the arrival of drugs at the market place from abroad by interdiction at sea, at borders and so on. The foundations of the system as a whole, however, are those measures aimed at neutralising the individuals involved in drug supply wherever they may be found. These measures include the investigation, arrest and punishment of these drug suppliers for a range of different offences, the identification and confiscation of their assets derived from drug trafficking and the elimination of money laundering. The techniques used to supply drugs and hide the profits of supply are constantly evolving, while the size of the profits to be made encourages participation. Any treaty hoping to suppress this activity must describe the different activities involved in the supply of drugs and the disposal of profits accurately and comprehensively and provide for punishment sufficient to deter offenders. The physical location of alleged offenders in many different jurisdictions creates perhaps the biggest problem for the application of supply reduction at the international level. An international legal basis is necessary for states to establish sufficient jurisdictional connection to prosecute alleged offenders and to provide for the extradition of the accused.

---

52 See generally K. Murji, 'Drug enforcement strategies' (1993) 32 *Howard Law Journal* 215-230.

to prosecute alleged offenders and to provide for the extradition of the accused. Allied problems include the location of witnesses and evidence in many different jurisdictions. Given the preclusion of one state from engaging in law-enforcement in the territory of another, international law must provide for states to assist each other at levels ranging from the operational to the formal in order to ensure the swift gathering and transfer of legally usable evidence.

The provisions in the drug conventions are there to make such actions possible, to provide the infrastructure, the expertise and the legal right for Parties to take these steps against drug supply. With the emphasis firmly on supply reduction, alternative strategies like demand reduction, which encourages users to stop using, and harm reduction, which emphasises that drugs must be used in a harmless manner whenever use occurs, are not pursued with any vigour at the international level. Unfortunately, however, for the advocates of supply reduction, the nature of international society limits international legal co-operation in regard to even this heavily supported policy.

1.4   SOVEREIGNTY LIMITATIONS ON THE APPLICATION OF DRUG PRO-
        HIBITION THROUGH INTERNATIONAL LAW

International law makes both international drug prohibition possible and limits its expression. Because there is no central source of sovereign international authority, international law relies on states themselves to apply this law. The drug conventions are not self-executing.[53] They provide a template for a system of domestic criminal drug law. One of the consequences of adopting a system of indirect control is that the transformation of the drug conventions into national law muddies the international expression of prohibition. States define offences differently, impose different penalties for similar conduct, establish jurisdiction on different grounds, grant or refuse extradition using different procedures and on different evidence, and base legal co-operation upon different forms of request. Crucial differences protected by sovereignty include the common law – civil law divide which manifests itself particularly in the reluctance of common law states to establish jurisdiction over anything other than territorial offences and in civil law states being unwilling to extradite their nationals. The UN's official *Commentary on the Single Convention on Narcotic Drugs, 1961* (hereinafter the *1961 Commentary*) points to the roots of the general divergence

---

53   See, for example, article 2(1), article 5(1) and article 5(9) of the 1988 Convention.

with regard to domestic criminal law and to the usual method resorted to in overcoming it in international law:

> Widely different moral, religious and cultural traditions are reflected in the differences that distinguish the systems of substantive and procedural penal law of individual nations and of groups of culturally related nations. It is therefore extremely difficult, and in some respects even impossible, to establish universally acceptable international rules to be implemented in the national penal systems. Attempts to overcome these difficulties have been made by adopting international provisions that are broad enough to leave escape clauses for the benefit of those Governments to which even such vague norms would be unacceptable.[54]

Escape clauses of this kind are, as we shall see, common in the drug conventions. They further confuse an already confused situation, but they are rationalised as a trade-off allowing for greater participation in international drug control. They do, however, point to the central weakness of the drug conventions – the reliance on states to mediate their provisions.

States do not only use sovereignty to resist commitment to elaborate provisions within the drug conventions, they also use it to resist external interference in the way they deal with illicit drugs. When the domestic inaction of a state creates legal havens for drug producers and traffickers, the rules of territorial sovereignty and non-intervention prevent interference with these havens. This point is well illustrated by the refusal of South American states to co-operate in the arrest and extradition of alleged drug traffickers to the United States. These states cloak themselves in their sovereignty, which sometimes leads to the United States abducting these traffickers. Supporters of abduction justify its international legality by arguing inter alia that the United States is specially affected by drug trafficking[55] and that it is acting in self-

---

54 *Commentary on the Single Convention on Narcotic Drugs, 1961* (New York, 1973) UN Publication Sales No. E.73.XI.1, p.425.

55 A. Fletcher, 'Pirates and smugglers: an analysis of the use of abductions to bring drug traffickers to trial' (1991) 32 *Virginia Journal of International Law* 233 at 236. He defends the US policy of selective abduction of drug traffickers on the basis that as a practical matter, the extraterritorial enforcement of domestic criminal law cannot in the case of drug trafficking 'effectively proceed by treating all nations as equals.' He argues, using the analogy of piracy, that international law treats similarly affected states differently from other states that are not affected.

defence in terms of article 51 of the UN Charter.[56] These claims may be disturbing, but they do indicate that it is impossible to use a law enforcement strategy to attempt to control the global drug-trade without either the unilateral derogation or the consensual mutual relaxation of state sovereignty. For obvious reasons, the international drug control system has adopted the latter approach. The Parties have agreed to countenance an encroachment of their sovereignty. That this is a grudging and limited agreement is well illustrated by the provisions within the drug conventions that safeguard sovereignty.

Article 2 of the 1988 Convention, apparently intended to safeguard the sovereignty of the Parties from the potentially intrusive obligations of the convention itself but not to derogate from those obligations, provides a good example of such a provision. Its title, 'Scope of the Convention', suggests a demarcation of obligation and the article was introduced precisely for the purpose of reassuring producer states and making them less hesitant to assume the 1988 Convention's obligations.[57] However, the UN's *Commentary on the United Nations Convention Against Illicit Traffic in Narcotic Drugs and Psychotropic Substances, 1988* (hereinafter the *1988 Commentary*) views article 2

---

56   A.D. Sofaer (State Department) before the Congressional Sub-committee on Civil and Constitutional Rights, 8 November 1989, in M.N. Leigh, 'Contemporary practice of the United States relating to international law: territorial jurisdiction' (1990) 84 AJIL 725 at 727 is quoted as stating: 'We are reaching the point ... at which the activities and threats of some drug traffickers may be so serious and damaging as to give rise to the right to resort to self-defense. The evidence of imminent harm from the trafficker's threats would have to be strong to sustain a self-defense argument. Arrests in foreign states without their consent have no legal justification under international law aside from self-defense. But where a criminal organisation grows to a point where it can and does perpetrate violent attacks against the United States, it can become a proper object of measures of self-defense.'

57   Article 2 was introduced by Mexico – see 'Report of the Review Group on the draft Convention' UN Doc. E/CONF.82/3 paras 14, 46 and 120 and Annexure II 'Revised text of the draft Convention against Illicit Traffic in Narcotic Drugs and Psychotropic Substances'. This very long proposed draft article evolved into the existing article 2. D.W. Sproule and P. St-Denis, 'The UN Drug Trafficking Convention: An Ambitious Step' [1989] CYBIL 263 explain at 266 note 18 that article 2 was among the most divisive at the Conference. They point out that article 2 was the result of Mexico's determination not to permit the Convention to be used to allow interference by consumer states in the domestic affairs of producer states. Article 2's wording, which includes wording from article 2 of the UN Charter and wording from the US/Mexico Mutual Legal Assistance Treaty, reassured the Mexicans and like-minded delegations. Sproule and St-Denis recognise the political necessity of such consensus building provisions but bemoan the uncertainty they create about the legal obligations established by the Convention.

merely as 'a statement of guiding principles for a correct interpretation and proper implementation of the substantive articles of the Convention'.[58] The problem is that article 2's broad wording allows it to operate as a general escape clause, which compounds the weakening effect of the escape clauses governing specific obligations.

The first sentence of article 2(1) explains that the purpose of the 1988 Convention is to promote international co-operation in the suppression of the international drug traffic in order to make suppression more effective. Unilateral action or inaction, by implication, contradicts the purposes of the Convention. Article 2(1)'s second sentence makes it clear that the 1988 Convention is not self-executing and must be transformed by the Parties into their domestic law, but with the caveat that this transformation must take place 'in conformity with the fundamental provisions of [the Parties] respective domestic legislative systems'. The Canadian co-sponsor of this provision noted that this does not mean that that the obligations assumed by the Parties pursuant to the 1988 Convention are subject to domestic law. Its purpose 'was to clarify that while Parties had assumed obligations, it was up to each of them to decide what laws they would require and what institutions they would need to establish to meet such obligations.'[59] Although it does not appear to be a true escape clause, nonetheless, the United States delegation, which was critical of the provision, felt that it might be used by Parties to avoid bringing their national legislation into line with the 1988 Convention.[60]

Article 2(2) is a more explicit safeguard clause. It obliges the Parties when carrying out the Convention's obligations to do so consistently with the principles of sovereign equality, territorial integrity and non-intervention.[61] As a general principle, all unauthorised law enforcement action within another state's territory, no matter how temporary or limited, is illegal. Parties engaging in such actions are not in any event engaging in actions authorised by the Convention. The *1988 Commentary* points out that the obligations in the Convention conform to these principles because they require Parties to make formal requests

---

58 (New York, 1998), UN Doc. E/CN.7/590, UN Publication Sales No.E.98.XI.5, p.41.

59 *United Nations Conference for the Adoption of a Convention against Illicit Traffic in Narcotic Drugs and Psychotropic Substances, Official Records, Volume II* (New York, 1991) UN Doc. E/CONF.82/16/Add.1, UN Publication Sales No. E.91.XI.1, p. 155 (hereinafter *1988 Records* vol. II). The *1988 Commentary* at 43 adheres to this interpretation.

60 *1988 Records* vol. II at 156.

61 Enshrined in article 2 paragraphs (1) and (7) of the UN Charter.

for co-operation and to be granted authorisation before acting in ways which intrude into the domain reserve of other states.[62]

Article 2(3) completes the picture by obliging Parties not to carry out in the territory of another Party either the exercise of extraterritorial jurisdiction or the performance of functions exclusively reserved to that other Party by its domestic law. These specific restrictions on the establishment and exercise of extraterritorial jurisdiction were considered justified because of the unorthodox enforcement practices of the United States for which legal exception had been claimed.[63] The Convention makes provision for the establishment of extraterritorial jurisdiction, but the Canadian co-sponsor of the provision notes that Parties would not be able to unilaterally extend their 'jurisdiction beyond their borders except as specifically agreed to in the Convention.'[64] Conducting hot pursuit operations on the land of another Party or engaging in investigations within the territory as a whole of another Party to the 1988 Convention, without that Party's consent, is clearly illegal.[65] However, the Parties to the Convention cannot rely on article 2(3) to invoke exclusive domestic jurisdiction in respect of the implementation of the Convention's provisions where such jurisdiction has been specifically excluded by agreement to these provisions.

In essence then, article 2 of the 1988 Convention emphasises that the drug conventions set up a system of indirect control and that international co-operation in terms of that system takes place within the limited derogation of sovereignty that states permit. Obviously, greater domestic action and more extensive international co-operation is possible. The drug conventions themselves urge states to go further. Thus article 24 of the 1988 Convention, entitled 'Application of stricter measures than those required by this Convention', provides that Parties may adopt 'more strict and severe measures than those provided by this Convention' if they believe such measures are necessary to prevent or suppress the illicit traffic.[66] Some states hold such beliefs and adopt stricter domestic provisions and push for greater international co-operation. Nevertheless, it remains an open question whether the drug conventions can provide effectively for the suppression of drugs given the limitations of indirect application and limited international co-operation. Direct control by international law, however, offers another possible way of suppressing drugs, and it may

---

62   *1988 Commentary* at 45.
63   Gilmore supra note 7 at 3-4.
64   *1988 Records* vol. II at 155.
65   Offences established in terms of article 3 of the 1988 Convention.
66   See also article 39 of the 1961 Convention and article 23 of the 1971 Convention.

be that the drug conventions will serve as vehicles for the establishment of such direct control by helping to establish drug offences as international crimes.

1.5   TOWARDS DIRECT INTERNATIONAL CONTROL: DRUG OFFENCES AS INTERNATIONAL CRIMES

Many commentators either submit or simply assume that the offences in the drug conventions are international crimes.[67] Some are more cautious, suggesting that they are international crimes de lege ferenda,[68] while others simply deny that drug crimes are international crimes.[69] There is no settled definition of what constitutes an international crime, but a number of criteria have been suggested.

The first of these is that the offence must find its source and definition in an international convention.[70] The issue to be examined here is whether the drug conventions create precise enough obligations to form uniform, in the sense of identical or near-identical, domestic drug offences. If the conventions only set standards that harmonise domestic offences within broad parameters they would seem to provide little foundation for the claim that drug offences are international crimes.

A second defining criterion of an international crime is the establishment of extraterritorial jurisdiction. It has been argued that because all states are

---

67   M.C Bassiouni, 'International criminal law' in S.H. Kadish (ed.), *Encyclopedia of Crime and Justice* Volume 3 (Macmillan, New York, 1983) p. 901 at p. 902; M.C. Bassiouni, 'Characteristics of international criminal law conventions' in M.C. Bassiouni (ed.), *1 International Criminal Law: Crimes* (Transnational, Dobbs Ferry, 1986) p. 1; W.N. Gianaris, 'The new world order and the need for an international criminal court' (1992/3) 16 *Fordham International Law Journal* 88 at note 1; J.F. Murphy, 'International Crimes' in C.C. Joyner (ed.), *The United Nations and International Law* (CUP/American Society of International Law, Cambridge, 1997), p. 362 at p. 370; D. Oehler, 'Criminal Law, International' in R. Bernhardt (ed.), *Encyclopedia of Public International Law* Volume I (Elsevier, Amsterdam, 1992) p. 877 at p. 881; The Quito Declaration of 11/8/1984 signed by Bolivia, Colombia, Ecuador, Panama, Peru and Venezuela declared drug trafficking to be a crime against humanity.

68   A. Abramovsky, 'Extraterritorial abductions: America's "Catch and Snatch" policy run amok' (1991) 31 *Virginia Journal of International Law* 151 at 180.

69   Anderson supra note 10 at 27.

70   M.C. Bassiouni, 'Characteristics of international criminal law conventions' in M.C. Bassiouni (ed.), *1 International Criminal Law: Crimes* (Transnational, Dobbs Ferry, 1986) p. 2. He submits that it need not be declared to be an international offence in the convention.

harmed by the problems created by drugs and have a duty to co-operate internationally to control them, all states are under an international obligation to
combat drug criminality in compliance with the principle of subsidiary universality (the aut dedere aut judicare principle – the duty to extradite or
prosecute).[71] But it is doubtful whether such a duty exists independently of
the drug conventions in customary international law. The issue to be examined
here is whether the application of subsidiary universality and other principles
of extraterritorial jurisdiction within the drug conventions can provide a successful jurisdictional bridge to international status for drug offences.

A third criterion for classifying crimes as international is whether the
particular conventions proscribe the conduct because it: i) contains either an
international or transnational (cross-border) element; and ii) it is necessary to
take international steps against this conduct.[72] In order to contain an international element it would have to be shown that drug offences threatened international peace and security or are subject to universal opprobrium. This is a
tall order and at first glance it would seem easier to establish that drug offences
are transnational in that they affect the interests of more than one state. To
establish the second element, the necessity of taking international steps, it would
have to be shown that drug trafficking does require international co-operation
to enforce suppression.

It appears that these criteria actually distinguish between two kinds of
offences. If the drug conventions provide for precisely defined offences, extend
unrestricted universal jurisdiction over these offences, and express the belief
of the international community that these offences either threaten the state
system or are subject to universal opprobrium, then, it is submitted, the drug
conventions create international offences. But if they define the offences ambiguously, make restricted provision for extraterritorial jurisdiction, and appear
only to assume that these offences threaten transnational interests, then the drug
conventions only provide for transnational offences. They may be genuine international activities, but they would not be true international crimes.[73]

The definition of drug offences as international crimes represents a shift
from indirect to direct international control over these offences. States may resist
this development for various reasons, but the centrifugal forces at work in
international society as a whole have not left drug control untouched, and one

---

71   M.C. Bassiouni, 'The International Narcotics Control Scheme' in M.C. Bassiouni (ed.),
     1 International Criminal Law: Crimes (Transnational, Dobbs Ferry, 1986), p. 507.
72   Bassiouni supra note 70 at 2.
73   Anderson supra note 10 at 27.

of the purposes of this book is to investigate how far towards a system of direct international control over drug offences international society has progressed.

1.6   THE INDIVIDUAL IN THE SYSTEM

Preoccupation with developing international prohibition is driven by the perception that illicit drugs threaten states. It must not, however, be forgotten that the policy of prohibition threatens the interests of the individuals caught up in the web of national laws derived from international regulation in a variety of ways. The residents of urban areas are threatened through the use of police raids, curfews and warrant-less searches. Cultivators of land may be subject to eradication operations involving the use of herbicides. The rights of users are of course threatened by the criminalisation of private behaviour. Suppliers are, however, the main targets of the system. Suspected suppliers may be subject to detention without trial or the confiscation of property not proved to be linked directly to trafficking. Once arrested, offenders may be denied fair pre-trial proceedings and a fair trial. Allied to this is the potential denial of the general procedural rights of alleged offenders in proceedings leading to international criminal co-operation, such as the right to be informed of an extradition request, the right to be heard, and the right to legal assistance. Once convicted, offenders may not receive fair conditions of punishment and protection against cruel and unusual punishment for drug offences. In particular, states that apply the death penalty for trafficking threaten the right to life. All of these various individuals must be protected, principally through procedural due process rights, but in other ways such as the right to treatment for convicted drug addicts. Warnings have already been sounded about the apparent lack of concern in international drug control for human rights.[74] This book outlines the protections provided in the drug conventions for individuals and considers whether these conventions regard individuals as objects of negotiation between states, or as subjects of international law able to use international law to guarantee their protection from official abuse.

---

74   Norbert Gilmore supra note 21 at 356.

1.7   THE PURPOSE, STRUCTURE AND METHOD OF THIS BOOK

The examination of the penal aspects of the drug conventions that follows this introduction will try to assist in resolving various questions about the illicit drug control system. It will attempt to reveal more about the nature of the international "consensus" about drug control. It will endeavour to indicate how successful states have been at using sovereignty to retain some control over policing the supply and use of drugs within their territories. It will seek to expose any tendency to move away from a system of indirect international control to a system of direct control. It will also seek to show how, if at all, those individuals subject to the system are protected by the system. The primary purpose of this book is, however, to describe the scope and content of the technical rules of international law designed to suppress illicit drugs. In this way it is intended to serve as a resource for those interested in international drug control and international criminal law because amazingly, given the sustained dominance of illicit drugs as a social issue, there is a paucity of information on and analysis of the drug conventions.[75] The structure adopted in the book is fairly straightforward. Chapter Two recounts the historical development of the illicit drug control system and then the substance of the book is divided up along the lines of the four basic thrusts of the drug conventions.

The cornerstone of the system is the national criminalisation and punishment of different forms of conduct involved in the supply and use of drugs. Chapter Three of this book first examines the offences that the drug conventions require Parties to create in their national law. Although the conventions are mainly concerned with criminalising the supply of drugs and related activities such as money laundering, they controversially criminalise personal use offences, and close attention is paid to these provisions. This chapter also examines the penalties that the drug conventions require Parties to enact to complement these offences, as well as alternatives to penalisation such as treatment and rehabilitation permitted by international law.

The international drug control system depends, however, for its effectiveness on the establishment of national criminal jurisdiction over drug offences wherever committed and on the extradition of drug offenders to ensure that they do not escape prosecution. Chapter Four examines the provisions in the drug conventions that relate to the crucial issue of jurisdiction over drug offences, and looks particularly closely at the extraterritorial extension of such jurisdiction. It examines the provisions relating to extradition simultaneously because the

---

75   See note 9 supra.

provisions for jurisdiction and extradition are bound up with each other in the drug conventions.

The investigation, arrest and prosecution of drug offenders is the subject of an extensive range of provisions that ambitiously provide for effective and speedy co-operation between national authorities in the enforcement of illicit drug laws. Chapter Five investigates the general provisions for law enforcement co-operation in the sense of policing and prosecution of drug offenders. It covers the general provisions of the drug conventions that regulate drugs policing, operational co-operation and mutual legal assistance between states. Chapter Six, the longest chapter, is concerned with specific aspects of international law enforcement co-operation, such as confiscation of the proceeds of drug offences, the monitoring of precursor substances, and investigative techniques such as controlled delivery and law enforcement at sea.

The international drug control system provides for its own supervision by international organs. Chapter Seven sets out the supervisory structures of the system and the information gathering and oversight powers they exercise. This chapter examines the role of the various UN organs controlling or participating in the system, as well as intergovernmental organisations and the domestic organs of various influential states. It also examines the conventions' provisions for the resolution of disputes and the enforcement of the application of the international system against Parties and non-parties.

Before we begin examining the penal provisions of the drug conventions, it is necessary to point out the general method of investigation adopted in this book. The international drug control system is a creature of international treaty law. As this book examines the provisions of the relevant conventions – and is designed to be read together with the texts of the drug conventions – it is an exercise in the interpretation of treaties.[76] The drug conventions are products largely of compromise and are, as we shall see, saturated with textual ambiguity. Clarification of the meaning of these provisions frequently forces recourse to attempts to discover the intention of the Parties. For this reason, the drafting history of the provisions has been drawn on extensively to resolve ambiguity and obscurity and to avoid absurd and unreasonable results. But it is not always satisfactory to rely only on the intention of authors of conventions to which considerable numbers of states have later acceded. In the process of interpretation of the drug conventions regard is thus taken of the contemporary expectations of Parties to these treaties, as evidenced by their subsequent state

---

76 See generally articles 31 and 32 of the 1969 Vienna Convention on the Law of Treaties, 1155 UNTS 331.

practice.[77] Reference is made to domestic legislation, administrative measures and court decisions. But the use of state practice as an interpretative tool does not mean that this book is an exhaustive examination of the implementation of international drug control law; such a task is beyond its scope. In the same way, while this book draws upon the "soft law" of major policy instruments generated by the UN to interpret the "hard" law of the drug conventions, it is not a study of these instruments per se. These are tasks for another.

---

77 Article 31(3)(b) of the Vienna Convention allows recourse to state practice subsequent to the conclusion of a treaty as evidence of what was originally intended by its authors.

THE HISTORY OF THE INTERNATIONAL
LEGAL REGULATION OF DRUGS[1]

2.1   THE INTRODUCTION OF INTERNATIONAL DRUG CONTROL

Examination of the history of international drug control has been the subject of significant scholarly effort.[2] The aim of this chapter is not to revisit the history of drug control as a whole, but to chart the development of the international legal system for the suppression of illicit drugs in order to illustrate how historical events in the nineteenth and twentieth centuries have shaped political and legal responses to drugs.

The origins of this system can be traced back to the international rejection of the Indo-Chinese opium trade. The trade had flourished when European colonial powers and in particular Britain, realising the commercial possibilities, encouraged opium production in India for supply to China.[3] Although opium had been prohibited in China in the eighteenth century, the nineteenth century

---

1   Much of the substance of this chapter has already been published in the following three articles: 'The interrelationship between the development of domestic and international drug control law' (1995) 7 *African Journal of Comparative and International Law* 906-914; 'The international legal regulation of drug production, distribution and consumption' (1996) 29 *Comparative and International Law Journal of Southern Africa* 1-15; 'The historical development of international legal measures to suppress drug trafficking' (1997) 30 *Comparative and International Law Journal of Southern Africa* 1-21.

2   For a history of the early phases of the international legal regulation of drugs see L.E.S. Eisenlohr, *International Narcotics Control* (George Allen and Unwin, London, 1934); H.L. May, 'Narcotic drug control – development of international action and the establishment of supervision under the United Nations' (1948) 441 *International Conciliation* 303 at 320 et seq.; B.A. Renborg, *International Drug Control* (Washington, Carnegie Endowment for International Peace, 1947) 14-28; P.D. Lowes, *The Genesis of International Narcotics Control* (Librairie Droz, Geneva, 1966). For a general history of the regulation of drug use see B. Inglis, *The Forbidden Game* (Hodder and Stoughton, London, 1975).

3   See S.K. Chatterjee, *Legal Aspects of International Drug Control* (Nijhoff, Dordrecht, 1981), pp. 3-4.

"opium wars" with the colonial powers[4] forced China to accept legalisation of the trade in 1858.[5] However, negative reaction to the wars and the trade fed support for the anti-opium lobby in Europe and the United States. While the temperance movement objected to the use of opium on moral grounds, commercial interests wanted to break the colonial drug trade to China and replace it with more legitimate forms of trade. These arguments influenced official policy in the United States and although the United States had also profited from the opium trade, it threw its weight behind global prohibition[6] after its domestic opium problem led to the first federal drug control law.[7] Pressure from the anti-opium lobby eventually led to the phasing out of the licit Chinese opium trade.[8] By the turn of the century the many negative consequences of the use of more hazardous substances, such as heroin and cocaine, were also becoming apparent.[9] Pressure to prohibit all drug use except for approved purposes mounted and finally bore fruit during the early twentieth century when the foundations of the international drug control system were laid.

---

4   See E. Holt, *The Opium Wars in China* (Putnam, London, 1964) and B. Inglis, *The Opium War* (Hodder and Stoughton, London, 1976). Karl Marx gives a contemporary view of the trade in D. Torr (ed.), *Marx on China, 1853-1860* (Lawrence and Wishart, London, 1968).

5   The Treaty of Tientsin, signed at the end of the Second Opium War.

6   See A.H. Taylor, *American Diplomacy and the Narcotics Traffic, 1930-1939* (Duke UP, Durham, 1969), chapter 1.

7   See Lowes supra note 2 at 89-90; D.F. Musto, *The American Disease* (OUP, New York, 1987), p. 1 et seq. After 1860 there was a rapid increase in drug use in the United States, mainly because of large scale use of opiates in patent medicines, opium use by migrant Chinese workers, and the acquisition of the Philippines in 1898 which had a significant opium problem. The report of the Philippines Opium Committee into opium abuse revealed a major domestic narcotics problem. It recommended complete prohibition of opium importation into the Philippines, and in 1909 Congress passed this recommendation into the first federal drug control law, the Opium Exclusion Act of 9 February 1909.

8   The Chinese Imperial Edict of 1906 called for the eradication of opium within ten years, and after negotiation the Chinese and British agreed in 1908 to phase out the trade – see Lowes supra note 2 at 75.

9   See Inglis supra note 2 at 131.

2.2   EARLY LEGAL DEVELOPMENTS

The Shanghai International Opium Commission[10] was the first concrete step in the process of development of this system. After American prompting, thirteen states[11] with an interest in opium met in Shanghai in 1909 to exchange views on the opium problem. Participants resolved to suppress opium smoking, to limit its use to medical purposes, to control its export and to control its harmful derivatives, but no attempt was made to regulate penal law. Of very limited legal effect, the most significant feature of the Shanghai Commission was that it established the United States as the, at first unwilling, leader of international drug control.[12]

Under pressure from the anti-opium lobby to see the Shanghai Commission's resolutions transformed into legal obligations, the United States proposed an international legal solution to the opium problem. A conference was held in 1911 at the Hague, and it adopted the International Opium Convention on 23 January 1912 (hereinafter the 1912 or Hague Convention), the first multilateral international drug control treaty.[13]

The 1912 Convention made little provision for suppression of the illicit traffic in drugs. The Americans had proposed adoption of 'uniform provisions of penal laws concerning offences against any agreement entered into by the powers in regard to the opium production and traffic', but the proposal was dropped when the French objected that it would require an unacceptable alteration of domestic law.[14] Article 20, all that remained of the American initiative, provided:

> The Contracting Powers shall examine the possibility of enacting laws or regulations making it a penal offence to be in illegal possession of raw opium, prepared opium, morphine, cocaine and their respective salts, unless laws or regulations on the subject are already in existence.

---

10   See H. Wright, 'The International Opium Commission' (1909) 3 AJIL 648; H. Wright, 'The International Opium Commission (part 2)' (1909) 3 AJIL 827.

11   The UK, US, China, Austria-Hungary, France, Germany, Italy, the Netherlands, Portugal, Russia, Japan, Persia and Siam.

12   See Lowes supra note 2 at 192.

13   8 LNTS 187; in force only generally at the end of World War One. The conference was attended by delegates from China, France, Germany, the UK, Italy, Japan, the Netherlands, Persia, Portugal, Russia, Siam and the US. See H. Wright, 'The International Opium Conference (part 1)' (1912) 6 AJIL 865; H. Wright, 'The International Opium Conference (part 2)' (1913) 7 AJIL 109.

14   H. Wright, 'The International Opium Convention' (1922) 6 AJIL 865 at 869.

Although this modest first attempt to harmonise domestic law criminalising possession of opium failed, it represented the growing perception that effective domestic control of drugs was useless if illicit drugs could be obtained from other states that exercised little or no domestic control.[15] In 1914 the United States enacted the Harrison Act[16] in response to its adherence to the 1912 Hague Convention and to its burgeoning domestic drug problem.[17] This piece of domestic legislation had an enormous national and then international impact because it dealt comprehensively with the drug problem as one of national criminal law, unlike the approach in many other jurisdictions at the time where drugs were dealt with as a medical problem.[18]

2.3   INTERNATIONAL DRUG CONTROL UNDER THE LEAGUE OF NATIONS[19]

The institutionalisation of international drug control took a significant step forward when, upon its formation, the League of Nations assumed supervision of the execution of the 1912 Hague Convention. At the League's first meeting in 1920, the Advisory Committee on the Traffic in Opium and other Dangerous Drugs (hereinafter the Advisory Committee) was established with two functions: to collect and analyse information on the drug traffic, and to encourage compliance with the Convention.[20] Dominated from the outset by diplomats, politicians and police officers, it began a trend within a system that even today subordinates the role of health to policing, politics and international diplomacy.[21] Although formally only an advisory body, the Advisory Committee's formulation of policies with international implications helped to transform national administration of drugs into international administration of drugs.[22] It quickly established itself in the key role of campaigning against the illicit traffic,[23] regularly receiving information from states on cases of illicit trafficking and making an account of this traffic, together with suggestions for its suppression,

---

15   See Renborg supra note 2 at 86.
16   Act of Dec. 17, 1914 C.1, 38 Stat.785 as amended; 26 USC 4701-36.
17   W. B. Eldridge, *Narcotics and the law* (The University of Chicago Press, Chicago and London, 1967), p. 7.
18   See Musto supra note 7 at 282.
19   See generally Q. Wright, 'The Opium Question' (1924) 18 AJIL 281-295.
20   On the Advisory Committee's establishment see Eisenlohr supra note 2 at 43-60.
21   See Lowes supra note 2 at 188-189.
22   Chatterjee supra note 3 at 75.
23   See generally Renborg supra note 2 at 142-146.

to the League's Council. The Advisory Committee also played an important role in securing uniformly severe penalties for drug offenders with the aim of preventing states with inadequate penalties from becoming havens of the illicit traffic.[24] It could not, however, agree that drug trafficking should be considered an 'international crime' because it could not agree upon the definition of an international crime.[25]

Although the League struggled through the 1920s to limit the supply of raw opium,[26] in 1924-1925 a conference was convened in Geneva with the different goal of controlling the manufacture of drugs. It eventually produced the International Opium Convention signed at Geneva on 19 February 1925 (hereinafter the 1925 or Geneva Convention).[27] Of limited material scope,[28] the Convention set out an elaborate export/import authorisation scheme and added to the growing international drug control bureaucracy by establishing the Permanent Central Board (hereinafter the Board) to observe and supervise the international drug trade, which at the time was the main source of supply for the illicit traffic. The Board was given the power to recommend that Parties embargo exports of drugs to other Parties, which it identified as centres of the illicit traffic. With respect to penal law, article 28 of the 1925 Convention provided that each of the Parties

> agrees that breaches of its laws or regulations by which the provisions of the present conventions are enforced shall be punishable by adequate penalties including in appropriate cases the confiscation of the substance concerned.

Article 29 provided that the Parties would examine in the most favourable spirit the possibility of taking legislative measures to render punishable acts

> committed within their jurisdiction for the purpose of procuring or assisting the commission in any place outside their jurisdiction of any act which constitutes an

---

24 See Q. Wright supra note 19 at 287.

25 See Eisenlohr supra note 2 at 83 referring to a rejected Portuguese proposal made in 1930.

26 Producer states opted to rely on government monopolies to control production, and this approach was formalised in the two closed Agreements, the Agreement Concerning the Suppression of the Manufacture of, Internal Trade in, and Use of, Prepared Opium, signed at Geneva on 11 February, 1925, 51 LNTS 337, and the Agreement Concerning the Suppression of Opium Smoking, signed at Bangkok, 27 November 1931, 177 LNTS 373. See generally Q. Wright, 'The Opium Conference' (1925) 19 AJIL 559 at 563.

27 81 LNTS 317; in force September 1923.

28 Raw opium, coca leaves, manufactured drugs and cannabis.

offence against the laws of that place relating to matters dealt with in the present convention.

The 1925 Convention also provided in terms of article 22 that information on illicit exports and imports of drugs would be reported to the Board. Although limited, these first attempts to provide for uniformly heavy penalties, penalise extraterritorial offences and ensure the supply of useful information, identified areas of legal activity that were to be revisited by later instruments.

Despite the conclusion of the 1925 Convention, massive diversion of morphine in the mid-1920s indicated a breakdown in the control system and the supply of illicit drugs by the pharmaceutical industry.[29] The League called for a conference on the limitation of drug production in 1931.[30] The conference adopted the Convention for Limiting the Manufacture and Regulating the Distribution of Narcotic Drugs, signed at Geneva on 13 July 1931 (hereinafter the 1931 Convention).[31] With an enlarged material scope, the Convention was concerned mostly with the limitation of licit drug production. It created a new body of experts, the Drug Supervisory Body (hereinafter the Supervisory Body), which, armed with an estimate of the drug requirements of every state, had the task of preparing annual and supplementary statements on maximum permissible world drug requirements. The Board was given the power to enforce the system through the use of an embargo on the export of drugs to nations exceeding their estimates.[32] The 1931 Convention directed greater attention to the institutional management of the illicit traffic than previous conventions. Article 15 urged Parties to create special administrations to inter alia take 'all useful steps to ... suppress the illicit traffic' and to organise the campaign against drug addiction. Parties also undertook in terms of article 20(1) to supply the League's Secretary General with a list of names and addresses of persons or firms authorised to manufacture or convert drugs and the specific drugs involved, information of value to police authorities in tracing the sources of illicit drugs. The Convention encouraged law enforcement co-operation by obliging Parties to communicate important cases (in the sense of quantities seized or methods used) discovered by them to other Parties through the League's Secret-

---

29 See K. Bruun, L. Pan and I. Rexed, *The Gentlemen's Club* (University of Chicago Press, Chicago, 1975), pp. 223-225.

30 See Eisenlohr supra note 2 at 132-134.

31 139 LNTS 301; in force 9 July 1933. See generally Q. Wright, 'The Narcotics Convention of 1931' (1934) 28 AJIL 475-486.

32 Article 14(2).

ary General. Article 23, which codified the existing practice, obliged states to provide details on:

(a) The kind and quantity of drugs involved;

(b) The origin of the drugs, their marks and labels;

(c) The points at which the drugs were diverted into the illicit traffic;

(d) The place from which the drugs were despatched, and the names of shipping or forwarding agents or consignors; the methods of consignment and the name and address of consignees, if known;

(e) The methods and routes used by smugglers and names of ships, if any, in which the drugs have been shipped;

(f) The action taken by the Government in regard to the persons involved, particularly those possessing authorisations or licenses and the penalties imposed; and

(g) Any other information which would assist in the suppression of the illicit traffic.

An annual summary of these reports had been made from 1925, but from 1931 these reports became quarterly and were circulated ever more widely in order to use publicity to combat the illicit traffic.[33] When it came to the implementation of the new system, the Board succeeded in welding disparate national administrations into a co-ordinated whole, and in its determination of legitimate consumption was unafraid to enquire into the domestic affairs of parties to query over-consumption.[34] But after a time the 1931 Convention's lack of efficacy began to show: non-parties began to produce opium to meet illicit demand; illicit drugs were not destroyed after being seized; and the embargo system was not used against states violating their commitments.[35]

In 1931 the Advisory Committee established a Subcommittee on Seizures and Illicit Traffic with the aim of giving a firmer organisation to its campaign against the illicit traffic.[36] But the campaign faced many problems. When the campaign focused on illicit supply by authorised manufacturers, for example, they relocated, first to states willing to license their factories and ignore their operations, and then, when international attention caught up with them, to obscure parts of the world to set up clandestine factories. The latter proved far more difficult to suppress. The Advisory Committee, unable to intervene direct-

---

33   See Eisenlohr supra note 2 at 84-87.

34   See Eisenlohr supra note 2 at 171-177.

35   See Inglis supra note 2 at 175.

36   See Renborg supra note 2 at 143.

ly, could only try to facilitate effective national policing by information gathering and organising co-operation.[37]

More intrusive methods appeared to be necessary to deal with the increasingly clandestine nature of illicit drug supply. The police assessor on the Advisory Committee had already presented a comprehensive plan in 1930 for the reorganisation of national drugs policing.[38] It called for each state to establish a central bureau to both unify national control over the drug trade and enable international co-operation, and it proposed the establishment of a central bureau for the international control of the drug trade.[39] Significantly, the plan called for extradition arrangements for offenders against important drug laws.[40] Unwilling to embark on a major restructuring of domestic law and practice, the Advisory Committee responded negatively.[41] However, in 1933 a draft convention along similar lines to the plan was submitted to the Committee, and it was passed on to governments for comment. Finally, in 1936 a diplomatic conference on international penal measures against drugs was held.

2.4   THE 1936 GENEVA CONVENTION[42]

As we have seen, prior to 1936, only a few provisions of the existing conventions dealt directly with the criminal laws to be adopted by states. These provisions took the same approach: they named but did not define penal offences, they called for adequate penalisation and tried to deal with extraterritorial crime, and they encouraged law enforcement co-operation. In implementing them many states went much further than was suggested,[43] but only in 1936 did international society attempt major elaboration of international penal control over drugs. The establishment of the licit drug control system through inter-

---

37 See Renborg supra note 2 at 187.
38 In 1923 the Advisory Committee had appointed a police expert as an assessor on the Committee. See generally Eisenlohr supra note 2 at 109-118.
39 The International Criminal Police Congress (ICPC or Interpol), rebuffed initially by the Committee, was granted observer status in 1928 and representative status in 1931.
40 See Eisenlohr supra note 2 at 113.
41 See Eisenlohr supra note 2 at 114.
42 See generally J.G. Starke, 'The Convention of 1936 for the Suppression of the Illicit Traffic in Dangerous Drugs' (1937) 31 AJIL 31-43; Chatterjee supra note 3 at 168-190.
43 See W. Henrichs, 'Problems of competence in international law with regard to the punishment of narcotic drug offences and the extradition of narcotics offenders' (1960) 12 *Bulletin on Narcotics* 1 at 1-2 for an account of German implementation of these provisions.

national law had made this development possible because it marked the line between licit and illicit traffic, thus inviting the international community to endeavour to suppress the illicit traffic.[44]

However, to achieve concrete results, some relaxation of national sovereignty over criminal law was required. The draft convention presented by the ICPC delegates to the Advisory Committee assumed such a relaxation was possible.[45] When asked to comment, governments showed themselves to be more reluctant. They opposed the unification of domestic drug offences due to the diversity of these offences, differences in penalty scales and basic distinctions in matters of principle, although they did favour international agreement on the necessity for severe punishment of these offences. Measures for extradition were also controversial and necessitated the insertion of an escape clause in the draft convention under which a state might refuse to extradite if the offence was considered insufficiently serious.[46] Despite this reluctance and a particular lack of enthusiasm from the United States, which felt that emphasis should have been on implementation of existing provisions,[47] after various redrafts a diplomatic conference met from the 8-16 June 1936 in Geneva and adopted the Convention for the Suppression of the Illicit Traffic in Dangerous Drugs signed at Geneva on 26 June 1936 (hereinafter the 1936 Convention).[48]

The object of the 1936 Convention as stated in the Preamble was 'to strengthen the measures intended to penalise offences' contained in the existing drug conventions and to 'combat by the methods most effective in the present circumstances the illicit traffic in drugs and substances covered by the Conventions.' The Convention aimed to achieve this goal in respect of a list of drugs the scope of which could be varied in terms of article 1.

The first aim of the convention was to harmonise domestic drug offences and penalties. The key provision, article 2, ensured the enactment of domestic legislative provisions by each Party for the severe punishment, particularly by custodial sentences,[49] of a number of specific acts falling under the rubric of

---

44   See Starke supra note 42 at 32.
45   See Starke supra note 42 at 33.
46   See Starke supra note 42 at 34-35.
47   See Taylor supra note 6 at 290-291.
48   198 LNTS 300; in force 26 October 1939.
49   The interpretations clause of the Convention's Final Act noted that the Convention did not restrict Parties in their application of mitigating principles in sentencing. Although the United States was not enthusiastic about the 1936 Convention, the strengthening of criminal penalties was a subject 'particularly favoured' by Harry Anslinger, the US delegate and US Commissioner of Narcotics. See R. King, *The Drug Hang Up:*

'illicit drug trafficking',[50] including the intentional participation in, conspiracy in, attempts towards and preparatory acts towards the commission of these acts.[51] Article 3 obliged Parties exercising extraterritorial jurisdiction over article 2 offences to enact legislation for the punishing of their nationals at least as severely as if the offence had been committed in their own territory.[52] Article 4 specified that the commission of article 2 offences in different countries should be regarded as distinct offences.[53] Article 5 obliged Parties to punish severely the illicit cultivation, gathering and production of drugs but, due to state sensitivity about cultivation, only when their domestic law provided that such actions were criminal.[54] Article 6 provided that where Parties admitted the principle of international recognition of previous convictions, foreign convictions for drug offences should be recognised for the purpose of establishing habitual criminality.

Aiming at elusive traffickers hiding out in foreign jurisdictions, the Convention also made elaborate provision for jurisdiction and extradition. Article 7

America's Fifty Year Folly (CC Thomas, Springfield, 1972), p. 214.

50   They are: 'The manufacture, conversion, extraction, preparation, possession, offering, offering for sale, distribution, purchase, sale, delivery on any terms whatsoever, brokerage, dispatch, dispatch in transit, transport, importation and exportation of narcotic drugs' contrary to the existing conventions. Starke supra note 42 at 39 notes that an effort was made to find an elastic formula which would include all these activities but that would be extendable to new as yet unthought of ways of circumventing the control system. However, due to the vagueness of proposed formulae and government objections, the generic approach was discarded in favour of an exhaustive enumeration of illicit activities, an approach still followed today. The terms used are in themselves open to interpretation, and the fact that "illicitness" is defined by that which is not licit in terms of the licit control system, gives even greater flexibility. However, as Chatterjee supra note 3 at 173 notes, on a strict interpretation of article 2, actions not mentioned by the article are not illicit in terms of the Convention.

51   Starke supra note 42 at 39 notes that through its extension of criminality to conspiracy and attempt, the article had as its object the penalisation of traffickers 'who direct operations from countries which do not punish or do not punish severely complicity or criminal conspiracy in drug offences.'

52   Renborg supra note 2 at 150 notes that this provision had in mind China and India whose local laws were much more severe than the laws applied by the extraterritorial courts to foreign nationals which allowed foreigners to carry on the illicit traffic almost with impunity in these states.

53   Starke supra note 42 at 40 notes that this means that such acts are not to be regarded as an element accessory to a principal offence committed in another country, which avoids the consequence that such an offender may escape liability.

54   This sensitivity about cultivation is also illustrated by the fact that the provisions involving enforcement of the Convention did not apply to article 5.

provided for the situation where a person committed an offence in one Party and was found in another. If that person was a national of the finding Party and the finding Party did not extradite its nationals, it was obliged to prosecute him unless his extradition would have had to be refused for a reason directly connected to the charge (i.e. other than nationality). Article 8 provided that if such a person was a foreigner, he had to be prosecuted and punished as if he had committed the offence in the Party in which he had taken refuge. Extradition, however, had to have been requested and been refused for a reason not connected to the offence, and furthermore the law of the Party of refuge had to allow the prosecution of foreigners for offences committed abroad. Article 9 provided that all the offences under article 2 were extradition offences for the purposes of all existing extradition treaties between Parties. It also provided that where Parties did not recognise extradition as being conditional on the existence of extradition treaties or of reciprocity, such Parties undertook to recognise these offences between themselves as extradition offences. It further provided that extradition should be granted in conformity with the law of the Party to which the application was made, and that any Party to which an extradition order was made could refuse such order if its competent authorities considered that the offence in question was not sufficiently serious.

Finally, the 1936 Convention also made a number of separate provisions relating to law enforcement action and co-operation against the illicit traffic. Article 10 provided for the seizure and confiscation of drugs, substances and instruments intended for the commission of article 2 offences.[55] Article 11 provided that each Party had to set up a central drug control office for the supervision and co-ordination of the campaign against illicit drugs.[56] These offices were to remain in close contact with each other in order to share information that might facilitate prevention and prosecution of drug offences. Article

---

55 Renborg supra note 2 at 153 notes that article 10 was an endeavour to deprive traffickers of the means to carry out their trade, and that it had a very wide scope so as to include the financial resources of traffickers and all kinds of vehicles used for transporting drugs. Starke supra note 42 notes that a proposal made at the conference for the seizure of profits derived from drug trafficking foundered on problems of implementation.

56 Renborg supra note 2 at 93-94 notes that the central drug offices concept grew out of the Advisory Committee's preoccupation with establishing the central drugs administrations envisaged by article 15 of the 1931 Convention. Article 11(5) of the 1936 Convention provided that the powers of central police offices could be delegated to such a central drug administration. In addition, the Final Act of the 1936 Convention recommended that each Party should create specialised police services for the purposes of the Convention.

12 obliged the Parties to share information relating to proposed or ongoing drugs transactions, the identity and description of traffickers and to discoveries of secret drugs factories. Article 13 provided for further arrangements to facilitate communication and co-operation. These arrangements included making provision for the transmission of letters of request from one Party to another, something which was preferably to be done through direct contact between the competent authorities or central offices of each country or through contact between Ministers of Justice or through diplomatic channels. Article 16 obliged Parties to communicate to each other through the League Secretariat the laws and regulations promulgated to give effect to the Convention and annual reports on the working of the Convention.

The 1936 Convention was designed to provide the necessary support in the area of criminal law for the licit drug control system. Yet it received little general support and never became effective law.[57] Its many escape clauses indicate the hesitancy of the conference delegates. Delegations insisted on the inclusion of article 14 stating that participation of a Party in the Convention should 'not be interpreted as affecting that Party's attitude on the general question of criminal jurisdiction as a question of international law.' Another significant provision was article 15, which reads:

> The present Convention does not affect the principle that the offences referred to in Articles 2 and 5 shall in each country be defined, prosecuted and punished in conformity with the general rules of its domestic law.

Although these escape and safeguard clauses had been allowed in order to secure the adherence of recalcitrant states, they did not have the desired effect of encouraging participation.[58] Many states had strong objections to the substance of the Convention, objections that illustrate the kind of stumbling blocks the illicit drug control system would struggle to overcome in the next half century.

Criticisms of article 2, the article providing for penalisation of different forms of conduct, were legion. The American delegates to the Conference had pointed both to the difficulty of describing such offences in a manner that would accord with different domestic legal systems and to the inadvisability of dic-

---

57   B. Renborg, 'International control of narcotics' (1957) 2 *Law and Contemporary Problems* 86 at 102.

58   H.L. May, 'The evolution of the international control of narcotic drugs' (1950) 2 *Bulletin on Narcotics* 1 at 6.

tating the terms of legislation in such detail.[59] The enumeration of offences was also bound to omit some potential forms of illicit conduct. Interestingly, the 1936 Convention did not criminalise use;[60] Renborg notes the offences were 'all in the nature of illicit industrial and commercial transactions'.[61] A further criticism of article 2 was that it failed to provide acceptable definitions for inchoate offences. Conspiracy was included because of Canadian and American concerns about the prosecution of drug traffickers who promoted drug trafficking but did not personally handle the drugs.[62] However, this type of highly developed common law concept was unrecognised in states with civilian legal systems where even the punishment of 'preparatory acts' in terms of article 2(d) required uncomfortable changes to domestic law.[63] With regard to punishment, article 2 was criticised for failing to recognise that many states were constrained by their law to punishing the listed actions with administrative rather than judicial penalties.[64] A conflict also emerged between states adopting a harsh position on punishment for drug offences, the position that has since dominated, and states with more liberal punishment policies. Those states opposed to the stringent punishment regime advocated by article 2 were unwilling to impose the Convention.[65] A final criticism of article 2 is that it made no mention of the mental element required for article 2 offences other than requiring 'intention' for 'participation'. There had been some debate at the conference as to whether the words 'if wilfully committed' should be required for all article 2 offences. Those who favoured requiring wilfulness had pointed out that it would avoid Parties being obliged to punish negligent or inadvertent acts,[66] but the United States and Canadian delegates successfully opposed this stipulation arguing that it would render the successful prosecution of many drug offenders impossible.[67] The interpretation clause inserted into the Final Act ameliorated the exclusion of a specific fault element to some extent when it provided that the provisions of the Convention, and in particular articles 2 and 5, did not apply to offences committed unintentionally.

---

59 See Taylor supra note 6 at 293-294.
60 Possession appears inadequate for covering use in situations such as those in states that differentiate between possession for own use and possession for trafficking purposes.
61 Supra note 2 at 209.
62 See Taylor supra note 6 at 293.
63 Chatterjee supra note 3 at 181.
64 See Chatterjee supra note 3 at 180.
65 See Chatterjee supra note 3 at 180.
66 See Taylor supra note 6 at 293.
67 See Taylor supra note 6 at 293.

Articles 7, 8 and 9, dealing with the punishment of extraterritorial offences struggled to overcome the prevailing antipathy towards extradition and extraterritorial jurisdiction. Although article 7 obliged a Party to prosecute its nationals for extraterritorial offences if it did not extradite them, in terms of article 7(2) prosecution was not obligatory if, in a hypothetically similar case, the extradition of a foreigner could not be granted.[68] Article 8 allowed a Party to prosecute foreigners who had committed offences abroad and were found in its territory, but they could only do so if firstly, 'extradition had been requested and could not be granted for a reason independent of the offence itself.' Such a reason potentially included the amorphous political offence exception.[69] The second qualification to article 8's operation, that the 'law of the country of refuge considers prosecution for offences committed abroad by foreigners admissible as a general rule' rendered the article even more vulnerable, because it was doubtful at the time whether the law of many countries did so.[70] Article 9, the extradition article, was hamstrung by the simple fact that many states did not recognise the principle of prosecution of extraterritorial offences.[71] The provision in article 9(4) of a right to refuse extradition if the requested state felt the offence was not sufficiently serious maintained this trend of non-recognition. States would only extradite in serious cases and in 1936 many states felt that drug offences were not serious enough.[72] It was pointed out at the diplomatic conference that for articles 7 and 8 to function properly, all article 2 offences would have to become extraditable. Article 9 attempted to achieve this by including these offences in every extradition treaty concluded or to be concluded by the Parties, but it created too general an obligation for most states to stomach.

The provisions for law enforcement co-operation, articles 11, 12, 13 and 16, were ambitious but also had shaky foundations.[73] For example, article 11's provision for central offices of supervision ignored the fact that many states did not have the financial or technical capacity to meet this requirement. It required displacement of existing government structures, and did not address the practical problems of maintaining contact with all the relevant authorities in a state with a complex governmental structure. Strengths like the transmission

---

68 See Chatterjee supra note 3 at 184.
69 See Chatterjee supra note 3 at 184.
70 See Chatterjee supra note 3 at 185.
71 See Chatterjee supra note 3 at 185.
72 See statement of Swedish delegate – LN Doc. C.341.M216.1936.XI at 193 (annex. 2).
73 See Chatterjee supra note 3 at 186-187.

of letters of request provision in article 13 were undermined by escape clauses like that in article 13(8) which provided effectively that Parties were not obliged to use uniform methods and procedures to gather information and evidence. Following domestic procedures in such matters often rendered the information gathered legally useless in other jurisdictions.

In general terms, however, the problem was that the 1936 Convention was too complicated and too invasive. States without a drug problem did not want to get involved in a Convention demanding complicated administrative and legal measures,[74] and unlike previous drug control instruments, the 1936 Convention required the alteration of entrenched domestic principles,[75] not just the establishment of novel regulations. The 1936 Convention was the creation of police experts who planned far more serious inroads into national sovereignty than the level of political co-operation available in the League era made possible. By contrast to the attitude of the majority of states, the United States regarded the Convention as too soft on crime and never signed up to it.[76] Premature though it was, Renborg suggests that the 1936 Convention had 'the effect of making illicit drug trafficking a crime of international character, and the punishment and prevention of illicit traffic became the concern of the community of nations.'[77] The penal provisions of the later drug conventions have a surprisingly similar form and content because they are constructed to solve the same problems. In some respects they are less ambitious than the 1936 Convention.[78]

---

74 See Renborg supra note 57 at 102.

75 Chatterjee supra note 3 at 183.

76 The American delegation did not sign the Convention because in their own words 'the stipulations of the Convention do not tend in any increasing measure effectively to prevent or adequately punish the illicit traffic.' See King supra note 49 at 214.

77 Supra note 2 at 27.

78 Despite receiving little support from the international community, because many later conventions did not go as far in their provisions relating to control of illicit drugs, the 1936 Convention is still in force for the limited number of states which remain party to it and it remains open to new parties. Only article 9 of the 1936 Convention deeming the inclusion of drug offences in existing extradition treaties between Parties and providing that they should be regarded as extradition offences by states that grant extraction without treaty, was deleted by article 44(2) of the 1961 Convention and replaced by article 36(2)(b) which now makes this process voluntary.

2.5   THE UNITED NATIONS ASSUMES CONTROL

The Second World War resulted in a breakdown in international drug control, but after the war, with the establishment of the United Nations (UN), the international community began to redevelop the international drug control system under General Assembly and Economic and Social Council (ECOSOC)[79] authority. The Lake Success Protocol of 1946 enabled the conventions previously supervised by the League to be brought into the UN framework.[80] Although the UN's assumption of control did not change the constitution or functions of the Permanent Central Opium Board or Drug Supervisory Body, the UN Commission on Narcotic Drugs (CND), with the UN Division of Narcotic Drugs (DND) as its secretariat and executive arm, took over the role of the Opium Advisory Committee.[81] The CND continued the Advisory Committee's role as the international forum for drug control and established new roles for itself, such as the rendering of technical assistance to UN member states with drug problems. It also persevered with the campaign against the illicit traffic and took over as co-ordinator of the illicit traffic information network.[82] It focused its at-

---

79 In terms of its competence under article 1(3) of the UN Charter in solving problems of an economic, social, cultural, or humanitarian character.

80 Protocol amending the Agreements, Conventions and Protocols on Narcotic Drugs concluded at the Hague on 23 January 1912, at Geneva on 11 February 1925 and 19 February 1925, and 13 July 1931, at Bangkok on 27 November 1931 and at Geneva on 26 June 1936, signed at Lake Success, New York, 11 December 1946, 12 UNTS 179. The Protocol came into force in 1948.

81 The CND initially limited its membership to representatives of 15 UN member states. A 1961 increase to 21 made it possible for representation of states with drug addiction problems and for election of non-UN members. See DND, 'Twenty years of narcotics control under the United Nations' (1966) 18 *Bulletin on Narcotics* 1 at 6. A notable feature of CND membership has been the continuity and influence of certain personnel, illustrated by the fact that Harry Anslinger, US Commissioner of Narcotics from 1930 to 1962 and US representative to the 1931 and 1936 Conferences, was US representative on the CND from its establishment until 1970. See King supra note 49 at 214; Bruun et al supra note 29 generally.

82 From 1946 the DND prepared an annual illicit traffic survey setting out details of drugs seized including amounts, smuggling routes, countries of origin, methods of concealment, prices, penalties imposed by national authorities, nationality of traffickers, and nationality of ships carrying drugs. This survey, supplemented by states, served as the basis for the CND's discussion of the illicit trade – see H.L. May, 'Narcotic drug control' (1952) 485 *International Conciliation* 489 at 507-508.

tention on the development of methods for determining the sources of drugs[83] and on policing methods such as listing and circulating the names of suspect merchant vessels. In what has since become a familiar litany it continually urged states to increase their enforcement efforts, impose severe penalties on traffickers, empower their drug law enforcement agencies, facilitate the direct exchange of information between law enforcement authorities and meet their treaty obligations, particularly with respect to communicating information to the UN.[84]

Rapid legal development took place. The 1948 Paris Protocol extended existing controls to new, mainly synthetic, drugs outside the scope of the 1931 Convention.[85] It was a success, with all of the principal drug manufacturing states becoming party to it and many non-parties applying its provisions. The 1953 New York Protocol,[86] which established the principle of limitation of opium production, restricted the right to export to seven states, and provided the Board with comprehensive enforcement powers,[87] was a more difficult legal pill to swallow and did not enter into force until 1962. This lack of enthusiasm can to some extent be explained by the simultaneous development of the most extensive post-war drug convention, the 1961 Single Convention.[88]

2.6   THE 1961 SINGLE CONVENTION[89]

By the mid-1950s the volume of the illicit traffic was growing and drug supply and use patterns were evolving rapidly. Features of this evolution included the

---

83   See DND supra note 81 at 25-27. The US initiated the programme, and initially it supplied laboratory facilities and maintained a centre for information and sample exchange. After 1954 a narcotics laboratory was established in Geneva as part of the DND.

84   See DND supra note 81 at 28.

85   The Protocol Bringing under International Control Drugs Outside the Scope of the Convention of 13 July 1931 for Limiting the Manufacture and Regulating the Distribution of Narcotic Drugs, as Amended by the Protocol signed at Lake Success, New York, on 11 December, 1946, signed at Paris on 19 November 1948, 44 UNTS 277; in force 1 December 1949.

86   The Protocol signed in New York on 23 June, 1953 for Limiting and Regulating the Cultivation of the Poppy Plant, the Production of, International and Wholesale Trade in, and Use of, Opium, 456 UNTS 3; in force 8 March 1963.

87   See R.W. Gregg, 'The United Nations and the Opium Problem' (1964) 13 ICLQ 96 at 106.

88   See Gregg supra note 87 at 107.

89   See A. Lande, 'The Single Convention on Narcotic Drugs, 1961' (1962) 16 *International Organisation* 776-797.

introduction of drugs to new markets, the formation of multinational drug trafficking rings and the manufacture of drugs in hitherto undeveloped regions.[90]
The successful regulation of the licit drug trade resulted in almost total reliance
by the illicit traffic on illicit sources of supply,[91] yet the illicit traffic still
managed to supply an increasing variety of drugs to an expanding market. The
CND began to move towards a more developmental approach, as the true nature
of the problem became more apparent and legal measures proved ineffective
in extinguishing it.[92] At a political level, international drug control was heavily
influenced by the process of de-colonisation, which resulted in the political
dichotomy of developing producer and developed consumer states that still
polarises drug control today. Before de-colonisation, colonial powers with
colonial interests in drugs such as those interests Britain had in India, had borne
the brunt of most international drug control efforts. After de-colonisation, it
was the newly independent states that were to bear much of the burden of international drug control.[93]

Work on a new unified convention embracing the whole field of drug control
began in 1948.[94] On the 3 August 1948, ECOSOC adopted a CND resolution
requesting the UN Secretary General to prepare a draft convention to replace
the nine existing conventions.[95] The Convention was to have the following
objectives: limiting the production of raw materials; codifying the existing
multilateral drugs conventions into one convention; and simplifying the existing
control machinery.[96] Between 1950 and 1958 the convention went through
three drafts until the CND convened a plenary conference attended by a large
number of states with diverse interests,[97] which met in New York from the
24 January to the 25 March 1961. Finally, on the 30 March 1961, it adopted
the Single Convention on Narcotic Drugs (hereinafter the 1961 Convention).[98]

---

90   See DND supra note 81at 22.
91   See DND supra note 81at 22.
92   See DND supra note 81at 7.
93   See generally M.C. Bassiouni, 'Critical reflections on international and national control
     of drugs' (1990) 18 *Denver Journal of International Law and Policy* 311 at 312-315.
94   See R.W. Gregg, 'The Single Convention for Narcotic Drugs' (1961) 16 *Food Drug
     Cosmetic Law Journal* 187 at 194-195.
95   Resolution 159 IID (VII).
96   See DND supra note 81 at 44.
97   Representatives of 73 states attended the conference including representatives of all the
     major powers except Communist China. They were joined by representatives from the
     Board, the Supervisory Body, the FAO, WHO and Interpol. See generally I.G. Waddel,
     'International Narcotics Control' (1970) 64 AJIL 310 at 315-321.
98   520 UNTS 151; in force 13 December 1964.

The 1961 Convention adopts the indirect approach of the earlier conventions. It places the obligation on the Parties and then monitors the execution of that obligation. The material scope of the 1961 Convention is much wider than that of the previous conventions.[99] It consists of the division of narcotic drugs, based on an assessment of their properties, into four different schedules, and the application of different control regimes to the drugs in these schedules.[100]

The major thrust of the Convention is the regulation of agricultural production, manufacture, trade and consumption of the scheduled drugs.[101] The Convention requires the Parties to limit the production of all scheduled drugs, including opium, exclusively to medical and scientific purposes. It provides for government control of opium cultivation, indirectly limits the number of opium producing states, and limits opium exports to authorised states. Separate systems of control apply to coca bush, cannabis, poppy straw and to poppies cultivated for purposes other than opium production. The 1961 Convention recognises that limitation of agricultural production of drugs would always be a problem for poor states due to the economic, social and cultural importance of these drugs, by only requiring Parties to prohibit cultivation of opium poppies, coca bushes or cannabis plants if they consider it necessary to protect the public health and prevent diversion into the illicit traffic.[102]

In order to control drug manufacturing,[103] the 1961 Convention adopted the measures used in earlier conventions, including the licensing of manufacturers and the estimates system used by the 1931 Convention. These measures are complimented by a statistical returns system that enables an audit of Parties'

---

99   See generally Chatterjee supra note 3 at 344-355.
100 All the general control articles apply to Schedule I drugs in terms of article 2(1). In terms of article 2(2) less stringent provisions apply to Schedule II's list of four drugs not addictive in themselves but capable of being converted into addictive drugs. In terms of article 2(4) even less stringent provisions apply to the drug preparations in Schedule III. Schedule IV is a list of the drugs considered most dangerous, to which it is recommended in terms of article 2(5) that Parties apply special additional control measures, extending, if necessary, to prohibition of manufacture, traffic or use of the drugs, except for medical or scientific use. In terms of article 3 drugs can be added to or transferred from one schedule to another. The power is granted to the CND to determine if a drug should be controlled and if so to place it under a particular schedule, but in doing so it is obliged to consult with the WHO. See Annexure A: Substances Controlled, for an outline of this procedure.
101 See generally Chatterjee supra note 3 at 367-395.
102 See Gregg supra note 87 at 113.
103 See generally Chatterjee supra note 3 at 396-416.

estimates with the aim of restraining the manufacture and importation of drugs by Parties and revealing possible diversion of drugs into the illicit traffic.

The 1961 Convention controls the trade in drugs[104] by applying the principle that legal trade, both national and international, must always be authorised through licensing to distinguish it from illegal trafficking. At the local level, for example, prescriptions are required for the dispensation of drugs to individuals and drugs offered for sale must show the exact drug content by weight or percentage on the label. The 1961 Convention controls the international trade by licensing provisions and through reliance on the import/export authorisation system that requires a state authorising export of drugs to do so only upon receipt of an import certificate from the state of destination.

The 1961 Convention streamlined the drug control bureaucracy by abolishing the Permanent Central Opium Board and Supervisory Body and replacing them with the International Narcotics Control Board (INCB), a body of eleven independent experts entrusted with enforcing the Convention by, inter alia, supervision of the estimates system and statistical returns. The 1961 Convention provides the INCB with a number of ways of forcing Parties to comply with the Convention, including requests for information and explanations, public declarations that a Party has violated its obligations and two embargo procedures, one recommendatory and the other mandatory.[105]

Although significant progress was made in respect of the administration of licit drugs, when it came to the suppression of illicit drugs, international resistance tempered the 1961 Convention's provisions. The draft penal provisions were controversial and despite the inclusion of escape clauses to facilitate their general acceptance, they were rejected by the 1961 Conference. The penal measures eventually adopted are moderate and devised to avoid conflict with the different legal systems of the Parties.[106] Indeed, because they were so mild it was agreed that they would not replace the 1936 Convention for those states that chose to remain party to it and apply its stronger provisions among themselves.[107]

The 1961 Convention's penal measures (articles 35-36) include obligations to punish certain specified offences adequately on a scale commensurate with the seriousness of these offences as well as provisions in respect of jurisdiction,

---

104 See generally Chatterjee supra note 3 at 424-436.
105 See generally Chatterjee supra note 3 at 264-273.
106 See Gregg supra note 94 at 202.
107 In terms of article 44(2) only article 9 of the 1936 Convention is terminated, unless a Party notifies the Secretary General that it is still in force.

extradition and law enforcement co-operation, all of which are subject to the constitutional limitations and domestic law of the Parties. A novelty in the Convention is the obligation on Parties to give attention to providing facilities for medical treatment, care and rehabilitation of addicts (article 38). Given that most states are still party to the 1961 Convention, the analysis of these penal provisions forms part of the substance of this book, and will be dealt with below.

Returning to the general provisions of the 1961 Convention, although constituting the structure for the licit control system today, the Convention's obligations represent a compromise, and the Convention has had its critics, particularly in respect of the weak control of cultivation of drugs. The 1961 Convention embodies the general strategy of the developed drug consumer states to curtail and eventually eliminate the cultivation of drug producing plants, objectives that could only be achieved at some cost to the developing states where these plants were grown. Concerned about the cost, many developing states did not become party to the 1961 Convention. In response to this reluctance, the UN was forced to pay greater attention to the economic and technical capacities of states to apply international drug control law. In fact, quite early on in its tenure of the international drug control system the UN had recognised that the failure of governments to carry out their international obligations or their unwillingness to accept international obligations 'may be due more to lack of capacity rather than lack of desire.'[108] In 1956, all governments had been invited by ECOSOC to apply for technical assistance in the shape of expert advice, training, the holding of seminars and laboratory services. The UN set aside a budget for this assistance which soon extended to the out-posting of UN officers to facilitate co-operation and the co-ordination of regional meetings, missions and consultative groups. Alternative developmental methods of dealing with the drug problem, such as crop substitution, had also become popular with the UN during the 1950s and 1960s. However, the need for extra specially directed funding was patent and finally in 1970 the United Nations Fund for Drug Abuse Control (UNFDAC) was established to provide funding.[109] Significantly, UNFDAC enjoyed major financial support from the United States from the start.

---

108 L.M. Goodrich, 'New trends in narcotics control' (1960) 530 *International Conciliation* 181 at 188.

109 See J.W. Murphy, 'Implementation of international narcotics control: the struggle against opium cultivation in Pakistan' (1983) 6 *Boston College International. and Comparative Law Review* 199 at 230.

2.7   THE 1971 PSYCHOTROPIC CONVENTION[110]

In 1971 the international community took a further step in the expansion of the scope of international drug control. Until 1971, the international system only regulated narcotic substances. Psychotropic substances, stimulants of the central nervous system and hallucinogens, the abuse of which had become common in the 1960s as their variety and availability increased, fell outside the scope of existing instruments. With the option of amending the 1961 Convention rejected on the grounds that the 1961 Convention would become too complex, support for a new convention grew. In 1969, the CND adopted a draft convention, and a plenary conference held in 1971 in Vienna adopted the Convention on Psychotropic Substances, signed at Vienna, 21 February 1971 (hereinafter the 1971 Convention).[111]

The 1971 Convention applies a similar control system to psychotropic substances as the 1961 Convention does to narcotic substances. However, there are differences due to the heterogeneity of psychotropic substances and the different risks connected to their abuse and dependence producing potential. Controls also vary greatly among the groups of psychotropic substances as broken down in the four schedules annexed to the Convention.[112] The Convention does not limit the cultivation of plants from which psychotropic substances are made. The basic obligation imposed on the Parties is to limit the use of psychotropic substances to medical and scientific purposes. The manufacture, export and import of psychotropic substances is controlled through reliance on prohibition, strict supervision and licensing. The international trade in psychotropic substances is controlled by the import-export authorisation scheme. Parties are also obliged to provide information to the INCB on their control systems including an annual report regarding the implementation of the Convention, changes in their domestic law and reports on important seizures of drugs

---

110 See generally Bruun et al supra note 29 at 243-268; Chatterjee supra note 3 at 456-494.

111 1019 UNTS 175; in force 16 August 1976.

112 A. Noll, 'International treaties and the control of drug use and abuse' (1977) 6 *Contemporary Drug Problems* 17 at 19. The process for extending the scope of Convention is similar to that contained in the 1961 Convention. See Annexure A: Substances Controlled. K.F. Ryan, 'Globalizing the problem: The United States and international drug control' in E.L. Jensen and J. Gerber (eds), *The New War on Drugs: Symbolic Politics and Criminal Justice Policy* (ACJS and Anderson Publishing Co., Cincinatti, 1998), p. 141 at p. 148 makes the division of psychotropics into four schedules and has an obvious precursor in the US's Comprehensive Drug Abuse Prevention and Control Act of 1970.

and cases of illicit trafficking. The INCB functions in much the same way as under the 1961 Convention, concerning itself with the maintenance of statistics, appropriate operation of the export-import system, and keeping Parties informed of urgent situations. It retains investigative and embargo powers. However, the 1971 Convention does not provide for an estimates system of each Party's psychotropic substance requirements.

The Convention provides for measures for co-operation against the illicit traffic (article 21) and for criminal sanctions in national law (article 22). A major innovation was the inclusion of provisions relating to the abuse of psychotropic substances including provision for rehabilitation and social re-integration (article 20). The adoption of a more remedial approach was not surprising given the pressure for liberalisation of drug policy in certain states in the late 1960s and early 1970s. Nevertheless, it dissipated support for the Convention.[113] Again, these provisions are examined in detail in the body of this book because they remain binding on most of the member states of the international community.

As a whole the 1971 Convention was modelled on the 1961 Convention but because it was aimed at drug manufacturing states rather than agricultural states, its provisions are not as rigorous as those of the 1961 Convention. It had a mixed reception; some states had reservations about the efficacy of its provisions, but others appeared disturbed by the growing reach of international drug control provisions.[114]

2.8   THE 1972 PROTOCOL TO THE 1961 CONVENTION[115]

Despite the efforts of the international community catalogued above, the United States was dissatisfied with the measures for control of drugs, especially of opium. A conference held in March 1972 in Geneva considered a list of amendments to the 1961 Convention sponsored by thirty nations, and adopted the Protocol Amending the Single Convention on Narcotic Drugs, 1961, signed

---

113 See Bruun et al supra note 29 at 283.
114 Ryan supra note 112 at 148. The INCB noted in 1993 that some of the major manufacturing and exporting states had not yet become party to it or introduced control measures in respect of psychotropic substances – INCB, *Report of the International Narcotics Control Board for 1994* UN Doc. E/INCB/1993/1, p. 2.
115 See generally N.G. Gross and G.J. Greenwald, 'The 1972 Narcotics Protocol' (1973) 2 *Contemporary Drug Problems* 119-163.

at Geneva on 25 March 1972 (hereinafter the 1972 Protocol).[116] The 1972 Protocol does not make dramatic changes to the indirect system of control applied by the 1961 Convention. Rather it fine tunes existing provisions relating to the estimates system, data collection and output, and fortifies law enforcement measures and extradition. Following the 1971 Convention, it also makes greater provision for treatment, rehabilitation and preventive measures, but in this case for users of narcotic drugs. Importantly, the Protocol increases the INCB's monitoring and enforcement powers and strengthens its powers to suppress the illicit traffic.[117] The granting of this power to a purely technical body may have been the result of doubts about the utility of the cumbersome CND, the central policy organ, for suppressing the illicit traffic on a full time basis.

2.9   NEW CONCERNS AND NEW RESPONSES IN INTERNATIONAL DRUG CONTROL

When it came to practical effect, the 1961 Convention, 1971 Convention and 1972 Protocol were fairly successful in the regulation of the licit production, trade and consumption of drugs, although many developing states resisted. With regard to the suppression of the illicit traffic, some progress was also made. Parties moved away from the general criminalisation of drug related conduct in national penal codes[118] and enacted the specialised drug legislation dealing with all aspects of suppression of illicit drugs. But this shift did not result in the suppression of the illicit traffic.

Rather, as Western social attitudes to drugs became more relaxed in the 1960s and 1970s, drug use and drug supply grew, which resulted in turn in some amelioration of Western official attitudes. Domestic developments included the uncoupling, for the purposes of punishment, of the offence of possession from trafficking and the search for more effective non-penal methods of treating and rehabilitating drug users. This change in attitude resulted in a more elastic interpretation of international obligations by some states, but importantly, it

---

116 976 UNTS 3; in force 8 August 1975.
117 Gross and Greenwald supra note 115 at 125-126, note that until 1972 the INCB had been increasingly involved in monitoring the illicit traffic without a specific mandate to do so.
118 D. Cotic, *Drugs and Punishment* (UNSDRI, Rome, 1988), p. 113.

did not result in a fundamental change to either national or international drug policy.[119]

Developed consumer states reacted to the expansion of the variety of drugs available,[120] the growth in the number of users[121] and the increase in drug associated criminal activity by changing the emphasis of their drug control strategy from suppression of domestic drug trafficking to reduction of external supplies.[122] In 1969, President Richard Nixon of the United States took the further momentous step of declaring 'war' on drugs.[123] Already sceptical about the international community's willingness and ability to implement strict drug prohibition, the United States set up its own international drug control system to keep drugs out of its territory.[124] After reorganising and centralising its drug control agencies,[125] it developed a global Narcotic Control Action Plan which extended the international activities of its law enforcement agencies[126] and enforcement jurisdiction,[127] increased extradition of foreign drug traf-

---

119 Ratification of the 1971 Convention was unsuccessfully resisted because it imposed criminalisation of psychotropic substances – see Comment, 'The Convention on Psychotropic Substances: domestic consequences of ratification' (1978) 63 *Iowa Law Review* 950-974. Although it was argued that the US could legalise cannabis in spite of its obligations under the 1961 Convention, and strong efforts were made to decriminalise cannabis at the federal level, they did not succeed. See M.A. Leinward, 'The international law of treaties and United States legalization of marijuana' (1971) 10 *Columbia Journal of Transnational Law* 413-441.

120 The opiates and cannabis were joined by a host of other drugs, including amphetamines, barbiturates, cocaine, crack, benzine, solvents, LSD and mescaline.

121 M.C. Bassiouni, 'Transnational control of narcotics' (1972) *Proceedings of the American Society of International Law* 227 at 228 estimates that there were twenty million addicted or habitual drug users in at least seventy countries in 1972.

122 R. Clutterbuck, *Drugs, Crime and Corruption* (MacMillan, London, 1995), pp. 124-125.

123 E.A. Nadelmann, *Cops Across Borders: The Internationalization of U.S. Criminal Law Enforcement* (The Pennsylvania State University Press, University Park, Pennsylvania, 1993), p. 141.

124 See generally K. Fisher, 'Trends in extraterritorial narcotics control: slamming the stable door after the horse has bolted' (1984) 16 *New York University Journal of International Law and Policy* 353-413.

125 The Federal Narcotics Bureau was replaced by the Drug Enforcement Agency (DEA) in 1973. The DEA has pursued an aggressive anti-drugs policy in foreign jurisdictions since its inception.

126 Nadelmann supra note 122 at 3 notes that between 1967 and 1991, the number of US drug enforcement agents stationed abroad rose from about twelve in eight foreign cities to about 300 in more than seventy foreign locations.

127 See for example, the 1980 Marijuana on the High Seas Act 21 USC section 955(b) which potentially subjects any vessel on the high seas to United States jurisdiction.

fickers, and when that failed or proved impossible, increased reliance on ir-regular rendition or abduction.[128] The United States became heavily involved in the training and funding of foreign drug police,[129] it provided direct aid to foreign governments and greater contributions to UNFDAC and it switched its efforts from crop substitution to law enforcement initiatives such as crop eradication.[130] Importantly, it tried to guarantee the commitment of other states through bilateral drug control treaties.[131] This developed global supply reduc-tion strategy was bound eventually to find its way into a multilateral drug convention. That development took until 1988 because states took time to acclimatise themselves to this new supply reduction approach, and many states only supported further international development as a way of avoiding further unilateral action by the United States.[132]

The UN was the agent for the transformation of this new approach into general international consciousness. Law enforcement co-operation became a priority for the UN and significant developments included the establishment in 1974 by the CND of the Sub-commission on Illicit Drug Traffic and Related Matters in the Near and Middle East, and the Meeting of Heads of National Drug Law Enforcement Agencies (HONLEA), Asia and the Pacific.[133] By the late 1970s, UN organs were committed to organising and funding law enforce-ment programmes and providing a forum for increased international law enforce-

---

128 E.A. Nadelmann, 'The evolution of United States involvement in the international rendition of fugitive criminals' (1993) 25 *New York University Journal of International Law and Politics* 813 at 868.

129 Fisher supra note 124 at 405-407 notes that from 1971 to 1984 22 000 foreign police officials were trained by the DEA in the US, and that from 1973-1984 the US funded a substantial portion of the national police budgets of Mexico, Colombia, Peru, Bolivia, Ecuador, Jamaica, Haiti, Costa Rica, Panama, Pakistan, Turkey, Thailand and Burma.

130 See generally S.R. Murphy, 'Drug diplomacy and the supply side strategy: a survey of United States practice' (1990) 43 *Vanderbilt Law Review* 1259 at 1270-1277. She notes at 1272 that US crop substitution programmes became contingent on eradication of large amounts of the particular state's illicit crop, and through US pressure, UN aid programmes also became linked to drug control efforts.

131 By 1972, thirty such treaties had been concluded.

132 P. Green, *Drugs, Trafficking and Criminal Policy* (Waterside Press, Winchester, 1998), p. 36.

133 A global network of HONLEA meetings slowly developed: the Meeting of HONLEA, Africa, was established in 1985; the Meeting of HONLEA, Latin America and the Caribbean, in 1987; and the Meeting of HONLEA, Europe, in 1990.

ment co-operation.[134] A call for changes in legal assistance and extradition came in 1975, when the Fifth UN Congress on the Prevention of Crime and Treatment of Offenders recommended that consideration be given to the drafting of an international convention on judicial assistance and improved extradition for drug offences.[135] In 1976, ECOSOC urged Parties to the 1961 Convention to criminalise financial support of the illicit traffic.[136] The conclusion of the 1982 UN Convention on the Law of the Sea emphasised the need to control drug trafficking on territorial waters and on the high seas.[137] By this time, the United States was pushing for further development of the international drug control system in order to complement its bilateral efforts. The impact of growing drug use globally induced both developed and developing states to accept the American view that the problem was spreading.[138] The United States believed the problem should be solved by producer states and resorted to economic pressure to make them take action.[139] The UN's 1981 International Drug Abuse Control Strategy reflected American interests in using criminal law to suppress drug supply.[140] By the mid-1980s a new danger emerged in the shape of the threat to the global economy posed by the 'laundering' of

---

134 See Fisher supra note 124 at 408-410. He notes UNFDAC's large scale funding of law enforcement programmes in Afghanistan, Burma, Egypt, Malawi, Malaysia and Turkey in 1981. By this time Interpol was also becoming more heavily involved in drug law enforcement co-operation. An example is the SEPAT plan for analysis of the European drug problem in the 1970s by Interpol officers – see R. Littas, 'The SEPAT-plan and its development' (1979) *International Criminal Police Review* 101-104.

135 See Noll supra note 112 at 30.

136 In 1976, ECOSOC adopted Resolution E/Res/2002 (LX) 'urging governments to enact such legislation as may be necessary to make financial support, by whatever means, in furtherance of the offences set out in article 36(1) of the Single Convention a punishable offence and to co-operate with one another in exchanging information to identify drug traffickers committing such offences.'

137 Article 7 and article 108 respectively of the 1982 United Nations Convention on the Law of the Sea, 21 ILM 261.

138 M. Anderson, *Policing the World* (Clarendon, Oxford, 1989), p. 109 at p. 110 note 4 cites the example of Pakistan. An opium producer since the early 19th century, Pakistan reported its first case of heroin addiction in the 1980s. It was estimated by 1987 to have over half a million heroin addicts.

139 See generally Murphy supra note 130 at 1266-1270. Through the 1986 Anti-Drug Abuse Act the US amended its Foreign Assistance Act to the effect that states that did not co-operate with it in stopping the flow of drugs into the US would be decertified and forfeit all forms of foreign aid from the US.

140 See Ryan supra note 112 at 149.

billion dollar profits.[141] Greater international co-operation was touted by the international drug control lobby as the only method for successfully pursuing this dirty money, and states began to accept that this was indeed the case.

2.10   DEVELOPMENT OF THE 1988 UNITED NATIONS DRUG TRAFFICKING CONVENTION[142]

In the 1980s, with the growth of this global consciousness of the dangers of the illicit traffic,[143] the international community tried to do what it had failed to do in 1936 – produce a successful international convention aimed solely at suppressing the illicit traffic. The spotlight fell on the penal provisions of the 1961 and 1971 Conventions. In the early 1980s the CND convened a number of expert group meetings to discuss their adequacy. The focus was on their extradition provisions, but new measures for the seizure and confiscation of the proceeds of drug offences were also discussed.[144] Following a Venezuelan initiative, in 1984 the General Assembly directed ECOSOC to instruct the CND to prepare a draft convention.[145] The CND resolved that the convention should be concerned with law enforcement, and particularly with such matters as 'controlled delivery' and the 'identification, tracing, freezing and forfeiture of proceeds of drug trafficking'. A draft was circulated to governments for comment and in 1987 the CND considered these comments and the draft convention. ECOSOC then requested the DND to prepare a working document consolidating the first draft and the comments of governments and the CND upon that draft.[146] Controversial elements of this draft convention, such as the classification of drug trafficking as a crime against humanity within the jurisdiction of an

---

141 M.C. Bassiouni, 'The international narcotics control system' in M.C. Bassiouni (ed.), *1 International Criminal Law: Crimes* (Transnational, Dobbs Ferry, 1986), p. 507 at p. 522.

142 See generally the UN's *Commentary on the United Nations Convention Against Illicit Traffic in Narcotic Drugs and Psychotropic Substances, 1988* (New York, 1998) UN Doc. E/CN.7/590 (hereinafter the *1988 Commentary*), pp. 1-11.

143 This consciousness was reflected in instruments such as the 1984 Quito Declaration against Traffic in Narcotic Drugs signed by Bolivia, Colombia, Ecuador, Nicaragua, Panama, Peru and Venezuela (A/39/407), the 1984 New York Declaration against Drug Trafficking and the Illicit Use of Drugs signed by Argentina, Bolivia, Brazil, Ecuador, Peru and Venezuela (A/39/55 and Corr. 1 and 2 annex) and the 1985 Lima Declaration.

144 *1988 Commentary* at 2.

145 GA Resolution 39/141.

146 Resolution 1987/27 of May 1987.

international criminal court, failed the test of general acceptability by states and were omitted. But with growing international support the process of development of the Convention was now firmly on track. The CND was instructed by ECOSOC to prepare a new draft and in 1986 the CND recommended fourteen elements for inclusion in the draft.[147] These included provision for: definitions; seizure and confiscation of the proceeds of drug offences; extradition; precursor monitoring; control of commercial carriers; law enforcement co-operation; mutual legal assistance; controlled delivery; adequate sanctions for offences; interdiction of vessels on the high seas; eradicating illicit drug plant cultivation; control of free ports and free trade zones; control of illicit drug manufacturing equipment; and prevention of the use of the mail for trafficking. Under pressure from the General Assembly to deliver[148] the CND requested the DND convene an open-ended intergovernmental expert group to discuss the draft, which consisted only of substantive provisions. Endorsed by ECOSOC,[149] the Expert Group met from 29 June to 10 July and 5 to 16 October 1987 and again from 5 January to 5 February 1988. The subjects under discussion included comments made by governments and members of the CND and the preambular and implementing provisions. The CND reviewed the revised draft in early 1988, forwarded some articles for consideration to the forthcoming diplomatic conference but also submitted a draft resolution to the ECOSOC recommending further preparation before the holding of such a conference. ECOSOC made provision for the convening of a Review Group to review certain of the draft articles before the diplomatic conference.[150] The Review Group met from 27 June to 8 July 1988, and adopted a report including both settled articles as well as variations of controversial provisions, because many states had still noted their difficulties with provisions such as those for mutual assistance in law enforcement and the posting of liaison officers.[151]

While the "hard" law of international drug control was being developed, it was simultaneously being fleshed out in "soft" law. In June 1987 the UN Secretary-General convened a ministerial conference, the 'International Con-

---

147 Resolution 1 (S-IX) *Official Records of ECOSOC, 1986*, Supp. No.3 (E/1986/23) chap. X, section A.
148 GA Resolution 41/26.
149 Resolution 1987/27.
150 Resolution 1988/8.
151 Anderson supra note 138 at 116.

ference on Drug Abuse and Drug Trafficking'.[152] Delegates from 138 states to the 1987 Conference approved a wide range of recommendations, contained in the Comprehensive Multidisciplinary Outline of Future Activities in Drug Abuse Control. The Outline provides a broad framework for drug abuse control, and presages many of the provisions of the forthcoming convention.[153] It focuses on four main areas: prevention and reduction of demand for drugs; control of supply; suppression of trafficking; treatment and rehabilitation of addicts,[154] and sets specific targets and actions to be taken at national, regional and international levels.[155] But no particular order of priority is proffered and

---

152 The idea of an international conference on drug abuse was floated by the UN Secretary General in 1985. The same year the General Assembly adopted Resolution 40/122 setting the goals for the Conference as the adoption of a multidisciplinary outline of future steps to be taken at national, regional and international levels to combat drug abuse and illicit trafficking. See V. Kaufman, 'United Nations: International Conference on Drug Abuse and Illicit Trafficking' (1988) 29 *Harvard International Law Journal* 581-586.

153 Reprinted in 26 ILM 1638 (1987); *Declaration of the International Conference on Drug Abuse and Illicit Trafficking and Comprehensive Multidisciplinary Outline of Future Activities in Drug Abuse Control* (UN Publication St/Nar/14, UN Sales No. E.88.XI.1, New York, 1988); see also UN Secretariat, *Report of the International Conference on Drug Abuse and Illicit Trafficking, Vienna 17-26 June 1987* (UN Publication A/Conf.133/12, UN Sales No. E.87.I.18, New York, 1987).

154 The outline sets out 35 targets within these four major areas. The chapter on prevention and demand reduction suggests efforts be made to develop methodologies and to institute systems to assess the prevalence and trends of drug abuse on a comparative basis and to implement the necessary measures to reduce demand. The chapter on supply control promotes programmes and projects for integrated rural development activities, including crop eradication and substitution schemes, as well as the development and implementation of the necessary procedures to eliminate the supply of substances used in the manufacture of illicit drugs. The chapter on suppression of illicit trafficking offers suggestions for the development of mutual legal assistance through bilateral or multilateral treaties or arrangements, including extradition and ways of tracing, freezing and seizing drug profits. This chapter also contains suggestions for improving the dissemination of information to national and international law enforcement bodies and for further developing international financial, technical and operational co-operation on drug-related investigations. The final chapter is devoted to treatment and rehabilitation and suggests means to develop, promote and evaluate effective treatment techniques and to provide health professionals with information and training concerning the appropriate medical use of drugs.

155 For example, seven targets are presented with respect to demand prevention and reduction, viz.: assessment of the extent of drug misuse and abuse; organisation of comprehensive systems for the collection and evaluation of data; prevention of drug abuse through education; prevention of drug abuse in the workplace; prevention programmes by civic, community and special-interest groups; leisure-time activities in the service

each state is left to determine whether and how it wishes to employ the recommendations, taking into account its own political and economic requisites. A Political Declaration, announcing the priorities of states to be inter alia strengthening international co-operation, striving for universal accession to the drug conventions and recognising their responsibility to provide appropriate resources for elimination of the drug problem, was also adopted at the 1987 Conference.[156] Both the Outline and Political Declaration are as concerned with reduction of drug demand and the rehabilitation of users as they are with supply reduction. Significantly, however, the former concerns had to be left in the realm of soft law because the 1987 Conference was not willing to adopt these provisions in a formal legal instrument creating rights and obligations. By contrast, the Political Declaration recognised that mandatory treaty provisions were required to give content to the framework for the suppression of illicit drug trafficking provided by the 1987 Conference.[157] Two processes of development were going on, but only one was to receive legal sanction, a pattern of development that reflects the constricted focus and political strength of international prohibitionists.

Delegates to the 1987 Conference gave the development of the new convention support and ECOSOC decided to convene a diplomatic conference to settle the new convention.[158] The draft convention put to the plenary conference held in Vienna from the 25 November to the 20 December 1988 contained a wide range of national and international measures aimed at providing the international community with more effective weapons against the illicit drug traf-

---

of the continuing campaign against drug abuse; and programmes undertaken through public information media. Suggested courses of action at the national level to meet the first target, assessing the extent of drug abuse, include: reviewing current methodologies for epidemiological studies of drug abuse; reviewing present methods of data collection; and establishing central records for storing and evaluating data. At the regional and international level the possibilities include: comparative studies by regional organisations of drug abuse patterns; the establishment of formal agreements for international collaboration in the measurement of international drug abuse patterns; and technical assistance to states by international organisations such as the WHO, in the planning and carrying out of epidemiological surveys.

156 'Declaration of the International Conference on Drug Abuse and Illicit Trafficking' 26 ILM 1722 (1987).
157 26 ILM 1723 (1987).
158 Resolution 1988/8.

fic.[159] Attended by representatives from 106 states, a variety of intergovernmental and non-governmental organisations, and other observers, the 1988 Conference adopted, by consensus, the 1988 United Nations Convention Against
Illicit Traffic in Narcotic Drugs and Psychotropic Substances (hereinafter the
1988 Convention).[160] The Convention was open to ratification or accession
by states and regional economic organisations, and it came into force, very
rapidly, on 11 November 1990.

2.11   OVERVIEW OF THE 1988 CONVENTION[161]

The Preamble to the Convention, which serves as an aid to interpretation of
the Convention's substantive provisions,[162] has a number of separate strands,
representing to an extent the different concerns of different states. These different strands serve as a useful introduction to the Convention.

The first strand of the Preamble involves the general reasons for adopting
the Convention. Paragraph one of the Preamble recognises that the magnitude
of the international drug problem in all its forms, including both supply and
demand, is the Convention's major rationale because of the impact of this problem on society and even upon the sovereignty of states. Given that all but a
few of the provisions of the Convention are devoted to supply reduction this
seemingly general concern is not borne out in the substance of the Convention.

The Preamble's second strand relates to more specific problems confronted
by international society and sets out the Convention's specific responses to these
problems. Paragraph two recognises the importance of the need to protect social
groups particularly vulnerable to drugs, such as children.[163] Paragraph three
singles out the links between illicit drug trafficking and other forms of organised

---

159 *United Nations Conference for the Adoption of a Convention against Illicit Traffic in
Narcotic Drugs and Psychotropic Substances, Official Records, Volume II* (New York,
1991) UN Doc. E/CONF.82/16/Add.1, UN Publication Sales No. E.91.XI.1, p. 155
(hereinafter *1988 Records* vol. II), pp. 1-2.

160 UN Doc. E/CONF.82.15; UKTS 26 (1993). The procedure for adoption was somewhat
unusual: the two Committees of the Whole of the Conference submitted their work
directly to the Drafting Committee. It submitted the Convention to the Conference which
adopted it by consensus without consideration of its separate articles.

161 See generally D.P. Stewart, 'Internationalizing the war on drugs: the UN Convention
Against Illicit Traffic in Narcotic Drugs and Psychotropic Substances' (1990) 18 *Denver
Journal of International Law and Policy* 387-404.

162 Article 31 of the Vienna Convention on the Law of Treaties, 1115 UNTS 331.

163 See also article 3(5)(f) and (g).

crime which undermine the economies of states and threaten state sovereignty, but does not stipulate these other illicit activities.[164] Paragraph four recognises that 'illicit traffic is an international criminal activity' which must be suppressed as a priority. Paragraph five recognises the economic threat posed by the illicit traffic, particularly by the large profits of the illicit traffic which lead to the corruption of society at all levels including public and private enterprise. Paragraph six prescribes the medicine for this disease – depriving illicit traffickers of the proceeds of their criminal conduct and thus eliminating their main incentive for trafficking. This medicine is concretised in several of the Convention's substantive legal obligations relating to the combating of drug money laundering.[165] Paragraph seven is the only one of the Preamble's paragraphs solely concerned with the drug abuse problem. It articulates a desire to eliminate the 'root causes' of the problems of drug abuse including, somewhat anachronistically given the context, demand,[166] and, less surprisingly given the Convention's concern with trafficking, the enormous profits derived from the illicit traffic.[167] Paragraph eight introduces another law enforcement concern together with the technique for combating it, namely the monitoring of precursors, chemicals and solvents to prevent their ready availability to the traffic for the manufacture of drugs.[168] Paragraph nine of the Preamble identifies another aspect of law enforcement requiring attention in the Convention, namely, improving international drug law enforcement co-operation at sea.[169]

The final strand of the Preamble relates to the organisation and general purpose of the international drug control system. Paragraph ten recognises that the suppression of illicit trafficking is a collective state responsibility and that all states must co-operate to this end within the UN framework of international co-operation. Paragraph eleven recognises the UN's competence in international drug control and expresses the desire that international drug control organs

---

164 The *1988 Commentary* at 16 mentions arms trafficking, subversion, terrorism, fraud and points out that they include local as well as national organised criminal activities. See also article 3(5)(a) and (b) and article 9(1)(a).

165 See article 3(1)(a)(v), article 3(1)(b), article 3(1)(c)(i), article 3(4)(a), and article 5. For convenience sake I have situated most of the general discussion of this approach to drug money laundering in the discussion under article 5.

166 See article 14(4).

167 See article 5.

168 See article 12.

169 See generally article 17.

should remain within the UN family.[170] Paragraph twelve of the Preamble formally acknowledges and affirms the guiding role of the extant international drug control system created through the 1961 Convention, 1971 Convention and 1972 Protocol, but paragraph thirteen of the Preamble recognises the need to reinforce and expand this system to counter the illicit traffic while paragraph fourteen recognises the need for legal co-operation to this end.[171] Finally paragraph 15 expresses the desire of the Convention's authors to conclude an instrument effective in a practical legal sense against the illicit traffic in all its forms including those forms not previously confronted by international law. Paragraph 15 advocates a holistic approach but with a specific focus – a narrow concern with the illicit traffic – which mirrors the concern of the Preamble as a whole and makes the Preamble an appropriate introduction to the 34 articles and one annexure of the 1988 Convention.

The first substantive provisions of the Convention are found in the definitions section which provides specific definitions of terms used in the substantive articles of the Convention (these are examined in the body of this book) or confirms definitions used in the earlier conventions.[172] Perhaps the 1988 Convention's most significant substantive feature is article 2, entitled 'Scope of the Convention'. Discussed above in Chapter One, article 2, which asserts state sovereignty in the face of international obligation, is a sign-post to the tensions prevalent in international drug control – the tensions between supply reduction and demand reduction as dominant drug control strategies, the tensions between consumer states and supply states, and the tensions between intrusive international intervention and the bulwark of national sovereignty.[173] These tensions are also manifested in the rest of the provisions of

---

170 ECOSOC see article 22; CND see articles 12, 20 and 21; INCB see article 12, 22, 23 and 32; UNDCP see article 5, 7, 17, 20, 23, 27, 28, 29, 30, 31 and 34; ICJ see article 32.
171 See articles 5, 6, 7 and 11.
172 For example, 'cannabis plant' and 'coca bush' have the same definitions as in the 1961 Convention.
173 See foot-note 80 and the accompanying text. There were many examples of the tensions between consumer and producer states at the 1988 Conference. D.W. Sproule and P. St-Denis, 'The UN Drug Trafficking Convention: An Ambitious Step' [1989] CYBIL 263 point out that the Mexican delegation consistently tried to water down the Convention's obligations by replacing 'shall' with 'undertakes to propose ... to its competent legislative authorities' in several key obligations under the Convention, thus making these provisions non-binding (see, for example, Mexico's proposed definition of draft article 2(1) in 'Further proposals put forward at the Review Group meeting relating to the text of the draft Convention for consideration by the Conference' UN Doc. E/

the Convention. Because examination of these provisions forms the substance of this book, it is enough to point out here that they provide the structure for an extensive legal regime for the suppression of the illicit drug traffic. This regime includes new offences such as money-laundering, new forms of international co-operation in areas like confiscation, new obligations in the fields of extradition and jurisdiction, and new law enforcement techniques such as controlled delivery.[174]

The rest of the 1988 Convention is devoted to final provisions, of which most are standard,[175] although the following are worth singling out. Article 24 allows Parties to impose stricter measures if they are of the opinion that stricter measures are desirable or necessary for the prevention or suppression of the illicit traffic, and as long as they do not intrude on the national jurisdictions of other states. Article 25 makes it clear that the provisions of the Convention shall not derogate from any rights enjoyed or obligations undertaken by Parties under the earlier conventions, thus making it clear that the new Convention in no way affects or weakens existing international obligations assumed by Parties. Specific provision is made for overlaps in relevant articles.[176] Article 31 dealing with amendments and article 32 dealing with settlement of disputes are discussed in Chapter Seven below. One unfortunate omission is that there is no article dealing with reservations. The committee that dealt with this matter did not regard this deliberate omission as an invite to states to make reservations, but rather held that the issue was governed by the 1969 Vienna Convention on the Law of Treaties, which contains a broad provision to the

---

CONF.82/3 Annex IV).

174 See W.C. Gilmore, *Combating International Drug Trafficking: The 1988 United Nations Convention Against the Illicit Traffic in Narcotic Drugs and Psychotropic Substances* (Commonwealth Secretariat, London, 1991), p. 42.

175 Article 26 states that the Convention is open to signature by all states, Namibia as represented by the UN Council for Namibia, and regional economic organisations having competence in matters covered by the Convention. Article 27 makes provision for ratification, acceptance, approval or an act of formal confirmation. Article 28 makes provision for accession. Article 29 makes provision for entry into force (the Convention came into force 90 days after the deposit of the 20th instrument of ratification/accession). Article 30 provides for denunciation. Article 31 provides for amendments. Article 32 provides for settlement of disputes. Article 33 provides for the authentic texts of the 1988 Convention. Article 34 makes the Secretary General the depositary for the Convention.

176 Thus, for example, it is expressly provided in article 14 that measures taken to eradicate illicit cultivation shall not be less stringent than those provided in earlier conventions – see the *1988 Commentary* at 395-396.

effect that reservations that are not compatible with the object and purpose of the treaty are not permitted.[177] It left unanswered the problem of who determines what is or is not incompatible with the treaty. In the absence of a reservations provision some states seemed to feel that reservations were not permitted by the prevailing international law, while others felt they were, and some states immediately made reservations.[178] Finally, the 1988 Conference also passed three non-binding resolutions that are simply invitations to states to take certain actions. In anticipation of a long delay before application, resolution two urged states to provisionally apply the 1988 Convention because of the slowness of both the ratification process of states and the legislative process in states compared to the urgent need to take action against the rapidly growing drug use.[179]

Resolution two was overly pessimistic. The Convention has received the kind of support that the 1936 Convention did not get. It has been backed by the United States, the Commonwealth Heads of Government, and in early 1990 the General Assembly urged states to take the necessary steps to become party to it and to apply its provisions where practicable.[180] The first recommendation of the 1990 Report of the Group of Seven's Financial Action Task Force (FATF) was that 'each country should, without further delay, take steps to fully implement the Vienna Convention and proceed to ratify it.'[181] Many of the most important producer, transit and consumer states have signed the Convention and the ratification/accession process has been very rapid. The Convention came into force on 11 November 1990, and by 31 January 1997 one hundred and thirty eight states and regional IGOs such as the European Union had become party to it. In 1994, the INCB cautiously stated that it believed that the Convention had led to enhanced drug control.[182] Yet there have been complaints that states heavily involved in production and trafficking of drugs hastened to ratify

---

177 *1988 Records* vol. II at 316-317, 320-322.

178 *1988 Records* vol. II at 36-37.

179 Pakistan delegate's statement, *1988 Records* vol. II at 20.

180 See Gilmore supra note 174 at 42 citing UN General Assembly Resolution S-17/2/1990 'Political Declaration and Global Programme of Action', p. 6.

181 Recommendation One of the 'Financial Action Task Force on Money Laundering Report on 6 February 1990' in W.C. Gilmore (ed.), *International Efforts to Combat Money Laundering* (Grotius, Cambridge, 1992), p. 4 at p.15.

182 INCB, *Report of the International Narcotics Control Board for 1994* UN Doc. E/INCB/ 1994/1, p. 2.

the 1988 Convention without changing their practices or bringing their legislation into line with it.[183]

2.12   INTERNATIONAL DRUG CONTROL FROM 1987 TO THE PRESENT

The 1988 Convention and the 1987 Comprehensive Multidisciplinary Outline were the key elements in a major drug-control programme launched by the UN in the late 1980s.[184] While the 1988 Convention has spawned a number of regional international drug control agreements based very closely upon it,[185] the Outline has been used as the major policy guide by regional drug control organisations such as the Inter-American Drug Abuse Commission (CICAD) and national governments. Yet the UN felt that further support for its drug control efforts was necessary. Nineteen ninety saw the adoption by the General Assembly of a Political Declaration and Global Programme of Action on Drug Abuse Control, a call for government action in numerous areas with a view to attacking the drug problem at the national, regional and international levels using a variety of methods.[186] Nineteen ninety also saw the General Assembly

---

183 B. Leroy, 'The United Nations strategy' in G. Estievenart (ed.), *Policies and Strategies to Combat Drugs in Europe* (Nijhoff, Dordrecht, 1995), p. 27 at p. 37. E. Marotta, 'Drugs as a priority in co-operation in the fields of justice and home affairs' in G. Estievenart (ed.), *Policies and Strategies to Combat Drugs in Europe* (Nijhoff, Dordrecht, 1995), p. 369 at p. 372 complains of a weakening of the 'Vienna spirit' which drove the development of the 1988 Convention.

184 See generally Leroy supra note 183 at 30-32; R. Rolley, 'United Nations activities in international drug control' in S.B. Macdonald, B. Zagaris (eds), *International Handbook on Drug Control* (Greenwood Press, Westport, 1992), pp. 415-433.

185 See for example the 1990 South Asian Association for Regional Co-operation Convention on Narcotic Drugs and Psychotropic Substances reprinted in W.C. Gilmore (ed.), *Mutual Assistance in Criminal and Business Regulatory Matters* (Grotius, Cambridge, 1995), p. 185. The Convention Applying the Schengen Agreement of 14 June 1985 between the Governments of the States of the Benelux Economic Union, the Federal Republic of Germany and the French republic, on the Gradual Abolition of Checks at Their Common Borders, in force 19 June 1990, makes a number of direct references in chapter 6, entitled 'narcotic drugs', to Parties' obligations under the drug conventions.

186 UN General Assembly Resolution S-17/2/1990. The areas of focus included eliminating illicit demand for drugs; treatment, rehabilitation and social reintegration of drug addicts; control of drug supply; suppression of illicit trafficking; the illegal use of the banking system; strengthening judicial and legal systems; measures against the diversion of arms and explosives to traffickers; and the use of the existing resources and structures of the UN for drug control – see 'International co-operation against illicit drugs: Political

establish the System-Wide Action Plan on Drug Abuse Control, intended to serve as an instrument to co-ordinate the anti-drug abuse activities of the UN drug control organs and to strengthen co-operation in respect of drug control within the UN system as a whole.

Against the background of these plans and programmes and the UN's declaration of the 1990s as the 'United Nations Decade Against Drug Abuse', the UN undertook a significant restructuring of its international drug control machinery. The General Assembly made provision for the consolidation of the UN drug control system's administrative structures into a single structure with the general objective of more effective resource utilisation in order to meet the threat presented by the growing illicit drug trade.[187] The DND, the secretariat of the INCB and UNFDAC were integrated into the United Nations International Drug Control Programme (UNDCP), based in Vienna and headed by a Director-General. Responsible for implementing the policy decisions of the CND and ECOSOC, the UNDCP took over the treaty functions of the INCB's secretariat and the DND and the operational functions and the technical co-operation projects once executed by UNFDAC, the DND and the INCB's secretariat.[188] The financial resources of UNFDAC were placed under UNDCP control and became what is now referred to as the Fund of the UNDCP.

The CND and INCB were left intact and functioning in their treaty defined roles, but the General Assembly requested the CND to consider ways of improving its functioning as a policy-making body, and as a result, in 1991 the CND's mandate was enlarged by ECOSOC[189] and by the General Assembly.[190] In effect the CND became the governing body of the UNDCP with the power of approval over the budget and programme of the Fund of UNDCP. The CND was also mandated to monitor and review the implementation of the UN's drug control plans. In order to broaden the CND's representational base to keep pace

---

Declaration and Global Programme of Action' (1990) 16 *Commonwealth Law Bulletin* 929-931.

187 GA Resolution 45/179, 21 December 1990, entitled 'Enhancement of the United Nations structure for drug abuse control'.

188 One of the UNDCP's major tasks since the reorganisation has been to secure ratification and effective implementation by states of the drug conventions, particularly the 1988 Convention.

189 Resolution 1991/38.

190 Resolution 46/185 C.

with the global expansion of the drug abuse phenomenon, the number of representatives was increased.[191]

In November 1997 the UN's organs in Vienna were rearranged in a new management structure.[192] The UN Office for Drug Control and Crime Prevention (ODCCP) was established as the umbrella body with the purpose of bringing the UN's efforts against drug traffickers, terrorists, money launderers and other international criminals under one roof. Its director was placed in control of the UNDCP and of the Centre for International Crime Prevention (CICP), formerly the UN's Division for Crime Prevention and Criminal Justice, which deals with other offences of international importance and provides administrative services for the UN's Commission on Crime Prevention and Criminal Justice. While the UNDCP and CICP remain separate entities with separate resource bases, the ODCCP's task is to integrate approaches to fighting organised crime generally, and drug trafficking in particular, in the belief that there is no practical division between these activities. But budget shortfalls also dictated a leaner organisation in Vienna, and reorganisation has also been driven by the need to keep the UN's drug control organs at centre stage in international drug control as other non-UN organs, such as the G7's Financial Action Task Force (FATF),[193] have assumed a prominent role in drug control.

The UN capped its "Decade Against Drug Abuse" in 1998 by a Special Session of the General Assembly on International Drug Control[194] at which member states adopted a Political Declaration reasserting their strong commitment to drug control as a priority at national and international levels. The Declaration emphasises implementation of the 1988 Convention and other provisions of the drug conventions to reduce drug supply and demand.[195] The General Assem-

---

191 Membership in the Commission grew from 15 States in 1946 to 21 in 1961, 24 in 1966, 30 in 1972, 40 in 1983, and 53 in 1991.

192 The restructuring took place as a result of the UN Secretary General's reform proposals made in July of 1997; see UN Doc. A/51/950 Action 8.

193 The scale of money laundering has bolstered FATF's importance. FATF estimated in 1990 that $122 billion per annum was being generated from the sale of cocaine, heroin, and cannabis in the US and Europe alone, of which as much as $85 billion was available to be laundered – see 'FATF Money Laundering Report, 1990' in Gilmore supra note 181 at 6.

194 Held from 8-10 June. The origin of the session was ECOSOC Res. 1996/17 and GA Res. 51/64.

195 In terms of the Declaration members states agreed by 2003 to: i) establish new or enhanced drug reduction strategies or programmes; ii) establish or strengthen national legislation and programmes to combat the illicit manufacture of amphetamine type stimulants and their precursors; iii) strengthen multilateral, regional and bilateral co-

bly also adopted a Declaration on the Guiding Principles of Demand Reduction[196] and a Resolution on Measures to Emphasise International Co-operation to Counter the World Drug Problem. The laudable goal of these measures is a drug free world, but the decade of drug-abuse control was not an unqualified success. A 1998 evaluation of the 1990 System Wide Action Plan on Drug Abuse Control found that it had failed to meet its objectives.[197]

Greater concern in the 1980s and 1990s at the international level with enforcing global prohibition and supply reduction has been coupled with the resurgence of a tougher line on drugs domestically. In the United States, the flood of crack, a cheap smokeable form of cocaine and the spread of Aids through sharing hypodermic needles, resulted in massive increases in national funding for law enforcement. The 'war on drugs' has become a permanent feature of American foreign policy.[198] The many strategies of this war, from military intervention in drug producer states[199] to mutual legal assistance,[200] have outweighed any attention to 'demand reduction' which also took on a

---

operation against criminal organisations. By 2008 they agreed to: i) eliminate or significantly reduce manufacture, marketing and trafficking in drugs and diversion of precursors; ii) achieve significant and measurable results in demand reduction; iii) achieve significant and measurable results in the reduction of illicit cultivation.

196 This Declaration contains: i) standards to assist governments to establish demand reduction programmes by the target date; ii) standards to guide the setting up of effective prevention, treatment, and rehabilitation programmes and calls for adequate provision of resources for such programmes.

197 Expert Group Report, *Strengthening the United Nations Machinery for Drug Control* E/CN.7/1999/5, 7 December 1998, p. 8.

198 For an official US view see R.S. Williamson, 'International illicit drug traffic: the United States response' (1983) 35 *Bulletin on Narcotics* 33-48.

199 The US military and intelligence communities became increasingly involved in the 1980s. See Fisher supra note 24 at 391-400; L.A. Keig, 'A proposal for direct use of the United States military in drug enforcement operations abroad' (1988) 23 *Texas International Law Journal* 291-316. A high point of extraterritorial military involvement was Operation "Blast Furnace", involving the use in July 1986 of US armed forces in Bolivia against Cocaine laboratories and smugglers airstrips in Bolivia. It proved singularly unsuccessful, and was condemned, despite the Bolivian President's consent, as a violation of international law – see D.G. Wadler, 'Operation Blast Furnace: The United States involvement in Bolivia to put the heat on drug traffickers' (1987) 2 *Journal of International Dispute Resolution* 175-203. See also M.E. Welch, 'The extraterritorial war on cocaine: perspectives from Bolivia and Colombia' (1988) 12 *Suffolk Transnational Law Journal* 39-81.

200 See generally T.M. Catino, 'Italian and American co-operative efforts to reduce heroin trafficking: a role model for the United States and drug supplying foreign nations' (1990) 8 *Dickinson Journal of International Law* 415-440.

punitive character with the introduction of notions of 'user accountability'.[201] The United States has also remained committed to the internationalisation of the war on drugs in the 1990s[202] and polices the implementation of international instruments like the 1988 Convention through economic sanctions.[203] The rest of the developed world has tended to follow the American line, although some less enthusiastically than others.[204] In Europe, official policy has also hardened, with a trend towards broader and tougher sanctions, the enactment of stiffer penalties for possession and distribution, and laws designed to seize drug trafficker's assets and to prosecute drug trafficking conspiracies more effectively.[205] European regional organisations began to get involved in drug control from the early 1970s onwards, and their role in fostering a tougher approach to drug control has grown through the 1980s and early 1990s.[206] In the developed world generally the removal of internal border

---

201 'Zero tolerance' as William Bennet called it – see D. Baum, 'Tunnel vision: the war on drugs, 12 years later' (1993) 79 *American Bar Association Journal* 70 at 72.

202 S.A. Gardner, 'A global initiative to deter drug trafficking: will internationalizing the drug war work?' (1993) 7 *Temple International and Comparative Law Review* 287 at 315-316.

203 For example, the US determined that in 1994 and 1995 the Nigerian Government had not taken adequate steps to achieve full compliance with the goals and objectives of the 1988 Convention and imposed foreign assistance reductions on Nigeria – DEA *Nigeria Country Report* (1995).

204 States such as Canada have not been as committed to supply reduction as the United States. N. Gilmore, 'Drug use and human rights: privacy, vulnerability, disability, and human rights infringements' (1996) 12 *The Journal of Contemporary Health Law and Policy* 355 at 402 notes that while the US spent roughly 71% on supply reduction and 29% on demand reduction in the early 1990s, Canada's figures were 30% and 70% respectively.

205 Nadelmann supra note 122 at 197.

206 The Pompidou Group, set up in 1971, assumed a role in drug control (it has since been incorporated in the Council of Europe) – see generally C. Brule, 'The role of the Pompidou Group of the Council of Europe in combating drug abuse and illicit drug trafficking' (1983) 35 *Bulletin on Narcotics* 73. T.J. David, 'The British Government's international anti-drugs work' (1991) 17 *Commonwealth Law Bulletin* 1368 at 1372 describes the work of other European anti-drugs groups such as the TREVI Group, founded in 1975, as a loose inter-governmental structure to co-ordinate the fight against terrorism. Initiatives in the TREVI Group to examine the scope for developing a drugs liaison system monitoring developments in producer countries led to the European Drugs Intelligence Unit for the exchange of operational intelligence among EC members. In 1990 the European Convention on Money Laundering (30 ILM 148; in force 1 September 1993) was adopted and in 1991 a Directive on Money Laundering (EC Directive 91/308) was issued. The European Union has been involved in anti-drug production initiatives

restrictions, the ascription of drug trafficking to ethnic immigrant minorities, and the rise in the use of psychotropic substances, has seen greater emphasis on co-operation to enforce prohibition.[207]

The position in the developing world ranges from extremely punitive to mildly punitive prohibition. Whilst most states in Africa and South America have been ambivalent, some have accepted the role of proxies for the drug war.[208] Asian states have been some of the most eager advocates of the renewed war on drugs, and have in many cases taken an apparently much tougher stance than the United States.[209] One unforeseen consequence of the globalising of drug prohibition is that it has driven up illicit production in developing states. Fuelled by economic necessity due to the drying up of foreign economic aid in the post-cold war era, this rise in production has resulted in two disturbing trends: the increased use of drugs in these states, and an increase in corruption.[210]

Despite apparent global support for what has become in effect an international war on drugs, a war in which international law plays a key role, recent trends in agricultural production and synthetic drug manufacture, detection of illicit laboratories, drug seizures and demand all show steady increases in these

---

in the Caribbean (1995) and Asia (1997). Dissent from the war on drugs in Europe is exemplified by the 1990 Frankfurt Resolution by European Cities on Drug Control Policy (EDCP) calling for a revision of prohibitionist policies.

207 For an overview of the illicit drug trade in the 1980s and early 1990s see the 'Introduction' to Macdonald and Zagaris supra note 184 at 7-15.

208 Under the Clinton administration the US began to channel its producer country control efforts through the agency of local drugs police, with some success – see P.B. Stares, *Global Habit: The Drug Problem in a Borderless World* (Brookings Institution, Washington DC, 1996) at 45.

209 See S.L. Harring, 'Death, drugs and development: Malaysia's mandatory death penalty for drug traffickers and the international war on drugs' (1991) 29 *Columbia Journal of Transnational Law* 364-405. He notes that Malaysia's president, Dr Mahathir bin Mohamed sought out the chair of the 1988 Conference in order to promote Malaysia's tough anti-drugs stance, which includes the death penalty for drug traffickers and detention of suspects for up to two years without trial in terms of the Dangerous Drugs (Special Preventive Measures) Act 316 of 1985 (as amended in 1990).

210 R. Seccombe, 'Squeezing the balloon: international drugs policy' (1995) 14 *Drug and Alcohol Review* 311-316 notes the link between the introduction of drug control laws and the phenomenon of increased drug use in producer and transit states. At pp. 313-314 he gives as examples the rapid spread of heroin addiction in Pakistan from 1980 after the passing of the Prohibition Order of 1979 which restricted licit cultivation of opium.

activities.[211] In the 1990s agricultural drug production has become more sophisticated with greater yields from smaller crops and more potent plants, and the spread of refining facilities globally. Drug trafficking has adapted itself to modern commercial transport systems with heavy use of ship and vehicle-borne containers making for large-scale movement of drugs. Drug consumption, although fairly stable in the developed world is growing quite rapidly in the developing world.[212] The laundering of drug profits remains a major concern, as does the growth of transnational crime generally. The growing disparity of wealth between the developed and developing worlds, the globalisation of capitalism in the post-cold war era, the deregulation of the global economy, and the resurgence of ethnic conflict and nationalism have all contributed to the growing illicit drug trade.[213]

2.13   CONCLUSION

The history of the international regulation of drug control is really a history of the development of two parallel strategies to deal with a problem that in the modern era first became of international concern because of its impact in China, and then in America and then, gradually, globally. The first, the creation of the control system for the trade in licit drugs was initiated earlier than the second, the international control of illicit drugs. International law could only logically follow this pattern of development, as the definition of licit behaviour is an absolute precondition of the definition of illicit behaviour.

The system of commercial regulation of drugs was initiated by the Shanghai Opium Commission and developed by the conventions that followed. This development followed a three pronged approach: first, by confining the international drug trade to medical and scientific purposes; second, by confining the manufac-

---

211 A. Wells, *International drug control: recent developments, patterns and trends* (unpublished conference paper, New Delhi Global Drugs Law Conference, 1997) at pp. 4-6 sets out the now as usual alarming statistics. Taking just one drug, cocaine, his statistics indicate a doubling in size of the coca leaf crop between 1985-1994, a shift in laboratory sites to growing areas, steady increases in seizures of drugs and precursors, the tripling of global cocaine production since 1980 to around 900 tons and an estimated user population of between 30-45 million.

212 See generally Stares supra note 208 at 3-5.

213 S.E. Flynn and G.M. Grant, *The Transnational Drug Challenge and the New World Order: The Report of the CSIS Project on the Global Drug Trade in the Post-Cold War Era* (The Centre for Strategic and International Studies, Washington, 1993), pp. 2-3.

turing and then the agricultural production of drugs to the same purposes; third, by confining the consumption of drugs to the same purposes. The stress throughout was on the control of material. As May puts it, 'the Conventions should be considered as restrictive commodity agreements rather than health measures.'[214] This system is a system of indirect control; it relies on states to apply the law in good faith and then regulates the behaviour of these states. Economic sanctions in the form of embargoes are available against defaulting states, but it is by its nature a consent-based system that does not rely heavily on coercive/ extreme sanctions for its implementation, or else states simply would not comply. The system is generally regarded as functioning in a satisfactory manner.[215]

By the 1930s, the commercial regulatory system was already well established, and a brief switch in emphasis was made to developing measures to extinguish the illicit traffic which had grown up to serve drug users. Minor provisions to control the illicit traffic had been included in the early conventions, but the suppression of illicit activities by means of criminal law and enforcement really began with the abortive 1936 Convention. It failed because international society was not yet ready for the derogation of national sovereignty necessitated by the development of international rules controlling criminal activity. Further minor progress was made in the 1961 Convention as amended and in the 1971 Psychotropic Convention, but only in 1988 was another full scale attempt made to provide for legal regulation in this area with the conclusion of the UN Drug Trafficking Convention. It appears that the 1988 Convention has escaped the fate of the 1936 Convention because of the political support flowing from the greater scale and breadth of the drug problem today. Moreover, many of the provisions of international drug control law viewed with a great deal of suspicion in 1936, such as those that provide for extension of extraterritorial jurisdiction, extradition, and law enforcement co-operation, are not viewed with the same suspicion today as states have become more accustomed to co-operating in the suppression of crime. However, the presence of escape clauses in the drug conventions indicates that states are still wary of international drug control and jealous of their sovereignty. International society is only slowly becoming used to indirect international control of penal drug law.

---

214 Supra note 2 at 305.

215 INCB, *Effectiveness of the International Drug Control Treaties: Supplement to the Report of the International Narcotics Control Board for 1994* UN Doc. E/INCB/1994/1/Supp.1, p. 4.

The international drug control system has been a success as a commercial regulatory measure, but the strategy to extinguish the illicit drug problem has, at least thus far, failed. The system has tried for a century to balance two goals, viz.: making possible the supply of drugs for licit purposes, and suppressing the supply of drugs for illicit purposes. These goals may be irreconcilable and it may be that the system has served more to keep drug companies in business than to put illicit traffickers out of business. Enactment of severe laws and tighter law enforcement has always tended to be followed by a surge in the illicit traffic and a rise in illicit drug prices. It may be that efforts to extinguish illicit supply and use have failed because they attempt to control the lives of individuals, whereas licit regulation has succeeded because it depends upon influencing the conduct of government administrations, professionals and private enterprise.[216] The stock response to criticism of international prohibition's failure is that illicit drug supply and use would be far more widespread and would constitute a far greater menace to the whole world without international drug control.[217] But this response remains speculation.

---

216 See Bruun et al supra note 29 at 276-7.
217 See for example Renborg supra note 2 at 111.

OFFENCES AND PENALTIES

3.1   GENERAL

The international illicit drug control system functions to apprehend and successfully prosecute individuals who commit certain drug related offences wherever
they commit them, whatever their degree of complicity, whether they complete
these offences or not, and then to punish such offenders appropriately so that
they and others are deterred from engaging in such conduct. This chapter
examines whether the offences and the penalties set out in the drug conventions
are appropriate to these general functions. Adopting a common dichotomy, it
examines offences and penalties separately, although the articulation of offences
and penalties in the same provisions makes it necessary to examine them in
one chapter. But it is important to note at the outset that strictly speaking the
drug conventions do not create a system of international offences[1] and international penalties. They broadly describe a number of offences and suggest
a range of penalties, both offences and penalties to be defined and applied by
national legal systems. Thus international law initiates a top-down process that
results in the criminalisation and punishment of certain drug related conduct.
Although the definitions of offences and penalties are guided by both the ordinary meaning of the terms used in the drug conventions and the interpretation
given those terms by inter alia the UN and other Parties, each offence and each
penalty is essentially national in its content, and international only in general
character. The "offences" listed in the international conventions are not offences

---

1   The term offence is generally used here in preference to the term crime because of its
     consistent use in the drug conventions. Offence is as the *Commentary on the Convention
     on Psychotropic Substances, 1971* (New York, 1976) UN Doc. E/CN.7/589; UN
     Publication Sales No.E.76.XI.5 (hereinafter the *1971 Commentary*), explains at p. 348,
     a broader term than crime, and includes all violations of the criminal law no matter
     how serious.

at all, but are merely terms used to set out the obligations Parties assume to render certain conduct criminal, and so too with penalties. However, if a Party claims to meet its obligations under the conventions through a domestic offence or penalty that does not or only partly meets the definitions of offences or penalties laid down in the drug conventions, the Party in question may well be in breach of its international obligations. For convenience sake, the general terms offence and penalty have been used to describe these indirect legal obligations.

3.2   OFFENCES

3.2.1   Introduction

In essence, the illicit traffic involves the supply of drugs created by non-medical or non-scientific demand. Thus for the execution of a drug supply reduction strategy, the content of the definition of illicit drug trafficking is crucial. Flynn and Grant define drug trafficking as follows:

> At its heart, drug trafficking is a transnational business with five stages: (1) the production of the raw materials, (2) their refinement into the final product, (3) the transportation of the product to their markets, (4) wholesale and retail distribution within these markets, and (5) the investment/laundering of the profits.[2]

International society has made a major effort in the drug conventions to settle upon a series of definitions of conduct, which adequately cover the entirety of this process, from production through all the levels of engagement with the drugs until they are delivered to the user. It includes how profits are dealt with because they serve as the rationale for supply. Personal use offences fall outside the illicit traffic, but controversially are criminalised by the system mainly because of pressure from drug producer states on consumer states to do something about demand.

When defining these offences, the authors of the drug conventions tried to lay down international guidelines sufficient to determine a harmonious set of national drug offences facilitating international law enforcement co-operation

---

2   S.E. Flynn, G.M. Grant, *The Transnational Drug Challenge and the New World Order: The Report of the CSIS Project on the Global Drug Trade in the Post-Cold War Era* (The Centre for Strategic and International Studies, Washington, 1993), pp. vii-viii.

against drug offenders. The problem inherent in attempting to impose harmony by international agreement is the difference in national grammars of criminal law. Any attempt to impose harmony has to overcome the fact that states criminalise the same conduct in completely different ways. Conduct that may be the subject of a single offence in one state, may be the subject of more than one offence elsewhere, or may not be criminalised at all. Participation in offences may be broken up into various degrees in some states while others have not adopted sophisticated taxonomies. A major point of divergence is the criminalisation of conduct preparatory to an offence with, for example, some states having well developed notions of "conspiracy" utterly foreign to others.

When defining the drug offences the authors of the conventions had two options. They could withdraw from the problem of overcoming distinctive national grammars and choose generality, that is criminalising all conduct not defined as legal in terms of the international system. The alternative was to attempt to impose some degree of harmony by specifying the various forms of conduct to be criminalised. Generality presents few sovereignty obstacles for adoption. It results in an indeterminacy that makes for ease of passage into domestic law but for little international standardisation. Specificity has roughly the reverse effect, being more effective from the point of view of those who seek coherence within the system. The 1961 Convention, its amended version and the 1988 Convention opt for the latter approach while the 1971 Convention opts for the former. Political pressure for effective prohibition means that the international community has tended to take the more difficult option, but this does not mean that it has opted for perfect uniformity. To achieve this, Henrichs notes that the conventions would have to define 'the offences exhaustively, and in that way ... establish a system of definitions that would be uniform in the territories of all the states parties.'[3] The drafters of the drug conventions were forced to abandon strict uniformity, as it was unlikely to lead to either agreement or application. However, the conventions do attempt a limited specificity of definition of illicit conduct that demands more of Parties than generality. It introduces the potential for a measure of harmony, but realisation of that potential depends on actual enactment of the same or similar offences by Parties.

Specificity of definition demands a specific examination of each offence. Generally, in this chapter, the first step of this examination explores the basis for the criminal nature of the conduct, that is, the unlawfulness of each form

---

3   W. Henrichs, 'Problems of competence in international law with regard to the punishment of narcotic drug offences and the extradition of narcotics offenders' (1960) 3 *Bulletin on Narcotics* 1 at 7.

of conduct as generated by the international obligation itself and as potentially limited by the existence of constitutional and domestic safeguard clauses.[4] Next, it examines the nature of the conduct itself, that is, the various forms of conduct that describe unlawful actions relating to drugs. Finally, it examines the fault element required to establish criminal liability for the conduct.

3.2.2 The offences stipulated by the 1961 Convention as amended by the 1972 Protocol

3.2.2.1 General

The 1961 Convention focuses on the illicit traffic, which it defines as cultivation or trafficking contrary to its provisions.[5] Article 36, entitled 'Penal Provisions', is, for the purposes of the criminalisation of drug related conduct, the central article in the 1961 Convention. It is drafted in fairly general terms in order to make it more acceptable to a large number of states and so avoid the fate of the 1936 Convention.[6] It was not intended to be self-executing, even in Parties whose constitutions make provision for the self-execution of international treaties.[7] Article 36(4) provides that nothing contained in article 36 'shall affect the principle that the offences to which it refers shall be defined, prosecuted and punished in conformity with the domestic law of a Party.' Before turning to a consideration of the different offences, two points are worth noting.

First, it is important to recall that all the drugs included in Schedule I of the 1961 Convention are subject to all of the control measures under the Convention including the prohibitions on illicit conduct. The drugs included in Schedule IV may in terms of article 2(5) be subjected to a range of extra measures at the discretion of the Parties.

---

4   The former subject the Parties' obligations to the constitutional principles or basic concepts of their legal systems, the latter to their domestic law and other legal concepts and principles – see D.W. Sproule and P. St-Denis, 'The UN Drug Trafficking Convention: An Ambitious Step' [1989] CYBIL 263 at 270, notes 29 and 30.

5   Article 1(1)(l). The *Commentary on the Single Convention on Narcotic Drugs, 1961* (New York, 1973) UN Publication Sales No. E.73.XI, (hereinafter the *1961 Commentary*), notes at p.11 that the 'term "trafficking" not only includes all forms of trade and distribution, but also manufacture and "production", i.e. the "separation of opium, coca leaves, cannabis and cannabis resin from the plants from which they are obtained".'

6   Statement of the Canadian delegate – *United Nations Conference for the Adoption of a Single Convention on Narcotic Drugs, Official Records, Volume I* (New York, 1964) UN Doc. E/CONF.34/24, UN Publication Sales No. 63.XI.4 (hereinafter *1961 Records* vol. I), p. 122.

7   *1961 Commentary* at 440.

Second, article 36 adopts an enumerative method but it was designed to be considered against the background of the broad prohibitions set out in the Convention. In terms of article 2(5)(b), a Party may elect to prohibit the 'production, manufacture, export and import, trade in, possession or use of any [Schedule IV] drug except for amounts which may be necessary for medical and scientific research only', if it believes that the conditions prevailing within its territory render prohibition the most appropriate means of protecting the public health and welfare. At a more general level, in terms of article 4(1)(c) Parties are subject to the key obligation 'to limit exclusively to medical and scientific purposes the production, manufacture, export, import, distribution of, trade in, use and possession of drugs.' In addition, article 33 provides that 'the Parties shall not permit the possession of drugs except under legal authority'. However, these general prohibitions do not determine the precise obligations on Parties to criminalise certain forms of conduct. Article 2(5)(b) is optional. Article 33 allows possession under legal authority, leaving the question of unlawful behaviour largely undefined. The duty in article 4(1)(c) to limit to medical and scientific purposes the various forms of drug related conduct enumerated is a 'General Obligation' specifically 'subject to the provisions of this Convention'. As such it cannot bind Parties to criminalise these actions if they are not specifically criminalised in the provision dealing with offences, i.e. article 36. In essence unlawful forms of conduct are stipulated in article 36, but in deciding what is unlawful supply and so forth Parties must first, using the rest of the Convention for guidance, define what is lawful supply. The authors of the Convention undoubtedly hoped that the scheme they created would have no holes – the specific offences would complement the lawful conduct perfectly. Thus if the Convention regulated any particular form of conduct the Convention was designed to get the Parties to criminalise any failure to comply with that regulation. Thus, for example, in the case of the obligation in article 29(3) on all Parties to require manufacturers of drugs to apply for a permit to manufacture, the Convention was designed to get the Parties to criminalise the failure of a manufacturer to apply for a permit. Unlicensed manufacture would be unlawful 'manufacture' of drugs in terms of article 36(1). However, the problem arising from enumerating the unlawful forms of conduct in article 36(1) is that if an individual fails to obey a regulation stipulated in the Convention but such failure is not stipulated as an offence in terms of article 36(1), Parties are not obliged to criminalise that form of conduct. Moreover, the general prohibitions cannot oblige Parties to criminalise conduct in the absence of a specific obligation to do so. The most pertinent example of such a lacuna, discussed below, is possession of a drug for personal use.

3.2.2.2   Article 36(1)'s standard offences

Article 36(1), which is left unaltered by the 1972 Protocol,[8] specifies and pro-scribes various drug related offences that Parties are under a duty to criminalise in their national law. The provision anticipates that Parties 'shall adopt' the necessary measures, confirming that the obligation is not self-executing. The duty to criminalise such conduct has in most cases been executed through some form of drug control legislation, but a few Parties have insisted that they may also use administrative measures.[9]

Illicit or unlawful conduct is defined as being 'contrary to the provisions' of the 1961 Convention as a whole[10] or more specifically, drug related conduct for non-medical and non-scientific purposes.[11] However, to make sense it should read conduct contrary to the national legislation as, in strict technical terms, the Parties criminalise the conduct, not international law. Moreover, the precise contours of illicit conduct in each specific case is a question of the substance and execution of domestic drugs legislation because, as noted above, article 36(4) provides that these offences 'shall be defined, prosecuted and punished in conformity with the domestic law of a Party'. Article 36(1) makes it clear that the criminalisation of conduct is subject to each Party's 'con-stitutional limitations'.[12] However, although accepted in principle, the existence of constitutional limitations preventing a Party from implementing article 36(1)

---

8   Article 14 of the 1972 Protocol simply changes article 36(1) into article 36(1)(a) and adds a provision on rehabilitation as article 36(1)(b).

9   See, for example, Austria's declaration upon accession to this effect (1/2/1978) – *Multilateral Treaties Deposited with the Secretary General: Status as at 31 December 1996* (New York, 1997) UN Doc. St/Leg/Ser.E/15 (hereinafter *Multilateral Treaties Deposited* (1997)), at p. 282.

10   Article 1(1)(m).

11   Article 4(c).

12   The elaboration of this proviso in article 36(2) to 'subject to the constitutional limitations of a Party, its legal system and domestic law' indicates that article 36(1) supports the interpretation that the refusal to criminalise cannot be based on anything less than the constitution. On the difference between the two escape clauses, see *United Nations Conference for the Adoption of a Single Convention on Narcotic Drugs, Official Records, Volume II* (New York, 1964) UN Doc. E/CONF.34/24/ Add.1, UN Publication Sales No. 63.XI.5 (hereinafter *1961 Records* vol. II), at pp. 236-237.

seems doubtful[13] except in the case of 'possession' of drugs for personal use.[14]

With respect to the conduct criminalised, article 36(1) takes a two pronged approach, viz. it specifically enumerates different forms of conduct and, in addition, provides a general formula to cover actions contrary to the provisions of the 1961 Convention that are not enumerated. While article 1(1)(m) defines 'illicit traffic' generally as 'cultivation or trafficking in drugs', and article 4 (c) talks of limitation of the 'production, manufacture, export, import, distribution of, trade in, use and possession of drugs', article 36(1)'s enumeration allowed the drafters of the Convention to describe in some detail and fairly exhaustively the range of illicit conduct that can be associated with drugs.[15] It is not clear whether they anticipated Parties enacting separate offences with respect to each form of conduct listed, or whether they expected Parties to enact catchall offences that would criminalise all of the forms of conduct. Thus an offender who simultaneously engaged in cultivation, sale and transport, might in state A be liable for three different offences while in state B he might be liable for three counts of the offence of, for instance, 'drug trafficking'. In practice, most Parties have specifically criminalised most of the forms listed,[16] while a few have relied on generic terms to meet the obligation.[17] Ultimately,

---

13 Article 36(1)'s obligation may arguably conflict with rights to freedom of commercial activity but Parties appear to have been content to limit these rights in respect of drug trafficking offences. Federal states may have constitutional difficulties in implementing the obligation in article 36(1), but the *1961 Commentary* at 429 submits that they are obliged to obtain the necessary action by the legislatures of their component states/ provinces.

14 For examples of state practice see note 227 infra.

15 The enumeration of these activities closely follows the list in article 2(a) of the 1936 Convention.

16 For example, section 6(1) of the Austrian Narcotic Drugs Amendment Act of 1977, Bundesgesetzblatt No.1978/532, provides: 'Persons who wittingly and in violation of these provisions produce, import, export or trade in narcotic drugs in such quantities as to constitute a general danger to human life or health shall be guilty of an offence against the public health.'

17 In South Africa, for example, the Abuse of Dependence Producing Substances and Rehabilitation Centres Act 41 of 1971, made 'dealing' in drugs an offence (sections 2 and 3), and then defined dealing (section 1) as 'performing any act in connection with the collection, importation, supply, transhipment, administration, exportation, cultivation, sale, manufacture, transmission or prescription' of drugs.

the question of how the provision is applied is a domestic affair, but examination of the enumerated forms of conduct illustrates that they are quite distinct.[18]

The first five forms of conduct mentioned refer to steps in the creation of drugs. 'Cultivation', according to the definitions in article 1(1)(i), means exclusively 'the cultivation of the opium poppy,[19] coca bush[20] or cannabis plant.'[21] The 1961 Convention is not concerned with other plants. It is important to note that article 22 of the 1961 Convention permits but does not oblige Parties to prohibit the cultivation of these plants. Thus licit cultivation is possible, and the 1961 Convention regulates the licit cultivation of the opium poppy (article 23), coca bushes and coca leaves (article 26) and cannabis (article 28).[22] Article 36(1) is concerned with domestically unregulated, illicit, pro-

---

18   The *1961 Commentary* at 428 notes that some Parties penal codes may not consider some of these forms of conduct to be the conduct of principals, but only as secondary forms of participation as defined in article 36(2)(a)(ii).

19   'Opium' is defined in article 1(p) of the 1961 Convention as 'the coagulated juice of the opium poppy'; the 'opium poppy' is defined in article 1(q) as 'the plant of the species *Papaver somniferum L*'; while 'poppy straw' is defined in article 1(r) as 'all parts (except the seeds) of the opium poppy after mowing.

20   'Coca bush' is defined in article 1(e) of the 1961 Convention as 'the plant of any species of the genus Erythroxylon'; 'coca leaf' is defined in article 1(f) of the 1961 Convention as 'the leaf of the coca bush except a leaf from which all ecognine, cocaine or other ecognine alkaloids have been removed.'

21   'Cannabis' is defined in article 1(b) of the 1961 Convention as the 'flowering or fruiting tops of the cannabis plant (excluding the seeds and leaves when not accompanied by the tops) from which the resin has not been extracted, by whatever name designated'; 'cannabis plant' is defined in article (1)(c) as 'any plant of the genus cannabis'; while 'cannabis resin' is defined in article 1(d) as 'the separated resin, whether crude or purified, obtained from the cannabis plant'.

22   Cannabis provides a good example. Because cannabis plants were still cultivated in many states in 1961 such cultivation was not prohibited by the Convention; instead it was subject to a special regime. Article 28(2) specifically excludes cannabis cultivated for industrial purposes from the material scope of the convention. Article 28(1) provides that where a Party permits the cultivation of cannabis, it is obliged to apply the same system of controls that apply to the cultivation of opium. Article 22(1) provides that a Party is only obliged to prohibit cultivation when the prevailing conditions render it a suitable measure for protecting the public health and welfare and preventing the diversion into the illicit traffic. Most Parties have done so, which raises the interesting problem of whether they can repeal prohibition of cultivation relying on the implied discretion in article 22(1) or whether once taken this is an irreversible step unless the other Parties to the Convention agree. Cannabis seeds and leaves fall outside the scope of the definition of cannabis in article 1 although article 28(3) obliges Parties to adopt measures to prevent the misuse of and illicit traffic in cannabis leaves. K. Dawkins, 'International law and legalising cannabis' [1997] *New Zealand Law Journal* 281-282,

hibited cultivation. 'Cultivation' involves the fostering or nurturing of the growth of the plants while they are still in the ground; to cultivate in general legal parlance is to 'till, prepare for crops, manure, plough, dress, sow, and reap, manage and improve by husbandry'.[23] 'Production' according to article 1(1)(t) 'means the separation of opium, coca leaves, cannabis and cannabis resin from the plants from which they are obtained,' an agricultural operation as distinct from the industrial process involved in the manufacture of drugs.[24] 'Manufacture', according to article 1(1)(n), 'means all processes, other than production, by which the drugs may be obtained and includes refining as well as the transformation of drugs into other drugs.' 'Manufacture' is the industrial process complimentary but distinct from 'production'. It covers a wide range of substances and processes[25] but does not include the transformation of drugs into substances not covered by the Convention. No definition is given for 'extraction' under section 1 but it usually involves the derivation of drugs or the taking out of drugs from a substance; to extract is 'to draw out or forth'.[26] Nor does section 1 define the verb 'preparation', which usually involves the preparation of a substance for use as a drug; to prepare is 'to make ready'.[27] Specifically in the context of drug supply it may mean the mixing or compounding of one

---

ingeniously suggests that the Convention permits the decriminalisation of cultivation of small quantities of cannabis leaves and seeds for private use.

23   *Black's Law Dictionary* (3rd edn 1951), p. 454.

24   See *1961 Commentary* at 26. The *Commentary* points out at 27 that it follows from the limitation of the production of drugs to the plants listed that the separation of drugs from any other plants will be 'manufacture'. So too will the separation of any other drugs than those listed from the plants listed. The separation of drugs from poppy straw is not production and is covered by an entirely separate regime.

25   The *1961 Commentary* at 14-21 sets out in detail the various facets of the manufacturing process as contemplated by the 1961 Convention. It includes the refining of drugs, the transformation of drugs into their salts, the manufacture of isomers, esters and ethers of scheduled substances (if possible), and the conversion of drugs into other drugs. It notes that 'conversion' must include in certain circumstances the conversion of drugs into substances not classified as drugs under the 1961 Convention, although it is clear that the authors of the 1961 Convention did not intend to criminalise such manufacture because they did not consider these substances harmful. 'Manufacture' does not include fabrication of the preparations of drugs or the production of drugs from the plants defined in 'production', but includes the separation of any new drugs from those plants and from other plants. The *1961 Commentary* also notes at 428 that 'manufacture' covers 'extraction' and 'preparation' and explains the overlap because article 36(1) closely follows article 2(a) of the 1936 Convention.

26   *Black's Law Dictionary* (3rd edn 1951), p. 698.

27   *Black's Law Dictionary* (3rd edn 1951), p. 1344.

substance with one or more buffer substances or diluents and subsequent division into units or packaging for therapeutic or scientific use.[28] It is submitted, however, that preparation of a drug by a user for immediate use, for example the rolling of cannabis into a cigarette, is not preparation because if it were it would blur the distinction between drug supply, which is criminalised by article 36, and drug use, which is not. Domestic application of the defined forms of producing drugs is not coherent. While the forms appear to be specifically defined by article 36, they are used interchangeably in the domestic legislation that has resulted from observance of the 1961 Convention.[29]

'Possession' is a legal term of art in most jurisdictions. It usually includes an element of physical control and a consciousness of control, although it takes on a variety of forms, such as actual and civil possession, specific to certain situations.[30] When exploring the meaning of 'possession' in article 36(1) it is useful to begin by noting that 'use', or personal consumption of drugs, is not listed in article 36. Therefore, in spite of the fact that article 4 (c) of the Convention requires Parties to limit 'the use and possession' of drugs to medical and scientific purposes, no specific obligation exists under the 1961 Convention to punish unauthorised use in international law. Parties are free to choose whether to criminalise use or to rely on legal measures controlling the illicit traffic to control use indirectly.[31] The meaning of possession itself is more controversial. Article 4(1)(c) obliges Parties to limit possession to medical and scientific purposes, article 33 makes it clear that Parties must not permit the

---

28 The definition offered for the same term in the 1988 Convention by the *Commentary on the United Nations Convention Against Illicit Traffic in Narcotic Drugs and Psychotropic Substances, 1988* (New York, 1998) UN Doc. E/CN.7/590; UN Publication Sales No.E.98.XI.5, (hereinafter the *1988 Commentary*), p. 54. These further definitions have been incorporated into the examination of article 36(1) where appropriate.

29 For example, in domestic drugs law, conversion of one drug to another can mean 'production' and not manufacture – see sections 4 and 37 of the UK's Drug Trafficking Offences Act, 1986.

30 See *Black's Law Dictionary* (3rd edn 1951), p. 1325 et seq.

31 A. Noll, 'Drug abuse and penal provisions of the international drug control treaties' (1977) 19 *Bulletin on Narcotics* 41 at 44 argues that article 4 precludes the legalisation of drugs in the sense of making them freely available for non-medical and non-scientific use. But he notes that the 1961 Convention does not oblige Parties to achieve this goal through criminalisation of use or simple possession. They can do so through other legislative and administrative steps. Article 33 which provides that Parties 'shall not permit the possession of drugs except under legal authority' does not require penal sanctions, and the ambiguity of the rest of the Convention on simple possession means that it is arguable that possession for use is possession under legal authority.

possession of drugs except under legal authority and then only for medical and scientific purposes, and article 36(1) obliges Parties to make possession a punishable offence.[32] However, with regard to the obligation to criminalise possession a distinction has been made between possession for personal use (simple possession) and possession for trafficking.[33] As the thrust of the penal provisions of the Convention is the prohibition of drug trafficking, there appears little doubt that Parties are obliged to criminalise possession for trafficking. Some Parties have, however, taken the view that because the thrust of the Convention is the suppression of trafficking they are not obliged in terms of article 36 to criminalise simple possession.[34] This view is supported by the drafting history and context of article 36.[35] Criminalisation of simple possession amounting in effect to criminalisation of use blurs the distinction between criminal supply and non-criminal demand. It thus does not appear that article 36(1) obliges Parties to criminalise possession of drugs for personal use.[36] Anticipating that some Parties were likely not to criminalise simple possession, the *1961 Commentary* suggests a via media that has had a strong influence on state practice with respect to possession under the Convention:

---

32   These provisions flatly contradict the liberal interpretation of article 2(5)(b) that application of prohibition is optional when a Party is of the opinion that the conditions at home render legalisation the most appropriate means of protecting 'public health and welfare'.

33   Possession for trafficking would in this sense mean all forms of possession when the possessor had the intention of engaging in any of the other forms of conduct enumerated in article 36(1) or in any form of conduct contrary to the Convention other than personal use.

34   *1961 Commentary* at 112. An example is section 31 of South Australia's Controlled Substances Act, 1984, which makes simple possession of drugs an offence but then in section 35 provides for the diversion of alleged offenders to a drug assessment and aid panel rather than prosecution. Although formally the offence is retained, this amounts to de facto decriminalisation.

35   In the third draft of the Convention article 36, then draft article 45, was included in chapter 11 entitled 'Measures against illicit traffickers' before all chapter headings were deleted from the Convention. It is still included in that part of the Convention preceded by article 35 entitled 'Action against the illicit traffic' and followed by article 37 entitled 'Seizure and confiscation'. See *1961 Commentary* at 112.

36   A. Noll, 'International treaties and the control of drug use and abuse' (1977) 6 *Contemporary Legal Problems* 17 at 25. Some Parties such as the US have taken the more conservative view that it does, leading A.J. Currie, J.F. Decker and J. Van Der Vaart, 'International control of cannabis sativa' [1973] *Journal of Drug Issues* 240-255 to argue for amendment of article 36 to explicitly exclude possession of cannabis as an offence.

It has ... been pointed out, particularly by enforcement officers, that penalisation of all unauthorised possession of drugs, including that for personal use, facilitates the prosecution and conviction of traffickers, since it is very difficult to prove the intention for which the drugs are held. If Governments choose not to punish possession for personal consumption or to impose only minor penalties on it, their legislation could very usefully provide for a legal presumption that any quantity exceeding a specified small amount is intended for distribution. It could also be stipulated that this presumption becomes irrebuttable if the amount in the possession of the offender is in excess of certain limits.[37]

Such presumptions are fairly common in post-1961 domestic drug legislation[38] but they have become increasingly vulnerable to constitutional challenge.[39]

Actions involving drug-related conduct of a transactional nature are an essential part of trafficking and present less of a problem than possession. 'Offering' is not defined in article 1 but generally involves the tendering, the making available, the holding out of a drug to a potential consumer for acceptance or refusal; an offer is 'a proposal to do a thing'.[40] It is a step towards the transfer of the substance. Making the drug available without consideration, a step towards a donation which donation would be completed upon acceptance, is thus an offer.[41] 'Offering for sale' involves the tendering etc. of a drug to a potential purchaser for acceptance or refusal. 'Distribution' involves the dis-

---

37 *1961 Commentary* at 113.

38 See, for example, section 37 of the Malaysian Dangerous Drugs Amendment Act 390 of 1977 (amending the 1952 Act) which deems possession of more than 100gms of heroin or morphine (later 15gms), 200gms of cannabis or cannabis resin, 1kg of prepared opium, or 5kg of raw opium, enough to prove an intent to traffic.

39 Presumptions of trafficking based on possession of more than a certain amount of a drug have been found to be unconstitutional in a number of states. For example, see the Canadian decision of *R v Oakes* (1986) 50 CR (3d) 1, 24 CCC (3d) 321 (SCC) where the reverse onus provision of section 8 of the Narcotic Control Act, RSC 1985, c.N-1 was held to be inoperative because of the right of an accused to be presumed innocent under section 11(d) of the Canadian Charter of Rights and Freedoms. See the similar South African decision in *S v Bhulwana* 1995 (2) SACR 748 (CC). The then Chief Justice of India complained at an International Conference on Global Drugs Law held in New Delhi, 27 February 1997, that 'the basis of arriving at these amounts' as indicated in India's Narcotic Drugs and Psychotropic Substances Act of 1985, was 'uncertain'. But see *contra* the *Salabiaku* Case ECHR Series A vol. 141-A (1988), where a possession based presumption that the accused was smuggling in article 392(1) of the French Customs Code was held to be compatible with the presumption of innocence in article 6(2) of the 1950 European Convention on Human Rights, ETS 46.

40 *Black's Law Dictionary* (3rd edn 1951), p. 1233.

41 See the *1988 Commentary* at 55.

persal of drugs among consumers; to distribute is in its ordinary sense 'to deal or divide out in proportion or in shares'.[42] In the context of the illicit traffic a more appropriate sense of the word may be the commercial function of the 'distributor', the role of ensuring that drugs move through the chain of supply from manufacturer or importer to wholesaler or retailer.[43] 'Purchase' involves the buying of drugs; the 'transmission of property from one person to another by voluntary act and agreement, founded in valuable consideration.'[44] While it is clear that the purchase of drugs for resale must be criminalised under the 1961 Convention, it seems, following the argument relating to 'possession' for personal use, that Parties are not obliged in terms of article 36 to criminalise purchase of drugs for personal use. Article 36 is directed at illicit traffickers, those who make some profit from the trafficking of drugs, and purchasing for use cannot logically be regarded as trafficking.[45] 'Sale' involves the disposal of drugs for some consideration; 'an agreement by which one gives a thing for a price in current money and the other gives the price in order to have the thing itself'.[46] 'Delivery on any terms whatsoever' involves an 'act by which the res or substance thereof is placed within the actual or constructive possession or control of another'[47] on any terms whatsoever. This would seem to cover disposal of drugs to another without consideration, including giving drugs as a gift.[48] It would include delivery as the result of a sale, or an agreement in terms of which the receiver is to carry or transmit the drugs to some other place.[49] The words 'on any terms whatsoever' suggest that forms of constructive delivery such as the transfer of keys to a storage facility would also amount to a delivery in legal systems where these forms were recognised.[50] 'Brokerage' involves acting as a middleman or agent for either purchaser or seller in drug transactions and thereby facilitating the transaction.[51]

---

42 *Black's Law Dictionary* (3rd edn 1951), p. 562.

43 See the *1988 Commentary* at 55.

44 *Black's Law Dictionary* (3rd edn 1951), p. 1395.

45 The South African Appellate Division in *S v Solomon* 1986 (3) SA 705 held at 710B that purchasing for personal use was possession of drugs, not dealing in drugs.

46 *Black's Law Dictionary* (3rd edn 1951), p.1503.

47 *Black's Law Dictionary* (3rd edn 1951), p. 515.

48 This is how it was interpreted in section 1 of the South African Abuse of Dependence Producing Substances and Rehabilitation Centres Act 41 of 1971.

49 *1988 Commentary* at 55.

50 *1988 Commentary* at 55.

51 *Black's Law Dictionary* (3rd edn 1951), p. 241. The *1988 Commentary* at 55 points out that in some legal systems a broker will be liable for the main offence while in others a broker does not have possession; an agent in possession is a 'factor' not a 'broker'.

Given that illicit trafficking involves the movement of drugs within states and across international borders, article 36 tries to provide for forms of conduct involving all aspects of the transport of drugs. 'Dispatch' involves the sending off of drugs to a specific destination[52] while 'dispatch in transit' involves the sending off of drugs through the territory of a Party but either not to a destination within that Party's territory or to a destination of which the dispatcher or carrier are ignorant.[53] 'Transport' involves the conveying of drugs from one place to another[54] by any mode through any medium. It covers gratuitous carriage in addition to carriage for reward.[55] With respect to 'importation, and exportation', article 1(1)(m) of the 1961 Convention defines the import and export of drugs as the 'physical transfer of drugs from one State to another State, or from one territory to another territory of the same State.' What is contemplated here is the movement of drugs across either international boundaries or the internal frontiers in states where territories are treated as separate entities for the purposes of the import-export authorisation system of licit drugs.[56] The export and the import of the drugs are two separate actions taking place in two different jurisdictions. They have been held to be two separate offences even if they involve the movement by the same person of a consignment of drugs from one Party to another.[57]

Finally, article 36 provides a catchall provision to deal with forms of trafficking related conduct not contemplated by the framers of the Convention.[58] It obliges Parties to criminalise 'any other action which in the opinion of such

---

52   *Black's Law Dictionary* (3rd edn 1951) at p. 357 uses the words 'delivery' or 'discharge' of goods.
53   *1988 Commentary* at 56.
54   *Black's Law Dictionary* (3rd edn 1951), p. 1670.
55   *1988 Commentary* at 56.
56   *1961 Commentary* at 12-13.
57   See the decision in *Batkoun* (1988) 73 ILR 248. Batkoun transported 50kgs of heroin in his car from France to Canada. He was charged in both France and Canada, but although in Canada the charge of illegal importation of drugs failed through lack of proof of knowledge of the offence, in France he was convicted of illegal export of drugs in violation of article L627 of the Public Health Code. His ground of appeal in France was that the export and import of the drugs were a single offence and was now res judicata due to the Canadian decision. The French Appeal Court dismissed his appeal, holding that they were separate offences under French law and under international law. It stated at p. 251 that in article 36(1) 'the terms "importation and exportation of drugs" constitute two separate offences and not simply two different aspects of the same offence.'
58   *1961 Records* vol. II at 238.

Party may be contrary to the provisions of this Convention'. The list of proscribed forms of conduct is thus not a numerus clausus. Gaps may exist and the catch-all gives the Parties the discretion to extend the list of offences or not, but the Parties are obliged to act bona fide in this regard.[59] As all of the listed forms of conduct are trafficking related, it is arguable that any extension of the listed forms of conduct must be trafficking related, and that Parties are not obliged to criminalise simple possession or use in terms of this provision. The catchall seems practical, but it is also an admission by the authors of the convention that national uniformity is an aspiration. The failure to achieve uniformity results in systemic incoherence, which in turn causes difficulties for extradition because the double criminality rule insists that extradited crimes be recognised by both Parties.[60]

With respect to the fault or mental element of crime, article 36 has as a general principle, wisely it is submitted, adopted the rule that each of the proscribed acts must be 'committed intentionally', including those acts contrary to the Convention but not listed in the article.[61] This implies that the criminal conduct must be performed consciously, wilfully or knowingly.[62] How each Party defines such intention and whether they extend it to concepts such as constructive intention (dolus eventualis) or conscious recklessness is entirely a question of their domestic law. Negligence or objective standards of conduct, however, should only lead to criminal liability in exceptional circumstances. What this provision makes clear is that drug trafficking is not one of these.

3.2.2.3 Complicity, inchoate offences and 'financial operations' under the 1961 Convention

Article 36(2)(a)(ii) provides for criminal liability for non-perpetrators and for inchoate offences.[63] It obliges Parties to criminalise the participation of any

---

59 *1961 Commentary* at 428.

60 F. Malekian, *International Criminal Law: The Legal and Critical Analysis of International Crimes* Volume II (Uppsala UP, Uppsala, 1991), p. 182. An example of such an extension is the US's Racketeer Influenced Corrupt Organisations Act (RICO), 18 USC sections 1961-1968, providing for a major extension of criminal liability unpalatable to many states to which the US makes extradition requests.

61 The US delegation's objection that criminal offences included intention by definition was overridden in order to restrict the imposition of negligent/ and or strict liability to drug offences – *United Nations Conference for the Adoption of a Single Convention on Narcotic Drugs, Official Records, Volume I* (New York, 1964) UN Doc. E/CONF.34/ 24, UN Publication Sales No. 63.XI.4 (hereinafter *1961 Records* vol. I), p. 123.

62 The first adverb is mine, the second and third come from the *1961 Commentary* at 428.

63 The 1972 Protocol did not amend article 36(2)(ii).

persons other than the perpetrator in the commission of article 36(1) offences,[64] to criminalise inchoate or uncompleted forms of those offences and to criminalise the conduct of persons engaged in financial operations in connection with all illicit trafficking offences. This provision appears to be directed against organised crime. Conspiracy permits the prosecution of the entire drug trafficking operation rather than just those physically involved in moving the drugs, while the prosecution of those involved in financing reaches out to those who seldom have any contact with drugs at all, yet who make trafficking possible.[65] These provisions were novel to many states in 1961, and their unfamiliarity restricted the extent of the obligation in article 36(2).

Once again the Convention directs the Parties to criminalise the different forms of conduct. Once again, criminalisation is limited by the fact that in terms of article 36(4), article 36(2) is implemented indirectly through the Party's domestic laws and regulations enacted to carry it out. However, while article 36(2) of the 1961 Convention binds Parties to criminalise these forms of conduct, it is with the proviso that such criminalisation is 'subject to the constitutional limitations of a Party, its legal system and domestic law'. Article 36(2) is subordinate to each Party's constitution, which means that the remarks made above in respect of article 36(1) are equally pertinent here. But, in addition, article 36(2) is subordinate to other provisions of the domestic law and legal system not embodied in the constitution. Such subordination means that Parties whose domestic legal systems do not allow the criminalisation of inchoate offences and the participation of socii are not obliged to do so under the Convention. The Canadian delegate at the 1961 Conference rationalised this subordination on the basis that these forms of conduct were not considered as offences under certain legal systems or domestic laws and the Convention had to take account of differences in legal systems while simultaneously trying to ensure that all types of offence would be punished in all countries.[66] The *1961 Commentary* argues, however, that it was not intended to completely exempt such Parties from taking legislative action to implement the article, but only to provide that they were not obliged to change their basic legal principles

---

64 Socius criminis, particeps criminis, accomplice liability, aiders and abettors, whatever term a particular legal system uses, what is dealt with here are the participants in a crime who are not the actual perpetrators of the offence. These participants participate at different levels of engagement, hence degrees of complicity or participation. These offences were included in article 2 paragraphs (b), (c) and (d) of the 1936 Convention.

65 J.R. Barnett, 'Extradition treaty improvements to combat drug trafficking' (1985) 15 *Georgia Journal of International and Comparative Law* 285 at 307.

66 *1961 Records* vol. II at 236-237.

relating to complicity or inchoate offences in implementing article 36(2)(a)
(ii).[67] This distinction is fine and ignores the potentially greater breadth of
domestic law than the basic principles of the legal system.

Article 36(2)(a)(ii) describes two general categories of criminal conduct
relating to article 36(1)(a) offences. The division of the inchoate forms of
conduct into the separate forms of conspiracy, attempts and preparatory acts
reflects the strong influence of an Anglo-American criminal jurisprudence not
easily translatable into the domestic law of many states. Although the terms
do refer to distinct forms of conduct, some overlap is possible given different
domestic interpretation,[68] leading to the criticism that they are too similar to
be effective.[69]

'Conspiracy' is criminalised even though it is an offence peculiar to common
law systems. Usually taken to mean an agreement to engage in criminal activity,[70] its parameters vary depending on the jurisdiction. For instance, in many
states in the United States 'conspiracy' has a very wide ambit,[71] whereas in
some states its ambit is very strictly curtailed,[72] while at least prior to 1961
it was not recognised by civil law states as a separate offence.[73] Although

---

67　*1961 Commentary* at 430.

68　See, for example, the statement by the Norwegian delegate to the 1961 Conference to
the effect that in Norway 'conspiracy' was classified as a 'preparatory act', and
'preparatory acts' were not punishable – *1961 Records* vol. I at 126.

69　S.K. Chatterje, *Legal Aspects of International Drug Control* (Nijhoff, Drodrecht, 1981),
p. 445.

70　*Black's Law Dictionary* (3rd edn 1951) at p. 382 defines a conspiracy as '[a] combination
or confederacy between two or more persons formed for the purpose of committing,
by their joint efforts, some unlawful or criminal act or some act which is innocent in
itself, but becomes unlawful when done by the concerted actions of the conspirators,
or for the purpose of using criminal or unlawful means to the commission of an act
not in itself unlawful.'

71　S.A. Bernholz, M.J. Bernholz and J.N. Herman, 'International extradition in drug cases'
(1985) 10 *North Carolina Journal of International Law and Commercial Regulation*
353 at 377 complain that in the US, conspiracy is so vague that it fails to present a clear
charge to which a foreign judicial official could respond to in an extradition request.

72　For example, the Netherlands delegate to the 1961 Conference stated that conspiracy
was not punishable in Netherlands law except as a preparatory act in respect of the most
serious offences and only when execution had in fact begun – *1961 Records* vol. I at
123.

73　The *1961 Commentary* notes at 433 note 4 that this may be the reason why the French
and Spanish texts of the Convention do not use the direct translation of conspiracy
(*conspiration* and *conspiracion* respectively).

the *1961 Commentary* suggests that they should do so,[74] protected by the domestic law proviso in the opening paragraph of article 36(2), Parties are not obliged to criminalise conspiracy to commit drug trafficking offences. However, those Parties that do recognise it as a separate offence in their domestic law are obliged to punish any conspiracy to commit the offences listed in article 36(1)(a).

'Attempts' to commit offences are by contrast the most universally recognised inchoate crime. There is, however, a distinction between states that only consider an attempt to have begun when the stage of execution of the offence has actually been reached, and states that extend liability for attempts to include actions taken prior to this stage. For the former states the transfer of money to a cocaine broker before delivery of cocaine would amount to an attempted purchase of cocaine while a simple enquiry about the price of cocaine would not, but the latter group of states may consider both actions to amount to an attempted purchase of cocaine.[75] Parties are, of course, not obliged to change their legal definition of attempt because this provision is subject to the 'domestic law' proviso.

'Preparatory acts' are steps taken towards the perpetration of an offence that have not yet passed the stage of commencement of consummation, and are thus not regarded as attempts in many domestic legal systems.[76] In 1961 such acts were not generally criminalised.[77] Nonetheless, article 36(2)(a)(ii) obliges Parties to criminalise such acts if they are able to do so in terms of their legal systems and the *1961 Commentary* recommends that Parties which only punish preparatory acts carried out with the intention of committing serious offences should include drug trafficking offences among those serious of-

---

74   The *1961 Commentary* at 433. It notes that exempted Parties could do so by including what amounts to a conspiracy as a 'preparatory act'.

75   See generally the *1961 Commentary* at 432 et seq. The division is between the states that insist on objective proof of an offender's intention to carry out the completed offence through evidence of his having gone a considerable way towards the commission of the actual offence, and those that allow any evidence of a subjective intention to carry out the offence, however slight, to constitute sufficient evidence for conviction of an attempt.

76   *1961 Commentary* at 433.

77   Statement of the Netherlands delegate, *1961 Records* vol. I at 123.

fences.[78] In practice, these offences have been adopted by states that do not usually recognise such offences.[79]

'Financial operations' are regarded as inchoate offences because they must be connected to an article 36 offence or any other article 36(2)(a)(ii) offences.[80] Although financial operations are covered by the other provisions of article 36(2)(a)(ii), they were referred to expressly to draw the Parties' attention to them.[81] The provision was introduced to criminalise the conduct of individuals who financed drug transactions, yet it does not specify the nature of the link between the financial operation and the offence. This link could include a whole range of operations connected to the illicit traffic. A major lacunae that results from the characterisation of financial operations as a preparatory offence is the exclusion of money laundering which takes place after the fact of a completed article 36 offence.

With respect to degrees of complicity in drug offences, article 36(2)(a)(ii) refers only to 'intentional participation'. The *1961 Commentary* notes that the wording 'covers all kinds of complicity and accessory acts, which may in different countries be divided into different categories.'[82] Liability for these offences depends on there having been a principal offender, but it is left to the Party to decide whether that offender should actually have been apprehended and/or convicted.

Finally, it is important to note that as criminal liability attaches to the completed offences in article 36(1)(a) only if they are performed intentionally, the inchoate forms of conduct criminalised by article 36(2)(a)(ii) must also be performed intentionally for criminal liability to attach to them. The same logic applies to the various participants other than the actual perpetrator of the offences who must, to be held liable, have been acting intentionally.

---

78 *1961 Commentary* at 433.
79 For example, sections 15-25 of India's Narcotic Drugs and Psychotropic Substances Act, 1985, make an attempt to prepare to commit any of the offences under the Act an offence in itself, something not generally punishable under Indian law.
80 Statement of the Canadian delegate, *1961 Records* vol. I at 146.
81 This attention was justified on the basis that these operations often involved the biggest traffickers who were the hardest to bring to justice, and because judges were extremely cautious in cases where no drugs had been seized – Interpol representative's statement, *1961 Records* vol. II at 234.
82 *1961 Commentary* at 432.

3.2.2.4   The 1961 Convention's offences appraised

The offences in the 1961 Convention have served as the source for most existing domestic legislation suppressing drug trafficking.[83] Even notions of conspiracy have been accepted by civil law states.[84] The fact that article 36's obligations were neither particularly extensive nor progressive – they were meant to constitute a set of general principles rather than an extensive international penal code[85]- made compliance relatively easy. The adoption of the enumerative method had its limitations but it was effective in globalising the basic kinds of conduct the 1961 Convention seeks to criminalise. Despite article 36(4) reserving definition of the offences to the Parties, many Parties to whom specialised drugs legislation was new simply lifted the wording of article 36's offences and used it in their new laws. Escape clauses were not heavily used. The failure of article 36 from the law enforcement perspective was that it was not ambitious enough; in creating penal provisions that were modelled on those in the 1936 Convention it was unable to counter a rapidly evolving illicit drugs market and further modification of the international drug control system became necessary.

---

83   For example, Malaysia's Dangerous Drugs Act 234 of 1952 defines 'drug trafficking' in section 2 as 'manufacturing, importing, exporting, keeping, concealing, buying, selling, giving, receiving, storing, administering, transporting, carrying, sending, delivering, procuring, supplying, or distributing an dangerous drug'. Some states simply enacted one statute. Others, like the UK, criminalised the import and export of drugs under customs legislation (Customs and Excise Management Act of 1979) while leaving the rest of the offences in a special drug offences statute (Misuse of Drugs Act of 1971). The US, by contrast, enacted a plethora of legislation much more sophisticated than required by international law.

84   The French *Code de Sante Publique* art. L. 627 (1975) criminalises, exceptionally in French law, conspiracy to violate drugs laws. Paragraphs 2 and 3 of the law refer to the crimes of *association* or *entente* with a view to violating French drugs law, and render them as punishable as a completed offence. Negotiations for the purpose of obtaining, manufacturing or selling illicit drugs suffice to establish such an *association* or *entente*, even before agreement is reached among the parties – see generally C. Blakesly, 'Extraterritorial jurisdiction' in M.C. Bassiouni (ed.), *2 International Criminal Law: Procedure* (Transnational, Dobbs Ferry, 1986), p. 3 at p. 51 and cases cited at note 199.

85   Statement of the Yugoslavian delegate, *1961 Records* vol. II at 238.

3.2.3   *The offences stipulated by the 1971 Convention*

3.2.3.1   *General*

The 1971 Convention extends the material scope of existing international penal drug control provisions to include psychotropic substances. It makes provision for very similar offences to those contained in the 1961 Convention, following much the same scheme with separate provisions on specific drug offences and accessory offences. The central focus is once again on the illicit traffic, and article 22 contains the key provisions. As with article 36 of the 1961 Convention, article 22(5) makes it clear that article 22 was not intended to be self-executing. It provides that '[n]othing contained in this article shall affect the principle that the offences to which it refers shall be defined, prosecuted and punished in conformity with the domestic law of a Party.'

Following the model provided by article 36 of the 1961 Convention, article 22 must be read against the background of general prohibitions in the 1971 Convention. Article 7(a) operates as a general prohibition. It obliges Parties to 'prohibit all use except for scientific and very limited medical purposes by duly authorised persons' of the substances in Schedule I. The remainder of the article details the conditions of such lawful use. Unlike article 2(5)(b) of the 1961 Convention, there is no savings clause making the obligation dependent on the Party's own view of the 'prevailing conditions' in its territory and the requirement is obligatory.[86] Again, however, the specific prohibitions are in article 22. But unlike the 1961 Convention, article 22 is itself general in nature. By choosing a non-enumerative method, it renders all forms of conduct not regarded as lawful in terms of the Convention unlawful, and leaves it to the Parties themselves to specify each particular form of unlawful conduct.

3.2.3.2   *Article 22(1)(a)'s standard offences*

Article 22(1)(a) obliges Parties to criminalise all forms of intentional conduct contrary to the law or regulations adopted in pursuance of the 1971 Convention. Unlawful conduct is defined as conduct 'contrary to a law or regulation adopted [by a Party] in pursuance of its obligations under this Convention.'[87] Criminal-

---

86   For this reason dronabinol, a cannabinoid, had to be de-scheduled before Parties could allow prescription for medical purposes.

87   In the *United Nations Conference for the Adoption of a Protocol on Psychotropic Substances, Official Records, Volume II* (New York, 1973) UN Doc. E/CONF.58/7/Add.1, UN Publication Sales No.E.73.XI.4 (hereinafter *1971 Records* vol. II), p. 44 the Legal Adviser to the 1971 Conference explains that this provision differs from article 36(1)

isation is a matter of a Party's domestic law, as article 22(5) makes it clear that these offences 'shall be defined, prosecuted and punished in conformity with the domestic law of a Party.' As with the 1961 Convention, an escape clause is also provided by article 22(1)(a) itself, which makes article 22's obligations subject to the 'constitutional limitations' of the Party. Thus the 1971 Convention permits exceptions to the duty to criminalise conduct contrary to its obligations if to criminalise would be in violation of the Party's constitution, but the escape clause is not operative with respect to violations of other ordinary domestic law.[88]

With regard to conduct, the obvious difference between article 22(1)(a) and article 36(1) of the 1961 Convention is that the former does not enumerate specific offences. Adopting a general formula, it provides that intentional 'actions' contrary to laws or regulations adopted by Parties in pursuance of their obligations under the Convention shall be treated as punishable offences.[89] Although it does not use the terms specifically, in its use of the term 'actions' the article must be referring to 'illicit traffic' in drugs. 'Illicit traffic' is defined by article 1(j) as 'manufacture of or trafficking in psychotropic substances contrary to the provisions of this Convention,'[90] where 'trafficking' means all forms of unauthorised trade and distribution, while 'manufacture' is self-explanatory.[91] However, 'illicit traffic' is contrary to the provisions of the Convention, while article 22(1)(a) envisages actions contrary to the laws and regulations adopted by the Parties to apply the Convention, so they are not

---

of the 1961 Convention, which provides for criminalisation of conduct 'contrary to the provisions' of that Convention, because of the realisation in 1971 that in non-self-executing treaties such as the drug conventions the offences whose punishment they require must be contrary to national legislation and not to international law.

88 Constitutional challenge based on substance of offences is unlikely except perhaps in the case of simple possession. Federal states constitutionally incapable of enacting penal law are still bound to obtain the required enactment of legislation from their component provinces or states.

89 Although draft article 18 followed the enumeration of offences in article 36(1) of the 1961 Convention, the drafting committee decided to switch to the general formula because enumeration was regarded as 'cumbersome' and was not exhaustive in any event – see the comments of the Yugoslavian delegate and the legal adviser, *1971 Records* vol. II at 44.

90 The *1971 Commentary* at 25 notes that unlike under the 1961 Convention (article 1(1)(i)), the term 'illicit traffic' in article 1(j) does not cover the cultivation of plants from which psychotropic drugs can be obtained. It suggests, however, that cultivation may constitute an attempt or preparatory act in terms of article 22(2)(a) to commit an offence under article 22(1)(a).

91 *1971 Commentary* at 25.

necessarily coextensive in meaning.[92] But the UN's *Commentary on the Convention on Psychotropic Substances, 1971* (hereinafter the *1971 Commentary*)[93] assumes 'that the 1971 Conference intended that all actions in the illicit traffic should be punishable offences pursuant to article 22(1), subparagraph (a).'[94] It was not the intention of the drafters to define the specific forms of conduct that make up trafficking, but it is safe to assume that it was their intention that the Parties adopt measures criminalising different forms of conduct such as those set out in article 36(1)(a) of the 1961 Convention and the latter may serve as a useful guide in this context.[95] In practice, Parties have criminalised these forms of conduct relating to trafficking in psychotropic substances with varying degrees of specificity.[96]

The one form of conduct that does require comment in the context of article 22(1)(a)'s general formula is possession because it is unclear precisely what the provision demands of Parties. Whether 'use' and 'acquisition for use' must be criminalised depends on whether article 22(1)(a) demands that simple possession be criminalised.[97] It is useful to begin trying to discover what article 22(1)(a) obliges Parties to do by first asking whether other provisions in the Convention oblige Parties to criminalise possession. With regard to substances in Schedules II, III and IV it appears no such obligation exists. Article 5(3) does state that it is 'desirable' that their 'possession' not be permitted except

---

92 *1971 Commentary* at 26.

93 For the full citation see note 1.

94 *1971 Commentary* at 26.

95 See Noll supra note 31 at 47.

96 Thus, for example, Portugal's Act No.21 of 1977 in sections 19 to 21 renders the unauthorised purchase and sale of psychotropic substances an offence.

97 Article 5(2) limits the use of Schedule II, III, and IV substances to medical and scientific purposes. Article 5(1) limits the use of Schedule I substances as provided in article 7, which in turn prohibits their use except for 'scientific and very limited medical purposes'. It is arguable that in terms of the latter provision, use of Schedule I substances for any purpose is an action in violation of an obligation under the Convention and is thus in terms of article 22(1)(a) a criminal offence. However, article 7 is devoted to control of supply of such substances suggesting that prohibition of use only for the purposes of trafficking is contemplated. Article 7(b) requires that possession of such substances for use requires authorisation in terms of article 7(b). The *1971 Commentary* at 349 notes, however, that these limitations relate to the supplier and not the consumer. Use, together with acquisition for use are, according to the *1971 Commentary*, unauthorised actions, but they are not 'actions' contrary to the laws and regulations that a Party is obliged to adopt under the Convention. They both imply possession and whether they are unlawful in terms of the Convention depends on whether possession is an offence under article 22(1)(a).

under 'legal authority'.[98] But this provision leaves the decision in the hands
of the Party, and criminalisation of possession is not required by article 22(1)(a)
as article 5(3) is not a 'law or regulation' that the Parties are obliged to adopt
rendering such possession for use unlawful.[99] Some confusion is caused by
article 5(2)'s obligation on Parties to 'limit by such measures as it considers
appropriate the ... use and possession of' these substances, but in order to
reconcile this provision with article 5(3), appropriate measures must include
non-penal measures.[100] With regard to substances in Schedule I, special obligations are set out in article 7. Article 7(b) requires that possession be under
'special licence or prior authorisation'. It appears that there is an obligation
to prohibit possession of such substances where no such authorisation exists,
although it is arguable that the whole tenor of article 7 suggests that it refers
to possession for the purpose of trafficking.[101]

A more useful line of inquiry is to ask whether possession of psychotropic
substances is an 'action' in the sense that that term is used in article 22(1)(a).
If possession is simply a passive state of affairs, then it is difficult to regard
it as an 'action'. The *1971 Commentary* submits that possession in the sense
in which it is used in the Convention means more than just a state of affairs,
it means some form of positive action, for example, 'holding' a substance, 'preserving' it, 'hiding' it, 'moving it from one place to another'.[102] The *1971
Commentary* continues that according to this interpretation of 'action', possession for personal use of a Schedule I substance is an 'action' and an offence
under article 22(1)(a), and notes that this was the view of many participants

---

98 The original draft of this provision proposed prohibition of possession except under
    legal authority. It was changed because of the delegates' concerns that prohibition of
    these substances that were often the subject of youthful experimentation would be
    ineffective and counterproductive, as well as concerns about whether 'legal authority'
    meant refraining from proscribing possession or acting positively and providing for
    something akin to licensed possession – see *1971 Records* vol. II at 164-166. The
    compromise leaves each Party to deal with possession as it sees fit, but what exactly
    the desirable 'legal authority' means remains unclear.

99 *1971 Commentary* at 350.

100 Article 9 appears to require that such substances be dispensed only through medical
    prescription, but in order to reconcile article 5(3) with article 9, illicit purchase cannot
    be regarded as a criminal offence in terms of article 22(1)(a).

101 The provision reads: 'In respect of substances in Schedule I, the Parties shall: ... (b)
    require that manufacture, trade, distribution and possession be under special license or
    prior authorisation;'.

102 *1971 Commentary* at 351.

at the 1971 Conference.[103] However, a different view is defensible. Possession, as a state of affairs, must be created and changed by the positive conduct to which the *1971 Commentary* refers. It is arguable that in the context of the Convention this moving of the substance from one place to another, hiding it, preserving it, all beg the question – with what purpose? If the individual's purpose is to preserve it for personal use then it is arguable that the general purpose of the Convention, the suppression of supply, means that Parties are free to interpret such conduct as not being an 'action'. The context demands, however, that if the purpose with which the substance is preserved is supply, it is an 'action'. While article 22(1)(a) was intended to criminalise possession for supply, it is submitted that it was not intended to criminalise simple possession and by extension use and acquisition for use of Schedule I or for that matter any psychotropic substance.

A final comment on article 22(1)(a) is that, as with article 36 in the 1961 Convention, it insists that only 'intentional' 'actions' be criminalised.

3.2.3.3 Complicity, inchoate offences and 'financial operations' under the 1971 Convention

The provisions in article 22(2)(a)(ii) are identical to the provisions in the 1961 Convention's article 36(2)(a)(ii). They have been devised to criminalise the inchoate forms of, and the different degrees of complicity in, the standard offences provided for by article 22(1)(a). Parties are in terms of article 22(2)(a)(ii) under an obligation to render these forms of conduct unlawful. However, this obligation is subject to two restrictions. Article 22(5) provides generally that the substance and execution of the article is a domestic affair. More specifically, article 22(2)'s opening paragraph provides that the obligation to criminalise is subject to the Party's 'constitutional limitations',[104] 'legal system and domestic law'.[105] The *1971 Commentary* submits that the latter proviso was intended to ensure that Parties are not obliged to change their basic concepts of 'intentional participation', 'conspiracy', 'attempts' or 'preparatory acts' or to introduce such notions if they are foreign to their penal law.[106] This suggests that the provision is optional. It seems more likely that the authors

---

103 *1971 Commentary* at 351 citing *1971 Records* vol. II 164-166.
104 Parties with federal constitutions must ensure that constituent states or provinces enact the necessary laws and regulations.
105 'Domestic law' is apparently of wider ambit than 'legal system' and is thus a greater limitation on the obligation in article 22(2) – *1971 Commentary* at 356.
106 *1971 Commentary* at 356.

of article 22(2)(a)(ii) intended that Parties could choose to opt out if major changes to their domestic law were required.

With the aim of inter alia reaching those individuals who organise but do not actively take part in the chain of supply, article 22(2)(a)(ii) criminalises certain inchoate forms of conduct.[107] Although 'attempts' are the most widely accepted of these incomplete forms of conduct, the distinction between 'attempts' and 'preparatory acts' may be difficult to draw in the domestic law of many of the Parties.[108] While attempts refers only to the actual commencement of the execution of offences, preparatory acts refers to the devising or arrangement of the means or measures necessary for the commission of an offence up to but not including the threshold of the commencement of its execution.[109] A 'conspiracy' in the context of this provision is an agreement between two or more persons to commit an article 22(1)(a) offence jointly. In many states it is not regarded as a separate offence but simply as a 'preparatory act'.[110] 'Financial operations in connection with the offences referred to in this article' is a special form of inchoate offence included in the Convention's penal provisions, even though the other forms of inchoate conduct enumerated cover this conduct.[111] The provision is vague, however, as to the meaning of 'financial operations'. With respect to complicity, the phrase 'intentional participation' is a catchall that includes all forms of participation in the offences envisaged by article 22(1)(a). The demarcation of these forms is a domestic matter, but it includes participation after the fact.[112]

Finally, it is worth noting that negligence will not be sufficient to establish liability for participation, and nor will it suffice for liability for the various inchoate offences listed by article 22(2)(a)(ii). The fault element for all these forms of conduct is intention.

---

107 The *1971 Commentary* notes at 359-360 that while plants from which psychotropic substances are obtainable are not subject to the 1971 Convention, their cultivation may be regarded as one of the forms of inchoate offence set down if such cultivation is for use in illicit manufacture.

108 For example, 'preparatory acts' in terms of article 22(2)(a)(ii) appear to refer to conduct which in South African law is classified as an incomplete attempt.

109 *1971 Commentary* at 358.

110 *1971 Commentary* at 359.

111 *1971 Commentary* at 359.

112 *1971 Commentary* at 358.

3.2.3.4 The 1971 Convention's offences appraised

The adoption of offences in the 1971 Convention was necessitated by the narrow application of the 1961 Convention to narcotic substances, and the need to expand the material scope of drug trafficking offences to include the new psychotropic substances that were entering the illicit drugs market. The one distinguishing feature of article 22's standard offences, the use of the general formula for criminalisation, was unlikely to result in much change to domestic drug law. It left Parties to extend the application of existing domestic drug offences to psychotropic substances, and these offences had already been shaped by the enumeration in article 36(1) of the 1961 Convention. The effect of the more unusual obligations imposed by article 22(2)(a)(ii), combined with the identical obligations already imposed by article 36(2)(a)(ii) of the 1961 Convention, can be seen in the specialised drug legislation that began to emerge after the adoption of the 1961 and 1971 Conventions. This legislation provided for increased criminal responsibility for preparatory actions and attempted crimes, frequently transforming these preliminary phases into separate crimes.[113] It also enlarged the circle of criminal liability to include all persons who in some way or other induce, organise, assist, shelter or finance the illicit production, cultivation, trafficking, acquisition, possession and consumption of drugs.[114] In spite of these changes, new substances continued to enter the market, the market expanded rapidly in size and began to generate enormous profits. Some states reacted to the growing drug problem and its effect on the financial system by criminalising the acquisition, possession, transfer or laundering of the proceeds derived from the illicit traffic and by enlarging their jurisdiction to allow confiscation of illicitly derived property and proceeds. In doing so they went beyond the 1961 and 1971 Conventions and beyond international law. The 1988 Convention was the international community's attempt to make sure that other states followed suit.

3.2.4 The 1988 Convention's offences

3.2.4.1 General

The 1988 Convention attempts to suppress all of the different forms of activity involved in modern drug trafficking. Although the offences in the earlier con-

---

113 D. Cotic, *Drugs and Punishment* (UNSDRI, Rome, 1988), p.115.
114 See Cotic supra note 113 at 115.

ventions provide the foundation upon which the 1988 Convention builds,[115] the offences in article 3 of the 1988 Convention represent a major extension and elaboration of drug related crimes beyond the limited provisions of the 1961 and 1971 Conventions. The Convention's penal provisions are concerned with the 'illicit traffic' as a whole, which it states in article 1(m) 'means the offences set forth in article 3, paragraphs 1 and 2, of this Convention.'[116] These offences include most of the activities prohibited by article 36 of the 1961 Convention, plus a range of new offences, all of which are specifically enumerated and detailed in separate sub-paragraphs. The use of the word 'means' in the definition suggests that the list is closed and there can be no other forms of illicit traffic for the purposes of the Convention. The types of conduct listed in the main indicate the intention of the Conference to stipulate specific obligations as a way of combating the illicit supply of drugs. However, in response to the concerns of drug producer states that they would have to shoulder most of the burden of a Convention whose obligations had been drawn up and defined by drug consumer states, the 1988 Convention also criminalises the demand for drugs.[117]

---

115 For example, 'illicit traffic' in the 1988 Convention retains the definition given to it in the earlier conventions.

116 Draft article 1(i) originally defined 'illicit traffic' by enumerating most of the activities finally enumerated in the separate sub-paragraphs of article 3(1) of the Convention, and then draft article 2(1)(a) simply obliged Parties to criminalise this 'illicit traffic'. There followed a long dispute about the meaning of illicit traffic resolved in the Working Group of Committee I which agreed the existing expanded offences in article 3(1) and the definition of 'illicit traffic' finally settled as referring to those offences. Ironically, the term is rarely used in the Convention as most provisions refer to the specific offences in article 3. See the *United Nations Conference for the Adoption of a Convention against Illicit Traffic in Narcotic Drugs and Psychotropic Substances, Official Records, Volume I* (New York, 1994) UN Doc. E/CONF.82/16, UN Publication Sales No. E.94.XI.5 (hereinafter *1988 Records* vol. I), p. 4, pp.12-14, pp. 60-61, p. 107.

117 Draft article 1(i) did not include use or simple possession. Mexico proposed an expansive definition of 'illicit traffic' (*1988 Records* vol. I at 89), which included use, possession and purchase for possession. Western states argued that these actions did not form part of the illicit traffic. The adoption of article 3(2), the personal use offence, and the inclusion of this offence within the Convention's definition of illicit traffic in article 1(m), suggests that producer states were successful in equalising the burden. However, the fact that the words 'illicit traffic' were substituted by 'offences established in accordance with Article 3, paragraph 1' in order to make the distinction between supply offences to which the 1988 Convention's co-operation provisions applied and possession offences to which they did not apply, possible, suggests otherwise. 'Illicit traffic' was retained in articles 17 (illicit traffic by sea), 18 (free trade zones and free Ports) and 19 (use of the mails) because it made little difference to the actual effect of these articles.

More elaborate substance has not meant a change in the general principle that these provisions are applied indirectly. The fleshing out of these offences and the admission of appropriate defences to them remains a domestic affair. Article 3 is not self-executing. Article 3(11) provides that nothing in the article 'shall affect the principle that the description of offences to which it refers and of legal defences thereto is reserved to the domestic law of a Party and that such offences shall be prosecuted and punished in conformity with that law.'[118] It is also important to remember that the whole Convention labours under the restrictions contained in article 2(1) which provides that application of the Convention's obligations must be 'in conformity with the fundamental provisions of their respective domestic legislative systems.'

3.2.4.2 Supply related offences under the 1988 Convention

3.2.4.2.1 The offences created by article 3(1) of the 1988 Convention generally
The offences that Parties are obliged to create in terms of article 3(1) of the 1988 Convention relate to drug trafficking in all of its modern manifestations. For the purposes of the rest of the provisions in the Convention, these offences are the most important because it is to them that the provisions allowing confiscation (article 5), extradition (article 6) and mutual legal assistance (article 7) apply. However, article 3(1)'s opening paragraph makes it clear that the provision is not self-executing. It provides that each Party is responsible for adopting the necessary measures for the establishment of the enumerated "offences" as criminal offences under its domestic law. The *1988 Commentary* insists, however, that the offences must be established as criminal offences, not regulatory infractions or administrative offences.[119]

Article 3(1) is broken up into divisions and subdivisions in order to distinguish between the different forms of conduct involved. Article 3(1)(a) reiterates the standard drug trafficking offences relating to the production and supply of drugs set out in the earlier conventions with some extension. Article 3(1)(b)

Thus although it is literally possible to board and confiscate a ship in terms of article 17 on the basis of simple possession of drugs by someone on board, the content of the article makes this highly unlikely.

118 The 'Expert Group Report' in *1988 Records* vol. I at 16 supported the inclusion of this provision in the Convention on the basis that it was not a limitation clause covering all the provisions of article 3, but rather its objective was to 'indicate that the procedural modalities for the execution of [article 3's] obligation ... would be within the purview of [the Party's] respective domestic law.'

119 See the *1988 Commentary* at 50.

establishes new offences relating to property conversion and the laundering of the profits of trafficking. Article 3(1)(c) establishes offences involving the infrastructure of drug trafficking, inchoate offences, and criminal liability for complicity in drug trafficking offences. Significantly, while subparagraphs (a) and (b) of article 3(1) are mandatory and are not subject to any specific constitutional or domestic law safeguard clauses,[120] article 3(1)(c)'s obligation is subject to the constitutional principles and the basic concepts of the Parties' legal systems because of concerns about compatibility with the Parties' penal law.[121]

3.2.4.2.2 The standard trafficking offences

Article 3(1)(a)(i) enumerates forms of conduct that are unlawful when they are contrary to the provisions of the 1961 Convention, the 1961 Convention as amended and the 1971 Convention.[122] The earlier conventions thus describe both what is lawful and what is unlawful conduct with respect to drugs. In this way the 1988 Convention is integrated without contradiction[123] into the existing international drug control system, the terms of which are incorporated by reference into the 1988 Convention. Parties that are not subject to the earlier conventions are thus forced to have regard to them.[124] However, to constitute a violation of article 3(1) conduct must assume one of the forms listed.

The forms of conduct enumerated in article 3(1)(a)(i) include almost all of the forms of conduct enumerated in article 36(1) of the 1961 Convention,

---

120 Draft article 2 originally subjected the obligation to criminalise all offences to 'the constitutional limitations, legal system and domestic law' of the Parties. There was strong opposition to this limitation clause in the Expert Group because of the way it weakened one of the basic articles of the draft Convention and because it was not in conformity with the accepted practice in other international penal instruments – see *1988 Records* vol. I at 12 The suggestion at the Expert's meeting to subject some but not all of the offences to a limiting clause eventually evolved into the separate sub-set of offences provided for in article 3(1)(c) that are subject to a limiting clause.

121 See Sproule and St-Denis supra note 4 at 270.

122 Unlawful conduct is logically conduct contrary to the legislation transforming the earlier conventions into domestic law and not conduct contrary to the conventions themselves.

123 For example, the 1961 Convention permits the accumulation of Schedule II substances for retail purposes and their sale without prescription because of the licit trade in them. It follows that the authors of the 1988 Convention did not intend that the offering for sale of these substances should be criminalised by Parties to the 1988 Convention – see the *1988 Commentary* at 52.

124 *1988 Commentary* at 53.

now commonly applied crimes in domestic law.[125] The comments made in respect of article 36(1) above apply equally here and further definition of these forms of conduct by the *1988 Commentary* has been incorporated for convenience sake in the examination under article 36(1) above.[126] Article 3(1)(a)(i) does not repeat 'cultivation' which is dealt with separately in article 3(1)(a)(ii) and 'possession' and 'purchase' for trafficking purposes which are dealt with separately in article 3(1)(a)(iii). These offences are discussed below. Possession and purchase for personal use were excluded because the authors of article 3(1)(a)(i) saw them as unconnected to the main target of the Convention, the illicit traffic.[127] It is important to note that the fact that article 3(1)(a)(i) is not identical to these earlier provisions does not admit the possibility of derogation from the provisions for offences in the earlier Conventions; article 23 of the 1988 Convention does not permit such derogation.[128]

The mental element of criminal liability for article 3(1)(a) offences is clear; the opening paragraph of article 3(1) provides that these offences must be committed 'intentionally'.[129] The 1988 Convention provides further guidance in respect of the mental element. Article 3(3) states that '[k]nowledge, intent or purpose required as an element of an offence set forth in paragraph 1 of this article may be inferred from objective factual circumstances.' This provision does not refer to the level of proof required to establish fault but to the inferences that may be drawn from the evidence of fault and it requires no change

---

125 For a modern example, see section 6 of the Australian Crimes (Traffic in Narcotic Drugs and Psychotropic Substances) Act, 1990. This act anticipates that dealing in drugs will be an offence in Australian State law and section 6(1) reads: '(1) For the purposes of this Act, each of the following is a dealing in drugs: ... (b) the separation of opium, coca leaves, cannabis or cannabis resin from the plant from which they are obtained; (c) the manufacture, extraction or preparation of a narcotic drug or psychotropic substance; (d) ...; (e) the sale, supply, ... of a narcotic drug or psychotropic substance; (f) the importation into Australia, exportation from Australia, ... of a narcotic drug or psychotropic substance; ...'.

126 See the *1988 Commentary* at 54-56.

127 See the remarks of the chairman of the Working Group of Committee I – *United Nations Conference for the Adoption of a Convention against Illicit Traffic in Narcotic Drugs and Psychotropic Substances, Official Records, Volume II* (New York, 1991) UN Doc. E/CONF.82/16/Add.1, UN Publication Sales No. E.91.XI.1 (hereinafter *1988 Records* vol. II), p. 150.

128 Article 23 provides that the provisions of the 1988 Convention shall not derogate from any of the rights enjoyed or obligations endured under the earlier conventions.

129 *1988 Commentary* at 51. The *Commentary* notes that Parties are not obliged to consider mistakes of law in regard to these offences as valid excuses. They are of course free to choose to do so if compelled by their domestic law.

in the evidential procedures of Parties.[130] It means that direct proof such as a confession is not required and allows fault to be established circumstantially.[131] Although this method of establishing fault was unfamiliar to many states in 1988, some Parties have chosen explicitly to follow this approach.[132]

3.2.4.2.3 The cultivation offence

Article 3(1)(a)(ii) obliges Parties to criminalise the cultivation of the plants that are commonly used for the production of drugs. In terms of this provision it is the 1961 Convention and its amended version which defines what is lawful

---

130 *1988 Commentary* at 83.

131 This provision was introduced by the Netherlands delegation at the Conference to assist state authorities in establishing the knowledge requirement in the property handling offence (now article 3(c)(i)) – see *1988 Records* vol. I at 101. But the Netherlands delegate's explanation of the necessity for and purpose of this provision applies to all the offences in article 3 that require proof of intention: 'The basic question was, how to ascertain that someone could be considered as knowing that certain property was derived from crime. It could be assumed that the person did not need to know all the particulars of the crime committed. If it was necessary for it to be established in court that the person had actual knowledge, that would be tantamount to depending on a confession by the offender, which would obviously present insuperable difficulties. Some legal systems had incriminated acts of handling where negligence was involved; in other words the offender was criminally liable if in the circumstances he ought to have understood that the property was of criminal origin. In other legal systems it was possible, without expressly making such negligence criminal, to infer someone's knowledge from facts other than the confession of the offender. The term dolus eventualis was used in this respect, but it was very difficult to draw a distinction between that and culpa in the abstract. The proposed paragraph 1 bis [now paragraph 3] was designed to make it clear beyond doubt that, when appraising the evidence establishing knowledge, courts should not have to depend on the confession of the offender but could rely on objective facts from which the knowledge possessed by the offender might be inferred.' – *1988 Records* vol. II at 52-3.

132 For example, section 8A.(1) of the Australian Crimes (Traffic in Narcotic Drugs and Psychotropic Substances) Act, 1990, reads: 'If a particular knowledge, intent or purpose is an element of an offence against this Act, that knowledge, intent or purpose may be inferred from objective factual circumstances.'

cultivation of the specified plants.[133] Thus unlawful conduct is conduct contrary to their provisions.[134]

The provision demands the criminalisation of 'cultivation', but it links 'cultivation' directly to the provisions of the 1961 Convention. Article 3(1)(a)(ii) only makes provision for the criminalisation of cultivation of the opium poppy,[135] coca bush[136] or cannabis plant[137] for the purpose of producing illicit narcotics. Thus the list of plants is a numerus clausus and no new plants can be added without the amendment of the 1961 Convention as well as this provision. There were objections at the 1988 Conference to the inclusion of coca-leaf 'cultivation' as an offence on the basis that this went beyond the stipulations of the 1961 Convention.[138] Not surprisingly, Parties with a populace that has a historical or cultural interest in coca-leaf cultivation have made reservations to article 3(1)(a)(ii) because they feel that it does not distinguish sufficiently between licit and illicit cultivation.[139] Other Parties with no interest whatsoever in cultivation have found it easy to comply with this provision.[140]

Finally, the opening paragraph of article 3(1) provides that these offences must be committed 'intentionally', and article 3(3) provides that such intention can be inferred from the evidence.

---

133 Article 22 of the 1961 Convention permitted but did not oblige Parties to prohibit the cultivation of these plants. The 1961 Convention controls the licit cultivation of the opium poppy (article 23), coca bushes and coca leaves (article 26) and cannabis (article 28).

134 The 1971 Convention and the production of psychotropic substances are not mentioned, but the Soviet delegate suggested at the 1988 Conference that production of psychotropic substances is an offence under article 3(1)(a) – *1988 Records* vol. II at 30.

135 In terms of article 1(o), a 'plant of the species Papaver somniferum L' but no other narcotic yielding Poppy.

136 In terms of article 1(c) 'the plant of any species of the genus Erythoxylon'.

137 In terms of article 1(b) 'any plant of the genus Cannabis'.

138 See the reservation of the Bolivian delegate who stated that such criminalisation in his country would result in massive overcrowding of jails – *1988 Records* vol. II at 154.

139 For example, Peru reserved upon signature (20/12/1988), *Multilateral Treaties Deposited* (1997) at 305. Peru also reserved its position in respect of the scope of the 'illicit traffic' as defined in article 1 insofar as it refers to article 3(1)(a)(ii).

140 See again, for example, section 6 of the Australian Crimes (Traffic in Narcotic Drugs and Psychotropic Substances) Act, 1990. The Act makes dealing in drugs an offence and section 6(1)(a)(f) reads: '(1) For the purposes of this Act, each of the following is a dealing in drugs: (a) the cultivation of the opium poppy, coca bush or cannabis plant for the purpose of producing drugs'.

3.2.4.2.4 The offences of possession or purchase of drugs for the purposes of trafficking

Article 3(1)(a)(iii) obliges Parties to criminalise the possession or purchase of narcotic drugs or psychotropic substances for the purpose of any form of trafficking. 'Possession' in terms of this provision is rendered unlawful by reference through article 3(1)(a)(i) to conduct contrary to the 1961 Convention, its amended version and the 1971 Convention.

It was noted above that article 36(1) of the 1961 Convention has been interpreted as criminalising possession for the purposes of trafficking but not simple possession. Here that distinction is made clear: the criminalised form of conduct is possession, but it is a specialised form of possession because it must be coupled with an intention to carry out one or more of the trafficking offences listed in article 3(1)(a)(i). The 1988 Convention has two possession offences in order to distinguish between conduct to which the rest of the Convention's provisions on mutual assistance apply – possession for trafficking – from conduct to which these provisions do not apply – simple possession. The purchase of drugs without necessarily taking possession[141] for the same purposes must also be criminalised in terms of article 3(1)(a)(iii). This obligation is uncontroversial and Parties have responded accordingly.[142]

With respect to the mental element of criminal liability, the opening paragraph of article 3(1) provides that such possession must be intentional, while article 3(3) provides that this intention may be 'inferred from objective factual circumstances.'

3.2.4.2.5 The offences of manufacturing, transporting or distributing equipment, materials, precursor substances or essential chemicals knowing that they are to be used in drug trafficking offences

Article (3)(1)(a)(iv) is an innovative provision, intended according to the United States delegation to criminalise the conduct of 'those who knowingly supply

---

141 *1988 Commentary* at 57.

142 See for example, section 6 of the Australian Crimes (Traffic in Narcotic Drugs and Psychotropic Substances) Act, 1990. This act makes dealing in drugs an offence and section 6(1)(a)-(f) reads: '(1) For the purposes of this Act, each of the following is a dealing in drugs: ... (d) the possession of a narcotic drug or psychotropic substance for the purpose of the manufacture, extraction or preparation of another drug or substance; (e) ... possession for the purpose of sale or supply, of a narcotic drug or psychotropic substance; (f) ... possession for the purpose of such importation or exportation, of a narcotic drug or psychotropic substance.'

essential materials or chemicals to produce or cultivate illegal drugs'.[143] The existing conventions do not regulate the manufacture, transport or distribution of equipment, materials, precursor substances or essential chemicals. The 1988 Convention itself renders these forms of conduct in connection with these materials unlawful, but only if they are connected with 'the illicit cultivation, production or manufacture of narcotic drugs or psychotropic substances'.

This offence deals essentially with conduct relating to preparatory stages of the illicit creation of drugs and overlaps with article 3(1)(c)(iv) criminalising secondary participation in drug production. It involves the 'manufacture',[144] 'transport' and 'distribution', that is, the making, taking and dispersal of 'equipment', 'materials' or the 'substances' listed in the tables. Possession of these things is a separate offence under article 3(1)(c)(ii). Whether the 'equipment' and 'materials' mentioned fall in or out of the scope of the provision depends not so much on the definition of 'equipment' or 'materials' but on the purpose for which they are to be used, that is, illicit drug trafficking. Article 13 regulates the trade and diversion of these equipment and materials to the illicit traffic. The 'substances' listed in the tables are precursor substances or essential chemicals, substances that are frequently used in the illicit manufacture of narcotic drugs or psychotropic substances. Their diversion into the illicit traffic is regulated by article 12, but these substances are not contraband unless they are dealt with in preparation for the cultivation, production or manufacture of drugs, a necessary qualification given the licit commercial functions of these substances.

As with all the other offences governed by the opening paragraph of article 3(1), these offences must be committed 'intentionally'. However, these offences demand knowledge of a particular kind for criminal liability to follow. The provision itself requires that the alleged offender must have dealt with the materials and so on 'knowing that they are to be used in or for' the proscribed purposes. This implies prior knowledge of the illicit objective.[145] Article 3(3) provides that such knowledge may be inferred from the facts.

---

143 'Report of the United States Delegation to the United Nations Conference for the adoption of a Convention Against Illicit Traffic in Narcotic Drugs and Psychotropic Substances' from *United Nations Convention Against Illicit Traffic in Narcotic Drugs and Psychotropic Substances*, Senate Executive Report 101-15, 101st Congress, 1st Session, p.27.

144 'Manufacture' under article 1(1)(n) of the 1961 Convention 'means all processes, other than production, by which drugs may be obtained and includes refining as well as the transformation of drugs into other drugs'.

145 The 'Expert Group Report', *1988 Records* vol. I at 12.

Article 3(1)(a)(iv) extended the scope of criminal conduct and although Parties have transformed article 3(1)(a)(iv) into their domestic law,[146] it does not seem, at least in some Parties that have met their obligations, that prosecutions are common.[147] Other more zealous Parties have extended domestic criminal liability beyond that demanded by its provisions.[148]

3.2.4.2.6 The offences of the organisation, management or financing of drug trafficking

Article 3(1)(a)(v) is intended to suppress the illicit traffic's logistical backup and to criminalise the activities of individuals who may never come into contact with drugs, but without whom the illicit traffic could not operate at its present scale. It is designed to reach the highest levels of drug trafficking, levels not reached by the 1961 Convention because the 1961 Convention only addresses the financing of drug trafficking and subjects the obligation to criminalise financing to a domestic limitations clause.[149]

Article 3(1)(a)(v) renders the 'organisation, management or financing' of any of the forms of conduct criminalised by the earlier sub-paragraphs of article 3(1)(a) unlawful. What is unlawful conduct then depends on these earlier pro-

---

146 See, for example, section 6 of the Australian Crimes (Traffic in Narcotic Drugs and Psychotropic Substances) Act, 1990, which provides that dealing includes: '(1) (fa) the manufacture, transport or distribution of any substance listed in Table I or Table II in the Annex to the Convention or of equipment and materials' with the knowledge that they are going to be used for dealing.

147 A.N. Brown, 'Drug Trafficking and the control of precursor and essential chemicals: UK domestic law and practice' in H.L. MacQueen and B.G. Main (eds), *Drug Trafficking and the Chemical Industry: Hume Papers on Public Policy* Vol. 4, no.1, (Edinburgh UP, Edinburgh, 1996), p. 25 at p. 42 could discover no evidence of prosecutions under the relevant UK legislation.

148 The US's Chemical Diversion and Trafficking Act of 1988, 21 USC section 960(d) (1990) imposes criminal liability on any person who intentionally or knowingly imports or exports a listed chemical, or any person who reasonably believes that drug traffickers may divert and use a regulated chemical to produce illegal drugs and supplies it to them.

149 See 'Report of the US Delegation' supra note 143 at 27-28. The criminalisation of such conduct has been a priority in the US. D.P. Stewart, 'Internationalizing the war on drugs: the UN Convention Against Illicit Traffic in Narcotic Drugs and Psychotropic Substances' (1990) 18 *Denver Journal of International Law and Policy* 387 at 392 footnote 17 points out that this offence embraces specific US offences such as Racketeer Influenced Corrupt Organisations or RICO, 18 USC sections 1961-1968 (Supp. 1989); and Continuing Criminal Enterprises or CCE, 21 USC section 848 (Supp. 1989). Italian action against organised crime saw more general legislation being enacted, such as Decree No.309 of 9 October 1990.

visions. The 'organisation' of these other offences implies making arrangements for their execution, 'management' implies their administration, while 'financing' involves provision of pecuniary resources so that they may be carried out. Although these offences are accessory in nature, in that they depend on the commission of other drug offences, whether they depend on the apprehension or conviction of offenders for these primary offences appears to have been left to domestic law. Article 3(1)(c)(iv) deals in more general terms with forms of accessory liability but is limited by a chapeau.

Article 3(1)'s opening paragraph provides that these offences must be committed intentionally. Article 3(3) provides that such intention can be inferred from the facts.

Parties have responded positively to the general calls to take action against the organisational infrastructure of the illicit traffic and have enacted article 3(1)(a)(v) offences.[150] A criticism of this provision is that it appears to view the illicit traffic as a monolithic structure with a clearly defined leadership, when in fact it may operate as a chain of connected small-scale cells. Domestic legislation applying article 3(1)(a)(v) will probably, however, be adaptable to suppressing small as well as large-scale management.

3.2.4.2.7 Money laundering offences[151]
Mounting international concern about the use to which the financial system was being put for the "laundering" of the profits of drug trafficking, a concern expressed in paragraphs five and six of the Convention's Preamble, lead to article 3(1)(b)'s inclusion in the 1988 Convention.[152] With its origins in United States law,[153] article 3(1)(b) creates new offences[154] aimed at global curtail-

---

150 See again, for example, section 6 of the Australian Crimes (Traffic in Narcotic Drugs and Psychotropic Substances) Act, 1990, which provides that dealing includes: '(1)(fb) the organising, managing or financing a dealing in drugs'. See also article 222.34 of the French Penal Code.

151 The 1988 Convention does not use the term money laundering because of its novelty and because of difficulties of translation – *1988 Commentary* at 65.

152 See generally K.D. Magliveras, 'Defeating the money launderer – the international and European framework' (1992) 3 *Journal of Business Law* 161-177.

153 The money laundering provisions, subsequently repealed and replaced, were in the Anti-Drug Abuse Act of 1986, collectively called the Money Laundering Control Act (MLCA) of 1986 (as amended in 1988 and codified in 18 USC sections 1956 and 1957). See generally B.E. Hernandez, 'RIP to IRP – Money laundering and drug trafficking controls score a knockout victory over bank secrecy' (1993) 18 *North Carolina Journal of International Law and Commercial Regulation* 235 at 265-275.

ment of drug-money laundering, the attempt to convert, conceal, transfer or disguise the proceeds of illicit drug trafficking and render them reusable.[155] The authors of this provision sought not only to criminalise this conduct, but also to bring to bear for the first time the rest of the international drug control system against money laundering, allowing confiscation, mutual legal assistance and extradition of offenders.[156]

Article 3(1)(b) obliges Parties to render unlawful the 'conversion or transfer' of property or the 'concealment or disguise' of property in the circumstances specified. The tainted nature of this property stems from the fact that it is derived from article 3(1)(a)'s illicit trafficking offences. Thus article 3(1)(b)'s offences appear to be accessory in nature. However, use of terms like 'transfer' can be applied to someone who commits the original (predicate) offence. The Convention according to the *1988 Commentary* does not bind Parties to either one or other view.[157] If it is treated solely as an accessory offence it does not matter whether the offender in the predicate offence has been apprehended or convicted for the offender in the accessory offence to be found liable.[158] In some legal systems, if the same person is responsible for the predicate offence

---

154 The incorporation of this provision originally in draft article 3(2) and then in draft article 1(c) did not occur without resistance, some members of the Expert Group complaining that the ambiguous provisions were likely to lead to the criminalisation of bona fide business persons and unnecessarily limit free trade – see the *1988 Records* vol. I at 12. Yet their adoption at the 1988 Conference was not contentious – F. Rouchereau, 'La Convention des Nations Unies Contre le Traffic Illicite de Stupefiants et de Substances Psychotropes' (1988) 34 *Annuaire Francais de Droit Internationale* 601 at 603.

155 In money laundering jargon 'placement' involves the physical introduction of the drug proceeds into the financial system, through for example a cash deposit, 'layering' involves the disguising of the origins of the proceeds by creating complex layers of financial transactions, and 'integration' involves the integration of the layered funds back into the economy as legitimate funds. Friman notes: 'Methods used range from simple cash exchanges, cash smuggling, and purchases of bearer instruments (bearer bonds, money orders, cashiers checks, certificates of deposit) to routing funds by means of wire transfer through foreign banks, trusts, shell corporations and brokerage houses. Cross national differences in bank secrecy, tax, and monitoring regulations have offered launderers an array of opportunities to utilise bank transactions.' See H.R. Friman, 'International pressure and domestic bargains: regulating money laundering in Japan' (1994) 21 *Criminal Law and Social Change* 253 at 254.

156 See W.C. Gilmore, *Combating International Drug Trafficking: The 1988 United Nations Convention Against the Illicit Traffic in Narcotic Drugs and Psychotropic Substances* (Commonwealth Secretariat, London, 1991), p. 6.

157 *1988 Commentary* at 62. The *Commentary* does note however that the absence of guidance on this matter has caused difficulty for legislators.

158 Comment of the Jamaican delegate, *1988 Records* vol. II at 152.

and the laundering, he cannot be held liable for the laundering.[159] But other Parties provide in their law that the drug trafficker who launders his own profits can commit these offences.[160] In the past Parties established jurisdiction over the offence only if the predicate offence occurred within their territorial jurisdiction.[161] However, it was suggested at the 1988 Conference that the offences to which this offence is accessory must have been established and committed in the jurisdiction of a Party other than the one in which the offender commits this offence.[162] No territorial limitation is imposed by the text,[163] and it seems the purposes of the Convention would best be served by following modern practice where Parties apply the offence to laundering that takes place within their territory whether the predicate offence occurred within their territory or extraterritorially.[164] It is noteworthy that some Parties have gone further than required by article 3(1)(b) and criminalised money laundering if a link to any offence involving drugs, and not just article 3(1) offences, can be established.[165]

---

159 See, for example, Austria – *1988 Records* vol. II at 30. Article 3(11) would protect Austrian law in this regard.

160 See for example the position in the UK after the enactment of section 14 of the Criminal Justice (International Co-operation) Act, 1990.

161 See F. Taisch, 'Swiss statutes concerning money laundering' (1992) 26 *The International Lawyer* 695 at 697 setting out the pre-1990 position in Switzerland.

162 See the statement of the Netherlands delegate, *1988 Records* vol. II at 29.

163 *1988 Commentary* at 63.

164 See, for example, section 14 of Botswana's Proceeds of Serious Crime Act 19 of 1990 which makes it an offence to launder 'the proceeds of a serious offence, whether committed in Botswana or elsewhere'. See also the 1990 amendment to the Swiss Penal Code (article 305bis) which provides in subparagraph 3: 'The perpetrator shall also be punished if the principal offence has been committed abroad'. Recommendation 4(b) of the 'Report of the Caribbean Drug Money Laundering Conference, 1990' in W.C. Gilmore (ed.), *International Efforts to Combat Money Laundering* (Grotius, Cambridge, 1992), p. 25 at p. 26 is to the same effect. So is article 1 of the EU Directive on the Prevention of the Use of the Financial System for the Purpose of Money laundering, 10 June 1991, article 3 of the OAS Model Regulations Concerning Laundering Offences Connected to Illicit Trafficking and Related Offences, and article 6(2)(a) of the 1990 Council of Europe Convention on Laundering, Search, Seizure and Confiscation of Crime, ETS 141.

165 For example, the UK in its Drug Trafficking Offences Act, 1986. The Financial Action Task Force (FATF) in recommendation 5 of its 1988 Report recommended other states consider doing the same. Its reformulated recommendation 4 of 1996 states that countries should extend the criminalisation of money-laundering from drug money laundering to serious offences (FATF, *Annual Report*, 1995-1996, Paris, 28 June 1996, p.11). The *1988 Commentary* at 66 notes that there are difficulties with drug offence specific

In an effort to be comprehensive, article 3(1)(b) does not discriminate with respect to its personal scope. It appears to apply to any person, juristic[166] or natural, that engages in money laundering. Because of the breadth of the scope of conduct, the offence has been divided into two parts.[167]

Sub-paragraph (b)(i) relates to the 'conversion or transfer' of property derived from article 3(1) offences, that is, from the illicit traffic. Both conversion and transfer involve transfer of the title in the property, such transfer being of obvious use to drug traffickers seeking to launder their profits. 'Conversion' involves either the change or alteration of the condition of the property, e.g. sale of the property. 'Transfer' involves in its ordinary sense the conveyance or movement of property from one place or person to another in an unchanged form.[168] These terms are vague, but must include movement or conversion of property particularly money, the main target of these provisions, by electronic transmission.[169] The *1988 Commentary* opines that transfer involves criminalisation of the conduct of the transferor not transferee, and that while conversion could include both parties, the separate criminalisation in article 3(1)(c)(i) of 'acquisition' suggests that the recipient is not covered by article 3(1)(b)(i).[170] In essence, the *1988 Commentary* suggests that article 3(1)(b)(i) is aimed at the person who in a broad sense dispatches the property for laundering purposes.

---

laundering provisions such as proving that particular property is derived from drug trafficking where the person in question is involved in a broad range of criminal activities.

166 The *1988 Commentary* at 66-67 discusses the criminal liability of corporations, noting that the 1988 Convention is silent on this matter but that in 1990 FATF recommended imposition of liability on corporate entities and that Iceland has imposed such liability. See also article 14 of the OAS Model Regulations Concerning Laundering Offences Connected to Illicit Trafficking and related Offences, 1992; and Liability of Enterprises for Offences: Recommendation No.R(88) adopted by the Committee of Ministers of the Council of Europe on 20 October 1988 together with its Explanatory Memorandum (Strasbourg, Council of Europe, 1990). Liability of corporations is justified because of the byzantine complexity of many corporate structures and the consequent difficulties of individualising responsibility for laundering.

167 *1988 Records* vol. II at 151.

168 In its narrow legal sense it is an act by 'which the title of the property is conveyed from one person to another' – *Black's Law Dictionary* (6th edn 1990), p. 1497.

169 Draft article 1(j) defined 'laundering' as 'the concealment or disguise of the true nature, source, disposition, movement or ownership of proceeds and includes the movement or conversion of proceeds by electronic transmission.' – see UN Doc. E/CN.7/1987/2. Money can be rapidly transferred within and between jurisdictions electronically and converted into other currencies electronically.

170 *1988 Commentary* at 64.

The language of article 3(1)(b)(i) requires the conversion or transfer to be carried out with the specific purpose of either concealing or disguising the illicit origin of the property or assisting 'any person' (including by implication the accused himself) to evade the legal consequences of his involvement in the commission of an offence or offences. These purposes are limiting. For example, a bank that merely transfers funds which it knows to be property derived from an offence will not, absent either purpose, commit an offence under article 3(1)(b)(i).[171] It has been argued that knowledge of the source of these funds is a weak foundation for attributing either of these two purposes to the bank, and submits that to commit such an offence a bank would have to participate more actively in the scheme.[172] It does seem that purpose implies more than mere subjective recklessness or dolus eventualis, but the provision is ambiguous with regard to the extent of the knowledge required. It has been pointed out, for example, that article 3(1)(b)(i)'s provision that the conversion or transfer of money must be for the purpose of assisting an individual to 'evade the legal consequences of his actions' appears to make it an offence to convert or transfer property for the purpose of providing a legal counsel or defence to the accused.[173] The US delegation's answer to the dilemma was to interpret 'evasion' as implying a criminal purpose, and not legal avoidance through the bona fide representation of a defence attorney.[174]

Sub-paragraph (b)(ii) involves the intentional deception of others, especially law enforcement agencies, with knowledge of how the property was acquired illicitly, as to how the property was acquired or derived by the taking of measures to conceal or disguise its origins and the rights and interests in it. Thus the offender must have sought to disguise any of the listed characteristics, viz. its 'true nature', the essential quality of the property as being derived from trafficking; its 'source', the origin of the property in trafficking or its physical origin; its 'location', the site or place where the trafficking derived property is located; its 'disposition', the transfer, alienation or giving up of the property

---

171 D.E. Spencer, 'Bank liability under the UN Drug Trafficking Convention' (1990) 9 *International Financial Law Review* 16 at 17.

172 Supra note 171 at 17.

173 B. Zagaris, 'Developments in international judicial assistance and related matters' (1990) 18 *Denver Journal of International Law and Policy* 339 at 343-345. He suggests that legal counsel may be protected by article 5(8)'s protection of the rights of bona fide third parties in confiscation proceedings. He adds that article 3(1)(b)(i) seems only to forbid such transfer or conversion if the person is guilty, and that if it turns out he was not, then such conversion or transfer would not be an offence.

174 See 'Report of the US Delegation' supra note 143 at 28.

derived from trafficking; its 'movement', the change in position or location of the property; the 'rights with respect to' the property, the fact that the rights in the property are held by traffickers; and its 'ownership', the fact that traffickers have dominium in the property. There is no requirement that such concealment or disguise must have been made with the intention of facilitating the illicit trafficker in any way, which suggests that the offence has a very broad ambit. Nevertheless, again doubts have been raised as to whether article 3(1)(b)(ii) criminalises the conduct of a bank that merely transferred funds at the request of a trafficker that was its customer even with knowledge of the criminal origins of the funds.[175] However, the simple transfer of funds is a very efficient and rapid method of disguising their origins and it is arguable on a literal interpretation of the provision that any dealing by a bank or financial institution with the funds constitutes sufficient conduct for a violation of the offence.

Both the forms of conduct criminalised relate to 'property' which article 1(q) defines as 'assets of every kind, whether corporeal or incorporeal, movable or immovable, tangible or intangible, and legal documents or instruments evidencing title to, or interest in, such assets'. The *1988 Commentary* points out that it would have been more appropriate to use 'proceeds', defined in article 1(p) as 'any property derived from or obtained, directly or indirectly, through the commission of an offence established in accordance with article 3, paragraph 1'.[176] The indirect derivation of property from drug offences may cause problems for the implementation of this provision unless the suggestion of the *1988 Commentary* is followed and the reference to 'property' being 'derived from' drug offences is construed as property 'obtained directly or indirectly' from these offences.[177]

The opening paragraph of article 3(1) provides that these offences must be committed intentionally, while article 3(3) provides that such intention may be inferred from the 'objective factual circumstances'.[178] As noted, however,

---

175 Spencer supra note 171 at 17. He argues that a bank might be considered to conceal or disguise such property only if it helped, 'for example, the trafficker to set up a tax haven corporation with bearer shares and/or "nominee" directors or shareholders to which the bank would transfer the proceeds of an offence.'

176 *1988 Commentary* at 63.

177 *1988 Commentary* at 63.

178 Article 305bis of the Swiss *Code Penal* provides that knowledge for the offence of laundering may be established directly by showing actual knowledge or constructive knowledge, or indirectly by reckless disregard or wilful blindness. The position of law enforcement professionals appears to be that requiring proof of an actual intention as opposed to a suspicion by the launderer of the criminal origins of laundered funds would

these offences demand a special form of knowledge. Both require that the offender must have known that the property was derived from an article 3(1)(a) offence or offences, or from 'an act of participation'[179] in such an offence or offences. It is not clear precisely how much the launderer must have known about these other offences or acts. Clearly it must be awareness that the predicate offence falls within one of the broad categories of article 3(1)(a) offences even if precise details of the actual offence are unknown. Although some Parties resist the trend towards inference of intention from objective factual circumstances,[180] because of the practical difficulties of proving intention in money laundering prosecutions other Parties go as far as applying negligence as the mental element of laundering offences and the dominant international trend seems to be in this direction.[181]

---

make successful prosecution very difficult – see comments of Association of Chief Police Officers (ACPO) in House of Lords Select Committee on the European Communities, *Report: Money Laundering* (HL Paper 6, HMSO, London, 1990), p. 12.

179 The subjection of article 3(1)(c)(iv)'s criminalisation of participation to a chapeau recognises that some Parties will find it difficult to criminalise participation. The *1988 Commentary*, however, points out at 63 that article 3(1)(b) obliges Parties to criminalise laundering even if they don't recognise offences of participation. All that this provision requires is knowledge of 'an act' of participation, not 'an offence' of participation.

180 J. Castaignede, 'France' in N. Dorn (ed.), *Regulating European Drug Problems* (Kluwer, Hague, 1999), p. 103 at p. 111 notes that it was stated in a French Ministry of Justice Circular dated 10 June 1996 that the almost identical provision in the European Money-laundering Directive (article 1) appears too remote from French legal traditions and that the requirement of proving intent in French law meant that the prosecutor's duty was to provide evidence of such intent.

181 The US Money Laundering Control Act of 1986 (a new Bill was introduced on 29 April 1998) extends criminal liability to individuals and financial institutions that 'knew or would have reason to suspect' that 'the property involved in a financial transaction represents the proceeds of some unlawful activity.' The impact of this legislation is obvious in *US v Banque Leu (Luxembourg) SA*, CR.93.0607 (NDCal). The bank pleaded guilty to laundering 2.3 million dollars from drug sales on behalf of Colombians and agreed to forfeit the amount to US authorities and a further 1 million dollars to Luxembourg although US authorities had conceded that it had not known of the source of the deposits. The 1990 Council of Europe Convention on Laundering, Search, Seizure and Confiscation of the Proceeds of Crime, ETS 141, suggests but does not require negligence as the basis for its article 6(3)(a) laundering offence, as does article 2 of the 1992 OAS Model Regulations Concerning Laundering Offences Connected to Illicit Drug Trafficking and Related Offences and Recommendation 6 of the 1990 FATF Recommendations. Recommendation 33 of the 1990 FATF Recommendations is to the effect that national differences in this scienter element should not be allowed to affect the ability or willingness of states to provide each other with mutual legal assistance in regard to laundering.

Article 3(1)(b)'s criminalisation of money laundering is part of the 1988 Convention's broad strategy against the financial aspects of drug trafficking. Article 3(1)(c)(i), discussed below, criminalises another aspect of money laundering. Article 5(a) provides for confiscation of the proceeds of article 3(1) offences. Article 9(b)(ii) provides for co-operation in investigating and sharing information on laundering. Sub-paragraphs (d) and (e) of article 9(2) provide for training in uncovering laundering. Compliance with these provisions has not been perfect – for example, few African countries have criminalised money laundering[182] – but on the whole Parties have responded positively.[183] Some have enacted new legislation,[184] while others have amended their existing legislation to bring it into line with the provisions' requirements.[185] Indeed,

---

182 E.U. Savona and M. De Feo, *Money trails: international money laundering trends and prevention/control policies*, report prepared for the International Conference on Preventing and Controlling Money-Laundering and the Use of the Proceeds of Crime: a Global Approach, held at Courmayeur, Italy, from 18-20 June 1994, p. 97.

183 Recommendation 4 of the 1990 FATF Report calls for criminalisation of money laundering in accordance with the 1988 Convention. By 1990 money laundering was already an offence in most FATF states – see the 'FATF Money Laundering Report, 1990' in Gilmore supra note 164 at 15.

184 Magliveras supra note 152 at 174-177 records the rash of European legislation in the late 1980s and early 1990s criminalising money laundering.

185 The UK, for example, had to include specific provisions in the Criminal Justice (International Co-operation) Act, 1990, in order to bring section 24 of the Drug Trafficking Offences Act, 1986, into line with article 3. A. Dickson, 'Taking dealers to the cleaners' (1991) 141 *New Law Journal* 1068-1069 (part one of two part article) notes that while section 24 of the 1986 Act only prevented the laundering of proceeds by a third party and not by the drug trafficker himself and also required that there must be a retention of the benefit for the drug trafficker, article 3(1)(b) applied to both categories of persons and made laundering an offence no matter whom the money was intended to benefit. Section 14(1) of the 1990 Act, which brought English Law into line with article 3(1)(b)(i), made it an offence for a person to: '(a) Conceal or disguise any property which is, or in whole or in part directly represents, his proceeds of drug trafficking; or (b) Convert or transfer that property or remove it from the jurisdiction, for the purpose of avoiding prosecution of a drug trafficking offence or the making or enforcement in his case of a confiscation order.' Section 14(2) of the 1990 Act brought English law into line with article 3(1)(b)(ii) by creating offences committed by those who conceal, disguise, convert or transfer the property of a third person, knowing or having reasonable grounds to suspect that it is, or in the whole or in part directly or indirectly represents, another persons proceeds of drug trafficking. Section 14(3) of the 1990 Act, in line with article 3(1)(c)(i), made it an offence for a person to acquire property for inadequate or no consideration when he knows or has reasonable grounds to suspect that any property is, or in whole or in part directly or indirectly represents, another person's drug trafficking proceeds.

the 1988 Convention's provisions remain central to the generation of the broadest possible mobilisation to counter money laundering, a centrality attributable inter alia to it being the only treaty of global reach that criminalises this activity.[186]

The 1988 Convention's provisions are adequate, but they do not go as far as some would have liked. For example, they fail to criminalise negligent conduct in respect of money laundering and to clearly provide for the criminal liability of corporations as distinct from their employees.[187] In addition, they do not criminalise failure to report suspicious currency transactions (suspicion based reporting), currency transactions over certain thresholds (threshold reporting) or the purchase of certain types of highly mobile financial instruments such as bank cheques and payment orders. Nor do they criminalise the failure to keep correct records on the identification and reporting of the nature, sources, disposition, movement, and ownership of funds. Transaction reporting and record keeping requirements were first developed in the United States[188] and have since proved to be effective weapons against money laundering. Their strength

---

186 W.C. Gilmore, 'International initiatives' in R. Parlour (ed.), *Butterworths International Guide to Money Laundering Law and Practice* (Butterworths, London, 1995), p. 15 at p. 19. B. Zagaris and S.M. Castilla, 'Constructing an international financial enforcement subregime: the implementation of anti-money laundering policy' (1993) 19 *Brooklyn Journal of International Law* 871 at 908 state that the principle of criminalising money laundering derives primarily from the 1988 Convention.

187 Gilmore supra note 186 at 20-21.

188 In terms of section 5316 of the Currency and Foreign Transactions Reporting Act of 1970, 31 USC sections 5311-5324, the US Secretary of the Treasury promulgated regulations requiring banks and other financial institutions to submit detailed Currency Transaction Reports (CTRs) for all cash transactions greater than ten thousand dollars, and Currency and Monetary Instrument Reports (CMIRs) for cross-border transport of cash in excess of five thousand dollars. The Anti-Drug Abuse Acts of 1986 and 1988 (codified in scattered sections of 12 USC, 18 USC and 31 USC) extended these monitoring provisions from cash to bearer instruments of ten thousand dollars or more in value, and introduced new prohibitions against structuring multiple transactions to circumvent reporting requirements (see particularly 31 USC section 5324). In 1996 the US made it a legal requirement for financial institutions to file a Suspicious Activity Report (SAR) on transactions of five thousand dollars or more that involve potential money laundering or violations of the Bank Secrecy Act. See M.A. DeFeo, 'Depriving international narcotics traffickers and other organised criminals of illegal proceeds and combating money laundering' (1990) 18 *Denver Journal of International Law and Policy* 405; A.M. Grilli 'Preventing billions from being washed offshore: a growing approach to stopping international drug trafficking' (1987) 14 *Syracuse Journal of International Law and Commerce* 65-88; P. O'Brien, 'Tracking narco-dollars: the evolution of a potent weapon in the drug war' (1990) 21 *Inter-American Law Review* 637-677.

is that they focus on the cash deposit at the bank, the weak link in the money laundering chain. Once a deposit is accepted and the bank transfers the funds, the detection of tainted funds by other banks or government authorities becomes highly problematic, especially with electronic transfers. These objective mechanical rules apply whether or not the bank knows or suspects that the funds are tainted thus avoiding problems with proving a nefarious purpose. It has been suggested that the 1988 Convention should have gone further with regulation of professionals operating in the financial sector.[189] It should have imposed and criminalised the failure to adhere to 'know your customer' or 'due diligence' provisions,[190] suspicious transaction reporting requirements[191] and threshold reporting requirements.[192] But in 1988, agreement on monitoring and record keeping provisions for certain types of deposit was unlikely, because they are very costly to administer[193] and also raise difficult questions of criminal liability. Other elements to the creation of a hostile environment for money launderers such as the co-operation of financial institutions with supervisory financial reporting services and law enforcement agencies had to wait for general agreement on the preventative strategy which has been developed and implemented since 1988. Although there has been a lot of development at the inter-

---

189 See B. Zagaris, 'The emergence of an international anti-money laundering regime' in D. Atkins (ed.), *The Alleged Transnational Criminal* (Nijhoff, The Hague, 1995), p. 127 at p.156.

190 Article 305ter of the Swiss Penal Code provides: 'Any person who professionally accepts, keeps on deposit, manages, or transfers assets belonging to a third party, and fails to establish with all due diligence the identity of the beneficial owner, shall be punished by imprisonment up to one year's detention or a fine.' See also recommendation 12 of the 1990 FATF Recommendations.

191 See, for example, recommendation 16 of the 1990 FATF Recommendations. Section 31(1) of South Africa's Proceeds of Crime Act 76 of 1996 makes it an offence not to report a suspicion of laundering but provides that attorney-client privilege remains unaffected, an issue of some concern in other jurisdictions.

192 See, for example, Australia's Financial Transaction Reports Act, 1988, which provides in section 7 for threshold reporting of all transactions over 10 000 Australian dollars, in section 17B for reporting of all electronic fund transfers out of or into Australia, and in section 16 for suspicion based reporting.

193 R. Clutterbuck, *Drugs, Crime and Corruption* (MacMillan, London, 1995) reports that US banks make some six million CTRs per annum at a cost of seventeen dollars each. For this reason UK banks are opposed to currency reporting provisions – see UK Home Affairs Committee, *Report: Drug Trafficking and Related Serious Crime* vol. II (1989), p. 106.

national level in this area since 1988,[194] harmonisation of national laws has still not been achieved, and it is difficult to address the need to suppress money laundering without imposing undue burdens on the financial system. Resource and infrastructural problems mean that developments in "following the money", such as the extension of increasingly sophisticated obligations to all large-scale commercial enterprises regardless of their economic activity, seem destined at this stage to be isolated to compliant advanced jurisdictions, with the consequent removal of laundering to less compliant less advanced jurisdictions, and de facto policing of the latter by the former.[195]

3.2.4.2.8 Offences relating to the handling of property derived from drug trafficking

Article 3(1)(c)(i) criminalises various ways of handling property derived from drug trafficking. It is one of the four permissive provisions in the 1988 Convention. In other words, the Parties' obligation to implement is subject to the 'constitutional principles and the basic concepts' of their legal systems.[196] Although modelled on the limitation clause in article 36(2) of the 1961 Convention, the limitation clause in article 3(1)(c) is narrower, reflecting the desire

---

194 Article 3 of the 1991 European Union Directive on Prevention of Use of the Financial System for the Purpose of Money Laundering (Council Directive 91/308, OJ 1991 L166.77) imposes strict identification requirements on anyone opening a bank account or engaging in a transaction of over 15 000 ECUs. The 1992 OAS Model Regulations require financial institutions to record and verify information about their clients (article 10), make such information available on request to authorities (article 11), record cash transactions in excess of a specified amount and treat multiple cash transactions as a single transaction (article 12), and report suspicious transactions (article 13). Hernandez supra note 153 at 274 points out that the US has negotiated bilateral agreements with a number of states to enforce the adoption of US regulations with respect to reporting and record-keeping amounts in excess of ten thousand dollars, e.g. the Agreement between the United States and Venezuela Regarding Co-operation in the Prevention and Control of Money-Laundering arising from Illicit Trafficking in Narcotic Drugs and Psychotropic Substances, 5 November 1990, US Treaty Doc. No.43, 102nd Con., 1st Sess. (1991).

195 The global reach of organisations like FATF and financial intelligence agencies like the United States' financial security agency, FINSEC, is testimony to this trend toward dispersal.

196 Colombia has made an express declaration to this effect (10/6/1994 – *Multilateral Treaties Deposited* (1997) at 304).

of the delegates to reduce the emphasis on 'domestic law'.[197] 'Constitutional principles' were intended by the Convention's authors to mean written or unwritten basic principles that amount to something less than constitutional limitations. The Convention's authors wanted to avoid the situation where constitutionally enforced freedoms, such as the freedom of expression, provided insurmountable obstacles to criminalisation of the forms of conduct listed in article 3(1)(c).[198] Sproule and St-Denis explain that the reference to 'basic concepts' of their legal systems reflects the concerns of many delegates at the experts' meetings that these offences would conflict with such basic principles.[199] 'Basic concepts' was intended to reflect the differences in the penal legislation and judicial decisions of civil and common law systems in respect of the offences enumerated, for example, the differences in treatment of the offence of receiving criminal property.[200] The United States delegation noted that it was important to formulate offences that would not sweep innocent conduct such as a purchase by a bona fide purchaser for value within the definition of proscribed conduct particularly in states that did not grant prosecutors sufficient discretion to avoid such a result.[201]

Article 3(1)(c)(i) criminalises the acquisition, possession or use of property derived from or used in an article 3(1)(a) offence. The provision criminalises the conduct of people to whom a drug trafficker gives or sells his property, so that taking such property becomes an offence.[202] Article 3(1)(c)(i) requires knowledge of the origin of the property at the time of receipt, and therefore it is essential that the offender must have received the goods.[203] Limitation of 'acquisition' to simply taking possession may render 'possession' and 'use' redundant as the former action is a prerequisite for the latter actions.[204] Many

---

197 W.C. Gilmore, *Combating International Drug Trafficking: The 1988 United Nations Convention Against Illicit Traffic in Narcotic Drugs and Psychotropic Substances* (Commonwealth Legal Office, London, 1991, at p. 7 notes that the draft provision wording had been much closer to article 36(2) – see *1988 Records* vol. I at 77.

198 See generally the statement of the Netherlands delegate, *1988 Records* vol. II at 153.

199 Supra note 4 at 270. The Austrian delegation was 'strongly opposed' to the elimination of limitation clauses because certain of these offences were incompatible with Austrian law – *1988 Records* vol. II at 55.

200 Sproule and St-Denis supra note 4 at 270. See also the Working Group of Committee 1, *1988 Records* vol. I at 104.

201 'Report of the US Delegation' supra note 143 at 21.

202 Dickson supra note 185 at 1069.

203 *1988 Commentary* at 73.

204 *1988 Commentary* at 73.

states had already criminalised dealing in criminal proceeds,[205] but this offence seems to go further, because for one thing, it does not insist that the handler retain a benefit in the property.[206] The fact that it is very broadly drawn – it could involve the acquisition of any property or rights in property – may lead to absurd results.[207]

The opening paragraph of article 3(1) provides that this offence must be committed intentionally and article 3(3) provides that '[k]nowledge, intent or purpose required as an element of an offence set forth in paragraph 1 of this article may be inferred from objective factual circumstances.' Article 3(3) may prove of some assistance because the acquisition, possession or use must be with the specific knowledge that the property is either derived from an article 3(1)(a) offence or offences or from an act of participation in such offence or offences. The handler of the property must know at the time of receiving it that it constitutes proceeds of crime. A person who receives in good faith and then later learns of the criminal origin of the proceeds commits no offence. Thus a bank commits no offence if it accepts a deposit ignorant that it is tainted even if it later learns of its criminal origin. If, however, the handler of property once alive to these tainted origins deliberately conceals or disguises them from investigating authorities he will violate article 3(1)(b)(ii), the laundering offence proper. If he uses the knowledge he has acquired to make an unjustified profit for himself or another by converting the proceeds into other property or by transferring them, then he will violate article 3(1)(b)(i).[208]

Despite article 3(1)(c)(i)'s novelty and the potentially broad net of criminal liability that it creates, states have enacted this offence, finding it easier to accept after having criminalised laundering.[209]

---

205 For example, the US Anti-Drug Abuse Act of 1986, 31 USC section 5324.
206 Section 24 of the UK's Drug Trafficking Offences Act, 1986, did require the retention of a benefit but was amended after the 1988 Convention was concluded by the Criminal Justice (International Co-operation) Act, 1990 so as not to require one.
207 For example, the Japanese delegate pointed out that 'it could even cover the purchase of ... oranges at supermarkets.' -*1988 Records* vol. II at 153.
208 See the remarks of the Netherlands delegate – *1988 Records* vol. II at 52.
209 For example, section 6 of the South African Drugs and Drug Trafficking Act 140 of 1992, entitled 'Acquisition of proceeds of defined crime', reads: 'No person shall acquire any property, knowing that any such property is the proceeds of a defined crime.' Defined crimes include all of the offences laid down in article 3(1) of the 1988 Convention.

3.2.4.2.9 Offences relating to the possession of equipment, materials, precursor substances or essential chemicals to be used in the illicit cultivation, production or manufacture of drugs

While article 3(1)(a)(iv) obliges Parties to criminalise the manufacture, transport or distribution of materials used in drug trafficking offences, because of the controversial nature of criminalising possession of the commercial material to which it applies, article 3(1)(c)(ii) was dissociated from that provision in order to allow it to be subject to the constitutional principles and the basic concepts of the Parties' legal systems.[210]

Article 3(1)(c)(ii) anticipates that equipment, materials or the substances in Tables I and II will be used in the creation of drugs, and thus criminalises their possession if that is the purpose for which they are being held. The processes of creation, manufacture, cultivation and production were defined originally in the 1961 Convention.[211]

Finally, the opening paragraph of article 3(1) provides that these offences must be committed intentionally. However, the provision requires that the offender must have known that the material was being or was going to be used for the creation of drugs in any of the ways stipulated. The *1988 Commentary* points out that 'possession' implies an ongoing relationship with the material in question which suggests that the prescribed knowledge need not exist at the moment of gaining possession and can come into existence at a later stage.[212] A bona fide possessor who learns of these purposes and remains in possession thus becomes a mala fide possessor. Article 3(3) assists in proving such intention and knowledge because it provides that they can be 'inferred from objective factual circumstances.'

---

210 *1988 Records* vol. I at 14.
211 'Manufacture' under article 1(1)(n) of the 1961 Convention 'means all processes, other than production, by which drugs may be obtained and includes refining as well as the transformation of drugs into other drugs'; 'cultivation' according to 1(1)(i) 'means the cultivation of the opium poppy, coca bush or cannabis plant' and no other plant as the 1961 Convention does not deal with any other plant; and 'production' under article 1(1)(t) means 'the separation of opium, coca leaves, cannabis and cannabis resin from the plants from which they are obtained.'
212 *1988 Commentary* at 74.

In spite of the caution necessitating a separate offence subject to limitations, and in spite of the novelty of this provision particularly with regard to the material to which it applies, Parties have responded positively.[213]

3.2.4.2.10 Incitement or induction offences

Reaching way beyond the provisions of the earlier conventions, article 3(1)(c) (iii) is designed to penalise any act of 'overt encouragement which might induce persons to participate in any aspect of illicit drug trafficking.'[214] In reality, it covers the advocacy of drug use or supply through print and electronic media.[215] A novel provision, it is among those offences subject to the constitutional principles and the basic concepts of the Parties' legal systems.[216] Article 3(1)(c)(iii) criminalises the public incitement or induction, by any means, of others to commit any of the article 3 offences, both the serious offences of article 3(1) and the simple possession offence of article 3(2), or to use drugs illicitly (use itself not being an offence under article 3(2)). This offence is among those criminalising inchoate conduct; the inciter does not complete the drug offence himself, he encourages others to do so by some form of communication that must reach the mind of the incitee. It is immaterial whether the person being encouraged actually commits the offence. Inducement involves the introduction of someone to trafficking or using drugs by the offering of money or by 'any' other means. Whether or not the subject of induction actually does traffic or use drugs is irrelevant. Although ambiguous, it appears that both incitement and induction must be public. Non-public induction may constitute counselling in terms of article 3(1)(c)(iv).[217] 'Publicly' may mean at an occasion to which the public is invited or at a place open to the public or by a means of transmission receivable by the public such as radio, but it is undefined and domestic practice will probably determine what is meant by the term.[218]

---

213 Section 6 of the Australian Crimes (Traffic in Narcotic Drugs and Psychotropic Substances) Act, 1990, provides that dealing includes: '(1) (g) the possession of any substance listed in Table I or Table II in the Annex to the Convention or of any equipment or materials,' with the knowledge that they are going to be used for dealing.

214 See the remarks of Mexican delegate who introduced the original much more extensive version of this provision – *1988 Records* vol. II at 53.

215 *1988 Commentary* at 74.

216 The US delegation were concerned that it was unconstitutional obviously because it may impinge on rights to free speech – see 'Report of the US Delegation' supra note 143 at 28.

217 *1988 Commentary* at 74.

218 *1988 Commentary* at 74.

The opening paragraph of article 3(1) provides that these offences must be committed intentionally while article 3(3) provides that such intention 'may be inferred from objective factual circumstances.'

Again, despite its novelty, Parties have responded positively to this provision, broadening their legislation in respect of the incitement of drug offences.[219]

3.2.4.2.11 Inchoate offences and complicity

It is probable that the inchoate offences and degrees of complicity provided for in article 3(1)(c)(v) were uppermost in the minds of the authors of article 3(1)(c) when they subjected the provision to the constitutional principles and the basic concepts of the Parties' legal systems. Like article 36 of the 1961 Convention, these offences include concepts that are not yet universally recognised, such as 'conspiracy', hence the limitation.[220]

The inchoate forms of conduct criminalised includes 'attempts' and 'association or conspiracy', examined above under article 36 of the 1961 Convention and article 22 of the 1971 Convention. The only novelty here is the use of 'association' as an alternative to conspiracy. It implies a group of individuals actively associating with or sharing a mandate to commit article 3(1) offences. Association may have been used in order to overcome the difficulties of civil states with the precise meaning of conspiracy. The various degrees of complicity under article 3(1)(c)(v) include forms of participation, which involve some furthering or promotion of an article 3(1) offence committed by another. They potentially criminalise a broad range of conduct from actual involvement ('participation'), to assistance ('aiding' and 'abetting') to encouragement ('counselling'

---

219 Section 6 of the Australian Crimes (Traffic in Narcotic Drugs and Psychotropic Substances) Act, 1990, provides that dealing includes: '(2) (c) inciting to, urging or encouraging, any conduct that is, under subsection (1), a dealing in drugs. Incitement of drug offences was an offence in many jurisdictions prior to the 1988 Convention, e.g., section 17 of the UK's Misuse of Drugs Act, 1971. But these pre-1988 offences were limited by the narrow scope of then applicable drug trafficking offences.

220 See the 'Expert Group Report', *1988 Records* vol. I at 14. Although limited under both the 1961 and 1971 Conventions, the corresponding provision was not limited in the 1936 Convention and its limitation in the 1988 Convention has been questioned in the light of the seriousness of the conduct involved and particularly because it involved the brains behind drug trafficking – see the statement of the Indian delegate, *1988 Records* vol. II at 30, 53. But the US delegation noted that conspiracy offences are not titled the same in different states and do not have the same elements – 'Report of the US Delegation' supra note 143 at 28.

or 'facilitating').[221] The provision as a whole is intended to help prosecutors who cannot show actual sale and so on of drugs or laundering of proceeds by accused persons but against whom there is strong evidence of participation in an overall trafficking scheme. But it may go too far. Questions have been asked, for example, about whether the provision criminalises the simple transfer of funds during a normal banking transaction by a bank at the request of the customer when the bank knows the funds to be the proceeds of a drug trafficking offence.[222] It may be that some further active participation in an offence would be necessary, but upon a strict construction, however, such a transfer can be interpreted as facilitating the commission of one of the laundering offences or even the trafficking offences in article 3(1) and thus it falls under article 3(1)(c)(v).

In terms of article 3(1) these offences must be committed intentionally, and article 3(3) provides that such intention 'may be inferred from objective factual circumstances.'

In practice, law enforcement agencies are keen supporters of the utility of these offences for ensnaring drug trafficking "managers" who remain at a safe distance from their product, and in spite of the unusual nature of some of these provisions, Parties have enacted broad provisions in this regard.[223] The similar provisions in the earlier conventions may well have facilitated acceptance of this obligation in spite of the get-out clause. To those Parties that choose to rely upon the chapeau to avoid application of accessory liability, the *1988 Commentary* points out that the criminalisation of money laundering in article 3(1)(b) when such property is derived from 'an act of participation in' an article 3(1)(a) offence implies an obligation to extend liability beyond direct perpetration.[224]

3.2.4.3   Demand related offences under the 1988 Convention

It has been pointed out above that authoritative interpretations of the provisions of the earlier conventions held that possession for personal use was not conduct that Parties were obliged to criminalise. Subsequent state practice saw a variety

---

221 *1988 Commentary* at 75.
222 Spencer supra note 171 at 18.
223 Section 6 of the Australian Crimes (Traffic in Narcotic Drugs and Psychotropic Substances) Act, 1990, for example, provides that dealing includes: '(2) (a) a conspiracy or attempt to engage in conduct that is, under subsection (1), a dealing in drugs; (b) being a party to any dealing in drugs referred to in subsection (1); (ba) aiding, abetting, counselling or procuring, or being by act or omission in any way directly or indirectly knowingly concerned in, any conduct that is, under subsection (1), a dealing in drugs.'
224 *1988 Commentary* at 78.

of non-penal approaches being taken to personal use offences and these were within the spirit of this liberal interpretation of the earlier conventions.[225] Continuing in this spirit, early drafts of the 1988 Convention did not address the issue of personal use offences.[226] 'Illicit traffic' was defined so as to include most of the offences contained in article 36 of the 1961 Convention, but possession was limited to possession for the purpose of distribution. Successive drafts omitted simple possession reflecting the general view among delegations that the Convention was a tool for the suppression of what they considered to be the more serious aspects of the drugs problem rather than for criminalising trivial conduct like possession for personal consumption. The Mexican delegation, opposing the general view because it assigned responsibility for illicit drug suppression to the producer states, argued that the Convention should address all aspects of the illicit drug problem including personal use. Delegations opposed to the inclusion of a personal use offence, particularly delegations from consumer states like the United States, argued that it would be impractical to require Parties to render expensive and time-consuming legal assistance for relatively minor offences. As a compromise between the two positions, the Conference agreed that although a personal use offence should be added to the Convention, it should not be a subject of the expensive and logistically complicated obligations imposed by the Convention in respect of extradition, confiscation and mutual legal assistance. Article 3(2) is the net result.[227] It represents an apparent victory for the producer states in their dispute with consumer states about who is responsible for the drug problem. However, many producer states also have large numbers of consumers in their populations and therefore criminalising possession for use under the Convention

---

225 K. Krajewski, 'How flexible are the UN drug conventions?' in *Agenda and Delegates Materials Regulating Cannabis: Options for Control in the 21ˢᵗ Century: An International Symposium* (Release/Lindesmith Center, 1998), p. 8. It is interesting to note that the whole effort to criminalise consumption at the 1988 Conference was made on the assumption that it had not been established as an offence by either the 1961 or 1971 Convention, *1988 Records* vol. II at 151.

226 See generally Sproule and St-Denis supra note 4 at 269-270 citing UN Doc. E/CONF.82/ 3 20 July 1988 at 13 and UN Doc. E/CONF.82/C.1/SR.24 at 4.

227 Article 3(2) is not the only consumption related measure in the 1988 Convention. Article 14(4) also attempts to balance the distribution of obligations between producer and consumer states by providing that consumer states 'shall adopt measures aimed at reducing or eliminating elicit demand for narcotic drugs and psychotropic substances.' The wording of the provision as a whole suggests that these measures should be non-penal in nature.

is self-directed, although in reality its implementation is not generally a concern of the rest of the international community.

It is not surprising that article 3(2)'s controversial obligation is subject to the 'constitutional principles and basic legal concepts of [the Party's] legal system'. Thus Parties would not violate the Convention if their domestic courts held criminalisation of personal use to be unconstitutional.[228] Whether legis-

---

228 Courts have been active in this regard. Many of the earlier cases involved conflicts between criminalisation and general rights such as privacy and equality. The early land mark case on decriminalisation for constitutional reasons was the 1975 Alaskan decision of *Ravin v State* 537 F.2d 494 (1975) per Rabinowitz CJ with Doochover and Conner JJ concurring, where the State Supreme Court decided that the relative insignificance of cannabis consumption as a health problem in Alaskan society meant there was no reason to intrude on the citizen's right to privacy by prohibiting possession of cannabis by an adult for personal consumption at home. Possession in public, and purchase and sale were not constitutionally protected. In Hawaii, three out of five Supreme Court judges in *State v Kanter* 493 F.2d 306 (1972) concluded that an individual has a right to smoke cannabis. In 1994, the Colombian Constitutional Court, in Sentence No. C-221/94, Constitutional Court Gazette 1994 Special Edition (available at <www.drugtext.org/legal>) ruled that the domestic criminalisation of simple possession of small quantities of drugs in article 2 and article 51 of Law 30 of 1986 was unconstitutional primarily on the basis that it interfered with article 5 of the Constitution, the right to personal autonomy. By regulating the conduct of an individual, when that conduct did not affect others, the legislator was held to cross an ontologically prohibited frontier because, the court held, law is only bilateral, while morality is unilateral. In spite of the chapeau in article 3(2), and the Colombian Constitutional Court's opinion that the 1988 Convention distinguished between use and trafficking, the Court's declaration was considered to be 'not in conformity with the provisions of the international drug control treaties' by the INCB in its *Report of the International Narcotics Control Board for 1994* UN Doc. E/INCB/1994/1, p. 33. In Germany, criminalisation of cannabis under the Narcotics Act (Betäubungsmittelgesetz or BtMG) was considered unconstitutional by the Regional Court in Lübeck on the basis that as intoxicants such as alcohol were not criminalised it violated the principle of equality (article 3(1) of the Basic Law) and because becoming intoxicated fell within the principle of self-determination (article 2(1) of the Basic Law). The Federal Constitutional Court in the *Cannabis Decision,* BverfG NJW 1994, 1577 (available at <www.drugtext.org/legal>), held that the criminalisation of the sale or donation of cannabis in the Narcotics Act was constitutional. In addition, it held that criminalisation of conduct preparatory to the use of small quantities of cannabis products which does not endanger others, does not contravene the prohibition of excessive state interference, since the legislature has made it possible for the prosecution authorities to take account of any individual element of the wrongdoing by refraining from imposing a penalty (section 29(5) of the BtMG) or refraining from prosecution (sections 153 et seq. of the Code of Criminal Procedure). The court ruled that in the latter instances the prohibition on excessive interference with the personal freedom of an individual when that freedom does not harm others effectively requires that the prosecution authorities

lative decriminalisation of, for example possession of cannabis, could be seen

---

refrain from prosecuting such offences.

The right to freedom of religion has also been relied upon in domestic jurisdictions to try to justify judicial intervention. Its narrower scope may make it more appealing to the judiciary. But it does not have a universal appeal. In the United States in *Employment Division Department of Human Resources of Oregon, et al v Smith* [1990] 494 US 872, 108 Led 2(d) 876,the US Supreme Court decided a similar issue, the constitutionality of the prohibition of the possession and use of the hallucinogenic drug Peyote by members of the North American Church for sacramental purposes in terms of the free exercise of religion protected by the First Amendment to the Constitution. The majority held that the prohibition was not unconstitutional, although a significant minority dissented. Inferior US courts have consistently upheld the majority's position: *Olsen v Iowa* 808 F2d 652 (CA 1986 – marijuana use by Ethiopian Zion Coptic Church); *Commonwealth v Nissenbaum*, 404 Mass 575, 536 NE 2d 592 (1989 – marijuana use by Ethiopian Zion Coptic Church); *State v Blake*, 5 Haw App 411, 695 P 2d 336 (1985- marijuana use in practice of Hindu Tantrism); *Whyte v United States,* 471 A 2d 1144 (1982 – marijuana use by Rastafarians); *State v Rocheleau,* 142 Vt 61, 451 A2d 1144 (1982 – marijuana use by Tantric Buddhist); and *State v Brashear*, 92NM 622, 593 P2d 63 (1979 – marijuana use by non-denominational Christians). In Canada in *Regina v Kerr* [1986] 75 NSJ (2d) 305 (CA) the Nova Scotia Supreme Court upheld a conviction despite the defence that cannabis use was in accordance with the appellant's religious beliefs. In 1997 in *Forsythe v DPP*, The Gleaner, Kingston, 17 May 1997, the Jamaican Supreme Court rejected the appellant's argument that the statutory prohibition of possession of cannabis in Jamaica conflicted with his constitutional right to conscience and freedom of religion. However, in late 1999, in the *People of Guam v Guerrero,* Criminal Case No. 00001-91, August 1999, the Superior Court of Guam held that the importing of cannabis by a Rastafarian priest was protected by constitutional and statutory guarantees of freedom of the exercise of religion and against religious non-discrimination, and that the state had failed to demonstrate a compelling state interest in the denial of these rights. In a 1998 South African case, *Prince v President of the Law Society, Cape of Good Hope and Others*, 1998 (8) BCLR 976 (CPD) Friedman JP, Brand J, Hlophe J, the Cape Provincial Division of the High Court held that the Cape Law Society's decision that the applicant was not a 'fit and proper person' to be admitted as an attorney because of his two previous convictions for possession of cannabis and his avowed intention as a Rastafarian to continue to use the substance, assumed that such an action limited his constitutional right to freedom of religion, the prohibition against discrimination and the right freely to choose one's profession, but held that these rights could be reasonably limited in the circumstances. In doing so it relied heavily on South Africa's international obligations under the international drug conventions (at 985D-H). It rejected the argument that an exception could be made in respect of Rastafarians by holding that 'such an exception would be contrary to South Africa's obligations in terms of the international conventions to which it is a party (at 989A).' Amazingly, no mention was made of the chapeau in article 3(2) of the 1988 Convention. The decision was confirmed on appeal – *Prince v President of the Law Society, Cape of Good Hope and Others*, case no. 220/98, 25 May 2000, SCA.

to be part of the 'basic concepts' of a legal system and thus also escape article 3(2)'s obligation is unclear.[229] Cautious in spite of the limitation clause, some Parties have made reservations to article 3(2)'s criminalisation of personal use on constitutional grounds and because it conflicts with the basic concepts of their legal system.[230] Other Parties have stated that the basic concepts of their legal systems may alter, obviously anticipating that changes such as decriminalisation may occur in future.[231]

Article 3(2) criminalises possession, purchase and cultivation for use 'contrary to the provisions of the 1961 Convention, the 1961 Convention as amended or the 1971 Convention.' Once again the earlier conventions define by implication what is unlawful conduct. This may lead to the interpretation that Parties are able to retain the stance they had adopted to simple possession under the earlier conventions.[232] The *1988 Commentary* suggests, however, that to be consistent with the express inclusion of 'personal consumption' in article 3(2), 'contrary to the provisions' of the earlier conventions 'incorporates the schedules of controlled substances as well as the distinction under those conventions between licit and illicit consumption.'[233] However, given the ambiguities sur-

---

229 The INCB does not believe it can because the INCB stated that Italian legislation repealing the non-medical prohibition on drugs passed after a referendum in April 1993 was not in line with article 4(c) and 33 of the 1961 Convention or article 3(2) of the 1988 Convention – INCB, *Report of the International Narcotics Control Board for 1994* UN Doc. E/INCB/1994/1, p. 52.

230 Bolivia has made a reservation (20/8/1990) to the effect that article 3(2) is inapplicable in Bolivia to the extent that it may be interpreted as establishing 'as a criminal offence the use, consumption, possession, purchase or cultivation of the coca leaf for personal consumption'. It declares that such an interpretation 'is contrary to principles of its Constitution and basic concepts of its legal system which embody respect for the culture, legitimate practices, values and attributes of the nationalities making up Bolivia's population.' Bolivia justified the reservation on the basis of the historical use of coca leaf, pointing out that it is not a drug, its use does not cause significant harm, it is widely used for medicinal and industrial purposes, criminalisation of its consumption would result in a large part of the Bolivian population being criminals and its transformation into cocaine takes place using precursors that do not originate in Bolivia – *Multilateral Treaties Deposited* (1997) at 303. Colombia has only gone as far as declaring that article 3(2)'s obligation is conditional upon respect for its constitutional principles (10/6/1994) – *Multilateral Treaties Deposited* (1997) at 304.

231 See the declaration made by the Federal Republic of Germany (20/11/1993) – *Multilateral Treaties Deposited* (1997) at 304.

232 *1988 Commentary* at 81.

233 *1988 Commentary* at 81.

rounding the delimitation of lawful conduct under the earlier conventions,[234] as pointed out particularly in the discussion above of simple possession as an offence under the 1971 Convention, it is not easy to discern what conduct is rendered unlawful by article 3(2). One might question, for example, whether simple possession of a Schedule II psychotropic substance is an offence under article 3(2) when the 1971 Convention provides in terms of article 5(3) that it is only 'desirable' that the Parties do not permit possession except under legal authority of the substances in Schedule II. The precise material delimitation of the scope of article 3(2) requires careful investigation of the classification and attendant obligations of each particular substance under the earlier conventions.

The provision criminalises three forms of conduct associated with personal use of drugs although use itself is not criminalised. 'Possession' involves some form of control of the drug and knowledge of control but must be distinguished from 'possession' in article 3(1)(a)(iii) because in article 3(2) the purpose of possession is not drug trafficking, it is personal use. 'Purchase' involves the buying of drugs but once again it must be for the purpose of use and not drug trafficking, in order to distinguish it from 'purchase' in article 3(1)(a)(iii). Finally 'cultivation', which involves the nurturing of a plant from which drugs are produced, is also only criminalised by this provision if it is done with the purpose of use and not trafficking, in order to distinguish it from 'cultivation' in article 3(1)(a)(ii). Echoing the earlier commentaries, the *1988 Commentary* believes that the distinction of possession for use from possession for trafficking may be facilitated by threshold requirements such as possession of a specified mass of the drug in question,[235] but once again it must be pointed out that such provisions are constitutionally vulnerable. [236]

Article 3(2) makes it clear that the personal use offences must be 'committed intentionally'. There is no provision for inference of such intention from object-

---

234 The authors of article 3(2) must have had in mind the obligation on Parties in the earlier conventions to limit use and possession to medical and scientific purposes (article 4(c) of the 1961 Convention and article 5 paragraphs (2) and (3) of the 1971 Convention). But the extent of that obligation depends to a large extent on the type of substance involved and under which control regime it falls in terms of the general scope of control provisions (articles 2 and 3 of the 1961 Convention and article 2 of the 1971 Conventions), as well as the impact of any special provisions relating to that substance (such as article 28(3) of the 1961 Convention relating to the misuse of cannabis leaves).

235 *1988 Commentary* at 83.

236 See note 39 supra.

ive circumstances, a further indication of the absence of zealous support at the Conference for article 3(2).

The 1988 Convention's criminalisation of simple possession shows that demand reduction can involve the application of the criminal law. But whether the criminalisation of such conduct will achieve a reduction in demand is uncertain and it may be counter-productive in other ways. As Chatterjee points out, 'according to criminologists, social workers, medical practitioners and psychologists attribution of criminality to drug addicts may conflict with the process of therapy and treatment.'[237] Although a victory for drug producer states, the reality is that the developing states that sponsored article 3(2) seldom have the financial wherewithal to engage with users in any other way than treating them as criminals. When they are faced with large numbers of users developing states pragmatically often choose to ignore them. While most states in the developed world still criminalise possession, state practice in the developed world has shown a steady if narrow trend toward a limited legalisation or decriminalisation of personal use[238] and a much wider de facto decriminalisation of personal use. It seems unlikely that the massive invasion of individual rights associated with the draconian law necessary to suppress demand is possible in the developed world, given the growing tolerance of drug use.[239] Nevertheless, those Parties that actually remove all legal sanction from the possession of even small amounts of drugs violate article 3(2) and the 1988 Convention unless their actions fall within article 3(2)'s escape clause. The provision in article 3(4)(d) for treatment measures to be applied by Parties as an alternative or in addition to conviction or punishment only provides an escape route from violation of the 1988 Convention's obligation in article 3(2) to those Parties that criminalise and then choose as a matter of administrative policy

---

237 S.K. Chatterjee, *Drug Abuse and Drug Related Crimes* (Nijhoff, Dordrecht, 1989), p. 65.

238 In April 1993 the German Constitutional Court ruled that possession of small amounts of drugs need no longer be prosecuted – *Newsweek*, 4 July 1994. In November 1996, California legalised the use of cannabis for medical purposes and Arizona allowed doctors to prescribe any drug for medical treatment and approved treatment and not incarceration for illegal possession – *The Guardian*, 22 February 1997.

239 Thus, for example, while article 71(2) of the Second Schengen Agreement, 1990, required Parties to criminalise supply of drugs, article 7(5) only required Parties to apply measures to prevent and counteract demand, explicitly leaving the choice of measures to the Parties.

not to prosecute or punish.[240] It allows for the depenalisation of simple possession.[241] It has been suggested that a more principled alternative would be to combine the principle that self-destructive behaviour should not be the subject of punishment[242] and the expediency principle whereby a state introduces legislation but does not enforce it, to allow Parties to enact the article 3(2) offence and then use their administrative discretion not to apply it when no-one other than the user is threatened by use.[243]

3.2.4.4 The 1988 Convention's penal provisions appraised

While it has been argued that article 3(2)'s criminalisation of possession for personal use confirms that demand is a major part of the international drug problem,[244] the focus of the Convention's penal provisions is obviously on supply. Article 3(1) built upon the offences contained in the earlier conventions in order to facilitate domestic implementation of the new Convention.[245] However, article 3(1) broadened the scope of the earlier offences in response to the perceived international threat presented by traffickers who never handle drugs but organise, finance, and profit from international trafficking.[246] Com-

---

240 See B. Leroy, 'European legislative systems in relation to demand in 1993: recent developments and comparative study' in G. Estievenart (ed.), *Policies and Strategies to Combat Drugs in Europe* (Nijhoff, Dordrecht, 1995), p.112 at p.114.

241 This is the position in the Netherlands. The Dutch assert that they are in compliance with the 1988 Convention because although it requires criminalisation it says nothing about the scope of the required enforcement – Memorandum of the Minister of Health and the Environment, 'Drug Policy', 2nd Chamber of Parliament, 1999/2000, 24.077 No.71, at 24. Condemnation by fellow EU members like France is avoided by granting control over the issue to a local triangle of authority – the mayor, police chief and health committee, thus diffusing pressure to re-penalise. However, states that adhere strictly to the principle of legality, which obliges prosecution and punishment, find such an approach difficult to adopt.

242 This principle was used by the German Constitutional Tribunal in its 1994 decision decriminalising use. It was applied only to use, not possession, because possession can lead to supply.

243 Krajewski supra note 225 at 8-12.

244 Sproule and St-Denis supra note 4 at 291.

245 For non-parties to the earlier conventions this means major legislative action. The *1988 Commentary* at 60 suggests the adoption of UN model legislation for a single drug law and refers to UNDCP 'Model law on the classification and regulation of the licit cultivation, production and manufacture and trading of narcotic drugs, psychotropic substances and precursors', *Model Legislation* (June 1992), vol. 1.

246 W.N. Gianaris, 'The new world order and the need for an international criminal court' (1992/3) 16 *Fordham International Law Journal* 88 at 99.

mission by offenders of one or more of the offences relating to the 'illicit traffic' triggers the extensive provisions for co-operation in respect of the prosecution of offenders and law enforcement. These "core" offences are thus the keys to the rest of a system of international co-operation. But these keys do not always work smoothly. The necessity of accommodating the technical differences between the different criminal legal systems of states in the substance of the provisions, and the unwillingness of states to accept in practice the burdens imposed by international law, means ambiguity, limitation[247] and uneven application.

3.2.5   Conclusion – criticisms of the provisions for offences

The international provisions for drug offences have been examined in terms of three aspects of criminal liability, viz. unlawfulness, conduct and fault.

Drug associated conduct becomes unlawful through the translation into a Party's domestic law of its international obligations under the drug conventions, limited by the existence of the constitutional and domestic safeguard clauses in these conventions. Because of their status as international treaties creating delictual or tortious obligations among the Parties, the conventions do not have the same normative strength with respect to Parties as domestic legislation has with respect to its subjects. The existence of the limitation clauses and the broadness and ambiguity of the Conventions' provisions allows domestic encroachment on international obligations. This encroachment is not uniform from Party to Party and leads to irregular domestic drug offences.

With respect to the actual conduct criminalised, enumerating the forms of conduct has proved more popular than using a general formula. In result, international law has had a greater impact on the precise shape of domestic criminal law than it would otherwise have had. However, the detailing of these obligations still does not result in globally uniform drug offences. Each of the standard offences set out in the conventions involves attaching a particular verb, such as 'sale', to a noun, usually 'drugs' or some type of material used in the drug traffic, with the intention of covering most of the facets of demand and supply of illicit drugs. Whether this approach covers all the facets of 'illicit drug traffic' is a matter of interpretation. The drug conventions have on the whole left the

---

247 The Venezuelan delegate to the 1988 Conference illustrated this when he queried the application of the limitation clause only to article 3(1)(c); he said '[f]or the recognition of any offence, at least in Venezuela, it was a sine qua non that the domestic legal system must be respected.'- *1988 Records* vol. II at 152.

definition of these verbs and thus the definition of the content of the offences to the Parties. The official UN commentaries and the conference records only provide a supplementary guide for states about what the international community believes the contents of these offences should be. These offences were of course drafted with particular activities in mind, and as has been seen, it is not difficult to give a definition to each of them. But it is possible at the domestic level to construe each offence to mean something different. Loose definition of non-self-executing international penal provisions inhibits uniformity.[248] This point is most apposite to offences that Parties find difficult to adapt their law to, such as the inchoate offences, where wide domestic variation has necessitated the broadest of provisions. While these provisions successfully accommodate domestic variation they are not intended to[249] and they do not provide a specific and rigorous guide to the Parties on how to formulate their law. Internationally they make possible a common terminology, not content, harmony, not uniformity. In spite of this, these offences are broad in scope, covering much of the chain of supply of drugs and the laundering of profits, as well as controversial issues like use and possession. Even so, drug law enforcement "hawks" would like to see more. They would like to see the criminalisation of participation in organised criminal enterprises such as the 1982 Italian anti-Mafia laws,[250] criminalisation of failure to report suspicious financial transactions, criminalisation of tipping off a suspect that his or her affairs are subject to official scrutiny,[251] and criminalisation of corruption and particularly of international corruption of both private citizens and public officials.[252] The drug conventions do leave significant aspects of the international drug traffic unaddressed. They pay little attention to collateral problems of illicit trafficking, such as corruption, or narco-terrorism, or the illicit trade in weapons, all of which prop up the illegal traffic and make it more dangerous to police. But

---

248 Cotic supra note 113 at 100 footnote 10 points out, for example, that while in Japan forty two offences relate to drug production in four separate laws, in the Cote d'Ivoire there is only one such offence.

249 The *1988 Commentary* at 60 emphasises the flexibility left to Parties in implementation. The *Commentary* submits that it is unnecessary to mention each specific category of article 3(1)(a) offence and that what should be aimed for rather is comprehensive coverage.

250 Article 416bis of the Italian Penal Code.

251 See, for example, article 8 of the EC Directive on Prevention of the Use of the Financial System for the Purpose of Money Laundering, 10 June 1991.

252 See generally P. Williams and E.U. Savona (eds), *The United Nations and Transnational Organized Crime* (Frank Cass, London, 1996), p. 134.

it is more practical to address these issues in separate instruments in order to avoid making the drug conventions even more unwieldy, and because they are also collateral to non-drug related offences, and internationally specific steps have been taken against these practices.[253]

The mental element of criminal liability for drug offences suffers from the same problems of definition as the conduct element. While it appears to be precisely defined by being limited with respect to all the international drug offences to 'intention', no effort to define intention is made, thus inviting domestic variation. While Parties are allowed through the rules of treaty interpretation to interpret these provisions in accordance with their own practice, they can in terms of the conventions apply stricter measures of criminal fault such as negligence or no-fault liability to drug offences.

It is clear that the broad implementation of offences and not their accurate definition has been the focus of international law. Encouraging implementation has become the main task of the international drug control organs, although they have been supported by regional organisations through agreements like the Schengen Convention.[254] Wells notes that 'while the general level of legis-

---

253 In the last decade, for instance, there has been a flurry of anti-corruption activity. In December 1996 the UN General Assembly adopted 'The UN Declaration on Corruption and Bribery in Transnational Commercial Activities', GA Resolution 51/191, 36 ILM 1043. In 1996, the OAS adopted the Inter-American Convention Against Corruption, 35 ILM 724. The Convention's preamble expresses deep concern about the 'steadily increasing links between the corruption and the proceeds generated by illicit narcotics trafficking which undermine and threaten legitimate commercial and financial activities and society at all levels.' The Convention, which is aimed at improving the Parties' domestic mechanisms for prevention, detection and eradication of corruption also envisages international co-operation in this regard (article 2). It adopts a range of measures to achieve this aim including conduct standards, the criminalisation of acts of national and transnational corruption, and the full gamut of support measures including mutual assistance, extraterritorial jurisdiction, extradition, seizure and confiscation of property, and removal of bank secrecy. The Convention envisages progressive development of action against corruption and is an important feature of the OAS's Inter-American Program of Co-operation in the Fight Against Corruption. In 1997, the OECD adopted a Convention on Combating Transnational Bribery of Foreign Public Officials In International Business Transactions in 1997, (1998) 37 ILM 1, which criminalises the making of bribes and develops international co-operation in this regard.

254 Convention Applying the Schengen Agreement of 14 June 1985 between the Governments of the States of the Benelux Economic Union, the Federal Republic of Germany and the French Republic, on the Gradual Abolition of Checks at Their Common Borders, in force 19 June 1990. Article 71 paragraphs (1)-(2) provide that contracting parties undertake, in compliance with the drug conventions, to prevent and punish the sale, export and supply of drugs. In terms of article 71(5) Parties shall do all in their

lative implementation of the more "classical" trafficking activities has been broadly satisfactory, it has been much less so with the newer offences relating to the crucial facilitating or support activities of money laundering and illicit precursor supply.'[255] There has never been an exhaustive investigation of the extent to which Parties have established drug trafficking offences[256] but it does appear that the standard trafficking offences relating to illicit cultivation, production, manufacture, trafficking, possession for trafficking and so on set out in all three of the major conventions are fairly commonly legislated by states, although offences relating to incitement to traffic and purchase for traffic are not as common.[257] The international obligations to criminalise inchoate conduct such as attempts and conspiracy, as well as all forms of participation in drug production and supply not only by principals but also by accomplices, appear to have been complied with by states.[258] Some of the more abstract trafficking related offences, most of which were introduced in the 1988 Convention, such as holding of equipment, trafficking in precursors, money laundering, receiving and or possessing the proceeds of trafficking are not as commonly

---

power to 'prevent and combat' illicit demand using whatever measures they choose.

255 A. Wells, *International Legal and Policy Framework* (unpublished conference paper, New Delhi Global Drugs Law Conference, 1997), p. 13.

256 INCB, *Report of the International Narcotics Control Board for 1994* UN Doc. E/INCB/ 1994/1, p. 6.

257 Wells supra note 255 reveals in Appendix E the UNDCP's broad survey of domestic legislation penalising drug offences. While some of this information is outdated and many Parties that may well have enacted these offences have not supplied the UNDCP with information, it does reveal broad trends:

Trafficking Offences (out of 91 states)

Illicit cultivation (1961;1971;1988)	82
Production/manufacture (1961;1971;1988)	90
International trafficking (1961;1971;1988)	91
Domestic trafficking (1961;1971;1988)	91
Trafficking by users (1961;1971;1988)	90
Incitement of trafficking (1988)	41
Possession of drugs for trafficking (1961;1971)	88
Acquisition of drugs for trafficking (1961;1971)	65

Cotic supra note 113 notes that surveys of the legislation and practice of 31 selected states from three major areas, Europe, Africa/Asia, and South America reveals that most states are carrying out their international obligations to punish drug production and supply (he discusses Europe at p. 22, p. 34; Africa/Asia at p. 65; Latin America at p. 93).

258 Cotic supra note 113 at 99.

legislated.[259] Personal use offences, laid down clearly in the 1988 Convention, are commonly legislated, although state practice is inconsistent.[260] It appears that the 1988 Convention's new offences are not as widely implemented as the offences introduced by the older conventions, which indicates that the general process of indirect application of international drug crime is slow. With regard to the actual prosecution of all offences information is limited, but it appears from the practice of states that personal use offences still account for

---

259 See Wells supra note 255 who gives the following figures in Appendix E:

Trafficking Related Offences (out of 99 states)
Possession/holding of equipment (1988)	43
Trafficking in precursors (1988)	33
Organisation/financing/direction of traffic (1961;1971;1988)	71
Laundering (1988)	43
Receiving/possessing/trafficking property/proceeds (1988)	44
Regulatory offences (licit activities) (-)	53
Aggravating circumstances (1988)	47

260 See Wells supra note 255 who gives the following figures in Appendix E:

Use and related offences (out of 97 states)
Use (-)	66
Possession/holding/acquisition for personal use (1988)	75
Incitement to use (-)	57
Facilitating use (-)	74
Convenience prescriptions (-)	65
Use of falsified prescriptions (-)	49

Cotic supra note 113 reveals the ambivalence of state practice with respect to possession, particularly in Europe (at p. 46) where some states adopt a much more repressive approach than others, and most states distinguish possession for use and possession for gain. Only two states do not incriminate possession for personal use – Denmark and the Netherlands. In Africa/Asia (at p. 80) possession was equalised with trafficking and production, and there was little legislation allowing for lighter punishment. In Latin/America (at p. 94) a distinction was made between possession for use and possession for trafficking, although all states criminalised possession.

the vast majority of prosecutions,[261] followed by general trafficking offences, with relatively few prosecutions of the 1988 Convention's new offences.[262]

The dilemma of those attempting to formulate an international criminal law of drugs is that more specific provisions aimed at establishing globally uniform law may result in non-compliance with conventional obligations and no law at all. The key is the willingness of states to adapt entrenched principles to suit new international legislation. Although a degree of harmony does appear to have been established, the growth of a shared perception by most nations that no other alternative is possible would be necessary to move the system to greater uniformity. A change in the political dynamic impacting on the drug conventions would have to occur. At present producer states want consumer states to take more responsibility for the drug problem and thus they have forced the criminalisation of personal use offences. But consumer states focus on supply, and their political dominance means that producer states carry much of the burden of international obligations directed at the illicit traffic. Uniformity of state practice is not likely to flow from provisions that reflect these divisions in opinion on who bears responsibility for the drug problem. The criminalisation of supply and demand is seen by Rouchereau to be logical in terms of effective drug prohibition, which must fight both production and use.[263] But if we are to look beyond international prohibition to the possibility of treating drug use primarily as a social and medical problem while maintaining an umbrella of legal protection over users through the prohibition of supply, then a new logic will have to emerge.

---

261 This is true for example, in respect of Australia – see S. Allsop and R. Nicholas, 'Harm minimisation' in *Souvenir Brochure of the International Conference on Global drugs Law* (Indian Law Institute, New Delhi, 1997), p. 22 at p. 23.

262 Prosecution of these offences in jurisdictions such as the US where they have been in place for some time is common, but in less sophisticated jurisdictions or those untouched by money laundering and so on prosecution appears uncommon.

263 Supra note 154 at 603.

3.3   PENALTIES

3.3.1   Introduction

May records that the Turkish Sultan Murad IV (1612-1640) forbade the use of opium on pain of death.[264] Yet until relatively recently in historical terms, drug use and drug trafficking either went unpunished or punishment was sporadic and varied enormously in nature and severity. The advent of international regulation, however, prompted a general call for more uniformly severe punishment. Commenting on the need for the 1936 Convention, Bailey remarked that penalties for drug traffickers should neither be merely pecuniary nor consist only of short terms of incarceration, and that the heavy profits made by traffickers should mean heavy prison sentences.[265] In the post-war period, international attitudes to punishment of drug traffickers have generally followed this line.[266] Thus, for example, when a 1961 CND Resolution called for 'adequate' sentences this was interpreted by many CND members as severe punishment.[267] The drafters of the 1961 Convention were also motivated by the desire to punish drug offenders heavily.[268]

The problem confronted by the international community in its effort to harmonise punishment was that similar offences were punished completely differently. A UN study of the sentencing policies of selected states in 1972 concluded that there was an 'obvious lack of a common international view on

---

264 H.L. May, 'The evolution of the international control of narcotic drugs' (1950) 2 *Bulletin on Narcotics* 1 footnote 1.

265 S.H. Bailey, *The Anti-Drug Campaign: An Experiment in International Control* (PS King, London, 1935), p. 115.

266 US practice has been very influential. In 1953, Anslinger and Tompkins in the *Traffic in Narcotics* (Funk and Wagnalls, New York) advocated the following approach which gained widespread legislative approval in the US: for traffickers they advocated maximum sentences with no probation, parole or suspension of sentence, minimum sentences of five years except for informers, no plea-bargaining for lighter sentences, prosecution of every case and maximum sentences for sale to minors; for addicts they supported lengthy probation periods with enforced submission to hospital treatment, enforced monthly medical examinations as a probation condition, regular reports after discharge and comprehensive follow up care.

267 See K. Bruun, L. Pan and I. Rexed, *The Gentlemen's Club* (University of Chicago Press, Chicago, 1975), p. 238.

268 See, for example, the various statements of delegates in the *1961 Records* vol. II at 238 et seq.

the subject.'[269] The study noted vastly different concepts of what constitutes fit punishment for a particular offence, but ascribed these differences to differences in local conditions rather than differences in principle. The study urged harmonisation of legislation on drug penalties, but Bruun et al commented that the CND's pursuit of uniformity was effectively a pursuit of greater severity.[270] A later UN study revealed that trafficking and production offences were more likely to receive severe punishment than simple possession, and in respect of both types of offences, the quantity and harmfulness of the drugs involved[271] played a large role in determination of sentence, with some states differentiating between hard drugs such as heroin, cocaine, opium and morphine, and soft drugs such as cannabis and its products.[272] But this study also revealed that harsh legislation and maximum sentencing provisions were not usually applied, and in most states authorities applied a great number of suspended sentences and fines.[273] Unsurprisingly, given this history and the expansion of the drug market, the emphasis of the international system today is on the severe punishment of producers and traffickers. Severe sentences are intended to function mainly as a deterrent, but coupled with prosecutorial discretion they also act as a law enforcement tool against the illicit traffic.[274]

Up until the 1960s, the CND regarded the reasons for demand for drugs or the causes, treatment and rehabilitation of drug dependency as falling beyond its strict technical competence.[275] Heavily reliant on the WHO Expert Committee for guidance with regard to the treatment and care of addicts, the CND was also unsure about the extent of drug dependence. In 1954 the CND sponsored an ECOSOC Resolution which called for more information from states about

---

269 Memorandum on Penal Sanctions for Narcotics Offences, 1972 MNAR/3/72.

270 Supra note 267 at 239.

271 For example, Afghanistan's Law on Combating Drugs, 1991, punished the production of cannabis as follows: less than 50gms of cannabis with less than three months imprisonment; 50gms-1kg with a short term of imprisonment of more than three months; 1-10kgs with a long term of imprisonment; more than 10kgs with from 7 years to life.

272 Cotic supra note 113 at 118. For example, in Vietnam the import or export of opiates may in terms of Decree No. 008-TT/SLU result in the death penalty in certain circumstances, while the most severe penalty for the same conduct in respect of cannabis is forced labour for life.

273 Cotic supra note 113 at 12, 119.

274 In many common law systems plea-bargaining is used to pressurise the accused into co-operating with the police in informing on their colleagues.

275 DND, 'Twenty years of narcotics control under the United Nations' (1966) 18 *Bulletin on Narcotics* 1 at 40-1.

addiction.[276] The Resolution showed the heavy influence of law enforcement agencies and a distinct bias against outpatient treatment. The growth in interest in the CND in the treatment of drug dependency was finally matched in the positive international law by provision being made in the 1961 Convention for the treatment of drug dependency. However, the international drug control system has always remained politically sensitive about alternative measures such as the treatment of offenders[277] International recognition that the problem also has a medical and a social nature, and the adoption by the international system of measures which to some extent recognise that the criminal law cannot provide a total solution to the problem, has not resulted in a fundamental shift away from prohibition and punishment. The emphasis has been on integrating these "softer" measures into the prohibitionist penal legal system either as alternatives to conviction and punishment, or in addition to conviction and punishment.[278]

Against this background, let us turn to a discussion of the punishment provisions of the drug conventions.

3.3.2   Penalty provisions under the 1961 Convention

3.3.2.1   General
The 1961 Convention's penalty provisions attempt to complement those for offences. They represent an uneasy compromise between the international system's emphasis on severe punishment for illicit drug traffickers, the major thrust of the penalty provisions of the 1936 Convention and of CND statements up until 1961, and new, at least in 1961, concerns about the purpose and nature of punishment.

3.3.2.2   Penalties for article 36(1) offences
Article 36(1) of the 1961 Convention obliges Parties, subject to their constitutional limitations,[279] to provide in their legislation or through administrative

---

276 Resolution 548E (XVIII), 12 July 1954.
277 See, for example, the *1988 Commentary* at 88.
278 See generally B. Rexed, K. Edmonson, I. Khan and R. Sansom, *Guidelines for the Control of Narcotic and Psychotropic Substances: In the Context of the International Treaties* (WHO, Geneva,1984), pp. 101-120.
279 It is important to recall that article 36's provisions are not self-executing; article 36(4) makes it clear that they are to be 'punished in conformity with the domestic law of a Party.'

measures[280] for two standards of punishment. The general standard provides that all the forms of drug related conduct enumerated in article 36(1) shall be 'punishable offences'. How Parties choose to punish offenders is their affair. The special standard provides that 'serious offences shall be liable to adequate punishment particularly by imprisonment or other penalties of deprivation of liberty.' There are three variables here, all to be defined by the Parties. First, the Parties determine whether or not such an offence is 'serious' and thus liable to punishment by imprisonment or some other form of deprivation of liberty. Obviously, what is a 'serious' offence may be viewed differently in different legal systems; thus the selection of offences themselves will almost certainly be different. Second, the obligation to apply 'adequate' punishment to these 'serious' offences does not stipulate what is adequate. Fundamentally different attitudes at the 1961 Conference towards punishment forced the use of the phrase 'adequate punishment' instead of 'severe punishment'.[281] In result, however, different Parties may apply different punishments for essentially the same offences[282] or essentially the same punishments for different offences. The *1961 Commentary* tries to repair the damage by submitting that

> in order to be "adequate" for the fight against serious offences of the illicit traffic, the penalties must be sufficiently severe to have the desired deterring effect under the special conditions of the country in which they are imposed. This idea is also embodied in the requirement that the "adequate punishment" should be meted out "particularly by imprisonment or other penalties of deprivation of liberty". The imposition of fines alone would in no case constitute an "adequate" punishment for serious offences of the illicit traffic.[283]

---

280 Austria declared upon accession to the 1961 Convention that article 36(1)'s obligation 'may also be implemented by administrative regulations providing adequate sanction for the offences enumerated therein' (1/2/1978).

281 Despite the fact that article 2 of the 1936 Convention used the phrase 'severely punishing', use of 'severe' was opposed at the Conference because degrees of severity might differ widely from state to state and because 'severe' carried overtones of retributive punishment which some delegates rejected as a legitimate purpose of punishment. See *1961 Records* vol. II at 234-239, and particularly the remarks of the executive secretary of the Conference at 237.

282 See the opinion of the Soviet delegate, *1961 Records*, vol. II at 238.

283 *1961 Commentary* at 429.

Of course Parties are not obliged to follow this suggestion, and ultimately the determination of appropriate punishment remains with them.[284] Whether a Party which tended, for example, to only fine traffickers of small quantities of drugs would be in violation of this article is difficult to say, because it would have to be shown that the Party was obliged to regard the offence as serious before it could be argued that the punishment was inadequate. The third variable is how the Parties interpret 'imprisonment or other penalties of deprivation of liberty'. In its broad sense 'imprisonment' includes all forms of 'deprivation of liberty'. The additional wording 'or other penalties of deprivation of liberty' refers to incarceration other than imprisonment.[285]

It is clear that these provisions, both general and special, apply to illicit trafficking offences. They do not apply to personal use offences, as 'use' is not listed in article 36(1), and 'possession' and 'purchase' in article 36(1) have been restrictively interpreted as limited to possession or purchase for the purpose of trafficking.[286] The 1961 Convention does not therefore require the imposition of harsh penal sanctions on users.[287] In reply to Parties that argue that article 36 does oblige the criminalisation of personal use offences, the *1961 Commentary* points out that Parties may 'undoubtedly choose not to provide for imprisonment of persons found in such possession, but to impose only minor penalties such as fines and even censure' and thus in effect not to treat possession for personal use as a 'serious' offence under article 36(1) deserving of imprisonment or other 'adequate punishment.'[288] Parties may choose to impose punishment for simple possession or use in terms of article 39's provision for the adoption of stricter measures, and many Parties still do so with custodial sentences. Possible alternatives include confiscating the illicit substance, cautioning or fining the users, or, recognising their problem as a health issue,

---

284 A fairly typical example of implementation is provided by section 6(1) of the Austrian Narcotic Drugs Amendment Act of 1977, Bundesgesetzblatt No. 1978/532, which provides that the offence of trafficking is per se regarded as serious enough to warrant adequate punishment by a short to medium term in prison. Coupled with aggravating circumstances, notably group involvement, the seriousness of the offence increases the adequate punishment to a maximum of ten years incarceration. The option of an additional rather than alternative fine up to 225 000 schillings, indicates the seriousness with which the offence is viewed.

285 The wording follows article 2 of the 1936 Convention. The *1961 Commentary's* suggestion at 429 that it includes labour and re-education camps is passe.

286 Noll supra note 36 at 24 thus argues that criticism of the 1961 Convention by those who favour the decriminalisation of use and possession of drugs is misdirected.

287 Noll supra note 31 at 44.

288 See *1961 Commentary* at 112.

diverting them to treatment and rehabilitation. Parties are becoming more flexible in their punishment of use and simple possession.[289]

3.3.2.3 Penalties for complicity, inchoate offences and 'financial operations' under the 1961 Convention

Article 36(2)(a)(ii) provides that the various inchoate offences and degrees of complicity 'shall be punishable offences as provided in paragraph 1'. Thus the remarks made with respect to the punishment of article 36(1) offences apply equally here because the same dual system of punishment applies. Parties are thus obliged to punish, for example, the attempted sale of a drug, and should they regard sale of a drug as a serious offence they are obliged to punish such attempted sale 'adequately'. The *1961 Commentary* notes that if the completed or principal offences are serious, then adequate punishment of the inchoate or accessory offences means 'imprisonment or other penalties of deprivation of liberty.'[290] In practice, however, many domestic legal systems punish several of the categories of offenders dealt with in this provision, for instance accomplices, more lightly than the perpetrator of an offence, and the proviso in respect of domestic law in article 36(2) allows such distinctions to continue to be made.

3.3.2.4 Recidivism under the 1961 Convention

Article 36(2)(a)(iii)[291] obliges the partial recognition of foreign penal judgments with respect to recidivists; individuals who habitually relapse into illicit drug trafficking. The term 'convictions' must be taken to include both conviction and sentence in Parties where these are two separate processes and proof of both conviction and sentence is required to establish recidivism.[292] In practice recidivism is regarded as an aggravating factor on punishment and frequently as a condition for the classification of the offender as a habitual criminal to

---

289 See A. Fraser and M. George, 'Cautions for cannabis' (1992) 8 *Policing* 88 at 91 and the cases cited there. They note that British Courts are likely to impose non-custodial sentences for simple cannabis possession and that custody is only considered after the fourth or fifth conviction.

290 *1961 Commentary* at 434.

291 Rooted in article 6 of the 1936 Convention, this provision was left unchanged by the 1972 Protocol.

292 See the remarks of the US delegate, *1961 Records* vol. I at 123.

whom special restrictions apply.[293] Bassiouni complains that the obligation
in article 36(2)(a)(iii) is 'without regard to the rights of the offender in such
cases and fails to set forth the basis for such co-operation between states with
respect to the recognition and consequences of foreign penal convictions.'[294]
The amplification of article 36(2)(a)(iii) is a domestic concern and one subject
to the 'constitutional limitations of a Party, its legal system and domestic law'.
This means in practice that a Party is not required to take into account foreign
convictions of an alleged offender if its constitution, legal principles or domestic
criminal law (the widest of the three) precludes it from doing so.[295] In many
states, at least in 1961, this was the case.[296] The legal provisions for aggravating punishment in many such Parties may well, however, be sufficient
to cover foreign convictions.[297]

3.3.2.5 Confiscation as punishment

Article 37 of the 1961 Convention, entitled 'Seizure and Confiscation', provides
for the seizure and confiscation of any drugs, substances and equipment used
in or intended for the commission of any article 36 offences. The other function
of these methods is in law enforcement, and the article is discussed at length
in Chapter Six on specific law techniques. However, confiscation also functions
as a punishment with the aim of depriving the offender of his ill-gotten gains
and the means to continue his criminal activities.[298] Article 37 appears to
oblige Parties to ensure that drugs, substances and equipment used in drug

---

293 *1961 Commentary* at 434. Cotic supra note 113 at 110-112 discusses recidivism in respect
of drug offences in 31 states. He notes that in addition to being an aggravating factor,
it also functions to increase both maximum and minimum legal limits for punishment
and sometimes to eliminate the possibility of the waiving or suspension of prosecution.

294 M.C. Bassiouni, 'The International Narcotics Control Scheme' in M.C. Bassiouni (ed.),
1 International Criminal Law: Crimes (Transnational, Dobbs Ferry, 1986), p. 507 at
p. 519.

295 *1961 Commentary* at 430.

296 Henrichs supra note 3 at 7 notes that in German law in 1960 recidivism was only applied
in exceptional cases, and the courts invariably took the view that foreign convictions
could not establish it.

297 *1961 Commentary* at 434.

298 Thus in Belgian Law a 'special confiscation' under section 4(6) of the Drugs Act, 1921,
which applies sections 42 and 43 of the Belgian Penal Code, is an accessory sentence
which cannot be imposed in isolation but must be combined with a principal punishment
– C. Van Den Wyngaert, *Strafrecht en strafprocesrecht in hoofdlynen* (Maklu, Antwerp,
1994), p. 317.

offences are subject to confiscation[299] as a type of non-custodial punishment with both deterrent and retributive effect. Domestic provision for confiscation of these forms of material is common in practice.[300] Confiscation of the proceeds of drug trafficking as a punishment had not been envisaged in 1961.

3.3.2.6   Alternatives to punishment in the 1961 Convention

While the 1961 Convention contains the first multilateral treaty provision for the treatment of drug dependency, it is not indicative of a dramatic change in international policy. Draft article 47(2) firmly rejected ambulatory treatment of addicts, called for 'the compulsory treatment of drug addicts in closed institutions' and urged member states with a serious drug 'addiction' problem and the economic means to do so to provide such facilities. Some states at the 1961 Conference objected to this approach on the basis that health matters were within the jurisdiction of local authorities.[301] Others objected to the specification of compulsory treatment in a closed institution that they regarded as restricting the use of other potentially effective methods.[302] The Conference

---

299 Seizure is not applicable as it is a pre-conviction process and thus cannot serve as a punishment. Most domestic legislation allows for a confiscation order to be made by a court or competent authority on sentence following conviction, although confiscation prior to conviction is possible, for instance when a potential first offender is released on warning.

300 For example, section 6(3) and (4) of the Austrian Narcotic Drugs Amendment Act of 1977, Bundesgesetzblatt No. 1978/532, provide: '(3) The objects used in the punishable act [trafficking] or the proceeds there from shall be declared confiscated if they are owned by the offender or an accomplice or accessory to the offence or if they were owned by such persons at the time of seizure. In other cases, they may be declared confiscated. Similarly, materials and apparatus used for manufacture and processing may be declared confiscated, and also vehicles used for transport other than vehicles owned by a public transport undertaking if the owner of the vehicle was aware it was to be misused for unlawful purposes. (4) If the objects or their proceeds cannot be seized or declared confiscated, a fine equal to the value of such objects or their proceeds shall be imposed.'

301 L.M. Goodrich, 'New trends in narcotics control' (1960) 530 *International Conciliation* 181 at 219.

302 The US strongly supported draft article 47(2) requiring Parties 'to use their best endeavours to establish facilities for the compulsory treatment of drug addicts in closed institutions'. It argued that such isolation was not punitive, that it was necessary because drug addiction was contagious as addicts tended to convert others, and that treatment at liberty had failed where it had been tried – *1961 Records* vol. I at 103. Canada, the UAR, China, India and Iran also supported compulsory commitment – *1961 Records* vol. I at 103-106. Yet an obligation to provide for compulsory commitment was rejected because the 1961 Conference was unwilling to prescribe a particular method of treatment

acted cautiously, and adopted article 38, entitled 'Treatment of Drug Addicts'. Article 38 does not detail precisely how Parties should implement the measures recommended. While it uses the terms 'drug addict' and 'drug addiction', the article's scope is not limited to narcotic drugs that cause physical dependence. It applies to all narcotic drugs subject to the 1961 Convention.[303]

Article 38(1) only obliges the Parties to give regard to the provision of facilities for treatment, care and rehabilitation. According to its authors the term 'medical treatment' refers to 'necessary therapeutic treatment' and the phrase 'care and rehabilitation' must be understood very broadly.[304] The *1961 Commentary* notes the difficulty sometimes of distinguishing between 'care' and 'rehabilitation', and suggests

> that the term 'care' includes such psychiatric, psychoanalytical or psychological treatment of the addict as may be necessary after he has been withdrawn from the drugs which he abused. The word 'rehabilitation' covers such measures as may be required to make the addicts physically, vocationally and otherwise fit for living a normal life as useful members of society (cure of diseases, physical rehabilitation of disabled addicts, vocational training, supervision, accompanied by advice and encouragement, of a perhaps gradual transition to a normal self-reliant life etc.).[305]

Article 38(2) recommends that Parties establish an adequate infrastructure for the effective treatment of drug addicts, but only if they have a serious drug problem and their economic resources permit them to establish such an infrastructure. The identification of the drug problem as serious is at the Parties' discretion,[306] and Parties that use scarce resources for other tasks do not act

---

as valid under all conditions and for the duration of the operation of the Convention – *1961 Records* vol. I at 103-114. Lack of resources was a significant factor in the rejection of compulsory commitment – see the statement of the Greek delegate, *1961 Records* vol. I at 105. The delegate from the Netherlands remarked that 'closed institutions' sounded like 'prisons', highlighting for some the repugnancy of the penal nature of commitment – *1961 Records* vol. I at 109.

303 *1961 Commentary* at 446. Cannabis is the obvious example of a drug that does not produce physical dependence but which does fall under article 38.

304 *1961 Records* vol. II at 283 footnote 19.

305 *1961 Commentary* at 447.

306 The *1961 Commentary* at 448 suggests that it would be desirable for Parties to establish such an infrastructure even were the addiction problem not 'serious', and the New Zealand delegate made the point that all drug addiction was 'serious' – *1961 Records* vol. I at 107.

contrary to the recommendation.[307] The phrase 'adequate facilities for the effective treatment' allows Parties to use whatever methods their medical authorities may consider appropriate.[308] The term 'treatment' must include what is termed in article 38(1) 'medical treatment, care and rehabilitation'.[309]

Article 38 was regarded as an innovation that suggested that all facets of control were being addressed at the international level. However, while the article extended regulation over the medical aspects of drug use, no mention was made of other methods of control such as education. Treatment and so on was also regarded by most states as the province of the wealthy states. It was pointed out at the time that article 38 would have little concrete effect except in states with adequate resources to undertake the expensive task of institutional care and rehabilitation.[310] Interestingly, a proposed amendment to draft article 47 by Byelorussia characterising the drug problem as a socio-economic problem and calling for measures to address it as such was rejected by the 1961 Conference.[311]

Development of international drug control was still at an early stage in 1961. The Conference's energies were devoted to reinforcing the policy of prohibition through establishing uniform penal provisions. The 1961 Convention does not even go so far as linking the provisions for penalisation of drug offences in article 36 with the provisions for other measures to be applied against drug use as envisioned by article 38.[312] That linkage had to wait until 1971.

---

307 *1961 Commentary* at 447.

308 *1961 Records* vol. I at 110 and 114. Resolution II of the Conference did declare, however, that one of the most effective methods of treating addiction was in a hospital with a drug free atmosphere and urged Parties having a serious addiction problem to provide such facilities if they had the means – *1961 Records* vol. II at 316.

309 *1961 Commentary* at 446.

310 See R.W. Gregg, 'The Single Convention for Narcotic Drugs' (1961) 16 *Food Drug Cosmetic Law Journal* 187 at 203.

311 The proposed draft read: '1. The Parties consider that the most important prerequisite for the prevention and eradication of drug addiction is the consistent application by States of measures aimed at improving the economic and social well-being of the people, raising its cultural level and providing medical services that are available to all segments of the population.' – *1961 Records* vol. II at 49. The amendment's strongest opponent was the US which rejected as political philosophy the idea that measures aimed at improving the economic and social well-being of the people was the most important prerequisite for eradication of drug addiction, and threatened not to ratify the convention if the amendment was included – *1961 Records* vol. II at 111.

312 Noll supra note 31 at 45-46.

3.3.3   Penalty provisions under the 1971 Convention

3.3.3.1   General

The most innovative provisions dealing with drug offenders in the 1971 Convention were those relating to their treatment and rehabilitation. Adopting an almost identical structure with respect to the punishment of drug offences as that in the 1961 Convention, the 1971 Convention does not develop international law any further in this regard.

3.3.3.2   Penalties for article 22(1)(a) offences[313]

As with the 1961 Convention, a dual punishment regime is envisaged by the 1971 Convention, viz. 'punishable offences' and 'serious offences ... liable to adequate punishment'. How punishable offences are to be punished is not stipulated by article 22(1)(a), and this remains an area of domestic discretion. It is assumed that punishable offences are not serious, but exactly what sort of offences the authors of the Convention envisaged is unclear. While the *1971 Commentary* argues that Parties must criminalise possession of Schedule I substances under article 22(1)(a), it notes that Parties need not treat such offences as serious offences and may limit themselves to 'fining the offender, or even to only censuring or admonishing him'.[314] If one accepts that use and possession for use of any substances are not criminalised by the 1971 Convention, then the question of their conviction and punishment is entirely a domestic affair.

With respect to the selection of 'serious offences' for 'adequate punishment', the *1971 Commentary* suggests that they should be identified on the basis of their 'potential for causing, directly or indirectly, damage to the health of people other than the offender, particularly of people residing in other countries than that in which the offence is committed.'[315] The *1971 Commentary* appears to have transnational trafficking in mind and suggests that Parties are not required to consider as a serious offence the possession of a small amount of a psychotropic substance for sale by users to finance their own dependency, or even for the purpose of supplying a friend without consideration.[316]

---

313 It is important to note that article 22's provisions are not self-executing; article 22(5) makes it clear that they are to be 'punished in conformity with the domestic law of a Party.'

314 *1971 Commentary* at 351.

315 *1971 Commentary* at 348.

316 *1971 Commentary* at 352.

Article 22(1)(a) requires such 'serious' offences to be punished by 'adequate' penalties. The *1971 Commentary* notes that what is adequate punishment may be construed differently by different Parties; deterrence will only be achieved if 'it includes imprisonment or another form of deprivation of liberty.'[317] However, use of 'particularly' in the provision suggests that while its authors may have had imprisonment in mind for serious offences, they envisaged that other forms of punishment would be used. The addition of the wording 'or another penalty of deprivation of liberty' to imprisonment, clarifies that confinement need not necessarily be in a prison.

3.3.3.3   *Penalties for complicity, inchoate offences and 'financial operations' under the 1971 Convention*

Article 22(2)(a)(ii) provides that the various forms of secondary participation and inchoate conduct listed 'shall be punishable offences as provided in paragraph 1'. The requirement of adequate punishment by imprisonment or some other form of deprivation of liberty applies to these forms of conduct criminalised under article 22(2)(a)(ii) if they are serious. The *1971 Commentary* points out that although 'preparatory acts' are not punished by incarceration in many Parties unless undertaken for the purpose of committing a few very serious offences, the offences in article 22(1)(a) should be considered among the most serious. Likewise if Parties only punish conspiracies as 'preparatory acts', or only punish conspiracies to commit very serious offences, or only punish 'attempts' at serious offences. In all these situations the *1971 Commentary* suggests that article 22(1)(a) offences are serious, conspiracies or attempts to commit them must be punished, and the limitation clause will not avail these Parties.[318] It is submitted, however, that while inchoate forms of and complicity in article 22(1)(a) offences may be punished as severely as choate offences and principal offenders, some gradation of punishment, depending on proximity to actual perpetration of the offence, is an adequate response to this provision. As with 'financial operations', the grading of such offences for punishment depends not so much on a broad categorisation of all such offences as serious as upon the facts of the individual case.

3.3.3.4   *Recidivism under the 1971 Convention*

Identical to the recidivism provision in article 36(2)(a)(iii) of the 1961 Convention, article 22(2)(a)(iii) enables foreign convictions to be taken into account

---

317   *1971 Commentary* at 352.
318   *1971 Commentary* at 358-359.

in determining the severity of punishment. While this may be done through declaration of the offender as a habitual criminal, it may only be in aggravation of sentence, depending on the circumstances and the Party's domestic law. This provision's subjection to the limitation clause means that a Party cannot be obliged to consider foreign convictions for the purpose of determining recidivism if its domestic penal law does not permit it to do so.[319] The *1971 Commentary* submits that Parties in this situation may rely on the provisions of their penal law allowing for consideration of aggravating circumstances in punishment to cover foreign convictions.[320]

3.3.3.5   Confiscation as a punishment under the 1971 Convention

Article 22(3) of the 1971 Convention provides for the seizure and confiscation of 'any psychotropic substance or other substance, as well as any equipment, used in or intended for the commission of' article 22 offences. As noted above, confiscation, although it functions as a form of punishment, is discussed under law enforcement in Chapter Six.

3.3.3.6   Alternatives to punishment under the 1971 Convention

Article 22(1)(b) grants Parties the discretion to implement measures such as treatment, education, and rehabilitation as alternatives to conviction and punishment or in addition to conviction and punishment, no matter how serious the offence, as long as the offender is a drug abuser.[321] Article 20 sets out various provisions facilitating this alternative regime. While these alternatives specifically apply to article 22(1)(a) offences, by implication they must also apply to the accessory forms of these offences set out in article 22(2)(a)(ii).

The development of these provisions can be traced to the early 1970s, when punitive and retributive methods of dealing with drug offenders were giving way at the national level to alternative approaches to dealing with the problem. The provisions in the 1971 Convention go further in this direction than those in the 1961 Convention. The use throughout the 1971 Convention of the terms drug 'dependence' and drug 'abuser' rather than 'addiction' and 'addict' reflect

---

319 *1971 Commentary* at 356.
320 *1971 Commentary* at 360.
321 The Mexican delegate to the 1971 Conference did suggest that 'a clear distinction should, however, be drawn between drug addicts, for whom measures of treatment were suitable, and traffickers, who should be liable to imprisonment', a sentiment echoed by the Brazilian delegate – *1971 Records* vol. II at 30.

this more enlightened attitude.[322] Yet the 1971 Convention remains primarily penal-sanctions oriented and only secondarily treatment-rehabilitation conscious, something illustrated by its failure to make pharmacological distinctions between different drugs when it comes to distinguishing different methods of treatment for their abuse.[323]

Article 22(1)(b) establishes a clear link between article 22's penal and alternate measures. It provides that when abusers of psychotropic substances have committed article 22(1)(a) offences, the Parties may provide, either as an alternative to conviction or punishment or in addition to conviction or punishment, for an obligation on abusers to undergo measures of treatment, education, aftercare, rehabilitation and social reintegration in conformity with article 20(1). Parties were at liberty before the conclusion of the Convention to apply such measures in addition to punishment. Article 22(1)(a) serves to remind them that these measures may be advisable.[324] Substitution of such measures, although also entirely at the Parties' discretion, is more contentious. It is controversial in respect of the types of offences to which it can apply. It has been argued that article 22(1)(b)'s measures deal with drug abusers, and are not intended to apply to traffickers.[325] The *1971 Commentary* expands its application to the 'minor offences' of

> unauthorised possession of substances in Schedule I for personal consumption, unauthorised sale of comparatively minor quantities of psychotropic substances for the purpose of obtaining the financial means required to support the seller's dependence on such substances, or unauthorised supply of small amounts of a psychotropic substance to a friend abusing it, with or without consideration.[326]

It is submitted, however, that substitution is not limited to these minor offences, and that no general rule denying substitution to traffickers can be extracted from article 22(1)(b); each case must be dealt with by the Party concerned on its merits. Substitution also controversial with respect to the level of abuse to which it can be applied. The *1971 Commentary* submits: (i) that article 22(1)(b) applies

---

322 It was only in 1967 that the WHO Expert Committee proposed to the CND that the term 'drug dependence' be substituted for the terms 'drug addiction' or 'drug habituation' thus resolving some of the problems associated with differentiating between drugs producing physical as opposed to psychological dependence.

323 Bassiouni supra note 294 at 521.

324 *1971 Commentary* at 354.

325 Noll supra note 31 at 48; see also the French delegate, *1971 Records* vol. II at 30.

326 *1971 Commentary* at 353.

to frequent and not occasional abusers of psychotropic substances, i.e. to dependency; and (ii) that substitution would only be justified if it could reasonably be hoped that the abuser will not only be cured of his dependence but would not commit a serious offence again.[327] However, on the wording of the provision the Party is able to employ substitution under any circumstance to any abusers of a psychotropic substance. Moreover, occasional abusers of potent substances may need treatment, while making substitution conditional on hope of the abuser being cured and on his not committing another serious offence unrealistically links substitution to speculation about the effectiveness of treatment and the commission of further possibly unrelated offences.

A problem integral to substitution is deciding the stage in the legal process at which it should occur, that is, should it apply after conviction, or after prosecution but before conviction, or after arrest but before prosecution? Article 22(1)(b) only establishes that an offence must have occurred. The *1971 Commentary* opines that Parties should divert an offender after prosecution has been instituted, reasoning that during the process of prosecution the Party will be able to decide on the appropriateness of substitution.[328] It is submitted, however, that Parties retain the discretion to substitute at pre-prosecution stages of criminal proceedings. Substitution may well, for example, be appropriate at the arrest stage when the offence is obviously not serious.

Article 22(1)(b) provides for measures of 'treatment' and so on 'in conformity with paragraph 1 of article 20'. The two provisions must be read together. Article 20, entitled 'Measures Against the Abuse of Psychotropic Substances', can be seen as an updated version of article 38 of the 1961 Convention. Its provisions are general and operate as guidelines rather than obligations.

Article 20(1) deals with the measures to be applied to abusers of psychotropic substances. These measures are aimed first at the 'prevention' of the abuse of psychotropic substances. They include appropriate socio-economic control measures in addition to the penal and administrative control measures in the Convention.[329] Co-ordination of efforts across various disciplines at the national and international levels is envisaged,[330] but these measures need

---

327 *1971 Commentary* at 353-354.
328 *1971 Commentary* at 353.
329 Contra the *1971 Commentary* at 334 which includes all the 1971 Convention's control measures among these preventative measures, an interpretation abandoned by the *1972 Commentary* in its interpretation of the identical provision in article 38(1) of the amended 1961 Convention. The latter interpretation is to be preferred as article 20 is clearly a provision for alternative measures.
330 *1971 Commentary* at 334.

only be taken if they are 'practicable'. Practicability depends on the resources available to the Party and on the importance of its drug problem relative to other social problems.[331] The standard of the 'measures' available will depend generally on the socio-economic conditions prevailing in a Party and specifically on the treatment infrastructure available, conditions that are bound to vary enormously.[332]

'Identification', 'treatment', 'education', 'after-care', 'rehabilitation' and 'social reintegration' form stages in the restoration of the abuser's well being. It must be noted, however, that the meanings of these terms are not the subjects of strict agreement and that the dividing lines between them are not always clear. Their definition must thus be tentative, as must the suggested sequence of their application. However, the blurring of the timing and content of these stages presents no practical problem and indeed reinforces the main thrust of article 20(1) which is the application of all practicable measures for the successful restoration of abusers at any time.[333]

'Identification', the *1971 Commentary* suggests, means the identification of groups of potential abusers as well as individual abusers.[334] Nothing is said about which steps should to be taken in the 'early identification' of such groups/individuals, but the Netherlands delegate to the 1971 Conference suggested that such steps should have the character of public health measures, and penal measures should be avoided at this stage as they would hamper the process of rehabilitation and social reintegration.[335]

'Treatment' can mean the entire process of restoration, but the *1971 Commentary* suggests that in article 20(1) it means 'the process of withdrawal of the abused substances, or where necessary of inducing the abuser to restrict his intake of substances liable to be abused to such minimum quantities as are medically justified in the light of his personal condition.'[336]

The *1971 Commentary* suggests that 'education' in article 20(1) means the education of actual abusers, classes in schools, and special groups prone to

---

331 *1971 Commentary* at 331.
332 Chatterjee supra note 69 at 482.
333 *1971 Commentary* at 333.
334 *1971 Commentary* at 334.
335 *1971 Records* vol. II at 20.
336 *1971 Commentary* at 332. Whether such treatment should be enforced through commitment to an institution or be voluntary is not specified. States have tended to regard enforced admission as an exceptional procedure limited to situations where there is no other suitable treatment and the risk presented by the abuser both to himself and others demands his removal from society.

substance abuse about the harmful consequences of substance abuse, and not the education of the general public in these matters.[337] This restrictive interpretation is rooted in the apprehension that education of the general public will encourage drug use.

'After-care', the *1971 Commentary* suggests, consists of psychiatric, psychoanalytical or psychological measures necessary after withdrawal or restriction (in the case of a maintenance programme) of the intake of psychotropic substances.[338] Such measures may also be necessary during treatment.

'Rehabilitation', the *1971 Commentary* suggests, consists of measures designed to make the former abuser

> physically, vocationally, morally and otherwise fit for living a normal life as a useful member of society (cure of diseases, physical rehabilitation of disabled persons, vocational training, supervision, accompanied by advice and encouragement, measures of gradual progress to a normal self-reliant life, etc.).[339]

'Social integration' overlaps considerably with rehabilitation, but the *1971 Commentary* suggests that while rehabilitation refers to the development of the personal qualities of the abuser, social integration refers to the measures designed to make it possible for the abuser to live in a better environment and would cover such measures as a suitable job, appropriate housing and the opportunity for the abuser to leave the environment which nurtured his abuse for one less likely to do so.[340] Such a change of environment will also prevent the abuser from being stigmatised.

Article 20(2) should be seen as an effort to iron out differences in the rehabilitative capacity of states by promotion of the training of personnel involved in the process of restoring abusers. It is concerned with the professional skills training of the personnel dealing with the treatment (in the generic sense) of abusers, that is, mainly health-care professionals.[341] It states that the Parties shall as far as possible 'promote' such training. Promotion does not necessarily mean direct engagement in training, but implies the support or encouragement of such training appropriate to a particular Party's abuse problem and its educational infrastructure. Promotion 'as far as possible' depends on the means

---

337 *1971 Commentary* at 333.
338 *1971 Commentary* at 332.
339 *1971 Commentary* at 332.
340 *1971 Commentary* at 332.
341 *1971 Commentary* at 334.

available to a particular Party and the seriousness of the threat of abuse relative to other demands on those means.[342] Although training centres for rehabilitation and preventive education have been set up,[343] the heavily qualified nature of this recommendation indicates that the authors of the 1971 Convention did not expect too much to come of it.

Article 20(3) deals with the promotion of an understanding of the drug problem by those who handle users and by the general public. The goal of the first part of this provision is the promotion of a broad grasp of the multi-faceted nature of the problem by personnel whose work brings them into contact with it but who are not directly involved in treatment.[344] The second part of article 20(2) provides that such a broad understanding is also to be promoted, where appropriate, on the part of the general public 'if there is a risk that abuse of such substances will become widespread'. This promotion is essential for the formation of informed public opinion and the adoption of adequate drug policies, but it is interesting that it only becomes obligatory when the problem reaches epidemic proportions.[345] While couched as an obligation, this provision does not actually oblige a government of a Party to engage directly in promotion of knowledge about drug abuse; such a government may do so but can legitimately promote the educative work of private individuals and organisations.[346] There is no qualification on article 20(3)'s requirements in terms of practicability, but it appears that the authors of the provision expected Parties only

---

342 *1971 Commentary* at 335. The delegate from the Holy See to the 1971 Conference made a fruitless effort to urge the deletion of 'as far as possible' on the basis that states should be bound to take steps such as moral and social reconstruction to deal with the causes rather than just the symptoms of drug abuse – *1971 Records* vol. II at 20.

343 C. Yodmani, 'The role of the Association of South East Asian Nations in fighting illicit drug traffic' (1983) 35 *Bulletin on Narcotics* 97 at 99 notes that ASEAN set up training centres for rehabilitation in Malaysia and preventive education in Thailand after 1979.

344 These personnel include all those to whom article 20(2) applies but, in addition, persons engaged in any aspect of drug control or whose work is only partly concerned with drug control such as police officers, social workers, psychologists, judges, probation officers, prison officers, doctors, religious workers etc., in fact anyone involved in the restorative process in any way.

345 The *1971 Commentary* notes at 335 that this qualification was motivated by the fear of spreading substance abuse through the promotion of the 'morbid curiosity of psychologically weak persons'; see the comments of the Interpol delegate to the 1971 Conference – *1971 Records* vol. II at 22.

346 *1971 Commentary* at 336.

to do what could reasonably be expected of them in the light of the seriousness of their abuse problem and the means available to them for education.[347]

The measures in articles 22(1)(b) and 20 of the 1971 Convention are a modernisation of the measures in the 1961 Convention. Their shortcomings are patent: article 22(1)(b) falls within the general prosecutorial framework of the 1971 Convention's measures against the illicit traffic, while article 20 is hamstrung by inter alia constant reference to the capacity of Parties, which capacity the Parties are free to determine themselves. The former embodies the colonisation of alternative measures of dealing with drug use by the penal process; the latter signifies a failure to meaningfully divert resources away from punishment. These provisions do not represent a dramatic departure from previous international practice with respect to the treatment of users.

3.3.4 Alternatives to punishment inserted in the 1961 Convention by the 1972 Protocol

Article 36(1)(b), inserted by article 14 of the 1972 Protocol into the 1961 Convention, provides Parties with the discretion to implement measures such as treatment, education, and rehabilitation as alternatives to conviction and punishment or in addition to conviction and punishment, no matter how serious the offence, but only when the person who has committed the offence is an 'abuser of drugs'. While these alternatives specifically apply to article 36(1)(a) offences, by implication they must also apply to the additional forms of these offences set out in article 36(2)(a)(ii). Provision for Parties to set up facilities to make such alternative regimes available was made in article 38 of the Convention, and this article was elaborated upon by the 1972 Protocol. Using the 1971 Convention as a model, the 1972 Protocol amended, in terms of articles 14 and 15, the 1961 Convention, replacing the short article 38 with two provisions. The intention of the Swedish Government, which introduced these amendments, was that the 1961 Convention should be revised to bring it into line with modern views and to ensure that persons addicted to narcotics could receive the same treatment as psychotropic abusers.[348] It would also help to

---

347 *1971 Commentary* at 336.

348 The *1971 Commentary* at 347 notes, however, 'that as long as the Protocol is not accepted by all Parties to the unamended Single Convention, Parties to its amended text which are simultaneously Parties to its unamended text are not able to make use of the choice because of their continued obligation under the unamended text to those Parties thereto that have not accepted the Protocol.'

create 'a proper balance between control measures, law enforcement and so on, on the one hand, and therapeutic and rehabilitative activity on the other.'[349]

Article 36(1)(b) is a recommendation closely following the wording of article 22(1)(b) of the 1971 Convention. Treatment and so on 'may' serve as an alternative or as an addition to the conviction and punishment for the criminal offences listed in article 36(1)(a).[350] The measures listed, viz. 'treatment, education, after-care, rehabilitation and social reintegration', are steps in the general process of reintegration of the drug user. Their precise meaning is examined below in the discussion of article 38(1). Using treatment as an addition to conviction and punishment has always been within the Parties discretion. But Parties are now also given the discretion to substitute these measures for conviction and punishment for all offences.[351] Again the UN takes the view that substitution can be used only in respect of 'minor offences' such as selling small amounts of drugs for the purpose of getting money necessary to support a habit, or supplying with or without consideration small amounts of a drug to a friend abusing it.[352] On its face, however, the provision allows substitution for a range of offences from the most serious case of drug trafficking to cases of simple possession.[353] Moreover, while article 36(1)(b)'s alternatives are clearly not intended to apply to non-users, the *1972 Commentary* goes too far when it states that they may not be applied to occasional drug users but only to frequent drugs users which it classifies as those users dependent on drugs.[354] For one thing, education can be of enormous benefit to non-dependent users when it prompts them to choose to stop using drugs. The *1972*

---

349 See the Explanatory Memorandum presented to the 24th Session of the CND where the amendments were first proposed – *United Nations Conference to consider amendments to the Single Convention on Narcotic Drugs, Official Records, Volume I* (New York, 1974) UN Doc. E/CONF.63/10; UN Publication Sales No.E.73.XI.7. (hereinafter *1972 Records* vol. I), p. 4.

350 *1972 Commentary* at 77.

351 The *1972 Commentary* at 78 qualifies enthusiasm for substitution by pointing out that it is not possible by Parties to both the 1961 Convention and the 1972 Protocol because of their continued obligation to Parties to the 1961 Convention which have not accepted the 1972 Protocol.

352 *1972 Commentary* at 77.

353 Although it has been submitted above that the 1961 Convention does not demand conviction and punishment of simple possession of drugs, if the view were taken by a state that it does, article 36(1)(b) allows the substitution of conviction and punishment of simple possession with treatment.

354 *1972 Commentary* at 77.

Commentary's submission that in the light of the purpose of article 36 substitution should be made 'only if it can reasonably be hoped that the drug-dependent offender would not only be cured of his dependence, but would also not again commit a serious offence,'[355] must also be rejected. While it is true that national legislation often allows substitution only once or for a strictly limited number of times, with any reversion being subject to conviction and punishment, that decision falls entirely within the Parties' discretion and speculation about cures and the commission of other serious offences may not always be a good reason for a Party to limit substitution.

The use of these measures as a substitute for conviction and punishment raises the question of when in the legal process such substitution should take place. The *1972 Commentary* states that Parties are bound to prosecute and may only divert an offender to treatment and so on before conviction, reasoning that it is during the trial that the decision as to the suitability of diversion is best made.[356] It is submitted, however, that the Parties retain the discretion to divert at any stage of criminal proceedings. Diversion may well be appropriate at the arrest stage when it is patent that the offence is not serious.

The amended article 36(1)(b)'s attempt to characterise the drug problem as social and medical as well as criminal is complemented in the 1972 Protocol by the amendment of article 38. The new article 38, with the new title 'Measures against the abuse of drugs', closely follows article 20 of the 1971 Convention. Article 38(1) provides that the Parties 'shall give special attention to and take all practicable measures' for certain stated ends. The provision's use of 'shall' obliges Parties to 'give special attention' to these ends, but the measures that they 'shall' use to achieve these ends are qualified by the requirement that these measures be 'practicable'. The provision, recognising that different situations prevail in different Parties, does not involve a binding obligation to take specified concrete steps. It becomes a question of the capacity of a Party to implement the steps to be taken to observe the principles outlined, and should that capacity exist, the priority to be given by the Party to this implementation in the light of other demands on their resources earmarked to address social problems.[357]

---

355 *1972 Commentary* at 77.
356 *1972 Commentary* at 77.
357 *1972 Commentary* at 84. It submits that governments need not engage directly in the implementation of these measures and may leave their implementation to private facilities. In the plenary session of the 1972 Conference, certain states that doubted their capacities to implement these provisions were referred to the UN for financial help.

The first of the ends article 38(1) mentions is drug abuse 'prevention'. By prevention the authors of article 38(1) mean measures other than administrative control measures or penal sanctions. The *1972 Commentary* states that prevention means

> 'all practicable economic and social measures capable of changing a social atmosphere or subcultural conditions responsible for the development of personality traits finding expression in the abuse of narcotic drugs.'[358]

The remaining ends of article 38(1) constitute stages within a comprehensive treatment programme for drug users. 'Early identification' of drug abuse may apply to both individual users and groups especially prone to use.[359] 'Treatment' of abusers appears to mean either the withdrawal of drugs from the user or restriction of intake through, for instance, a maintenance programme.[360] 'Education', according to the *1972 Commentary*, seems limited to education about the harmful consequences of drug abuse and not to the propagation of a general understanding of the problems of drug abuse; it is directed at drug abusers and target groups such as school children, and not to the education in these matters of the general public.[361] Again the education of the general public in these matters is of obvious importance and again an irrational fear of education is manifest. 'After-care', the *1972 Commentary* opines, consists of 'psychiatric, psychoanalytical or psychological measures' to treat users from whom drugs have been withdrawn or users subject to a maintenance programme.[362] 'Rehabilitation', according to the *1972 Commentary*, covers measures to make the individual abuser

> physically, vocationally, morally and otherwise fit for living a normal life as a useful member of society (cure of diseases, physical rehabilitation of disabled persons, vocational training, supervision accompanied by advice and encouragement, measures of gradual progress to a normal self-reliant life, etc.).[363]

    1972 Records vol. II at 18.

358 *1972 Commentary* at 86.

359 The *1972 Commentary* suggests at 86 two methods to make such identification possible, viz. inspection of prescriptions retained by retail distributors of drugs and a reporting system based on that used for the reporting of communicable diseases.

360 *1972 Commentary* at 84.

361 *1972 Commentary* at 86.

362 *1972 Commentary* at 77.

363 *1972 Commentary* at 85.

'Social reintegration', by contrast, the *1972 Commentary* suggests, refers to measures intended to make it possible for the rehabilitated abuser to live in an environment most favourable to him. These may include provision of employment, housing, and the movement of the abuser away from the environment which nurtured the abuse or from one likely to stigmatise that abuse.[364]

For practical reasons and because there was little agreement in 1972 as to these details, article 38(1) does not detail to which types of drug abuse and when and how treatment should be applied. These matters are left entirely up to the Parties.[365] The Parties are also left to decide whether treatment should be voluntary or compulsory.[366] The categories of treatment are not easily distinguishable and may overlap.[367] It suggests that by overlapping the stages the authors of the provision were encouraging the application of 'all practicable measures' necessary for the successful treatment of abusers.[368] Finally, article 38(1) provides for the co-ordination of Parties' efforts to these stated ends, which implies both intra-national and international co-ordination.[369]

Article 38(2) provides that the Parties shall as far as possible 'promote' the training of personnel in treatment, education, aftercare, rehabilitation and social reintegration of drug abusers. It contemplates the promotion of training of those personnel directly engaged in alternative methods of dealing with drug users, but it can be broadly interpreted to indicate the training of any person engaged in the application of penal measures to drug offenders in these alternative methods. The *1972 Commentary* suggests that the 'promotion' of training by the Parties means the encouragement and support of this training, and that the Parties may support private initiatives and are not obliged to engage in governmental training programmes.[370] Once again the obligation is a question of the capacity of the Party to implement the training and the priority it can

---

364   *1972 Commentary* at 85.

365   Many different approaches were espoused at the Conference; see, for example, the French delegate's comment that epidemiological study, search for causes of abuse, and treatment of abuse varied because little was known and there was a lot of disagreement in and between states – *1972 Records* vol. II at 183.

366   An Argentinean proposal that it should be compulsory was rejected – *1972 Records* vol. II at 182-185.

367   *1972 Commentary* at 85.

368   *1972 Commentary* at 85-86.

369   At the national level, what is contemplated is the special administration pursuant to article 17 of the 1961 Convention.

370   *1972 Commentary* at 88.

give to the training in the light of the seriousness of its drug abuse problem and other social demands on its training capacity.[371]

Article 38(3) provides that the Parties shall assist persons whose work requires them to gain an understanding of the problems of drug abuse and prevention, but only to the extent that the Parties' have the capacity to do so. These 'persons' include those engaged directly in the treatment of abusers, and persons involved in any aspect of the penal or administrative control of drug abuse.[372] The Parties are also required to promote such understanding among the general public but only if there is a risk that drug abuse will become widespread, something left to the Parties to assess. The *1972 Commentary* suggests that such a promotion is also required if drug addiction has already become widespread.[373] The *1972 Commentary* submits that there is no difference between 'promote' and 'assist' as they are used in the two obligations in article 38(3); they mean the same as 'promote' in article 38(2) which implies that governments are not obliged to engage in training or publicity directly and may rely on promoting private activities engaged in such training and publicity.[374] Although there is no express limitation of practicability in respect of the second obligation under article 38(3), the *1972 Commentary* submits that its drafting history implies a limitation of practicability on the second obligation as well.[375]

The 1972 Protocol's provisions on alternatives to conviction and punishment reflect a modest shift from a purely administrative/penal regime to a more multidisciplinary approach to the drug problem. This shift was already in evidence from the adoption of similar provisions of the 1971 Convention. However, the 1972 Protocol goes further by making provision in article 16 for a new article 38bis entitled 'Agreements on Regional Centres'. As it is only 'desirable', this article does not impose any legal obligations on Parties. Nor does article 16 directly recommend that the Parties promote the establishment of regional

---

371 *1972 Commentary* at 88.
372 The *1972 Commentary* states at 87 that these include judicial officers, police officers, prison wardens, doctors and religious workers who deal with drug abusers, even though their work may not be concerned entirely with drug abusers.
373 *1972 Commentary* at 87. At pp. 87-88 the *1972 Commentary* explains that the linking of the obligation to potential or actual widespread abuse is based on the assumption of the officials of some governments that the promotion of knowledge about drugs in states where their abuse is rare may actually lead to their abuse through the arousal of the curiosity of 'psychologically weak' persons.
374 *1972 Commentary* at 88.
375 *1972 Commentary* at 88-89.

centres; it simply provides that Parties should engage in such promotion if they consider it desirable as part of their action against the illicit traffic.[376] Together with a desire on the part of the Party, the undertaking of promotion of such centres must also have due regard to their constitutional, legal and administrative systems. Such promotion is not made subject to these systems because strict domestic limitation appears unnecessary given what is being promoted. A Party may have recourse to the technical advice of the INCB and other specialised agencies in promoting these agreements, but this does not preclude it from seeking advice elsewhere.[377] The promotion of these agreements is to be made 'with other interested Parties in the region' which covers all Parties in the region including those that can benefit, those with something to offer and even non-parties.[378] Precisely what is to be promoted is couched in vague terms. The article envisages the promotion of agreements contemplating the development of regional centres and not the immediate setting up of such centres. The aim of these centres is to engage in scientific research and education aimed at combating all aspects of the drug abuse problem.[379] Yet the *1972 Commentary* suggests that they also be used for

> such operational activities as the development of regional policies for the campaign against drug abuse, the exchange of police information, or more generally the co-ordination of the illicit traffic work of the enforcement services of the States of the region and forming a centre of international information on problems of drug abuse.[380]

This interpretation of the provision is symbolic of the colonisation by the law enforcement of the attempt in the 1972 Protocol to put in place a multi-disciplinary approach to drug control. This is not to detract from the value of regional centres to Parties that lack the individual resources or competencies to mount effective multidisciplinary programmes against drug abuse. States sig-

---

376 *1972 Commentary* at 90.
377 *1972 Commentary* at 91.
378 *1972 Commentary* at 91.
379 The *1972 Commentary* at 91-92 mentions sociological, economic, medical (including pharmacological and psychiatric), psychological, chemical, legal and governmental (including policing) aspects of the drug problem.
380 *1972 Commentary* at 92.

nified their intention to set up regional centres,[381] but the first real progress occurred in 1993 with the European Union's establishment in Lisbon of the European Monitoring Centre on Drugs and Drug Addiction (EMCDDA).[382] It is concerned with the gathering and analysis of reliable data on the full range of drug problems and the strategies being developed to cope with them in Europe.

3.3.5   Penalty and related provisions under the 1988 Convention

3.3.5.1   General

A 1988 UN study revealed a simple pattern in drug crime punishment.[383] States took similar approaches to the illicit trafficking offences, considering these crimes the most serious and providing the harshest punishment for them.[384] With regard to illicit possession and use, however, state practice varied enormously. Some states only punished such conduct when it was done with the intention of trafficking while others punished it per se, varying the sentence according to the intention.[385] It is not surprising that delegates to the 1988 Conference were clearly divided on the issue of appropriate punishment for use.[386] Nordic and European civil law states favoured flexible provisions allowing for alternatives to incarceration such as treatment, rehabilitation and aftercare for drug users, while producer states such as Mexico were concerned that this approach would signal that demand offences were not serious com-

---

381 C.N. Cagliotti, 'The role of the South American Agreement on Narcotic Drugs and Psychotropic Substances in the fight against illicit drug trafficking' (1983) 35 *Bulletin on Narcotics* 83 at 86 notes that the 1973 South American Agreement on Narcotic Drugs and Psychotropic Substances (ASEP) contemplates such a centre.

382 Established in terms of Council Regulation 1302/93.

383 Cotic supra note 113 at 116-119.

384 Cotic supra note 113 at 113. The study revealed an average punishment of five years imprisonment, and a range of ten to fifteen years imprisonment for the more serious offences. The most common maximum penalty was ten years, with variations reaching twenty years, twenty-four years, life imprisonment and death. Many states had accepted the idea of a petty trafficking offence to which much less severe punishments, such as six months imprisonment, applied, although there was variation of the maximum up to five years.

385 Cotic supra note 113 at 117 notes that determination of the motive for possession becomes a key issue, and states rely either on possession of a stipulated threshold mass to invoke a presumption of intent to traffic, or simply leave the determination of motive in the hands of the court.

386 See Sproule and St-Denis supra note 4 at 271 footnote 31.

ponents of the drug trafficking problem.[387] The fact that article 3(4)(d) allows treatment and rehabilitation to be used as alternatives to conviction and punishment in respect of article 3(2)'s personal use offences indicates a small victory for the former states. General support for a harsh regime for article 3(1) offenders is clear. Article 3(5) provides for factors aggravating article 3(1) offences while article 3(4)(b) allows treatment only 'in addition' to the penalties provided for in article 3(4)(a), except in the minor cases as provided for in article 3(4)(c). Further emphasis of the seriousness of these offences in the eyes of the authors of the Convention is evident from the fact that article 3 also directs the criminal justice systems of the Parties to take steps to ensure that article 3(1) offenders are prosecuted and punished by limiting plea-bargaining, parole and statutes of limitation and by ensuring alleged offenders appear in court. Parties uncertain about the viability or legal validity of the 1988 Convention's punishment provisions can rely on article 3(11) which makes it clear that these provisions are not self-executing by providing that article 3 offences shall inter alia be prosecuted, defended and punished according to the Party's domestic law.

3.3.5.2   *Penalties for article 3(1) offences*
The intention of article 3(4)(a) is to ensure that the offences established by article 3(1) are punished by penalties that take into account their 'grave nature'. The provision appears to accept that such offences are in and of themselves always 'grave' and there can be no instances when they describe relatively minor infractions of the law.[388] The enumeration of the punishments indicates

---

387 Draft article 2(2) had obliged Parties to punish adequately through imprisonment, fines and/or forfeiture the supply related offences in draft article 2(1).

388 Draft article 2(1) had qualified all the offences listed therein as 'serious' but the 'Expert Group Report', *1988 Records* vol. I at 12 notes that several experts suggested that the adjective be deleted since the offences described therein could include minor cases. Although there is no other obligation in the provision stating expressly that these are serious offences that must be punished severely, various experts recommended inter alia that the applicable sanctions should be sufficiently stringent to achieve a deterrent effect and that the penalty provisions should go further than those in the 1961 and 1971 Conventions. Only at the end of the experts' discussion of the draft article was the clause 'grave nature of the offences' agreed upon as the basis for emphasising how seriously the offences were to be viewed for punishment purposes, and it was agreed to delete 'serious' because such offences were inherently serious.

how seriously these offences are viewed.[389] The forms of punishment enumerated are not a numerus clausus. Other forms are possible at the discretion of the Party, but it would seem that they would have to be of a penal nature and not in the nature of treatment or rehabilitation as separate provisions exist for such measures. The enumerated forms are not necessarily cumulative; they function as alternatives or in combinations. Turning to the other extreme of the punishment spectrum, given international condemnation of the use of capital punishment, the exclusion of reference to the death penalty in article 3(4)(a) must have been deliberate.[390] But the absence of express condemnation of such use in this provision indicates the unwillingness of its authors to take positive steps to protect basic human rights.

The first enumerated form is 'imprisonment or other forms of deprivation of liberty'. The Convention does not limit the form of incarceration to imprisonment. It contemplates other forms but does not specify these forms. Such forms may include custodial measures such as house arrest or curfew and non-custodial measures such as electronic monitoring,[391] but they may not, however, include repugnant forms such as re-education camps.[392] The provision does not lay down a minimum period of confinement. Draft article 2(1)(a) obliged Parties to incarcerate offenders for a 'substantial period of time', but this requirement was absorbed into the demand that Parties take into account the 'grave nature' of drug offences when incarcerating offenders, a demand that must of necessity reflect on the place and duration of their incarceration.

The second form of punishment is 'pecuniary sanctions'. These include fines and other punishments of a pecuniary nature. In practice, fines are likely to be applied to the economic offences under article 3(1)(b)[393] and may operate as an alternative to confiscation of the specific assets derived from the illicit traffic.

The third form is 'confiscation', defined by article 1(f) of the 1988 Convention as including forfeiture where applicable, and meaning 'the permanent de-

---

389 Some of the experts were opposed to this enumeration because of the difficulties of application to diverse legal systems, but their suggestion of a broad non-specific provision was rejected – see 'Expert Group Report', *1988 Records* vol. I at 12.

390 The *1988 Commentary* at 98-99 points to the problems for international co-operation posed by capital punishment particularly by the death penalty exception to extradition, but rather lamely does not condemn its use outright.

391 *1988 Commentary* at 86.

392 *1988 Records* vol. I at 13 contra the *1988 Commentary* at 85.

393 For example, article 30bis of Switzerland's *Code Penal* makes money laundering punishable by up to five years in prison and a maximum fine of one million Swiss francs.

privation of property by order of court or other competent authority.' Article 5, discussed in chapter six, contains extensive provisions designed to oblige Parties to deter drug traffickers by enacting legislation for the purposes of confiscating profits, assets, and benefits derived from illicit drug trafficking. These provisions also allow for the identification, tracing, freezing and seizure of this property. Although confiscation was used in state practice before 1988,[394] the Convention's sophisticated provisions have served as the means for introducing it into the domestic practice of most states.

States have responded to article 3(4)(a) as a whole by increasing penalties for familiar trafficking offences and imposing harsh penalties for new offences such as money laundering.[395] Article 3(4)(a) does not provide any guidance on other forms of civil or criminal penalties which have been attached in state practice to drug offences[396] or on civil reparation by drug offenders to their victims.

3.3.5.3   Factors aggravating the punishment of article 3(1) offences

The UN's 1987 Comprehensive Multidisciplinary Outline suggested that states take certain aggravating circumstances into account in connection with sentencing and parole.[397] It is thus not surprising that article 3(5) provides a list of factors which a Party is obliged to allow its courts or competent authorities to take into account in deciding whether an offence is to be regarded as par-

---

394   For example, the US Money Laundering Control Act of 1986, 18 USC sections 981-982.

395   The 'FATF Money Laundering Report, 1990' in W.C. Gilmore (ed.), *International Efforts to Combat Money Laundering* (Grotius, Cambridge, 1992), p. 4 at p. 12 reports that the penalties in member states for laundering offences 'are heavy fines, imprisonment up to 20 years, and sometimes prohibitions against engaging in certain professions.'

396   Articles 19-20 and 28-38 of the Italian Penal Code, for example, allow a) deprivation of political rights and a ban on holding public office; b) a ban on exercising a professional or artistic occupation; c) civil incapacity, involving a form of guardianship, d) a ban on exercising supervision over legal persons or enterprises; e) incapacity for contracting with public authorities; f) suspension of forfeiture of parental rights; g) the publication of the guilty verdict. Other statutes allow h) the withdrawal of a drivers license; i) restriction on travelling abroad – see M.L. Cesoni, 'Italy' in N. Dorn (ed.), *Regulating European Drug Problems* (Kluwer, Hague, 1999), p. 181 at p. 184. Another popular option is expulsion of convicted foreign drug offenders, e.g. article 34 of the Portuguese Drugs Law of 1993 (as amended) – see M.P. Machado, 'Portugal' in Dorn supra at 235.

397   Paragraph 274 – *Declaration of the International Conference on Drug Abuse and Illicit Trafficking and Comprehensive Multidisciplinary Outline of Future Activities in Drug Abuse Control*, UN Publication St/Nar/14, UN Sales No.E.88.XI.1, (New York, 1988), p. 61.

ticularly serious. It is not a numerus clausus but serves as a strong guide to
the kind of factors regarded as aggravating by the 1988 Conference. While this
innovative provision is obviously designed to ensure that domestic legal systems
treat drug offences seriously, it fails to specify the purposes for which courts
or other competent authorities should take these factors into account.[398] It
appears that it must be for sentencing, but the provision did not specify that
this was the case in order to leave the Parties with complete freedom of action.[399] This ambiguity may be due to the fact that aggravating factors are
a common law concept; the courts in common law countries are left with the
discretion to apply them or not with or without express legislation to that effect.
In the civil law tradition, however, the courts, while competent to apply ex-
tenuating factors, cannot apply aggravating factors without legislative authority.[400] The use of these factors in sentencing has, however, also got human
rights implications relating to their proof. It is arguable, for example, because
of the serious implications for the accused, that provisions like article 3(5)(g)'s
reference to commission of an offence in a particular place should be part of
the definition of the offence and they should have to proved during the conviction process where the right to remain silent generally applies, rather than be
considered to be an aggravating factor on sentence where no such right may
apply. But given that they were not included in the definition of offences in
article 3(1) that does not seem to have been the intention of the authors of the
1988 Convention. In any event, under article 3(5) a Party's courts or competent
authorities retain their independence and are not obliged to take these factors
into account; the obligation is only mandatory on the Party to 'allow' or 'enable'
them to take these factors into account.[401] The 'courts' that are to take these
factors into account are judicial tribunals, but 'other competent authorities' is

---

398 Sproule and St-Denis supra note 4 at 271 footnote 32.
399 The Jamaican delegate recommended that the words 'in considering the sanction to be
     imposed on the convicted offender' should be inserted into the provision but they were
     not – *1988 Records* vol. II at 41. Parties have used this provision in other ways. For
     example, the South African Drugs and Drug trafficking Act 140 of 1992 originally
     contained in section 21(1)(a)(ii) a presumption of liability for the offence of 'dealing'
     in drugs based on possession of drugs on or within 100 meters of 'school grounds' which
     had its origin in article 3(5)(g). It was struck down as unconstitutional in *S v Bhulwana*
     1995 (2) SACR 748 (CC).
400 See the remarks in the 'Expert Group Report', *1988 Records* vol. I at 14.
401 See the remarks of the German (FDR) delegation – *1988 Records* vol. II at 41-42.

not as easily defined. It appears, however, that they must have criminal and sentencing jurisdiction.[402]

As for the factors themselves, their meaning is not plain.[403] For example, while it is plain in terms of article 3(5)(a) that it is an aggravation if an individual acts with others and these others are organised and involved in the offence, article 3(5)(a) does not define what an 'organised criminal group' is, or just how an offender 'belongs', to such a group. In the same way, while article 3(5)(b) makes it an aggravation for an individual to be involved in other 'international organised criminal activities', it does not define either the degree of 'involvement' or what types of activities may be classified as 'organised' and 'international'. It only stipulates that they must be 'other' than drug offences.[404] Both these provisions echo the Preamble's concern in paragraph 3 with the link between drug trafficking and organised crime, but the meaning of organised crime in international law is uncertain.[405]

Article 3(5)(c)'s reference to the offender's 'involvement in other illegal activities facilitated by the commission of the offence' is also vague. Although this appears to refer to the combination of drug offences with economic offences,[406] it can on its face mean involvement in any illegal activities facilitated by the commission of an article 3(1) offence. The use of 'illegal' includes activities that are regulated in some systems but which are not criminal.[407]

Article 3(5)(d) makes it an aggravating factor to 'use' 'violence or arms'. By necessary implication this must be in the commission of an article 3(1) offence. The *1988 Commentary* points out that the French text is not limited

---

402　See the statement of the Netherlands delegate – *1988 Records* vol. II at 42. In Ghana 'competent authorities' would thus include the special public tribunals set up to try drug offenders – *1988 Records* vol. II at 42.

403　The *1988 Commentary's* explanation at 90 that specific definition was not required as these are not definitional elements of an offence is unconvincing and no comfort to an offender whose sentence may depend on proof of the presence of these factors.

404　Remarks by various delegates indicate that international arms smuggling and terrorism were contemplated, but there was no agreement on what these activities meant or on the inclusion of a list of examples – *1988 Records* vol. II at 43-45.

405　The development of an International Convention for the Combating of Organised Crime may settle precisely what organised crime is, but as yet no settled definition exists in international law.

406　See the 'Expert Group Report', *1988 Records* vol. I at 15.

407　*1988 Commentary* at 91. It gives the example of gambling or prostitution, which in some systems are illegal but not criminal.

to use of firearms and thus 'arms' should be understood as broadly as possible.[408] The provision's reliance on very general terms is designed to ease
domestic acceptance by legal systems that have struggled in their domestic law
with defining these terms.[409]

The reference in article 3(5)(e) to an offender who 'holds a public office'
and who commits an offence in connection with that office defines neither the
meaning of a 'public office' or the nature of the link between offence and office.
These definitions are left to the Parties. This provision could usefully have been
applied by the authors of article 3 to holders of office in the private sector as
long as these offices indicated positions of trust and leadership and the offender's conduct involved an abuse of this position.[410] Such an extension
would have had a deterrent effect on drug traffickers with legitimate business
fronts.

Article 3(5)(f)'s reference to the 'victimisation or use of minors' is also
unduly limited. Echoing the concern of paragraph 2 of the Preamble with the
use of children in the supply of drugs and as a market for drugs, it could well
have been extended to physically or mentally handicapped persons.[411] The
fact that the age of minority and the definition of victimisation[412] is also left
to be decided in accordance with each Party's domestic law, is indicative of
the trend in the Convention to harmonisation rather than universalisation of
punishments.

Article 3(5)(g) is an unusual provision. It renders the commission of the
offence in a penal institution, educational institution, social service facility or
other place where school children or students go for education, sports or social
activities an aggravating factor. Partly echoing paragraph two of the Preamble's
concern with the protection of children, its aim appears to be to protect young
people whether at school, sport or play in inadequately supervised places. It
is the linking of penalty to place that is unusual. It could, literally interpreted,
result in the presence of the offender in one of the places being regarded as

---

408 *1988 Commentary* at 91 pointing out that the French text uses '*armes*' rather than '*armes*
       à feu'.
409 See *1988 Records* vol. II at 45.
410 See the remarks of the delegate from Papua New Guinea – *1988 Records* vol. II at 45-46.
       Article 14(1) of the OAS Model Regulations provides for the subjection to more severe
       sanctions of financial institutions and their staff members who participate in the illicit
       traffic.
411 See the 'Expert Group Report', *1988 Records* vol. I at 14.
412 The *1988 Commentary* at 92 gives using a minor as a messenger as an example.

aggravating even if the institution was empty of members of the target group.[413] Much of the provision's wording is vague, for example, its reference to the 'immediate vicinity' of the institutions mentioned.[414] Whether 'educational facility' includes tertiary educational facilities is uncertain, but the reference to 'students' implies that it does. 'Other places to which school children and students resort for educational, sports and social activities' includes museums, cinemas, theatres, recreational areas, tourist areas,[415] sports stadia and venues. This provision also exists to deter the sale of drugs in penal institutions and social service facilities such as rehabilitation centres where drugs are often freely available. However, whether prisoners and recipients of social services deserve the same protection as children was questioned; some Conference delegates felt the eradication of drug trafficking from penal institutions was utopian while others saw drugs as a problem impeding the rehabilitation of prisoners and deserving of action.[416]

Article 3(5)(h) is very specific, which may render it inapplicable in certain states. It renders 'prior convictions' and particularly convictions for similar offences whether foreign or domestic an aggravating factor. There is, however, a domestic limitation clause attached to this particular obligation because the domestic law of some states does not always allow them to take prior convictions into account on sentence.[417] It is noteworthy that the Convention makes no specific provision, unlike the earlier conventions, for taking foreign convictions into account for the purposes of establishing recidivism, but article 3(5)(h) does allow foreign convictions to impact on punishment.[418] The con-

---

413 The *1988 Commentary* at 93 does not see how geographical approximation alone can be given much weight.

414 The Mexican delegate explained the necessity of this wording because when traffickers were unable to enter schools they 'accosted young people in areas close-by' – *1988 Records* vol. II at 44.

415 See the remarks of the Argentinean delegate, *1988 Records* vol. II at 50.

416 See the remarks of the Netherlands delegate and the Mexican delegate respectively, *1988 Records* vol. II at 47.

417 See the remarks of the German delegate (FDR), *1988 Records* vol. II at 42.

418 Draft article 2(5) was such a recidivism provision but was deleted by the Expert Group because of practical and legal difficulties with it. Article 3(5)(h)'s reference to prior convictions whether foreign or domestic as an aggravating circumstance was included instead – *1988 Records* vol. I at 13, 16. Recidivism is not a universal concept, but the provision does allow Parties to take into account previous convictions which can then be used to establish recidivism or habitual criminality of drug offenders if the Party seeks to do so. Section 31 of the Indian Narcotic Drugs and Psychotropic Substances Act, 1985, for example, provides that previous convictions can be used as a basis to

victions taken into account are not necessarily limited to those for similar offences; they include any prior conviction.

A rather striking omission for the list of aggravating factors, given its currency in domestic practice, is the nature and the quantity of the drugs involved.[419] In practice, Parties are likely to apply the aggravating factors listed in article 3(5) as they see fit, give them the legal content they deem appropriate, and add to them as they see fit. Many are already contained in general domestic law[420] and do appear to be having some influence on state practice.[421]

3.3.5.4   Plea-bargaining

Article 3(6) was included in the Convention to ensure that Parties which allow prosecutorial discretion and thus by extension use of the technique of "plea-bargaining" do not allow abuse of this discretion to undermine the deterrent effect of drug related penalties.[422] The Mexican delegate who proposed this provision justified it as follows:

> [He] said it should be borne in mind that there were great numbers of dealers selling drugs to consumers, whereas the organisers were far fewer in number. He knew that the bargaining technique was favoured in some countries, but statistics he had seen showed that the technique was used generously and in a manner that was not always justified by the need to apprehend and prosecute the major criminals. It was sometimes used because there were not enough courts to try all the offenders

---

enhance the punishment of offenders, and for the purposes of the section any conviction under any corresponding law outside India shall be treated on a par with, and regarded as, a conviction in India.

419   See, for example, the UK case of *R v Aramah* (1983) CLR 271-273.

420   See, for example, in the US the sentencing guidelines in 18 USC section 3553 and chapter 3.

421   For example, F. Taisch, 'Swiss statutes concerning money laundering' (1992) 26 *The International Lawyer* 695 at 700-701 discusses the factors enacted in the Swiss Penal Code which render the crime of money laundering more serious. Article 305bis provides in subparagraph 2 that 'a case is severe ... if the perpetrator: a) acts as a member of a criminal organisation; b) acts as a member of a gang, formed with the purpose of continued money laundering.'

422   See Sproule and St-Denis supra note 4 at 271. Guidelines in respect of prosecutorial discretion had already been recommended at a number of international expert meetings affiliated with the UN, e.g. European Seminar of Non-Prosecution organised by the Helsinki Institute for Crime Prevention and Control, 22-23 March 1986.

arrested, or not enough prisons to hold them. The result was that battalions of dealers went back to the streets to deliver drugs to consumers.[423]

Common law states such as Canada and the United States countered that, apart from being fundamental to their legal systems, prosecutorial discretion induced "little fish" to co-operate in catching "big fish" through concessions such as reduction of sentence.[424] The justification for plea-bargaining is that it facilitates a rational prosecution policy by recognising the need to prioritise the use of resources and reach the upper echelons of the illicit trafficking organisations through their minions.[425] However, plea-bargaining can undermine the enforcement of drug laws and their deterrent effect on traffickers or users whether they are potential offenders, offenders not yet in custody or offenders already in custody. Thus article 3(6) provides as a compromise that Parties shall endeavour to ensure that plea-bargaining and other forms of prosecutorial discretion are exercised to maximise the effectiveness of law enforcement measures in respect of article 3 offences and to maximise the deterrence of the commission of article 3 offences. The exact scope of 'discretionary legal powers' in article 3(6) remains undefined, but they can be taken to mean 'such discretionary acts as dismissal of criminal action, diminishing of charges, their modification, transaction regarding the reduction or modification of sanction, concession of immunity or any other form of bargaining.'[426] The provision appears to hit both the traditional plea-bargain in which a prosecutor and defence counsel agree to have the defendant plead guilty to a lesser charge in return for foregoing the right to a trial, and the practice in some common law states[427] of law enforcement agents arresting or threatening prospective informants and then offering them a deal in exchange for co-operation in making a

---

423 *1988 Records* vol. II at 49. The Mexican proposal would have done away entirely with plea-bargaining for drug offences – *1988 Records* vol. I at 90. See also the similar sentiments of the Colombian delegate, *1988 Records* vol. II at 49.

424 Sproule and St-Denis supra note 4 at 271 footnote 33.

425 *1988 Commentary* at 94.

426 See the Statement of the Philippines delegate, *1988 Records* vol. II at 62.

427 Such deals may be illegal in civil law states where they violate the rule of compulsory prosecution requiring prosecution of anyone known to have committed an offence. E. Nadelmann, *Cops Across Borders: The Internationalization of U.S. Criminal Law Enforcement* (The Pennsylvania State University Press, University Park, Pennsylvania, 1993), p. 218 notes, however, that police in many European states now openly pursue such practices, and laws have been altered accordingly – see section 31 of the German Narcotics Law.

case against other traffickers ("flipping").[428] Such a deal may involve not proceeding with the arrest or arranging with the prosecutor to drop charges, and thus may involve the co-operation of a prosecutor or judge. The provision is also wide enough to be applied to the granting of bail.[429]

Compliance with article 3(6) will restrict what law enforcement officials regard as one of the most important sources of drug intelligence available. Although the provision fetters prosecution policy, the degree to which it does so is uncertain. The most logical method for ascertaining the degree to which the discretion should be curtailed in a particular case would be to weigh up the interest of the state in the prosecution of the particular individual against the interest in the supply of intelligence he or she offers to provide. It has thus been argued that the Parties' discretionary legal powers are wider with respect to the prosecution of use offences under article 3(2) as opposed to illicit drug trafficking offences under article 3(1).[430] However this provision is applied, it seems unlikely that it will ever have any real impact, as it is monitored almost entirely by the same officials who use plea-bargaining and prosecutorial discretion.[431]

---

428 See Nadelmann supra note 427 at 215.

429 The understanding of the US delegate, *1988 Records* vol. II at 57.

430 See the statement of the Netherlands delegate, *1988 Records* vol. II at 30, where he points out that the Convention already adopts a softer approach to the punishment of simple possession in article 3 paragraphs 4(d) and 11. The Netherlands made a reservation to this effect upon signature and upon acceptance (8/9/1993) – *Multilateral Treaties Deposited* (1997) at 305, the latter pointing out that it only accepts article 3(6) insofar as it accords with Dutch criminal policy and legislation.

431 S.B. Ellington, 'United States v. Noriega as a reason for an international criminal court' (1993) 11 *Dickinson Journal of International Law* 451 at 472 notes that during Manuel Noriega's trial the prosecution granted some type of immunity or leniency to twenty of the testifying drug dealers. In the BCCI case, charges were dropped against the corporation under a plea-bargaining agreement and the BCCI paid $14 million in drug forfeiture money, something criticised by the US Senate Foreign Relations Committee's Subcommittee on Narcotics and Terrorism as 'merely turning over the profits of drug trafficking to the federal government' in exchange for the ending of criminal liability – see Clutterbuck supra note 193 at 112-113.

3.3.5.5 Parole for article 3(1) offences

Article 3(7) is an innovative provision[432] designed to ensure that Parties do not allow parole[433] to become a convenient means for article 3(1) drug offenders to avoid completing the long terms of imprisonment or some other form of deprivation of liberty appropriate to the gravity of drug offences contemplated by article 3(4), especially where one or more of the aggravating factors enumerated in article 3(5) were present. In this regard, the provisions in article 3(6) with respect to limitation of prosecutorial discretion when plea-bargaining and in article 3(8) with respect to extended statute of limitations periods, are both intended to ensure that the offender receives an appropriate punishment and that its deterrent effect is not undermined by domestic practice. The provision does not require, however, that parole be deferred for every article 3(1) offender in every case. Parties are simply obliged to ensure that when courts or competent authorities consider granting parole they take into account in terms of article 3(4) the gravity of conviction for these offences as well as in terms of article 3(5) the presence of any aggravating factors. The courts/authorities retain the discretion to grant parole in any event. Whether this requires a Party to change its domestic legislation dealing with parole is not clear, but it appears not.[434] Some Parties have declared that they will apply it only in accordance with their legal systems.[435]

---

432 Introduced in draft article 2(7), the Mexican delegate believed that the provision in its final form had been watered down. He stated that 'in the Mexican legal system the eventuality of early release or parole of the offenders in question was totally ruled out' – *1988 Records* vol. II at 56.

433 The provision applies only to parole and not to release on bail before trial, although the CND had drawn attention to the fact that drug traffickers are wealthy enough to make bail payments and obtain release – see the comment of the Indian delegate, *1988 Records* vol. II at 57. Bail may, however, be covered by the restrictions in article 3(6).

434 The Netherlands delegate at the Conference did not feel that the provision required a change in its relevant legislation to accommodate 'the concerns expressed by the terms' of this provision – *1988 Records* vol. II at 30. The Netherlands made reservations to this effect upon signature and upon acceptance (8/9/1993), the latter pointing out that it only accepts article 3(7) insofar as it accords with Dutch criminal policy and legislation.

435 Colombia (10/6/1994) – *Multilateral Treaties Deposited* (1997) at 303 declares that it will use discretion in this regard, somewhat ambiguously 'taking into account the benefits of its policies regarding the indictment of and collaboration with alleged criminals.'

3.3.5.6   Statutes of limitation

Article 3(8) obliges Parties to ensure that statutes of limitation are not used to provide a means for offenders to avoid punishment. It envisages two situations, viz. Parties have a qualified obligation to (a) establish a 'long' statute of limitations period for the commencement of article 3(1) prosecutions, and (b) an even 'longer' statute of limitations period where the alleged article 3(1) offender has evaded justice. The word 'long' indicates that the drafters of the Convention had in mind an 'extensive time limit',[436] but just how 'long' remains unspecified. The establishment of a 'longer period' was originally designed to discourage the flight of offenders from the administration of justice whether within a Party or between Parties. This provision for extension where evasion takes place does not imply the complete abandonment of statutes of limitation.[437] It appears to require some positive act upon the part of the accused to evade prosecution and not simply the mere non-prosecution of the accused, or it would make nonsense of the purpose of a statute of limitations.[438]

As noted, the Parties' obligation is qualified. The inclusion of the wording 'where appropriate' sugared this particular legal pill for most delegations because it appears to render the provision hortatory.[439] This conclusion differs from that of the chairman of Committee I who felt the words did not offer 'Parties the opportunity of not fulfilling the obligations established by the paragraph; the qualification was merely intended to take account of cases where no improvement of the existing national measures was required.'[440] The provision is presumably inapplicable if a Party either does not impose a statute of limitation on drug offences or at all. For such Parties the decision to proceed or not will presumably be made on a case by case basis taking into account practical considerations such as the availability of witnesses and evidence and the reasonableness of the chance of conviction. It is not clear whether 'establish' means the creation of new legislation where Parties do have either general or

---

436 See the understanding of Committee I, *1988 Records* vol. II at 57.

437 Colombia has made it clear in a declaration (10/6/1994) – *Multilateral Treaties Deposited* (1997) at 304, that it understands that the provision 'does not imply the non-applicability of the statutory limitation of penal action.'

438 *1988 Commentary* at 95.

439 See Sproule and St-Denis supra note 4 at 271. The 'Expert Group Report', *1988 Records* vol. I at 16 notes that because the introduction of a special prescription for a particular category of offences was incompatible with some legal systems an escape clause was introduced.

440 See *1988 Records* vol. II at 58.

specific drug offence statute of limitation provisions. The Netherlands' delegate to the Conference did not feel that satisfaction of the provision required a change in its relevant legislation dealing generally with statutes of limitation on serious offences.[441]

3.3.5.7 *Presence of alleged offenders and offenders at court*

Article 3(9) obliges each Party to take appropriate measures, consistent with their legal systems, to ensure that a person charged with or convicted of an article 3(1) offence, who is found within its territory, is present at the criminal proceedings. The original draft article 2(8) included the sentence: 'In this regard the Parties shall bear in mind the large sums of money available to traffickers when setting bail.'[442] The Expert Group deleted the sentence because there was disagreement about whether bail should be available at all for article 3(1) offences, and if it were available, whether its grant should be regulated by the Convention or remain entirely a domestic concern.[443] What is left of the provision is restricted to an obligation to ensure a person charged with or convicted of an article 3(1) offence is present at 'criminal proceedings' but only if the offender is found in the territorial jurisdiction of the Party.[444] The exact nature of such proceedings is left undefined and will depend on the nature of the Party's criminal process, but the provision does not deal with extradition, which is dealt with by article 6. It does not preclude, according to the *1988 Commentary*, trials in absentia.[445] The Parties are obliged to take 'appropriate measures'

---

441 See *1988 Records* vol. II at 30. See also the statement of the Austrian delegate and Barbadian delegate to similar effect. The Netherlands made a reservation to this effect upon signature and upon acceptance (8/9/1993) – *Multilateral Treaties Deposited* (1997) at 305. In the latter reservation it points out that it only accepts article 3(8) insofar as it accords with Dutch criminal policy and legislation. The US delegation considered the US's five year statute of limitations for non-capital drug offences together with provisions to suspend the running of the limitation period when an indictment is filed (18 USC section 3282), where a person flees justice (18 USC section 3290), and to allow evidence to be obtained from abroad (18 USC section 3292), to be sufficient to meet its obligations under article 3(8) – see 'Report of the US Delegation' supra note 143 at 31.

442 See *1988 Records* vol. I at 4.

443 See the 'Expert Group Report', *1988 Records* vol. I at 16.

444 The scope of draft article 2(8) was not limited to the territorial jurisdiction of the arresting Party. The Expert Group restricted its scope because some states could not accept a universal scope of application – see the 'Expert Group Report', *1988 Records* vol. I at 16.

445 *1988 Commentary* at 96.

to ensure the alleged offender's presence at proceedings which assumedly means arrest and/or detention, and the refusal of bail if there is no reasonable prospect that he or she will attend trial. It is important to note that the provision has an in-built limitation clause, as the measures have to be 'consistent' with the Party's 'legal system'.

3.3.5.8   The punishment of the personal use offence under the 1988 Convention

The 1988 Convention's provisions for punishment are directed almost entirely at the drug trafficking offences in article 3(1). The 1988 Convention's only direct reference to punishment for the personal use offence in article 3(2) is the provision in article 3(4)(d) which allows Parties to 'provide either as an alternative to conviction or punishment, or in addition to conviction or punishment' for measures such as education and treatment. The Convention thus anticipates that Parties will punish such offenders, but not in every case. It does not stipulate the form such punishment will take, although the separation of article 3(4)(a)'s provision for the punishment of grave article 3(1) offences by imprisonment from the provision in article 3(4)(d) suggests that incarceration is not expected, although this remains at the discretion of the Party. Clearly cautioning of users or their diversion out of the criminal justice system is both possible and desirable under this provision, and this issue is discussed in greater detail below.

3.3.5.9   Alternatives to punishment for article 3 offences

3.3.5.9.1 Introduction

The sixteen years between 1972 and 1988 did not see any remarkable development of positive international law when it came to a multidisciplinary approach to drug control. Such development was left to the "soft" law[446] that culminated in the 1987 *Comprehensive Multidisciplinary Outline of Future Activities in*

---

446 For example, in 1976, the CND recommended and ECOSOC passed Resolution E/Res/ 1934 (LVIII) on 'Measures to reduce illicit demand for drugs'. In the belief that supply reduction could not be effective without demand reduction, ECOSOC recommended that states take all possible measures to reduce abuse and to provide treatment facilities for addicts. It requested WHO with the aid of UNFDAC to provide financial and technical assistance to governments to provide treatment and rehabilitation. The resolution recommended that states incorporate measures for prevention and treatment in their integrated health programmes, and urged appropriate international organisations to provide world-wide exchange of information on prevention/treatment and research.

Drug Abuse Control.[447] In chapter one the Outline sets out a number of de-mand reduction measures that were not translated into positive legal obligations in the 1988 Convention. These include measures for assessing the size and nature of the drug problem that each state faces.[448] The Outline identifies the workplace as a significant area for drug abuse and suggests steps to both publicise the risks of such usage and to identify and treat it when it occurs.[449] The community is considered a resource in the war against drugs, and the Out-line targets for support prevention programmes by civic, community, special interest groups and law enforcement agencies that stress the risks involved and provide facilities for treatment and so on.[450] Leisure time is also identified as critical in drug usage and alternative leisure time activities are targeted as a way of coaxing especially young people away from drug usage.[451] Finally, the media is targeted as having a particularly important role to play in en-couraging drug usage and the Outline suggests that guidelines be drawn up for the portrayal of drug usage in the media.[452]

Chapter four of the Outline begins by suggesting the development of a national policy towards treatment.[453] To this end it proposes the establishment of a national body to co-ordinate a national treatment programme. It recom-mends that this task be pursued by making an inventory of available methods of treatment and rehabilitation.[454] As part of this inventory the Outline makes recommendations with respect to the evaluation of funding and apportionment of resources, the evaluation of available material and manpower and the evaluation of the effectiveness of the different treatment methods. Then it goes on to tackle the thorny problem of which treatment programmes to adopt in

---

447 Supra note 397.
448 Target 1, 'Assessment of the extent of drug misuse and abuse', recognises the difficulties of collecting data on drug use. Identifying the problems associated with using data from sources such as the police, it recommends that a comprehensive system of data-collection be developed utilising sophisticated methodologies for gathering and analysing informa-tion from as many sources as possible to give a more accurate reflection of the nature of the problem faced – supra note 397 at 12-15. Target 2, entitled 'Organisation of comprehensive systems for the collection and evaluation of data', focuses on the nature of the actual data collection system used and the skills of those who run it – supra note 397 at 16-18.
449 Target 4, supra note 397 at 22.
450 Target 5, supra note 397 at 23-25.
451 Target 6, supra note 397 at 26.
452 Target 7, supra note 397 at 27.
453 Target 29, supra note 397 at 74.
454 Target 30, supra note 397 at 76.

what circumstances, and suggests a selection of appropriate treatment program-mes.[455] In doing so it tries to meld the role of government, the community, the family and the individual into an appropriate treatment programme. It recommends training for personnel working with drug addicts, both basic and specialised.[456] It targets, rather vaguely, the reduction of diseases and infections transmitted through drug-using habits.[457] It also targets care for drug-addicted offenders within the criminal justice and prison systems, and suggests the studying of this part of the prison population.[458] Finally the Outline focuses on the social reintegration of users who have undergone treatment and rehabilitation, and urges the adoption of the programme most cost-effective to the community.[459]

The scope and detail of the recommendations is impressive, but they betray the underdevelopment of the official non-criminal justice response to drug use and the harm it causes. The recommendations tend to vagueness when, for example, they deal with difficult issues such as HIV communicated shared needle use – the provision of free needles by the authorities is not mentioned as a possible tactic. They anticipate drug control remaining in government hands and envisage the international function to be co-ordinating rather than directing national authorities. The fact that the Outline places such emphasis on the gathering and analysis of data at the national level indicates how impoverished demand and harm reduction policies are at the national level because of the absence of an empirical basis with which to work.

Although they required further development, only a skeleton of these recommendations was transformed into "hard" law in the 1988 Convention. As the United States delegation to the 1988 Conference notes: 'Domestic and international strategies for reducing the demand for illegal drugs are, for the most part, not the subject of the Convention.'[460] No alternatives to punishment were contained in the original draft convention, on the basis that its purpose was suppression of the illicit traffic. Alternative provisions were only introduced after concerns were raised that their absence would mean that Parties would no longer regard similar provisions in the amended 1961 Convention (article 36(1)(b)) and the 1971 Convention (article 22(1)(b)) as binding.[461]

---

455 Target 31, supra note 397 at 78.
456 Target 32, supra note 397 at 80.
457 Target 33, supra note 397 at 82.
458 Target 34, supra note 397 at 83.
459 Target 35, supra note 397 at 85.
460 'Report of the US Delegation' supra note 143 at 26.
461 *1988 Records* vol. I at 13 and 15.

3.3.5.9.2 Punishment alternatives in article 3(4)

The 1988 Convention follows the pattern of the earlier conventions by integrating entirely optional alternatives to punishment into the punishment provisions. Article 3(4) sub-paragraphs (b) and (c) provide for 'treatment, education, aftercare, rehabilitation or social reintegration' in addition to punishment for article 3(1)'s supply related offences, and in minor cases as an alternative to punishment, while article 3(4)(d) provides for these measures to be used both in addition to and as alternatives to punishment for article 3(2)'s demand related offences.

Article 3(4)(b)'s measures are not limited to drug abusers; they apply to all offenders convicted of and punished for an article 3(1) offence. Because these measures are aimed at drug traffickers and the authors of the provision felt that it was inappropriate to substitute them for the conviction or punishment of major traffickers, Parties have the discretion to apply these measures only in addition to and not as alternatives to punishment.[462]

Substitution for punishment is only possible with regard to article 3(1) offences in, as contemplated in article 3(4)(c), 'appropriate cases of a minor nature'. This provision accepts that not all article 3(1) offences are by definition 'grave', but the definition of minor offences is left to the Parties. By implication it must exclude any offence considered 'particularly serious' because it exhibits any of the factual circumstances set out in article 3(5). The wording of the measures suggested emphasises that measures for drug abusers differ from those for ordinary offenders, which implies that this provision has in mind article 3(1) offenders who are themselves drug users and who are engaging in trafficking in order perhaps to finance their own drug usage.

Article 3(4)(d)'s provisions are alternative or additional measures, but they are limited to article 3(2) offenders – possessors, users or purchasers for personal use. A separate sub-paragraph to this effect was necessitated by the criminalisation of the aforementioned activities.[463]

The measures suggested in all three provisions, viz. 'treatment, education, aftercare, rehabilitation or social reintegration of the offender', are intended not to be exhaustive but rather only indicative of the measures which the Parties

---

462 See the 'Expert Group Report', *1988 Records* vol. I at 15.

463 The Netherlands delegation understood that the discretion afforded by article 3(4)(d) to either punish or treat users made the Parties' discretionary powers with respect to the offence in article 3(2) wider than the Parties' discretionary powers with respect to the offences in article 3(1) – *1988 Records* vol. II at 30.

may provide.[464] 'Treatment' implies the withdrawal of the drugs from the user or the enforced restriction by the user of his intake to a maintenance dosage. It may include drug-maintenance such as methadone treatment, but detoxification usually implies withdrawal. Individual or group counselling may be used to support treatment, which may also involve outpatient day care, day support, in-patient care or therapeutic community support.[465] A variety of other treatments are suggested by the *1988 Commentary* including acupuncture, behaviour modification, family therapy, relapse prevention training and the development of coping and interpersonal skills.[466] 'Education' implies the education of both special target groups such as users where education may take place during treatment and the education of the general public in this regard. 'Aftercare' implies measures of a psychiatric, psychoanalytical or psychological nature used to treat users from whom drugs have been withdrawn or users subject to a maintenance programme. In a penal context it may also mean the phase of supervision and counselling following discharge from a custodial sentence to enable adjustment to society.[467] 'Rehabilitation' is the process designed to render the formerly drug dependent individual physically, vocationally, morally and otherwise fit for living a normal life as a useful member of society. This may involve the cure of diseases, physical rehabilitation of disabled persons, vocational training, supervision accompanied by advice and encouragement, measures of gradual progress to a normal self-reliant life, and so on. 'Social reintegration', finally, refers to the measures taken to allow the rehabilitated drug abuser to live in an environment most favourable to him. These measures may include provision of employment, housing and ideally the movement of the abuser away from the environment which nurtured the abuse or from one likely to stigmatise that abuse. The *1988 Commentary* suggests that community service may be considered a valid method of social reintegration.[468] More controversially, it has been suggested that the decriminalisation of small amounts of cannabis for personal use could be defended as the 'social reintegration' of a class of persons presently subject to prohibition.[469]

Although abuse is the main target of these measures and dictates their nature, none of the three sub-paragraphs limits their application to drug abusers so these

---

464 See the 'Expert Group Report', *1988 Records* vol. I at 15.
465 *1988 Commentary* at 87.
466 *1988 Commentary* at 87.
467 *1988 Commentary* at 87-88.
468 *1988 Commentary* at 89.
469 Dawkins supra note 22 at 283.

measures may extend beyond the medical and social problems of abusers to measures for the treatment of offenders in general.[470] The list of measures is not a numerus clausus and Parties are free to use whatever other methods are judged to be appropriate to the particular circumstances of the offender.[471] These measures may overlap in terms of their content and the stages in the process at which they are applied. All of these measures may be applied in terms of article 3(4)(b) to traffickers[472] and in terms of article 3(4)(d) to simple users, but in respect of the minor trafficking offences in article 3(4)(c) only 'education, rehabilitation or social reintegration' apply, while 'treatment and aftercare' apply when these offenders are users. Parties should apply the measures that are indicated in each particular case.

Their wording implies the stage in the trial process at which the measures in all three provisions may be applied. They operate additionally and/or alternatively to 'conviction or punishment', which tends to imply that they only become operative after the alleged offender has been prosecuted. The authors of the provisions obviously felt that such a decision is best made when more about the offence is known. However, it is not clear whether a charge must have been put to the accused, whether the accused must have entered a plea, or whether evidence must have been led. It is submitted that diversion at an early stage in the criminal process should be available if it is appropriate to the circumstances of the particular case, and this includes diversion after arrest only in the case of police cautions. Diversion at the stage of enforcement of a sentence may also be a viable option in many cases.[473]

The provisions in article 3(4) relating to alternatives to punishment were an afterthought, a late attachment to a law enforcement convention. They reflect in the positive law the conservative interpretation given to the similar but more broadly worded provisions in the earlier conventions. Discretion is retained by the Parties as article 3(4)'s provisions are only recommendations, but their

---

470 *1988 Commentary* at 88.
471 *1988 Commentary* at 89.
472 The provision obviously contemplates that such traffickers should be users or else it is redundant.
473 The *1988 Commentary* at 87 gives as an example of the former option conditional discontinuation of criminal proceedings under condition of attending a treatment programme or a treatment order pronounced by a prosecuting magistrate (e.g. the *injonction thérapeutic* in accordance with article 628-1(1) and governed by articles L 355-15 to L 355-17 of the French Public Health Code), and as an example of the latter option transfer from prison to an institution or therapeutic community (e.g. L 628-3 CSP of the French Public Health Code).

general tone is much more restrictive than that of the earlier provisions, indicative of the swing in the 1980s to a more strongly prohibitionist approach to drug control. State response has been uneven. For example, a 1995 survey of European states, most of them Parties to the 1988 Convention,[474] discovered that some had specific provisions for using treatment as an alternative to repression,[475] others had no specific provisions but still used treatment as an alternative in terms of their general laws,[476] while other states had specific legal provisions for compulsory treatment.[477] Information on application by developing states is very difficult to come by.

3.3.5.9.3 Demand reduction in the 1988 Convention

Other than the provisions in article 3(2) criminalising simple possession and article 3(4) providing for alternatives to penalisation, the 1988 Convention is not concerned with drug use. Article 14(4) contains the only other reference to the user. Aimed at correcting the imbalance between supply reduction and demand reduction measures in the 1988 Convention,[478] article 14(4) echoes the sole paragraph in the Preamble concerned with demand as a cause of drug abuse, paragraph seven. It is, however, contained within article 14, the bulk of which sets out the general provisions in the 1988 Convention aimed at source reduction. Its position is symbolic of the position of demand in the Convention as a whole,[479] which is even weaker than in the earlier conventions. It is not surprising that article 14(4) is subject to article 14(1) which makes it clear that

---

474 Conducted by Leroy supra note 240 at 121-124.

475 Germany, Spain, France, Greece, Ireland, Italy, Luxembourg and Portugal all provide for treatment measures as an alternative to punishment to be handed down at any stage of the procedure, viz.: before the start of proceedings; instead of starting on the initiative of the prosecutor; at the pronouncement of sentence by the court; after judgment; and when enforcing a penalty at either the prosecutor's or judge's discretion – Leroy supra note 240 at 121.

476 Belgium, Denmark, the Netherlands and the UK all rely on their ordinary law to encourage or compel users to seek treatment, usually through suspension of sentence during probation and by suspending sentences coupled with tests or conditional discharge – Leroy supra note 240 at 122.

477 Spain, Italy, Denmark, France, Luxembourg and Portugal all provide for the compulsory treatment through hospitalisation etc. on the order of a judicial official outside of criminal proceedings. States such as Germany, France, Greece, Ireland and Italy also provide for the compulsory committal of offenders in criminal proceedings – Leroy supra note 240 at 123-124.

478 Statement of the Mexican delegate, *1988 Records* vol. II at 304.

479 This provision was not contained in the original draft convention, but was included at the Review Group stage – *1988 Records* vol. I at 83.

the demand reduction measures that Parties take as a result of article 14(4) 'shall not be less stringent' than the demand reduction measures under the earlier conventions.

Article 14(4) recognises that 'prevention, treatment and rehabilitation' of offenders are valid forms of demand reduction. The notable exception is education, which was mentioned in earlier drafts, but omitted here.[480] While the Parties are obliged to adopt measures aimed at demand reduction, the measures they choose are at their discretion. They may have reference to the recommendations of the UN, its specialised agencies and most significantly the 1987 'Comprehensive Multidisciplinary Outline'. Article 14(4) is the strongest attempt in the 1988 Convention to enforce UN policy with respect to demand reduction. But article 14(4) remains a recommendation because there was a strong sense at the 1988 Conference that it was not the business of the Convention to spell out the measures to be used by the Parties, and reference to the Outline did not mean that a Party was obliged to follow its recommendations.[481] The provision's optional nature serves as the escape route for Parties unwilling to address the roots of the domestic demand for drugs. Nonetheless, it is submitted that Parties that have a drug demand problem must address that problem, using the "soft" law of the Comprehensive Multidisciplinary Outline as a guide, and taking into account the seriousness of the problem and the reasonableness of devoting their resources to the 'elimination or reduction' of demand. If not, they will not be acting bona fide with regard to article 14(4). The final sentence of article 14(4) urges Parties to enter into formal agreements or informal arrangements aimed at reducing or eliminating demand.

The only other provision of the 1988 Convention that touches upon alternative approaches to drug control is article 14(3)(a) which makes reference to rural development programmes when it expands on its general invitation to Parties to co-operate in eradication of illicit drug bearing plants. By referring to integrated rural development programmes 'leading to economically viable alternatives to illicit cultivation' crop substitution is necessarily implied. It also notes that factors such as market access, resource availability and prevailing socio-economic conditions should be taken into account before rural development programmes are implemented. But this provision is optional, and in the context of the 1988 Convention, is focused on suppression of the illicit cultivation through law enforcement action.

---

480 See the 'Expert Group Report', *1988 Records* vol. I at 26.
481 *1988 Records* vol. II at 304.

3.3.6   Conclusion – criticisms of the provisions for penalties and alternatives

The international illicit drug control system is striving for uniformity of punishment of drug offences. State practice does not suggest that uniformity has been achieved, but it reveals a general trend towards severity.[482]

Heading the list in terms of severity is capital punishment. The death penalty for drug offences is the source of many of the official executions taking place today.[483] Cheaper than the law enforcement measures necessary to achieve sustained results against the illicit traffic, it is often used by developing states as a sop to international pressure for greater drug control because they can ill-afford the levels of drugs-policing being called for by developed states.[484] There is little uniformity in its use; it may depend on the particular drug involved, on previous convictions, or on the nature of the offence.[485] Its use has provoked outrage[486] while its efficacy has also been trenchantly criticised as a pointless and symbolic application of the drug war model to drug con-

---

482 Wells supra note 255 sets out in Appendix E the UNDCP's tables of the penalties states have applied to drug offences and although outdated and patchy, it does serve as a useful source of comparison across and within states.

483 It is available in over twenty states and has been used in eight Asian countries for drug related offences. See, for example, S.L. Harring, 'Death, drugs and development: Malaysia's mandatory death penalty for drug traffickers and the international war on drugs' (1991) 29 *Columbia Journal of Transnational Law* 364-405. Harring notes that the Malaysian Dangerous Drugs Act 234 of 1952, was amended by Act 293 of 1975 to make the death penalty possible for drug trafficking and then by Act 553 of 1983 to include section 39B making the death penalty for drug trafficking mandatory. From 1975-1990 approximately 300 traffickers were sentenced to death and 104 hanged.

484 I. Okagbue, *The Death Penalty as an Effective Deterrent to Drug Abuse and Drug Trafficking: Myth or Reality* (Nigerian Centre for Advanced Legal Studies, Lagos,1991), pp.22-23.

485 Supra note 484 at 20-21. She notes that while the death penalty is usually limited to trafficking offences, the definition of trafficking is stretched to include presumptive trafficking based on possession of small amounts of drugs, e.g. section 37 of Malaysia's Dangerous Drugs Act, 1952, or includes the simple giving of drugs for no consideration, e.g. section 2 of Singapore's Misuse of Drugs Act, 1973.

486 M. Anderson, *Policing the World* (Clarendon, Oxford, 1989), pp. 113-114 at footnote 1 notes the outcry in the West when it has been used on Westerners has led to complaints of double standards by the executing states who point out that the West complains they do nothing about drugs but when they do something they are subject to criticism.

trol.[487] Given the general international protection in human rights instruments of the right to life, imposition of the death penalty cannot be regarded as being called for by the drugs conventions' provisions for adequate punishment. This should, however, have been explicit in the 1988 Convention.

The most common punishments for trafficking involve some form of incarceration. Most states do not distinguish legislatively between the punishments they apply to the various trafficking offences, although the punishments for cultivation offences and for incitement are sometimes lighter. The range of terms of imprisonment varies from the trifling to life. Many states apply quite lengthy minimum terms. There has been an upward escalation in imprisonment in most countries for trafficking.[488] The merits of these measures have not been demonstrated.[489] Although long terms of imprisonment are expensive and have little deterrent value, they remain popular because they are expressive

---

487 See Okagbue supra note 484 at 21 et seq. She argues that its deterrent effects are questionable because of the huge profits made available to poor people and the amount of violence implicit in the drug trade already, that retribution provides little ground for its use because most drug transactions are consensual, and that the cost of someone's life outweighs the costs to society of drug trafficking and use. Its effectiveness against traffickers when applied by hesitant courts seeking cast-iron cases before they apply it is questionable. Harring supra note 483 at 404-405 points out that Malaysia's "mandatory" death penalty is not mandatory as so many trafficking arrests lead to dispositions other than death, and that its application has not affected Malaysia's high levels of drug dependence or trafficking.

488 N. Dorn, K. Murji and N. South, *Traffickers: Drug Markets and Law Enforcement* (Routledge, London, 1992), p.184 et seq. set out the modern British approach which provides a good example. The Misuse of Drugs Act, 1971, increased the maximum penalties for trafficking from 10 to 14 years and the Controlled Drugs (Penalties) Act, 1985, increased the maximum penalty to life. The Appeal Court in *R v Aramah* (1983) CLR 271-273 held that supply of heroin has to be punished by three years to life depending on the degree of involvement, amount of trafficking and value of drugs being handled. In the 1980s trafficking of a kilogram of heroin/cocaine (a class A drug under the Drug Trafficking Offences Act, 1986) generally got the offender ten years. Several such consignments or larger amounts was awarded with fourteen years plus. Trafficking in a few kilograms of amphetamines (a class B drug) was awarded with five years. On how international pressure forced sentences up in the UK see R. Fortson, 'Sentencing drug offenders' in P. Green (ed.), *Drug Couriers: A New Perspective* (1996), p. 80.

489 In fact, they have been counterproductive. Commenting on the effect of minimum sentences in the Indian Narcotic Drugs and Psychotropic Substances Act, 1985, the Chief Justice of India remarked in 1997 that their net result is a low conviction ratio – Speech by Chief Justice A.M. Ahmadi at the New Delhi International Conference on Global Drugs Law, 27 February 1997.

of societal disapproval of drug trafficking. This symbolism has driven these sentences upward culminating, for example, in life imprisonment in the UK.[490]

Financial penalties, especially fines, have grown steadily in importance as an alternative to imprisonment, a growth made possible by the growth of a money economy and general prosperity in consumer nations.[491] States apply fines either as an alternative or in addition to imprisonment and these are also usually quite weighty, with the range varying from zero to very large amounts. Some states apply minimum fines. Fiscal penalties are frequently used for trafficking related offences such as laundering. Whether they are equally effective against impoverished peasants and wealthy traffickers is debatable. Many states have also introduced asset confiscation as a punishment.[492] Attractive because it encourages law enforcement to be self-financing, the negative aspect of confiscation is its effect on innocent parties whose property gets mixed up with the proceeds of the illicit traffic.

Other punishments available for supply related offences include the closure of businesses and the suspension or removal of licenses from individuals in whose business premises drugs were being trafficked or used. Corporal punishment is also applied, often by states that apply capital punishment.[493] Aggravating factors are provided for by some states and not by others. Involvement of minors is the most popular of these factors but the range is wide and includes involvement of women, the mentally handicapped, civil servants, banks or professionals, serious health risk, use of violence or intimidation, involvement of organised crime or gangs, involvement of large quantities of drugs, previous offences, and occurrence of the offence in an educational, sporting, cultural or military facility.

With respect to personal use offences, penal and fiscal punishments remain popular. Maximum terms are fairly long and minimum terms are sometimes provided for.[494] The tariffs for fines can be high. In a few states the death

---

490 Dorn et al supra note 488 at 198.

491 Dorn et al supra note 488 at 179.

492 There has been some debate in US courts over whether civil forfeiture (where confiscation does not follow from conviction but is the result of a separate civil action against the thing itself) is a punishment or not. Blackmun J in *US v Austin* 509 US 601 at 611-618 believed that it was but the Supreme Court in *US v Ursery* 518 US 2367 held it was not, although it changed its mind in *US v Baijakajan* (1998) US Lexis 4171.

493 Section 39A of Malaysia's Dangerous Drugs Act 234 of 1952 makes provision for mandatory whippings for those convicted under the Act.

494 For example, from 4-20 years in Costa Rica in terms of Law No.2257 of 1991.

sentence applies. However, in some states such conduct is not criminalised and in others only administrative sanctions apply.[495]

Demand reduction measures emphasising preventive and health care steps backed up by administrative[496] or penal sanctions, although commonly used particularly for personal use offences in more developed states, may be completely unavailable in less developed states. Alternatives to convictions such as police cautions,[497] diversions and conditional discontinuances[498] are becoming more popular in developed states.[499] The emphasis is moving beyond fines, suspended sentences, parole, and probation to the use by administrative and multi-disciplinary tribunals of a range of sanctions, such as non-institutional detention, weekend detention, community service orders, and other short-term measures of deprivation of liberty.[500] Other such sanctions include temporary prohibitions on freedom of movement and of association and temporary withdrawal of rights and benefits such as passports and driving licenses.[501] The UN recommends the use of non-custodial measures and the provision of medical, psychological and social treatment programmes in appropriate cases.[502]

A range of anomalies disturb the general picture of heavy prison sentences and heavy fines for trafficking, and lighter punishment or treatment for personal

---

495 For example, in Spain fire-arm and driving licenses may be suspended.

496 Germany, for instance, imposes a range of administrative fines the amounts of which are decided by the administrative body involved. Section 32 of the Narcotics Code is just one of many enabling provisions – see generally L. Bollinger, ' Germany' in N. Dorn (ed.), *Regulating European Drug Problems* (Kluwer, Hague, 1999), p. 133 at p. 135.

497 Possessors are separated from their drugs and warned but never formally enter the criminal justice system.

498 Users who go forward to trial are given the option of attending a community-based programme instead of imprisonment.

499 N. Dorn and K. Murji, 'Low level drug enforcement' (1992) 20 *International Journal of the Sociology of Law* 159 at 163-165.

500 The development of specialised 'drug courts' to deal with user offenders by implementing combinative strategies of treatment, rehabilitation, counselling etc. combined with progressive incarceration and other forms of punishment in operation immediately upon conviction, has become popular in the US – see J. Tauber, 'A systems participants glossary of a drug court' in *Souvenir Brochure of the International Conference on Global drugs Law* (1997), pp.159-166.

501 Wells supra note 255 at 12.

502 *Eighth United Nations Congress on the Prevention of Crime and Treatment of Offenders, Havana 27 August-7 September 1990*, UN Pub. Sales No. E.70.V.5, chp. 21 section C.1.

use offences, that appears to be called for by international law. In practice, actual tariffs vary widely, as do the conditions of imprisonment which range from forced labour to incarceration in open prisons. Aggravating factors can in some states result in the death sentence, in others no provision is made for them at all. The differentiation in article 36 of the 1961 Convention and article 22 of the 1971 Convention between the punishment of 'serious' trafficking offences and those not serious is difficult to identify in domestic legislation.[503] Some states apply draconian penalties to personal use offences.[504] Flexible procedures in the criminal process, such as plea-bargaining, allow offenders to make deals with the state in order to avoid heavy tariffs while simultaneously guaranteeing high conviction rates. Early parole relieves the pressure of over-crowded prisons. Hovering in the background is a palpable gap between paper law and implemented law. Implementation is subject to the economic resources at the disposal of Parties. For many incarceration costs too much.

The loose framework for punishment in the earlier drug conventions did not result in global uniformity of punishment and although the 1988 Convention stiffened the system, its impact was dissipated by the hortatory nature of many of the provisions. These flaws have been ascribed to the political dynamic at the Conference and in particular the need for delegations from developing states to show their own governments that consumer states have been "forced" to as-sume partial responsibility for the international drug problem.[505] While the punishment provisions are general in order to provide for flexibility of national interpretation,[506] this generality is a further flaw. Distinction of the different types of involvement in trafficking from international to local would have made it possible for international law to be more responsive to the actual nature of the illicit traffic. No distinction is made, for example, between "mules" who do not own the drugs they transport for others and the traffickers who do. "Mules" are subject to equally severe penalties despite the difference in their importance to the chain of supply and despite the fact that many more of them are apprehended. On the other hand, the crude distinction between users and suppliers for the purposes of sentencing is not reflected in reality because

---

503 One indicator may be the heavier punishment meted out to international traffickers than to domestic traffickers, but a survey of legislation reveals that only 26 states out of 91 make such a distinction – see Wells supra note 255 at Appendix E.

504 The Nigerian Indian Hemp Amendment Decree no.27 of 1984 set a minimum of 4 years imprisonment for possession of cannabis.

505 Sproule and St-Denis supra note 4 at 271-272.

506 *1988 Commentary* at 97.

traffickers are often users, and this distinction requires urgent re-examination.[507] The lack of precision in the drug conventions' punishment provisions also makes international co-operation in respect of punishment difficult. In principle, recognition of other Parties' punishment limits is essential.[508] In practice, Parties to the conventions have avoided recognising other Parties' punishment limits for drug offences.[509] The international provisions on punishment, having grown organically and in a reactive way, exhibit little coherence. They reflect an incoherent international punishment policy. The system aims at suppression, apparently through deterrence, although implicit in the continued thrust towards more and more severe punishment for traffickers is a desire for retribution.

The thrust of international policy is clear in regard to the integration of therapeutic alternatives into the system The 1961 Convention focused on criminal repression. The 1971 Convention and the 1972 Protocol adopted a moderately holistic approach then in vogue at a national level. The 1988 Convention swung back to repression and de-emphasised alternatives. At all times, however, the international drug control system has remained primarily penal-sanctions oriented and only secondarily treatment-rehabilitation directed. Efforts to integrate these two approaches as equal partners in the drug conventions have been unsuccessful. This uneasy relationship reflects the uneasy relationship at the national level between treatment programmes and the criminal justice system.[510] Although law enforcement agencies have, because of the obvious limitations of the punitive approach, turned increasingly to treatment pro-

---

507 See R. Henham, 'Criminal justice and sentencing policy for drug offenders' (1994) 22 *International Journal of the Sociology of Law* 223.

508 J. Meyer, 'The vicarious administration of justice: an overlooked basis of jurisdiction' (1990) 31 *Harvard International Law Journal* 108 at 116 points out, for instance, that when jurisdiction is taken on the basis of the aut dedere aut judicare principle, the state taking jurisdiction should not inflict a punishment greater than that imposed by the state where the offence was committed because: i) at the time of commission the offender did not know the criminal law which is now applied to his conduct; and ii) the state taking jurisdiction is in principle standing in for the state where the offence was committed.

509 For example, while section 20 of the UK's 1971 Misuse of Drugs Act allows the prosecution in the UK of someone who assists in or induces the commission of a drug offence in another Party to the 1961 or 1971 Conventions, the English courts have held that the maximum sentence under the corresponding law is irrelevant to the sentences passed in the UK (*R v Faulkner and Thomas* (1976) 63 Cr.App.R 295).

510 See generally H. Ghodse, *The Criminal Justice System and the Treatment of Drug Misuse* (unpublished paper, New Delhi Global Drugs Law Conference, 1997).

grammes through referral schemes, the difference in goals – abstinence as opposed to health – makes working together difficult.[511] Structural demand reduction measures beyond treatment and rehabilitation are even less palatable. Unlike treatment and rehabilitation, these measures do not assume that society is healthy, and are thus even less likely to be acceptable to the international drug control establishment.

A great deal of work needs to be done to raise the profile of alternative approaches to the drug problem in black letter international law, if the existing orthodoxy is to change. A number of problems beset this task. A prominent difficulty is that there is a paucity of information about the extent to which Parties actually do provide alternatives to punishment.[512] The extent of the application of these measures is simply unknown.[513] Another related issue is the capability of the majority of Parties and especially those from the developing world to implement therapeutic and demand reduction measures. This is a question of the economic resources and the priority to be attached to these programmes. At present, credible treatment programmes are beyond the reach of most developing states,[514] and the supply of technical assistance through the UN is an inadequate substitute. The international community cannot demand that states devote greater resources to these measures because states are not legally obliged to do so. The international community chose to relegate therapeutic measures to the status of recommendations in the conventions. It failed at the 1987 Ministerial Conference to confirm the demand reduction measures of the Comprehensive Multidisciplinary Outline as legally binding. And the international community remains of that opinion. In June 1998, the General Assembly's Special Session on Countering the World Drug Problem held in

---

511 Ghodse supra note 510 at 3 and 5.
512 See the INCB, *Report of the International Narcotics Control Board for 1994* UN Doc. E/INCB/1994/1, p. 6 where it stated that it did not know the extent to which Parties made provision for such alternatives.
513 Something the INCB admitted in 1995 in *Effectiveness of the International Drug Control Treaties: Supplement to the Report of the International Narcotics Control Board for 1994* UN Doc. E/INCB/1994/1/Supp.1, p. 22.
514 See, for example, the situation in Nigeria – *DEA Nigeria Country Report* (DEA, Lagos, 1995). The DEA comments that the Nigerian National Drug Law Enforcement Agency's demand reduction programme 'primarily consists of distribution of posters with anti-drug slogans and an occasional newspaper article.'

June 1998[515] again recognised the need for such measures and again chose to leave them in the realm of soft law, while emphasising their articulation with law enforcement.[516] The INCB believes that 'demand reduction methods ... cannot be "standardised" by legal documents.'[517] The reason for this, it has been argued, is that to be successful demand reduction strategies must be socio-culturally sensitive to the norms of the community to which they are being applied.[518] Perhaps a more compelling reason why demand reduction cannot be translated into binding international law at present is that it implies a withdrawal of authority and funding from the enforcement of prohibition.

The drug conventions have been criticised for not defining precisely the scope and main characteristics of the alternatives they recommend. Treatment and rehabilitation are curative methods that assume that society is healthy but which have been criticised as having little long-term effects on demand.[519] The INCB fears that this leaves open the possibility for Parties to adopt 'interpretations that would not be in line with the spirit of the conventions.'[520] The organs of the international drug control system do not welcome other policies beyond supply and demand reduction, such as harm reduction. The INCB sees the absence of implementation of either penal or alternative methods

---

515 The Declaration on the Guiding Principles of Drug Demand Reduction, apart from exhorting the adoption of the measures in article 14(4) of the 1988 Convention, contains standards to assist governments to establish drug demand reduction programmes by 2008 and standards to guide governments to set up prevention, treatment and rehabilitation programmes. It also calls for the provision of adequate resources for such programmes. The Political Declaration adopted simultaneously calls for UN member states to 'achieve significant and measurable results in demand reduction', while the Resolution on Measures to Enhance International Co-operation to Counter the World Drug Problem contains an Action Plan on International Co-operation and Alternative Development (Part E). See generally GA Press Release GA/9423 10 June 1998.

516 The 1998 measures emphasise the application of the existing features of the international supply reduction system – extradition, mutual legal assistance etc. Thus, for example, when it addresses alternative development programmes for areas under illicit cultivation, Part E of the Action Plan on International Co-operation on the Eradication of Illicit Drug Crops and Alternative Development urges governments to ensure that such measures are complimented by law enforcement measures – see GA Press Release GA/9423.

517 INCB supra note 512 at 4. The INCB does not believe that a demand reduction treaty can be agreed upon – supra note 512 at 6.

518 Ghodse supra note 510 at 7.

519 R. Rodd, 'The politics of failure: a perspective on the war on drugs' in *Souvenir Brochure of the International Conference on Global drugs Law* (Indian Law Institute, New Delhi, 1997), p. 52 at p. 57.

520 INCB supra note 512 at 6.

to users as an entry point of de facto legalisation, which it regards as undesirable.[521] The paradigm is fixed, supply and demand reduction, in an
unequal relationship, with all else excluded.

---

521 INCB supra note 512 at 21.

JURISDICTION AND EXTRADITION

4.1 GENERAL

In Chapter Four we are concerned with examining the legal foundations necessary for national courts to entertain legal proceedings in respect of persons alleged to have committed the drug offences set out in Chapter Three. This examination covers the provisions in the drug conventions that set out the grounds for establishing jurisdiction over these alleged offenders, and because jurisdiction and extradition are inextricably entwined in the drug conventions, it also includes within its scope the provisions in the drug conventions for the extradition of alleged offenders. These provisions are among the most important in the drug conventions because they provide for the responsibility of states for drug offences that occur extraterritorially and for access to drug offenders in foreign locations. If drug control was a purely national concern these provisions would be unnecessary; the establishment of extraterritorial jurisdiction and the exercise of that jurisdiction through extradition are what make the drug control system created by the drug conventions international.

4.2 INTRODUCTION TO JURISDICTION OVER DRUG OFFENCES

Fundamental to the international drug control system is the establishment of criminal jurisdiction over drug offences and drug offenders. It is the logical precursor of the exercise of that jurisdiction through prosecution, adjudication and punishment if the alleged offender is within the state's custody, or of extradition followed by the normal criminal process if he or she is in the custody of some other state. States in their national drug laws prescribe the reach of these laws (prescriptive or legislative jurisdiction), their courts apply this legislative jurisdiction in individual drugs cases (judicial jurisdiction), and their drug law enforcement arms enforce this legislative or judicial jurisdiction (executive or enforcement jurisdiction). The aim of the discussion of jurisdiction in this chapter is to examine what the drug conventions stipulate about the reach of prescriptive national jurisdiction over drug offences, especially the extraterritorial reach of national jurisdiction.

According to strict principle national jurisdiction is determined exclusively by international law and not by national interest.[1] It follows that if state laws reach beyond the boundaries prescribed by international law – respect for foreign sovereignty and territorial integrity – they engage in a wrongful establishment of jurisdiction. In this context, the exercise of criminal jurisdiction is ordinarily territorial and only extraordinarily extraterritorial.[2] Thus when a drug offence occurs within a state's territory and the offender is taken into custody in that territory, the normal criminal process of that state will run its course and the situation presents no legal problems for the international community. Difficulties occur, however, when the drug offence occurs extraterritorially, or the offender is in another state, or both. It is not surprising then that one of the aims of the drug conventions is to ensure that '[i]llicit traffickers do not escape prosecution and punishment solely on the technical ground of lack of local jurisdiction in the country in which they may be found.'[3] This aim exists because, absent the drug conventions, there is confusion over the extent of extraterritorial jurisdiction in respect of drug offences, with a range of positions being adopted between the two extremes of those who argue that jurisdiction is strictly territorial and those who argue that a permissive rule exists allowing a state to exercise its power over drug offences perpetrated in the territory of other states.

---

1 F.A. Mann, 'The doctrine of jurisdiction in international law' (1964-I) 113 *Recueil des Cours* 9 at 10. In a later piece, 'The doctrine of international jurisdiction revisited after twenty years' (1984-III) 186 *Recueil des Cours* 19 at 20, Mann reiterates the co-terminacy of national jurisdiction with sovereignty and rejects the view espoused in the US that extraterritorial criminal jurisdiction is a question of the reasonable interests of states. The problem is obvious with respect to drug traffickers over whom the US may claim jurisdiction on no other basis than its general interest in suppressing drug trafficking. Following Mann, a closer connection is required.

2 The PCIJ made this clear in the *Lotus Case*: 'Now the first and foremost restriction imposed by international law upon a state is that – failing the existence of a permissive rule to the contrary – it may not exercise its power in any form in the territory of another state.' (1927) PCIJ Reports Series A No.10.

3 See the *Commentary on the Convention on Psychotropic Substances, 1971* (New York, 1976) UN Doc. E/CN.7/589; UN Publication Sales No.E.76.XI.5 (hereinafter the *1971 Commentary*), p. 346.

It is useful at this point to examine what the existing principles of extra-territorial jurisdiction[4] offer to states trying to establish extraterritorial jurisdiction over drug offences. The utility of these principles to a state is a function of the breadth of their scope of application in relation to the persons and conduct they cover. The legal validity of a state's reliance upon them is primarily a question of the closeness, legitimacy and intimacy of a state's connection with the alleged offender and offence.[5] The burden of proof lies with the state claiming or disputing jurisdiction,[6] and it has also been suggested that establishment of such jurisdiction should not be unreasonable.[7]

"Subjective territoriality" allows a state to prosecute drug traffickers who operate extraterritorially but who complete one or more of the elements of the relevant offence within the territory of a state.[8] Popular because it is available against offenders of any nationality,[9] the requirement of a territorial occurrence of an element of the offence restricts its application.

---

4   See on these principles generally M. Akehurst, 'Jurisdiction in international law' (1972/3) 46 BYIL 145 at 152-162; D.W. Bowett, 'Jurisdiction: changing patterns of authority over activities and resources' in R.S.J. MacDonald and D.M. Jhonston (eds), *The Structure and Process of International law* (Nijhoff, Dordrecht, 1983), p. 555 at pp. 558-564; Mann (1964) supra note 1 at 82-94; and D. Oehler, 'Criminal Law, International' in R. Bernhardt (ed.), *Encyclopedia of Public International Law* Volume I (Elsevier, Amsterdam, 1992), p. 877 at pp. 878-879.
5   Mann (1964) supra note 1 at 93.
6   Akehurst supra note 4 at 167.
7   C.L. Blakesly, 'United States jurisdiction over extraterritorial crime' (1982) *Journal of Criminal Law and Criminology* 1109 at 1112 citing section 403 of the Third Restatement of US Foreign Relations Law.
8   A. Puttler, 'Extraterritorial application of criminal law: jurisdiction to prosecute drug traffic conducted by aliens abroad' in K.M. Meesen (ed.), *Extraterritorial Jurisdiction in Theory and Practice* (Kluwer, London, 1996), p. 103 at p. 106 comments that while no sufficiently close link can be established between a Dutch hashish dealer and the German clients who buy from him in the Netherlands when he does not know or care what they do, the situation changes and Germany has jurisdiction if he gives it to German nationals who smuggle it into Germany for him because a constituent element of the crime of importing drugs, the bringing of the drugs into Germany, takes place within Germany.
9   See Blakesly supra note 7 at 1108-1132. For example, the US Anti-Drug Abuse Act of 1986 (18 USC sections 1956(a) and (c) and 1957(f)) criminalises any US banking transaction involving the proceeds of foreign drugs offences. At a more general level, article 693 of the French *Code de Procedure Penal* provides that any offence is deemed to have been committed in France when 'an act compromising one of its elements is accomplished in France.'

"Objective territoriality" (the "effects" principle) allows a state to assume responsibility where only the effect of the drug offender's extraterritorial action is felt by a state on its territory. The exercise of jurisdiction on this basis is available against all nationalities. This principle is open to extravagant interpretation, and it has thus been argued that its application should be limited to situations of actual rather than intended effects, particularly in the case of inchoate offences,[10] and moreover, only to conduct which has a primary, direct and substantial effect on the state concerned.[11] The determining issue for application will in each case be the effects of consumption of drugs involved on the individuals and society of the state claiming jurisdiction.[12]

The "protective principle" provides a potential ground for asserting extraterritorial jurisdiction if drug trafficking is construed as a threat to the economic and security interests of a state. It has been used by some states against extra-

---

10   S.A. Bernholz, M.J. Bernholz and J.N. Herman, 'International extradition in drug cases' (1985) 10 *North Carolina Journal of International Law and Commercial Regulation* 353 at 370-371 examine the US's extension of jurisdiction over extraterritorial drug conspiracies through application of objective territoriality. They give as an example *United States v Ricardo* 619 Fed.2d 1124 (5th Cir. 1980), where the US District Court determined it had jurisdiction over defendants charged with conspiracy to import marijuana, even though the conspiracy took place outside the US and was thwarted before any marijuana was imported. The court ruled that US drug conspiracy laws had extraterritorial reach as long as the defendant intended to violate those laws and to have the effects occur within the US (at 1128-1129). Blakesly supra note 7 at 1145 argues that when harm is intended but no harmful effect actually occurs on the asserting state's territory, objective territoriality cannot be a basis for asserting jurisdiction because an inchoate offence, that remains inchoate, has no effects. Yet Akehurst supra note 4 at 154 footnote 2 notes that many states have extended their jurisdiction over externally committed inchoate offences where the primary intended effect would have been felt within their jurisdiction had the offence been consummated. For example, in 1986 the US passed 21 USC section 959 (1986) extending its jurisdiction over foreign nationals exporting drugs to the US. Section 959(d) renders it 'unlawful for any person to manufacture, or distribute a controlled substance ... intending that such substance be unlawfully imported into the United States'.

11   See Akehurst supra note 4 at 154, Mann (1984) supra note 1 at 34.

12   Proving deleterious effects upon which to base jurisdiction may be difficult. For example, Puttler supra note 8 at 108 notes that Germany's taking jurisdiction over Dutch cannabis dealers on the basis of the effects on the physical and mental health of German cannabis consumers is difficult because of the lack of conclusive evidence of physical effects and the controversy surrounding evidence of mental effects.

territorial trafficking,[13] and is available against any nationality, and even in situations where harm is only intended and no effect is felt on a state's territory.[14] Puttler notes, however, that the principle may not be used to impose a state's drug policy abroad. Its purpose must be to safeguard the political independence, security or governmental functions of the asserting state, and that in reality the primary effect of even large-scale drug crimes is not to threaten the state in this way.[15]

Resort to "nationality" ("active personality") to justify extraterritorial jurisdiction over a state's own citizens who commit any type of drug offence is common in civil law states but uncommon in common law states, although that is changing. An application of the general principle that a state may prescribe that its nationals abroad should not commit generally recognised criminal offences, nationality is obviously not available against foreigners. Nationality

---

13 Most national penal codes recognise the principle generally, but its specific application to drug offences is less common. The US Maritime Drug Law Enforcement Act, 46 USC section 1902, uses the wording 'specific threat to security' as a basis for extraterritorial jurisdiction. Blakesly supra note 7 at 1147-1149 notes that in *US v Brown* 549 F.2d 954 (4th Circ. 1977), where the defendant was convicted of a conspiracy to import heroin by army mail into the US from Germany, although jurisdiction was ostensibly based on an extension of territoriality, it was in fact based on the protective principle. Puttler supra note 8 at 108 notes that the German Bundesgerichtshof (34 BGHSt 334, 339) has based jurisdiction over a Dutch cannabis dealer operating in the Netherlands on the protective principle. The court held that the dealer had violated German interests by having sold over many years a considerable amount of hashish to German nationals who had taken the drug to Germany to consume it or resell it.

14 See, for example, the *United States v Biermann* 678 F.Supp 1427 (1988) at 1445 where the US District Court held that the protective principle as contained in 46 USC section 1903 enabled the extension of US jurisdiction over foreign vessels carrying drugs where only a threat of harm to the US and not an actual harmful effect could be shown.

15 Supra note 8 at 109. She notes that court decisions relying on this principle have not discussed whether external drug trafficking in fact threatened the security of the prosecuting state or its state functions. She comments at p. 110 in respect of the German courts' reliance on this principle to assert jurisdiction over Dutch nationals dealing in cannabis, that while sale of hard drugs followed by their import into Germany may arguably cause drug abuse and addiction of a considerable part of the population thereby corrupting the government or destabilising the social order, there is no evidence to show that sale of soft drugs will do so. C. Kallenbach, '*Plomo o plata*: irregular rendition as a means of gaining jurisdiction over Colombian drug kingpins' (1990) 23 *New York University Journal of International Law and Politics* 169 at 210 argues that this principle can be used to assert US jurisdiction over Colombian drug traffickers because of the violations of US borders, the poisoning of the US population and the full scale military effort required to combat drug trafficking.

is used against drug criminals in practice,[16] but is not as common as it appears.[17]

"Passive personality", justifying extraterritorial jurisdiction by a state over drug offenders because the victims of their actions are its citizens, is potentially available against offenders of any nationality.[18] It has not, however, been commonly resorted to, because the circumstances in which the injury inflicted by the accused is of sufficient weight to justify the application of passive personality are unclear. Moreover, establishing such a connection where the abuser of drugs takes the substance voluntarily is difficult. It is usually resorted to only in circumstances when it is the only way for any state to establish jurisdiction.[19]

"Universal jurisdiction" would allow all states to have jurisdiction over any drug offence committed anywhere at anytime by anyone,[20] even in situations where the domestic law of the state establishing jurisdiction did not outlaw the conduct in question and in spite of any extradition requests.[21] Universality would apply to drug offences if they were classified as international offences stricto sensu, that is, offences in international not national law.[22] Drug of-

---

16   For example, the US Anti-Drug Abuse Act of 1986, 18 USC sections 1956(f) and 1957(a) and (d), criminalises any transaction in proceeds knowingly derived from drug offences by an American person or entity outside the US. In *Public Prosecutor v Gunther B and Manfred E* (1976) 71 ILR 247 the Austrian court extended its jurisdiction on the basis of the nationality principle in article 36(1) of the Austrian Criminal Code over two Austrian citizens caught in Bulgaria who had purchased hashish in Afghanistan and were returning with it by car to Austria.

17   A.M. Surena in a panel discussion on the 'International drug traffic' (1990) 84 *American Society of International Law: Proceedings* 1 at 2 complains that 'only a few states will prosecute their nationals for offences committed against the interests of a third state.'

18   Some states apply the principle generally (e.g. German Penal Code section 7(1)), and some states do not (e.g. the US) – see C.L. Blakesly and O. Lagodny, 'Finding harmony amidst disagreement over extradition, jurisdiction, the role of human rights, and issues of extraterritoriality under international criminal law' (1991) 24 *Vanderbilt Journal of Transnational Law* 1 at 24.

19   Law Reform Commission of Canada, *Extraterritorial Jurisdiction* (Working Paper 37, LRC Canada, Ottawa, 1984), p. 10.

20   See generally K.C. Randall, 'Universal jurisdiction under international law' (1988) 66 *Texas Law Review* 785-841.

21   See G. Gilbert, 'Crimes *sans frontiers*: jurisdictional problems in English law' (1992) 63 BYIL 415 at 423 footnote 61.

22   E.M. Wise, 'The obligation to extradite or prosecute' (1993) 1&2 *Israel Law Review* 268 at 269.

fenders would, like pirates,[23] have to be considered hostes humanis generis, the enemies of all mankind, because of their moral and practical condemnation. There is support for this position both academically,[24] in state practice[25] and de lege ferenda in international law,[26] but there is also opposition.[27] The history of international drug control illustrates that the drug conventions did not

23 See A. Fletcher, 'Pirates and smugglers: an analysis of the use of abductions to bring drug traffickers to trial' (1991) 32 *Virginia Journal of International Law* 233-264. At 263-264 he explores the analogy with piracy and shows the link between the interests and capacity of affected states and the internationalisation of drug offences. European states developed the international crime of piracy because of their shared need and capacity to protect their maritime trading interests. Drug consumer states have developed their extraterritorial policing and prosecution of drug crimes because their social order is threatened by drug use and they believe supply interdiction is how it must and can be dealt with.

24 See, for instance, Y.Z. Blum, 'Extradition: a common approach to the control of international terrorism and the traffic in narcotic drugs' (1978) 13 *Israel Law Review* 194 at 197; M.C. Bassiouni in *International Crimes: Digest/Index of International Instruments 1815-1983* (1985), p. LVI; S.K. Chatterjee, *Legal Aspects of International Drug Control* (Nijhoff, Dordrecht, 1981), p. 525. Mann (1964) supra note 1 at 95 implies that the status of drug offences as international crimes comes from their being covered by treaties evidencing the general agreement of states to suppress them. See also the American Law Institute, *Third Restatement of the Foreign Relations Law of the United States* (1987) sections 404 and 423.

25 Section 6(5) of the German Penal Code reads: 'Irrespective of the law of the place where the offence was committed, German criminal law is applicable to the following offences committed abroad: ... (5) illicit traffic in narcotic drugs.' The German Federal Supreme Court has held in the *Universal Jurisdiction over Drug Offences Case* (1979) 74 ILR 166 that section 6(5) bases jurisdiction for prosecution of illicit traffic in all kinds of controlled drugs on the principle of universality. In *DPP v Doot* [1973] AC 807 Lord Wilberforce noted obiter that the prevention of the narcotics trade falls under the principle of universality in international law (at 803D). In *US v Marino Garcia* 679 F.2nd 1373 at 1382 n.16 the US Court noted: 'It may well be that the time has arrived when the Congress of the United States should by appropriate legislation include drug trafficking in the same category as slave trafficking and piracy and authorise prosecution of drug trafficking on the high seas as offences against the Law of Nations'.

26 Article 14 of the International Penal Law Treaty of Montevideo gave the state captor jurisdiction over drug trafficking. Although later erased, draft article 2 of the 1988 Convention stated that drug trafficking was an 'international crime against humanity' – see ECOSOC Res. 39/141.

27 In the *United States v James-Robinson* 515 F. Supp. 1340 at 1344 n.6 (1981) the US District Court found that drug trafficking is not a crime justifying universal jurisdiction. See also R. Linke, J.H. Epp and E. Kabelka, *Extradition for Drug-Related Offences* (UN, Austria, 1985) who state at p. 62 that drug offences are not yet recognised as offences to which universality applies.

crystallise a pre-existing customary international rule creating an international drug offence to which universal jurisdiction applied and it is unlikely that such a rule has grown up independently of the drug conventions. The only potential source for such an offence is thus the drug conventions themselves.[28]

More appropriate to drug offences, the application of "subsidiary universality"[29] is achieved through application of the aut dedere aut judicare principle.[30] This principle is applied to international offences lato sensu – offences of international concern that states are under an obligation, usually created by treaty, to prosecute. It functions to overcome problems with extradition in general but usually with the non-extradition of nationals, and holds that where an extradition request is rejected for whatever reason, the requested state is under a duty to assume jurisdiction itself and prosecute the alleged offender.[31] It is thus dependent on the existence of double criminality.[32] Some states make provision for its operation in their domestic law,[33] while others are less familiar

---

28 Article 38 of the Vienna Convention on the Law of Treaties makes it clear that a rule set out in a convention can subsequently pass into custom. See also the *North Sea Continental Shelf Case* ICJ Reports 1969, p. 3.

29 The term subsidiary universality was coined by A.R. Carnegie in 'Jurisdiction over violations of the laws and customs of war' (1963) 39 BYBIL 402 at 405. This form of extraterritorial jurisdiction is subsidiary not to other forms of jurisdiction, but to extradition. It is also commonly referred to as the "representative or vicarious administration of justice".

30 See generally Wise supra note 22 at 268-287; M.C. Bassiouni and E.M. Wise, *Aut Dedere Aut Judicare: The Duty to Extradite or Prosecute in International Law* (Nijhoff, Dordrecht, 1995), pp. 1-74. They explain that the principle aut dedere aut punire, meaning extradite or punish, as formulated by Grotius in *De Jure Belli Ac Pacis*, Book II, Chap. XXI para. IV(1) (1624) must be reformulated as aut dedere aut judicare to assume the offender's innocence.

31 M.C. Bassiouni, 'Characteristics of international criminal law conventions' in M.C. Bassiouni (ed.), *1 International Criminal Law: Crimes* (Transnational, Dobbs Ferry, 1986), p. 1 at pp. 8-9 submits that the choice between extradition or prosecution is the requested state's, but notes that the requested state is obliged to prosecute only if it validly cannot extradite. Wise supra note 22 at 272 submits that the obligation to prosecute is not contingent on a request for extradition nor on an offer of extradition being refused.

32 The offence must be punishable in both states, jurisdiction over the offence must be able to be established on the same basis, and the offence must not be open to more severe punishment in the requested state than in the requesting state.

33 The principle is popular in Europe. Section 7(2) of the German Penal Code, for example, allows Germany to assert its jurisdiction to prosecute drug related conduct committed abroad. The requirements are that the law of the state where the offence took place must regard the conduct as a punishable offence, and the offender must not have been

with it. It has not always worked well in practice[34] and has been criticised for overlooking the logistical and legal difficulties of prosecution outside the territory of the state where the crime is committed.[35] The requested state may, for instance, be unwilling or unable to prosecute for political or legal reasons, and if it does prosecute, it may do so inadequately because its interests are not at stake, and as a result it may tax relations with the already disappointed requesting state.[36] Extradition is preferred by some for these reasons, yet it has been argued that such criticisms are not apposite if drug offences are

---

extradited because no application had been made or extradition was not feasible, although German law would usually permit such extradition.

34 The US has had problems with the principle. A. Abramovsky, 'Extraterritorial abductions: America's "Catch and Snatch" policy run amok' (1991) 31 *Virginia Journal of International Law* 151 at 207 notes for example, that article 9(2) of the United States – Mexico Extradition Treaty, 31 UST 5056, allows for the requested Party, where it denies an extradition request, to submit the case to its own authorities for prosecution provided they have jurisdiction. In drug consumer states, such jurisdiction is commonly based on nationality (as they are commonly civil law states). Abramovsky notes that 'this process has not worked well in practice because the US has often been disappointed by both the law of prosecution of the relator and the slowness of the Mexican legal process', a frustration which has lead to illegal and irregular rendition.

35 Bowett supra note 4 at 564. These difficulties include language problems and problems with getting evidence and witnesses from one state to another. A strong argument against the application of subsidiary universality to drug offences is that its operation will be intolerable if they vary from state to state; the range of criminal conduct would be too great for any person to comprehend and guide his conduct accordingly – see Akehurst supra note 4 at 165 citing Brierly (1928) 44 LQR 154 at 161. Only globally uniform drug offences would alleviate this problem, and such uniformity does not exist. The splintering of prosecutions with some accused in the requesting state and others in the refusing requested state is also undesirable because no complete picture of the offence emerges to allow a court to attribute liability and penalties in an appropriate manner – see K. Prost, 'Breaking down the barriers: international co-operation in combating transnational crime' in *Souvenir Brochure of the International Conference on Global drugs Law* (Indian Law Institute, New Delhi, 1997), p. 44 at p. 52.

36 F. Patel, 'Crime without frontiers: a proposal for an international narcotics court' (1990) 22 *New York University Journal of International. Law and Politics* 709 at 720-721. Patel submits that intimidation of officials such as judges and law enforcement officers is also a problem in some states, as is the lack of a serious commitment by certain states to stopping drug trafficking. She cites the examples of intimidation of judges in Colombia, and the lack of commitment by states such as Bolivia. E.A. Nadelmann, 'The evolution of United States involvement in the international rendition of fugitive criminals' (1993) 25 *New York University Journal of International Law and Politics* 813 at 856 explains that most prosecutions are unsuccessful unless senior officials of the requesting state show a strong interest in the foreign prosecution.

regarded as universal threats and implies that states must simply make a greater effort.[37] For drug offences, the drug conventions can be the only source of a duty to extradite or prosecute because, absent a treaty undertaking, by the nineteenth century most states and scholars accepted that there was no customary legal duty either to extradite or to take legal action against an offender from another state.[38] Although the adoption of subsidiary universality in an increasing number of treaties has lead to greater attention being paid to its possible customary legal status,[39] the crucial issue for those who support its application to drug offences is whether the drug conventions create a duty to extradite or prosecute.[40]

---

37 Blum supra note 24 at 199.

38 R.S. Clark, 'Offences of international concern: multilateral state treaty practice in the forty years since Nuremberg' (1988) 57 *Nordic Journal of International Law* 49 at endnote 115; see also B. Swart, 'Refusal of extradition and the United Nations Model Treaty on Extradition' (1992) 23 NYIL 175 at 214; Wise supra note 22 at 279.

39 Bassiouni and Wise supra note 30 at 5. They note at p. 20 that the assertions about the customary status of the aut dedere aut judicare principle may take three progressively wider forms, viz.: i) it may be a customary rule with respect to a particular offence defined in a particular treaty (e.g. the offence of importation in article 36 of the 1961 Convention); it may be a customary rule with respect to a whole class of international offences (e.g. the drug offences in the drug conventions); or it may be a rule that applies to all international offences (including drug offences). The authors note at p. 21 that in practice it is the latter broad categorical assertion that is most commonly advanced. The argument, put crudely, is that the duty flows out of the common interest that all states have in the suppression of international offences. It is a duty owed to the international community, the civitas maxima. The authors conclude at p. 68, however, that state practice does not support the customary status of the principle, and its customary status depends rather on the postulated existence of the civitas maxima. While Bassiouni supports the validity of this postulate, Wise does not. In his earlier piece (supra note 22 at 282) Wise is critical of over reliance on the authority of the civitas maxima to create a theoretically coherent system of international offences to which the principle aut dedere aut judicare applies, when in fact reality denies this.

40 Supporters include Abramovsky supra note 34 at 180; Blakesly supra note 7 at 1141; Blakesly and Lagodny supra note 18 at 35; B. Penney in Panel discussion 'Drugs and small arms: can law stop the traffic?' (1987) 81 *American Society of International Law: Proceedings* 44 at 46; Kallenbach supra note 15 at 211. The legal adviser of the US State Department said in 1989: 'Certain forms of criminal activity have been subject to universal jurisdiction ... [A]greements deal with international drug dealers and create an obligation on parties to prosecute or extradite these criminals.' – A.D. Sofaer before the US Congressional Subcommittee on Civil and Constitutional Rights, 9 November 1989, recorded in M.N. Leigh, 'Contemporary practice of the United States relating to international law: territorial jurisdiction' (1990) 84 AJIL 725-729. Most of the commentators cited do not discriminate between subsidiary universality and universality

The attitude of states to these principles of extraterritorial jurisdiction depends on a range of factors. Differences in the severity of drug policy may result in the situation where a state that wants jurisdiction, does not have it, while a state that has it, does not want it.[41] States pursuing prohibition more vigorously may be inclined to have recourse to principles other than territoriality or nationality, although by doing so they implicitly reject the competence of other states. Civil law states tend to have broader jurisdictional principles allowing them to take greater extraterritorial jurisdiction while common law states are more restricted, and prefer extradition. There is, however, a general reluctance to establish extraterritorial jurisdiction. It is explained by the belief that prosecution in a jurisdiction other than that in which the offence took place is undesirable because no harm has been suffered in that jurisdiction and because effective prosecution will depend on overcoming language problems and problems with gathering both inculpatory and exculpatory evidence.[42] The result of different views on jurisdiction is that drug offenders who find themselves in a state other than the one in which they committed their offence frequently escape prosecution and punishment.[43]

A major thrust of this chapter is an examination of the jurisdictional provisions in the drug conventions, in order to discover whether they oblige Parties to extend their establishment of jurisdiction beyond the territorial and if so to what extent. The extension of jurisdiction must flow from the conventions themselves because the principles of prescriptive jurisdiction examined above do not provide an effective means for the assertion of extraterritorial jurisdiction over drug offences due to the controversy and uncertainty surrounding the limits in customary international law of the rights of states to legislate with extraterritorial effect[44] and because of the negative attitude of states to

---

stricto sensu.

41 A good example of this situation is the prosecution of Dutch nationals for dealing in cannabis derivatives in the Netherlands by German courts on the basis of extraterritorial jurisdiction in situations where the Dutch authorities, pursuing decriminalisation, decline to prosecute – see Puttler supra note 8 at 103-121.

42 *United Nations Conference for the Adoption of a Single Convention on Narcotic Drugs, Official Records, Volume I* (New York, 1964) UN Doc. E/CONF.34/24, UN Publication Sales No. 63.XI.4 (hereinafter *1961 Records* vol. I), p. 123.

43 The *Commentary on the Single Convention on Narcotic Drugs, 1961* (New York, 1973) UN Publication Sales No. E.73.XI, (hereinafter the *1961 Commentary*), p. 426.

44 See *Commentary on the United Nations Convention Against Illicit Traffic in Narcotic Drugs and Psychotropic Substances, 1988* (New York, 1998) UN Doc. E/CN.7/590; UN Publication Sales No.E.98.XI.5, (hereinafter the *1988 Commentary*), p.100, W.C. Gilmore, *Combating International Drug Trafficking: the 1988 United Nations Convention*

establishing such jurisdiction. Before examining jurisdiction in the context of the conventions, however, it is necessary to introduce the associated concept of extradition.

4.3   Introduction to the Extradition of Drug Offenders

Extradition is the legal process whereby the criminal justice system of one state gains access to witnesses and suspects from, or in, another state.[45] As was noted above, there is no general duty to extradite. Extradition of drug offenders is based in practice either upon treaty or upon reciprocity. The drug conventions thus either modify existing extradition treaties or existing extradition legislation. Their difficulty is laying down rules that will overcome the problems with extradition in modern state practice.

The primary impediments to the extradition of drug offenders are political in nature. In cases of concurrent jurisdiction, most extradition treaties recognise that the proper jurisdiction of the requested state is a valid ground for denying extradition.[46] But states are generally reluctant to give up jurisdiction over persons within their territory. They may resist extradition as a matter of national pride because of the perception that it questions the integrity of their judicial system. They may also perceive foreign courts as being biased, either systematically because of the unfamiliarity of language, customs and procedures, or against their citizens in particular.[47] The refusal by many civil law states to allow the extradition of their nationals for constitutional reasons or because of their domestic law is regarded as one of the chief legal obstructions to extradition in drug cases.[48] Many existing extradition treaties compensate for

---

Against Illicit Traffic in narcotic Drugs and Psychotropic Substances (Commonwealth Secretariat, London, 1991), p. 10.

45   See generally M.C. Bassiouni, *International Extradition and World Public Order* (1974), p. 1 et seq.; for extradition in respect of drug offences see generally Linke et al supra note 27.

46   See, for example, article 7(1) of the 1957 European Convention on Extradition, 359 UNTS 273.

47   Patel supra note 36 at 718.

48   Abramovsky supra note 34 at 155 note 10 points out that this is a particular problem in the US's drug war with Latin American states because several of the latter refuse to extradite for constitutional or other legal reasons. He gives the example of Colombia where in 1986 the Supreme Court declared that the 1979 extradition treaty with the US was unconstitutional and unenforceable, but notes that in terms of the Colombian Court's decision in *In re Aravelo* 10 Ann. Dig. 329 (1942) such offenders could be prosecuted

this and do not oblige states, including common law states, to extradite nationals.[49] But some states will not extradite nationals for other reasons, including the threat posed and the influence wielded by illicit drug cartels[50] and because extradition requests emanate mostly from consumer states perceived by the requested producer states as the real cause of the drug problem.[51]

Secondary obstacles to extradition are more technical. Most common law states require the existence of an extradition treaty to effectuate extradition although the civil law practice of relying solely upon domestic law grounded upon reciprocity or comity is growing in popularity. A simple problem common with older extradition treaties is that they frequently do not apply to drug offences. It is a result of following an enumerative approach to extradition in these treaties, i.e. listing extraditable offences. Such treaties are by definition

---

in Colombia under article 7 of its Penal Code.

49 For example, in terms of article 9(1) of the 1978 US-Mexico Extradition Treaty, 31 UST 5056, 5059, neither state is obliged to extradite its nationals.

50 The Colombian drug traffickers' war on extradition is well documented. See for example, R.M. Bin, 'Drug Lords and the Colombian Judiciary: A story of threats, bribes and bullets' (1986) 5 *UCLA Pacific Basin Law Journal* 178-182. She describes how the *narcotrafficantes* threat of "silver or lead" resulted in the death of sixty Colombian judges from 1982 and 1987 and how only twelve out of one hundred and thirty extradition requests by the US were granted until in 1987 the Colombian Supreme Court declared the legislation ratifying the extradition treaty with the US unconstitutional. In the early 1990s Colombia actually introduced a government leniency programme allowing reduced punishment for suspects who helped further drug law enforcement, a prohibition on extradition, exemptions from photographs and further sentence reductions for good behaviour. Pablo Escobar, a major trafficker, was jailed in a customised jail when he surrendered in terms of the programme – see S.A. Gardner, 'A global initiative to deter drug trafficking: will internationalising the drug war work?' (1993) 7 *Temple International and Comparative Law Review* 287 at 304-305. In the post-Escobar era (he was killed in late 1993) Colombian officials called for legalisation, commented that the flow of drugs to the US was heavier than ever despite all the lives lost in the war on drugs, and tried plea-bargaining with major traffickers – *Time*, 11 April 1994. In 1997 it was reported that senior officials in Mexico and Colombia were seeking to end the drug cartels reign of terror 'by removing the threat of extradition to the US, and offering reduced sentences for traffickers who turn themselves in.' They believed that extradition of drug traffickers sparks the criminal violence and that official counter violence backed by the US destabilises their countries – *The Guardian*, 16 April 1997. Late in 1997 the Colombian President signed into force legislation permitting extradition of drug traffickers with the exception of those already serving sentences in Colombian jails – *The Guardian*, 17 December 1997.

51 Patel supra note 36 at 718. See also ABA's Task Force 'Report' (1993) 27 *International Lawyer* 258 at 263.

limited and require constant updating. This dilemma can be avoided by the adoption of evaluative or eliminative approaches. They make extraditable all offences to which a minimum punishment, such as imprisonment for more than one year, applies in both Parties. Treaties that follow the eliminative method have the advantages of neither requiring constant updating to include new drug offences nor requiring restriction to serious drug offences as they are already restricted to serious offences by definition.

The general principles of extradition law may also be relied upon by states to refuse or challenge extradition once granted. These principles include the principle of speciality, that the extradited offender is to be tried only with the offence for which he is extradited and not surrendered to third states,[52] and the principle of double criminality, requiring that the offence for which the offender is being extradited must be an offence in both states.[53] Double jeopardy may also hamper extradition.[54] The political and fiscal offence excep-

---

52 Kallenbach supra note 15 at 175.
53 See generally L. Gardocki, 'Double criminality in extradition law' (1993) 1&2 *Israel LR* 288-296; and Bernholz et al supra note 10 at 353-382. New offences for which there is no corresponding offence in the law of other states such as the US's racketeering offences under RICO also cause problems for extradition. This has led to the general practice of not insisting upon terminological correspondence but considering all acts or omissions in deciding whether there is correspondence – *1988 Commentary* at 159. The principle of double criminality is sometimes interpreted as requiring that the elements that provide jurisdictional basis for the prosecution of the offence must be recognised in both states. In *Republic of France v Moghadam* 617 F. Supp. 777 (D.C. Cal. 1985) the US District Court in California denied France an extradition request when France's jurisdiction over the alleged drug offender was based upon French nationality. The court insisted in effect that French jurisdiction had to be based on subjective or objective territoriality, grounds for extraterritorial jurisdiction recognised by the US. By contrast, the UK now recognises that other states establish jurisdiction on different grounds and still grants their extradition requests (section 2 of the Extradition Act, 1989, c.33). A.B. Campbell, 'The Ker-Frisbie doctrine: a jurisdictional weapon in the war on drugs' (1990) 23 *Vanderbilt Journal of Transnational Law* 385 at 402 explains that, in addition, the rapid development of new drugs can also cause problems for double criminality as they are developed faster than extradition treaties can take account of them, i.e. they may be included within the list of scheduled drugs in the requesting state but not in the requested state when the extradition request is made.
54 See Linke et al supra note 27 at 53 et seq. Double jeopardy, or non bis in idem, means that once a criminal charge has been adjudicated upon by a court having jurisdiction to hear it, that adjudication is final and may be pleaded in bar to any subsequent prosecution for the same offence. While double jeopardy does operate in the international context through treaty law and its presence in extradition treaties means that requested states are able to refuse extradition requests if the subject of the request has been tried

tions to extradition, where states refuse to extradite for what they consider to be political or fiscal offences, also present problems.[55] Differences in extradition procedures constitute the biggest obstacles to international co-operation in drug control. Civil law states generally only require the issuance of a warrant of arrest from a judicial authority and a copy of the laws under which an offender is to be prosecuted to substantiate an extradition request. Common law states, on the other hand, have traditionally insisted upon the requesting state presenting a prima facie case before an extradition request will be granted. The latter approach has been troublesome for extradition from common law to civil law states, as civil law states have been unable in many instances to generate the level of proof required.[56] The reverse is not true,[57] although to be fair, nationals of common law states are exposed to extradition while those from civil law states are not. Where the system does work, speed, a necessity when prosecuting traffickers, is often difficult to achieve.[58] For example, Anderson points out that while most states regard Interpol's issuing of a red notice as an international warrant for arrest with the assurance that a request for extradition will automatically follow, and issue an arrest warrant immediately, some states still require further evidence to be presented before an arrest warrant will be issued. Such evidence may require the presence of witnesses, and as rogatory commissions are not common, the whole system can be slowed down

---

and punished already, it does not appear that customary international law prohibits international double jeopardy. Some states prosecute their nationals for crimes committed abroad and for which they have already been convicted – see the cases cited by L.C. Green, 'International crimes and the legal process' (1980) 29 ICLQ 567.

55   See Patel supra note 36 at 729. The political offence exception applies to drug offences usually when such trafficking is connected to fund-raising activities in support of political activities, but Linke et al supra note 27 at 27 reject this as a valid ground for refusing extradition. The fiscal offence exception usually applies to drug offences when they are classified as customs offences under domestic law. Linke et al argue that such offences are in reality drug offences and refusal to extradite would be counter-productive.

56   On the disadvantages of the latter approach – it is time consuming and costly and has led to the modern trend to reduce the standard – see generally P. Coggins and W.A. Roberts, 'Extraterritorial jurisdiction: an untamed adolescent' [1991] *Commonwealth Law Bulletin* 1391 at 1403; and Linke et al supra note 27 at 41-45.

57   Patel supra note 36 at 728.

58   It can be slowed up, for example, by the insistence in many states that the requesting state must be represented at the extradition hearing by a legal practitioner from the requested state, and the refusal of the courts in many states to admit certain kinds of evidence such as confessions, searches or electronic surveillance, common in drug trafficking prosecutions in for instance the US, in extradition hearings – see Surena supra note 17 at 5.

dramatically.[59] Built, as the system is, upon respect for the sovereignty of the criminal justice systems of each participating state, the international system must respect the procedural rules of each state relating to extradition. Some extradition treaties such as the 1957 European Convention on Extradition[60] have attempted to eliminate the differences in these procedures, but not every state is party to such a multilateral treaty. While states have taken domestic measures to iron out differences in extradition,[61] problems still remain.

Another example of divergence in practice relates to the extradition of individuals who may face capital punishment.[62] States that have abolished the death penalty usually refuse to extradite to countries where it remains a competent sentence for drug trafficking.[63] It has been suggested that this principle be applied to life and indeterminate sentences of imprisonment[64] and

---

59 M. Anderson, *Policing the World* (Clarendon, Oxford,1989), pp. 30-31. At p. 31 he points out the importance of "letters rogatory" and "rogatory commissions". "Letters rogatory" are a form of introduction of an investigator seeking assistance in gathering evidence in a foreign jurisdiction to a competent legal authority. "Rogatory commissions" are vehicles by which the results of a foreign enquiry can be brought home by the requesting state and used as evidence in its courts.

60 359 UNTS 276; ETS 24.

61 In the UK, the Criminal Justice Act, 1988, c33, provides for a simple procedure of endorsing the foreign arrest warrant, without examination of the merits of the prosecution's case. This dispenses with the requirement of making a prima facie prosecution case, first in respect of the members of the European Union and then in respect of other states when deemed appropriate.

62 See generally C.R. Roecks, 'Extradition, human rights, and the death penalty: when nations must refuse to extradite a person charged with a capital crime' (1994) 25 *California Western International Law Journal* 189-234.

63 Anderson supra note 59 at 32. States may grant extradition conditional upon a guarantee that the death penalty will not be imposed – see article 11 of the 1957 European Convention on Extradition. It is worth noting the principle laid down in the decision in *Ng v Canada* Comm. No. 469/1991, UN Doc. CCPR/C/09/D469/1991 (1993) where the UN Human Rights Committee held that Canada had breached its obligations under the 1966 International Covenant on Civil and Political Rights 999 UNTS 171 when it extradited Charles Ng, a British subject, to the US for trial for a capital offence without obtaining assurances that the death penalty would not be carried out. Applied to drug related cases, the decision serves to bar the granting by states party to the 1966 Covenant of extradition requests where the possibility of execution exists in the requesting state and no guarantees are given that it will not be carried out.

64 See footnote 12 to article 4(d) of the UN's 1990 Model Treaty on Extradition GA Res. 45/116 UNGAOR 45th Sess. UN Doc. A/Res/45/116 (reprinted 30 ILM at 1412). See also L. Sheleff, 'The "penological exception" to extradition: on ultimate penalties, human rights and international relations' (1993) 1&2 *Israel Law Review* 310-338 particularly at 322-323.

degrading forms of punishment such as corporal punishment,[65] and it has been applied to severe fixed sentences of imprisonment for drug traffickers.[66] Taking a more conservative view, Linke et al argue that the severity of sanctions involving deprivation of liberty should not be and is not usually accepted as a ground for refusing extradition.[67] They point out that excessively lenient punishment may also be an obstacle to extradition especially where the elimination method applies and the requesting Party has not put in place legislation allowing the punishment of serious drug offences with severe sanctions (a maximum penalty of imprisonment of at least one year).[68]

Some problems that states requesting extradition of drug offenders face are purely practical and flow directly from the corrupting influence of drug traffickers. For example, law enforcement agents in the requesting state often fear that corrupt officials in the requested state will alert the extradition target or manufacture "legal" grounds for refusing the request.[69]

Given that all of these reasons for the malfunctioning of extradition apply to the burgeoning drug traffic, it is not surprising that certain states have turned to other methods to obtain the custody of alleged drug offenders. Nadelmann[70] explains that while extradition is popular with the United States because it avoids ineffective prosecutions and punishments by local officials (processes in which United States law enforcement agents are unable to participate), extradition is also vulnerable to corruption, hence the steadily increasing popularity

---

65 See the 1981 Inter-American Convention on Extradition.
66 See, for example, the Quebec Court of Appeals refusal in *United States v Jamieson* 93 CCC 3d 265 (Que. CA. 1994) to extradite alleged drug trafficker Daniel Jamieson to the US State of Michigan where he would face a minimum sentence of twenty years imprisonment with no option of parole. In Canada Jamieson's conduct would be punishable by five years imprisonment. J. Leeson, 'Refusal to extradite: an examination of Canada's indictment of the American legal system' (1996) 26 *Georgia Journal of International and Comparative Law* 641 at 643 notes that the presiding judge ruled that sending Jamieson to Michigan would violate his human rights in terms of section 12 of the Canadian Charter of Rights and Freedoms which protects against cruel and unusual punishment. In *United States of America v Jamieson* [1996] 1 SCR 465 an appeal by the US Government was allowed by the Canadian Supreme Court.
67 Supra note 27 at 33.
68 Supra note 27 at 34.
69 Abramovsky supra note 34 at 155 footnote 12 gives as an example an incident where corrupt Mexican officials allowed a target to bribe his way out of an airport after his jet had been surrounded by Mexican police.
70 E.A.Nadelmann, 'The Drug Enforcement Agency in Latin America: the ins and outs of working around corruption' (1989) 62 *Police Journal* 157 at 166-167.

of extraterritorial abductions[71] and irregular renditions[72] as a substitute for extradition.[73] Although not violative of international law per se, an irregular rendition such as deportation is an unsuitable substitute for extradition because it is a unilateral act used to protect domestic public order rather than the result of bilateral agreement to surrender a fugitive, and it may expose the alleged offender to abuse without any of the protections available to him under an extradition treaty.[74] While unilateral abductions are not common,[75] they are not

---

71   The removal for trial of an alleged offender from another state without any consultation with responsible officials of that state's government.

72   The removal of an alleged offender from another state with its tacit approval or acquiescence.

73   Nadelmann supra note 36 at 857-882 provides an account of the evolution, institutionalisation and growing popularity of irregular rendition in the US. Abramovsky supra note 34 at 151-210 describes in detail the granting of in personam jurisdiction following the Ker-Frisbie doctrine (*Ker v Illinois* 119 US 436 and *Frisbie v Collins* 342 US 519) to US courts over foreign defendants in drugs related cases in disregard of the method used to bring the defendant before court. Abramovsky notes that "catch and snatch" received the sanction of the US Justice Department in 1989. The most infamous of the string of drugs cases following the doctrine is the *US v Alvarez-Machain* 112 US 2188 (1992) where the US Supreme Court allowed the acquisition of jurisdiction over the offender despite his abduction, the fact that he was a Mexican citizen, the existence of an extradition treaty between the US and the asylum state Mexico, and the strong protests of the Mexican government at the violation of international law. The District Court had found that the abduction was a unilateral substitution for extradition which violated treaty law (*US v Caro Quintero* 745 Fed. Supp. 599 at 609). The Court of Appeals (946 F.2d 1466 (9th Cir. 1991)) had affirmed the finding that jurisdiction was improper because of Mexico's protest, but the Supreme Court reversed the decision, holding the abduction did not prohibit trial in the US for a violation of its criminal law. For a defence of US practice see Fletcher supra note 23 at 256 who argues that '[e]xtradition treaties do not exist to protect the sovereignty of the contracting states. They exist in respect of the sovereignty of the contracting states.' But extradition treaties do not protect sovereignty, general international law does, and it is the violation of international law that is crucial here. Interestingly, Fletcher cites the State Department position in 1989 that drug trafficking's threat to domestic security justifies action in self-defence permitting violation of territorial integrity under article 51 of the UN Charter. In other jurisdictions abductions and irregular renditions have been rejected as a basis for the founding of jurisdiction because they are regarded as an abuse of process – see, for example, the decision of the UK's House of Lords in *R v Horseferry Road Magistrates Court, ex parte Bennet* [1994] 1 AC 42. The decision in *Alvarez-Machain* is the legal apotheosis of the drug war model of drug control.

74   See T. Stein, 'International law and extradition relations between the United States and Germany' (1990) 31 *Harvard International Law Journal* 12 at 12-14.

unknown, and aside from their potential human rights violations,[76] they are violations of international law because the abduction violates the sovereignty and territorial integrity of the asylum state which may lead to reprisals and to the discontinuance of international co-operation in international drug control generally.[77] Military action is the next absurd step when abduction fails.[78]

---

75 E.A. Nadelmann, *Cops Across Borders: The Internationalization of U.S. Criminal Law Enforcement* (Pennsylvania State University Press, University Park, Pennsylvania, 1993), p. 8.

76 M.C. Bassiouni, *International Extradition: United States Law and Practice* 2ed (1987) at pp. 223-224 submits that abduction violates the human rights protected in the UN Charter, the 1948 Universal Declaration of Human Rights, 3 UNGAOR 71, (article 3 – protection of life, liberty and security of a person, article 9 – protection from arbitrary arrest, detention or exile) and the 1966 International Covenant on Civil and Political Rights, 999 UNTS 171 (article 9(1) – protection from arbitrary arrest). Taking an opposing view, Kallenbach supra note 15 at 211-213 argues that irregular rendition/ abduction does not violate these rights as they are guaranteed once the alleged offender is brought to court. His argument ignores the fact that the process of irregular rendition/ abduction is itself part of a process to which these rights must attach. O. Lagodny, 'Legally protected interests of the abducted alleged offender' (1993) 1&2 *Israel Law Review* 339 at 345 et seq. lists protection from the death penalty and inhuman treatment associated with it, intolerably severe punishment, possible torture, possible unfair trial and the violation of family relationships through refusal of jail visitation rights as rights protected by an extradition hearing in the requested state which are not protected in the case of an abduction. Certainly traditional protections such as double criminality are not available to the abductee, and nor is judicial review of the extradition process in the courts of the country in which he or she was situated.

77 Abramovsky supra note 34 at 194 and 195. H.F. Woltring and J. Greig, 'State-sponsored kidnapping of fugitives: an alternative to extradition?' in D. Atkins (ed.), *The Alleged Transnational Criminal* (Nijhoff, The Hague, 1995), p. 115 at p.119 report that a survey undertaken by Canada of other states reactions in the wake of the *Alvarez Machain* debacle reveals that states regard the use of abduction as a violation of their sovereignty and international law, and that they believe that the abducted persons should be returned and that the courts should either rectify such situations or decline jurisdiction.

78 The US invasion of Panama is an example of the use of force to acquire jurisdiction over a drug trafficker. See generally S.B. Ellington, 'United States v. Noriega as a reason for an international criminal court' (1993) 11 *Dickinson Journal of International Law* 451-475. For critical views see D.B. Boggis, 'Exporting United States drug law: an example of the international legal ramifications of the "war on drugs"' (1992) 1 *Brigham Young University LR* 165; K.T. Landis, 'The seizure of Noriega: a challenge to the *Ker-Frisbie* doctrine' (1991) 6 *American University Journal of International Law and Policy* 571-607; F.Y.F. Ma, 'Noriega's abduction from Panama: is military invasion an appropriate substitute for international extradition?' (1993) 13 *Loyola of Los Angeles International and Comparative Law Journal* 925-953. For a sympathetic view see Campbell supra note 53 at 390-392. The invasion was justified by President Bush as

International provisions increasing Parties' obligations in respect of extradition present one way of overcoming many of the problems that lead to states taking the law into their own hands. These provisions must, however, be limited to protect the operation of fundamental principles of extradition such as double criminality. Entrenched legal differences and the lack of a political consensus about responsibility for the drug problem dictate that extradition will also be subject to domestic limitation clauses. In the drug conventions extradition has to be a compromise between extension of the criminal law's reach within the structure of international co-operation and the necessity of protecting established principles of international procedural justice and national sovereignty. Closer examination of the conventions' provisions will reveal their effectiveness as a tool for exercising jurisdiction over the illicit traffic.

4.4   JURISDICTION AND EXTRADITION UNDER THE UNAMENDED 1961 CONVENTION

4.4.1   General

Article 36(2) of the 1961 Convention lays down the basic scheme of the drug conventions with respect to jurisdiction: it invokes the territorial principle of jurisdiction, and then extends jurisdiction, either obligatorily or at the Parties' discretion, to make it possible for them to extradite or prosecute on the basis of subsidiary universality. Thus, while the Convention only urges extradition, it obliges Parties to take jurisdiction and prosecute offences committed extra-territorially, that is, the subsidiary universality principle partly urged, partly obliged.

Before commencing examination of article 36(2), it is important to recall that the Convention's provisions are subject to the primacy of the domestic law both through article 36(4) which insists that application of the penal law in article 36 is by means of domestic criminal law,[79] and through the opening paragraph of article 36(2) which subjects article 36(2) to 'the constitutional

---

self-defence but condemned as a violation of international law by the UN General Assembly in Resolution 240, 44 UNGAOR Supp. (No.49) (1989).

79 Article 36(4) provides that: 'Nothing contained in this article shall affect the principle that the offences to which it refers shall be defined, prosecuted and punished in conformity with the domestic law of a Party.' It appears that this provision serves as a limitation clause with respect to jurisdictional issues as they fall under the general term prosecution.

limitations of a Party, its legal system and domestic law'.[80] Chatterjee observes that these provisions mean that in practice 'the self-execution of any of the provisions of Article 36 is an exception, rather than a rule.'[81] It has been argued, however, that the reference to domestic legal systems is indispensable because the Convention only touches upon a few aspects of extradition and the legal systems of the Parties import the principles of extradition law such as double criminality.[82] The primacy of domestic law on questions of jurisdiction is given explicit recognition in article 36(3) which subjects article 36 'to the provisions of the criminal law of the Party concerned on questions of jurisdiction.' According to its author the purpose of this provision was to 'make it quite clear that the provisions of the criminal law of the Parties would prevail on points of jurisdiction.'[83] The *1961 Commentary* responds that article 36(3) does not mean that the Parties are under no obligation to change their law in order to implement article 36's provisions of a jurisdictional nature, pointing out that this would make provisions such as article 36(2)(a)(iv) dealing with the prosecution of offences committed extraterritorially entirely ineffective, something which the Convention's authors could not have intended.[84] It suggests instead that article 36(3) merely emphasises the limitation on the obligation of Parties to implement provisions such as article 36(2)(a)(iv) already provided by the subjection in terms of the opening paragraph of article 36(2) of all its provisions to the domestic legal principles of the Party.[85] It has been argued that article 36(3) has a more precise content – that it is not intended to deal with the jurisdictional competencies of national courts or authorities, but rather with the territorial or extraterritorial jurisdiction of Parties under international law.[86] Thus the purpose of article 36(3) is to make it clear that the development of the detailed application of the obligations of particularly article 36(2)(a)(iv) is a domestic affair, while at the same time preserving the right

---

80 The Indian delegate felt that this limitation clause rendered article 36(2)'s provisions 'pious hopes' while the legal adviser to the conference disagreed and stated that 'it placed on countries the obligation to take various measures unless they were prevented from doing so by constitutional or legal difficulties', *United Nations Conference for the Adoption of a Single Convention on Narcotic Drugs, Official Records, Volume II* (New York, 1964) UN Doc. E/CONF.34/24/ Add.1, UN Publication Sales No. 63.XI.5 (hereinafter *1961 Records* vol. II), p. 243.

81 Supra note 24 at 445.

82 Linke et al supra note 27 at 12.

83 Chilean delegate, *1961 Records* vol. II at 244.

84 *1961 Commentary* at 439.

85 *1961 Commentary* at 439.

86 Linke et al supra note 27 at 12.

of Parties to exercise rules of international jurisdiction either more extensive or more restrictive than those contained in the 1961 Convention. This allows Parties to elect to either exercise even greater extraterritorial jurisdiction or to restrict their jurisdiction to the territorial.[87] It seems that reluctance by the Parties to the Convention to be bound to international jurisdictional provisions has lead to a multi-layering of escape clauses, and to a potential multi-layering of jurisdiction which in turn may lead to the escape of drug offenders from states reluctant to exercise jurisdiction, and to contentious claims of extended jurisdiction by zealous Parties.

4.4.2   Territorial jurisdiction over distinct offences in terms of the 1961 Convention

Article 36(2)(a)(i) provides that each article 36(1) offence, 'if committed in different countries, shall be considered as a distinct offence'.[88] The provision recognises that the acts enumerated in article 36(1) are for the purpose of claiming territorial jurisdiction independent of one another. Thus it appears that if someone is, for instance, selling drugs in state A and has to transport them through state B to get to state A, he will be subject to the criminal jurisdiction of both state A and state B – in state A he will be liable for selling and in state B for transportation.

Although this provision allows each Party to establish jurisdiction over drug trafficking offences committed within its territory, it has been argued that it was not meant to oblige every Party through which drugs were transported from the state of origin to the state of destination to establish a distinct offence.[89] The purpose of this provision is to provide a solution to situations where a Party's penal law defines a number of the offences in article 36(1) as parts of a single offence, say illicit traffic. For example, in certain Parties the brokerage of a drug may be an offence accessory to the principal offence of sale of the drug, and the court competent to try the principal action – sale – may in terms of that Party's law be the only one having jurisdiction over the accessory action – brokerage. This provision prevents an offender in such a situation from escaping prosecution on the basis that only an accessory part of the offence

---

87   Linke et al supra note 27 at 12.
88   A similar provision was included in article 4 of the 1936 Convention.
89   Linke et al supra note 27 at 54 referring to the *1971 Commentary's* interpretation at 357 of the identical provision in article 22(2)(a)(i) of the 1971 Convention.

of trafficking had occurred within the particular Party's jurisdiction, because it obliges that Party to consider the accessory part of the offence as a distinct offence.[90]

The *1961 Commentary* points out that the provision was neither meant to violate the principle of double jeopardy nor prescribe a particular method of dealing with the cumulation of offences nor ensure the cumulative punishment of article 36(1) offences 'which form elements of a single crime of illicit traffic and are committed by the same person in different countries.'[91] The purpose of the provision was to empower each Party to prosecute within its own jurisdiction any drug trafficker who operates in that jurisdiction, despite the fact that he or she may well have operated in the Party "next door", that is, it establishes territorial jurisdiction.[92] Yet the provision may violate the double jeopardy principle[93] and it is included among those subject 'to the constitutional limitations of a Party, its legal system and domestic law', which means that a Party

> is not required to consider offences enumerated in paragraph 1 as distinct crimes if committed in different countries to the extent that doing so would be incompatible with the prohibition of double jeopardy in its domestic law.[94]

Multiple extradition requests in respect of one offender may also result, but conflicts can be avoided by allowing one state to proceed with all the main charges or by agreeing to re-extradition, taking into account the need not to violate double jeopardy principles.[95] A further problem is that because the provision allows many potential claims to territorial jurisdiction, it may be used as a reason for refusing extradition by the many states not permitted to extradite persons over whom they have jurisdiction. It has been argued that it was not the intention of the Convention's drafters to provide for an obstacle to extra-

---

90 *1961 Commentary* at 431.
91 *1961 Commentary* at 431; see also *1961 Records* vol. II at 241.
92 See *1961 Records* vol. II at 241.
93 M.C. Bassiouni, 'The International Narcotics Control Scheme' in Bassiouni MC (ed.), *1 International Criminal Law: Crimes* (Transnational, Dobbs Ferry, 1986), p. 507 at p. 519; see also Linke et al supra note 27 at 54.
94 *1961 Commentary* at 430.
95 Linke et al supra note 27 at 9. The possibility also exists of transit states claiming jurisdiction on the basis of this provision and denying extradition, but at p. 39 Linke et al note that in practice there is a tendency to waive the claim to jurisdiction especially when a later extradition request to the transit state is possible.

dition and that in general concurrent jurisdiction is not inevitably a reason for refusing extradition, particularly when the requesting Party may be in a better position to prosecute, something recognised by the Convention which makes no provision for the refusal of extradition on the basis of territoriality.[96]

Despite these arguments and the official assurances of the *1961 Commentary*, it is noteworthy that when a similar provision was introduced in the draft 1988 Convention it was deleted because it was felt that the earlier versions proved unworkable, their purpose was not clear and they amounted to a violation of the double jeopardy principle.[97]

4.4.3   Territorial and extraterritorial jurisdiction under the 1961 Convention

Article 36(2)(a)(iv) involves firstly an obligation[98] on Parties to prosecute serious drug offences that occur within their territory, no matter what the nationality of the offender and apparently whether or not the offender is actually in that territory. This is a straightforward application of territorial jurisdiction. What makes an offence 'serious' remains undefined but the qualification does imply that Parties are not under an obligation to punish minor offences such as personal use offences that occur within their jurisdictions.

As an alternative to prosecution on the basis of territorial jurisdiction,[99] the second part of the provision obliges a Party that has apprehended a serious drug offender to prosecute him for his extraterritorial offence, whether or not

---

96 Linke et al supra note 27 at 10.

97 See the 'Expert Group Report', *United Nations Conference for the Adoption of a Convention against Illicit Traffic in Narcotic Drugs and Psychotropic Substances, Official Records, Volume I* (New York, 1994) UN Doc. E/CONF.82/16, UN Publication Sales No. E.94.XI.5 (hereinafter *1988 Records* vol. I), p. 16.

98 The operative term 'shall' obviously does not mean that the Parties are under an obligation to prosecute every single potential drug offence; their authorities retain the discretion to prosecute only if sufficient evidence is available to make a successful prosecution reasonably possible.

99 The authors of the provision assumed that a preference had been given to territorial jurisdiction in recognition of the principle that the state in whose territory an offence was committed should have the first choice to prosecute, and that the Party in whose territory the offender was found should take proceedings only if the former Party had not asked for his extradition – see the remarks of the Hungarian delegate, *1961 Records* vol. I at 125, and the explanation of the Egyptian delegate, *1961 Records* vol. II at 247. However, the structure of the provision appears to make the options alternatives and nothing more, something also implied by the fact that the provision accepts that the requested Party can validly decline to extradite to a Party having territorial jurisdiction.

he is a national of that Party, if it refuses to extradite him. This extension of jurisdiction is based on the aut dedere aut judicare principle. It is the most contentious of article 36's jurisdiction provisions because states find it difficult to prosecute offences committed abroad unless they have some connection to the offender or offence such as nationality, subjective or objective territoriality, the protective principle, or even passive personality, enabling the establishment of extraterritorial jurisdiction. The problem with this provision is that it ignores the need for such a connection. Not surprisingly, the proviso in the opening paragraph of article 36(2) subjecting this obligation to a Party's other laws makes it dependent on whether those laws permit the exercise of extraterritorial jurisdiction.[100] It is also subject to two specific qualifications.

The first specific qualification is that the Party in whose territory the offender is found is only obliged to prosecute provided extradition to the state where the offence occurred is not acceptable to it.[101] The phrase 'application is made' does appear to insist that a formal extradition request must actually be made and refused before the requested Party is obliged to take jurisdiction, but the wording is ambiguous enough to leave the situation unclear when the Party with custody of the alleged offender wants to take jurisdiction but no extradition request is made.[102] And no extradition request may be forthcoming because article 36 of the 1961 Convention does not provide for a strict obligation to request extradition at all.[103] The provision is broad because it does not place any constraints on the reasons why the requested Party finds extra-

---

100 Bassiouni and Wise supra note 30 at 14.
101 Linke et al supra note 27 at 11-12 point out that the fact that extradition must in terms of the provision be unacceptable, means that a Party cannot free itself from an existing agreement to extradite by taking jurisdiction itself. At p. 40 they note that the necessity for a refusal to extradite narrows the general principle of subsidiary universality which does not always require the state with primary jurisdiction to make an application for extradition before the state with subsidiary jurisdiction may prosecute.
102 See Puttler supra note 8 at 114. The relevance of her example of unwilling Dutch officials not requesting the extradition of one of their nationals from Germany in order to prevent the German courts from establishing jurisdiction, is obvious. Linke et al supra note 27 at 11 argue that in reality there are situations where the taking of jurisdiction will be necessary even though no formal extradition request is made. See, for example, the *Drug Offences Jurisdiction Case* (1991) 86 ILR 550 where Austria took jurisdiction over an offence committed in Switzerland by an offender apprehended in Austria, despite the fact that Switzerland had not made a formal extradition request, on the basis that had such a request been made Austria would have had to refuse it as the offender was its national.
103 Linke et al supra note 27 at 8. They note that neither article 22(2)(a)(iv) of the 1971 Convention nor article 36(2)(a)(iv) of the 1972 Protocol change this position.

dition impossible.[104] If conformity to its law requires it to reject the extradition request then it must establish jurisdiction. Constitutional provisions against the extradition of nationals in civilian states provide the most common legal grounds for refusing extradition. The provision thus, somewhat indirectly, gives preference to the jurisdiction of these Parties over their own nationals.[105] It tacitly recognises nationality jurisdiction. Other reasons for declining extradition may include the fact that the requesting Party and requested Party are not bound by an extradition treaty and the requested Party requires such a treaty for extradition.[106] The provision does not apply either to Parties whose domestic law does permit extradition of nationals but who simply choose not to extradite or to extradition from non-parties.[107] The *1961 Commentary* opines, however, that to exclude such cases from the scope of the provision would not accord with its object and purpose which the *1961 Commentary* suggests is only to free a Party from the obligation to prosecute offenders if it is able to and does actually extradite them.[108]

The second qualification on subsidiary universality under article 36(2)(a)(iv) is that the Party in whose territory the offender is found is only obliged to prosecute him if he has not already been prosecuted and judged, whether convicted or acquitted, in another state. This qualification avoids double jeopardy.[109]

The *1961 Commentary* attempts to shore up the holes in article 36(2)(a)(iv)'s obligation to extradite or prosecute by noting that even when Parties are precluded by their domestic law from both extraditing and prosecuting, the spirit of the provision and the general obligations on Parties to collaborate in suppressing the illicit traffic in terms of article 4(1)(b) and article 35 paragraphs (b) and (c) binds them not to allow their territories to be used as bases for the illicit traffic or as refuges for illicit traffickers and requires them to expel or deport alien traffickers in these circumstances.[110] As pointed out above, however,

---

104 Unlike article 8 of the 1936 Convention which provides for jurisdiction only if extradition fails because of a reason independent of the offence, such as lack of reciprocity, absence of diplomatic relations or the impossibility of extraditing a national.

105 *1961 Commentary* at 435.

106 Linke et al supra note 27 at 11.

107 *1961 Commentary* at 436.

108 *1961 Commentary* at 436.

109 The *1961 Commentary* at 436 suggests that offenders who have been convicted abroad but who have not yet been punished should be either extradited or tried again. Extradition is the better option. Retrial would be a violation of the double jeopardy principle. Linke et al supra note 27 at 55 argue that it would not be in the spirit of this provision if a Party relied on it to refuse extradition for the purpose of serving out a sentence.

110 *1961 Commentary* at 436.

subjecting an alleged offender to unilateral action of this kind exposes them to the potential violation of their procedural and human rights and deprives them of the protections of the general principles of extradition.

Should the Party that refuses extradition establish and exercise jurisdiction, the Convention is not clear on whether it should apply its own law or that of the Party where the offence occurred. However, the choice would belong to the prosecuting Party and would depend on whether its law authorised the application of foreign laws.[111]

Chatterjee regards article 36(2)(a)(iv) as a 'rather bold step which proved to be unworkable in the 1936 Convention', but that it reinforces the idea that the authors of the 1961 Convention intended to give 'international recognition to certain types of crimes.'[112] Subsidiary universality, even in this qualified form, was opposed by common law states that would have preferred a system based on extradition.[113] It was left to the United Nations to convince those states that had difficulties extraditing their nationals to recognise the seriousness of the international drug threat and establish subsidiary universality. The *1961 Commentary*, for example, points out that states prosecute piracy and currency forgery no matter where they are committed and argues that the 'deterioration of the international drug situation since 1961 when the Single Convention was concluded' should convince Parties of the need to prosecute extraterritorial drug offences.[114] It argues that the domestic law safeguard clause in the opening paragraph of article 36(2) does not stand in the way, because the domestic law of all states permits the trial of particularly dangerous crimes committed abroad among which must be included serious offences of illicit trafficking.[115] The application of escape clauses to the provision indicates, however, that in 1961 international society was not prepared to give unqualified support to the ap-

---

111 The Legal Advisor to the 1961 Conference, *1961 Records* vol. I at 145-146.
112 Supra note 24 at 438 referring to articles 8 and 9 of the 1936 Convention.
113 One of the major objectors at the 1961 Conference to the extension of jurisdiction extraterritorially through subsidiary universality was the US delegation which stated: 'To prosecute a person [extraterritorially] would not be conducive to the best administration of justice and might prevent him, for financial and other reasons, from obtaining witnesses and evidence.' The delegation went on to note that if the provisions on extradition were adequate the prosecution provision would be superfluous – *1961 Records* vol. I at 123. Ultimately, the prosecution provision was necessary because the extradition provision was not binding.
114 *1961 Commentary* at 435.
115 *1961 Commentary* at 435.

plication of subsidiary universality.[116] Article 36(3)'s subjection of all questions of jurisdiction to a Party's criminal law implies that a Party is not prevented from exercising extraterritorial jurisdiction on some other jurisdictional basis, something that they regard as important to ensure that serious drug offences do not go unpunished.[117]

State practice since 1961 indicates that while many states do not prosecute extraterritorial offences,[118] some Parties do prosecute extraterritorial drug offences, relying either generally on the Conventions[119] or explicitly on article 36(2)(a)(iv).[120] Some Parties have gone so far as to state that the 1961 Convention's provisions generally support application of universality to drug offences.[121] But many states establishing extraterritorial jurisdiction prefer to rely on some connection between themselves and the offender beyond his mere

---

116 As a result of these safeguards, Clark supra note 38 at 58 states that although the provision looks like a universal jurisdiction provision, and universal jurisdiction is probably acceptable, 'its exercise is far from obligatory.'

117 Linke et al supra note 27 at 9.

118 For example, neither the Canadian Narcotic Control Act RSC 1970 c. N-1 and the Food and Drugs Act RSC 1970 c. F-27 created an extraterritorial offence.

119 See, for example, the *Thailand Drug Offences (Jurisdiction) Case* (1991) 86 ILR 587 where a Danish court held that it had jurisdiction over a Danish national who committed drug trafficking from Thailand to the US partly on the basis that Denmark, Thailand and the US were all party to the 1961 Convention.

120 See, for example, the *Drug Offences Jurisdiction Case* (1991) 86 ILR 550 where the Austrian Supreme Court confirmed the conviction of an Austrian national for trafficking drugs in Switzerland on the basis of article 36(2)(a)(iv). It stated that in terms of the article Austria is obliged to prosecute the offender even though he was apprehended in Austria and provided that an extradition request from a foreign state had been rejected and the offender had not been prosecuted and convicted. The court noted that no such prosecution and conviction had occurred in Switzerland, and then held that any request by Switzerland for extradition would have to be rejected since the accused was an Austrian national (at pp. 551-552).

121 The German Federal Supreme Court in *Universal Jurisdiction over Drug Offences Case* (1979) 74 ILR 166, 168-169, confirmed the conviction of a Dutch national who sold cannabis in the Netherlands to Germans for resale in Germany on the basis that article 6(5)(b) of the German Criminal code establishing universal jurisdiction over drug trafficking offences accorded with Germany's obligations under the 1961 Convention. The Court held that article 36(2)(a)(iv) appears to support subsidiary universality, but warned that 'it was not entirely clear that this is the case since liability to prosecution in the place where the offence was committed is not expressly made a precondition for prosecution in the state where the offender has been arrested.' The Court noted academic support for the application of universality in serious cases and that article 36(3) protected Germany's application of its own criminal norms, and concluded that international law did not in any event deny the application of universality.

presence in their territory.[122] The failure of article 36(2)(a) is that it does not expressly regulate and thus guide the many states that find themselves in the muddled middle ground between strict territoriality and subsidiary universality.

4.4.4   Extradition provisions in the 1961 Convention

Article 36(2)(b) states that it is desirable that the offences in article 36 should either be included in existing or future extradition treaties between Parties or be recognised as extraditable by Parties that do not rely on treaties or reciprocity. It follows the pattern established in article 9 of the 1936 Convention, the most significant difference being that the words 'it is desirable' make it a recommendation.[123] This explains why the 1936 provision is still operative for Parties to both Conventions that choose to allow it to remain in operation.[124] Drafts of the provision had bound Parties to either include drug offences as extradition crimes in existing treaties or recognise drug offences as extradition crimes.[125] The 1961 Conference, however, recognising the dif-

---

122 A good example is the prosecution of the Panamanian dictator, Manuel Noriega – see Ellington supra note 78 at 451-475 commenting on *United States v Noriega* 746 F. Supp. 1506 (S.D. Fla. 1990). Although he never actually entered the US while involved in the conspiracy to import drugs with which he was charged, the Court found that his co-conspirators had and it considered him to have committed their acts within the US (at pp. 1513-1514). It also found that the statutes he was charged with violating were intended to apply extraterritorially (at p. 1515), a finding supported by the fact that some specifically state that importation of drugs into the US is illegal which showed a clear legislative intent to apply them extraterritorially, e.g. the Drug Abuse Protection Act, 21 USC sections 952 and 959(c).

123 Despite its recommendatory nature, on accession (4/11/1997) Vietnam reserved on article 36(2)(b). Austria (16/12/1998), Sweden (14/12/1998), UK (17/12/1998) and Finland (15/1/1999) have all objected to the reservation – see *Multilateral Treaties Deposited with the Secretary General: Status as at 30 April 1999* (New York, 1999) UN Doc. St/Leg/Ser.E/17.

124 In terms of article 44(2) of the 1961 Convention, article 9 of the 1936 Convention was terminated and replaced by article 36(2)(b) of the 1961 Convention as between Parties to the 1936 Convention which became Parties to the 1961 Convention, but article 9 continues to be in force in respect of those Parties to both Conventions which notify the UN Secretary General that they wish to continue to be bound by it. France (19/2/1969), Liechtenstein (31/10/1979) and Switzerland (23/1/1970) all made reservations keeping article 9 in force – see generally *Multilateral Treaties Deposited with the Secretary General: Status as at 31 December 1996* (New York, 1997) UN Doc. St/Leg/Ser.E/15, pp. 283-284 (hereinafter *Multilateral Treaties Deposited* (1997)).

125 Draft article 45(3), *1961 Records* vol. II at 17.

ficulties states would have in accepting mandatory extradition of drug offenders, despite criticism[126] made extradition optional.[127] It also limited the recommendation to include trafficking offences among extradition crimes in two ways: first, the Party may refuse to arrest the offender or grant extradition where its authorities do not consider the offence to be 'sufficiently serious';[128] second, extradition must be 'in conformity with the domestic law' of the requested Party.[129]

In effect, the provision recommends that the illicit trafficking offences set out in article 36 of the 1961 Convention must be included as extradition crimes in existing or future extradition treaties between any of the Parties[130] and be recognised as extradition crimes between any of the Parties that do not make extradition conditional on the existence of a treaty or on reciprocity.[131] The recommendation does not apply to the following situations: Parties that do make extradition conditional upon reciprocity, Parties that unilaterally grant extradition to other Parties which do not comply with the recommendation[132] and extradition to non-parties.[133] These lacunas prompt the *1961 Commentary* to suggest that all Parties should grant extradition to Parties and non-parties alike in all cases where it is necessary in order to prosecute or punish major illicit traffickers.[134]

In practice, in their post-1961 extradition treaties many states did not specifically include drug offences as extraditable offences, but relied on them being offences under both states' domestic laws. The absence of uniform or

---

126 *1961 Records* vol. II 242-243 (Mexico) and vol. I at 146 (UK).
127 See the discussion in the ad hoc committee on draft article 45, *1961 Records* vol. II at 241-242.
128 The provision does not specify what makes an offence serious enough to make it extraditable – see the remarks of the Greek delegate, *1961 Records* vol. I at 127. It is probable that a minimum period of incarceration is what is meant here.
129 For example, the application by the requested state of its own statute of limitations to bar extradition.
130 Nadelmann supra note 36 at 830 comments that efforts in the early 1970s to extradite Latin American drug traffickers were 'stymied by the fact that thirty-six treaties, including most of those with Latin American governments, made no mention of drug violations, having mostly been negotiated before World War I.
131 *1961 Commentary* at 437.
132 This is due to the fact that article 36(2)(b) recommends that the offences of the illicit traffic be recognised as extradition crimes 'as between any of the Parties' – *1961 Commentary* at 437.
133 *1961 Commentary* at 437.
134 *1961 Commentary* at 437.

at the very least substantially similar drug offences in every Party remained a problem for double criminality.[135]

4.4.5   The 1961 Convention's jurisdiction and extradition provisions considered

The 1961 Convention's provisions on jurisdiction and extradition lay heavy emphasis on the exercise of territorial jurisdiction over drug crimes, but they also allow a tentative extension beyond the territorial toward the exercise of universal jurisdiction. However, the 1961 Convention does not provide for the extension of territorial jurisdiction except under the aut dedere aut judicare provision, leaving any other such extension to the Parties' national law.[136] Moreover, these provisions contain internal limitations and are subject to general limitations that render them all but non-binding. The optional provision on extradition recognises the hesitancy of the international community in 1961 to begin to cast drug offences in the same light as offences such as piracy. The 1961 Convention's provisions give little or no direction on difficult issues such as concurrent jurisdiction,[137] the basis for claiming extraterritorial jurisdiction, the duty to request extradition[138] and so on. Their resolution of these issues was left to particular extradition treaties, to general international law, to politically expedient processes such as deportation and expulsion. The 1961 Convention's provisions as a whole were a limited response to the international

---

135 While correspondence of the purpose of the offence and not simply correspondence of the essential elements is at issue, correspondence of the elements is important. For example, Bernholz et al supra note 10 at 358-361 illustrate that the more sophisticated US offences such as Continuing Criminal Enterprise (CCE) 21 USC section 848(b) (1982), while containing drug related conduct within them, go beyond the jurisdictional elements contained in national drug offences in other Parties derived from article 36(1) and are therefore not extraditable because they do not satisfy double criminality.

136 Linke et al supra note 27 at 63.

137 Although, as Linke et al supra note 27 at 65 point out, when more than one Party claims jurisdiction, although article 36(2)(a)(iv) does prioritise territoriality it does not prohibit extradition to other states, such as the state of nationality, on the basis of ordinary principles of extraterritoriality. It does not, however, give any guidance as to how such other claims would be ranked.

138 Linke et al supra note 27 at 65 note that the only option left to them in cases where no extradition request is made by a state having jurisdiction is to urge the detaining Party to offer extradition, and to base jurisdiction on the refusal to take up the offer, or if all else fails simply as a matter of expediency to expel the alleged offender to a state having jurisdiction. The latter option is undesirable from the point of view of protection of the alleged offender's rights.

drug problem and the particular problems of dealing with extraterritorial drug offenders.

4.5   JURISDICTION AND EXTRADITION UNDER THE 1971 CONVENTION

4.5.1   General

Article 22(2) of the 1971 Convention is almost identical to article 36(2) of the unamended 1961 Convention.[139] There were various reasons why article 36(2) was used as a model. The authors of article 22(2) felt that the 1961 Convention had 'stood the test' and that the situation had to be avoided where offenders were treated differently according to the type of substance with which they were involved. They were also aware that Parties to both Conventions wanted to avoid having to enact separate legislation to regulate narcotics and psychotropic substances.[140] Article 22(2) adheres to the basic scheme of the 1961 Convention. It provides for the territorial jurisdiction of the Party in whose territory the offence was committed, and then urges Parties with custody of extraterritorial offenders to extradite and, if such extradition is impossible, it obliges them to take jurisdiction and prosecute the offender.

As with the 1961 Convention, article 22's provisions on jurisdiction are subject to the primacy of domestic law. The limitation clause in the opening subparagraph of article 22(2) subjects them to 'the constitutional limitations of a Party's legal system and domestic law'. The general limitation clause in article 22(5) asserts that the 'prosecution' of drug offences shall be in conformity with the domestic law of the Parties. Finally, article 22(4) subjects article 22 'to the provisions of the domestic law of the Party concerned on questions of jurisdiction.' The latter limitation, which closely follows article 36(3) of the 1961 Convention, all but makes the Convention's obligations with respect to jurisdiction illusory. The extreme view is that without the Parties' assent no modification of their law on jurisdiction can take place.[141] Yet the *1971 Commentary* holds that it does not mean that Parties are never required to change

---

139 The only difference being the wording of the sub-paragraph 2(a)(i).
140 See the Danish delegate's statement, *United Nations Conference for the Adoption of a Protocol on Psychotropic Substances, Official Records, Volume II* (New York, 1973) UN Doc. E/CONF.58/7/Add.1, UN Publication Sales No.E.73.XI.4 (hereinafter *1971 Records* vol. II), p. 32.
141 See the Danish delegate's statement, *1971 Records* vol. II at 35.

their law in order to carry out obligations like that in article 22(2)(a)(iv) to prosecute serious drug offences even if they are committed extraterritorially because that would render the provision ineffective, something that could not have been the intention of its authors. The *1971 Commentary* submits instead that article 22(4) frees Parties from the obligation to apply the rules flowing from article 22(2)(a)(iv)'s obligation to the extent that they are incompatible with its general concepts in the field of criminal jurisdiction.[142]

4.5.2 Territorial jurisdiction over distinct offences in terms of the 1971 Convention

Article 22(2)(a)(i) is substantively the same as article 36(2)(a)(i) of the 1961 Convention, providing that article 22 offences committed in different countries shall be considered distinct and therefore the comments made above apply equally here. The limitation clause in the opening subparagraph of article 22(2) means that a Party need not meet this obligation to the extent that doing so would violate the domestic prohibition of double jeopardy.[143] The *1971 Commentary* states that the purpose of article 22(2)(a)(i) appears to be to give domestic courts territorial jurisdiction in some cases in which they might otherwise not have it and in particular 'over every act of intentional participation in principal acts of offences committed abroad, even though in principle it assigns jurisdiction over accessory acts to the courts in whose districts the related principal acts were committed.'[144] Thus if X brokers in state B the sale of drugs in state A, the criminal courts of state B may ordinarily have no jurisdiction over his conduct if it is regarded as accessory to the sale taking place in state A and the jurisdictional rule in state B is that the court that tries the principal conduct is the only court competent to try the accessory conduct. But if, under article 22(2)(a)(i) the brokerage and sale carried out in the two states are regarded as two separate offences, both states A and B would have territorial jurisdiction over the conduct committed in its territory.[145] Despite this interpretation, this provision has the potential to cause problems of double jeopardy, and as noted above, a provision to this effect in the draft 1988 Convention was cut because it had proved impractical in the earlier conventions.

---

142 *1971 Commentary* at 368-369.
143 *1971 Commentary* at 356.
144 *1971 Commentary* at 357.
145 See the *1971 Commentary* at 357.

4.5.3   Territorial and extraterritorial jurisdiction under the 1971 Convention

Article 22(2)(a)(iv) of the 1971 Convention is identical to article 36(2)(a)(iv) of the 1961 Convention and the comments made above apply equally here. Although couched as an obligation, the operation of this provision is limited. The operation of the limitation clause in the opening subparagraph of article 22(2) means that a Party need not prosecute criminal acts abroad, particularly minor offences, if its domestic law normally does not extend its jurisdiction extraterritorially.[146] The *1971 Commentary* submits that a Party could not rely on this limitation clause if the drug offence is very serious and the Party already extends its jurisdiction through universality or protection over other offences of 'equal gravity.'[147] The validity of this submission depends, of course, on the Parties accepting that drug offences are of equal gravity to offences such as piracy.

The provision firstly obliges Parties to exercise jurisdiction over nationals and foreigners who commit serious drug offences within their territory. It does not define what serious offences are, but implies that Parties are not under an obligation to prosecute non-serious offences. It assumes that the Party will be able to either arrest the offender within its territory or obtain his extradition from another state.[148] The *1971 Commentary* notes that even though the provision does not explicitly oblige Parties to obtain the extradition of an offender from abroad, it submits that Parties should in the spirit of the provision seek extradition in all cases where they are aware that the offender has not been prosecuted or subject to alternative measures of treatment and there is no prospect that she will be.[149]

Secondly, as an alternative to extradition, the provision obliges Parties to exercise jurisdiction over nationals and foreigners if they are found within the Party's territory even if they committed a serious drug offence extraterritorially. It provides for that extension on the basis of the principle of nationality for nationals and subsidiary universality, the obligation to prosecute where extradition is impossible, in respect of foreigners.

The second obligation is subject to two conditions. The first is that the obligation to prosecute only exists 'if extradition is not acceptable in conformity with the law of the Party to which application is made.' The *1971 Commentary*

---

146 *1971 Commentary* at 356.
147 *1971 Commentary* at 361.
148 *1971 Commentary* at 362.
149 *1971 Commentary* at 362.

assumes that this means that the requested Party is only relieved of the obligation to establish jurisdiction if extradition was acceptable to it and has actually been carried out to the state where the offence took place or to the state of whom the offender is a national.[150] Non-parties are of course not subject to any obligation.

The second condition on the second obligation, the proviso that the obligation is only operative if the 'offender has not already been prosecuted and judgement given', upholds the principle against double jeopardy. This proviso would also apply where the offender has been prosecuted and then instead of being punished has been subject to the alternative measures provided for in article 22(1)(b), but would not apply when the offender has been prosecuted, sentenced and has then absconded before serving his sentence.[151]

The *1971 Commentary* suggests that the spirit of the provision demands that a Party which can neither prosecute nor extradite an offender should not allow the offender to take refuge in its territory but should expel or deport him or her.[152] However, unilateral action of this nature would expose the alleged offender to abuse of her rights without any of the protections of formal extradition arrangements and is highly undesirable.

Like earlier provisions, article 22(1)(a)(iv) does not provide expressly for any ground of extraterritorial jurisdiction other than nationality and subsidiary universality. However, recognition in the provision that not all states view drug offences as serious enough to establish extraterritorial jurisdiction over foreigners without their being some kind of nexus between them and the offender, would have undermined the principle of subsidiary universality's application to drug offences. The provision is legally ambitious but practically certain to disappoint.

---

150 *1971 Commentary* at 362. Based on the provision against manifest unreasonableness in interpreting conventions in article 32(b) of the 1969 Vienna Convention on the Law of Treaties, the *1971 Commentary* also assumes that a Party which extradites the offender to a state which is not a party to the 1971 Convention would be freed of its obligation to prosecute. It notes that the state to which the offender is extradited must have the jurisdiction to try him, or it would defeat the purpose of the provision.

151 *1971 Commentary* at 363. Further on the question of the applicability of the proviso to sentencing, Chatterjee supra note 24 at 484 argues that this proviso runs counter to the provision in article 22(2)(a)(ii) which makes it possible to take foreign convictions into account when establishing recidivism. The recidivism provision, however, relates to different sentences for different convictions, not conviction and sentence for the same offence which bar further prosecution and sentence in terms of this proviso.

152 *1971 Commentary* at 364.

4.5.4   Extradition under the 1971 Convention

Article 22(2)(b) of the 1971 Convention follows the approach of article 36(2)(b) of the 1961 Convention and the comments made in the latter's respect are equally applicable here. In simple terms, it provides that it is desirable that the drug 'crimes'[153] in article 22(1) and 22(2)(a)(ii) be included in extradition treaties as extraditable offences by Parties that use extradition treaties in such circumstances, and be recognised as extraditable by Parties that do not require the existence of extradition treaties in order to extradite. In spite of efforts at the 1971 Conference to make its application mandatory,[154] article 22(2)(b) is a recommendation. Nonetheless, Parties have made reservations in its regard.[155] Article 22(2)(b) does not apply to Parties that do not require an extradition treaty but which make extradition conditional on reciprocity. Nor does it apply to the situation where a Party does not require the existence of an extradition treaty but is unilaterally willing to extradite offenders to other Parties that have the same general policy in respect of extradition but do not extradite drug offenders.[156] The provision also does not appear to apply to relations with non-parties. Parties may refuse to follow the provision's recommendation when their competent authorities do not consider the offence for which the extradition request is being made to be 'sufficiently serious'. Unfortunately, 'sufficiently serious' is left undefined.

Bassiouni is deeply critical of the provision because it is only a recommendation and because of its escape clause. He comments on the 1971 Convention:

> Recognising the principle of "universality" by allowing any state wherein the
> offender may be found to prosecute for the offence as an alternative to extradition,

---

153 The term 'crimes' is used here in preference to offences apparently to denote the serious nature of these breaches because extradition is only granted in such serious cases – see the statement of the legal advisor, *1971 Records* vol. II at 45.

154 See *United Nations Conference for the Adoption of a Protocol on Psychotropic Substances, Official Records, Volume 1* (New York, 1973) UN Doc. E/CONF.58/7; UN Publication Sales No.E.73.XI.3 (hereinafter *1971 Records* vol. I), p. 98 and vol. II at pp. 32-33. Unlike the 1961 Convention, the 1971 Convention makes no provision for the optional retention of article 9 of the 1936 Convention.

155 Myanmar does not consider itself bound by article 22(2)(b) (20/6/1994 – *Multilateral Treaties Deposited* (1997) at 304); no other Parties objected to this reservation within 12 months in terms of article 32(3) so it has been deemed to be permitted.

156 See the *1971 Commentary* at 365. This second lacuna is caused by the requirement that the offences must be recognised as extradition offences 'as between any of the Parties.'

it nonetheless only suggests the "desirability" to make it an extraditable offence. No wonder so few treaties contain such violations in their list of extraditable offences.[157]

4.5.5   *The 1971 Convention's jurisdiction and extradition provisions considered*

While extending their scope to include psychotropic substances,[158] the 1971 Convention's provisions on jurisdiction and extradition are no stronger than those in the 1961 Convention. Internal and general limitation deprives them of force. Largely based on territorial jurisdiction, their extension of extra-territorial jurisdiction appears more ambitious than it actually is. Although the authors of the 1971 Convention adopted subsidiary universality over drug offences, in practice the international community was as unlikely in 1971 to embrace universal jurisdiction over drug offences as it was ten years previously. But nor were states enthusiastic about the alternative, extradition, their lack of enthusiasm evident in the hortatory nature of the 1971 Convention's extradition provision.

4.6   EXTRADITION UNDER THE 1972 PROTOCOL'S AMENDMENTS TO THE 1961 CONVENTION

4.6.1   *General*

The 1972 Protocol stiffened the 1961 Convention's provisions on extradition. Article 14 of the 1972 Protocol replaced the weak provision in article 36(2)(b) of the 1961 Convention with a new, stronger, article 36(2)(b). The aim of the amendment's American sponsors was to make drug offences automatically extra-ditable and thus to facilitate extradition between states whose bilateral extra-dition treaties did not mention drug offences or between states that did not have such treaties at all.[159] The Israeli delegate explained that the 'new provisions

---

157 Supra note 93 at 519.
158 Thus, for example, article 2(3) of the 1974 US-Australia Extradition Treaty, 27 UST 957, lists as extraditable 'offences against the laws relating to narcotics, dangerous drugs or psychotropic substances.'
159 The US initiated the process of amending article 36 through submission to the CND's 24th session of new provisions making extradition of drug offences mandatory along the lines of those contained in article 9 of the 1936 Convention and article 8 of the 1970

represented an important step in the multilateralisation of the modern international law of extradition, which was necessary in the light of the development of the resources of modern criminals.'[160] But the 1972 Conference was circumspect and the amended article 36(2)'s provisions on extradition remain subject to the primacy of domestic law through the general limitation clause in article 36(4) and to the limitation clause in the opening paragraph of article 36(2) which guarantees the existing rights of the Parties with respect to extradition. Thus, for example, Parties that do not in terms of their domestic law extradite their nationals, would not in terms of the amended article 36 be obliged to do so.[161] Moreover, article 36(3) provides that on questions of jurisdiction domestic criminal legal provisions are paramount.

4.6.2   Drug offences deemed extraditable in terms of existing and future extradition treaties

A response to the failure to provide for extradition of drug offences in early bilateral extradition treaties and the continued exclusion of drug offences from new extradition treaties, the new paragraph (2)(b)(i) is an ex lege fiction that deems the drug offences in article 36 to be extradition offences for the purposes of all existing extradition treaties without the necessity of amending these treaties and compels their inclusion in all future extradition treaties.[162] This automatic extension of treaty rights and obligations takes effect without the necessity for any declaration, notification or special agreement, and such an action would only have a declaratory effect.[163] In effect, the first sentence

---

Hague Convention for the Suppression of Unlawful Seizure of Aircraft, 860 UNTS 105 – see *United Nations Conference to consider amendments to the Single Convention on Narcotic Drugs, Official Records, Volume I* (New York, 1974) UN Doc. E/CONF.63/10; UN Publication Sales No.E.73.XI.7 (hereinafter *1972 Records* vol. I), pp. 3-4. The passage of these amendments through the CND and the Conference was resisted on the basis that a multilateral convention dealing with drug control should not serve as the basis for extradition usually regulated by bilateral extradition treaties.

160 *United Nations Conference to consider amendments to the Single Convention on Narcotic Drugs, Official Records, Volume II* (New York, 1973) UN Doc. E/CONF.63/10/Add.1; UN Publication Sales No. E.73.XI.8 (hereinafter *1972 Records* vol. II), p. 203.

161 Brazil declared upon ratification of the Protocol that the amended article 36 did not oblige Parties 'with laws against extradition of nationals to extradite them.' (16/5/1973 – *Multilateral Treaties Deposited* (1997) at 295).

162 Article 36(2)(b)(i) closely follows the wording of article 8(1) of the 1970 Hague Hijacking Convention, and reproduces the substance of article 9(1) of the 1936 Convention.

163 Linke et al supra note 27 at 4-5.

of the provision amends all bilateral or multilateral extradition treaties between or among the Parties to such treaties that are Parties to the 1961 Convention and which are in force at the time when extradition of the drug offender is requested.[164] The second sentence of the provision obliges Parties to include article 36 offences in any bilateral or multilateral extradition treaty concluded among them. Thus there is no obligation if one or more Parties to the extradition treaty is not a Party to the 1961 Convention.[165] However, if the Parties to such a treaty were Parties to the amended 1961 Convention they would be obliged to treat these offences as extradition offences because these offences would be deemed under the first sentence of the provision to be included as extraditable offences in that 'existing' extradition treaty.[166] Extradition relations with non-parties to both the extradition treaty and the 1961 Convention are not covered by this provision.

Article 36(2)(b)(i) is an ambitious provision with a potentially enormous scope. In practice article 36 offences are added to the list of extraditable offences in enumerative extradition treaties only if states agree that the offence is sufficiently serious. Eliminative extradition treaties rendering offences with a penalty of a certain severity extraditable by definition only include serious drug offences. For this reason the *1972 Commentary* suggests that only sufficiently serious violations of article 36 offences need to be deemed extraditable offences in any extradition treaty existing between the Parties to the 1961 Convention.[167] Linke et al point out, however, that Parties are free to declare less serious offences extraditable.[168]

The limitation clause in the opening paragraph of article 36(2) does not exempt Parties from meeting their obligation but it does mean that they are not required to change their constitutions or take actions incompatible with the basic principles of their legal system or domestic law on the matter.[169] The other provisions of article 36(2)(b) make it clear that extradition need only be granted in conformity with the law of the requested Party.[170] In practice, Par-

---

164 See *Commentary on the 1972 Protocol Amending the Single Convention on Narcotic Drugs, 1961* (New York, 1976) UN Doc. E/CN.7/588, UN Publication Sales No.E.76.XI.6 (hereinafter *1972 Commentary*), p. 79.

165 The *1972 Commentary* at 79.

166 *1972 Commentary* at 79.

167 *1972 Commentary* at 79-80.

168 Supra note 27 at 5.

169 *1972 Commentary* at 80.

170 *1972 Commentary* at 80.

ties have found the legal fiction in the new article 36(2)(b)(i) a useful legal tool for updating old extradition treaties to include drug offences.[171]

4.6.3   Extradition of drug offences where an extradition treaty is necessary but not in existence

The novel provision in article 36(2)(b)(ii) does not impose a legal obligation on any of the Parties. It gives Parties that make extradition conditional on the existence of a treaty the option of considering the amended 1961 Convention as the legal basis for extradition if they receive an extradition request for an article 36 offender from another Party to the 1961 Convention with which they do not have an extradition treaty.[172] Thus extradition on this basis remains discretionary, and in terms of the second sentence of the provision requested Parties are free to subject the extradition to the legal conditions they think fit. This provision, which follows the wording of article 8(2) of the 1970 Hague Convention for the Suppression of Unlawful Seizure of Aircraft, departed significantly from extradition practice in 1972. The British delegation to the CND's discussion of the proposed amendments commented:

> That provision had been included in the 1970 Convention to ensure that a hijacker of an aircraft would not escape being brought to justice by taking refuge in another country. The United Kingdom Government had agreed to that provision, making it clear that such an agreement represented a wholly exceptional departure from normal extradition practice. However alarming the problem of drug abuse might be, it could hardly be compared to the dangers to which the unlawful seizure of

---

171   In *Arnbjornsdottir-Mendler v United States* 721 F.2nd 679 (9th Cir.1983) a binding but old US-Denmark extradition treaty was updated by the fiction in the amended 1961 Convention to allow an extradition to take place to Iceland. The US delegation to the 1988 Conference noted that this fiction has been very useful in supplementing old bilateral extradition treaties that do not allow the extradition of drug offenders. They gave as an example the US-Costa Rica treaty which, although negotiated at the turn of the century, has been effectively updated because both states are party to the 1961 Convention and the 1972 Protocol to enable the extradition of more than 20 drug offenders between 1982 and 1988 – 'Report of the United States Delegation to the United Nations Conference for the adoption of a Convention Against Illicit Traffic in Narcotic Drugs and Psychotropic Substances' from *United Nations Convention Against Illicit Traffic in Narcotic Drugs and Psychotropic Substances* Senate Executive Report 101-15, 101st Congress, 1st Session, p.50 footnote 3.

172   In spite of its entirely optional nature, Cuba still declared that it only extradited on the basis of treaty (14/12/1989 – *Multilateral Treaties Deposited* (1997) at 295).

aircraft subjected innocent victims. It was necessary to make it clear that the United Kingdom would be most unlikely to take up the option ... if it were adopted by the plenipotentiary conference.[173]

One of the central themes of the development of international drug control law is patent in the British delegate's concerns – general acceptance of the ever greater inroads into state sovereignty demanded by the international drug control system is dependent on the perceived gravity of the threat that illicit drugs present. In 1985, it was suggested that given the threat from serious cases of drug trafficking states should either take up the option of using the amended 1961 Convention as an extradition treaty or enter into bilateral extradition treaties.[174] But back in 1972, there was little consensus that the threat was sufficiently serious to warrant exceptional international legal provisions to deal with it.

4.6.4 *Extradition of drug offences where an extradition treaty is not required*

Article 36(2)(b)(iii)[175] obliges Parties that do not require an extradition treaty to effect extradition to recognise drug offences as extraditable offences.[176] Again this is a very broad provision. In order to restrict it, it has been suggested that it does not oblige Parties that extradite on the basis of reciprocity to provide for the extradition of all article 36 offences.[177] It has been submitted that only a general possibility of extradition should be provided for 'sufficiently serious'

---

173 *1972 Records* vol. I at 47.
174 Supra note 27 at 6.
175 Based on article 8(3) of the 1970 Hague Hijacking Convention, and to a certain extent on article 9(2) of the 1936 Convention.
176 Linke et al supra note 27 at 7 note that this provision applies to all cases of extradition on a non-contractual basis. They note that although it is arguable that extradition in such situations is not subject to reciprocity because the 1961 Convention as amended does not mention reciprocity as a condition for extradition, it follows from general state practice and the conditions provided by the requested Party that it is always possible to invoke lack of reciprocity in order to refuse extradition. The unamended 1961 Convention in article 36(2)(b) mentions reciprocity, as does article 22(2)(b) of the 1971 Convention. They note, however, that reciprocity would exist in principle if both Parties to the extradition were Parties to the 1961 Convention as amended as both Parties would be under article 36's obligation to criminalise and recognise as extraditable serious drug offences.
177 Linke et al supra note 27 at 4.

drug offences punishable by imprisonment or other forms of deprivation of liberty in conformity with state practice which in principle reserves extradition for cases that really justify the measure. Parties are, however, left free by the 1961 Convention to declare less serious offences extraditable.[178] The words 'between themselves' make it clear that the provision only applies to Parties. Chatterjee notes that subparagraph (iii) of the new article 36(2)(b) ensures that 'both the recognition of an extraditable offence and extradition itself shall be subject to the conditions established by the law of the requested party.'[179] What is recognised here are the grounds for refusing extradition contained in a Party's substantive law.[180]

4.6.5   Limitations on extradition

The new sub-paragraph (b)(iv) of article 36 does two things: it subjects extradition to the law of the requested Party, and grants a right of refusal of extradition to the requested party if their competent authorities do not consider the offence 'sufficiently serious'. Subjecting extradition to the law of the requested Party envisages requirements of a procedural nature such as the production of documents and satisfaction of evidential tests such as the prima facie rule.[181] The right of refusal in respect of minor offences recognises the British and Canadian delegation's objections to the provisions for mandatory extradition when the CND met to discuss them before the 1972 Conference because they appeared to make extradition of personal use offenders mandatory.[182] The criteria by which the competent authorities are to determine the degree of seriousness of the offence are not spelled out and this remains an area of domestic discretion.[183] Gross and Greenwald argue, however, that the content of the qualification must on the basis of its negotiating history and extradition practice be considered finite, and note that it

> would not be possible for a Party to maintain in good faith that it was ... permitted
> [by this qualification] to refuse extradition of an individual otherwise liable to

---

178 Linke et al supra note 27 at 4.
179 Supra note 24 at 439.
180 Linke et al supra note 27 at 10.
181 Linke et al supra note 27 at 10.
182 *1972 Records* vol. I at 47. Canada still reserved in respect of article 36(2)(b)(i)-(iii) (5/8/1976 – *Multilateral Treaties Deposited* (1997) at 295).
183 See *1972 Records* vol. II at 27-28 where the possibility of setting out such criteria was raised then dismissed as impractical.

extradition who was charged with an offence that carried a penalty under its own laws of, for example, 10 or 20 years imprisonment.[184]

4.6.6   The 1972 Protocol's extradition provisions considered

In spite of the more extensive obligations in article 36(2)(b), many governments were uncertain whether the language in the Protocol provided sufficient authority to extradite.[185] The overlapping domestic safeguard clauses so emphasise the subjective control of the extradition process by the requested state that they enfeeble the new extradition provisions. Yet even these protections were not enough for some Parties who made reservations with regard to the new provision.[186] The scope of the provision is ambiguous. It relates to the drug offences in article 36(1) and article 36(2)(a)(ii) but does not distinguish between the extradition of serious offences and minor offences and does not mention at all the extradition of offences associated with drugs such as drug connected violent crimes.[187] Article 36(2)(b)'s provisions are also by no means inclusive of extradition in all states. Non-parties are excluded and article 36 does not make provision for states that are willing to be unilaterally bound by the principle of extradition, although not on a treaty basis, but with or without any condition of reciprocity.[188] An unfortunate consequence of the 1972 Protocol's elaboration of extradition was that narcotic drugs and psychotropic substances were no longer treated equally from the point of view of extradition. Although the Protocol's provisions did have some practical effect,[189] this point emphasises the piecemeal development of drug offence extradition. Largely the project of states such as the United States that preferred extradition to the extension of universal jurisdiction, it was resisted by the international community.

---

184 N.G. Gross and G.J. Greenwald, 'The 1972 Narcotics Protocol' (1973) 2 *Contemporary Drug Problems* 119 at 152.

185 Nadelmann supra note 75 at 413.

186 For example, India (14/12/1978 – *Multilateral Treaties Deposited* (1997) at 295).

187 Linke *et al* supra note 27 at 8 argue that provision should have been made for the extradition of offences such as property crimes used to obtain drugs, offences involving drug related violence and drug related fiscal offences.

188 Chatterjee supra note 24 at 446.

189 Nadelmann supra note 36 at 861 notes that omissions in existing bilateral extradition treaties were to some extent rectified by the provision in the 1972 Protocol allowing it to be the basis for extradition requests.

The 1961, 1971 and 1972 instruments can be seen as a slow and uneven progression towards an extension of universal jurisdiction and a facilitation of extradition, these two thrusts sometimes complementing, sometimes conflicting with each other. By 1972, it still could not be said that the drug conventions represented more than a very restrained attempt to put into place a system of universal jurisdiction for drug offences because at an international level drugs were still not regarded as a sufficiently serious threat to warrant such a response. While the enactment of specialist drug legislation generally resulted in the expansion of national jurisdiction for certain drug offences committed abroad,[190] the attempts of consumer states to encourage producer states to apply the aut dedere aut judicare principle to drug crimes soured.[191] Stronger efforts were made by consumer states in respect of extradition. But these developments were mainly bilateral as there was a distinct lack of enthusiasm for mulitalteralism. Nadelmann notes that while many governments were slow to ratify the 1972 Protocol and some were uncertain whether it provided adequate authority to extradite, by contrast the 'negotiation of new bilateral treaties required the time and resources of a very small number of officials with experience in extradition matters.'[192] The revision of antiquated bilateral extradition treaties was undertaken and new treaties were adopted[193] because al-

---

190 D. Cotic, *Drugs and Punishment* (UNSDRI, Rome, 1988), p. 114.

191 E.A. Nadelmann, 'The role of the United States in the international enforcement of criminal law' (1990) 31 *Harvard International Law Journal* 37 at 70 gives as an example, the creation by US officials in 1975 of Operation JANUS, a systematic effort by the US government, confronted by growing numbers of violations of US drug laws by Mexican drug traffickers, to help Mexican criminal justice officials to vicariously prosecute drug traffickers for violations of US drug laws. He notes that in the late 1970s, Operation JANUS was phased out, because it had largely failed.

192 E.A. Nadelmann, 'The evolution of United States involvement in the international rendition of fugitive criminals' (1993) 25 *New York University Journal of International Law and Politics* 813 at 831.

193 The US, for example, concluded six bilateral extradition treaties between 1960 and 1969, but sixteen between 1970 and 1978 – see K. Fisher, 'Trends in extraterritorial narcotics control: slamming the stable door after the horse has bolted' (1984) 16 *New York University Journal of International Law and Politics* 353 at 366-7. J.R. Barnett, 'Extradition treaty improvements to combat drug trafficking' (1985) 15 *Georgia Journal of International and Comparative Law* 285 at 285-315 reports that the US concluded a number of new bilateral extradition treaties in 1984 with states with which it already had such treaties, mainly because of the need to include drug offences among the extraditable offences and to improve the operation of extradition with these states through the following measures: providing that inchoate and preparatory offences constitute extraditable offences; making provision for the avoidance of the requested state's statute

though the existing multilateral drug conventions filled in some of the gaps in the older bilateral treaties, they proved too limited in scope to avoid the general need for new extradition treaties.[194] By the early 1980's, extradition requests for drug offences had grown enormously.[195] However, in spite of the rash of new treaties, extraditing drug traffickers remained problematic due to legal difficulties, the lack of political will in producer states and the machinations of the traffickers themselves.[196]

4.7   JURISDICTION AND EXTRADITION IN THE 1988 CONVENTION

4.7.1   Jurisdiction under the 1988 Convention

4.7.1.1   Introduction
Recognising the need for a more comprehensive approach to the establishment of jurisdiction over drug offences, the framers of the 1988 Convention attempted to provide for one. At the 1988 Conference certain delegations pushed for an extension of jurisdiction beyond the territorial because they felt that extradition was not an effective tool in the fight against the global illicit drug traffic.[197]

---

of limitations; making provision for more stringent measures with regard to the extradition of nationals if legally possible; and clarifying extradition procedures, documentation and evidence requirements.

194 Nadelmann supra note 75 at 411.

195 Barnett supra note 193 at 286 notes that in the 1960s the number of extradition requests involving the US seldom exceeded twenty per annum. By 1978, however, the number reached one hundred, and in 1984 the US expected more than four hundred, approximately one third of which would relate to drug offences.

196 See, for example, the history of the operation of the 1979 Extradition Treaty between the US and Colombia, discussed by J.P. Kelley, 'United States – Colombian extradition treaty: efforts to prosecute drug lords' (1990) 14 *Suffolk Transnational Law Journal* 162-182. Kelley notes that the Treaty became a key instrument in the US's bilateral drug law enforcement strategy, even providing for the extradition of Colombian nationals if the alleged offence is punishable in both states and its consummation occurs in the US. But the chaotic events in Colombia caused by the campaign waged against the judiciary by the cartels inhibited the success of the treaty, with the treaty being declared unconstitutional in 1986 and 1987 and then being renewed by Presidential decree in 1989.

197 See, for example, the statement by Sweden on behalf of the Nordic states, *United Nations Conference for the Adoption of a Convention against Illicit Traffic in Narcotic Drugs and Psychotropic Substances, Official Records, Volume II* (New York, 1991) UN Doc. E/CONF.82/16/Add.1, UN Publication Sales No. E.91.XI.1 (hereinafter *1988 Records*

However, because of divergence in opinion on the appropriate grounds for the establishment of jurisdiction, the 1988 Convention still follows the basic scheme of the earlier conventions by allowing for the obligatory assertion of territorial jurisdiction and then the optional extension of jurisdiction. Article 4, entitled 'Jurisdiction', is two-tiered. The basic difference between article 4(1) and article 4(2) is that the former directs the establishment of jurisdiction on the basis of territoriality but includes extraterritorial jurisdiction on the basis of nationality and other more unusual factors, while the latter contemplates the Party establishing jurisdiction because it finds the alleged offender, who may well have committed his offence elsewhere, within its extended territorial jurisdiction, and it refuses to extradite inter alia because of nationality.

The jurisdiction provisions in the 1988 Convention recognise the primacy of domestic law. Article 4(3) provides that the Convention 'does not exclude the exercise of any criminal jurisdiction established by a Party in accordance with its domestic law.' This means that in the situations where the Convention allows the extension of a Party's jurisdiction, such jurisdiction cannot exclude the exercise of domestic criminal jurisdiction which has been established by a Party according to its own law. As significant, however, is article 2(3) which provides that '[a] Party shall not undertake in the territory of another Party the exercise of jurisdiction and performance of functions which are exclusively reserved for the authorities of that other Party by its domestic law.' Thus when a Party exclusively reserves jurisdiction for its own authorities in its territory no other Party may exercise concurrent jurisdiction. Both provisions involve the reservation of jurisdiction by a Party when other Parties may potentially want to exercise jurisdiction. The *1988 Commentary* submits, however, that article 4(3) in particular should not be regarded as a carte blanche for any Party to establish any kind of extraterritorial jurisdiction and points out that such extension is a sensitive matter governed by the rules of customary international law.[198] It is, however, a glaring omission in the 1988 Convention that while it anticipates the possibility of concurrent jurisdiction, it does nothing to resolve conflicts of jurisdiction. As the United States delegation points out, 'it does not resolve the inherent question of which Party's assertion of jurisdiction is preferred when there is an overlap of competing jurisdictions'.[199]

---

vol. II), p. 118.

198 *1988 Commentary* at 116.

199 'Report of the US Delegation' supra note 171 at 34. The report explains that if X transports drugs from state A to state B, he commits an article 3(1) offence in state A (exporting) and in state B (importing). Both states must establish territorial jurisdiction,

4.7.1.2 Mandatory jurisdiction based upon territoriality and analogous grounds

Article 4(1)(a) obliges Parties to take measures to establish jurisdiction over article 3(1) drug offences committed within their territory and on board vessels flying their flag or aircraft registered under their law. It thus obliges Parties to establish territoriality and a standard form of quasi-territoriality over their ships and planes. The introductory wording of the provision obliges Parties to establish their jurisdiction, not to exercise it once it is established, an obligation reserved to article 6 on extradition and prosecution.[200] The offender need not actually be located on the Party's territory or flag vessel or registered aircraft when it establishes its jurisdiction; the offender's location is only a question of whether the Party is able to exercise that jurisdiction. Establishment of jurisdiction does not mean that the Party concerned may choose not to exercise jurisdiction if, for instance, it feels that it would be more appropriate to extradite the accused to a state where the bulk of his offending conduct allegedly occurred.[201] The provision gives no guidance about which elements of an offence must have occurred within a Party's territory, aircraft or vessel before an offence can said to have been 'committed' there.[202] That is an issue of domestic criminal law. The provision also makes no reference to the nationality of the offender; all offenders who commit article 3(1) offences within the territory, in its legally extended sense, of a Party, fall within its jurisdiction.

In order to establish the nationality of vessels and thus make the establishment of jurisdiction by the Party over its own vessels uncontroversial, article 4(1)(a)(ii) uses the expression 'flying its flag' in preference to 'registered'. Registration is an unreliable means of establishing the nationality of a vessel and an unreliable basis for the establishment of jurisdiction because in practice the flag that a vessel is flying may not reveal its correct registration. A vessel flying one state's flag may well be registered in another state as many states allow vessels registered with them to fly the flags of other states. The 1982 United Nations Convention on the Law of the Sea[203] provides in article 91(1)

---

and the article does not give primacy to either one or the other's right to prosecute. The *1988 Commentary* at 101 points out that customary international law also provides no solution but notes that the prohibition on double jeopardy may prevent concurrent exercise of jurisdiction in certain circumstances.

200 See generally the discussion in Committee I of the Conference where the 'exercise' of jurisdiction was deleted from the draft provision – *1988 Records* vol. II at 120-121.
201 *1988 Commentary* at 102.
202 *1988 Commentary* at 102.
203 21 ILM 261.

that the nationality of a vessel is that of a state whose flag it is entitled to fly. For the purposes of article 4(1)(a)(ii), however, a vessel is considered to belong to the state whose flag it flies and if that state is a Party to the Convention it is obliged to take jurisdiction over that vessel.[204] The flag being flown is the relevant criterion in the matter of jurisdiction because it allows the assumption, based on visual identification, of a genuine connection between the state and vessel.[205] The vessel must fly the flag of the Party establishing its jurisdiction at the time of the commission of the offence. If not, the Party will not have jurisdiction.

The same principle applies to a Party establishing jurisdiction over an aircraft. The aircraft must be registered with the Party at the time of the offence, something that may be difficult to establish given the modern practice of the exchange of aircraft between airlines. Multiple registration of aircraft may give problems but implies concurrent jurisdiction in this context.[206]

Article 4(1)(a) reflects long-established state practice and thus should not require significant alteration of Parties' domestic law.[207] The *1988 Comment-*

---

204 A suggestion at the 1988 Conference by the Jamaican delegate to the effect that article 4(1)(a)(ii) read a vessel 'entitled to fly its flag' was rejected, *1988 Records* vol. II at 119.

205 See the statement of the German Democratic Republic's delegate, *1988 Records* vol. II at 119. The grant of a flag of convenience is in international law not an administrative formality and does not mean that the state granting such flag is not obliged to guarantee that it possesses a genuine link with the vessel concerned – 'Report of the ILC on its Eighth Session' (1956) II *Yearbook of the ILC* at 279 cited in H. Nordquist (ed.), *UN Convention on the Law of the Sea: A Commentary,* vol. III, p. 107. Vessels that fly the flags of states that they are not entitled to fly are considered stateless in terms of article 92(2) of 1982 United Nations Law of the Sea Convention. However, for the purposes of the establishment of jurisdiction in terms of the 1988 Convention vessels 'flying the flag' include those entitled to fly the flag and those not so entitled but which in fact are doing so. Parties to the Convention are in terms of article 4(1)(a)(ii) obliged to establish jurisdiction over such vessels. This leaves vessels not flying any flag in a curious position in that they are not covered by either article 4(1)(a)(ii)'s mandatory provision or article 4(1)(b)(ii)'s optional provision for the establishment of jurisdiction. The establishment of jurisdiction over such vessels is, however, contemplated by the 1988 Convention because article 17(2) allows Parties interdicting such vessels to request assistance for that purpose. It is not, however, obligatory.

206 The *1988 Commentary* at 103 refers to the practice of multi-state airlines and the International Civil Aviation Organisation's controversial decision (doc. 8743-C/978 at 26) to allow the establishment of joint or international registration.

207 See Gilmore supra note 44 at 10. For an example of the extension of jurisdiction to aircraft and ships see the Australian Crimes (Traffic in Narcotic Drugs and Psychotropic Substances) Act 1990. It provides in section 10 that dealing in drugs on board an

ary does, however, note that Parties are not constrained by international law to limit themselves to subjective territoriality and may also legislate for objective territoriality which it believes particularly appropriate to article 3(1)(c)(iv)'s inchoate offences.[208] It also suggests that Parties should consider whether their laws adequately provide for the establishment of jurisdiction in their territorial sea.[209] Article 4(1)(a)'s weakness is that it gives no guidance on competing claims to jurisdiction, particularly in the case of offences that occur within another Party's territorial sea or airspace.

4.7.1.3   Optional jurisdiction based upon nationality/habitual residence, authorisation over foreign vessels or the effects principle

Article 4(1)(b) provides for three separate[210] permissive grounds for the establishment of jurisdiction. The first of these is 'active personality'. Despite attempts during the drafting process to make article 4(1)(b)(i) mandatory,[211] the 1988 Convention does not oblige Parties to establish jurisdiction over extraterritorial article 3(1) drug offences committed by their nationals or habitual residents.[212] Allowing it to remain optional has been criticised,[213] but the fact that it has been left optional does not mean that there is consensus that drug trafficking offences differ from offences where international law renders

---

Australian aircraft 'in flight' is an offence and defines 'in flight' in section 7. It provides in section 11 that dealing in drugs on board an Australian ship 'at sea' is an offence and then defines 'at sea' in section 8. Both the definitions of Australian planes in flight and of ships at sea extend beyond situations where the vehicle is still within a very broadly defined physical Australian territory, and are intended to extend jurisdiction over offences committed on these modes of transport outside Australian territory stricto sensu. See also W.C. Gilmore, 'Drug trafficking by sea: the 1988 United Nations Convention against illicit traffic in narcotic drugs and psychotropic substances' (1991) 15 *Marine Policy* 181 at 191.

208 *1988 Commentary* at 104. It does not explain how inchoate offences can have objective effects.

209 *1988 Commentary* at 104-105. It cites as an example article 113-2 of the French Penal Code and refers to article 6(b) of the 1988 Convention for the Suppression of Unlawful Act against the Safety of Maritime Navigation, (1988) 207 ILM 676.

210 The *1988 Commentary* at 106 notes that the view that they are cumulative is not supported by the *travaux preparatoires* as each ground was developed in isolation.

211 See, for instance, the Nordic and Israeli amendments to draft article 2bis, *1988 Records* vol. I at 108-109.

212 See Gilmore supra note 44 at 10.

213 See D.W. Sproule and P. St-Denis, 'The UN Drug Trafficking Convention: An Ambitious Step' [1989] CYBIL 263 at 275.

the assertion of jurisdiction on the nationality principle obligatory.[214] Rather there is no consensus that the relationship of an offender and the country to which he belongs or in which he has habitual residence provides a justifiable basis for jurisdiction. While assertion of jurisdiction on the basis of the active personality principle may be acceptable to many civil law states,[215] common law states are firmly wedded to the territorial principle and the Conference recognised that they find it difficult to establish extraterritorial jurisdiction over, for example, their own nationals. These states were apprehensive about the difficulties involved in securing convictions for extraterritorial offences committed in a country whose procedure and rules of evidence were completely different from their own and they feared that acquittals would produce double-jeopardy bars to further prosecution. They preferred to rely on extradition to transfer the offender to the territorially competent state.[216] But the common law states had more than practical objections to a mandatory provision for active personality jurisdiction. Their opposition was largely a response to the adamant refusal of civil law states to accept any provisions requiring the extradition of nationals.[217] Nonetheless, some common law states have decided to take the option.[218]

---

214 See, for example, article 6(1)(c) of the 1988 Convention for the Suppression of Unlawful Acts Against the Safety of Maritime Navigation, 27 ILM 668 at 676.

215 See, for example, article 689 of the French Code of Criminal Procedure.

216 See *1988 Records* vol. II at 121-122.

217 Sproule and St-Denis supra note 213 at 275.

218 See, for example, the Australian Crimes (Traffic in Narcotic Drugs and Psychotropic Substances) Act, 1990. The Explanatory Memorandum for the 1989 Bill which preceded the Act explains that the Bill was drafted so as to apply to Australian nationals apprehended in Australia who committed drug offences outside Australia that would be offences in Australia. Section 12 of the Act, entitled 'Dealing in drugs outside Australia', reads: '12 (1). A person is guilty of an offence against this section if: (a) the person engages, outside Australia, in conduct that is dealing in drugs; and (b) the conduct constitutes an offence against the law of a foreign country; and (c) the conduct would constitute an offence against a law in force in a State or Territory if it were engaged in by the person in that State or Territory. (2) A person may be charged with an offence against this section only if: (a) the person is present in Australia; and (b) if the person is not an Australian citizen: (i) no steps have been taken by the foreign country referred to in paragraph (1)(b) for the surrender of the person to that country; or (ii) proceedings taken by that country under the *Extradition Act 1988* have not resulted in the person being surrendered to that country.' Australia thus extends extraterritorial jurisdiction over nationals without the necessity of an extradition request and refusal, i.e. on the basis of nationality, but in respect of non-nationals on the basis of subsidiary universality.

'Nationality' is undefined in the Convention. Cases of dual or multiple nationality raise the possibility of multiple legitimate jurisdictional claims. 'Habitual residence' of the offender has been included in article 4(1)(b)(i) as an optional ground for the establishment of jurisdiction even though it is not as well established in international or domestic practice. It too is undefined.[219] While some Parties treat habitual residents in the same way as nationals for extradition purposes, others treat them as aliens, and some do not know how to treat them, as they do not recognise the concept. Sproule and St-Denis comment that different interpretations of habitual residence might lead to disputes between Parties.[220] In spite of these ambiguities some Parties have applied this option,[221] but others have reacted more cautiously. Although the provision is optional, the Philippines has declared that it does not consider itself bound by it.[222]

Article 4(1)(b)(ii) permits the establishment of jurisdiction within the framework of the law enforcement scheme provided for in article 17. Article 17 provides for the consensual interdiction of a foreign flag vessel exercising freedom of navigation on the high seas. Article 4(1)(b)(ii) provides that jurisdiction may be established only if it exercised on the basis of the agreements or arrangements referred to in article 17 paragraphs 4 and 9. These agreements permit a Party that has received prior authorisation to board and search such a vessel and to take suitable action upon the discovery of evidence of illicit trafficking. Article 4(1)(b)(ii) takes this process to its logical conclusion by allowing the interdicting Party to establish jurisdiction when a drug offence has occurred on the vessel without the necessity of having to establish a jurisdictional nexus between its territory and the offence.[223] Although resort to article 17(4) to interdict a vessel is futile if a Party chooses not to take the option to extend its jurisdiction in terms of article 4(1)(b)(ii) as no criminal charge will

---

219 The *1988 Commentary* at 106 cites a resolution of the Committee of Ministers of the Council of Europe (72(1) annex) which suggests that in determining habitual residence account should be taken of duration and continuity of residence and other factors of a personal or professional nature that point to a durable link between person and residence.

220 Supra note 213 at 276. The Moroccan delegation expressed a reservation with respect to this provision – *1988 Records* vol. II at 31.

221 See, for example, section 5(1) of Thailand's 1991 Act on Measures for the Suppression of Offenders in an Offence Relating to Narcotics cited by the *1988 Commentary* at 109.

222 7/6/1996 – *Multilateral Treaties Deposited* (1997) at 305.

223 'Report of the US Delegation' supra note 171 at 37.

eventuate,[224] relatively few Parties have enacted legislation to establish such jurisdiction.[225] Article 4(1)(b)(ii) says nothing about the vessels belonging to non-parties although establishment of jurisdiction over their vessels is legally possible with their consent.[226] Another lacuna in article 4(1)(b)(ii) is that it says nothing about establishing jurisdiction over stateless vessels even though article 17(2) provides for the interdiction of such vessels.[227] Article 4(1)(b)(ii) supplements earlier provisions for coastal state maritime jurisdiction. The 1958 Convention on the Law of the Territorial Sea and the Contiguous Zone[228] provides in article 19(d) for the criminal jurisdiction of the coastal state over a foreign ship passing through its territorial waters if it is necessary for the suppression of the illicit traffic in narcotic drugs. Article 27 of the 1982 United Nations Convention on the Law of the Sea[229] reproduces this provision but with the addition of 'psychotropic substances' to 'narcotic drugs'. The non-derogation clause in article 17(11) means that coastal state jurisdiction remains governed by these provisions of the international law of the sea.

Article 4(1)(b)(iii) is an attempt to prevent the importation of illicit drugs by giving Parties the option of establishing jurisdiction using the effects or objective territoriality principle over conspiracies occurring outside their territory. Article 4(1)(b)(iii)'s operation is dependent upon the criminalisation in article 3(1)(c)(iv) of certain forms of inchoate conduct and complicity, although the latter obligation is subject to domestic limitation. Such offences, treated as principal offences in their own right, would usually fall under the jurisdiction

---

224 The *1988 Commentary* at 109-110. W.C. Gilmore, 'Narcotics interdiction at sea: the 1995 Council of Europe Agreement' (1996) 20 *Marine Policy* 3 at 6 notes that the 1995 Council of Europe Agreement, Implementing Article 17 of the UN Convention Against Illicit Traffic in Narcotic Drugs and Psychotropic Substances, ETS 156, has, by obliging Parties to apply jurisdiction over offences on the vessels of other Parties in article 3(3), significantly improved on article 4(1)(b)(ii) of the 1988 Convention.

225 The *1988 Commentary* at 110. It gives as an example the UK's Criminal Justice (International Co-operation) Act, 1990, c.5, sections 18-21 and schedule 3.

226 This is the position adopted by the US in its Maritime Law Enforcement Act, 46 USC 1903.

227 The *1988 Commentary* at 110 discusses recent developments in this area, noting that it is regarded as a matter requiring attention by recommendation 13 of the Working Group on Maritime Co-operation, endorsed by CND Resolution 8(XXXVIII) Official Records of ECOSOC, 1995, Supp. no.9, E/1995/25, chp.XII, sec.A. Article 3(3) of the 1995 Council of Europe Agreement obliges Parties to establish such jurisdiction over stateless vessels.

228 15 UST 1607.

229 21 ILM 261.

of the Party in whose territory they were committed. However, article 4(1)(b)(iii) allows the optional extension of a Party's jurisdiction over these offences committed outside its territory when they are committed with a view to committing an article 3(1) offence within its territory. Thus the provision allows Parties to establish extraterritorial jurisdiction over offences of complicit participation and inchoate conduct that occur outside a party's territory when they are committed with the intent of committing principal offences inside its territory. An extraterritorial conspiracy to import drugs whether or not they actually arrive within a Party's territory would be an example. As noted in the introduction to this chapter, the extension of the effects principle from actual to intended effects is logically difficult,[230] but this is what article 4(1)(b)(iii) has done. When it is unclear in which state the inchoate offence will be completed or the principal offence will occur then no Party may establish jurisdiction as the offence must be 'with a view to' commission of an offence in a particular party's territory.[231] Despite the fact that the provision is a legal innovation requiring alteration of a Party's domestic law,[232] Parties have responded positively.[233]

---

230 See Blakesly supra note 7 at 1145.

231 *1988 Commentary* at 107-108.

232 Gilmore supra note 44 at 12 notes that judiciaries in common law jurisdictions have been adopting a creative approach to jurisdiction to allow a greater reach to the criminal law over drug trafficking. A classic example is the 1990 case of *Somchai Liangsiriprasert v United States Government* [1990] 2 All ER 866 where the Privy Council, in an appeal from Hong Kong, directed its attention to conspiracies carried out entirely abroad. Lord Griffiths, speaking for a unanimous Board stated: 'Unfortunately in this century crime has ceased to be largely of local origin and effect. Crime is now established on an international scale and the common law must face this new reality. Their Lordships can find nothing in precedent, comity or good sense that should inhibit the common law from regarding as justiciable in England inchoate crimes committed abroad which are intended to result in the commission of criminal offences in England. Accordingly, a conspiracy entered into in Thailand with the intention of committing the criminal offence of trafficking in drugs in Hong Kong is justiciable in Hong Kong even if no overt act pursuant to the conspiracy has yet occurred in Hong Kong [at 878].' This position was adopted by the UK's Court of Appeal in *R v Sansom and Others* [1991] 2 All ER 145.

233 See, for example, sections 13 and 14 of the Australian Crimes (Traffic in Narcotic Drugs and Psychotropic Substances) Act, 1990. Section 13, entitled 'Dealing in drugs outside Australia with a view to commission of an offence in Australia' provides: '13. A person is guilty of an offence against this section if the person engages, outside Australia, in conduct that is dealing in drugs with a view to the carrying out: (a) in Australia; or (b) on board an Australian aircraft in flight outside Australia; or (c) on board an Australian ship at sea; of a dealing in drugs that constitutes an offence against a law of the Com-

The provisions of article 4(1)(b) allowing for the optional establishment of jurisdiction all have particular difficulties that may discourage Parties from applying them. They are also potentially problematic in other more general ways. International co-operation is endangered when for instance an extradition request is made and it cannot be shown that one of the Parties establishes prescriptive jurisdiction over the particular offence.[234] Moreover, they potentially overlap. Thus, for example, if Party X's national engages in a conspiracy to import an illicit drug into Party Y and is apprehended before completion of the conspiracy on the high seas on board a vessel flying the flag of Party Z, all three Parties, if they have taken the relevant option, will be able to exercise jurisdiction. Article 4(1)(b) does not rank such claims, a recipe for legal confusion and inaction.

4.7.1.4   Mandatory jurisdiction over alleged offenders found within a Party's territory when extradition is refused because of territoriality or nationality

Article 4(2)(a) obliges a Party to establish jurisdiction over a person who has allegedly committed an article 3(1) offence and who it finds within its territory, if it refuses an extradition request or would have done so had one been made. Article 4(2)(a) thus provides the jurisdictional basis for the obligation to prosecute or extradite in article 6(9), with which it must be read. However, unlike other international conventions[235] which provide for the subsidiary form of universal jurisdiction any time that extradition is refused, article 4(2)(a) limits the application of the aut dedere aut judicare principle and thus the establishment of jurisdiction to situations when the Party refuses to extradite because the offence has occurred on its territory, or on board a ship flying its flag, or on an aircraft registered under its law, or because the offender is one of its nationals. Should the Party's refusal to extradite be based on some other

---

monwealth, of a State or of a Territory.' Section 14, entitled 'Conspiracy etc. outside Australia to commit an offence inside Australia' criminalises the conduct of: '14. A person who, by conduct engaged in outside Australia: conspires, or attempts to carry out in a State or Territory; or (b) aids, abets, counsels or procures, or is in any way directly or indirectly knowingly concerned in, or party to, the carrying out in a State or territory of; a dealing in drugs.'

234   *1988 Commentary* at 109. As pointed out above, the principle of double criminality requires that the elements that provide jurisdictional basis for the prosecution of the offence must be recognised in both states.

235   Gilmore supra note 44 at 13 notes that the 1988 Convention adopted a less ambitious scheme than those adopted for hijacking and terrorism.

reason it will not be under an obligation to establish jurisdiction and may well decline from doing so in spite of the optional provision in article 4(2)(b). Refusal on the basis of territoriality is common and it is notorious that civil law states do not extradite their nationals because of constitutional impediments[236] but generally establish extraterritorial jurisdiction over their nationals. Yet in spite of pressure from, for instance, the Nordic delegations,[237] delegates to the 1988 Conference from common law states were not prepared to assume an unqualified obligation to classify drug trafficking offences as falling under subsidiary universal jurisdiction.[238] The British delegate to Committee I of the Conference explained:

> Extradition ... had its part to play [in bringing drug traffickers to justice]. No country wished to become a safe haven for drug traffickers, but every country with the ability in its law to extradite persons had established certain rules and conditions for extradition. For instance, extradition was commonly barred where there was a previous acquittal or conviction, precisely because there could be no prosecution. In such cases there was no point in taking up the time of the prosecuting authorities to consider prosecution. The same applied when the reason for refusal to extradite was that there was no evidence. A blanket obligation to prosecute when there was no extradition would therefore be meaningless. The grounds for refusal had to be examined because they would demonstrate the prospects of pursuing the offender within a given system. The United Kingdom favoured extradition as a means of bringing criminals to justice. Its own criminal jurisdiction was founded on the offence being committed within its territory. She believed that the state where the crime was committed was by far the best place for a person to face trial, and the United Kingdom always favoured extradition in those cases and had no problem whatsoever about extraditing its own nationals for that purpose. It therefore had no need to assume universal jurisdiction although it had done so in special cases of terrorism and hijacking. The United Kingdom did not, however, desire universal jurisdiction for drug trafficking, not because the offence was any less serious, but because the nature of the caseload and of the individual cases was so different. It was through extradition and mutual legal assistance under the proposed convention that her country could improve its international contribution to combating drug trafficking offences. Requesting states would not thank the United Kingdom for failure to obtain a conviction in cases where it had not been able to extradite, if the result was that any state which later had an opportunity to prosecute was barred from doing so by the double jeopardy rule triggered by an acquittal in the United

---

236 See, for example, article 16(2) of the German Basic Law.
237 See *1988 Records* vol. II 136.
238 See *1988 Records* vol. II at 136-140.

Kingdom. Those states which, as a matter of principle, did not extradite their own nationals invariably had jurisdiction on the basis of nationality. It was therefore logical for them to submit the case to their competent authorities for the purposes of prosecution. Those states could then deal with the evidential and procedural problems in the way provided by their own legal system, which presumably allowed extraterritorial prosecution of that kind. In the view of her delegation a universally applicable system of prosecution and jurisdiction could not be achieved through the Convention. The constitutional safeguards in the proposal of the Nordic countries ... did not help, because the issue at stake was not constitutional or legal principles but long-established criminal policy, which was unlikely to be modified and was not an obstacle to improved international co-operation in bringing drug traffickers to trial and securing their conviction.[239]

What this long extract makes clear is that mandatory subsidiary universal jurisdiction over drug offences is rejected by common law states not because drug offences are less serious than offences to which such mandatory subsidiary universality applies, but because the legal bars to extradition in common law states also operate to bar prosecution for extraterritorial offences in the same circumstances and because the nature of the case load and of individual drug offences was so different from offences where mandatory subsidiary universality was applied.[240] The former reason rings a little hollow given the general relaxation of extradition formalities in common law states. The latter is more convincing. The central argument of supporters for the extradition of drug offenders in preference to the establishment of extraterritorial jurisdiction is that trial in the place where the offence is committed best addresses the objective of bringing drug traffickers to justice because it is the place where the greatest harm flows from the criminal acts in question and the place where the best case can be made. The United States delegation concludes that 'a realistic appraisal of the feasibility of prosecution in a state which has not gathered the evidence in a form and procedure admissible in its courts mitigates against successful prosecution in virtually every instance.'[241] The approach of common law states – territoriality coupled with universal extradition – does, however,

---

239 *1988 Records* vol. II at 137.

240 Echoing the UK's position, the US delegation also opposed such mandatory universal jurisdiction, noting that 'the nature of its domestic legal system prevented [it] from doing so in the present instance', and that the number of cases brought to trial under international conventions that did provide for such jurisdiction 'was infinitesimally small in comparison with the number of cases brought in respect of [drug] offences', *1988 Records* vol. II at 138.

241 'Report of the US Delegation' supra note 171 at 35-36.

face legal and practical hurdles of its own. Its biggest problem is one of perception; producer states perceive that consumer states simply want to use the international drug control system to get their hands on foreign drug traffickers. Given the history of international drug control and the obvious political concerns of states like the United States with drug supply reduction, there is a great deal of substance to this perception. But the case-load argument does indicate that drug crime is not of the same practical dimensions as the crimes already subject to universal jurisdiction. It is so common that effective mandatory universal jurisdiction over it would imply a massive burden on Parties and the necessity for the restructuring and accommodation of all national criminal justice systems into a coherent international unit. As the United States delegate put it: 'If all countries had the same legal system, then cases could be transferred from one country to another with the same facility as was currently enjoyed by drug traffickers in their movements.'[242] International society was not in that position in 1988. It did not have the general political will to pursue drug supply reduction as zealously as the major drug consumer states.

Article 4(2)(a)(i)'s obligation on Parties to take jurisdiction on the basis of the presence of the alleged offender on their territory when they have refused extradition because the offence was committed on their territory, or on a vessel flying its flag, or on an aircraft registered under its law, assumes that they will have established jurisdiction under article 4(1)(a)'s obligation to establish jurisdiction on the basis of this extended territoriality. Article 4(2)(a)(i) is saved from redundancy if one accepts the explanation by the Netherlands's delegation to Committee I that it is different from article 4(1)(a) because while the former provides for grounds for establishing jurisdiction, the latter deals with grounds for refusal of extradition and thus with the exercise of jurisdiction already established.[243]

---

242 *1988 Records* vol. II at 138-139.
243 *1988 Records* vol. II at 142. J.J.E. Schutte, 'Extradition for drug offences: new developments under the 1988 UN Convention Against Illicit Traffic in Narcotic Drugs and Psychotropic Substances' (1991) 62 *Revue Internationale de Droit Penal* 135 at 144 makes the same argument. He notes that while the 1988 Convention deals to a certain extent with the exercise of jurisdiction, it leaves it largely to domestic law as evidenced by provisions like article 3(11). He argues that the exception is article 6(9) where the exercise of jurisdiction in cases where extradition is refused 'is addressed by way of an obligation under international law.' Article 4(2) repeats article 4(1)'s reference to the establishment of territoriality and the flag because 'the exercise of such jurisdiction becomes an obligation under international law only in cases where a request for extradition from another Party ... has been refused.'

Article 4(2)(a)(ii) is, however, an advance over article 4(1)(b)(i) because it obliges Parties to establish jurisdiction over their nationals when they refuse to extradite them because these persons are their nationals, while article 4(1)(b)(i) only makes the establishment of jurisdiction over nationals optional. Thus the potential loophole left when a Party unwilling to extradite its nationals has not established its jurisdiction over extraterritorial offences committed by its nationals is closed by this obligation. It has been argued that article 4(2)(a)(ii) also obliges Parties that have established jurisdiction over all the crimes of their nationals, to actually exercise that jurisdiction.[244] The Philippines, apparently in reaction to the ambiguous boundaries of this obligation, has declared that it does not consider itself bound by article 4(2)(a)(ii).[245] It is interesting to note that no provision is made for the obligatory establishment of jurisdiction on refusal of extradition of a habitual resident.

4.7.1.5   Optional jurisdiction over alleged offenders found within a Party's territory where extradition is refused for reasons other than territoriality or nationality

Article 4(2)(b) provides for the optional establishment of jurisdiction by a Party which finds an alleged article 3(1) offender on its territory and then chooses to refuse an extradition request for reasons other than those enumerated in article 4(2)(a). They could, for instance, include the fact that the alleged offender is facing the death penalty or a penalty more severe in the requesting Party than in the requested Party.[246] Other reasons may be that the requested Party fears that once extradited the alleged offender will not in fact be prosecuted or perhaps will not be punished severely enough. Article 4(2)(b) provides for an optional ground for establishing jurisdiction not provided for in the other optional grounds for establishing jurisdiction in article 4. When a Party chooses to establish jurisdiction on this basis, article 6(9) requires that it submit the case to its competent authorities for prosecution unless requested not to do so by the Party making the extradition request in order for the latter to preserve its 'legitimate jurisdiction'.

The provision is optional largely because common law delegations to the 1988 Conference would not accept anything closer to an obligation to establish subsidiary universality over drug offences other than the narrowly circumscribed provision in article 4(2)(a). Article 4(2)(b) exists because certain mainly civil

---

244 Schutte supra note 243 at 145.
245 7/6/1996 – *Multilateral Treaties Deposited* (1997) at 305.
246 Factors contained in the original draft article 2bis or suggested as amendments thereto.

law delegations, in the words of the Chairman of Committee I, 'wishing to expand the scope of the principle aut dedere aut judicare, preferred that no specific relevant grounds for refusal of extradition be singled out as calling for application of that principle.'[247] It is interesting to note that progressive common law jurisdictions such as Australia have made provision for the un-restricted establishment of extraterritorial jurisdiction over non-nationals on the basis of the aut dedere aut judicare principle.[248]

4.7.1.6   The 1988 Convention's jurisdictional provisions in conclusion
The 1988 Convention's provisions on jurisdiction do not represent a massive departure from existing practice. They are an improvement over the jurisdictional provisions in the earlier conventions if only because they clarify jurisdiction over drug offences. They emphasise territoriality and extend it on either an optional or very limited basis. Their most obvious inadequacy is that they make no provision for ranking competing claims to jurisdiction, and customary international law provides no adequate solution either.[249] Article 4(1), for example, generally allows the establishment of jurisdiction by more than one Party at a time over the same offence. Potential jurisdictional conflicts abound. These provisions also fail to resolve the conflicting approaches of civil and common law states to reliance on subsidiary universality for the prosecution of drug offences committed in other states. Although the 1988 Convention does not oblige Parties to establish jurisdiction over nationals or to extradite them, in order for the system to be effective against drug traffickers civil law states have to establish jurisdiction while common law states have to extradite them. Finally, with respect to protections of individuals, the jurisdictional provisions of the 1988 Convention compare poorly to the earlier conventions' provisions. For example, while article 36(2)(a)(iv) of the 1961 Convention subjects jurisdiction based on subsidiary universality to the absence of double jeopardy, article

---

247 *1988 Records* vol. II at 140.
248 See section 12(2) of the Australian Crimes (Traffic in Narcotic Drugs and Psychotropic Substances) Act, 1990, which provides that Australia will establish jurisdiction over extraterritorial dealing in drugs in the case of non-nationals if '(i) no steps have been taken by the foreign country referred to in paragraph 1(b) for the surrender of the person to that country; or (ii) proceedings taken by that country under the *Extradition Act 1988* have not resulted in the person being surrendered to that country.' Thus it does not stipulate that the refusal to extradite must be based on the territoriality of the offence and it does not apply to nationals who are covered by another provision.
249 Gilmore supra note 44 at 12.

4(2) does not.[250] Extension of the domestic criminal reach of states through international law should have been linked to express provisions for the protection of individual human rights.

4.7.2   Extradition under the 1988 Convention

4.7.2.1   Extradition under the 1988 Convention generally

Although the 1988 Convention's extradition provisions were developed in response to the growth in drug trafficking, in order to encourage state adherence to the 1988 Convention they are not a major advance on the limited provisions of the 1961 and 1971 Conventions.[251] Article 6, entitled 'Extradition', reflects a desire to protect established principles in the field of extradition rather than a response to the perceived necessity of arriving at bold solutions to the problems of prosecuting drug traffickers.[252] The bold solutions that were suggested at the 1988 Conference failed to clear the hurdles of sovereignty, the protection of nationals and the retention of discretion with regard to requests from politically suspect states.[253] Following precedents established in anti-terrorism conventions,[254] article 6 does not try to establish an extradition treaty that creates obligations to extradite but rather, like the earlier drug conventions, tries to make extradition possible using existing domestic legislation and existing or future bilateral and multilateral extradition treaties.

Article 6(5), which subjects extradition 'to the conditions provided for by the law of the requested Party or by applicable extradition treaties, including the grounds upon which the requested Party may refuse extradition', reflects this cautious approach to extradition.[255] There is, for example, no specific

---

250 Puttler supra note 8 at 114 points out in the context of her example about German prosecution of Dutch drug traffickers that this means that the German court would not have to take into account any previous trial in the Netherlands or failing that any maximum sentence awarded under Dutch law.

251 See the 'Expert Group Report', *1988 Records* vol. I at 19.

252 Sproule and St-Denis supra note 213 at 277-278.

253 'Report of the US Delegation' supra note 171 at 48.

254 For example, article 8 of the 1970 Hague Convention for the Suppression of Unlawful Seizure of Aircraft, 860 UNTS 105.

255 Draft article 4(5) made it clear that a requested Party would not be able to refuse extradition on the basis that a) the offender was its national, or b) if the offence was committed outside the territory of the requested Party but was intended to have or had effects within its territory, or c) if the offence was political in character. After pressure from states whose constitutions or domestic law precluded the extradition of nationals, states that rejected the effects principle and states that wanted to retain the political

exclusion of nationality as a ground for refusing extradition. It has been submitted, however, that on the principle of pacta sunt servanda article 6(5) should
not be seen as a way of invoking grounds of refusal which may have been
recognised in a Party's domestic law but which have not been recognised by
the applicable extradition treaty.[256] In cases of extradition requests by Parties
that still apply the death penalty, however, caution may be justified.[257] Moreover, article 6(5)'s breadth allows Parties to subject extradition requests to the
general principles of extradition such as those of double criminality and
speciality, which ensures respect for these procedural due process provisions
and may perhaps halt their erosion in state practice.[258] It has been submitted
that article 6(5) may also allow Parties to refuse extradition when an offence
is not particularly serious.[259] The justification for this interpretation is that
the domestic law of Parties recognises that there should be a certain measure
of proportionality between the seriousness of the offence and whether it should
be extraditable, and while proportionality was not that important with regard
to offences such as hijacking, it may be different for drug offences. This ground
of refusal was expressly recognised in the earlier drug conventions.[260] Article
6(5)'s waiving of international control over the domestic grounds for a refusal
to extradite is limited to the extent that article 3(10) regulates the political and
fiscal exceptions to extradition. Article 6(5) must be overridden by article 3(10)
unless its conditions for refusal are part of the constitution or fundamental laws
of the requested Party.

---

offence exception, these restrictions were dropped – see the 'Expert Group Report',
1988 Records vol. I at 19, 36-37.

256 Schutte supra note 243 at 139.

257 Sproule and St-Denis supra note 213 at 279 footnote 58.

258 Double criminality has been eroded by the prosecution of drug offenders in the US using
the Continuing Criminal Enterprise Statute (CCE), 21 USC section 848(b), a unique
offence made up of five separate elements. Kelley supra note 196 at 177-179 notes that
Colombian drug traffickers extradited to the US under this statute claim that it violates
double criminality because it is uniquely American, but the US courts have decided
that such prosecutions do not violate the principle because they were within the con-
templation of the Parties to the treaty, justifying this conclusion because of the importance of CCE prosecutions to the drug war (*US v Lehder-Rivas* 688 F.Supp 1523, 1527-
1528 (MD Fla 1987).

259 Schutte supra note 243 at 139-140.

260 Schutte supra note 243 at 139.

4.7.2.2   Limitation of the political and fiscal offence exception

It is appropriate to discuss article 3(10), the 1988 Convention's limitation of the political and fiscal offence exceptions in this context because although it is a general provision directed at other forms of interstate co-operation and for that reason was left in article 3, it is usually associated with extradition.[261] Article 3(10) provides that for the purposes of co-operation in terms of the Convention and particularly in terms of articles 5, 6, 7 and 9, article 3 offences shall not be considered as fiscal or political offences or regarded as politically motivated. However, this is without prejudice to the Parties' constitutional limitations and fundamental domestic law. Article 3(10) is an attempt to limit, although not to extinguish, the application of the political or fiscal offence exception to extradition in respect of the drug trafficking offences set out in article 3(1) (and to confiscation in terms of article 5, mutual legal assistance in terms of article 7 and general law enforcement co-operation in terms of article 9). It is an attempt to ensure that Parties act in good faith.[262]

The political offence exception is still common in extradition treaties and in state practice generally[263] and has been used to foil drug related extradition requests.[264] The roots of article 3(10) are to be found in provisions in multilateral schemes that close this potential escape route for offenders whose offence is not of a political nature.[265] Although there was resistance to the introduction of article 3(10) on the grounds that it would prejudice the right of asylum and the protection of refugees, during the drafting stage there was considerable

---

261 See Sproule and St-Denis supra note 213 at 272.

262 See the 'Review Group Report', *1988 Records* vol. I at 65.

263 See generally Panel, 'Extradition and the political offence exception' (1987) 81 *American Society of International Law: Proceedings* 467-483.

264 The extradition request of the Colombian Jorge Luis Ochoa on drug charges to the US from Spain was initially turned down by the Spanish *Audiencia Nacional* because of its 'political context'. The National Court noted that granting of the request could possibly aggravate Ochoa's situation because of 'political considerations'. These appeared to stem from the US's allegation that Ochoa was connected to alleged cartel trafficking activity in Nicaragua which connection the court found unconvincing, given the then prevailing animosity between the US and Nicaragua. See S.Y. Okera, 'International extradition and the Medellin cocaine cartel: surgical removal of Colombian cocaine traffickers for trial in the United States' (1992) 13 *Loyola of Los Angeles International and Comparative Law Journal* 955 at 965 footnote 80.

265 The substance of Article 3(10), introduced by the Jamaican delegation, can be traced to the Commonwealth Scheme for the Rendition of Fugitive Offenders, (1986) 4 *Commonwealth Law Bulletin* 1124, and the Scheme for Mutual Legal Assistance in Criminal Matters within the Commonwealth, (1986) 4 *Commonwealth Law Bulletin* 1118 – see *1988 Records* vol. II at 59.

support for such a provision.[266] Many delegations to the Conference held the view that drug-related offences should not be considered to be political[267] because to do so would be to provide a legal shield for offenders and undermine extradition as well as the other forms of co-operation contemplated by the Convention. It is arguable that actions carried out in a political context but with the purpose of personal or private material gain such as the trafficking of drugs cannot be considered as falling within the exception in any event. Conversely, rebel groups in the developing world that use drug trafficking as a source of funding may counter that they have a legitimate claim to the exception and especially so if they believe that supporting the supply of drugs to the developed world is simply one way of prosecuting a political struggle.[268] Nevertheless, the UN has expressed concern about the growing link between illicit trafficking and terrorism[269] and the prevailing view seems to be that no drug or laundering offence under the 1988 Convention should be considered a political or fiscal offence.[270] Blakesly warns, however, that '[t]he political offence exception often functions as a repository for human rights protections. It could be limited, if human rights protections were placed directly into extradition treaties.'[271]

---

266 See, for example, the 'Review Group Report', *1988 Records* vol. I at 61. In Committee I the French delegate put the case for those who supported the deletion of the provision. He pointed out that it attempted to depoliticise drug offences and that as such it ran counter to French law which in article 5 of the 1927 Law on Extradition provides that no-one shall be extradited for a political crime or for political purposes. He also noted that the French Constitution provided for a right of political asylum – *1988 Records* vol. II at 57-58. The Nordic delegations 'did not accept any restriction on their absolute freedom to assess which offences were political or politically motivated' and reserved their position on article 3(10) – *1988 Records* vol. II at 169.

267 See the 'Expert Group Report', *1988 Records* vol. I at 19, 37.

268 The obvious example is M19 in Colombia. The US delegation interpreted article 3(10) to mean that 'if a Party recognises a limitation to its obligation to co-operate for offences committed for political reasons, such as drug trafficking to raise money for a political group, that limitation shall not apply.' See 'Report of the US Delegation' supra note 171 at 32.

269 GA Resolution S-17/2, annex.

270 See the opinion of experts in the 'Explanatory Report on the Council of Europe's Convention on Laundering, Search, Seizure and Confiscation of the Proceeds from Crime' in W.C. Gilmore (ed.), *International Efforts to Combat Money Laundering* (Grotius, Cambridge, 1992), p. 192 at p. 224.

271 C.L. Blakesly, *Terrorism, Drugs, International Law and the Protection of Human Liberty* (Transnational, Ardsley-on-Hudson, 1992), p. 270.

The fiscal offence exception was included in the Convention to deal with Parties that refuse to co-operate because of their perception that the problem is of a fiscal rather than of a criminal nature.[272] Many states classify drug offences as offences against customs legislation[273] and many states still exclude these offences from extradition on the basis of the fiscal offence exception.[274] The fiscal offence exception is particularly significant in the context of drugs related money-laundering and is thus important in respect of extradition for the offences in article 3 sub-paragraphs (1)(b) and (1)(c)(i).

The provision in article 3(10) is itself limited in a number of ways, which suggests that it is no more than a declaration of principle that will not have much practical effect.[275] The most important limitation is the 'constitutional' and 'fundamental domestic law' safeguard clause. The provision forces Parties to only use either the political or fiscal offence exception when fundamental breaches of its basic law would be involved. The United States delegation stated:

> [T]he constitutional law of a few states requires that the courts of those states determine whether or not an offence is a political offence. At the insistence of those states, the paragraph is qualified ... . It is understood, however, that the courts of those states will be guided by the principle contained in the paragraph of not viewing Article 3 offences as political, politically motivated or fiscal offences.[276]

It is likely that in practice such Parties will treat each case on its merits.[277] A further limitation on article 3(10) is that it does not exclude the political offence exception where the request as opposed to the offence is politically motivated. Sproule and St-Denis note:

---

272 There was some resistance in the Review Group to the inclusion of the fiscal offence exception on the basis that it was not yet settled internationally that fiscal offences were non-extraditable – see the 'Review Group Report', *1988 Records* vol. I at 65.

273 Historically, the legal regulation of drugs has been carried out by taxing licit supplies and prosecuting those who supply without the relevant proof of taxation.

274 The Commonwealth Extradition Scheme recognises this in clause 2(3) which specifically mentions fiscal offences as extraditable, but only where the requested state's law allows extradition, which implies that when the law is silent, fiscal offences are not subject to extradition.

275 Sproule and St-Denis supra note 213 at 274.

276 'Report of the US Delegation' supra note 171 at 32.

277 Sweden has made a declaration (22/7/1991 – *Multilateral Treaties Deposited* (1997) at 306) in respect of article 3(10) to the effect that its constitutional legislation on extradition implies that when deciding whether a specific offence is political, 'regard shall be had to all the circumstances in each individual case.'

Although most delegations were willing to support the notion that a drug-related offence should be punished notwithstanding that it was politically motivated (for example, to finance a liberation movement), few were prepared to concede that states should be required to co-operate when a request made pursuant to a Convention offence was only a cover to apprehend and persecute an individual for political reasons.[278]

4.7.2.3   Discrimination as a ground for refusing extradition

Article 6(6) is a "non-discrimination" clause that also serves to ameliorate article 3(10)'s attempt to restrict the availability of the political offence exception to extradition in drug trafficking cases.[279] It provides that when a requested state considers an extradition request, it may refuse to comply 'where there are substantial grounds leading its judicial or other competent authorities to believe that compliance would facilitate the prosecution and punishment of any person on account of his race, religion, nationality or political opinions, or would cause prejudice for any of those reasons to any person affected by the request.' The Jamaican delegate to the 1988 Conference who proposed the provision stated that

> even in the case of an offence not deemed to be political, the Convention should provide that if a requested State has substantial grounds to believe that action on its part would facilitate prosecution of a person on the grounds of his race, religion, nationality or political opinions, it might refuse to comply with the request for extradition.[280]

The key phrase in the provision is 'substantial grounds'. Although there is no guidance on what these grounds are and when they become substantial, it appears that there must be objective evidence flowing from the request itself or in the general practice of the requesting Party from which the requested Party's judicial or other competent authorities can draw the inference that there is a

---

278 Supra note 213 at 273-274.

279 Schutte supra note 243 at 140 argues that article 6(6)'s insertion is illogical. He argues that because the 1988 Convention is not an extradition treaty in its own right and relies rather on existing or future extradition treaties or domestic law, it follows that the conditions under which extradition is granted are governed by those treaties or that domestic law. The same criticism can be applied to article 3(10) itself.

280 *1988 Records* vol. II at 167. Provisions along these lines are present in the Commonwealth Scheme for the Rendition of Fugitive Offenders, (1986) 4 *Commonwealth Law Bulletin* 1124, the 1977 European Convention on the Suppression of Terrorism, ETS 90, and in the domestic extradition laws of numerous states.

reasonable prospect that the offender will be prejudiced because of his 'race, religion, nationality or political opinions' before an extradition request can be refused. The reference to 'judicial and other competent authorities' can be construed as meaning that the Parties are obliged to ensure that their judicial authorities or other branches of government are given the power to determine whether potential human rights abuses preclude extradition.[281]

4.7.2.4   Extradition limited to article 3(1) offences
Article 6(1) restricts the material scope of the Convention's extradition provisions to the offences in article 3(1). The 1988 Convention does not create extradition relations in respect of offences of possession, purchase or cultivation for personal consumption in terms of article 3(2). Article 6(1) avoids the direct limitation of extradition to offences that Parties consider 'sufficiently serious', the limitation found in the earlier provisions.[282] Although article 6(1) updated existing extradition treaties by extending their range to the "new" money laundering offences in article 3(1), it is a shortcoming of article 6(1) that it applies to all article 3(1) offences even if they are not serious while it does not apply to drug offences established by Parties outside of the terms of article 3(1), even if such offences are serious. This shortcoming is compensated for by the fact that most Parties will not extradite for trivial offences, that is, usually offences punishable by a term of imprisonment of less than one year. However, article 6(1) has been criticised for perpetuating the enumerative approach to extradition in the drug conventions and for thus being unresponsive to changes in the drug traffic and the offences designed to attack it.[283] But the alternative would have been for the Parties to agree to be bound to enact and extradite

---

281   The US delegation to the 1988 Conference interpreted this provision as giving Parties the full discretion to determine which branch of government was to make these kinds of decisions – *1988 Records* vol. II at 32.

282   The Expert Group discussed the desirability of developing common standards concerning the criteria for drug offences to be considered sufficiently serious to justify extradition. Although finally abandoned because of their diversity and because they could serve as a further way of avoiding extradition, several thresholds of punishment were suggested varying from deprivation of liberty for a maximum term of one year to at least two years. A minimum sentence of four months was suggested where extradition was requested in respect of a person already convicted. Relying on imprisonment itself as the mark of the gravity of an offence was considered dubious in spite of the fact that many bilateral extradition treaties defined extraditable offences as those punishable under the laws of both states by imprisonment for more than a stipulated period. See the 'Expert Group Report', *1988 Records* vol. I at 35.

283   Patel supra note 36 at 726.

offences falling within a very broadly defined catch-all offence, such as 'illicit traffic', which would almost certainly have presented double criminality problems in practice. The fact that the offences must be 'established by the Parties' means that they must be established by both Parties, thus satisfying the requirement of double criminality.[284] Article 6(5)'s provision that extradition remains subject to the conditions provided for by domestic law and applicable extradition treaties also secures double criminality. This principle may become important in respect of extradition of article 3(1)(c) offences because they are subject to the constitutional principles and basic concepts of the legal systems of each Party concerned, and thus may be enacted to different degrees by different Parties.[285]

4.7.2.5   Article 3(1) offences included in existing and future extradition treaties
Article 6(2) places two unqualified obligations on Parties.[286] In its first sentence it provides for the legal fiction that the offences to which it applies shall be deemed to be extraditable offences for the purposes of existing extradition treaties. Thus all existing extradition treaties between (bilateral) or among (multilateral) Parties are amended to include article 3(1) offences. In its second sentence it obliges Parties to include these offences as extraditable offences in every new extradition treaty concluded between or among them. This obligation is irrelevant to states party to extradition treaties that obligate extradition of all offences carrying a threshold prison sentence.[287] The scope of treaties following an eliminative approach will simply be extended in practice. Some states that follow an enumerative approach have, however, already adapted their practice to follow the approach laid down in article 6(2).[288] Article 6(2) extends extradition generally, but this extension is significant as a means for introducing article 3(1)'s newer economic offences into the scope of extradition

---

284   See the 'Review Group Report', *1988 Records* vol. I at 64.
285   Schutte supra note 243 at 137. He gives as examples the different definitions in different legal systems of notions of attempt, conspiracy, facilitating and counselling under article 3(1)(c)(iv).
286   As an obligation it follows the example set in the 1972 Protocol and not the optional provisions in the earlier conventions. But while article 36(2) of the 1972 Protocol is subject to a safeguard clause, article 6(2) of the 1988 Convention is not.
287   Schutte supra note 243 at 137.
288   For example, the US allows the amendment of all existing bilateral extradition treaties to which it is party by multilateral treaties like the 1988 Convention in order to include new offences in the list of extraditable offences, and pursues a policy that includes drug and money laundering offences as extraditable offences in all future treaties to be negotiated – 'Report of the US Delegation' supra note 171 at 50.

treaties because many states do not recognise that economic crimes such as money laundering are extraditable in terms of existing extradition treaties.

4.7.2.6   The 1988 Convention functioning as an extradition treaty

Article 6(3) applies to that minority of Parties that require in terms of their domestic law a treaty or legislative basis to grant extradition. It gives such Parties the option to use the 1988 Convention as a basis for extradition. It distinguishes between Parties in two distinct positions.

The first sentence of article 6(3) applies to Parties that have detailed legislation catering for the technicalities of extradition but require the existence of a bilateral or multilateral treaty to make extradition possible. For these Parties, article 6(3) adopts the common approach of providing that the Convention may serve as the basis for extradition when the Parties' extradition law depends on the existence of a treaty and there is no such treaty. The provision is not mandatory.[289]

The second sentence of article 6(3), an innovation not contained in other multilateral criminal law conventions, applies to those Parties able to rely on a treaty basis for extradition but which rely on the provisions of the extradition treaty to provide guidance in respect of all its technical details.[290] It obliges these Parties, if they intend using the Convention as the legal basis for extra-

---

289   Many delegations wanted a mandatory provision – see the 'Expert Group Report', *1988 Records* vol. I at 19. But as Sproule and St-Denis supra note 213 at 278 footnote 53 observe, most common law states do not extradite in the absence of a treaty. They note that in Canada section 35(1) of the Extradition Act R.S.C. (1985) chp.E-23 allows extradition without a treaty where so declared by proclamation. Due to this provision and the Canadian policy of selective extradition relations, the Canadian delegation supported an optional rather than mandatory article 6(3). In Committee I the US delegation noted that it could not accept mandatory wording because the US adhered to a policy that extradition was agreed on a bilateral and not a multilateral basis – *1988 Records* vol. II at 99. The US made it clear in an understanding made upon ratification (20/2/1990 – *Multilateral Treaties Deposited* (1997) at 305) that it shall not consider the Convention as the legal basis for extradition of citizens to any country with which it does not have a bilateral extradition treaty. The permissive wording of article 6(3) means that Parties requiring the existence of an extradition treaty for extradition can refuse to extradite to Parties with which they do not have an extradition treaty on the basis that they choose not to recognise the 1988 Convention as an extradition treaty. Parties that do not require extradition treaties would in the same situation be obliged to extradite under article 6(4) unless it is recognised that article 6(4) only obliges such Parties to create the conditions for extradition in their domestic law and that they retain the discretion to extradite or not.

290   *1988 Commentary* at 156.

dition, to consider enacting the relevant enabling legislation as neither article 6 nor the 1988 Convention as a whole provide for such detail.[291] It is only an obligation to appraise the necessity for such legislation, but it must be complied with in good faith, and sceptical Parties have complied with it.[292]

4.7.2.7 The obligation on Parties not requiring the existence of an extradition treaty for extradition to recognise drug trafficking offences as extraditable

Article 6(4) obliges the vast majority of Parties that rely on their national law as a basis for extradition or which extradite on the basis of comity to recognise article 3(1) offences as extraditable. Article 6(4) only requires these Parties to create the legal possibility of extradition but does not affect their discretion in granting or even dealing with an extradition request from other Parties.[293] They have the same measure of discretion as the Parties covered in article 6(3). Obviously this obligation only applies when both Parties to the request are Parties that do not require a treaty base for extradition. Parties that do not in their domestic law permit extradition without a treaty but do not wish to use the 1988 Convention as an extradition treaty in terms of article 6(3) would be advised to change their domestic law so as to permit ad hoc extradition because most states do not have extradition treaty relations with one another.[294]

---

291 See Schutte supra note 243 at 139.
292 The UK, one of the states opposed to making the provision mandatory, complied with it by adding the 1988 Convention to the list of international instruments contained in article 22 of the Extradition Act, 1989, c.33 , and by making the Extradition (Drug Trafficking) Order, 1991 (SI 1991 No.1701), that makes provision for extradition with respect to Parties to the 1988 Convention but with which no general extradition arrangements have been established.
293 Schutte supra note 243 at 138. He notes that states that grant extradition entirely on the basis of their domestic law reserve for themselves the right to do so at their discretion. They cannot be called to account for how they do so under international law because their granting of extradition is not a question of international law.
294 W.C. Gilmore, 'International action against drug trafficking: trends in United Kingdom law and practice through the 1980's' (1991) 17 *Commonwealth Law Bulletin* 287 at 291 points out that section 3(3)(b) of the 1989 UK Extradition Act, 1989, c.33, empowers the Secretary of State to make special extradition arrangements for particular cases with states with which the UK has no general extradition agreements.

4.7.2.8 Expediting and simplifying extradition

Article 6(7) urges Parties to explore the possibility of speeding up extradition processes and of streamlining the evidentiary requirements insisted upon during these processes.

Whether expediting extradition procedures necessarily includes the simplification of procedures such as the detailed identification procedures that some Parties apply to extradition is uncertain, but the application of the different verb 'simplify' to evidentiary requirements suggests that alteration of the procedural law is not anticipated. In Europe abandonment of the diplomatic channel as the conduit for communication of extradition requests in favour of direct contact between ministries of justice or designated central authorities has avoided unnecessary delays.[295] The use of modern means of communication such as the facsimile or internet has great potential in this regard, as does the use of a summary procedure when the individual concerned does not contest the extradition.[296] Better information on other Parties' extradition procedures may assist in speeding up the process. More fundamental reform such as change to basic principles like the non-extradition of nationals is more controversial.

The simplification of evidentiary requirements does envisage their alteration and reduction. It is aimed primarily at the prima facie rule still applied in many common law jurisdictions which makes the granting of an extradition order conditional upon the requesting state presenting evidence of the same weight as that sufficient to justify the commission of the alleged offender to trial if the offence had been committed in the territory of the requested state.[297] Article 6(7) reflects the common view in civil law jurisdictions that common law requirements such as the prima facie rule make the process of extradition difficult and sometimes impossible.[298] Co-operation in this regard can be

---

295 *1988 Commentary* at 164.

296 *1988 Commentary* at 164. Technological innovation is provided for in the Agreement between the Member States of the EC for the Simplification and Modernisation of the Ways of Transmitting Extradition requests, 26 May 1989, the summary procedure in various instruments including the 1995 Convention on Simplified Extradition Procedure Between the Member States of the European Union.

297 At the Expert Group Meeting it was suggested that a valid arrest warrant or an executory judgment of the requesting state should replace the requirement, but these proposals were rejected – see the 'Expert Group Report', *1988 Records* vol. I at 20, 38 respectively.

298 Gilmore supra note 44 at 2. He points to the allowance for the possibility of dispensing with the *prima facie* requirement in the Commonwealth Scheme for Rendition of Fugitive Offenders, (1986) 4 *Commonwealth Law Bulletin* 1124, between members on the basis of bilateral agreements, and the gradual abolition of this requirement in the UK on a

achieved through, for example, the prosecuting authority in the requesting Party sending a record of the evidence and an attested declaration that in its opinion there is sufficient evidence to prosecute. But while more permissive evidentiary and procedural requirements for extradition would assist in the fight against drug trafficking, common law states fear that such relaxation would compromise their administration of justice, and are reluctant to alter their domestic legislation. Recently, however, many common law states have relaxed their strict rules governing the admission of evidence provided in support of an extradition request, some lowering the threshold, others abandoning it entirely, but these rules still present an obstacle to effective international co-operation.[299]

4.7.2.9   Ensuring the presence of the subjects of extradition requests at extradition proceedings

The object of article 6(8) is to expedite the procedure for the extradition of drug traffickers. It provides that a requested Party may take measures to ensure the alleged offender is actually available when these proceedings begin. A requested Party must be satisfied that the circumstances warrant such action and that they are urgent, and only need act in response to a request from the requesting Party. The specific measure mentioned is taking into custody, while the other measures remain at the Parties' discretion. In effect, article 6(8) provides for provisional arrest prior to the presentation of the formal extradition request. It relies on Parties' domestic law to set out such details as which authority may order the arrest, the length of time the person may be detained, and the possibilities of bail and/or conditional release, as well as the right to legal assistance. Speed and efficiency seem to be the watchwords when developing the content of these procedures[300] but reliance on domestic protection of the individual's rights in this context is dangerous when domestic law may

state by state basis by the Extradition Act, 1989, c.33, as evidence of awareness of these problems. But in 'International action against drug trafficking: trends in United Kingdom law and practice through the 1980's' (1991) 17 *Commonwealth Law Bulletin* 287 at 290-294 he gives an idea of how slow this change is in the face of resistance to "extradition on demand" despite the official desire for increased extradition.

299 D. Stafford, *International Legal Co-operation Against Serious Crime: Inter-legal Systems Issues Impacting on International Co-operation* (unpublished paper, New Delhi Global Drugs Law Conference, 1997), p. 3.

300 *1988 Commentary* at 167.

be totally inadequate.[301] Article 6(8) may be used as a vehicle to abuse human rights because it does not specify what test must be satisfied before a suspect is to be taken into custody – the simple say so of the requesting state may be sufficient – and it does not specify the length of time the suspect can be held before being released if no request is forthcoming. Part of the explanation for the absence of detail is that article 6(8) is irrelevant when extradition treaties already exist between the Parties setting out detailed rules governing provisional arrest or when a state extradites on the basis of its domestic law as that law will govern provisional arrest.[302] Article 6(8) is only relevant to those states that require a treaty basis for extradition and who are going to rely on the 1988 Convention to provide that basis and who in respect of provisional arrest, are going to rely on article 6(8).[303]

4.7.2.10 The obligation to prosecute where extradition is refused

Article 6(9) is an aut dedere aut judicare provision – the Party who finds an alleged offender in its territory must either extradite or prosecute him – of a sophisticated kind. A crucial provision, it tries to reconcile an attempt to eliminate all safe havens for drug traffickers created by legal limitations on their extradition with an attempt to prevent drug traffickers from profiting by possible conflicts of jurisdiction between Parties.[304] It is thus not surprising that article 6(9) is subject to the exercise by the requested Party 'of any criminal jurisdiction established in accordance with its domestic law'. Thus if the requested Party chooses not to respond to an extradition request but decides in its own right to exercise jurisdiction already established, that choice overrides its obligation under this provision. On the other hand an extradition request may not actually be forthcoming; as with the earlier conventions the 1988 Convention contains no obligation to request extradition and the Party in whose territory the accused resides may be forced to look for some other basis to establish and exercise extraterritorial jurisdiction. But Schutte warns against the implication that a Party is free to establish any kind of extraterritorial jurisdiction it chooses, and points out that the 'right of states to establish and

---

301 See, for example, the complaint by M.C. Bassiouni in 'Extradition: the United States model' in M.C. Bassiouni (ed.), 2 *International Criminal Law: Procedure* (Transnational, Ardsley-on-Hudson, 1986), p. 405 at p. 410 that someone can be held in the US for forty five days on the basis of a two line telex without the requesting state having to show probable cause.

302 Schutte supra note 282 at 142.

303 Schutte supra note 282 at 142.

304 See Schutte supra note 282 at 142.

exercise national jurisdiction is by definition limited by rules and general principles of public international law.'[305]

Article 6(9) must be read with article 4(2) which provides for the establishment of jurisdiction when the alleged article 3(1) offender is found on the Party's territory and it refuses to extradite. Both these provisions were the subjects of long and tortuous debate in Committee I of the 1988 Conference. It is important to recall, however, that as article 4(2) does not lay down a blanket obligation to establish jurisdiction upon refusal to extradite, there can be no blanket obligation to prosecute under article 6(9). Article 6(9) is only a partial translation into legal obligation of the aut dedere aut judicare principle. The sequence of events contemplated by the combined obligations of the two articles is as follows: refusal to extradite, establishment of jurisdiction (mandatory or optional) and then prosecution (mandatory). Because the establishment of jurisdiction in article 4(2) is made mandatory or optional depending on the grounds for refusal to extradite, in article 6(9) that distinction is carried through even though in both situations prosecution is mandatory once jurisdiction has been established.

Article 6(9)(a) sets out the first part of the two-part approach. It obliges a requested Party to prosecute an alleged offender found within its territory where it refuses to extradite him because of one of the grounds set forth in article 4(2)(a), that is, where the requested Party is obliged to establish its own jurisdiction through territoriality or nationality. Article 6(9)(a)'s wording makes it clear that the obligation to prosecute only arises when the other Party has in fact presented an extradition request that has been refused. The grounds in article 4(2)(a) obliging a Party to establish jurisdiction imported into article 6(9) as grounds for refusal of extradition are: first, when the offence was committed in its territory or on one of its flag-ships or registered aircraft, and second, when extradition is refused because the individual is a national of the requested state. Despite efforts before and at the Conference, there is no provision in the Convention obliging a Party to extradite its own nationals.[306]

---

305 Supra note 243 at 143.

306 The 'Review Group Report', *1988 Records* vol. I at 66. Thus the reservation made upon ratification by Colombia (20/12/1988 – *Multilateral Treaties Deposited* (1997) at 303) to the effect that it is not bound by article 3, paragraphs 6 and 9, and article 6, because they contravene article 35 of its own Political Constitution which prohibits the extradition of Colombians by birth, was redundant. The US, in response to the Colombian reservation declared (23/10/95 – *Multilateral Treaties Deposited* (1997) at 307) that it understands Colombia's reservation as only applying to extradition of Colombian nationals by birth, and objects to extension beyond this category of persons. Colombia

The majority of states, many of them within the civil law tradition, were opposed to any provision, even a hortatory provision, to this effect. Civil law states argued that their refusal to extradite their nationals is counterbalanced by their willingness to assert jurisdiction over their nationals wherever their location and that in any event article 6(9) would ensure the prosecution of offenders.

The provision obliges the requested Party, where it refuses to extradite for the above mentioned reasons, to 'submit the case to its competent authorities for the purposes of prosecution'. Conference delegates appeared to be of the opinion that this meant that although a requested Party was obliged to submit the case to its competent authorities, these authorities retained the discretion not to prosecute if they felt that no case could be made against the alleged offender.[307] In other words what is laid down here is an obligation to exercise jurisdiction and an obligation to submit for prosecution, not necessarily to prosecute; the formula preserves prosecutorial discretion in those Parties where it exists. Nonetheless, the provision has been criticised for apparently restricting that discretion.[308]

Requested Parties are obliged to submit the case for trial if extradition is refused 'unless otherwise agreed with the requesting Party.' The Chairman of Committee I of the 1988 Conference explained that this 'would allow the two states concerned, after consultation between themselves, to decide that prosecution in the requested state was not the appropriate method of administering justice in the case in question.'[309] Although refusal of the extradition request will in the normal course of events trigger the prosecution of the offender by the requested Party, such consultation was felt necessary to avoid the requesting Party turning to illegal rendition of the offender if it felt strongly that it should

---

withdrew its reservation on 30/12/1997. Despite their redundancy, Venezuela (16/7/1991 – *Multilateral Treaties Deposited* (1997) at 306) and Myanmar (11/6/1991 – *Multilateral Treaties Deposited* (1997) at 305) have made similar declarations/reservations to article 6 rejecting it as a basis for the extradition of nationals.

307 See, for example, the Jamaican delegate's statement – *1988 Records* vol. II at 146.

308 The Netherlands's delegate comments in *1988 Records* vol. II at 127 that 'International drug trafficking was unlike terrorism or hijacking in that the requested Party might decline to extradite a person and also wish not to submit the case ... to its competent authorities because it wished to track down the whole organisation of which the person formed a part. A requirement to submit the case to the competent authorities would end the person's usefulness to any investigation.'

309 *1988 Records* vol. II at 131. The Expert Group felt that one instance where an alternative to the obligation to prosecute might be agreed upon was when the Parties decided instead to enforce a foreign sentence under article 6(10) – see the 'Expert Group Report', *1988 Records* vol. I at 38.

prosecute him,[310] or to allow the requesting Party the option of waiting for the alleged offender to move to another Party which might agree to extradition.[311] For practical reasons such as co-operation in the supply of evidence, the requesting Party's support of the prosecution by the requested Party will be necessary. Agreement to waive prosecution rather than unilateral demands for and refusals of prosecution is also a good idea against the background of a refusal to extradite based on territoriality or nationality.[312] This wording does not, however, in any way prevent the requested Party from exercising jurisdiction in such a case, even if the requesting Party objects and does not provide that support.[313] A Party is obliged to prosecute if an extradition request is made and refused on one of the grounds set forth in article 4(2)(a) without any necessity of the requesting Party actually asking for such prosecution or agreeing to it, which means that the provision to prosecute is mandatory.[314] Moreover, the requested Party, because of the limitation clause in the opening sentence of article 6(9), retains the right to establish its criminal jurisdiction at any time and on any domestic grounds even if, as noted, no extradition request is made.

Article 6(9)(b) contains the second part of the extradite or prosecute provision in the 1988 Convention. Article 4(2)(b) permits but does not require Parties to establish their jurisdiction over serious drug trafficking offences 'when the alleged offender is present in its territory and it does not extradite him to another Party.' The reasons for the refusal to extradite are not laid down in

---

310 See the Netherlands delegate's explanation, *1988 Records* vol. II at 131.

311 Schutte supra note 243 at 146 notes that this would be particularly apt where the person sought is a member of a criminal organisation, the other members of which are standing trial in the requesting Party. The prosecution in isolation of the single member in the requested Party would be impractical and inappropriate in such a situation.

312 Schutte supra note 243 at 146.

313 Gilmore supra note 44 at 20. The provision does not make the obligation to prosecute or extradite subject to international agreement as to which Party is the most appropriate to try a specific case. Once provision is made for the obligatory prosecution of offenders where extradition is refused, conflicts of jurisdiction are bound to arise from which drug traffickers may benefit. While trial in absentia or simply waiting for the offender to return to its or another more co-operative Party's territory may present themselves as options to the requesting Party should it wish to pursue the matter, they would be subject to a double jeopardy bar.

314 This is in line with similar provisions in article 7 of the 1971 Montreal Convention for the Suppression of Unlawful Acts against the Safety of Civil Aviation, 10 ILM 1151, and article 10 of the 1988 Convention for the Suppression of Unlawful Acts against the Safety of Maritime Navigation, 27 ILM 672.

article 4(2)(b), but it is assumed that they would be other than the potential establishment of jurisdiction because of territoriality or nationality set out in article 4(2)(a).[315] Thus article 4(2)(b) anticipates the establishment of a broad jurisdiction by those Parties that choose to rely on it. However, when extradition is refused and the requested Party opts to establish jurisdiction, on whatever basis other than territoriality and nationality, article 6(9)(b) obliges it to exercise its jurisdiction by submitting the case to its competent authorities for the purposes of prosecution[316] 'unless otherwise requested by the requesting state for the purposes of preserving its legitimate jurisdiction.' The condition that the requesting Party must not have asked the requested Party to refrain from prosecution differs from that attached to article 9(6)(a) because it is dependent on a unilateral request by the requesting Party. Although it does not give a right to a requesting Party to veto the establishment of jurisdiction by a requested Party in accordance with its domestic law,[317] a requested Party, if it chooses to exercise jurisdiction, cannot argue that it does so in terms of an international obligation if the requesting Party, which may have a much stronger case against the alleged offender, objects. Sproule and St-Denis note:

> This provision, most strongly advocated by the United States delegation, is aimed at preventing the creation of so-called "double jeopardy havens" or countries that would knowingly or unwittingly advantage traffickers by trying and acquitting them or by imposing an excessively lenient sentence for offences over which a second country would not only have jurisdiction but would have a better case against the offender. Such action, by virtue of the rule against double jeopardy, would insulate the trafficker from potentially more severe punishment in the second country.[318]

The condition implies that the requesting Party may have a more legitimate jurisdiction than the requested Party not only in its own view but also under international law.[319] It also means that jurisdiction based on territoriality and nationality is seen by international law as more legitimate than the other unspecified grounds of jurisdiction contemplated by article 4(2)(b) and used as a basis for the obligation of the refusing requested Party to exercise jurisdiction in terms of article 6(9)(b). In this way the 1988 Convention appears to

---

315 In fact, nationals and non-nationals would be treated alike under article 4(2)(b) and article 6(9)(b).

316 They retain prosecutorial discretion.

317 *1988 Commentary* at 169.

318 Supra note 213 at 278-279.

319 See Schutte supra note 243 at 147-148.

recognise an order of priority of jurisdiction starting with territoriality and nationality.[320]

Article 9(6)(b) provides a way of avoiding the double jeopardy rule,[321] and may well be useful in other ways,[322] but in many cases the reasons for refusing extradition at the same time constitute an obstacle to the requested Party's own exercise of jurisdiction, such as the absence of double criminality, prosecutorial immunity under the requested Party's law due to time limitations, double jeopardy, diplomatic status of the alleged offender, insufficiency of evidence etc.[323]

Although article 6(9) as a whole is not particularly onerous, it appears to be most applicable where a requested party refuses extradition on the ground that the accused is one of its nationals. This may be the reason that the Philippines has declared that it does not consider itself bound by article 6(9).[324]

4.7.2.11 The obligation to carry out sentence where the extradition of a convicted offender is refused

Article 6(10) is an innovation that recognises that extradition is frequently sought not only to establish jurisdiction over alleged offenders, but to regain control over convicted offenders who have escaped and returned to their country of nationality.[325] It is an effort to avoid the difficulties associated with re-prosecution of the offender and the potential disparity in his re-sentencing where an extradition request is made, refused, and the requested state assumes jurisdiction. It provides that if extradition is refused because the offender is a national of the requested Party, the requested Party must 'consider', but only if its law so permits and if the requested Party makes application, enforcing the offender's

---

320 Schutte supra note 243 at 148 opines that this may be the beginning of a development of a balanced theory of jurisdiction in international criminal law which leads to a ranking of concurrent jurisdictional claims over certain offences.

321 Sproule and St-Denis supra note 213 at 278 footnote 56 note that attempts to avoid the rule by characterising the transport of drugs through several states as separate offences are unlikely to succeed given the interpretation of earlier drugs conventions.

322 See Gilmore supra note 44 at 21 who refers to the Australian Explanatory Memorandum on the Crimes (Traffic in narcotic Drugs and Psychotropic Substances) Bill, 1989, (1989) at 7. He notes Australia's plan to use this provision as the basis for prosecution inter alia where an extradition request has been refused because the requesting Party has not given satisfactory undertakings that the death sentence would not be imposed or carried out.

323 Schutte supra note 243 at 147 footnote 11.

324 7/6/1996 – *Multilateral Treaties Deposited* (1997) at 305.

325 See generally the 'Expert Group Report', *1988 Records* vol. I at 38.

sentence or what remains of it. The transfer of the sentence is subject to the law of the requested Party, but the enforcement of the transferred sentence is subject to the conditions provided for by the law of the requesting Party. The provision is an innovation and domestic limitation is understandable. The safeguard clause recognises that the domestic law of the requested Party would have to be in a position to accept the enforcement of foreign sentences in order to apply the provision.[326] The enforcement of foreign criminal judgments is not well established, but the whole scheme is conditional on appropriate domestic legislation being in place, on the extradition request being made and being refused, and on the requested Party choosing to enforce the sentence.[327]

Article 6(10) is an attempt to close a loophole in the law.[328] Its advantages are that it avoids jurisdictional conflicts, it assists a Party enforcing the sentence to avoid double jeopardy bars raised against retrial and it avoids the difficulties associated with trial in a jurisdiction different from that in which the offence was committed.[329] The Netherlands delegate to the 1988 Conference denied that the provision was a way of introducing universal jurisdiction through the back door.[330] Article 6(10) does not impose obligations on Parties that cannot adapt their domestic law accordingly. However, some cautious Parties have reaffirmed that its application must be made in terms of their domestic law,[331] while others have declared that they do not consider themselves bound by it.[332]

---

326 For example, the Swiss Federal Law on Judicial Assistance in Criminal Matters, 1981, provides in section 94(1) for the execution of criminal judgments of foreign courts, but only if: i) the judgment is final and enforceable in the requesting state; ii) the offender is resident in Switzerland or charged there with a serious offence; iii) the offence of which the offender has been convicted is also an offence in Switzerland; and iv) the execution of the sentence is precluded in the requesting state. The Swiss Federal Office takes the decision as to whether to accept or reject such a request, but its decision must be confirmed by a court before execution is carried out.

327 Schutte supra note 243 at 149.

328 Chapter 5 of the 1990 Schengen Convention allows for the transfer of execution of criminal judgments.

329 Netherlands delegate, *1988 Records* vol. II at 165.

330 *1988 Records* vol. I at 166.

331 Colombia (10/6/1994 – *Multilateral Treaties Deposited* (1997) at 304) has declared that it will only apply the provision and execute foreign sentences if its constitutional and other legal norms are observed.

332 The Philippines (7/6/1996 – *Multilateral Treaties Deposited* (1997) at 305).

4.7.2.12 Encouraging the conclusion of extradition treaties and agreements

Whilst not an obligation, article 6(11) is a forcefully worded provision which encourages Parties to conclude bilateral and multilateral agreements to enhance the effectiveness of extradition. It was intended by its authors to encourage Parties to enter into extradition agreements that covered situations not contemplated by article 6.[333] Article 6 is not an extradition mini-convention; it is reliant on existing and future extradition treaties or domestic extradition law as the case may be, and this is why article 6(11) appeals to Parties to enlarge their existing extradition relations through bilateral and multilateral agreements to make extradition possible and where already possible, more effective.[334]

4.7.2.13 Prisoner transfer agreements

Article 6(12) is a permissive provision encouraging Parties to enter into international prisoner-transfer agreements. These agreements may be bilateral[335] or multilateral,[336] ad hoc or general. Like extradition these agreements involve the inter-state transfer of persons, but in this case of persons who have already received a criminal sentence which they have not completed. The aim of this provision according to its authors is to encourage states to be more favourably disposed to the extradition of their nationals because it guarantees that their nationals will be returned to them for the serving of sentence.[337] It enhances effective imprisonment while also serving humanitarian purposes because it avoids the problems associated with the incarceration of foreign drug of-

---

333 See the 'Expert Group Report', *1988 Records* vol. I at 39.

334 Schutte supra note 243 at 149. The 1991 UN Model Treaty on Extradition UN GA Res. 45/116 provides a model.

335 See, for example, the 1985 UN Model Agreement on the Transfer of Foreign Prisoners, annexed to the Report on the Seventh UN Congress on the Prevention of Crime and the Treatment of Offenders, 1985, UN Publication Sales No.91.IV.2.

336 This provision was largely the result of the efforts of western European delegations who have had a positive experience with the 1983 European Convention on the Transfer of Sentenced Persons, ETS 112; see the 'Expert Group Report', *1988 Records* vol. I at 39.

337 See the 'Expert Group Report', *1988 Records* vol. I at 39. In the Netherlands it has had the desired effect – article 4(2) of the Netherlands Extradition Act makes provision for the extradition of nationals if the Minister of Justice is satisfied that the offender may be able to serve his sentence in the Netherlands.

fenders.[338] Rehabilitation is also best facilitated in the offender's home country.[339]

Article 6(12) applies to individuals sentenced to imprisonment or other forms of deprivation of liberty for article 3(1) offences. Precisely what qualifies as a form of deprivation of liberty is not stated, but it would not apply to repugnant forms of incarceration such as confinement in a labour or re-education camp. It applies to prisoners who are to be transferred back to 'their country'; it does not stipulate the legal relationship that they must have with this country. It is assumed that they include nationals, citizens and perhaps habitual residents, but the position of other persons who enjoy some legal status in that country is unclear.[340] Nor is mention made in the provision of the requirement of the prisoner's[341] or state of nationality's consent. These matters, and others such as the duration of the sentence that qualifies and which state (sentencing or administering or both) may initiate transfer, have been left to the particular agreements. As many of the offenders in foreign jails are there for drug related reasons and they require treatment this provision is potentially of wide effect,[342] and prisoner transfers are taking place,[343] but some consumer states

---

338 Schutte supra note 243 at 149 points out that foreign prisoners present special problems leading to differentiation in prison regimes due to their different nationality and language, absence of relatives and friends, absence of a home when released etc.

339 *1988 Commentary* at 173.

340 By contrast, para.4(1)(a)(ii) of the Commonwealth Scheme for the Transfer of Convicted Offenders speaks of 'close ties' of a kind that may be recognised by the state taking transfer.

341 Some delegations to Committee I, for example the Spanish delegation, strongly supported a provision requiring the consent of the prisoner, but it was decided to leave it to the Parties to individually decide on whether consent was required according to their own practice – *1988 Records* vol. I at 111-113. The 1985 UN Model Agreement requires the consent of the prisoner to avoid using the process as one of disguised extradition and because of variation in prison conditions from country to country – *1988 Commentary* at 174.

342 Schutte supra note 243 at 150.

343 *The Economist*, 14 June 1997, reports the return to the UK to finish her sentence of Sandra Gregory on 5 June 1997 from Thailand, where she had been sentenced to twenty-five years for drug-smuggling, and that the numbers of prisoners generally transferred back to the UK were rising, albeit slowly. The level of co-operation is well illustrated by the fact that Ms Gregory was released before completing her sentence after the King of Thailand gave his permission to UK authorities to let her go. Under the 1976 US-Mexico Treaty on the Execution of Penal Sentences, 28 UST 7399, TIAS No. 8718 (in force 11/11/1977), 537 Americans and 920 Mexicans returned to serve sentences in their native states between 1977 and 1990 – Abramovsky supra note 34 at 207. The 1991 UN Model Treaty on the Transfer of Supervision of Offenders Conditionally

appear more comfortable entering such agreements with other consumer states than with producer states.[344]

4.7.2.14 The 1988 Convention's extradition provisions in conclusion

From the point of view of effectiveness against the illicit traffic, article 6 is only a moderate improvement on the extradition provisions in the earlier conventions. Sproule and St-Denis provide a catalogue of examples of its cautious nature when they state that the

> political offence provision is essentially preserved; there is no obligation to extradite nationals; the principle of double criminality is preserved by the obligation of all parties to adopt Convention offences; the rules against double jeopardy and that of speciality are not derogated from by the inclusion of the domestic safeguard clause; and even the hortatory provisions included in earlier drafts that encouraged Parties to extradite their nationals have been removed.[345]

Under the circumstances this caution was not unexpected. The Conference delegates were not ad idem about the fundamentals of extradition, never mind about innovations such as prisoner transfers. As the United States delegate to Committee I of the Conference pointed out, article 6 attempts to strike a balance between two different approaches to extradition, viz. between states that do extradite their nationals and states that do not.[346] The balance struck is an uneasy one. Compromised extradition provisions do not provide efficient methods for acquiring the custody of drug offenders and will not stop the trend towards illegal rendition of such offenders. In this context, Colombia has made the following declaration:

> Colombia declares that it considers contrary to the principles and norms of international law, in particular those of sovereign equality, territorial integrity and non-intervention, any attempt to abduct or illegally deprive of freedom any person within the territory of one state for the purpose of bringing that person before the courts of another state.[347]

Sentenced or Conditionally Released, GA Res. 45/119, may provide a useful model.

344 P. Green, *Drugs, Traffiicking and Criminal Policy* (Waterside Press, Winchester, 1998) at p. 168 reporting on the UK's position.

345 Supra note 213 at 279-280.

346 *1988 Records* vol. II at 115.

347 Reservation upon ratification (10/6/1994 – *Multilateral Treaties Deposited* (1997) at 304).

The 1988 Convention's provisions, flawed as they are, do not sanction such methods. It was clearly the intention of the authors of these provisions that the surrender and acquisition of offenders must be accomplished exclusively in a manner that does not violate state sovereignty.[348] Whether anything but the dismantling of the barrier preventing the extradition of nationals can protect the sovereignty of states in which major traffickers are present is, however, debatable.

It is significant that sovereignty is the motivation for restriction of extradition. Protection of individual human rights is only incidental to the protection of sovereignty. The drug conventions' extradition provisions objectify individuals; they are not granted rights of their own. International law leaves them to be protected, if at all, by a municipal law that it simultaneously pressurises into eliminating domestic legal impediments to co-operation.[349] Yet alleged offenders may well face an unfair trial, torture or inappropriate sanctions in the requesting Party, a situation about which the requested Party may have little information and less concern. The content of the drug conventions certainly has not been influenced by the trend in international and national law to create new human rights based, individual-oriented, bars to extradition.[350] Extradition is a powerful weapon against drug traffickers, a weapon that scares them,[351] but it must be used justly, not unjustly, and international drug control law lags behind general international human rights law in this regard.

---

348 Nevertheless, on accession (4/11/1997) Vietnam reserved on article 6. Austria (16/12/1998), France (16/12/1998), Germany (16/12/1998), Italy (18/12/1998), Sweden (14/12/98), UK (17/12/1998) and Finland (15/1/1999) have all objected in the strongest terms to the reservation, stating that it is contrary to the object and purpose of the Convention and should not be permitted – see *Multilateral Treaties Deposited with the Secretary General: Status as at 30 April 1999* (New York, 1999) UN Doc. St/Leg/Ser.E/17. Given that the general object and purpose of the 1988 Convention is to bring extraterritorial drug offenders to justice, the objections of these Parties must be valid and the Vietnamese reservation invalid in terms of articles 19 and 20 of the Vienna Convention on the Law of Treaties.

349 For example, Stafford supra note 299 at 4 argues that concerns with human rights abuse in foreign jurisdictions that underpin the application of strict rules in common law states in respect of extradition requests cannot be valid if punishments are uniform in requesting and requested states. But simple uniformity of punishments does not guarantee human rights protections unrelated to punishment that may be provided for in the requested state but not in the requesting state.

350 See Blakesly supra note 271 at 283 and footnote 514 where he gives as an example articles 697-726 of the 1988 Italian *Codice di Procedura Penale* based on the 1950 European Convention on Human Rights, 213 UNTS 221.

351 Okera supra note 264 at 968.

4.8   JURISDICTION AND EXTRADITION IN CONCLUSION

The drug conventions rely for jurisdiction on the principle of territoriality. They extend jurisdiction beyond the territorial cautiously. The potentially most expansive form of extraterritorial jurisdiction over drug offences is universal jurisdiction in the strict sense. Bassiouni argues that its establishment across all states over drug offences would break down the vertical barriers that protect traffickers allowing them to be completely suppressed.[352] However, examination of the drug conventions reveals that they do not create an international drug crime to which universal jurisdiction applies. The authors of these conventions did not intend them to create international crimes and Parties to them do not generally regard these conventions as creating international crimes. These conventions establish territorial jurisdiction over domestic drug offences and set out conditions for the establishment of jurisdiction over extraterritorial offences in limited cases.[353] They provide for the primacy of domestic law on criminal jurisdiction[354] whereas universal jurisdiction is unconditional and unlimited by domestic law. Nor do the drug conventions assist drug offences to qualify as crimes in customary international law to which universal jurisdiction applies. The drug conventions introduced new crimes to the world and cannot be said to have crystallised a rule of custom internationalising drug offences. Most states in their practice do not treat them as international crimes and they do not believe them to be international crimes. With this level of support, to argue that they are obligations erga omnes or that they are ius cogens norms of international law is absurd.[355] The conventions themselves provide poor evidence of consistent and uniform state practice or of opinio juris. Their authors were reluctant to commit themselves on questions of criminalisation and jurisdiction. This reluctance is borne out by the limitation clauses in the conventions making it clear that participation in a convention cannot be interpreted as affecting a Party's attitude on the issue of the limits of criminal

---

352 Supra note 93 at 518.

353 See, for example, article 36(2)(a)(iv) of the 1961 Convention and article 4(2)(b) of the 1988 Convention.

354 See, for example, article 36(3) of the 1961 Convention and article 4(3) of the 1988 Convention.

355 Erga omnes obligations are obligations on all states because of the legal interest of all states in the substance of these obligations – see *in re Barcelona Traction, Light and Power Co. (Belgium v Spain)* 1970 ICJ 4 at 33, while ius cogens norms are peremptory norms of international law – see article 53 of the Vienna Convention on the Law of Treaties.

jurisdiction. Moreover, while there may be international consensus about the criminalisation of some forms of conduct relating to drug trafficking,[356] such as exporting or importing drugs, there is no consensus about others, such as conspiracy to export or import or, for that matter, conduct relating to "soft" drugs such as cannabis. The way states view the effect of different weights of drugs being smuggled also injects uncertainty into the question of the status of a particular crime.[357] This diversity of practice and opinion is reflected in the domestic limitation clauses applicable to the more controversial forms of conduct criminalised in the drug conventions. The drug conventions recognise that drug offences may be transnational in nature and may require international co-operation for suppression, but to conclude that these offences are crimes in international law to which universal jurisdiction applies is to go too far. Whether these conventions, despite their limited effect, even serve as a clear basis for the development of such a rule, is controversial. States, jealous of their sovereignty, do not consider drug offences present a threat grave enough to the international legal order to force them to abandon the requirement of juris- dictional connection between criminal and prosecuting state. Before such a connection can be abandoned, it is submitted that an absolutely uniform drug crime and punishment regime would have to exist internationally, implying universal agreement on drug control policy. That is not presently the case.

The alternative is universality by the back door – through the application of the principle of subsidiary universality of jurisdiction to drug offences. The size of the threat posed by international drug trafficking and the elusive nature of its organisers is used to justify the application of the principle of subsidiary universality in national criminal legislation and the punishment of violators irrespective of their nationality or the place of their crime.[358] There are various types of aut dedere aut judicare provisions in international criminal conventions, and it appears that the provisions in the drug conventions fall largely within the same conditional type – they appear to follow the 1929 Convention for the Suppression of Counterfeiting.[359] Unlike unconditional types such as that con-

---

356 See Puttler supra note 8 at 117 who states that while every state may agree that selling heroin is an international crime to which universal jurisdiction applies, the same cannot be said of the sale of small quantities of hashish.

357 While some states view the weight of drugs as going to sentence, others view it as a way of distinguishing between serious and less serious offences.

358 Bassiouni supra note 93 at 521.

359 112 LNTS 371 (articles 8 and 9). See also the 1950 Convention for the Suppression of Traffic in Persons and the Exploitation of the Prostitution of Others, 90 UNTS 271 (article 9).

tained in the 1970 Hague Hijacking Convention, this type does not oblige the Parties to be prepared to take jurisdiction in every case in which an offender is not extradited.[360] This type of provision allows the Parties to have different approaches to the establishment of subsidiary universality, and to choose not to establish such jurisdiction even when they refuse extradition. It recognises that states may not want to establish this type of extraterritorial jurisdiction in every case and particularly with regard to crimes committed abroad by foreigners. Thus, for example, article 6(9) of the 1988 Convention provides that if extradition is refused on the ground of nationality, the refusing Party must submit the case for prosecution, but in the case of refusal of extradition of non-nationals, a Party is not obliged to establish extraterritorial jurisdiction. Only if it chooses to establish extraterritorial jurisdiction over non-nationals is it obliged to prosecute them if it refuses to extradite them. Thus a Party's stance on extraterritorial jurisdiction conditions its application of subsidiary universality to drug offences. A negative attitude to unconditional subsidiary universality and unconditional extradition can be traced in all of the drug conventions. The 1936 Convention's provisions were vague and accompanied by escape clauses in order to secure the adherence of states that would not accept stipulations different to their national law. The 1961 Convention took over the extradition provision from the 1936 Convention but diluted it. In 1972, however, there was a reversion to the more stringent extradition provisions of the 1936 Convention. Yet states continued to display a negative attitude towards implementation of these provisions.[361] The 1988 Convention attempted to overcome this reluctance by bridging the fundamental gap between civil and common law states on jurisdiction and extradition.

Both civil and common law states are, absent international legal obligation, in most cases unwilling to establish extraterritorial jurisdiction over aliens with whom they have no greater connection than the alien's presence in their territory. They are, however, legally able, and usually, although not always, willing to extradite aliens. Nationals present a more complicated problem. Civil law states prefer to prosecute their nationals at home. They are usually able, although not always willing, to establish and exercise extraterritorial jurisdiction on the basis of nationality. Civil law states will usually not extradite their nationals, because in most cases they are constitutionally prevented from doing so. Common law states believe that drug offences for practical reasons should be prosecuted where they occur. They will not prosecute their nationals for

---

360 Bassiouni and Wise supra note 30 at 12.
361 See Chatterjee supra note 24 at 439.

offences committed abroad, but they will extradite their nationals. Civil law states that support an international no-hiding place policy for drug offenders advocate the use of subsidiary universality for a number of reasons. They argue that it will oblige civil law states to establish and exercise extraterritorial jurisdiction over their nationals who commit extraterritorial drug offences when such states are reluctant or unable to invoke nationality as the basis for such jurisdiction, and are unable to extradite these nationals. The inviolability of the nationality exception to extradition will be respected, and the prosecution of extraterritorial drug offences achieved. Subsidiary universality is also held to be a solution to situations where a requested state, either civil or common law, is unwilling to extradite an alien for whatever reason. Common law states that support international drug control advocate the use of "universal" extradition; they oppose application of universal jurisdiction,[362] and support the extradition of all offenders no matter what their nationality. The aut dedere aut judicare principle becomes an area of contest; the common law states emphasise dedere at the cost of judicare and the civil law states emphasise judicare at the cost of dedere. The 1988 Convention is something of an awkward compromise between these two positions which tries to achieve the difficult task of obliging Parties if they don't give up to prosecute and if they don't prosecute to give up, but achieves neither particularly adequately because of the necessity of limiting both kinds of obligations in order to keep both groups happy. It protects the inviolability of the nationality exception to extradition, thus meeting the concerns of civil law states. And while it obliges Parties that refuse to extradite on the basis of nationality to establish jurisdiction and prosecute, it does not oblige them to establish jurisdiction over aliens if they refuse to extradite them. It thus meets the concern of the common law states opposed to unlimited subsidiary universality because they feel it is ineffective. But it leaves the 1988 Convention a weakened legal instrument that may extend jurisdiction and extradition to a certain extent in respect of drug offences but certainly does not lead to an unqualified subsidiary universality. While it may allow Parties to establish jurisdiction over extraterritorial drug offences, it does not oblige them to do so. As Schutte states:

---

362 The US delegation to the 1988 Conference reported on the need to overcome any domestic hurdles to the extradition of US nationals because: '[i]n the view of the general US policy favouring extradition of nationals to the country where the greatest harm has been suffered because of the commission of criminal acts, and against creating "universal" jurisdiction, we believe it preferable to eliminate situations in which we cannot extradite our nationals rather than create jurisdiction to prosecute them because we cannot extradite them.' – 'Report of the US Delegation' supra note 171 at 53.

It is to be stressed that the Convention does not contain the obligation to establish criminal jurisdiction on the basis of the so-called principle of universality, or any other rule of extraterritorial jurisdiction. In this respect, it has not followed the pattern of previous conventions in other areas of criminal law, such as the conventions on hijacking, hostage taking, other forms of terrorism, torture, etc. It has however, remained in line with the 1961 Single Convention on Narcotic Drugs, the 1961 Convention as amended by the 1972 Protocol and the 1971 Convention on Psychotropic Substances, which in their turn do not contain the obligation for States Parties thereto, to establish criminal jurisdiction over the offences covered by those instruments on the basis of universality.[363]

In practice, many states still fail to either extradite or prosecute drug offences committed abroad[364] and many states fail to enact the domestic legislation necessary to allow jurisdiction to be established on this basis. There is no great prospect for change. Civil law states resist change to the rule against the extradition of nationals,[365] and it is unlikely that significant numbers of common law states are going to begin establishing and exercising extraterritorial jurisdiction on the basis of nationality. As long as states are unwilling to make major alterations to their criminal justice systems, a compromised subsidiary universality seems unavoidable. However, it cannot be ignored that many common law states, and particularly the United States, see themselves as the ultimate victims of drug traffickers and particularly of foreign drug traffickers, and they are unwilling to surrender the option of prosecuting such traffickers at home, hence their opposition to universal jurisdiction for drug offences and their support for universal extradition. By contrast, many major supply states are through historical accident civil law states. Constitutional barriers make it difficult for these states to extradite alleged drug traffickers who are their nationals, and political pressure and duress compound these difficulties. Thus the state of international drug control law in this area reflects the political state

---

363 Supra note 243 at 145.
364 Nadelmann supra note 191 at 75 notes that the US officials still consider application of vicarious prosecution as contrary to US legal norms and, more to the point, unnecessary.
365 Nadelmann supra note 191 at 75. Myanmar has expressly reserved (11/5/1993 – *Multilateral Treaties Deposited* (1997) at 305) the right not to be bound by article 6 of the 1988 Convention in so far as its nationals are concerned. The growing popularity of this exception is the cause of some concern, especially when states do not assert jurisdiction either – see Stafford supra note 299 at 4. Prost supra note 35 at 52 notes, however, that previously unwilling states have recently allowed extradition of their nationals on condition that service of sentence is in the state of nationality.

of affairs that underpins it. A no-hiding place from international law is not the priority of consumer states – their priority is a no-hiding place from their domestic law. And the producer states are still willing to provide such a hiding place in such circumstances, for a variety of reasons.

The existing international provisions provide, at best, for quasi-universality of jurisdiction and quasi-universality of extradition. In practice, drug traffickers are likely to slip between these two stools. All that is left to catch them are the provisions for extraterritorial jurisdiction in international law. Some of these, for example, nationality, extended territoriality to ships and aircraft, and the effects principle, are recognised by the drug conventions, while others, for example the protective principle, are not. Extravagant interpretations of these principles by states that seek to establish legally justifiable connections between themselves and drug offences committed extraterritorially remain unchecked by the drug conventions. Customary international law provides no guide to the ranking of these principles where there are conflicts of jurisdiction and states are not likely to agree upon such ranking given that the interest of consumer states in the global supply reduction policy is not shared by producer states. The drug conventions have not intervened effectively into the area of extraterritorial jurisdiction over drug offenders by ensuring that most states recognise and rank the same connections between offender and state taking jurisdiction. Consensus on policy is a necessary precondition of a regulated and effective "no hiding place" approach to drug offences. This massively qualified "no hiding place" approach in the drug conventions is further qualified by the practical considerations of the quantity of state adherence to the conventions and by the quality of the implementation of their obligations by Parties. The potential danger is that consumer states may consider it a poor substitute for bilateral or unilateral action against the illicit traffic.

GENERAL LAW ENFORCEMENT COOPERATION

5.1   DRUG LAW ENFORCEMENT UNDER INTERNATIONAL LAW: NATIONAL
       CO-ORDINATION AND INTERNATIONAL CO-OPERATION

At a general level, the international drug control system guides Parties in the policing and prosecuting of drug offenders whether that process is purely domestic or has extraterritorial implications. Territorial policing, although legally uncomplicated as it is an exercise of domestic sovereign power, is an area of international concern because at the national level drugs policing not only suffers from a lack of co-ordination, it suffers from all the problems of modern policing. It is often the case that disorganised, poorly trained, poorly paid and poorly motivated law enforcement officers find themselves facing organised, well rewarded, highly motivated and corruptive illicit traffickers. International intervention to reorganise national policing focuses on training and organisation. It aims to centralise or co-ordinate national drugs policing and the responsible national organs and give them the expertise to deal with national drug problems. This intervention has been driven by the perception that efforts to suppress drug trafficking are weakened by the isolation of different law enforcement organs within and among states. Co-ordination of law enforcement organs at the national level is considered essential to enhance the effectiveness of drug law enforcement. Centralisation of control at the national level is regarded as the best method to achieve national co-ordination.[1] This implies centralisation of supervision over investigations and prosecutions, and centralisation of the storage and transfer of all information relating to the suppression of drug trafficking. The main reason for this reorganisation and training is to enable

---

1   The *Commentary on the Single Convention on Narcotic Drugs, 1961* (New York, 1973) UN Publication Sales No. E.73.XI, (hereinafter the *1961 Commentary*), p. 415.

national organs to co-operate internationally through the creation of a uniform domestic approach to drugs policing.

Extraterritorial law enforcement presents the international drug control system with a more difficult problem. International enforcement of domestic drug law encroaches upon state sovereignty because it involves extraterritorial action such as the collection of evidence abroad. Unilateral law enforcement action by one state in the territory of another is a violation of territorial sovereignty and of customary international law.[2] This principle is clearly articulated in the 1988 Convention. Article 2(2) asserts the principle of non-intervention in the domestic affairs of other states while article 2(3) prohibits any Party from undertaking 'in the territory of another Party the exercise of jurisdiction and performance of functions which are exclusively reserved for the authorities of that other Party by its domestic law.' International law enforcement is thus dependent upon international co-operation. Before the conclusion of the 1961 Convention Interpol listed the essentials of effective international drug law enforcement co-operation as co-ordination of preventive action at the national level, direct co-operation between the agencies responsible for co-ordination, and the speediest possible transmittal of legal papers required for prosecuting offenders.[3] These priorities have not changed.

At the international level, law enforcement co-operation is difficult to both agree upon in principle and to implement.[4] At the tactical level law enforcement methods preferred by some, such as the recruitment of informants and plea-bargaining for information, are frowned upon by others.[5] Yet many novel methods have been adopted by the drug conventions. They are discussed in Chapter Six. At the strategic level, where the gathering of information abroad works in tandem with the extension of jurisdiction and extradition, states heavily committed to supply reduction have more or less successfully coaxed disinterested states into joining in the effort to reduce supply. But they continue to

---

2   W.C. Gilmore, 'Introduction' in W.C. Gilmore (ed.), *Mutual Assistance in Criminal and Business Regulatory Matters* (Grotius, Cambridge, 1995), p. 11 at p. 12.

3   UN Doc. E/CONF.34/1 add draft article 44 of the 1961 Convention, comparing it unfavourably with the 1936 Convention.

4   See, for example, J. Benyon, L. Turnbill, A. Willis and R. Woodward, 'Understanding police co-operation in Europe: setting a framework for analysis', in M. Anderson and M. Den Boer (eds), *Policing Across National Boundaries* (Pinter, London, 1994), p. 46 at p. 49.

5   E. A. Nadelmann, 'The role of the United States in the international enforcement of criminal law' (1990) 31 *Harvard International Law Journal* 37 at 49 referring to US versus European practice.

struggle with states that provide national sanctuaries for the production of drugs, for the investment of illicitly gained funds and for the refuge of wanted offenders.[6]

The problem facing all states pursuing extraterritorial drug criminals has been obtaining information and evidence and getting access to witnesses extra-territorially.[7] In principle, law enforcement co-operation of this kind is divided hierarchically. At the lower level we find police co-operation that falls outside of judicial responsibility and entirely within executive jurisdiction. At the upper level, we encounter legal assistance, assistance in the gathering of information and admissible evidence, processes that fall within judicial jurisdiction. The exact parameters of each field of responsibility varies from state to state and it is therefore important for states to get as much information as possible about the division of responsibility in other states from whom they request co-opera-tion.

If the police or customs or a similar agency require operational assistance, that is, some form of non-compulsory assistance, then assistance is usually ob-tained by operational networking. Direct police co-operation is regarded as a useful method to avoid legal and political hurdles. This chapter maps the areas of general police co-operation provided for by the drug conventions.

However, national difference is not easily overcome by direct co-operation. Police forces wishing to gather evidence abroad have a problem that cannot be solved by contacting witnesses and document holders directly as they are under no obligation to help. If the executive or judiciary require formal mutual assistance, that is, some form of compulsory power to be exercised by the requested state, then formal requests for assistance are necessary.[8] Judicial orders, search and seizure orders, service of process and arrests of suspects all require a high degree of formality to overcome the problems associated with applying the criminal law of one state in another. The orthodox method, based on comity, has been the issue of letters rogatory by a judicial officer in the requesting state addressed through the executive arm to a judicial officer in the requested state, requesting the supply of public/private records and/or actual testimony within the latter's control. But this process which includes transmittal through diplomatic channels wastes time, it may not be available in respect of a particular offence, the issuing agency may not be recognised, it may not

---

6   See K. Bruun, C. Pan and I. Rexed, *The Gentlemen's Club* (University of Chicago Press, Chicago, 1975), p. 276.

7   D. McClean, *International Judicial Assistance* (Clarendon, Oxford, 1992), p. 174.

8   Gilmore supra note 2 at xiv.

overcome bank secrecy or similar restrictions on the production of evidence and it is usually expensive.[9] Frustrated, the United States resorted to highly controversial unilateral measures,[10] while at the same time putting a lot of effort into developing more expeditious procedures within the context of bilateral Mutual Legal Assistance Treaties (MLATs). MLATs encourage international co-operation in respect of all the facets of law enforcement work. They overcome the problem of non-recognition in civil law states of rogatory requests made by prosecutors in common law states by resorting to central authority mechanisms that play a substantive role in making, receiving and executing requests. One of the major purposes of this chapter is to examine how the authors of the drug conventions, driven by the desire to provide for rapid and effective international co-operation in drug law enforcement, have tried to transcend the use of conventional formal means of legal assistance by providing for more flexible forms of mutual legal assistance in the international pursuit of drug offenders.

5.2   LAW ENFORCEMENT CO-OPERATION UNDER THE 1961 CONVENTION

5.2.1   The nature of the obligation in article 35

In order to make it more acceptable than the 1936 Convention,[11] the drafters of the 1961 Convention diluted the provisions for operational co-operation in article 35, entitled 'Action Against the Illicit Traffic'. Article 35 is qualified by its introductory paragraph, which provides that Parties may take due regard of their constitutional, legal and administrative systems when applying the article. It has been argued that this means that a Party is not under an obligation

---

9   See J. Knapp, 'Mutual legal assistance treaties as a way to pierce bank secrecy' (1988) 20 *Case Western Reserve International Law Journal* 405 at 409-410.

10   See generally P. Coggins and W.A. Roberts, 'Extraterritorial jurisdiction: an untamed adolescent' (1991) 17 *Commonwealth Law Bulletin* 1391 at 1401-1402. Because of the inefficiency of letters rogatory the US resorted to unilaterally i) compelling defendants in drug trafficking cases to sign a consent form releasing foreign banks from secrecy obligations, and ii) enforcing court subpoenas on foreign banks with local branches to provide the required information. W.C. Gilmore, 'International action against drug trafficking: trends in United Kingdom law and practice through the 1980's' (1991) 17 *Commonwealth Law Bulletin* 287 at 295 notes that many states considered these unilateral actions to be violations of international law.

11   Paragraphs (1) and (2) of article 44 make the more exacting provisions of the 1936 Convention available should a Party so choose.

to implement the provisions of article 35 if they are incompatible with its constitutional, legal and/or administrative system.[12] However, the *1961 Commentary*, pointing to the difference between 'having due regard' used here and 'subject to' used in the qualification of article 36 paragraphs 1 and 2, submits that the introductory paragraph of article 35 was not intended to free Parties from article 35's obligations but rather to indicate 'the freedom of Parties to choose for the execution of the provisions of article 35 such as administrative arrangements, procedures and methods as are in conformity with their constitutional, legal or administrative systems, that is, having "due regard" to these systems.'[13] The *1961 Commentary's* interpretation is supported by the wording of the provision and by the fact that such clauses, the purpose of which is to inter alia protect federal constitutional arrangements, must leave the essence of the obligation intact.

5.2.2   *National law enforcement co-ordination under the 1961 Convention*

Article 35(a) obliges Parties to provide for national co-ordination of 'preventive and repressive action'. 'Preventive action' includes co-operation and exchange of information on the policing of drugs in the widest sense as well as on drug research. The *1961 Commentary* gives as examples of such action,

> the maintenance of lists of suspected traffickers, the communication of information regarding the methods used by traffickers to conceal and to transport drugs, the purchase of police equipment needed for the campaign against the illicit traffic, arrangements to facilitate the common use of such equipment by different police units and the training of enforcement officers.[14]

Although the use of the terms 'preventive and repressive' implies that the activities of these agencies must not be purely administrative and they must have a law enforcement aspect,[15] alternative measures, such as treatment of users,

---

12 S.K. Chatterjee, *Legal Aspects of International Drug Control* (Nijhoff, Dordrecht, 1981), p. 444. It was felt necessary to mention 'administrative systems' because paragraphs (b) and (c) of draft article 44 dealt with criminal justice administration, see *United Nations Conference for the Adoption of a Single Convention on Narcotic Drugs, Official Records, Volume II* (New York, 1964) UN Doc. E/CONF.34/24/ Add.1, UN Publication Sales No. 63.XI.5 (hereinafter *1961 Records* vol. II), p. 259 generally.

13 *1961 Commentary* at 416-417.

14 *1961 Commentary* at 418.

15 See the comments of the Interpol representative, *1961 Records* vol. II at 255.

are part of the preventive and repressive processes, and it is submitted that these measures would have to be included in the actions to be co-ordinated.[16]

Article 35(a) is not specific about the organs whose actions are to be co-ordinated nationally because of their dissimilarity from Party to Party and the different constitutional, legal and administrative systems prevailing within Parties. It is obvious, however, that the object of this provision is the co-ordination of drugs policing within states. This is especially so in situations where there is no national police force and policing is the function of sub-national entities, but is also the case where a national police force does exist but sub-national police forces are not subject to its authority.[17] The organs co-ordinated include specialised drug law enforcement agencies, the national police, the local police, the customs authorities and personnel not directly involved in law enforcement, such as scientists specialising in drugs,[18] as well as therapists in drug use treatment programmes.

The nature of the co-ordinating mechanism is prescribed by article 35(a) only to the extent that it must be 'appropriate' to the purpose of 'preventive and repressive action against the illicit traffic'. It must have law enforcement functions, but may have other functions.[19] Depending on the particular Party's constitutional, legal and administrative system, it may take various forms. It may be a system of liaison among law enforcement and other concerned organs, or a periodic joint meeting of governmental departments responsible for such organs, or a permanent inter-ministerial committee, or a special organ charged solely with co-ordination.[20] Through the terms 'may usefully', article 35(a) leaves it to the discretion of the Parties as to whether or not to designate an 'agency' with the task of co-ordination. Such an 'agency' need not be created specifically for co-ordination; it need only be 'appropriate' and may thus be constituted, as is common practice, by an existing government department or

---

16 But contra see the *1961 Commentary* at 418.

17 *1961 Commentary* at 417.

18 See Chatterjee supra note 12 at 434.

19 For this reason the 1961 Conference used the term 'appropriate agency' in preference to 'enforcement agency', see *1961 Records* vol. II at 41. Thus for example, Pakistan's Narcotics Control Board (PNCB), created in 1973, is a department of Pakistan's Ministry of the Interior. As the primary federal drug agency in Pakistan, it is involved in all aspects of drug control, including law enforcement, crop substitution, and treatment and rehabilitation of addicts. It is also the co-ordinating mechanism for UN drug related aid programmes – see generally J.W. Murphy, 'Implementation of international narcotics control: the struggle against opium cultivation in Pakistan' (1983) 6 *Boston College International and Comparative Law Review* 199 at 228-229.

20 *1961 Commentary* at 418.

by an interdepartmental committee. The *1961 Commentary* suggests that a 'central office' along the lines of that set out in the 1936 Convention would most usefully acquit this task.[21] Article 35(a)'s special provision for an agency for co-ordinating law enforcement action must be seen in the context of article 17's general obligation on the Parties to 'maintain a special administration for the purpose of applying the provisions of the Convention.' As it is concerned with co-ordination of the work of the various national agencies involved in drug control, the special administration under article 17 may be the same one envisaged by article 35(a), but this is not required by the 1961 Convention.[22] Such a 'special administration' may imply a group of national agencies responsible for applying the 1961 Convention as a whole.[23] One of these agencies may be the optional agency envisaged by article 35(a).

The setting up of such an agency is discretionary because in 1961 many states did not have a single body to co-ordinate action. But the qualification seriously weakens the 1961 Convention's provisions for law enforcement, particularly when the Party in question had no national police force and measures against the same kinds of offences were being taken by several distinct agencies.[24] National co-ordination is an essential prerequisite of international co-operation, and after 1961 a lot of international effort went into getting Parties to set up these central agencies.[25]

---

21 *1961 Commentary* at 418 referring to articles 11 and 12 of the 1936 Convention.

22 Under articles 15 and 11 of the 1936 Convention one central organisation was responsible for all these tasks. An attempt to combine the articles at the 1961 Conference was abandoned – see *United Nations Conference for the Adoption of a Single Convention on Narcotic Drugs, Official Records, Volume I* (New York, 1964) UN Doc. E/CONF.34/24, UN Publication Sales No. 63.XI.4 (hereinafter *1961 Records* vol. I), at p. 122 and *1961 Records* vol. II at 40-41, 249-253.

23 See *1961 Records* vol. II at 253 generally. This is, for example, the position in Finland where the Police, Customs, Criminal Courts, and National Agency for Medicines share authority in this area – see A. Kinnunen, 'Finland' in N. Dorn (ed.), *Regulating European Drug Problems* (Kluwer, The Hague, 1999), p. 87.

24 See the remarks of Interpol's delegate, *1961 Records* vol. II at 249.

25 C.N. Cagliotti, 'The role of the South American Agreement on Narcotic Drugs and Psychotropic Substances in the fight against illicit drug trafficking' (1983) 35 *Bulletin on Narcotics* 83 at 93 lists the then existing national co-ordinating agencies in South America. The UN Secretary General has published a list of competent national authorities under all of the drug conventions – *Competent National Authorities under the International Drug Control Treaties* UN Doc ST/NAR.3/1993/1.

5.2.3   International law enforcement co-operation under the 1961 Convention

Article 35, paragraphs (b), (c) and (d) are special provisions relating to international co-operation. Article 35(b) requires that the Parties provide mutual assistance to each other in the suppression of drug trafficking, while article 35(c) requires that the Parties co-operate with each other and with the relevant international drug control organs in this regard. Questions have been asked as to why the drafters of the Convention chose to include such synonymous phrases as 'assist each other' and 'co-operate closely' in paragraphs (b) and (c) of the same article.[26] Article 35(b) provides for a general obligation on the Parties to co-operate in the fight against illicit trafficking, while article 35(c) applies this general co-operation to a particular facet of the fight, viz. to the need to maintain 'a co-ordinated campaign against the illicit traffic,' something which experience has shown requires a permanently organised international structure that includes other Parties and international drug control organs.[27]

Neither paragraph (b) nor (c) specifies the content of this international co-operation against the illicit traffic. The *1961 Commentary* is hesitant to submit that there is an obligation on Parties to provide technical assistance to other Parties to fight the illicit traffic, although it feels that rendering such assistance is in the spirit of article 35.[28] It does, however, submit that Parties are as a result of the obligation to co-operate 'bound to make all efforts within their power to prevent their territory from becoming a base of operation of the illicit traffic in other countries, or a place of refuge of drug smugglers.'[29] Parties appear to be under an obligation to maintain a system of general law enforcement assistance which would include sharing intelligence, assisting in preparation for investigation and prosecution, assisting in preparation for an extradition request,[30] assisting in the training of other Parties' agents in new law enforce-

---

26 Chatterjee supra note 12 at 435.
27 *1961 Commentary* at 419.
28 *1961 Commentary* at 420-421.
29 *1961 Commentary* at 421.
30 R. Linke, H.J. Epp and E. Kabelka, *Extradition for Drug Related Offences* (UN Publication St/Nar/5, Austria, 1985), pp. 8-9, explain that any state making the decision to extradite can only do so if it has been informed about the relevant facts (arrest of offender, his identity and nationality, the seizure of drugs etc.) by the state in which he has been found. The arresting state will usually invite states having jurisdiction over the offence to request extradition. They submit that all of this information including the formal invitation to extradite corresponds to the obligations to co-operate in article 35(b) and (c), and it should be exchanged expeditiously to speed up the extradition process.

ment techniques and sharing scientific or therapeutic knowledge which may impact on law enforcement. In practice, Parties have based mutual legal assistance on article 35(b),[31] international seminars for the training of law enforcement agents have taken place[32] and regional training centres have been set-up.[33]

In article 35(c) the expression 'competent international organisations' must be taken to mean the non-governmental, inter-governmental and international organisations operating in the field of international drug control. The drafters of the 1961 Convention had in mind the specialised agencies of the UN and non-governmental agencies such as Interpol.[34] Chatterjee submits that the UN

---

31   See, for example, the Exchange of Notes between the United Kingdom and the United States Concerning Co-operation in the Suppression of the Unlawful Importation of Narcotic Drugs into the United States, 1982 UKTS 8, Cmnd 8470. The Exchange of Notes, which mentions the 1961 Convention in its preamble, permits US authorities to board and search for drugs British vessels on the high seas in the Gulf of Mexico, the Caribbean and Eastern Seaboard. If drugs are found the vessels may be seized and taken to the US where the drugs are liable to forfeiture and the crew to stand trial – see J. Siddle, 'Anglo-American co-operation in the suppression of drug smuggling' (1982) 31 ICLQ 726-747. Another example is *R v Crown Court at Southwark, ex parte Customs and Excise Commissioners; R v Crown Court at Southwark, ex parte BCCI* [1989] 3 All ER 673 where a reviewing court quashed conditions attached to a production order made in terms of section 27 of the Drug Trafficking Offences Act 1986 which prevented clients' files (including General Manual Noriega' of Panama), seized by customs officers investigating the Bank of Commerce Credit and Industry (BCCI) money laundering scandal, from leaving the Southwark Crown Court's jurisdiction without its permission. The review court noted that the UK was a party to the 1961 Convention and held that in terms of the UK's obligations under article 35 to co-operate with other Parties in the international fight against the drug traffic, such information must be available to officials in the US investigating the BCCI.

32   For example, Cagliotti supra note 25 at 92 refers to the Second Latin American Training Seminar for Instructors in the Fight Against Drug Abuse and Illicit Traffic held in Peru in 1984 under the auspices of the South American Agreement on Narcotic Drugs and Psychotropic Substances (ASEP). Assisted by the UN, eleven South American states sent participants who were lectured by experts from various national police forces and international drug control organs.

33   C. Yodmani, 'The role of the Association of South East Asian Nations in fighting illicit drug traffic' (1983) 35 *Bulletin on Narcotics* 97 at 99 notes that ASEAN set up a regional training centre for anti-drugs law enforcement in Thailand in 1979. Training co-operation crosses ideological barriers – British Customs trains Cubans Customs – UK Foreign and Commonwealth Office Press Release, 9 October 1998.

34   See the statements of the Yugoslavian, Polish, Turkish and French delegates – *1961 Records* vol. II at 254. There was some dispute at the 1961 Conference over whether the provision only requires Parties to co-operate with international organisations of which

as a whole is included since the CND and INCB are only subordinate bodies of ECOSOC.[35]

Article 35(d) provides that Parties are under an obligation to ensure international co-operation is conducted expeditiously between 'appropriate agencies'. Read with article 35(a), it may appear that Parties are required to ensure international co-operation between their 'appropriate agencies' only if they have opted to create such an agency. But the *1961 Commentary* submits that the terms do not have the same meanings in both article 35(a) and (d) and that in terms of article 35(d) the Parties are obliged to engage in international co-operation with any of another Party's government services dealing with a problem of the illicit traffic, whatever its form.[36] The emphasis here is on two things: i) the expeditious communication of information between the co-operating services of different Parties; and (ii) the giving of urgent attention to the request by the service once it has been received. The method and route of communication is not specified but it appears that international co-operation between the services must be routed according to the constitutional, legal or administrative systems of the Parties. One of Interpol's major objections to the draft article 44 that became article 35 was that it made no provision for the direct international co-operation between law enforcement agencies.[37] Attempts to provide expressly for such direct co-operation were rejected; as the Yugoslavian delegate noted, 'the different administrations in Yugoslavia could not communicate direct with foreign administrations; that was done through the

---

they are members. It was argued that co-operation between a Party which is not a member of the UN and the UN drug control organisations is not required by the provision on the basis that no Party should be required to co-operate with an organisation to which it does not belong – see *1961 Records* vol. II at 255. The Executive Secretary of the Conference submitted, however, that article 35(c) does oblige non-UN members to co-operate with the UN and its organs – see *1961 Records* vol. II at 254. The *1961 Commentary* at 420 understandably supports this view and seeks to reinforce it by reference to article 5 which obliges all Parties to recognise the UN's competence in international drug control. Parties may be obliged to co-operate with the UN through their general contractual obligation under the 1961 Convention. However, whether 'competent' implies membership in addition to competency in the field of drug control is arguable; the stricter view based on international principle would tend to suggest that it does. Voluntary co-operation is of course not precluded. There is no obligation under article 35(c) to co-operate with the national organisations of other states involved in drug control.

35   Supra note 12 at 435.
36   *1961 Commentary* at 421.
37   *1961 Records* vol. I at 122.

Ministry of Foreign Affairs.'[38] Nonetheless, the *1961 Commentary* suggests that where direct correspondence is compatible with the systems of the Parties concerned it would be an expeditious manner of co-operation. Direct and personal correspondence makes for article 35(d)'s 'close' co-operation, and the *1961 Commentary* suggests that diplomatic channels should be avoided.[39] It also suggests that where an article 35(a) 'appropriate agency' has been designated by a Party it should be the agent of correspondence, and in cases of unfamiliarity with the organisational structure of a foreign state or where no contact had previously been had with the drug control agencies of that state, Interpol may serve as a useful intermediary to make for expeditious handling of a case.[40]

Article 35(e) deals with the international transmission of legal papers. It provides that Parties shall do so expeditiously, but they retain the right to insist upon using diplomatic channels. Requests for transmittal of legal documentation from one state to another are common in illicit drug trafficking cases. Effective international co-operation demands speedy transmittal. Slow transmittal of such documents may well lead to the failure to prosecute alleged drug traffickers because of the legal inability of one Party's criminal justice system to retain such an alleged criminal in custody until the papers arrive.[41] Article 35(e) does not create a legal obligation to render mutual legal assistance. It regulates one small aspect of mutual legal assistance between Parties, viz. Parties are expected to ensure the expeditious international transmission of papers for the purposes of prosecution to the bodies designated by requesting Parties.

The *chapeau* in the opening paragraph of article 35 means that the Parties retain the right to insist that these papers be sent to them through diplomatic channels, but they remain free to choose more expeditious methods, unless the transmission of the particular papers is already regulated by, for instance, an extradition treaty in force. The *1961 Commentary* notes that communication to the corresponding Party of the identities of the bodies designated to receive these papers will speed up the process, and suggests that communication through article 35(a)'s 'appropriate agency', or prosecutor to prosecutor communication, or prosecutor to Justice Minister communication, or Justice Minister to Justice

---

38 *1961 Records* vol. II at 249.
39 *1961 Commentary* at 422.
40 *1961 Commentary* at 421-422.
41 See the example given by the Interpol representative – *1961 Records* vol. II at 257.

Minister communication may all make transmittal of legal papers more speedy.[42]

The 'papers' transmitted include requests for mutual legal assistance and requests for the arrest of a person whose extradition is demanded in terms of article 36(2)(b).[43] Reports by such a requesting state feeding back on the results of the legal assistance rendered and replies to extradition requests should also, by extension, be subject to the obligation of speedy transmittal.

The 'bodies' to which these papers would be transmitted could include courts, government departments responsible for prosecution and the like. These papers must be 'for the purposes of prosecution' and they include papers for any legal action against the illicit traffic, whether initiated by a judge or prosecutor.[44] Whether they include papers solely for police investigations where prosecution is not yet a consideration is uncertain. They do appear to include papers in cases where prosecution is impossible because the criminals have not been apprehended or the like, but where the court must still decide on the seizure or confiscation of drugs, substances or equipment used in or intended for the use in commission of drug offences.[45]

The limitations of mutual legal assistance circa 1961 are well illustrated by article 35(e); the direct transmission of legal documents between courts or prosecutors remains limited to bilateral legal assistance agreements. The lack of a commitment in article 35 to provide the greatest measure of assistance in criminal proceedings has been criticised.[46] Aware of its shortcomings, the *1961 Commentary* suggests that in accordance with article 35's obligations to co-operate Parties should either establish treaty relations or enact the necessary domestic legislation to make provision for mutual legal assistance in cases of illicit drug trafficking.[47]

5.2.4   Law enforcement co-operation under the 1961 Convention in review

Article 35 provides in the main for the co-ordination of national drug policing and the regulation of international police co-operation. Bassiouni, critical of

---

42 *1961 Commentary* at 423.
43 *1961 Commentary* at 422-423.
44 *1961 Commentary* at 423.
45 *1961 Commentary* at 423.
46 Linke et al supra note 30 at 49. They note that a much greater level of commitment was required by the other suppression conventions.
47 *1961 Commentary* at 422.

article 35, argues that 'invaluable co-operation between enforcing agencies is relegated to a personal exchange of confidences between agents or agencies who have developed some form of working relationship; instead it should be institutionalised, and such relations formalised.'[48] Informal co-operation has been shown to be effective and formalising it was to become the main aim of legal development in international drugs policing.[49] The limited nature of article 35 and the chapeau in the opening paragraph indicate that in 1961 the international regulation of national law enforcement co-ordination and international law enforcement co-operation was still only in its infancy. The authors of article 35 attempted to speed up the use of existing inefficient forms of legal co-operation, such as letters rogatory. Much work still had to be done, particularly in establishing a general obligation to render more rapid and direct forms of mutual legal assistance. A further shortcoming of article 35 is that it does not oblige Parties to co-operate with non-parties, although this weakness is remedied to a certain extent by article 4(b)'s obligation on Parties to co-operate with other states including non-parties in the implementation of the 1961 Convention.[50]

5.3 LAW ENFORCEMENT CO-OPERATION UNDER THE 1971 CONVENTION

5.3.1 The nature of the obligation in article 21

The fact that article 21 of the 1971 Convention, entitled 'Action Against the Illicit Traffic', is modelled closely on article 35 of the 1961 Convention, indicates that there was little development in the field between 1961 and 1971. Article 21(b) only adds a specific instance of co-operation to the general obligation on Parties in article 35(b) to co-operate in the campaign against the

---

48 M.C. Bassiouni, 'The International Narcotics Control Scheme' in M.C. Bassiouni MC (ed.), *1 International Criminal Law: Crimes* (Transnational, Dobbs Ferry, 1986) p. 507 at p. 522.

49 Informal links can operate in the most difficult of political circumstances. J. d'Oliveira, *International Mutual Legal Assistance and other Forms of International Legal Co-operation* (unpublished conference paper, New Delhi Global Drugs Law Conference, 1997), discusses at pp.7-9 the relationship between South Africa and India in combating the import of methaqualone from India to South Africa. He notes significant successes in the interdiction of supplies, but points out that most of the co-operation which made this possible has been informal because apartheid made co-operation impossible.

50 *1961 Commentary* at 419.

illicit traffic by obliging Parties to inform 'other Parties deeply concerned' of certain cases of the illicit traffic. Thus the comments made above in respect of article 35 of the 1961 Convention are generally apposite to article 21. Article 21's introductory paragraph subjects article 21 to the Parties' constitutional, legal and administrative systems. Parties will be freed of its obligations if it is found to be incompatible with these systems, something that weakens article 21 considerably.[51] The *1971 Commentary* submits, however, that no Party could find the broadly defined provisions of the article incompatible with these systems.[52] It notes that the authors of the provision, by using the phrase 'having due regard to', appear to have contemplated Parties implementing article 21 in different ways in order to make it compatible with their respective 'constitutional, legal and administrative systems'.[53]

5.3.2   National law enforcement co-ordination under the 1971 Convention

Article 21(a) obliges Parties to make domestic arrangements for co-ordinating preventive and repressive action against the illicit traffic. According to the *1971 Commentary* such action includes

> the maintenance of lists of illicit traffickers, establishment of specialised police units, training of police officers concerned with cases of the illicit traffic, communication to all police units concerned of information on the methods used by traffickers to conceal and to transport their contraband, and purchase of equipment which may be necessary for the special needs of the fight against the illicit traffic.[54]

Article 21(a) does not specify how each Party is to regulate intrastate co-operation. It only suggests[55] that an agency be designated for such co-ordination without specifying which agency is to be designated as the co-ordinating agency. Such decisions would depend on the constitution and/or the

---

51 Chatterjee supra note 12 at 493.
52 See the *Commentary on the Convention on Psychotropic Substances, 1971* (New York, 1976) UN Doc. E/CN.7/589; UN Publication Sales No.E.76.XI.5 (hereinafter the *1971 Commentary*), p. 338.
53 *1971 Commentary* at 338.
54 *1971 Commentary* at 339.
55 This appears to be because of the inability of developing states to fund such an agency – see the remarks of the Russian delegate, *United Nations Conference for the Adoption of a Protocol on Psychotropic Substances, Official Records, Volume II* (New York, 1973) UN Doc. E/CONF.58/7/Add.1, UN Publication Sales No.E.73.XI.4 (hereinafter *1971 Records* vol. II), p. 26.

legal and administrative system of the Party concerned. Article 21(a) should
be read with article 6 which emphasises the desirability of Parties establishing
a special administration for the purposes of applying the Convention and which
notes that it can be the same institution established for these purposes under
the 1961 Convention. The co-ordinating agency envisaged by article 21(a) could
be the same body as this special administration, but it may also be a part of
a formation of interested bodies or an organisational arrangement, that make
up the special administration. The designation of responsibility and organisational structure will depend on the Party. Designation of such an agency will
be simple in a Party that has a national police force with authority over local
police forces, in other words, in situations where law enforcement, including
drug law enforcement, is organised hierarchically. But designation of an agency
is probably more necessary, and more difficult, where subordinate governmental
units (such as states in a federation, provinces, cities etc.) exercise police powers
and are not subject to the authority of a national police force.[56] Whatever the
mechanism used by the Parties to ensure internal co-ordination of drug law
enforcement action, the *1971 Commentary* submits that each Party must ensure
'continuous co-operation and exchange of information among the police units
involved in order to make possible the effective handling of individual criminal
cases.'[57] National co-ordination is essential for the international co-operation
envisaged by the rest of article 21, and particularly for smooth and speedy
communications in the international drug control system.[58]

5.3.3   International law enforcement co-operation under the 1971 Convention

Paragraphs (b), (c) and (d) of article 21 provide for a system of co-operation
at the international level among state organisations and international control
organs to keep each other informed about the illicit traffic.

Article 21(b) places a general duty on Parties to assist each other against
the illicit traffic, and then specifies that this can be done by the immediate
transmission of a copy of an article 16(3) report on the discovery of a case of
illicit traffic or a seizure to the other Parties 'directly concerned'. The Turkish
delegate to the 1971 Conference who was responsible for this part of the provision, explained that it was aimed at the situation where the information had
been provided to the Secretary General but there had been delays in the pro-

---

56   *1971 Commentary* at 339.
57   *1971 Commentary* at 339.
58   *1971 Commentary* at 339.

vision of information to Parties concerned 'and in particular to ensure that a Party of whose country the traffickers were nationals or in whose country the substance had originated was informed of seizures promptly.'[59] The *1971 Commentary* suggests that such information should also be communicated to non-parties 'directly concerned'.[60] The method to be used for the transmission of this information is the diplomatic channel unless the Parties have designated 'competent authorities' for this purpose. With the aim of avoiding the diplomatic channel, the *1971 Commentary* suggests the designation of a government unit (such as the agency envisaged by article 21(a)) able to act expeditiously in the transmission and reception of information to and from the law enforcement agencies having jurisdiction over the cases involved.[61]

Article 21(c) expands upon article 21(b)'s general obligation on the Parties to co-operate in the suppression of illicit drug trafficking. While they both refer to international co-operation, article 21(c)

> specifies that co-operation should be close, should include co-operation with 'competent' international organisations of which the Parties concerned are members and should be carried out 'with a view to maintaining a co-ordinated campaign against the illicit traffic.[62]

In order to achieve a universal and coherent system of international co-operation Parties should co-operate with non-parties. A permanently maintained international organisational structure is also crucial to co-operation. In this context, 'competent international organisations' must include intergovernmental bodies such as the UN's drug control organs[63] and non-governmental organisations such as Interpol engaged in suppression of the illicit traffic.

With respect to the content of the co-operation envisaged by article 21(c) (and (b)), the *1971 Commentary* notes that at the very minimum the Parties are obliged to take all practical steps to prevent their territories from being used as a base of operation for the illicit traffic into other countries and/or as a refuge

---

59 *1971 Records* vol. II at 24-25.
60 *1971 Commentary* at 340.
61 *1971 Commentary* at 340.
62 *1971 Commentary* at 341.
63 Parties to the 1971 Convention do not appear to be bound to co-operate with the UN drug control agencies if they are not members of the UN. The *1971 Commentary* at 341-342 submits, however, that the authors of the 1971 Convention intended that non-UN members should co-operate with it, and even if they are not legally obliged to do so by the Convention it is within the spirit of the 1971 Convention that they do so.

for traffickers.[64] Requiring Parties to provide technical assistance to other Parties under this provision or any of those relating to international co-operation in article 21 is controversial, but the effective participation of poorer states in the campaign to suppress the illicit traffic and the satisfaction of the purpose of these provisions may depend on such assistance.[65]

Article 21(d) obliges Parties to ensure that co-operation between the 'appropriate agencies' be carried out speedily. Such agencies are not only those envisaged by article 21(a); they include any of a Party's agencies dealing with an illicit trafficking problem that requires or can give international assistance.[66] The provision anticipates both a rapid means of communication and the urgent attention of the various agencies to the communication of information. The *1971 Commentary* suggests that direct correspondence between law enforcement agencies, or correspondence through an article 21(a) 'appropriate agency', or direct contact between law enforcement officers could in appropriate cases result in the expeditious communication envisaged by article 21(d) and the close co-operation envisaged by article 21(c).[67]

Article 21(e) provides for the conditions under which transmittal of legal papers should take place internationally, i.e. the speedy transmittal of such papers to the bodies designated by the Parties.[68] It does not impose any obligation to render international legal assistance. The rules governing the Parties' relations in matters of legal assistance will be found elsewhere, usually in bilateral treaties or within a Party's domestic law. Article 21(e) was intended to 'ensure that, ... traditional forms of legal assistance would continue' and not be supplanted.[69] However, the *1971 Commentary* does submit that the international co-operation envisaged by paragraphs (b), (c) and (d) of article 21 includes making provision for international legal assistance in respect of drug offences through conclusion of mutual legal assistance treaties, or modification of existing treaties, or enactment of appropriate legislation.[70]

Proposals for the direct transmission of documents between the competent authorities of the Parties were rejected, and the text allows for such transmission

---

64 *1971 Commentary* at 342.
65 *1971 Commentary* at 342.
66 *1971 Commentary* at 342.
67 *1971 Commentary* at 343.
68 Although article 21(e) does not apply to relations with non-parties, the *1971 Commentary* at 345 suggests that it would be in the spirit of the 1971 Convention if it were so applied.
69 The Austrian delegate explaining his introduction of the amendment that resulted in paragraph (e) – *1971 Records* vol. II at 23.
70 *1971 Commentary* at 343.

only between the bodies designated by the Parties.[71] In order to speed up the
transmittal of such documents, the *1971 Commentary* suggests that direct
prosecutor to prosecutor, or court to court, or prosecutor to Justice Ministry,
or Justice Ministry to Justice Ministry communication should be authorised,
and that channelling the papers through the Justice Ministry or an article 21(a)
'appropriate agency' would speed up such transmission.[72] The right of the
Parties to use the diplomatic channels is expressly reserved but such use will
be slower than more direct transmittal of the documents. The documents must
be for use in 'judicial proceedings', which implies that investigations wholly
under police control are not covered by the provision, although police investigations under the guidance of a judge or magistrate would be covered. As
to the meaning of 'legal papers', the *1971 Commentary* explains:

> The term 'legal papers' covers requests for judicial assistance, reports on the results
> of assistance which has been rendered, including in particular copies of the records
> of requested evidence which has been taken, requests for extradition and replies
> thereto. It includes not only papers relating to the actual or possible prosecution
> of illicit traffickers, but all papers concerning any judicial proceeding in matters
> of the illicit traffic, e.g. the seizure or confiscation of psychotropic substances or
> of other substances or equipment used in or intended for offences of the illicit
> traffic.[73]

The expeditious transmission of legal papers implies not only using a speedy
method of transmission, but also an obligation to ensure the speedy taking of
the necessary steps to prepare the papers such as: the hearing of witnesses or
the taking of evidence, arrest of suspects, processing of extradition requests
and the seizure of contraband or material used in or intended for use in the
trafficking of psychotropic substances.[74] The actual method of transmission
will probably be prescribed in international legal assistance treaties to which
the Party is also party, but to accord with article 21(e) this method will have

---

71 Austrian amendment, *United Nations Conference for the Adoption of a Protocol on
    Psychotropic Substances, Official Records, Volume I* (New York, 1973) UN Doc. E/
    CONF.58/7; UN Publication Sales No.E.73.XI.3 (hereinafter *1971 Records* vol. I), p.
    95. The *1971 Commentary* at 344 notes that papers have to be addressed to the bodies
    designated for their receipt, and that Parties must notify each other of the appropriate
    addresses through the UN Secretariat.
72 *1971 Commentary* at 344.
73 *1971 Commentary* at 343-344.
74 *1971 Commentary* at 344.

to be the most expeditious constitutionally, legally and administratively possible.[75]

5.3.4   Law enforcement co-operation under the 1971 Convention in review

Because article 21 of the 1971 Convention largely mirrors article 35 of the 1961 Convention, many of the criticisms of article 35 are apposite to article 21. It too is concerned mainly with co-ordination of national drug policing and the regulation of international police co-operation. As with paragraphs (b) to (e) of article 35 of the 1961 Convention, it is controversial whether paragraphs (b) to (e) of article 21 of the 1971 Convention create a legal obligation on one Party to provide such mutual legal assistance to another party in the campaign against the illicit traffic. Unwilling to rely on the argument that such an obligation is certainly in the spirit of both provisions, supporters of a legal obligation to render mutual assistance in drug trafficking matters paid a lot of attention to this issue in the preparation of the 1988 Convention.

5.4   LAW ENFORCEMENT CO-OPERATION UNDER THE 1988 CONVENTION

5.4.1   Introduction

The period between 1971 and 1988 saw a massive increase in extraterritorial law enforcement action by consumer states such as the United States. The 1961 and 1971 Conventions neither authorise nor prohibit extraterritorial policing[76] and in particular the extraterritorial enforcement of domestic judicial orders for the production of evidence.[77] The innovative measures for law enforcement

---

75 *1971 Commentary* at 344.

76 D.B. Boggis, 'Exporting United States drug law: an example of the international legal ramifications of the war on drugs' (1992) 1 *Brigham Young University Law Review* 165 at 168.

77 See, for example, *In re Grand Jury Proceedings Bank of Nova Scotia* 740 F.2nd 817 (1981) at 830-831 where the US Circuit Court held that the 1961 Convention neither requires the US to issue foreign Grand Jury subpoenas to obtain financial records in another state (in this case the records of a Branch of the Bank of Nova Scotia operating in the Cayman Islands and allegedly involved in money laundering) nor does it require the Cayman Islands to defer to such a subpoena. But the subpoena was allowed on the principle that the 1961 Convention was not intended to restrict the enforcement of drug trafficking laws or restrict how states choose to apply those laws.

co-operation introduced through the 1988 Convention are an attempt to institute
bilateral developments in a multilateral treaty while at the same time restraining
unilateral excess. Law enforcement co-operation under the 1988 Convention
is far more sophisticated than that contemplated by the 1961 or 1971 Conventions. It takes a number of shapes including innovative forms of mutual legal
assistance in drug matters, transfer of proceedings and co-operation with respect
to transit states. At the same time the 1988 Convention provides for general
police co-operation of the kind provided for in the earlier drug conventions.
We turn first to examine the detailed provisions for mutual legal assistance.

5.4.2   Mutual legal assistance under the 1988 Convention

5.4.2.1   Introduction
Mutual legal assistance in respect of drug offences was first introduced via
bilateral mutual legal assistance treaties (MLATs). These treaties enabled states
to assist each other in ways beyond just the facilitation of formal legal requests
for the delivery of information. Bilateral arrangements (both formal and informal) for assistance in drugs policing have proliferated because of the perceived slowness of using Interpol channels.[78] Development has been bilateral
for a number of reasons. It does not have to reflect the lowest common denominator of agreement amongst a group of states. States are free to choose their
treaty partners and are not obliged to provide information to unfriendly or un-
trustworthy states. Finally, legal diversity such as the common law/civil law
fracture makes multilateral MLATs difficult to agree upon and to enforce.[79]

---

[78] M. Anderson, *Policing the World* (Clarendon, Oxford, 1989), p. 29.

[79] E.A. Nadelmann, 'Unlaundering dirty money abroad: U.S. foreign policy and financial
      secrecy jurisdictions' (1986) 18 *Inter-American Law Review* 33 at 74. An example of
      the latter problem is that while civil law states require judicial authorities to issue letters
      rogatory, MLATs bind civil law states to accept inquiries emanating from the procuracy
      alone.

The United States advocated this legal innovation[80] and the benefits of MLATs encouraged other states to enter into them.[81]

In the context of multilateral international drug trafficking control, the MLAT revolution almost began at the 1961 Conference when the delegation from the Netherlands attempted to introduce a provision for mutual legal assistance into what eventually became article 35.[82] The attempt failed, and although the UN's 1987 Comprehensive Multidisciplinary Outline targets mutual judicial and legal assistance,[83] international drug control had to wait until 1988 before a sub-

---

80 For a survey of the negotiation history and content of US MLATs see E.A. Nadelmann, 'Negotiations in criminal law assistance treaties' (1985) 33 *American Journal of Comparative Law* 467-505; and A. Ellis and R. Pisani, 'The United States treaties on mutual assistance in criminal matters' in M.C. Bassiouni (ed.), *2 International Criminal Law: Procedure* (Transnational, Dobbs Ferry, 1986), pp. 151-179. It is important to note that these agreements were aimed at facilitating procedural co-operation on a broad front and not just in respect of drug trafficking/ money laundering, although the latter activities were the most significant reasons for the US's diplomatic efforts. A good example of a late 1980s MLAT is the Mutual Legal Assistance Co-operation Treaty between the US and Mexico, signed on 9 December 1987, 27 ILM 445. It makes provision for mutual assistance in: i) the taking of testimony or the statements of witnesses; ii) the provision of documents, records and evidence; iii) the execution of requests for searches and seizures; iv) the serving of documents; and v) the provision of assistance in procedures regarding the immobilisation, security and forfeiture of the proceeds, fruits and instrumentalities of crime. See, generally, B. Zagaris and J. Resnick, 'The Mexico-U.S. mutual legal assistance in criminal matters treaty: another step towards the harmonisation of international law enforcement' (1997) 14 *Arizona Journal of International and Comparative Law* 1-96.

81 See W. Gilmore, *Combating International Drug Trafficking: The 1988 United Nations Convention Against Illicit Traffic in Narcotic Drugs and Psychotropic Substances* (Commonwealth Secretariat, London, 1991), p. 23.

82 Its amendment to draft article 45 read: 'Parties shall ... 1(b) render each other, within the framework of the existing treaties or practice, mutual assistance in the widest sense to enable the most appropriate Party to try the offences specified in sub-paragraph (a)' – see *1961 Records* vol. II at 46. The background to this amendment was undoubtedly European experience in multilateral mutual assistance on which see generally D. McClean, 'Mutual assistance in criminal matters: the Commonwealth initiative' (1988) 37 ICLQ 177-190 who examines the origins and development of multilateral mutual legal assistance from the conclusion of the 1959 European Convention on Mutual Assistance in Criminal Matters, ETS 30.

83 Target 20, *Declaration of the International Conference on Drug Abuse Control and Illicit Trafficking and Comprehensive Multidisciplinary Outline of Future Activities in Drug Abuse Control*, UN Publication St/Nar/14, UN Sales No.E.88.XI.1, (New York, 1988).

stantive provision on mutual legal assistance was incorporated into an international drug convention.

5.4.2.2   Article 7's provisions for mutual legal assistance

Article 7, entitled 'Mutual Legal Assistance', is a comprehensive attempt to provide for mutual legal assistance in international drug control. The use of the term 'legal' throughout the article indicates that it contemplates judicial assistance or assistance in investigations leading to judicial proceedings.[84] It does not contemplate purely administrative assistance, which is catered for by article 9.[85] Because many states were either not familiar in the 1980s with the concept of mutual legal assistance or not party to an MLAT, article 7 also provides a fairly detailed guideline for the development of bilateral MLATs as well as facilitating mutual legal assistance in the absence of an MLAT for those states requiring the existence of a treaty to give effect to such assistance. Some of article 7's authors favoured a loose provision limited to the laying down of a principle of international co-operation in this field because of the incompatibility of their legal systems and practices. But those that favoured a detailed approach setting out a specific mechanism for mutual legal assistance won out, indicative of the intensity of the international pressure to harmonise drug control law in the late 1980s.[86] Nevertheless, because of resistance the article is not as detailed as bilateral MLATs. It focuses on the key elements of mutual legal assistance and omits detailed procedures for providing such assistance, which details are left to the Parties to formulate.

---

84   D.W. Sproule and P. St-Denis, 'The UN Drug Trafficking Convention: An Ambitious Step' 1989 CYBIL 263 at 286 note the preference of common law states for the term mutual legal assistance, and of civil states for mutual judicial assistance, a reflection of the fact that in common law states such functions are performed by law enforcement officers while in civil law states they are carried out by judicial officers.

85   See the 'Expert Group Report', *United Nations Conference for the Adoption of a Convention against Illicit Traffic in Narcotic Drugs and Psychotropic Substances, Official Records, Volume I* (New York, 1994) UN Doc. E/CONF.82/16, UN Publication Sales No. E.94.XI.5 (hereinafter *1988 Records* vol. I), p. 40; the 'Review Group Report', *1988 Records* vol. I at 67-68; statement of the French delegate, *United Nations Conference for the Adoption of a Convention against Illicit Traffic in Narcotic Drugs and Psychotropic Substances, Official Records, Volume II* (New York, 1991) UN Doc. E/CONF.82/16/Add.1, UN Publication Sales No. E.91.XI.1 (hereinafter *1988 Records* vol. II), p.180.

86   See the 'Expert Group Report', *1988 Records* vol. I at 39.

5.4.2.3   Limitations on article 7

Before examining in detail the obligations to provide mutual legal assistance contained in article 7, it is appropriate to point out the limitations operative upon it. Political and fiscal offence exceptions have been extended to mutual assistance and are common in MLATs[87] and legal assistance legislation.[88] For this reason article 7 is also made subject to article 3(10)'s limitation of the political and fiscal offence exception, discussed in detail in Chapter Four, which attempts to limit the application of the political or fiscal offence exception to mutual assistance in terms of article 7. In response to the fact that the domestic laws of many states insist upon the application of principles such as double criminality to the gathering of evidence for prosecution in foreign jurisdictions,[89] article 7(12) provides that requests for assistance must be executed in accordance with the domestic law of the requested Party and article 7(15)(d) allows Parties to refuse assistance if it would be contrary to their legal system to grant it. Article 7 is also limited by the operation of existing international instruments concerned with mutual legal assistance. Article 7(6) recognises that the whole field of mutual legal assistance, including that in respect of illicit drug matters, was by 1988 already covered by an existing network of treaties,[90]

---

87   The 1986 Harare 'Scheme Relating to Mutual Assistance in Criminal Matters Within the Commonwealth', (1986) 12 *Commonwealth Law Bulletin* 1118, provides for refusal of co-operation if the request relates to 'an offence or proceedings of a political character.'

88   See, for example, section 4(3) of the UK's Criminal Justice (International Co-operation) Act, 1990.

89   L. Frei and S. Treschel, 'Origins and applications of the United States – Switzerland Treaty on Mutual Assistance in Criminal Matters' (1990) 31 *Harvard International Law Journal* 77 point out at 84, for example, that in terms of article 4(2) of the 1973 MLAT between Switzerland and the US (27 UST 2019), a US or Swiss magistrate 'may decree searches, seizures of evidence, summons and interview of witnesses, or releases of banking or business secrecy only if the offence described in the request was also a violation of the laws of the requested state' and note that any rule to the contrary would contradict Swiss public order.

90   W.C. Gilmore, 'International action against drug trafficking: trends in United Kingdom law and practice through the 1980's' (1991) 17 *Commonwealth Law Bulletin* 287 at 294-300 examines, for example, the evolution of US-UK relations with regard to the Cayman Islands, a secrecy haven used for laundering by drug traffickers. After legal debacles such as the *Bank of Nova Scotia* 740 F.2d 817 (1981) where the US fined the bank $1 825 000 for failing to produce records from offshore branches even though compliance with the grand jury subpoena would have violated secrecy laws in those jurisdictions, the US and UK concluded the limited 1984 Cayman Islands Narcotics Activity Agreement (cmnd 9344) which gave the US assistance in investigation and

and makes it clear that the operation of these instruments is not jeopardised by article 7. Thus article 7(6) provides that article 7 will not affect the obligations created by MLATs that already govern the particular situation or which may govern it in the future, even if only partly. The United States delegate pointed out that the provisions of article 7 should not be considered to be 'exclusive or "first-resort" provisions' where the Parties were capable of obtaining the same results more expeditiously by treaty or under their domestic law.[91] But nor can existing mutual legal assistance arrangements be used to frustrate the obligation to render mutual legal assistance under article 7 in respect of novel provisions such as the money laundering offences in article 3(1). The Netherlands delegate to the 1988 Conference explained:

> The inference to be drawn from [article 7] was that where such obligations went further than those envisaged in the draft convention, they would not be affected by the latter; and conversely, where they did not go as far as the provisions of the convention, the latter should be regarded as the basis for obligations to render legal assistance in criminal matters.[92]

According to the United States delegation, existing bilateral treaties are amended automatically by article 7 to make extended assistance possible.[93]

Article 7(7) specifically limits the application of the detailed procedural provisions of article 7 contained in paragraphs 8 to 19 if such procedures already exist in some other form. Article 7(7) provides that if there is no MLAT[94] between the Parties they shall use the procedure laid down in paragraphs 8 to 19 when dealing with requests for mutual legal assistance. If, however, the Parties are bound by an MLAT, the procedural provisions of that MLAT shall

---

prosecution through access to documentary evidence. Its success lead to the more comprehensive 1986 Cayman Islands Mutual Legal Assistance Treaty (cmnd 9862).

91 *1988 Records* vol. I at 181.

92 *1988 Records* vol. II at 180.

93 'Report of the United States Delegation to the United Nations Conference for the adoption of a Convention Against Illicit Traffic in Narcotic Drugs and Psychotropic Substances' from *United Nations Convention Against Illicit Traffic in Narcotic Drugs and Psychotropic Substances* Senate Executive Report 101-15, 101st Congress, 1st Session, p. 60.

94 A 'mutual legal assistance treaty' would not include in this context less formal arrangements such as the Commonwealth Scheme – see *Commentary on the United Nations Convention Against Illicit Traffic in Narcotic Drugs and Psychotropic Substances, 1988* (New York, 1998) UN Doc. E/CN.7/590; UN Publication Sales No.E.98.XI.5, (hereinafter the *1988 Commentary*), p. 185.

apply unless they agree to apply paragraphs 8 to 19 instead. In other words, they may choose to rely on the procedure laid down in those paragraphs irrespective of whether the provisions of that MLAT are broader or narrower in scope than those of the 1988 Convention.[95] The purpose of article 7(7) is thus to avoid the legal problems that would have resulted from obliging Parties to change to the procedures set out in paragraphs 8 to 19 of article 7 when they were already committed to particular procedures in their domestic law that they had put into place as a result of obligations under previous MLATs.[96] Article 7(7) recognises that the procedures in such an MLAT may well be more appropriate to relations between states that have made an effort to tailor their bilateral relations to their particular legal systems.[97]

5.4.2.4 Article 7's substantive provisions

The substantive obligations of article 7 apply generally to all requests for mutual legal assistance between the Parties. Article 7(1) sets out a general obligation to provide mutual assistance, article 7(2) provides a list of modalities of mutual assistance which article 7(3) notes is an open list, article 7(4) sets out an obligation to encourage the presence of persons to assist in proceedings and article 7(5) provides an obligation to remove bank secrecy.

Article 7(1) is the cardinal provision in the 1988 Convention obliging the Parties to grant each other mutual legal assistance.[98] It is a strong obligation, not weakened by any internal limitation clause. Article 7(1) specifies that assistance is to be provided for the criminal investigation, prosecution and adjudication of article 3(1)'s trafficking offences and not for the personal use offence in article 3(2). It is to be made available for all criminal proceedings except for confiscation, for which a separate mutual legal assistance regime is provided in article 5(4). The reference to investigations appears to make it clear that operational assistance can be requested at the police investigation stage prior to the actual institution of criminal proceedings.[99] The point at which an investigation actually begins is not specified by the provision. It is submitted that either an article 3(1) offence should have occurred or there should

---

95   Netherlands delegate, *1988 Records* vol. II at 180.
96   See Sproule and St-Denis supra note 84 at 206.
97   *1988 Commentary* at 185.
98   The language used here is taken from article 1(a) of the 1959 European Convention on Mutual Assistance in Criminal Matters, ETS 130.
99   Some delegations, particularly Austria, had reservations about an obligation to provide mutual legal assistance to purely police investigations – Report of the US Delegation supra note 93 at 59.

be reason to believe such an offence will occur before an investigation leading to prosecution and trial can be said to exist. The article contemplates assistance in the process leading up to and including judicial proceedings. Administrative proceedings fall outside its scope but provision is made for administrative co-operation in article 9.[100] The fact that the text refers to the 'widest measure' of assistance is intended to encourage broad and non-technical forms of assistance, including, but not limited to, the forms of assistance mentioned expressly in article 7.[101]

Article 7(2) details non-exhaustively forms of assistance that may be requested. It covers a wide range of investigation procedures and information gathering usually contained in bilateral MLATs and represents the core elements of mutual legal assistance.[102]

Looking more closely at this catalogue, article 7(2)(a) allows requests for the gathering of 'evidence or statements from persons'.[103] A distinction between 'statements' and 'evidence' appears to have been made because in common law systems 'statements' imply the taking of evidence under oath without which they would have no evidential value, and because making a false statement can lead to perjury.[104] The term 'evidence' effectively covers all other forms of oral evidence.[105] The provision is silent as to whether the 'persons' from whom this evidence is to be taken are compellable, that is, bound to testify

---

100 See the 'Expert Group Report', *1988 Records* vol. I at 39-40.

101 *1988 Commentary* at 178.

102 *1988 Commentary* at 201.

103 See, for example, section 3(1) of the UK's Criminal Justice (International Co-operation) Act, 1990. It provides that a judicial officer may issue 'a "letter of request" requesting assistance in obtaining outside the United Kingdom such evidence as is specified in the letter for use in ... proceedings or investigation.' Section 3(2) allows the accused to make such a request and section 3(3) the prosecuting authority. The request is sent to the Secretary of State for onward transmission in terms of section 3(4) to the court with jurisdiction in the foreign state or to the recognised authority for dealing with such requests in that state. Section 4 of the Act makes provision for the gathering of evidence for foreign jurisdictions within the UK. The UK will in terms of section 4(1) allow such requests from courts, prosecuting authorities or other authorities in respect of investigations or proceedings. Requests are routed through the Secretary of State who in terms of section 4(2) nominates a court in the UK for receipt of such evidence.

104 *1988 Records* vol. II at 174.

105 Its use was criticised at the 1988 Conference because in certain states it includes items seized from persons, but was preferred to the term 'testimony' because it includes expert evidence – see the statements of the Japanese and Israeli delegates for the former position and the Italian and Australian delegates for the latter position, *1988 Records* vol. II at 174.

or produce evidence, and also says nothing about the testimonial privileges that they enjoy. These are thus issues of the domestic law of the requested Party, which also lays down the conditions for the taking of oral testimony.[106]

Article 7(2)(b) allows requests for the 'effective service of judicial documents'. Details of the particular procedure for the mode of service and proof of service may be stipulated by the requesting Party in terms of article 7(10)(d) in order to satisfy its legal requirements. The requested Party will in terms of article 7(12) comply but only to the extent not contrary to its domestic law as that law governs execution of requests for assistance.[107]

Article 7(2)(c) allows requests for the execution of searches and seizures.[108] These include searches of premises, land, vehicles, vessels and aircraft.[109] The objective of such searches and seizures must be the obtaining of evidence for prosecution and not just the confiscation of the material searched for or seized. Again the procedure adopted will be in accordance with the requesting Party's law but only to the extent permitted by the law of the re-

---

106 The *1988 Commentary* at 201 notes that these details include the taking of oaths or affirmations, the participation of legal representatives, the use of cross-examination or judicial questioning, penalisation of perjury and witness protection.

107 *1988 Commentary* at 179. See, for example, sections 1 and 2 of the UK's Criminal Justice (International Co-operation) Act, 1990, which provide respectively for the service of foreign process in the UK and the service of UK process abroad. Section 1 provides a useful example of the kind of procedure used to put article 7(2)'s provisions into domestic operation. Section 1(1) provides that the section comes into operation when the UK's Secretary of State receives from a foreign state's government or authority either i) a summons or some other process requiring a person to appear as a defendant or witness in criminal proceedings in that state or ii) some other document recording a decision of a criminal court in that state, together with a request that it be served on someone in the UK. Section 1(2) provides for personal or postal service while section 1(3) provides that service of such process imposes no obligation under the law of the UK to comply, i.e. failure to comply is not contempt of court in the UK. Section 1(4) provides that upon service such process shall be accompanied by a notice explaining section 1(3), and informing the person upon whom the notice is served that he may wish to seek advice about the possible consequences of failing to comply with the process under the law of the state which issued it, and that under that state's law he may not be accorded the same protections accorded to witnesses in the UK. Section 1(5) deals with receipt or failure to serve.

108 See, for example, section 7 of the UK's Criminal Justice (International Co-operation) Act, 1990, which makes provisions for the granting of search warrants to British police upon a foreign authority's request to the Secretary of State.

109 See the widely supported remarks of the Canadian delegate – *1988 Records* vol. II at 174.

quested Party. Guidance on the domestic detail required may be had from other international instruments.[110]

Article 7(2)(d) which allows requests for the examination of 'objects and sites' is ambiguous and overlaps with article 7(2)(c), but its inclusion was justified on the basis 'that it represented a useful form of mutual legal assistance particularly for reconstituting offences committed in the territory of other States or for verifying evidence based on the interview of witnesses.'[111] No detail of the content of the report that will flow from such a request is provided.

Article 7(2)(e) allows requests for the provision of certain information and evidentiary items. It is intended to include the kind of material not available under any of the other sub-paragraphs.[112] Thus it would not include material in the hands of private persons subject to search and seizure under article 7(2)(c). However, provision of these forms of material may be hit by article 7(12) as the domestic law of Parties may in certain cases prevent information or objects from leaving national territory.

Article 7(2)(f) allows requests for original documents and records, or certified copies. These documents may include bank, financial, corporate or business records. They need not necessarily be in the hands of the requested Party when the request is made. Some delegations to the 1988 Conference stated that they would have difficulty in providing assistance in this regard and in regard to article 7(2)(g) unless criminal proceedings had been instituted against a suspected offender.[113]

Article 7(2)(g) provides for requests for the 'identification or tracing of proceeds, property, instrumentalities and other things' for the purposes of evidence. The inclusion of 'tracing' was regarded 'as useful for evidentiary

---

110 See, for example, article 17 of the 1990 UN Model Treaty on Mutual Assistance in Criminal Matters, GA Res. 45/117, which provides for delivery of materials acquired through search and seizure and the protection of bona fide third parties.

111 See the 'Review Group Report', *1988 Records* vol. I at 69.

112 *1988 Commentary* at 180.

113 See the statement of the Austrian delegate supported by the Jamaican, Saudi Arabian, Israeli and Mauritian delegates, *1988 Records* vol. II at 177. Lebanon has made a reservation regarding article 7(2)(f) (11/3/1996) to which France (7/3/1997), Germany (21/3/1997), UK (10/3/1997), Finland (24/4/1997), Italy (24/4/1997), Netherlands (11.3.1997), Sweden (7/3/1997), Austria (11/7/1997) and Greece (18/7/1997) have all objected – see *Multilateral Treaties Deposited with the Secretary General: Status as at 30 April 1999* (New York, 1999) UN Doc. St/Leg/Ser.E/17. Given that mutual assistance in the pursuit of drug traffickers is one of the major aims of the 1988 Convention, Lebanon's reservation must be considered contrary to the object and purpose of the 1988 Convention and thus invalid.

purposes in cases where proceeds from drug trafficking were transmitted from one country to another by electronic means.'[114] This provision appears to relate to the provision in article 5 for seizure and confiscation, yet explicit reference to seizure and confiscation was excluded from article 7(2)(g) because of article 7's limited objective of investigation and prosecution.[115] Whether such requests can be made for the purpose of article 5 seizures or confiscations is thus unclear, but it seems illogical not to permit requests for such purposes as prevention of the dispersal of such material is one of the objectives of the 1988 Convention.

Assistance with regard to the modalities in article 7(2) appears mandatory. Parties cannot limit this list, but article 7(3), which provides that article 7(2) is not a numerus clausus, makes it clear that they may extend this list to 'any other forms of mutual legal assistance' permitted by their domestic law. Other forms of assistance may include the verification in laboratories of the illegal nature of substances seized,[116] monitoring of telecommunications, access to computer systems, and the identification and/or location of persons, something not explicitly provided for in article 7(4) which is discussed below.[117] Some Parties that have made specific domestic provision for assistance of the kind envisaged in article 7(2) have specifically left open the possibility of other forms of assistance being rendered.[118]

Article 7(4) obliges Parties to facilitate or encourage the presence or availability of persons to assist in investigations or proceedings. Triggered by a request from another Party,[119] this provision anticipates the requested Party

---

114 Statement of the US delegate, *1988 Records* vol. II at 177.

115 See the 'Review Group Report', *1988 Records* vol. I at 69.

116 Something mentioned under paragraph 257 of Target 20 of the 1987 Comprehensive Multidisciplinary Outline – *Declaration of the International Conference on Drug Abuse and Illicit Trafficking and Comprehensive Multidisciplinary Outline of Future Activities in Drug Abuse Control*, UN Publication St/Nar/14, UN Sales No.E.88.XI.1, (New York, 1988), p. 61.

117 See, by contrast, article 1(2) of the 1986 US-UK Cayman Islands MLAT (cmnd 9682) which specifies this form of assistance as does paragraph 1(3)(a) of the 1986 Harare Scheme for Mutual Assistance in Criminal Matters, (1986) 12 *Commonwealth Law Bulletin* 1118.

118 See, for example, section 31 of South Africa's International Co-operation in Criminal Matters Act 75 of 1996.

119 There is no obligation on a Party to facilitate the travel of a person in custody within its territory who demands permission to travel to another Party in order to be present at a deposition being taken there in connection with a criminal case against them – Report of the US Delegation supra note 93 at 60.

encouraging the availability of persons, both at large and in custody,[120] for
evidentiary purposes, but not for the execution of sanctions.[121] Such encouragement may range from arranging for a simple interview to simplifying
obstacles to travel, such as the requirements of witnesses for travel documents
or permission of someone in custody to travel.[122] This obligation falls on both
Parties. Thus a requesting Party would have to, for example, assure the requested Party that a travelling prisoner would be secure and kept in appropriate
conditions. Article 7(4) is limited by the constraints of the requested Party's
'domestic law and practice' and by the fact that the requested Party requires
the consent of the person concerned. With regard to the former safeguard, many
of the matters may fall within the discretion of administrative authorities.[123]
The latter safeguard applies to persons in custody and at liberty. These limitations are also backed up by the safe conduct provision in article 7(18) for
persons giving evidence. It has been argued that paragraphs 4 and 18 of article
7 weaken the 1988 Convention as an effective weapon against the illicit traffic,
because they only encourage and do not compel expert and lay witnesses to
testify in a requesting Party. If key witnesses choose not to appear the prosecution's case may be destroyed. It has therefore been pointed out that these
provisions compare badly to existing bilateral MLATs which make provision
for the compulsion of witnesses from one state to testify in another.[124]
However, inclusion in a multilateral treaty of "international subpoena" provisions
doing away with the requirement that witnesses consent to give evidence in

---

120 Section 5(1) of the UK's Criminal Justice (International Co-operation) Act, 1990,
    provides for the transfer of prisoners to give evidence or to be identified in or assist
    through their presence in the investigation of an offence, but the prisoner's consent is
    required in terms of section 5(2). Section 6 provides for the reverse procedure but once
    again the foreign state's prisoner must consent in terms of section 6(3).
121 See the 'Expert Group Report', *1988 Records* vol. I at 40.
122 Report of the US Delegation supra note 93 at 60.
123 *1988 Commentary* at 183.
124 T.M. Catino, 'Italian and American co-operative efforts to reduce heroin trafficking:
    a role model for the United States and drug supplying foreign nations' (1990) 8 *Dickin-
    son Journal of International Law* 415 at 437. She prefers the international subpoena
    provision in the 1982 US MLAT with Italy which in article 15 makes provision for
    the compulsion of a witness where: i) there is no reasonable basis to deny it; ii) the
    witness would be compellable in similar circumstances in the requested state; and iii)
    the central authority of the requesting country certifies that the witness's testimony is
    material. Failure to appear if ordered results in the same sanctions as are usually applied
    to such failure in the requested state.

another Party was not politically practical in 1988, when states were still being introduced to the concept of mutual legal assistance.[125]

By 1988 bilateral MLATS had already proved to be a powerful means for penetrating financial secrecy laws. Although there was some resistance before and during the 1988 Conference to provide as a part of legal assistance for the mandatory withdrawal of the curtain of bank secrecy, the conclusion of article 7(5), which provides that a Party may not refuse mutual assistance on grounds of bank secrecy, reflects the general concern that delegates felt about the employment of bank secrecy as a justification for refusing assistance.[126]

An area where article 7(5) is particularly significant is the identification and confiscation of the illicit proceeds of drug trafficking in terms of article 5 of the 1988 Convention. This process faces enormous difficulties due to the penetration of the licit financial system by illicit funds. The Canadian delegate to the 1988 Conference noted that it was appropriate 'for the purposes of the confiscation measures contemplated in the Convention, ... to have access to bank records in order to investigate drug trafficking offences.'[127]

The US Attorney General described the extent of the obligation article 7(5) imposes on Parties as follows:

---

125 See McClean supra note 82 at 186. UK legislation requires the consent of any prisoner held in the UK before such transfer will be made – section 5(2) of the Criminal Justice (International Co-operation) Act, 1990. So does article 19 of the 1992 Inter-American Convention on Mutual Assistance in Criminal Matters.

126 See generally W.C. Gilmore, 'International initiatives' in R. Parlour (ed.), *Butterworths International Guide to Money Laundering Law and Practice* (Butterworths, London, 1995), p.15 at p. 24. He notes that the Nigerian delegate pointed out the importance of access to bank records in the investigation and deterrence of traffickers – see *1988 Records* vol. II at 178. Some delegates to the Expert Group which reviewed the draft convention opposed the inclusion of this provision on the basis that it was too sensitive to be dealt with by an international convention and was a matter of domestic law – see the 'Expert Group Report', *1988 Records* vol. I at 40; see generally Committee I's records in *1988 Records* vol. II at 178-179. However, the provision reflects developments in domestic law and bilateral relations. In 1987, for example, the Swiss Banker's Association and its member banks developed new rules (Agreement on Due Diligence of 1 July 1987) and practices on limiting bank secrecy. O. Dunant and M. Wassmer, 'Swiss bank secrecy: its limits under Swiss and international laws' (1988) 20 *Case Western Reserve Journal of International Law* 541-575 examine Switzerland's bilateral relations with the US and its own efforts at self-regulation in detail, and conclude at pp. 574-575 that while it still preserves bank secrecy, it has provided itself with the means to participate in international co-operation, and note that every request for assistance made by the US in 1987 in terms of their 1975 Mutual Assistance Treaty was accepted.

127 *1988 Records* vol. II at 178.

First, it is an obligation to enact implementing legislation, if necessary, to modify domestic bank secrecy laws to permit execution of requests for bank records under the Convention. Second, with respect to an individual request for bank records under the Convention, it obliges a requested Party to grant the request, if the only basis for refusing would be bank secrecy laws.[128]

The first part of this statement implies action on the part of the requested Party. The original version of article 7(5) obliged Parties to empower their courts to order records to be made available, but this is provided for now by article 5(3) read with article 5(4)(c), which together allow for such court orders to carry out the obligations of an international treaty. In the second part of the statement, the US Attorney General is pointing out that a requested Party cannot use bank secrecy as a reason for refusing mutual legal assistance in terms of article 7(15). Thus a potential conflict between article 7(15) and article 5's provision for confiscation is also avoided.[129]

In order to achieve the purpose of article 7 as a whole, article 7(5) is an exception to the general approach of article 7 summed up in article 7(12) which provides that assistance will be rendered in accordance with the domestic law of the requested Party, and which makes it plain that the requested Party is under no duty to contravene its own laws in order to give assistance. With respect to bank secrecy the 1988 Convention overrides domestic law[130] and other MLATs that permit bank secrecy.[131] Lebanon reserved on article 7(5) but its reservation has been objected to by a number of Parties and the legality of the reservation must be questionable given that the clear object and purpose of the 1988 Convention is to expose drug traffickers and money launderers to prosecution and confiscation of illicit assets.[132]

---

128 *United Nations Convention Against the Illicit Traffic in Narcotic Drugs and Psychotropic Substances,* Senate Executive Report 101-15, 101st Congress, 1st Session, p. 185.

129 See the statement of the Japanese delegate, *1988 Records* vol. II at 179.

130 See McClean supra note 7 at 177.

131 See McClean supra note 7 at 177-178 that an 'extensive interpretation of the provisions that the Convention is not to "affect" the obligations under other treaties could rob it of all significance where the countries concerned were parties to a general mutual assistance treaty.'

132 Lebanon (11/3/1996) to which France (7/3/1997), Germany (21/3/1997), UK (10/3/1997), Finland (24/4/1997), Italy (24/4/1997), Netherlands (11.3.1997), Sweden (7/3/1997), Austria (11/7/1997) and Greece (18/7/1997) have all objected – see *Multilateral Treaties Deposited with the Secretary General: Status as at 30 April 1999* (New York, 1999) UN Doc. St/Leg/Ser.E/17.

5.4.2.5   Article 7's procedural provisions

The procedures set out in article 7 paragraphs 8 to 18 detail the steps necessary for the successful request and grant of effective assistance. They settle issues such as which organs may make requests, the formal requirements of a request, the information it must contain, requests for additional information, legal restrictions, limits of use and confidentiality, grounds and reasons for refusal, postponement, safe conduct for witnesses and payment. These procedural obligations are limited by article 7(7) which provides that they will not apply if a request for mutual legal assistance is made by a Party to which the requested Party is already bound by an existing mutual legal assistance treaty. In such a case 'the corresponding provisions of that treaty shall apply unless the Parties agree to apply paragraphs 8 to 19 of this article in lieu thereof'.

Article 7(8) identifies the authorities that may handle requests for assistance and the methods they may use to transmit requests. There was strong interest at the 1988 Conference in providing for a central authority through which all requests for mutual assistance would flow and which would co-ordinate and monitor the progress of requests. Experience showed the value of such an authority.[133] In the requested state, central authorities reduce delay in the receipt and transmission of a request as they provide a direct entry point into the foreign legal system. They also provide easily accessible information in respect of the relevant legislation and execution process. In requesting states, a central authority ensures that requests are in a usable form and contain sufficient information to allow for their execution and that the most urgent and significant requests are made first. Unfortunately, article 7(8), in order to accommodate current practice in matters of legal assistance, allows for the possibility of more than one authority to process requests. It obliges each Party to designate an 'authority', or 'authorities' where necessary,[134] to be responsible for and have the power to execute requests for legal assistance. The designation of a single authority would centralise the process and make it more

---

133   See generally K. Prost, 'Breaking down the barriers: international co-operation in combating transnational crime' in *Souvenir Brochure of the International Conference on Global drugs Law* (Indian Law Institute, New Delhi, 1997), p. 44 at pp. 47-48.

134   The designation of more than one authority caters for the situation in federal states or in states where mutual assistance in criminal matters is in the purview of various jurisdictions – see the 'Review Group Report', *1988 Records* vol. I at 70. While it has been criticised, the US delegation to the 1988 Conference points out that this provision allows states which have dependent territories to designate a separate authority for that territory thus making possible direct communication with the territorial authority responsible for executing requests – Report of the US Delegation supra note 93 at 61.

efficient, especially in the case of a Party which has more than one agency competent on drug issues.[135]

The provision adopts a flexible approach to the identification of these authorities, similar to that of article 35(e) of the 1961 Convention. The designated authority(ies) will be the one responsible for executing the request. When a requested authority does not have the necessary information or is not legally competent to provide it, that authority will be obliged to transmit the request to the competent authority together with a request to provide the requesting Party with the information. For requests through the diplomatic channel the designated authority would have to be the Ministry of Foreign Affairs. But if not, it may be a law enforcement agency with the necessary authority, for example, a national police drugs unit. The identity of the designated authority or authorities must be communicated to the UN Secretariat.[136]

Although article 7(8) provides that designated 'authorities' will transmit requests to each other and communicate with each other, it does not specify

---

135 Prost supra note 133 at 48 states: 'It is critical to note that the establishment of a central authority for mutual assistance does not require the creation of an elaborate structure that is resource intensive. The models for successful central authorities are as varied as the number of states that have created them. The possibilities range from a central authority created by statute, to a group of officials carrying out delegated functions within an establishment department, to a person who, by practice, is responsible for co-ordinating all such requests. There are, or course, advantages and disadvantages to each method. For example, legislated central authorities have the authority of statute, and can better control and influence the execution of requests. Legislation also provides an opportunity to clearly define the functions of the central authority. On the other hand, legislation is costly and resource heavy and provides only limited flexibility to an authority which may be required to change and adjust as the practice of mutual assistance develops. For smaller countries with limited resources, it may be more realistic to establish a central authority by practice or as a delegated authority of a minister.' Whatever the arrangements, the *1988 Commentary* at 205 notes that it will be important that the designated authority can provide information on its country's legal requirements for the execution of requests to other Parties and any follow-up information required. It should also function to review requests before they are made. In practice, it seems that a central authority may function as little more than a glorified post-box, ensuring requests are correctly addressed – see C. Murray and L. Harris, *Mutual Assistance in Criminal Matters* (Sweet and Maxwell, London, 2000), p. 17.

136 The UN regularly publishes a list of these authorities including their address, telephone and facsimile numbers and whether they permit urgent requests through Interpol – see *Competent Authorities under the International Drug Control Treaties* issued by the UNDCP in the ST/NAR series. For example, the UK has notified that 'The authority designated by the United Kingdom under article 7, paragraph 8 is the Central Authority, C7 division, Home Office, 50 Queen Anne's Gate, London, SW1H9AT.'

the method of such transmission or communication and the Parties will decide upon it.[137] Direct communication is possible, but article 7(8) reserves the right of a Party to use the diplomatic channel. Parties may also agree, in urgent circumstances, if it is possible, to use Interpol.[138] Article 7(8) does not contemplate a rigid approach which uses direct communication between law enforcement agencies or Interpol at the investigation stage, and which always switches to diplomatic channels once criminal proceedings have begun. The alleged virtues of the diplomatic channel are assurance that the request reaches the competent service and provision of facilities for translation and mail servicing.[139] But article 7(8) anticipates the use of the fastest method and it has been observed that diplomatic channels should be avoided at both the trial and investigation stage as they are notoriously slow and inefficient, do not function smoothly in all regions, and smaller states have a limited network of diplomatic representation.[140]

Finally, article 7(8) says nothing about the agencies that may initiate a request through the central authority. In practice, law enforcement agencies or public prosecutors or judicial authorities may initiate a request for assistance.[141] In principle, it seems possible for such requests to be initiated by private prosecutors or even the defence in a criminal case.

Article 7(9) sets out the formal requirements for a valid request. It provides that requests are to be in writing in the language(s) acceptable to the requested Party.[142] The UN Secretariat will provide information as to the acceptable languages, as Parties are obliged to notify it of such.[143] The *1988 Commentary* notes that in most cases the national language of the requested Party should be used. In situations where it is unfamiliar, the *Commentary* encourages the choice of a language used in international communication.[144] Requests for

---

137 Suitable telecommunications equipment will be a necessity.
138 This possibility was included to develop Interpol's role in the struggle against drug trafficking – see the Chinese delegate's statement, *1988 Records* vol. II at 183.
139 The 'Review Group Report', *1988 Records* vol. I at 70.
140 See the 'Review Group Report', *1988 Records* vol. I at 70.
141 See, for example, article 4 of the 1986 Harare Scheme Relating to Mutual Assistance in Criminal Matters. The *1988 Commentary* at 205 notes that the designation of a person in each agency responsible for generating requests and to serve as a contact person helps the system to function effectively.
142 Writing includes telex messages, telegrams, faxes and electronic mail.
143 This will be especially necessary where the Party concerned has more than one official language.
144 *1988 Commentary* at 187. It also notes the enormous practical importance of adequate translation facilities.

the service of documents requiring the appearance of persons before the author-ities of the requesting Party must be transmitted in a reasonable time before the scheduled appearance.[145] Oral requests may be made, but only with the agreement of the Parties and only if the circumstances are urgent, and they must be confirmed in writing.[146]

Article 7(10) sets out the information that a request must contain. Article 7(10)(a) insists upon the indication in the request of the identity of the authority making the request, but does not require any further detail on that authority. Article 7(10)(b) requires the setting out of the substance and character of the investigation, prosecution or procedure to which the request relates, and the identity and functions of the authority conducting the investigation, prosecution or proceeding. This information is intended to give the requested Party some notion of the capacity in which this authority is acting.[147] This authority may be the designated authority contemplated by article 7(10)(a), but it may be some other agency. Article 7(10)(b)'s information will be used in practice by Parties' authorities to decide whether they will grant the request.[148] Article 7(10)(c) requires a summary of the relevant facts of the matter in all cases except requests for the service of judicial documents. In the latter instance delegates to the 1988 Conference regarded summaries as inappropriate.[149] Some states consider fact-summaries as cumbersome, but others regard them as essential in practice.[150] Article 7(10)(d) requires a description of the assistance sought

---

145 This is particularly the case where the right to a speedy trial applies, but the onus is on the prosecution in the requesting Party to anticipate what information they will need and the date by which it must be available, and make their request for assistance in good time.

146 Although written requests are standard practice in MLATs, certain treaties such as the International Convention on Mutual Administrative Assistance for the Prevention, Investigation and Repression of Customs Offences, adopted in Nairobi in 1977, provide for the possibility of oral requests to expedite the exchange of information between parties in urgent circumstances. Nonetheless, there was some resistance at the 1988 Conference to oral requests – see generally *1988 Records* vol. II at 185.

147 See the 'Review Group Report', *1988 Records* vol. I at 71.

148 See, for example, section 4(2) of the UK's Criminal Justice (International Co-operation) Act, 1990, which requires the Secretary of State to be satisfied '(a) that an offence under the law of the country or territory in question has been committed or that there are reasonable grounds for suspecting that such an offence has been committed; and (b) that proceedings in respect of that offence have been instituted in that country or that territory and that an investigation into that offence is being carried on there' before granting a request for assistance.

149 See the statement of the French delegate, *1988 Records* vol. II at 186.

150 See the 'Review Group Report', *1988 Records* vol. I at 71.

and details of any particular procedure the requesting Party would like followed. Following procedures compatible with the law of the requesting Party is necessary to make the information usable within the requesting Party.[151] Article 7(10)(e) requires, if possible, the identity, location and nationality of any person concerned. Such persons include not only accused persons but also any person whose testimony might be required.[152] It would be essential for the requested Party to be informed as to whether such persons were suspects or only witnesses as it 'could affect the way any interview with them was conducted and the legal validity of the information gained.'[153] Article 7(10)(f) requires the request to set out the purpose for which the evidence and so on is being requested, in order 'to enable the requested Party to gain an appreciation of the circumstances surrounding the request for their assistance.'[154] Knowledge of the purpose of the request also assists the requested Party in deciding on any potential violation of article 7(13) which prevents a requesting Party from using evidence for investigations and prosecutions other than that stated in the request.

Article 7(11) caters for the situation where the requested Party wants information other than that provided for in article 7(10). It allows a requested Party to ask for additional information if it appears necessary to execute or facilitate the request. Such a situation may occur where the original request did not contain information necessary to execute the request,[155] or where the material circumstances change after the request is made but before it is executed.[156] Time will be saved if in consequence of the requirements of article 7(10) a copy of the court order or judgment relevant to the request and the applicable provisions of the criminal law accompany the initial request.[157] Information on matters such as the length of time available for compliance and confidentiality requirements should also be provided.

---

151 The *1988 Commentary* at 189 gives as examples the administration of oaths to witnesses, the taking of verbatim records of witness interviews etc.
152 Statement of the Chairman of Committee I, *1988 Records* vol. II at 186.
153 Statement of the Netherlands delegate, *1988 Records* vol. II at 187.
154 Statement of the Jamaican delegate, *1988 Records* vol. II at 187.
155 The *1988 Commentary* at 190 gives as an example a request that does not contain a specific piece of information necessary for the grant of a judicial order to execute a search warrant.
156 The *1988 Commentary* at 190 gives as an example a situation where a request is made to trace property and the person believed to be holding the property leaves the country concerned.
157 Statement of the Colombian delegate, *1988 Records* vol. II at 187.

The principle restrictive provision on requests is article 7(12). It provides firstly that requests for assistance shall be executed 'to the extent not contrary to the domestic law of the requested Party'. It is obvious from the provisions of the rest of article 7 that requests will be executed within the restrictions of each Party's domestic law. However, in order to be effective, the execution of a request has to provide information in a form functional to the requesting Party hence article 7(12)'s further provision that the requests shall be executed 'where possible, in accordance with the procedures specified in the request.' The authors of this provision did not want insistence by the requested Party that requests be executed in a manner that suited it to frustrate the production of evidence effective in the requesting Party. In order to suit the requesting Party's procedural rules and requirements for admission of evidence, the provision requires the requested Party to follow the procedures specified in the request to the extent that these rules are not contrary to its domestic law even though they may not be required by that domestic law. Only if the procedure requested by the requesting Party conflicts with the law of the requested Party may the latter validly substitute these procedures with its own. Thus, for example, in a situation where the requesting Party had requested that a witness be both examined and opportunity be given for cross-examination in order to ensure the admissibility of the testimony in its courts, if the requested Party then disallowed cross-examination it would render the information dysfunctional. In terms of article 7(12), however, cross-examination would have to be allowed unless it conflicted with the domestic law of the requested Party, in which circumstances the request would be pointless anyway. The *1988 Commentary* urges discussion to avoid conflict,[158] but the example illustrates that article 7(12) also functions to clarify potential conflicts between the legal systems of the Parties as quickly as possible. States in practice do grant authority to their courts to assist foreign tribunals and allow the taking of evidence according to the practice of the requesting state.[159]

Article 7(13) imposes restrictions on the uses to which the information or evidence furnished by the requested Party may be put. This obligation may be cumbersome, as requesting Parties will often not be aware of all the purposes for which the information might be used. But the problem disappears when the obligation is made dependent upon the purpose for which the information is to be used. Article 7(10)(b) requires the requesting Party to state the purpose

---

158 *1988 Commentary* at 191.
159 See, for example, the broad authority to do this given to US courts by 28 USC section 1782.

for which the information is necessary, and article 7(13) provides that the requesting Party may not transfer to another Party,[160] or itself use, the information given it by the requested Party for any purpose other than that stated in the request without the latter's prior consent.[161] Thus disclosure in public of the information for the requested purpose is possible, but the onus is firmly on the requesting Party if it wishes to depart from the purpose laid down in the request. It has been suggested by the Jamaican delegate to the 1988 Conference that article 7(13) introduces the concept of speciality to the practice of mutual legal assistance. He said

> that he interpreted the paragraph as meaning that if information was requested for the purpose of dealing with a particular type of offence, it should not be used without the consent of the requested Party for dealing with any other type of offence. The Convention stipulated elsewhere that drug-related offences should not be considered as fiscal offences [article 3(10)], for otherwise the requested country might deny the request. Some countries might, however, agree to provide assistance in the case of drug-related offences notwithstanding their general policy, and it therefore seemed clear that if a Party wished to use information for any purpose other than in connection with a specific offence it had to seek the consent of the requested Party.[162]

Thus article 7(13) limits the usage of materials, information or evidence for purposes other than those requested, and only establishes an obligation of confidentiality on the requesting Party with respect to improper usage of the information. Improper usage occurs when the requested Party would not have granted the request in the first place.[163]

An obligation of confidentiality is imposed on the requested Party by article 7(14), which gives the requesting Party the right to ask that the 'fact and substance' of the request be kept confidential except to the extent necessary to execute it. The requested Party must inform the requesting Party immediately if it cannot comply. While article 7(14) recognises the need to protect sensitive

---

160 It was clearly understood by the delegates to Committee I that transmit meant transfer to another Party, *1988 Records* vol. II at 190 and 192.

161 See, for example, section 3(7) of the UK's Criminal Justice (International Co-operation) Act, 1990, which provides that 'evidence obtained by virtue of a letter of request shall not without the consent of an [appropriate foreign state's] authority ... be used for any purpose other than that specified in the letter.' The subsection also provides for the return of the documents unless the authority indicates that it is unnecessary.

162 *1988 Records* vol. II at 190.

163 *1988 Commentary* at 193.

investigative information, it also recognises that it may be impossible to keep such information confidential[164] and leaves it up to the requesting Party to decide whether to proceed with the request if confidentiality is breached.

Neither article 7(13) nor article 7(14) deal with the situation where a Party withholds important information on the illicit traffic from another Party. The Jamaican delegate pointed out that a Party would not be in breach of either paragraph if it refused to hand over information it considered to be highly confidential unless the requesting Party guaranteed not to disclose it.[165] The Barbadian delegate 'hoped that countries with superior intelligence agencies would provide small countries such as Barbados with all the information needed to put the Convention into effect.'[166] Unfortunately, the 1988 Convention contains no obligation to that effect.

Article 7(15) sets out the authorised grounds for refusing a request. It must be read together with article 3(10)'s limitation of the political and fiscal exception, which excludes political and fiscal grounds as grounds of refusal. Grounds for refusal do not change article 7's mandatory provisions to discretionary provisions.[167] The enumeration of the grounds for refusal is framed in such as way so as to protect the essential interests of the requested Party.

Article 7(15)(a), which provides that the request may be refused if it does not conform to the provisions of article 7, helps in particular to ensure requests conform to the procedural provisions of the article.

Article 7(15)(b) protects national interests by allowing refusal if the requested Party considers execution of the request 'likely to prejudice its sovereignty, security, *ordre public* or other essential interests.' What is protected here are state interests, not the interests of individuals.[168] On ratification of the 1988 Convention, the United States interpreted article 7(15)(b) to mean that it

> shall deny a request for assistance when the designated authority, after consultation with all appropriate intelligence, anti-narcotic, and foreign policy agencies, has specific information that a senior government official who will have access to

---

164 The requested Party's law may, for instance, provide for public notification of any confiscation procedure.
165 *1988 Records* vol. II at 33.
166 *1988 Records* vol. II at 33.
167 Report of the US Delegation supra note 93 at 64.
168 *1988 Commentary* at 195.

information to be provided under this treaty is engaged in or facilitates the production or distribution of illegal drugs.[169]

But this is just one narrow example of the national interests that potentially fall under the protection of article 7(15)(b). These interests could conceivably include economic interests, security interests and interests relating to internal public order. The provision is so broadly worded that it provides a blanket opt-out provision undermining mutual legal assistance under the 1988 Convention.

Article 7(15)(c) provides that legal assistance may be refused in cases where the requested Party would not be able to comply with such a request in criminal investigations or proceedings under its own jurisdiction. In effect, it means that the requested Party cannot be asked to go further at the behest of the requesting Party than it can within the confines of its law.[170]

Article 7(15)(d) allows refusal if the request is contrary to the domestic law, legal procedure or local practices relating to legal assistance of the requested Party. This appears to cover a situation where domestic legislation provides for specific grounds for refusal. In most states such a refusal might occur if it was known that the object of the request might be prosecuted on the grounds of race, religion or political opinion.[171] Other potential grounds for refusal may include: double jeopardy – the fact that the request relates to conduct for which the suspected or alleged offender has already been acquitted or convicted in any state; absence of double criminality – the fact that the request is not based on an offence recognised in the requested Party; and the death penalty exception – the potential imposition of the death penalty in the

---

169 20/2/1990 – *Multilateral Treaties Deposited with the Secretary General: Status as at 31 December 1996* (New York, 1997) UN Doc. St/Leg/Ser.E/15, p. 306 (hereinafter *Multilateral Treaties Deposited* (1997). Mexico objected to this declaration by the US because it considered the declaration a unilateral claim to justification for denying legal assistance to a requesting Party which ran counter to the Convention which amounted to a reservation – (10/7/1990) *Multilateral Treaties Deposited* (1997) at 307. However, given that article 7(15)(b) protects national interests and given that the US declaration is intended to prevent information landing in the hands of illicit traffickers, it is difficult to see how the US declaration is contrary to the purpose of the 1988 Convention.

170 Statement of the Netherlands delegate, *1988 Records* vol. II at 193. An example would be where the requesting Party requested the taking of a body-sample but the requested Party's law did not provide for the taking of such samples. See, for example, 28 USC section 1782 which provides that a US court may not, in response to a foreign request, compel a person 'to give his testimony or a statement or to produce a document or other thing in violation of a legally applicable privilege.'

171 Statement of the Netherlands delegate, *1988 Records* vol. II at 193.

requesting Party in the absence of guarantees that it will not be carried out. The shortcoming of the provision is that it does not insist that requests be refused in these circumstances, thus leaving the protection of the individual to the whim of the requested Party. The *1988 Commentary* suggests that as the liberty of the individual is directly at issue, grounds for refusal do not include grounds familiar in extradition, such as the involvement of a national of the requested Party.[172] If giving information on a national is contrary to domestic law, legal procedure or local practice, it renders article 7 largely ineffective.

Article 7(16) obliges a requested Party to provide reasons for refusing mutual legal assistance. Article 7(16) does not make clear the form which the refusal should take, but it is submitted that it should be a prompt, detailed, written answer in order to allow the requesting Party to assess whether the refusal is valid in terms of article 7(15) or to modify its future requests so that they succeed. The *1988 Commentary* suggests consultation before refusal, in the hope that refusal due to legal differences, funding etc. can be overcome.[173]

Article 7(17) provides for the postponement of a request for assistance. The decision to postpone lies with the requested Party. It can only be based on the ground that the request interferes with an ongoing investigation, prosecution or proceeding. If it were on some other ground the requested Party would have to seek justification elsewhere in the Convention or risk being in violation of its obligation under article 7. If the requested Party does defer, it is under a duty to consult with the requesting Party to ascertain whether the request can be met, but it may impose prerequisites. McClean submits that resort to this provision should be rare if the authorities of Parties communicate properly and agree upon strategies for handling cases.[174]

Article 7(18) is a safe conduct provision that restricts the power of the requesting Party over persons from a requested Party who consent to assist it evidentially.[175] The first sentence of article 7(18) indemnifies such a person from criminal proceedings resulting from any act or omission for which they were liable that occurred before they voluntarily entered the territory of the requesting Party to assist it. This provision is designed to encourage 'witnesses, experts, or other persons who consent to give evidence' to make themselves

---

172 *1988 Commentary* at 208.
173 *1988 Commentary* at 210.
174 Supra note 7 at 178.
175 It is modelled on article 12 of the 1959 European Convention on Mutual Assistance in Criminal Matters, ETS 30.

available to the requesting Party for the purpose of assisting in judicial proceedings,[176] especially as most states have no legal means of compelling their citizens to respond to a summons from a foreign court.[177] Such persons 'shall not be prosecuted, detained, punished or subjected to any other restriction of personal liberty'. Although it does not appear to apply to civil proceedings,[178] Some Parties have in practice guaranteed criminal immunity for non-payment of civil debts.[179] The second sentence of article 7(18) provides that its protection may be waived by such a person voluntarily remaining in the territory of the requesting Party for fifteen days or any agreed period after being informed that he is free to go, or by returning to that territory freely. Although article 7(18) does not make provision for the communication of the limits of the safe conduct to the person concerned, it would be essential to do so.[180] Some Parties have made reservations to this provision to the effect that they will not grant immunity unless either the person in question or the article 7(8) authority of the requested Party specifically requests such immunity, and will in any event refuse to grant it if to do so would not be in the public interest.[181] The provision does not protect the person from any offence such as perjury committed while he is in the territory of the Party.[182]

Article 7(19) attempts to deal with the vexed question of who pays for legal assistance. On the principle that no state should be asked to defray expenses incurred outside its territory, article 7(19) makes provision for the ordinary costs of a request for legal assistance to be borne by the requested Party without consultation. Thus the ordinary costs of, for instance, the service of documents, will be borne by the requested Party. However, this is 'unless otherwise agreed by the parties concerned', which provides for situations where there is an imbalance of requests between Parties. Flexibility is introduced by provision

---

176 See the 'Review Group Report', *1988 Records* vol. I at 71.
177 Statement of the Federal Republic of Germany, *1988 Records* vol. II at 196.
178 Committee I deleted an explicit reference to civil proceedings because it made the provision confusing and too broad in scope – *1988 Records* vol. II at 196-197.
179 See, for example, section 12 of South Africa's International Co-operation in Criminal Matters Act 75 of 1996 which provides: 'No witness residing in a foreign state and who attends a court or tribunal in the Republic shall, while so attending, be liable to be arrested in the Republic on any civil warrant for debt or on a criminal charge for the commission of an offence incurred or allegedly committed in the Republic, before his or her arrival in the Republic for the purpose of his or her attendance of such court or tribunal.'
180 *1988 Commentary* at 198.
181 The UK (28/6/1991) – *Multilateral Treaties Deposited* (1997) at 306.
182 Report of the US Delegation supra note 93 at 65.

being made in the second sentence for consultation between the Parties to resolve who will bear 'substantial or extraordinary' costs and the terms and conditions of the execution of such requests, a practical necessity considering the
vast differences in the capacities of the Parties and the kinds of requests they
are likely to make. The reference to 'substantial' costs allows the Parties to
consult to work out a scale of costs involved in executing an expensive request,
and who will pay for what.[183] 'Extraordinary' costs might include the fees
for expert witnesses, the cost of translation and transcription and personal travel
allowances.[184]

In conclusion, it should be clear that while they provide a fairly exhaustive
guide as to how to implement legal assistance, the procedural provisions set
out in article 7 tend to allow Parties to follow established procedures. The
danger, McClean notes, is that 'sufficient weight will not be given to the intention to make a real advance in the level of co-operation in the drugs field,
and that pre-existing practices and attitudes will be relied upon unthinkingly:
"It is something we have never done."'[185]

5.4.2.6   The further development of mutual legal assistance in drug enforce-
               ment

Article 7(20) obliges Parties to consider, if necessary, the conclusion of further
bilateral or multilateral agreements or arrangements that would serve the purposes of, give practical effect to, or enhance article 7. By recognising that many
Parties may still desire to conclude MLATs in addition to the 1988 Convention,
this provision complements article 7, paragraphs (6) and (7), which recognise
that many Parties had already concluded MLATs relating to drug control prior
to 1988.[186] The UK Home Office describes the solution adopted in article
7(20) as follows:

> By paragraph 20, the Parties are to consider the possibilities of bilateral or multi-
> lateral agreements to give effect to or enhance the provisions of the article, and

---

183 Statement of the Canadian delegate, *1988 Records* vol. II at 198.
184 Proposal of the US delegate, *1988 Records* vol. II at 197.
185 Supra note 93 at 178.
186 The 1991 UN Model Treaty on Mutual Assistance in Criminal Matters GA Res. 45/117
     serves as a useful model.

if such an agreement is in force the procedures specified therein shall prevail over the normative procedures specified in Article 7.[187]

States have concluded bilateral and regional MLATs on the model provided by article 7.[188] But Gilmore warns that Parties to the 1988 Convention 'cannot rely upon existing or future bilateral agreements to dilute the obligation to provide assistance in relation to Article 3(1) offences, including money laundering, or to evade the bank secrecy obligations contained in Article 7(5).'[189]

5.4.2.7 *Mutual legal assistance under article 7 concluded*

Article 7 provides for a comprehensive mutual legal assistance system for drug trafficking although it does not include mutual assistance in respect of confiscation because of the inclusion of appropriate provisions within article 5. Article 7 allows for the possibility of direct and informal co-operation and Parties have responded by enacting the necessary legislation to enable them both to request such assistance more easily and to respond to requests more effectively than was the case under the orthodox formal procedures.[190] However, implementation of the scheme has been poor. For example, in spite of the obligation in article 7(8), many Parties have yet to designate authorities to deal with requests for assistance.[191] The obvious reason is lack of resources, but entrenched legal difference and lack of enthusiasm are also problems.

---

187 Home Office Criminal Justice (International Co-operation Bill): *Explanatory Memorandum on the Proposals to Implement the Vienna Convention Against the Illicit Traffic in Narcotic Drugs and Psychotropic Substances* (1989), p. 29 cited by Gilmore supra note 81 at 25.

188 For example, the Southern African Development Community (SADC) Protocol on Combating Illicit Drug Trafficking of 1996, SA Foreign Affairs File NV101517/96, makes provision in article 5 for such assistance and it closely follows the forms of assistance provided for in article 7(2) of the 1988 Convention.

189 Supra note 81 at 25.

190 A good example is the UK's Criminal Justice (International Co-operation) Act, 1990, which, in a much more simple procedure than the long winded rogatory commission procedure, provides in section 3 for a presiding officer, upon application by either prosecution or defence, to simply send a letter of request to a foreign authority describing the evidence being sought and asking them to provide it. Section 4 of the Act provides that the Secretary of State may upon receipt of a request to obtain evidence in the UK from a foreign country's authorities, appoint a UK court to take such evidence.

191 See Prost supra note 133 at 48.

Article 7 has left significant legal barriers to assistance in place. It does not enforce sufficient coherency between Parties' legal systems. For one thing, article 7 does not provide enough guidance to Parties to understand each other's laws.[192] The key problem of requests for investigative assistance from common law states to civil law states being issued by prosecutorial authorities rather than judicial authorities as required in civil law, is not directly addressed by the article. Article 7 could have provided for the acceptance of a request if it emanates from a competent authority regardless of its status, or for the requesting Party to define the authority as competent, or for the requested Party to deem the authority to be a 'judicial authority'.[193] A further problem may be that the Parties requesting information may not get the evidence they request in a form they are able to use. Article 7 should have provided for an obligation on Parties to enact the necessary domestic legislation to ensure that the reception of foreign evidence is actually possible.[194] Differences in investigative and prosecutorial powers are also considered major obstacles to assistance. It has been pointed out that as assistance is dependent on the same investigative and prosecutorial powers being available to the requesting Party as are usually available to the requested Party to deal with its own concerns, it is important that the requested Party's powers of investigation and prosecution should be as wide ranging and effective as possible. A Party that does not legally permit the interception of telephone and telegraphic communications cannot, for example, make this service available to a requesting Party's investigating agency.[195] This is not an argument for greater policing resources so much as for greater legal resources. It has been suggested that article 7 should have provided for the designing of implementing legislation for mutual assistance in respect of all investigative measures presently available. The danger implicit in such a greatest legal capacity approach is that more sophisticated states, once the enabling laws are in place in the poorer states, will not provide the equip-

---

192 D. Stafford, *International Legal Co-operation Against Serious Crime: Inter-legal Systems Issues Impacting on International Co-operation* (unpublished conference paper, New Delhi Global Drugs Law Conference 1997), p. 7. She suggests that Parties establish central authorities staffed by lawyers who have learned the fundamentals of foreign criminal justice systems to avoid misunderstandings that will jeopardise investigations.

193 Measures already adopted by some civilian states – see Prost supra note 133 at 49.

194 Stafford supra note 192 at 6 points out that this is particularly the case with the admission of foreign documentary evidence including the statements of witnesses when the witness cannot attend the trial personally. She suggests that courts be given the discretion to admit such evidence provided it is in the interests of justice.

195 See Stafford supra note 192 at 6.

ment and training to perform wiretaps, but will simply do it for their less sophisticated "partners". Extraterritorial law enforcement by consumer states is made easier; reciprocity is practically unlikely. From a purely utilitarian viewpoint it would have been ideal if article 7 had brought all states into line,[196] but such an approach would have been incompatible with many legal systems and would have failed to satisfy the diversity of opinion at the 1988 Conference on the policy of international drug control.

Law enforcement utility is not, however, the only purpose of transnational criminal justice. Article 7 is also vulnerable to the criticism that it is ambiguous enough to allow the Parties to apply a fairly draconian system that ignores individual rights. Based as it is on existing MLATs, article7 provides no detail with regard to testimonial privileges, due process guarantees and evidentiary protections such as the hearsay rule, or protections such as the application of double criminality. Thus, like existing MLATs, it may be tilted against alleged offenders in a way that many domestic laws would not countenance.[197] One obvious way in which it is so tilted is that it provides no mechanism for alleged drug offenders to have access to information in other states. Such information may well be essential to their defences particularly in common law jurisdictions where the prosecutor is under no duty to gather exculpatory evidence, and their trials may be unfair if they have no access to it. The *1988 Commentary* points out that the tenor of the discussion at the 1988 Conference on this issue was that that the 1988 Convention 'was for the use of the Parties and was not designed to confer rights on private persons.'[198] The matter has been left to the Parties' domestic law. The *1988 Commentary* continues, however, that if Parties choose to make a request on behalf of an accused person or even a third party, such a request would 'be properly made under the Convention'. It would be transmitted to the designated authority in terms of article 7(8) and executed under article 7(12).[199] Some domestic legislation has made the mechanisms enacted as a result of article 7 available to both defence and prosecution.[200]

---

196 See Catino supra note 124 at 415-440 who prefers the much more rigorous Italian-American treaty.

197 See Ellis and Pisani supra note 80 at 179.

198 *1988 Commentary* at 191.

199 *1988 Commentary* at 191.

200 For example, while section 3(1) of the UK's Criminal Justice (International Co-operation) Act, 1990, provides for the provision of evidence from a foreign state to be used in the UK, section 3(2) provides that a letter of request for the obtaining of evidence outside the UK may be made not only by a prosecuting authority but also, 'if proceedings have been instituted, by the person charged in those proceedings.'

But article 7 should have included specific rules for the protection of standards in the issuance of search warrants and so forth. Article 7 also says nothing about the rights of accused persons to suppress or exclude evidence or to impede the execution of a request for mutual legal assistance and it is clear that the 1988 Convention creates no rights of this nature.[201] These rights may exist in either requesting or requested Party or both, but they may not. The 1988 Convention was an opportunity to disperse both efficient law enforcement regimes and human rights protections globally. The emphasis was on the former, the latter was ignored.

5.4.3   Transfer of proceedings in terms of the 1988 Convention

Transfer of proceedings is a relatively new method of legal co-operation which was included in the 1988 Convention as a method ancillary to those set out in article 7 in order to provide a solution to situations where one jurisdiction may be more suitable for prosecution than another.[202] It provides a solution to problems of the exercise of concurrent jurisdiction frequently associated with international drug trafficking such as the situation where the bulk of evidence against someone already on trial in state X emerges in state Y. In these circumstances it is logical to transfer proceedings to state Y. Transfer of proceedings, in its contemporary form, is not a form of extradition, because it takes place mostly in situations where the alleged offender still remains in the state in which the offence was committed.[203] The proceedings, not the person, are

---

201 *1988 Commentary* at 191.

202 The article was included at the instigation of the Netherlands delegation who saw merit in co-operative measures such as those that had been set down in the 1972 European Convention on the Transfer of Proceedings in Criminal Matters, ETS 73 – see the 'Expert Group Report', *1988 Records* vol. I at 40.

203 The UK Home Office noted: 'The idea is to provide an alternative to extradition where, for example, the offender is in country A and the evidence is in country B' – 'Ratification of the UN Convention Against Illicit trafficking in Narcotic Drugs and Psychotropic Substances: Contents' in House of Commons, Home Affairs Committee, *Drug Trafficking and Related Serious Crime* H.C. Paper 370-II 1988-89, p. 161 – see Gilmore supra note 81 at endnote 99.

transferred.[204] Transfer of proceedings also allows the consolidation of proceedings against traffickers.[205]

Article 8, entitled 'Transfer of Proceedings', does not oblige Parties to transfer proceedings, but simply indicates that they should consider the possibility of doing so. It is limited in scope to article 3(1)'s trafficking offences. Transfer of proceedings must only take place if the requested Party considers it to be 'in the interests of a proper administration of justice'. This implies two duties. The requested Party will have to assess the purpose for which the request is made and the judicial process to which it will surrender the prosecution of the alleged offender. The requesting Party will have to prove that the purpose for which it is prosecuting the offender and the procedure used is in the proper interests of the administration of justice. Various factors that can be taken into account in this decision, viz. the gravity of the offence and the likely sentence, the position of the suspect, that is, his whereabouts and whether he can be extradited, and the nature of the case, that is, the presence of accomplices and so on.[206] The 1991 UN Model Treaty on the Transfer of Proceedings in Criminal Matters provides a detailed model for those states that feel it necessary to base the transfer of proceedings on an international treaty.[207] Parties have declared that they understand the provision will not be used in such a way as to impair the constitutional guarantees available to a defendant.[208]

5.4.4   General police co-operation in terms of the 1988 Convention

5.4.4.1   Introduction
The inclusion of provisions for mutual legal assistance in the 1988 Convention did not prevent the adoption of more familiar provisions relating to police co-operation at a less formal level. Indeed, there is a deliberate overlap between the provisions for mutual legal assistance in article 7 and those contained in article 9, which is entitled 'Other Forms of Co-operation and Training'. This overlap occurred, according to the United States delegation, because of the wide variance among states as to which forms of assistance can be provided directly

---

204 J. Schutte, 'Transfer of criminal proceedings: the European system' in M.C. Bassiouni (ed.), 2 *International Criminal Law: Procedure* (Transnational, Dobbs Ferry, 1986) 319 at 320 emphasises that it is the file that is transferred. The suspect remains at liberty unless extradited. Deportation coupled with transfer is illegitimate.

205 *1988 Commentary* at 213.

206 Schutte supra note 204 at 331.

207 GA Res. 45/118.

208 Colombia (10/6/1994) – *Multilateral Treaties Deposited* (1997) at 303.

by law enforcement officials and which forms require compulsory measures to be taken by courts.[209] The United Kingdom's Home office comments on article 9:

> This article is designed to preserve and enhance forms of co-operation that may exist on a less formal basis than the mutual legal assistance referred to in Article 7. It provides that Parties shall co-operate more closely with each other in matters of intelligence in investigating offences. It also calls on them to facilitate co-or-dination of the work of their competent agencies and promote exchange of staff, to carry out suitable training programs and to assist one another in their training and research programs.[210]

Article 9 envisages co-operation among police, customs, prosecution authorities or judicial authorities, as the case may be, depending on the domestic arrange-ments in respect of law enforcement. Article 3(10)'s limitation of the political and fiscal offence exception discussed in Chapter Four also applies to article 9. It provides that article 3 offences are not to be considered as fiscal or political offences for the purpose of co-operation in terms of article 9.

5.4.4.2   The general duty to co-operate under article 9(1)

The first sentence of article 9(1) establishes the general obligation on Parties to co-operate internationally with the purpose of enhancing the effectiveness of 'law enforcement action' against article 3(1)'s drug trafficking offences. Again, it does not apply to article 3(2)'s personal use offence. 'Law enforcement action' assumedly includes but extends beyond article 7(1)'s formal co-operation in the investigation and prosecution of specific crimes. Although article 9(1) appears to be an exercise in formalising existing informal co-operation, given the extent of possible forms of co-operation the obligation in article 9(1) is subject to a domestic safeguard clause that insists it must be 'consistent with [the Parties'] respective domestic legal and administrative systems'. Many states have legal difficulties with sharing information with foreign law enforcement

---

209 The US delegation gives as an example the fact that the US permits the taking of a statement from a person who consents to be interviewed without a court order, while other states require all such statements to be taken only by order of the courts – Report of the US Delegation supra note 93 at 58.

210 Home Office Criminal Justice (International Co-operation Bill): *Explanatory Memor-andum on the Proposals to Implement the Vienna Convention Against the illicit Traffic in narcotic Drugs and Psychotropic Substances* (1989) at 29 cited by Gilmore supra note 81 at 25.

officials and with the operation of these officials within their territories.[211] Parties are of course free to engage directly is such co-operation and they can do so with the help of international law enforcement organisations like Interpol and regional organisations like the European Police Organisation, Europol.[212]

5.4.4.3 Specific forms of co-operation under article 9(1)

Article 9(1)'s subordinate paragraphs list specific modalities of co-operation. The sentence introducing these specific obligations makes it clear that they may, but do not have to be, carried out either through formal bilateral or multilateral agreements or informal bilateral or multilateral arrangements.[213] The Parties are free to choose the method of implementation that suits them. All of these specific obligations are also subject to article 9(1)'s domestic safeguard clause.

Article 9(1)(a) provides that the Parties must set up and sustain 'channels of communication' between their drug law enforcement agencies or services. These links must facilitate secure and speedy information exchange in respect of all facets of article 3(1) offences, including, if both Parties feel it is relevant, links with any other crimes.[214] Speed is of the essence in investigating drug offences, but so is the need to prevent the compromising of investigations by leaking information. The 'competent agencies and services' contemplated here include the centralised co-ordinating agencies established by states under article 35(a) of the 1961 Convention and article 21(a) of the 1971 Convention, as well as situations in Parties where many agencies or services are involved in co-operation and the exchange of information.[215] Close collaboration between the law enforcement community and the authority to be designated as a contact point for mutual legal assistance in terms of article 7(8) is also encouraged.[216] The types of information to be exchanged are not specified because it was intended that they be determined by mutual agreement between the Parties,

---

211 *1988 Commentary* at 225.

212 The nature and role of these and other organisations is examined in Chapter Seven.

213 See the Netherlands delegate's statement, *1988 Records* vol. II at 275.

214 The specific forms of co-operation do not, given the exclusion in article 9(1)'s first sentence, apply to the personal use offence in article 3(2).

215 See the 'Expert Group Report', *1988 Records* vol. I at 20. Such agencies may include police and customs agencies. The UK delegate made it clear that his delegation viewed this article as binding Parties' authorities as well as the authorities in territories for which Parties were responsible – *1988 Records* vol. II at 33.

216 *1988 Commentary* at 227.

but they must include information on all aspects of drug trafficking offences.[217] The means of communication is also not specified and will depend
on the operational needs of the Parties, but telecommunications will make for
direct and speedy co-operation.[218] The provision gives Parties the option of
increasing the scope of the information to cover other linked offences. Linked
offences are not stipulated but they must include the organised crimes recognised in paragraph 3 of the Preamble as being of major international concern.
They do not include the personal use offence in article 3(2) as article 9 focuses
on serious organised crime.

Article 9(1)(b) addresses the forms of investigative assistance to be provided
by the Parties. It creates an obligation on the Parties to engage in international
co-operation when investigating article 3(1) offences[219] that have 'an inter-

---

217 See the statements of the Netherlands, Brazilian and French delegates, *1988 Records*
vol. II at 278. Types of information were listed in draft article 6(a)(i)-(iv) and included:
the identity, whereabouts and activities of known or suspected traffickers; the methods
employed by traffickers; the movement of proceeds derived from or used by the illicit
traffic; and the ownership and utilisation of means of transport suspected of being used
in the illicit traffic. The list was excised because it was bound to become obsolete and
was incomplete – see the 'Expert Group Report', *1988 Records* vol. I at 20. Cuba
proposed an amendment to article 9(1) obliging any Party which adopts drug control
measures in the vicinity of the border of another Party with which it does not have an
agreement about law enforcement co-operation, to supply information to that Party so
that it may prevent such measures from having damaging consequences on its territory
as a result of attempts by traffickers to evade surveillance or pursuit – *1988 Records*
vol. II at 295. This amendment was rejected on the basis that it was adequately covered
by article 9(1)(a) – see the statement of the US delegate, *1988 Records* vol. II at 296.
218 The *1988 Commentary* at 228 refers to article 44(1) of the Schengen Convention as
an example of intimate and extensive co-operation. It details telephone, radio and telex
links as well as equipment exchange and standardisation.
219 Article 9(1)(b) through the term 'concerning' appears to make the conduct of enquiries
into the matters in (i), (ii) and (iii) conditional on the existence of an article 3(1) offence.
The US delegation stated that this was not the intention of Committee II who drafted
the provision. It held that the true intention of the provision's authors was to provide
for the conduct of enquiries involving article 3(1) offences, as well as for separate and
unrelated enquiries into the items marked (i), (ii) and (iii) – see *1988 Records* vol. II
at 33. Such an interpretation would, however, strain the syntax of the provision and
render the colon superfluous, and cannot be supported. On the other hand, the *1988
Commentary* at 219 points out that the obligation to co-operate in conducting enquiries
into article 3(1) offences does not imply, and cannot due to the safeguard clauses in
article 3 imply, that Parties are under an obligation to establish article 3(1) offences.
The implication is that article 9(1)(b) does not create an obligation when a Party chooses
not to establish such an offence.

national character'. It refers to drug trafficking offences that are not purely domestic.[220] Although the precise meaning of the term 'enquiries' is ambiguous, it appears to mean police or prosecution investigations whether formal or informal. The subject matter of these enquiries is listed and includes in terms of sub-paragraphs (i), (ii) and (iii) of article 9(1)(b), respectively: 'the identity, whereabouts and activities' of 'persons suspected of being involved in' an article 3(1) offence;[221] the 'movement of proceeds of property[222] derived' from these offences;[223] and the 'movement of narcotic drugs, psychotropic substances, substances in Table I and Table II of the [1988] Convention and instrumentalities[224] used or intended for use in such offences'. The *1988 Commentary* notes that this list of subjects of enquiry is not exhaustive and may include other forms of enquiry.[225] Although not mentioned in this provision, it was clear at the 1988 Conference that delegates envisaged the use of Interpol and other international law enforcement communication systems and offender databases when providing these forms of assistance.[226]

One of the most controversial provisions in the 1988 Convention is article 9(1)(c) which creates an obligation to establish joint teams in order to carry

---

220 Statement of the Netherlands delegate, *1988 Records* vol. II at 278.

221 These persons would include suspects in the legal sense, i.e. persons suspected of an actual offence, and known traffickers under preventative surveillance.

222 The *1988 Commentary* at 220 points out that given that the definition of proceeds in article 1(p) includes property derived from article 3(1) offences this provision is tautological.

223 Article 3(1) criminalises the laundering of drug crime proceeds, article 5(4)(b) provides for measures to trace, freeze and seize the proceeds of drug trafficking for the purpose of confiscation, and article 7(2)(g) allows for the mutual legal assistance for the identification or tracing of proceeds, property, instrumentalities or other things for evidentiary purposes. However, the actual investigation of money laundering is only dealt with directly under article 9(1)(a)(ii). Moreover, it only requires the transmission of information on the 'movement' of proceeds, which implies geographical movement or some change in their nature such as conversion. Considering that law enforcement co-operation in regard to money laundering is a crucial part of the general international action against money laundering, this may be regarded as inadequate in detail. See, by contrast, section D of the 1990 FATF Recommendations which is devoted to strengthening international co-operation, and which goes into detail on such subjects as the exchange of information relating to suspicious transactions (recommendation 32).

224 These could include vehicles as well as the materials and equipment referred to in article 13.

225 *1988 Commentary* at 219-220. It gives as an example of something that does not fit comfortably under the present list inspections in loco to look for characteristic features of the modus operandi of a suspected offender.

226 See the statement of the Chinese delegate, *1988 Records* vol. II at 275.

out 'all measures that would enhance the effectiveness of law enforcement action in this field'.[227] Because of the controversial nature of joint operations and the need to respect sovereignty, domestic law limits the obligation.[228] Moreover, it only exists in 'appropriate cases'. Without guidance from the provision, it is assumed such an 'appropriate case' will exist when both Parties to the joint team agree it exists. Factors influencing such a decision include effective law enforcement as well as the need to protect operational and personal security. With regard to the legal status of these teams once established, article 9(1)(c) provides that a Party's officials participating in a joint team shall act as authorised by the appropriate authorities of the territorial Party, but with the caveat that in all such cases, the Party involved must ensure full respect for the sovereignty of the territorial Party.[229] The establishment of 'joint teams' implies that the territorial Party may have to consent in principle to operations by the law enforcement personnel of another Party in its territory. It would have been better had it been made explicit that such operations should not be conducted without the express consent of the territorial Party. This situation is, however, covered by article 2(3)'s provision protecting territorial sovereignty. With regard to the conduct of the operations themselves, the *1988 Commentary* argues that adherence to operational guidelines rather than detailed instructions is more practical than specific authorisation, although such specific authorisation seems to be implied.[230] In practice, joint teams are much more likely to be effective in situations where regional organisations have jurisdiction over external border policing because they will be established on a permanent basis and subject to clear mutual control.[231] They may be particularly effective in the gathering of intelligence.[232] The inherent danger of establishing joint teams

---

227 *1988 Commentary* at 222.

228 Jurisdictional conflict may make joint teams impossible. Thus, for example, the Colombian delegate reserved its position on the creation of joint teams because it pointed out that in Colombia investigations were under the control of an independent judiciary legally incapable of such co-operation – *1988 Records* vol. II at 280.

229 This would include the situation where the joint team operates in the territory of a third party – *1988 Commentary* at 222.

230 *1988 Commentary* at 222.

231 F. Rouchereau, 'La Convention des Nations Unies Contre le Traffic Illicite de Stupefiants et de Substances Psychotropes' (1988) 34 *Annuaire Francais de Droit Internationale* 601 at 610 gives the example of Europe under the EU.

232 New Zealand did not find the obligation in article 9(1)(c) problematic because of its experience of joint intelligence gathering as a member of the Foreign anti-Narcotics Community (FANC) in Thailand – House of Representatives Justice and Law Reform Committee, *Report on International Treaty Examination of the United Nations Conven-*

is, however, that they should come to be regarded by officials as the right to police in another state with a license to use methods not permitted domestically.

The provision of samples of drugs and other substances is useful as evidence in prosecutions. In addition, the scientific profiling of drug samples in order to identify their source, scale of production, individuals involved, has also become a useful source of intelligence on the illicit traffic.[233] Article 9(1)(d) makes provision for the supply by Parties to each other, when required, of 'necessary quantities of substances' for analytical purposes. The *1988 Commentary* notes that 'substances' is broad enough to include narcotics, psychotropics and tabled substances as well as any other substance relevant to investigations such as colourants and bulking agents.[234] Article 9(1)(d) does not require an exchange of samples. The Parties will have to agree between themselves whether the provision of samples will be automatic or on a case by case basis. Samples will have to be of suitable quality.

Article 9(1)(e) obliges Parties to encourage co-ordination between their law enforcement agencies and services. It more specifically obliges Parties to encourage the exchange of personnel and other experts, including the posting of liaison officers. There was a great deal of support at the 1988 Conference for the use of liaison officers who are regarded as an extremely valuable law enforcement tool.[235] The delegate from Cameroon at the 1988 Conference noted: 'Indeed, it was difficult, in the framework of ICPO/Interpol, to obtain precise information or co-ordinate activities without such officers, who provided immediate and invaluable on-the-spot information.'[236] Whether such an exchange of personnel will be unilateral or reciprocal will depend on the Parties involved. Wealthier Parties are obviously more able to send personnel abroad. Reciprocity is impractical and unlikely to be requested, given the supply reduction thrust of the international system as a whole. Although not strictly necessary, the *1988 Commentary* opines that the personnel and experts exchanged should be directly connected with law enforcement agencies or services.[237]

---

tion Against Illicit Traffic in Narcotic Drugs and Psychotropic Substances 1988, 3 September 1998, p.4.

233 *1988 Commentary* at 229.

234 *1988 Commentary* at 222-223.

235 See generally statements in Committee II, although Colombia reserved its position on this provision, as its legal system made no provision for such officers – *1988 Records* vol. II at 286.

236 *1988 Records* vol. II at 287.

237 *1988 Commentary* at 223.

5.4.4.4   National training obligations under article 9(2)

Article 9(2) creates a general obligation on each Party to begin, elaborate or enrich training programmes for its law enforcement and other personnel including customs personnel[238] engaged in the suppression of article 3(1) offences, to the extent it is thought necessary. These programmes are to be 'specific' to each particular agency; that is, each training programme must be appropriate to that agency in its particular role. They involve the training of those involved not just in the detection of trafficking offences but in their suppression, and the bias must be towards suppression as a whole.[239] While article 9(2) does not set out a training course in detail, it provides an obligatory curriculum in sub-paragraphs (a) to (h). This curriculum is not a closed list. Sub-paragraph (a) requires instruction in the methods used in the detection and suppression of article 3(1) offences. As these offences have become more sophisticated, so has their investigation, and so too must the training their investigators receive. Sub-paragraph (b) requires training in the routes and methods used by suspected article 3(1) offenders, particularly in transit states,[240] and instruction in suitable countermeasures. Sub-paragraph (c) requires training in observation of the international trade in narcotic drugs, psychotropic substances and the substances in Table I and Table II. Sub-paragraph (d) requires training in the detection and monitoring of the movement of: proceeds and property derived from narcotic, psychotropic and tabled substances; and instrumentalities used or intended for use in the commission of article 3(1) offences. Such training is, together with the training envisaged in sub-paragraph (e), necessary because of the provision in article 5 of the 1988 Convention for the seizure and confiscation of these proceeds and property. Sub-paragraph (e) requires instruction in the methods used for the transfer, concealment or disguise of such proceeds, property and instrumentalities. Sub-paragraph (f) requires training in the collection of evidence. Sub-paragraph (g) requires training in control techniques in free trade zones and free ports. Sub-paragraph (h) requires training in modern law enforcement techniques. Although all of the subjects mentioned are law enforcement techniques, sub-paragraph (h) is a catchall to ensure training in any unspecified technique. Areas of training not specified include drug identification, presentation of evidence and

---

238 Specific mention was made of customs personnel to ensure that they would receive the specified training – see the statement of the US delegate, *1988 Records* vol. II at 283.
239 Draft article 6(2) was amended by the 'Expert Group' to make this clear – see the 'Expert Group Report', *1988 Records* vol. I at 21.
240 Defined by article 1(u), see below under article 10.

drug testing and analysis[241] (the latter being a particular problem in developing states), and training in foreign laws and languages.[242] A shortcoming of article 9(2) is that it does not provide for comparative legal training, something that certainly delays mutual assistance.

The major problem with article 9(2) is that it obliges Parties to engage in national law enforcement training when many are unable and unwilling to devote scarce resources to it. It is an area where technical assistance has to be provided by the developed world to developing states. The skills imbalance was recognised by the Commonwealth Caribbean Conference on the International Drug Conventions which stated in 1989:

> Training should be recognised as a human resource development exercise that commences with the identification of training needs. These should be determined collectively by Heads of Narcotics Units and be reviewed regularly. Training should be conducted on a national and regional basis. The regional training of trainers is an important aspect of this process. The utilisation of experienced officers in the training process is also emphasised, and practical hands-on experience should be provided wherever possible. Training should be seen as a dynamic process involving evaluation and retraining on a continuous basis. Provision must also be made for study tours for senior staff to work alongside experienced officers in more developed countries with similar drug problems and systems.[243]

Much work is done.[244] However, experience in the Commonwealth indicates that very different approaches have been adopted in different regions and that drug related training programmes have not been well co-ordinated with the basic training of the law enforcement agencies concerned.[245] In order to overcome the temptations of the illicit traffic, the training of law enforcement personnel in the skills required to interdict the illicit traffic must be built on an adequate basic training and on institutional integrity. It has therefore been argued that

---

241 See the 'Commonwealth Caribbean Conference on the International Drug Conventions and drug abuse' (1989) 15 *Commonwealth Law Bulletin* 1005 at 1007.

242 The UK's Home Affairs Committee *Report: Drug Trafficking and Related Serious Crime* (1989) vol. II at 66-67 noted that such training was a priority among UK police if they were to co-operate effectively with other police forces.

243 'Commonwealth Caribbean Conference on the International Drug Conventions and drug abuse' (1989) 15 *Commonwealth Law Bulletin* 1005 at 1007-1008.

244 The UNDCP issues an annual International Calendar of Drug Law Enforcement Training Events.

245 T. Oppenheimer, 'Drug abuse control: mutual assistance between members of the Commonwealth' (1990) 16 *Commonwealth Law Bulletin* 979 at 986-987.

institutional development should be supported rather than the organisation of ad hoc training projects.[246] Article 9(2) does not address these problems specifically, although it recognises implicitly the woeful inadequacy in practice of many states' law enforcement personnel.

5.4.4.5   International co-operation in training and research under article 9(3)
National inadequacy is the main reason for article 9(3)'s provision for mandatory international co-operation in the planning and implementation of both research and training programmes. These programmes appear limited to those designed to share the kinds of expertise referred to in article 9(2). However, this apparent limitation of scope is really an attempt to ensure that training programmes concerned with law enforcement co-operation and assistance are given special attention.[247] In practice, regional training institutions have been established for training in the prevention and detection of drug and other forms of transnational crime.[248]

Article 9(3) also provides for the optional use of regional and international discussion on problems of mutual concern including the particular problems and requirements of transit states,[249] when such discussion is appropriate. This provision as a whole contemplates the use of conferences and seminars to stimulate co-operation. It recognises that some Parties have far more highly developed levels of law enforcement expertise than others do, and hopes that they will share it. However, Parties with greater capacity are seldom willing to make such expertise available to others without attaching conditions that serve their own law enforcement objectives. Many law enforcement agents also doubt the functional value of discussion and particularly of multi-disciplinary discussion. They consider "talking shop" to be of little use in their primary task of gathering information of actual consequence and they tend to be cynical about the value of listening to advocates of alternative approaches such as rural-

---

246 Oppenheimer supra note 245 at 986-987.
247 See the statement of the US delegate, *1988 Records* vol. II at 285.
248 A significant development is the International Law Enforcement Academy (ILEA) established with US sponsorship in Hungary in 1994 to train law enforcement officers from Central and Eastern Europe. By contrast, drug law enforcement training in the Caribbean is spread over three institutions: the Regional Drug Law Enforcement Training Centre in Jamaica, the Centre Interministériel de Formation Anti-Drogues in Martinique and the Police Training College in Barbados.
249 Defined by article 1(u), see below under article 10.

development and health care measures.[250] However, international contact does lead to informal relations that improve co-operation within the system.[251]

5.4.4.6 International police co-operation under article 9 concluded

Article 9's main function is to provide for international co-operation in investigations prior to the conclusion of a legal case against a specific drug offender. The ambiguous nature of article 9 is a condition of its subject matter, and an obvious shortcoming. Article 9 could usefully have provided express guidance on the application of principles like double criminality to police co-operation. It would have been a helpful clarification for both police and potential accused, as the operation of these principles can have a direct impact on policing.[252] When it comes to the specific obligations, article 9 provides for less in the realm of police co-operation than many of the developed Parties with major drug consumption problems would have liked. Trying to get global agreement on powers such as the right of hot-pursuit of drug traffickers across borders[253] would have been impossible in 1988 for political reasons, but the capacity of poorer states was the obvious limitation on a more ambitious scheme for co-operation. This capacity determines the effectiveness of extraterritorial drug supply reduction. Article 9(2)'s provisions for training are obviously an attempt to rectify the imbalance in capacity. But provisions like article 9(1)(c)'s obligation to establish joint law enforcement teams implicitly recognise the continued incapacity of producer state drug law enforcement. One might cynically suggest that they constitute an attempt to substitute direct policing for policing by proxy, when the latter is impossible. It is not surprising that some of the producer states continue to hide behind the shield of the legally autonomous jurisdiction of

---

250 Anderson supra note 78 at 114-115.

251 Anderson supra note 78 at 115.

252 For example, before membership of a criminal organisation was made illegal in Japan in 1992, Japanese police had been successfully sued by Yakuza gang members for revealing their Yakuza status to foreign police forces – C. Sterling, *Crime Without Frontiers* (Little and Brown, London, 1994).

253 Benelux and Nordic arrangements go much further in the realm of law enforcement co-operation than the drug conventions, providing for hot pursuit etc. See generally C. Mulder and B. Swart, 'Sub-regional arrangements: the Benelux Countries' in M.C. Bassiouni (ed.), *1 International Criminal Law: Crimes* 2nd edn (Transnational, Ardsley-on-Hudson, 1999), pp.393-400.

their judicial authorities over drug offence investigations to law enforcement co-operation.[254]

5.4.5 Article 10's provisions for international co-operation and assistance for transit states

In addition to article 9's provisions for general co-operation, provision is also made for co-operation with respect to transit states. Article 10 entitled, 'International Co-operation and Assistance for Transit States', was included in the 1988 Convention to meet the special concerns of transit states as part of an overall comprehensive strategy to achieve co-operation against the illicit traffic. A 'transit' state is defined in article 1(u) of the 1988 Convention as 'any State through the territory of which illicit narcotic drugs, psychotropic substances and substances in Table I and Table II are being moved, which is neither the place of origin nor the place of ultimate destination thereof.' Many of these states are developing countries, many coterminous with major producer or consumer states, many have limited financial and material resources, and many have weak law enforcement infrastructures. They are vulnerable to the negative economic impact of the reliance on revenues generated from drug transit and to the corruptive influence of bribes used to "smooth" drug transit. Technical and financial assistance is necessary, and the view of transit states is that this burden must be borne by consumer states because drug consumers cause the flow of drugs through transit states. The problem with the concept 'transit state', is that most states are affected by drug production and consumption, so in theory there are very few purely transit states. But as the Soviet delegate to the 1988 Conference explained, for a state to be considered a transit state, in terms of article 1(u)'s definition, '[i]t would ... be necessary ... simply to determine that that State was neither the place of origin nor the place of ultimate destination of a given illicit shipment.'[255]

---

254 For example, Colombia made a reservation to article 9(1) upon signature (20/12/1988), substantially repeated at ratification (10/6/1994), which reads as follows: 'Colombia formulates a reservation to article 9, paragraph 1, of the Convention, specifically sub-paragraphs (b), (c), (d) and (e) thereof, since its legislation does not permit outside co-operation with the judiciary in investigating offences nor the establishment of joint teams with other countries to that end. Likewise inasmuch as samples of the substances that have given rise to investigations belong to the proceedings, only the judge, as previously, can take a decision in that regard.' – *Multilateral Treaties Deposited* (1997) at 303.

255 *1988 Records* vol. II at 288.

Article 10(1) establishes a general obligation on Parties to collaborate in aiding transit states either directly or through competent international or regional organisations.[256] Unlike the definition of transit states, however, which can apply to any state and not just to states vulnerable to transit traffic,[257] the provision recognises that there exist developing states in need of assistance and support and singles them out as recipients of this aid. It obliges Parties to render them this aid, as far as a Party is capable, through technical co-operation programmes focusing on interdiction and other related activities. Related activities include a broad range of activities such as training programmes and other forms of assistance.[258]

Article 10(2) gives Parties the option of undertaking the provision of financial assistance to transit states either directly or through competent international or regional organisations. Recognition of the peculiarly parlous circumstances of transit states makes this one of the only provisions referring directly to the granting of technical assistance in the 1988 Convention's law enforcement provisions. The 1988 Conference was not prepared to commit to a general obligation to provide technical assistance. Indeed, even article 10(2) makes the supply of financial assistance conditional upon it being used for the purpose of augmenting and strengthening the transit state's drug control infrastructure in order to make that infrastructure effective. Such assistance may include, for example, provision of X-ray machinery, vehicles and communications equipment.

Finally, article 10(3) gives Parties the further option of agreeing, either formally or through an informal arrangement, to strengthen the usefulness of international co-operation pursuant to article 10, and it allows Parties to take into consideration financial arrangements in this regard. This provision was regarded as necessary at the 1988 Conference to allow for the plugging of loopholes in the 1988 Convention.[259] No rigid formula is laid down for the financing of co-operation, which is left to the Parties to work out for themselves. Although attempts at the 1988 Convention to ensure that each Party involved

---

256 International organisations include the UN's drug control organs and Interpol, while regional organisations include ASEAN, the OAS, the EU and the like.

257 The Argentine delegate failed in an attempt to introduce into the definition of transit state the idea that it meant states adversely affected by the transit of drugs. To a certain extent article 10(1) compensates for this omission, see *1988 Records* vol. II at 290-291.

258 See the statement of the Indian delegate – *1988 Records* vol. II at 291.

259 See the statement of the Indian delegate – *1988 Records* vol. II at 291.

share the burden of the cost of law enforcement failed,[260] this provision and article 10(2) recognise that funds will have to be made available to poorer Parties in order for them to carry out effective programmes of interdiction.[261]

Article 10 acknowledges that transit states face a particular problem and that the solution to this problem depends on a commitment by other Parties. However, its hortatory provisions for financial assistance do little more than recognise the problem. Isolating the problems of transit states seems irrational given the poverty of many other Parties within the system. Moreover, the assumption that there is such an identifiable group that will always have unique problems is under attack today. The *1988 Commentary* points out that events since 1988 have shown that drug traffickers switch trafficking routes at will to avoid interdiction and that almost any state can become a transit state.[262]

5.4.6   Law enforcement co-operation under the 1988 Convention in review

The 1988 Convention, being a dedicated suppression convention, has introduced an ambitious scheme of law enforcement co-operation into international law, with detailed provisions for mutual legal assistance, transfer of proceedings, general police co-operation and assistance for transit states. This scheme is an attempt to overcome the barriers between different national systems of law enforcement, barriers that protect drug traffickers from criminal justice. Articles 7, 8 9 and 10 of the 1988 Convention constitute an attempt to create an institutional base to detect, investigate and prosecute transnational drug crime. Building upon this foundation is the task of Parties.

In practice, many Parties remain unable to give effect to the obligations for co-operation provided in the drug conventions. It remains, for instance, very difficult to get evidence that is admissible from other jurisdictions. Stafford believes that while there are many reasons for this the most pressing is the lack of human and financial resources.[263] Smaller states and developing states see their international obligations as being lower in priority than pressing domestic issues. Some may simply avoid developing international co-operation regimes because they fear the associated financial burden.[264] Those that engage in

---

260 See the Netherlands' amendment to draft article 6bis (article 10) in UN Doc. E/Conf.82/ C.2/L.30 which was rejected in Committee II – *1988 Records* vol. II at 292.
261 See the statement of the Mauritanian delegate – *1988 Records* vol. II at 292.
262 *1988 Commentary* at 232.
263 See Stafford supra note 192 at 3.
264 See Stafford supra note 192 at 3.

legal development often do not devote sufficient resources to implement these new laws. States that benefit directly from the illicit traffic and are consequently subject to many requests for assistance balk at co-operation. Even if a will to engage in co-operation exists, it may be hampered by an unwillingness to use unaccustomed methods and procedures. Effective law enforcement requires the abandonment of existing practice and in some instances principle, and awareness of the need to overcome these barriers must permeate through all levels. Experience shows that an investigation may progress well until trial and then fail due to the latter's lack of enthusiasm.[265] The international provisions can be used to encourage awareness, desire and flexibility, but it is difficult to impose these qualities through international law.

Part of the problem is that while the provisions for law enforcement co-operation in the 1988 Convention appear on paper to treat all Parties in the same way, in reality, in respect of law enforcement, the Parties are not all equal. They have different law enforcement capabilities and objectives and articles 7, 8, 9 and 10 have an in-built bias serving the interests of those Parties with large-scale internal drug consumption problems and large-scale external law enforcement programmes. Although the 1988 Convention's provisions demand technical assistance in order to make co-operation a reality, the Convention does not provide for obligatory financial assistance. Bilateral financial assistance remains the preferred incentive to be used by developed Parties to get recalcitrant developing Parties to co-operate. The hidden coda is that developing Parties are "free" to negotiate their own price. Developing Parties that choose

---

265 See the examples of DEA investigations recounted from personal experience by M.A. Fredericks, 'Counter-narcotics law enforcement co-operation: a necessity' in *Souvenir Brochure of the International Conference on Global drugs Law* (Indian Law Institute, New Delhi, 1997), p. 29 at pp. 30-31. He recounts how in State A the whole of the government apparatus co-operated with the DEA in deporting a known trafficker to a third state from which he was extradited to the US (there being no extradition treaty in existence between the US and State A). In State B, by contrast, a joint investigation by a local law enforcement agency with the DEA into another suspected trafficker revealed that he was out on bail from a prior charge laid six years previously, and when he was brought before the court on a new charge, he was released again on bail. Fredericks states: 'In the latter instance described, it was obvious to me that the counterpart law enforcement agency was aware, committed, and co-operative. Somewhere in the prosecution or judiciary, however, the ball appears to have been dropped.'

to insist on reciprocity are open to charges of violation of their treaty obligations and have no choice but to hide behind constitutional limitations.[266]

5.5   GENERAL LAW ENFORCEMENT CO-OPERATION IN CONCLUSION

This chapter has examined the provisions of the drug conventions dealing with national co-ordination and international co-operation in drug law enforcement. National co-ordination has been a priority because it is felt to serve the two-fold purpose of creating more effective national drug law enforcement while simultaneously laying the foundations for more effective international co-operation. The drug conventions embrace centralised control as the solution to problems of national coherency, but they can do no more than point the way to the Parties. Such re-organisation faces many hurdles including bureaucratic inertia, entrenched systems and the shortage of funding. However, the proliferation of national drugs police, dedicated divisions of the procuracy and ministerial level control, does indicate a measure of success in this regard.

The bulk of the law enforcement provisions in the drug conventions are, however, directed at international co-operation. A device suggested by Benyon et al for the analysis of general international police co-operation can be adapted to offer a useful framework for categorising the different levels of law enforcement co-operation demanded by the drug conventions.[267] The law enforcement provisions of the drug conventions can themselves be classified as the fruits of co-operation at the macro-level. They embody international legal agreement settled by senior government officials leading to the harmonisation of national law. These officials have in the drug conventions attempted to resolve some of the fundamental issues facing drug law enforcement, such as applying one state's drug control laws in another state. They have tried to achieve political consensus as a precondition for action. And to some extent they have been successful. The earlier Conventions introduced the concept of international co-operation in drug law enforcement, and the 1988 Convention has developed this concept significantly.

---

266 Colombia has declared: 'A request for reciprocal legal assistance will not be met when the Colombian judicial and other authorities consider that to do so would run counter to the public interest or the constitutional or legal order. The principle of reciprocity must be observed.' (10/6/1994) – *Multilateral Treaties Deposited* (1997) at 303.
267 Supra note 4 at 50.

The same pattern of development is evident at the meso-level of law enforcement co-operation. In the fields of police and legal co-operation this level is concerned primarily with operational structures, practices and procedures; the day to day framework of policing and prosecuting/adjudicating.[268] The drug conventions and particularly the 1988 Convention provide detailed direction in this regard. They set up broad structures and mechanisms for police co-operation. In the field of legal assistance they centralise authority to make communication easier, and attempt to overcome legal and administrative obstacles to the transmission of information and evidence to Parties investigating and prosecuting drug offences. In a sense, the 1988 Convention attempts to make up for the shortcomings of the 1961 and 1971 Conventions by institutionalising informal police co-operation while informalising orthodox methods of legal assistance. Yet these systems are not perfect from the point of view of effective law enforcement. They do not go as far, for example, as the Schengen Convention,[269] which in the field of police co-operation provides that police from one Party may engage in the observation and hot pursuit of suspected drug traffickers in another Party (articles 40 and 41), and in the field of legal assistance allows the use of the postal service to send documents (article 52) and encourages direct transmission of requests between judicial authorities (article 53).[270] Nor however, are the meso-level systems in the drug conventions perfect from other points of view. Most significantly, they do not provide due process guarantees to individuals caught up in the system. And with respect to the sovereignty of drug producer states, formality was at least a notional guarantor of sovereignty and reciprocity within a system where incapacity undermines formal equality.

Law enforcement co-operation at the micro-level is concerned with the actual investigation of specific offences and the prevention and control of actual crimes.[271] The drug conventions cannot provide much guidance or assistance in this regard because they are examples of macro-level co-operation. Put graphically, the kind of detailed obligations that a United States Drug Enforce-

---

268 See Benyon et al supra note 4 at 53.
269 Convention Applying the Schengen Agreement of 14 June 1985 between the Governments of the States of the Benelux Economic Union, the Federal Republic of Germany and the French Republic, on the Gradual Abolition of Checks at Their Common Borders, in force 19 June 1990.
270 The European Union's new Draft Convention on Mutual Assistance in Criminal Matters, 1999/C/251/01, 14 July 1999, goes even further, providing for the use of high-tech methods such as giving evidence by video link.
271 See Benyon et al supra note 4 at 55.

ment Agency official might want of an international instrument obliging the Bolivian police to assist him in a particular investigation are not available in the broadly drawn drug conventions. All the drug conventions can do is provide some direction as to the domestic authorities that might be of help, and the UN Secretary-General has obliged by publishing data on the competent national authorities under the drug conventions.[272] However, Chapter Six's analysis of specific law enforcement measures indicates that many tactics developed at the micro-level by organisations such as the DEA, have fed back up the system to become enshrined in the drug conventions themselves.

---

272 *Competent National Authorities under the International Drug Control Treaties* UN Doc. ST/NAR.3/1993/1.

SPECIFIC LAW ENFORCEMENT MEASURES

6.1   GENERAL INTRODUCTION

As well as making provision for the general law enforcement co-operation discussed in Chapter Five, the drug conventions also make extensive provision for the adoption by states of specific law enforcement measures. Some of these measures, such as limited forms of seizure and confiscation, were introduced into international drug control law in the earlier conventions. However, reluctant to interfere with domestic criminal law, then considered a precious domestic domain, the authors of the 1961 and 1971 Conventions provided for little regulation of the day to day tactics and methods of operational police work. Between 1971 and 1988 new techniques were developed at the operational level by the law enforcement agencies of consumer states, particularly the United States, that had proved effective in the interdiction of the supply of drugs. Controlled delivery, for example, allowed law enforcement agencies to reach beyond the couriers of drugs to arrest the individuals in control of drug trafficking operations, while 'going after the money' allowed the seizure and confiscation of the proceeds of drug offences and made law enforcement pay. Given the obvious utility of these measures, it seemed a simple task to get all states to adopt the same arsenal of tactics in a global attempt to respond to all the facets of the drug traffic. However, a number of problems beset this task. In 1988, many of these methods were still unfamiliar to Parties. They were also incompatible with the economic interests of important states, as in the case of the monitoring of the chemical and other substances used in the manufacture of drugs, which promised to prove very expensive to the chemical industry. Finally they were incompatible with the domestic criminal law of some states because they involved the derogation of established principles of that law, as in the conflict between the principle of legality demanding prosecution and controlled delivery. The 1988 Convention was used as a vehicle to familiarise states with these methods and to overcome the political and legal reluctance of many states to embrace them. It provided the legal foundation for the deployment of these measures globally. These specific law enforcement measures, which all have national and international aspects, are examined below.

6.2   SEIZURE AND CONFISCATION

6.2.1   Introduction

As noted in Chapter Three above, although they function as a punishment, seizure and confiscation also function as law enforcement measures. They assist in the investigation of offences, they are used to gather evidence for the trial of alleged drug offenders and in their modern role they are used to undermine the economic base of the illicit traffic. Typically a two step process is involved. The first provisional step of taking possession of the material involves procedural measures such as identification, tracing, freezing and seizing. These measures are necessary preliminaries to the second concluding step, which involves confiscating and/or forfeiting the material. The first step may be an administrative decision based on suspicion, while the second is usually a judicial decision based on proof.[1] Both steps necessarily precede disposal of the material. While simple in principle, the mechanics of this process often become complex due to the nature of the property to be confiscated. As we shall see, the earlier drug conventions contemplated the confiscation of drugs and material used in the commission of drug offences. The 1988 Convention reproduces this process, but then extends it to include the confiscation of the assets derived from illicit trafficking.

6.2.2   Seizure and confiscation under the 1961 Convention

Article 37 of the 1961 Convention, entitled 'Seizure and Confiscation', renders any drugs, substances and equipment used in or intended for the commission of any article 36 offence liable to seizure and confiscation. Article 37 is unclear in a number of respects.

It is uncertain whether the article only binds Parties to legally empower their authorities to engage in seizure/confiscation, leaving the decision to seize/

---

1   In Spanish, for example, a distinction is made between *embargo*, a precautionary measure, and *comiso*, the penalty of confiscation that transfers ownership to the state.

confiscate to these authorities,[2] or whether it creates a duty on Parties to engage in seizure/confiscation.[3] The latter appeared the stronger view at the 1961 Conference, and article 37 would not be very meaningful if it did not provide for such an obligation.[4] However, Parties do exercise a discretion in practice,[5] and the practical interpretation is that article 37 only obliges Parties to provide for the legal mechanism to enable seizure/confiscation. Most Parties also allow the exercise of the discretion of the judicial arm in deciding whether such seizure/confiscation is legally possible in terms of that state's domestic law. Although a confiscation decision need not in terms of article 37 be a judicial decision, and nor is it necessary that it be proved that the owner of the material did not consent to the material's illicit use, both of these measures are recommended by the *1961 Commentary*.[6]

There is also some uncertainty about the kinds of material to which article 37 applies. It applies disjunctively to 'drugs, substances and equipment' that have been used or were intended for use in an article 36 offence.[7] The quantity of drugs or substances, or the type of equipment, is not stipulated. The provision's potentially broad scope is a possible source of dispute. It was suggested at the 1961 Conference that it applied to the equipment of illicit laboratories

---

2   The view of the Yugoslav delegate, see *United Nations Conference for the Adoption of a Single Convention on Narcotic Drugs, Official Records, Volume II* (New York, 1964) UN Doc. E/CONF.34/24/ Add.1, UN Publication Sales No. 63.XI.5 (hereinafter *1961 Records vol. II*), p. 246.

3   The view of the German (FRG) delegate, see *United Nations Conference for the Adoption of a Single Convention on Narcotic Drugs, Official Records, Volume I* (New York, 1964) UN Doc. E/CONF.34/24, UN Publication Sales No. 63.XI.4 (hereinafter *1961 Records vol. I*), p. 128, and the Danish and FRG delegates and the Legal Advisor, *1961 Records* vol. II at 246.

4   The *Commentary on the Single Convention on Narcotic Drugs, 1961* (New York, 1973) UN Publication Sales No. E.73.XI, (hereinafter the *1961 Commentary*), pp. 442-443.

5   Garde points out, for example, that a small-time Danish drug trafficker going to Amsterdam in his own car would be unlikely to have it confiscated by Danish authorities even though they are entitled to do so in terms of section 75(2) of the Danish Criminal Code – see P. Garde, 'Denmark' in N. Dorn (ed.), *Regulating European Drug Problems: Administrative Measures and Civil Law in the Control of Drug Trafficking, Nuisance and Use* (Kluwer, The Hague, 1999), p. 67 at p. 69.

6   *1961 Commentary* at 444.

7   It does not apply to poppy straw or the leaves of the cannabis plant unaccompanied by tops because they are not drugs – article 1(1)(r) and (b). It does apply to the drugs in Schedule I and II and to all preparations including those in Schedule III because it is not one of the provisions from which the drugs in Schedule II or the substances in Schedule III are excluded.

and to vehicles used for the illicit transport of drugs.[8] But some delegates were also of the opinion that it did not apply to vehicles,[9] and the *1961 Commentary*, interpreting the Spanish and French versions of the text, feels that it cannot include vehicles or at least large vehicles such as rail stock, large boats or aeroplanes.[10] State practice tends to exclude real property, large vessels and aircraft from confiscation.[11] It is easy to justify the confiscation of a drug-laden light-plane flying an irregular route, but difficult to justify the confiscation of a large commercial aircraft flying a regular route because drugs are found on board. Given the use of such commercial transport by drug traffickers, there may also be a case for an obligation to seize a large transport plane found carrying drugs on an irregular route, or a persistent violator flying a regular route.[12]

With regard to the disposal of the drugs, substances and/or equipment confiscated, some delegates to the 1961 Conference felt that this material should be destroyed while others believed that it should be sold if it were not integral to the illicit drug trade.[13] The decision is left to the Party but it depends on

---

8   See the statement of the Mexican delegate, *1961 Records* vol. I at 128.

9   *1961 Records* vol. II at 246.

10 *1961 Commentary* at 444.

11 For example, section 37(1)(a) of the Bermudan Misuse of Drugs Act, 1972, excludes premises, ships exceeding 250 tons gross and aircraft from forfeiture. Section 56(1)(a) of Hong Kong's Dangerous Drugs Ordinance, 1969, also excludes trains from forfeiture. Taking a different approach, Singapore allows forfeiture of any ship, hovercraft, aircraft or vehicle except when used for a regular passenger service or used without the owner's consent – section 25(a) and (b) of the Misuse of Drugs Act, 1973. Some jurisdictions permit the confiscation of immovable as well as movable property, e.g., France in terms of Decree 95-322 of 17 March 1995.

12 See, for example, *Customs and Excise Commissioners v Air Canada* [1991] 1 All ER 570 where the English Court of Appeal upheld the seizure, made in terms of section 141(1) of the UK's Customs and Excise Act 1979, of an Air Canada airliner at London after cannabis resin was found on board when it landed at Heathrow. The Court of Appeal pointed out that there was a case for excluding larger aircraft from seizure and confiscation but that was a matter for Parliament, not the courts. The proceedings were in rem, so the absence of mens rea on the part of the airline was considered irrelevant. The decision was held not to be a violation of property rights by the European Court of Human Rights in *Air Canada v. Commissioners of Customs and Excise*, (1995) 20 EHRR 150 because it was not disproportionate to the UK's aim of encouraging Air Canada to improve its security given the way security had lapsed, the history of lapses and the value of the drugs found.

13 See the *1961 Records* vol. I at 128 generally.

the nature of the material.[14] Illicit drugs with no medical value must be destroyed; illicit drugs with medical value can be utilised by the confiscating Party; and material not in itself of an illicit nature can be sold to defray expenses. In practice, most domestic legislation leaves the decision in the hands of the court that authorised confiscation.[15]

One final problem is whether the Parties are obliged to make provision for return of the material if the possessor is either not charged, or if charged, found not guilty. The overriding consideration in such situations must be the nature of the material. Material not contraband in itself may be returned, while material that is contraband should not be returned. With respect to the confiscation of drugs in possession for personal use, even if a Party chooses not to regard such conduct as criminal under the 1961 Convention, it appears to be obliged to confiscate such drugs because article 33 obliges Parties not to permit non-medical/scientific possession. An ancillary consideration may be the purpose for which the material is being held. If the seizure/confiscation is operating as a punishment, then if the possessor is not guilty of any offence, material that can be lawfully possessed must be returned. However, if the seizure/confiscation is part of an ongoing investigation then Parties should not be obliged to return such material.

6.2.3   Seizure and confiscation under the 1971 Convention

Article 22(3) of the 1971 Convention provides that any psychotropic substance or other substance, as well as any equipment, used in or intended for the commission of any of the offences in article 22(1) or 22(2) shall be liable to seizure and confiscation. As with article 37 of the 1961 Convention, article 22(3) is ambiguous in a number of respects.

Article 22(3)'s phrase 'shall be liable to seizure and confiscation' can be read to mean either that the Parties are legally bound to seize and confiscate the material concerned or that the Parties are bound to ensure that this material is open to seizure and confiscation. The *1971 Commentary* prefers the former

---

14 See the statement of the Legal Advisor, *1961 Records* vol. I at 148. The exception is confiscated opium which if exported can in terms of article 24(2)-(4) of the 1961 Convention only be exported to another Party.

15 For example, section 28(1) of the Antiguan Misuse of Drugs Act, 1973, provides that anything forfeited shall be 'either destroyed or dealt with as the court may order.'

interpretation, arguing that it accords with the purpose of the provision and the intentions of its authors.[16] State practice supports the latter interpretation.

With regard to the objects open to seizure in terms of article 22(3), it applies primarily to psychotropic substances and substances used for the perpetration of an article 22(1) or article 22(2) offence. It has been suggested that the provisions of article 22(3) also apply to preparations of psychotropic substances.[17] 'Equipment' is vague. The Hungarian delegate stated that it meant 'any substance, plant or the like which might be used in the manufacture of a psychotropic substance.'[18] The United States delegate explained that under 'the term "equipment", ... his Government would consider itself authorised to seize and confiscate any vehicle, lorry, vessel or aircraft which had been used for the illicit transportation of psychotropic substances.'[19] The *1971 Commentary*, however, states that vehicles especially large vehicles such as rail stock, large boats and aeroplanes are not 'equipment'.[20] In practice the former definition seems to have been adopted.

The 1971 Convention does not restrict the way Parties may dispose of confiscated psychotropic substances or insist that they be destroyed. It appears that all substances, preparations and equipment seized will be returned to the alleged offender if found not guilty[21] unless lawful possession of such material is impossible.[22]

Like article 37 of the 1961 Convention, article 22(3) does not go beyond the insistence that drugs and instrumentalities involved in drug trafficking must be confiscated. In practice many states had already made provision for seizure and confiscation of the objects involved in crimes long before either the 1961

---

16   *Commentary on the Convention on Psychotropic Substances, 1971* (New York, 1976) UN Doc. E/CN.7/589; UN Publication Sales No.E.76.XI.5 (hereinafter the *1971 Commentary*), pp. 366-367.

17   S.K. Chatterjee, *Legal Aspects of International Drug Control* (Nijhoff, Drodrecht, 1981), p. 484.

18   *1971 Records* vol. II at 34.

19   *1971 Records* vol. II at 33.

20   *1971 Commentary* at 367; see also *1961 Commentary* at 444.

21   Chatterjee supra note 17 at 484.

22   The *1971 Commentary* at 368 submits that Schedule 1 substances found in the unauthorised possession of a user for his own consumption must be seized and confiscated by Parties because of the obligation in article 7(b) even if they do not regard such possession as an offence under article 22(1)(a).

or 1971 Convention was concluded.[23] What was new in state practice post-1971, was the seizure and confiscation of the proceeds of drug offences.[24]

6.2.4   Seizure and confiscation under the 1988 Convention

6.2.4.1   Introduction
By 1988, with the profits from the massive boom in illicit drug trafficking filling the world's banks, it was apparent that further development of the law of confiscation was necessary. This development took place within the context of the campaign against drug money laundering which began in the United States.[25] Beyond the general reason of countering the economic power of traffickers, various specific reasons for 'going after the money' are commonly offered. They include: i) it is the best way of deterring and punishing major traffickers who without profit aside from paying themselves cannot reinvest in production, pay employees, purchase weapons, bribe officials; ii) while drugs "busts" rarely lead to the major traffickers, the trail of profits – the "paper trail" – does; and iii) confiscation can make law enforcement pay for itself.[26] There are, however, difficulties with confiscating the proceeds of drug offences. In many cases the assets to be confiscated are many steps away from the original illicit drug transaction in a completely different form to the money paid for the illicit drug transaction and are practically impossible to link to the illicit drug transaction. Unfortunately, both article 37 of the 1961 Convention and article 22(3) of the

---

23 See, for example, article 58(1) of Switzerland's Code Penal, which has been in force since 1942.

24 For example, sections 60, 61 and 62 of the Indian Narcotic Drugs and Psychotropic Substances Act 61 of 1985 (as amended) provide for the confiscation of illicit drugs, illicit substances, goods used for concealing illicit drugs and substances and, going beyond the obligations of either the 1961 or 1971 Conventions, the proceeds of the sale of illicit drugs and substances.

25 See B.E. Hernandez, 'RIP to IRP – Money laundering and drug trafficking controls score a knockout victory over bank secrecy' (1993) 18 *North Carolina Journal of International Law and Commercial Regulation* 235 at 275-296 who charts the growth of national and international efforts against drug trafficking related money laundering. See also N. Kohler, 'The confiscation of criminal assets in the United States and Switzerland' (1990) 13 *Houston Journal of International Law* 1-38; D. McClean, 'Seizing the proceeds of crime: the state of the art' (1989) 38 ICLQ 334-360; E.A. Nadelmann, 'Unlaundering dirty money abroad: U.S. foreign policy and financial secrecy jurisdictions' (1986) 18 *Inter-American Law Review* 33-81.

26 See Nadelmann supra note 25 at 34.

1971 Convention are married to the conception that only property derived by the offender from the offence for which he was convicted could be legally confiscated. Neither make provision for the seizure of the proceeds of drug trafficking not immediately linked to a specific illicit transaction. Existing domestic legislation reflected this approach,[27] and when changes were made to secure the confiscation of assets derived from drug trafficking,[28] these changes did not fit comfortably under existing international provisions. Thus, for example, classification of money as 'material' under article 37 of the 1961 Convention is awkward. Calls were made for steps to be taken to bring the international position into line with the more advanced domestic jurisdictions.[29] The obvious limitations in only going after the money at the domestic level were also realised. McClean points out that '[t]he facility with which assets, particularly in the form of financial credits of some sort, can be passed across national boundaries means that an order enforceable only in the country of origin may be of limited value.'[30] While certain kinds of confiscation orders

---

27 McClean supra note 25 at 336 gives the useful example of section 27(1) of the English Misuse of Drugs Act, 1971, which allowed, according to Lord Diplock in *R v Cuthbertson* [1981] AC 470 at 484, the forfeiture of 'the drugs involved, apparatus for making them, vehicles used for transporting them, or cash ready to be, or having just been, handed over for them' but which, his lordship noted, did not 'serve as a means of stripping the drug traffickers of the total profits of their unlawful enterprises.'

28 W.C. Gilmore, *Combating International Drug Trafficking: The 1988 United Nations Convention Against Illicit Traffic in Narcotic Drugs and Psychotropic Substances* (Commonwealth Legal Secretariat, London, 1991), p. 13 describes how in the Drug Trafficking Offences Act, 1986, the British government made provision for the confiscation of the proceeds of drug trafficking. Apart from making the benefits of trafficking subject to forfeiture, it gave increased powers of seizure to the police and significantly, allowed the courts to register, upon application by a designated country, an external confiscation order. The initial impact of the 1986 Act was not impressive: in its first year of operation 17 money-laundering convictions resulted in the confiscation of 27.2 million pounds, while in 1989 of confiscation orders to the value of 7.9 million pounds only 1.1 million pounds was actually realised – less than one percent of estimated drug profits during that year according to R. Clutterbuck, *Drugs, Crime and Corruption* (MacMillan, London, 1995) at pp. 144-145.

29 The UN's DND commissioned two meetings of Experts in 1983 and 1984. The Expert Group on the Forfeiture of the Proceeds of Drug Crimes recommended that the existing drug conventions should be amended or supplemented by a treaty that would specifically address the issue of money laundering and asset forfeiture in order to provide a framework for the conclusion of bilateral MLATs, guidance in respect of domestic legislation and pressure on non-conforming states – see UN Doc. E/CN.7/657/Add.2.

30 McClean supra note 25 at 339.

were more effective in foreign jurisdictions than others,[31] domestic efforts were so disparate they made international co-operation extremely difficult.[32] Steps needed to be taken to develop confiscation in states where it was not being used, and to harmonise it in states where it was being used.

The delegates to the 1988 Conference responded by agreeing article 5 of the 1988 Convention. Entitled, 'Confiscation', it is designed to attack the international drug traffic by attacking the patrimonial benefits that accrue from it wherever they may be held. A novel and contentious provision, it serves, together with the criminalisation of money laundering in article 3(1) sub-paragraphs (b) and (c), as a way of reaching the trafficker and his profits. Article 5 makes provision first for measures to be taken at the domestic level to provide for confiscation on the Party's own behalf, and second for international co-operation to provide for identical measures on the application of another Party. In other words, article 5 enables the greatest number of states to use confiscation against traffickers and removes possible impediments to the recognition of confiscation orders of other states by ensuring that every state has such a mechanism in place.[33]

Article 5 is drafted in a flexible manner to avoid the necessity of expansive domestic law safeguard clauses.[34] However, article 5(9), is a general safeguard clause that provides that the measures referred to in article 5 shall be defined and implemented in accordance with and subject to the domestic law of a Party. In other words, article 5 is not self-executing, it is applied indirectly which means that some measure of domestic protection is provided. Concerns about attempts to avoid the novel obligations of the article by, for example, refusing to provide access to financial records thus preventing the tracing of laundered funds, resulted in article 3(10)'s limitation of the political and fiscal offence exception being applied to article 5.[35] Nevertheless, a Party would still be able

---

31 See McClean supra note 25 at 340 who describes the particular difficulties of enforcing forfeiture orders not linked to a conviction in foreign jurisdictions.

32 See generally Kohler supra note 25, who describes in detail the different confiscation procedures developed in the US and Switzerland prior to the 1988 Convention, and highlights the differences in procedure which made international co-operation in this regard so difficult.

33 D. McClean, International Judicial Assistance (Clarendon, Oxford, 1992), p. 179.

34 See the 'Expert Group Report', *United Nations Conference for the Adoption of a Convention against Illicit Traffic in Narcotic Drugs and Psychotropic Substances, Official Records, Volume I* (New York, 1994) UN Doc. E/CONF.82/16, UN Publication Sales No. E.94.XI.5 (hereinafter *1988 Records* vol. I), p. 31.

35 See the discussion in Chapter Four.

to refuse a request for financial records if there was no demonstrable link to the investigation or prosecution of an article 3 offence.[36]

6.2.4.2 Confiscation at the national level

Article 5(1) deals with measures for confiscation to be adopted by Parties at the national level. It is not encumbered by limitation clauses, an indication of the seriousness with which attacking the proceeds of drug trafficking at the national level was viewed by the 1988 Conference.[37]

The introductory sentence of article 5(1) does not impose a strict obligation to confiscate, but rather obliges the Parties to adopt the domestic legal steps necessary to 'enable' confiscation of the things mentioned in the sub-paragraphs at the national level. Early drafts of the provision specified in great detail the measures to be adopted,[38] but the final version leaves the Parties free to adopt whatever legal measures they deem fit to the task of confiscating these things.[39] This provision recognises that Parties have very different basic systems of confiscation, procedures for the taking of decisions to confiscate and procedural frameworks for such decisions.

Confiscation is defined in article 1(f) as meaning 'the permanent deprivation of property by order of a court or other competent authority.' The Chairman of Committee I noted that 'permanent deprivation' is used 'not so much to indicate the finality of deprivation as to distinguish the measure from provisional deprivation.'[40] Finality of deprivation depends on each Party's precise understanding of confiscation in terms of its own law. The definition's reference to

---

36   D.W. Sproule and P. St-Denis, 'The UN Drug Trafficking Convention: An Ambitious Step' 1989 CYBIL 263 at 274-275.

37   Sproule and St-Denis supra note 36 at 282.

38   Draft article 3(3)'s sub-paragraphs provided for the procedure and content of freezing/ seizure orders and confiscation orders, for the evidence to be taken into account in consideration of such orders and for measures to prevent intermingling with licit assets from adversely affecting such orders – see *1988 Records* vol. I at 4. Only the latter provision survived in article 5(6)(b), but the draft may serve as a useful model for domestic legislation.

39   These measures may include currency reporting requirements, "know your customer" measures for banks etc. More developed national systems have instituted a complex of laws and administrative measures aimed at relieving drug traffickers of their ill-gotten gains – see generally Hernandez supra note 25 at 235-304.

40   *United Nations Conference for the Adoption of a Convention against Illicit Traffic in Narcotic Drugs and Psychotropic Substances, Official Records, Volume II* (New York, 1991) UN Doc. E/CONF.82/16/Add.1, UN Publication Sales No. E.91.XI.1 (hereinafter *1988 Records* vol. II), p. 95.

the agency of confiscation indicates that while the authors of article 1(f) thought that most confiscation orders would be made by judicial authorities, they also anticipated the situation where some other lawful authority may be given this power by a Party's domestic law.[41] Article 1(f) does not dictate the nature of the proceedings that must be followed to enable confiscation. Any type of proceedings might qualify including proceedings linked to a criminal trial or proceedings independent of a criminal trial, so long as they enable confiscation. Although 'confiscation' is given priority because of its use in earlier conventions, article 1(f)'s definition caters for the different domestic approaches to confiscation by providing that it 'includes forfeiture where applicable'.[42] Article 1(f)'s definition expressly refers to the confiscation of property. However, it has been suggested that to make sense of article 5 such property must include the proceeds of crime.[43]

The targets of confiscation that are provided for in article 5(1)(a) are the proceeds derived from article 3(1) offences[44] or property of corresponding value to such proceeds. The Party must choose between the two options made available.

The first option makes provision for an asset-confiscation system. It focuses on confiscation of the proceeds of drug offences, i.e. the property derived from drug offences. Article 1(q) defines 'property' as 'assets of every kind, whether corporeal or incorporeal, movable or immovable, tangible or intangible, and legal documents or instruments evidencing title to, or interest in, such assets.' The Convention's authors wanted property to be formulated as broadly as possible so that nothing could avoid the net of article 5[45] and domestic legislation

---

41 See generally – *1988 Records* vol. II at 93-94.

42 The reference to forfeiture is necessary because while both terms are sometimes used to refer to the same process (see the 'Expert Group Report', *1988 Records* vol. I at 32), in some legal systems confiscation is a preliminary step following seizure and forfeiture is the final step (see the 'Review Group Report', *1988 Records* vol. I at 63), while in others the reverse applies (see the Iranian statement, *1988 Records* vol. II at 65). Generally, however, confiscation is used in Europe and forfeiture in the US to refer to the same process.

43 See *Commentary on the United Nations Convention Against Illicit Traffic in Narcotic Drugs and Psychotropic Substances, 1988* (New York, 1998) UN Doc. E/CN.7/590; UN Publication Sales No.E.98.XI.5, (hereinafter the *1988 Commentary*), p. 31.

44 Note that these offences have to be established in the Party's domestic law before confiscation is possible – see the 'Expert Group Report', *1988 Records* vol. I at 32.

45 See the US delegate's statement – *1988 Records* vol. II at 89. Unlike 'proceeds' its definition is not subject to any qualification. 'Assets of every kind' includes anything of value whether it is 'movable or immovable, tangible or intangible, corporeal or

has adopted correspondingly broad definitions of confiscatable property.[46] Article 1(p) defines 'proceeds' as 'any property derived from or obtained, directly or indirectly, through the commission of an offence established in accordance with article 3, paragraph 1'.[47] Property obtained 'directly' from drug offences may include the money paid for drugs, while property obtained 'indirectly' may include a motor vehicle purchased with that money.[48] Treating indirectly obtained property as proceeds for the purposes of article 5(1)(a) expands the net of confiscation to cover the various devices used by criminals to conceal proceeds, such as shell companies, which remove the proceeds from the formal entitlement of the original offender.[49] Some delegates to the 1988

incorporeal.' It includes 'incorporeal property' such as copyrights and patent rights in addition to corporeal property, because one of the aims of article 5 is to eliminate the sources of financing of the illicit traffic. It may include proceeds and thus be derived from an article 3(1) offence but this is not necessarily so. 'Legal documents or instruments' were included in the definition because they evidence title and their confiscation may be necessary. Moreover, although they are not regarded by some domestic legal systems as property, their confiscation serves in some legal systems as symbolic of the confiscation of the property they represent.

46   See, for example, section 38(1) of the UK's Drug Trafficking Offences Act, 1986, which defines property as including 'money and all other property, real or personal, heritable or moveable, including things in action and other intangible or incorporeal property.'

47   While the definition looks extensive in scope, compare it to article 1(a) of the 1990 Council of Europe Convention on Laundering, Search, Seizure and Confiscation of the Proceeds from Crime, ETS 141, 30 ILM 148, which defines proceeds as 'any economic advantage from criminal offences.'

48   *1988 Commentary* at 119.

49   See McClean supra note 25 at 339. The Australian delegate explained that reference to indirect derivation was necessary because before tainted property had intermingled with untainted property 'various steps might occur at law in its transmission – for example, the distribution of profits to shareholders by a company – and without the words "directly or indirectly" in the definition there would be no wording to cover those steps.' See *1988 Records* vol. II at 91. The definition is so broad, however, that although article 5(6)(c) expressly caters for the confiscation of income generated from the proceeds of an article 3(1) offence, it is arguable that the definition of property is broad enough to include it anyway. The United States delegation insisted that this is the case – see 'Report of the United States Delegation to the United Nations Conference for the adoption of a Convention Against Illicit Traffic in Narcotic Drugs and Psychotropic Substances' from *United Nations Convention Against Illicit Traffic in Narcotic Drugs and Psychotropic Substances* Senate Executive Report 101-15, 101st Congress, 1st Session, p. 40.

Conference were wary of this expansion.[50] One limiting factor is that article 1(p) requires at the least an indirect link to an offence, in the sense of a chain of transactions connecting the property to the offence. However, article 1(p)'s insistence upon this link does not cohere with the text of the Convention in certain instances[51] and the nature of the link is itself unclear. More specifically, the provision does not state expressly that a criminal offence by the owner or holder of the property must have been proved in court before confiscation is possible. In most jurisdictions confiscation orders are actions in personam, that is, they are criminal confiscation orders that enable only the confiscation of a convicted offender's assets derived from criminal actions. It is obvious that article 5(1)(a) anticipates confiscation of such property. Certain jurisdictions, however, allow actions in rem, that is, they allow the civil forfeiture of any property declared to be the proceeds of crime and the identity of the holder is immaterial unless he is able to establish he is bona fide.[52] The fact that

---

50   The French made a formal reservation during the Plenary with respect to use of the term 'indirectly', and the German delegation echoed their concern – *1988 Records* vol. II at 28.

51   The *1988 Commentary* at 36 cites two examples of incoherence. Article 3(1)(b) clauses (i) and (ii), and article 3(1)(c) use the phrase 'property derived from an offence'. Clearly the term 'proceeds' should have been used here. Article 5(1)(a) requires Parties to adopt such measures as may be necessary to enable confiscation of 'proceeds derived from offences established in accordance with article 3, paragraph 1'. The words 'derived from' incorporate the sense of the definition of 'proceeds' and are redundant.

52   McClean supra note 25 at 339. Prior to 1988, most states relied on criminal confiscation only, but some common law jurisdictions supplemented it with civil forfeiture because of the difficulties in proving offences and linking proceeds to offenders. B. Zagaris and E. Kingma, 'Asset forfeiture international and foreign law: an emerging regime' (1991) 5 *Emory International Law Review* 445 at 448-449 explain that the use in the US of civil in rem proceedings (e.g. 21 USC section 881(d)) to forfeit the proceeds of drug crime does not require the proof of an offence or conviction of an offender. As penal sanctions are not involved, criminal due process is not afforded to the property owner, forfeiture may occur without the benefit of a judicial proceeding, and once seized the property remains in the government's custody until title is determined. The burden of proof is on the claimant of the property. Zagaris and Kingma note that the divergent practice of other states is an obstacle to the favourable consideration of US requests for confiscation in other jurisdictions. The 1990 Council of Europe Convention on Money Laundering, ETS 141, attempts to overcome this problem by obligating Parties to assist on request whenever 'judicial proceedings' are pending. Paragraph 15 of the Council of Europe's Explanatory Memorandum on the Convention explains that the Convention applies to diverse decisions, by criminal courts, administrative courts and separate judicial authorities, to confiscate in civil and criminal proceedings totally separate from those in which the guilt of the offender is determined.

article 1(f) provides that confiscation 'includes forfeiture where applicable' suggests that the civil forfeiture proceedings used in certain jurisdictions requiring no link other than that the property be declared to be the proceeds of crime are also covered by this provision.[53] The *1988 Commentary* believes that both criminal and civil forms of confiscation are available under article 5(1)(a) and that 'the text does not prevent forms of confiscation that require no conviction.'[54] Legislation passed by Parties after the conclusion of the 1988 Convention confirms the availability of this choice.[55] It does not follow, however, that Parties to which civil forfeiture proceedings are completely foreign are under a legal obligation to enact legislation making them possible.[56] The use of 'where applicable' in article 1(f) suggests that the provision anticipates Parties only taking the steps appropriate to their legal systems. From an effective law enforcement point of view, the absence of an obligation to adopt civil forfeiture is compensated to some extent by the inclusion of the money laundering offences in article 3(1) because rendering the actual laundering of the proceeds of an offence means that the authorities can avoid having to link the assets to the actual trafficking of drugs.[57]

The second option provided for by article 5(1)(a) is a value-confiscation system. Such a system expands the confiscation net even further. It focuses not on the proceeds of the offence but on their value, and anticipates the confiscation from the offender of property, as broadly defined in article 1(q), cor-

---

53   The Convention's solution has been to make confiscation a generic term that includes notions of both forfeiture and confiscation in the narrow sense, so as to enable Parties to apply the process appropriate to their legal system – see the statements of the Chairman of Committee I, *1988 Records* vol. II at 65 and 95.

54   *1988 Commentary* at 120.

55   See, for example, section 22(3)(a) of the New South Wales Drug Trafficking (Civil Proceedings) Act 23 of 1990 which provides that the finding of a court upon which an asset forfeiture order is to be made 'need not be based on a finding as to the commission of a particular offence that constitutes a drug-related activity or a finding as to any particular quantity involved.'

56   This would present a problem for Greece, for instance, because confiscation of property of persons only suspected of trafficking is unconstitutional and a criminal conviction is necessary to enable confiscation – see M. Mavris, C.D. Spinellis and P. Zagoura, 'Greece' in Dorn supra note 5 at 165.

57   See McClean supra note 33 at 216 who notes that where a Party has criminalised money-laundering itself, the practical difference between confiscation orders and forfeiture orders is much reduced because while forfeiture orders seek to reach property held by third parties linked in some way to the primary offender but not themselves convicted of the primary offence, if such a third party can be convicted of money laundering a confiscation order can be applied to him and to any property he controls.

responding to the proceeds in value. Such property need not be linked, either directly or indirectly, to an offence;[58] it may in fact have been legally acquired. The investigating authorities are not claiming the proceeds of the crime nor are they concerned with property into which those proceeds have been transformed. Under this provision the law enforcement agencies do not have to waste time proving that the particular property to be confiscated is in some way related or linked to the crime at all. All they have to prove is ownership by the offender and that he has benefited from committing a criminal offence. It is useful in situations where the proceeds of the crime cannot be located, or have been transferred to a third party, or have been removed from the jurisdiction, or have been rendered worthless, or the like.[59] It is the 'value' of the benefit from crime that is crucial. In effect, this approach allows the state in question to exert a financial claim against the person against whom the order is made. If it is not paid, it may be realised in any property (no matter whether legally or illegally acquired) belonging to that person. The order is thus executed in a way similar to a court order for civil damages.[60] Article 5(1)(a) does not

---

58 Statement of the Chairman of Committee I – *1988 Records* vol. II at 66.
59 *1988 Commentary* at 139.
60 The British delegate to Committee I noted that British law provided for the substituted value approach and then gave as an example of its application a situation where 'if a trafficker had ownership of a one-eighth share in a race horse, the United Kingdom might confiscate from the trafficker's bank account the value of that one-eighth share,' – see *1988 Records* vol. II at 66 referring to the use of section 1 of the Drug Trafficking Offences Act, 1986. However, unlike a civil judgment, default on payment can lead to a heavy prison sentence (up to ten years under the 1986 Act). McClean supra note 25 cites at 345 sections 24 and 27 of the Commonwealth of Australia's Proceeds of Crime Act, 1987, as an elaborate example of how the value of the benefit is assessed. In assessing the amount of the pecuniary penalty to be imposed the court has regard to evidence on the following matters: 1) the value of the money and other property which came into the possession or under the control of the defendant (or of any person at the defendant's request) by reason of any of the offences of which the defendant was convicted; 2) the value of any other benefit provided for the defendant (or such other person) in these circumstances; 3) the market value of substances similar to the drugs involved in the offence or the amount ordinarily paid for carrying out the act in question; 4) the value of the defendant's property before and after the relevant offence or offences; and 5) the defendant's income and expenditure at those times. In addition, in terms of section 28 the court may also treat as the defendant's property anything subject to his effective control even if he has no interest or right in it, such as trusts, shares or debentures held by a corporation (the court may lift the corporate veil) or other property held through domestic or family relationships. Section 43 of the Belgian Penal Code also allows for such an approach. The monetary estimate of the value of the proceeds is based on all information available including the quantity of drugs trafficked – the gross profit

specify the details of the assessment process or define the necessary legal procedure.[61]

Article 5(1)(a) was drafted to accommodate the differing approaches to confiscation that have evolved in domestic legislation.[62] Some states only permit criminal confiscation of property directly acquired through proven criminal activities, a few also permit civil forfeiture of property indirectly acquired through suspected criminal activities, while others go even further and adopted the substitute of assets approach.[63] Delegates to the 1988 Convention regarded their adoption of measures to enable confiscation of proceeds, or of property of corresponding value, but not both, as satisfying article 5(1)(a)'s obligation,[64] and the *1988 Commentary* believes that this is the intention of the provision.[65] A potential problem is caused by article 5(4) requiring Parties to take legislative measures to enable them to deal with requests for co-operation under article 5. If the requested Party has only adopted a confiscation of assets approach will it be required to adopt measures to enable it to grant a request from a Party that only uses the substituted value option, and vice versa?[66] It seems logical that article 5(4)'s obligation in respect of international co-operation is limited by the choice offered in article 5(1)(a). Nonetheless, Parties have been quick to delimit their obligations in this respect. Panama has made a reservation to this provision to the effect that it does not consider itself obliged

---

is taken into account costs incurred by the offender by reason of the crime are ignored.

61 *1988 Commentary* at 119.

62 See Gilmore supra note 28 at 14.

63 While Portugal, for example, is not allowed in terms of its constitution to permit confiscation of property indirectly acquired – see *1988 Records* vol. II at 64, the UK allows substituted value confiscation orders in terms of section 38(1) of the Drug Trafficking Offences Act, 1986, and section 102 of the Criminal Justice (International Co-operation) Act, 1990. See also, for example, New South Wales' Drug Trafficking (Civil Proceedings) Act 23 of 1990, and see McClean supra note 25 at 341 for a summary of Commonwealth approaches.

64 The Italian delegation made it clear that their understanding of the provisions was that a Party which was only able in terms of its domestic law to apply one of the options would still be fulfilling its obligations under the Convention if it adopted only one of them in its law; see also the statements of Japanese delegate – *1988 Records* vol. II at 31.

65 *1988 Commentary* at 119.

66 This is the position under article 7(2)(a) of the 1990 Council of Europe Money Laundering Convention, ETS 141.

to apply the value confiscation system in so far as it contravenes its Constitu-tion.[67]

Article 5(1)(a) is a law enforcement measure. Driven by the successful ex-ample of the United States' domestic practice, it has been used to extend confis-cation to the proceeds of drug crime.[68] Article 5(1)(a) is, however, inherently invasive of individual rights. Remarking upon these provisions the Austrian delegate at the 1988 Conference drew attention to the necessity in Austrian law of proving links with concrete offences and the need to protect the rights to property, privacy and to be presumed innocent. The Philippines delegate noted their inconsistency with due process[69] and the Philippines later made a reservation to the effect that it does not feel itself bound by article 5(1)(a).[70] Article 5(9) does protect each Party's domestic application of article 5, but experience has shown that domestic legislation is not likely to protect individual rights.[71] Potential areas of abuse include interference with attorney-client privilege, authorities only having to satisfy civil burdens of proof,[72] as well

---

67   13/1/1994 – *Multilateral Treaties Deposited with the Secretary General: Status as at 31 December 1996* (New York, 1997) UN Doc. St/Leg/Ser.E/15, p. 305 (hereinafter *Multilateral Treaties Deposited* (1997)).

68   The progenitors of article 5(1)(a) are the provisions that the US has long had in place allowing civil and criminal forfeiture of property relating to drug trafficking and drug money laundering – see generally Kohler supra note 25 at 16-23. She notes at 17 that between 1970 and 1980 the US forfeited around two million dollars using the criminal forfeiture provisions in the Racketeer Influenced and Corrupt Organisation Act (RICO) of 1970 and the Continuing Crime Enterprise Statutes (CCE) (codified at 18 USC section 1961 and 1963 (1988)), while in 1980 alone the DEA confiscated 42 million dollars in assets using civil forfeiture provisions codified in 21 USC section 881. US legislation has been updated to allow under the 1988 Anti-drug Abuse Act forfeiture of any property involved in illegal transactions and any property 'traceable' to property involved in illegal transactions (see 18 USC section 981(a)(1)(a) and section 982(a)).

69   *1988 Records* vol. II at 31.

70   7/6/1996 – *Multilateral Treaties Deposited* (1997) at 305.

71   See, for example, C. Sallon and D. Beddingfield, 'Drugs, money and the law' (1993) *Criminal Law Review* 165-173 who complain that the UK's Drug Trafficking Offences Act, 1986, virtually eliminates the right to silence and trial by jury and question whether this takes us any closer to eliminating drug use.

72   See, for example, the application of confiscation in the UK's Drug Trafficking (Inter-national Co-operation) Act, 1990. Rather than satisfying the criminal standard of proof, the statute requires only that the prosecution satisfy the civil standard of proof for the confiscation order to be granted.

as the application of presumptions[73] and reverse onus provisions[74] of unusual severity. Unremarkably, article 5(7) invites the Parties to consider applying such reverse onus provisions. Fairness may also be the victim of the incredible complexity of resulting domestic confiscation legislation.

Article 5(1)(b) targets for confiscation the conventional targets set out in the earlier conventions,[75] viz.: 'narcotic drugs and psychotropic substances, materials and equipment or other instrumentalities used in or intended for use in any manner' in article 3(1) offences. These terms are with the exception of narcotic drugs and psychotropic substances undefined. 'Materials and equipment' are broad enough to extend to vessels, aircraft etc.,[76] but whether they include real property is more difficult to say. The United States delegation believes that 'instrumentalities' include all property used or intended for use in the offence.[77] The provision requires actual conduct – the materials etc. must be 'used in' – or preparatory conduct – the materials etc. must be 'intended for use in' – the commission of an offence.[78] The gloss 'in any manner' broadens

---

73 McClean supra note 25 at 345 cites as an example section 27(6) of the Commonwealth of Australia's Proceeds of Crime Act, 1987, which provides that in the case of 'serious offences' all the property of the defendant at the time of the application of a pecuniary penalty as well as all his property since the date of the earliest relevant offence (or within five years if that is the shorter period) is presumed, unless the contrary is proved, to be property that came into the possession or under the control of the defendant by reason of the commission of the offence or offences.

74 For example, Kohler supra note 25 at 20-21 explains that US laws permitting civil forfeiture, such as the Drug Abuse Prevention and Control Act of 1970, 21 USC section 881 (1988), depend firstly on the government showing probable cause for instituting the forfeiture proceeding. In doing so they can even rely on hearsay, and often do so because of the difficulty of getting direct evidence linking the assets to the illicit activity. Once probable cause has been established, the burden of proof shifts to the claimant to show by a preponderance of the evidence that the property is not subject to forfeiture or that he is an innocent owner. Section 881(d) of the Act requires the owner to show by a preponderance of the evidence that he was not involved in or aware of the unlawful conduct giving rise to forfeiture, and that he had taken all precautions that he could reasonably be expected to take to prevent the proscribed use of his property. This standard of 'exceptional innocence' contrasts with the standards of criminal forfeiture, and is very difficult to meet. Some of the more draconian features of the Act have been ameliorated by the Civil Asset Forfeiture Act of 2000, which inter alia strengthens the innocent owner defence.

75 See article 37 of the 1961 Convention and article 22(3) of the 1971 Convention.

76 See footnotes 11 and 12 supra.

77 Report of the US Delegation supra note 49 at 40.

78 In other words, drugs etc. used in the preparatory offences contemplated under article 3(1)(c).

the scope of the already very broad provision. The provision does not specify who must have an intention to use. The *1988 Commentary* notes that it will be up to the national legislator to decide whether it is limited to confiscation of materials held by a person intending to commit an offence or whether it extends to materials held by others that someone else intends to use to commit an offence.[79]

The eventual destiny of the contraband confiscated property is settled by article 14(5) of the 1988 Convention. According to the Indian delegation, the authors of article 14(5), it is 'intended to prevent any recycling of seized or confiscated substances on to the illicit market'.[80] It invites Parties to take the 'necessary measures' to engage in the destruction or lawful disposal of 'narcotic drugs, psychotropic substances and substances in Table I and Table II which have been seized or confiscated' by the Party's authorities as soon as is reasonably possible. The measures to be used are left to the Parties,[81] but they must ensure that the substances do not re-enter the illicit traffic. Article 14(5) also invites Parties to take the 'necessary measures' to ensure that quantities of the substances, duly certified by a government laboratory or the like as an illicit

---

79   *1988 Commentary* at 121.
80   See *1988 Records* vol. II at 307. It is in line with the recommendation in paragraph 267 of the Comprehensive Multidisciplinary Outline – see target 21 *Declaration of the International Conference on Drug Abuse and Illicit Trafficking and Comprehensive Multidisciplinary Outline of Future Activities in Drug Abuse Control* UN Publication St/Nar/14, UN Sales No.E.88.XI.1, (New York, 1988), at pp. 59-60.
81   The *1988 Commentary* at 308-310 notes that in-depth guidance in this process is available. It cites the reports of two Expert Groups on Pre-trial Destruction of Seized Narcotic Drugs, Psychotropic Substances and Precursor and Essential Chemicals, convened in 1989 and 1990 (see E/CN.7/1990/7Add.1). The 1989 meeting considered the legal implications and proposed practical measures for lawful disposal without hindering evidentiary requirements. The framework for implementation recommended included procedures to be used from the time of seizure until destruction such as the drawing up of inventories, the transportation, storage, sampling, expert analysis and urgent disposal. The 1990 Meeting examined the environmental impact of destruction itself. It recommended 'incineration' in an enclosed area with appropriate safeguards to prevent toxic gas release as the preferred process, but noted that recycling was a better option for certain precursors and essential chemicals although cost was a factor. The *1988 Commentary* at 310 notes that use of the substances to meet domestic needs is discouraged because of security reasons, the cost of reprocessing adulterated drugs and the need to suppress diversification of licit sources.

substance, are made available for evidential purposes.[82] Parties that lack this capacity may have to make provision for the export of the substance to a Party that does have such capacity and for the judicial recognition of foreign analysis.[83]

6.2.4.3   *Provisional measures at the national level*

Article 5(2) provides that each Party is obliged to authorise its competent authorities to put the article 5(1) confiscation procedure into practice at the national level through restraining measures designed to prevent criminals removing contraband, criminally derived property or property used to commit drug offences prior to confiscation. Like article 5(1), article 5(2) is not encumbered by a safeguard clause.

With confiscation as their aim, national authorities must be empowered to identify, trace and freeze or seize proceeds, property, instrumentalities or any other things referred to in article 5(1). Parties that adopt a value confiscation system will of course be obliged to provide for the taking of provisional measures on any realisable property. Article 5(2) does not set out in detail how this is to be done, leaving it to the Parties to work out their own methods, but article 1(l) does define 'freezing' or 'seizure' as 'temporarily prohibiting the transfer, conversion, disposition or movement of property or temporarily assuming custody or control of property on the basis of an order issued by a court or competent authority.' The United States delegation explained that in its view:

> 'Freezing' applied, for example, to bank accounts, which were in principle intangible entities, while 'seizure' applied to concrete objects, such as houses, boats, and so on. Whereas freezing referred to the prohibition of transfer, conversion or movement operations, seizure involved assuming custody or control of an object, often physical control.[84]

It appears from the 1988 Conference Records that different verbs were left in the provision to cater for the different domestic approaches of the Parties to

---

82   Thus, for example, while articles 87 and 88 of the Italian Presidential Decree Number 390 of 9 October 1990 provide for the destruction of confiscated drugs on an order from judicial authorities, samples may be requested by the Central Drug Control Unit, the Ministry of Health or the police.

83   *1988 Commentary* at 309.

84   *1988 Records* vol. II at 96.

freezing or seizure.[85] Domestic legislation enacted in response to this provision is particularly broad in scope.[86] The provision recognises that orders from judicial authorities or other competent authorities such as the customs or police, depending on the individual Party's domestic law, are required to serve as the basis for freezing or seizure. It is important to note that as defined, both are provisional processes. As such the emphasis is on speed of issue and authorities will usually not require the same level of proof from law enforcement agents for the granting of such orders as they do for the granting of final confiscation orders.[87] There are a number of gaps in article 5(2). The *1988 Commentary* points out that article 5(2) says nothing about the location of assets against which these provisional steps are to be taken, but notes that in practice Parties

---

85 See generally *1988 Records* vol. II at 67-68. For a review of Commonwealth legislation on freezing and seizure see McClean supra note 25 at 352-356 and 356-358 respectively. With respect to freezing, he discusses, for example, the UK's Drug Trafficking Offences Act, 1986, which provides in section 7(1)(c) that courts can order the freezing of property when they are satisfied that there is reasonable cause to believe that the defendant has benefited from drug trafficking. Material not usually admissible as evidence, such as hearsay, is admissible at this hearing. McClean notes that Canadian legislation provides much greater protection to those whose property may be affected by freezing including notice to persons appearing to have an interest in that property that it is to be frozen. With respect to seizure, McClean cites a developed example, the Commonwealth of Australia's legislation on search and seizure (Proceeds of Crime Act 1987 as amended). It provides for the search for tainted property of a person, including his clothing and other property in his immediate control, land and premises. It envisages warrants being issued in anticipation of the presence of tainted property within the next 72 hours. It allows for telephone applications when urgent, and for searches without warrant in emergency – defined as situations where action is necessary to prevent the concealment, loss or destruction of the property and in which the circumstances are so serious that immediate action without prior warrant is required. The Australian legislation also provides for additional far-reaching information gathering powers relating to the production of property tracing documents. These documents are used to locate, identify or quantify any of the defendant's property or to locate documents necessary for the transfer of the defendant's property, the search and seizure of property tracing documents etc.

86 See, for example, section 8(4) of Botswana's Proceeds of Serious Crime Act 19 of 1990, which allows a restraining order to be imposed on any person in order to prohibit him 'from dealing in any way with any property to which the order applies.' Restraining orders apply in terms of section 8(6) to '(a) property described in the order, being property (i) of the defendant, or (ii) received in connection with, or derived from, the commission of the offence and held by any person, other than the defendant in the order, or (b) all property of the defendant, whether described in the order or not, and including property acquired by the defendant after the making of the order.'

87 Depending on the domestic legal system they may only require a reasonable suspicion, or the issuing authority may not enter into the merits at all.

are only likely to be able to take steps against assets within their territories.[88] Where assets are located extraterritorially, a Party may make a freezing or seizure order with extraterritorial effect but it can only request foreign authorities to take action against these assets. Article 5(4)(b), discussed below, does not make law enforcement of such an order obligatory. Article 5(2) also says nothing about the control and care of assets once preliminary measures have been taken against them. The *1988 Commentary* points out the practical necessity of a functional asset-management regime for this purpose.[89]

6.2.4.4   *Removal of bank secrecy*

Bank secrecy has long served as a veil behind which the financial activities of drug traffickers have hidden from law enforcement authorities.[90] Generally speaking, in common law states violation of bank secrecy led only to civil remedies, while in civil law states such breach resulted in a criminal offence. Article 5(3), which is not subject to any safeguard clause, now ensures that bank secrecy will not obstruct the confiscation procedure.[91] The first sentence obliges Parties, in order to execute the measures referred to in article 5, to grant access to bank, financial or commercial records because it obliges Parties to empower their courts or other competent authorities to order the production or seizure[92] of these records. The second sentence of article 5(3) obliges Parties not to decline to act on grounds of 'bank secrecy'.

---

88   *1988 Commentary* at 121.
89   *1988 Commentary* at 141.
90   See Hernandez supra note 25 at 250 et seq. for a history of the clashes between the US and foreign sovereigns over bank secrecy provisions. The Panamanian Government prior to the removal of General Noriega was particularly zealous in the upholding of its bank secrecy laws in international drug trafficking investigations. The hardening of domestic secrecy provisions protects and fosters financial business for the jurisdiction involved, but attracts the attentions of money launderers and the US, usually resulting in the piecemeal lowering of secrecy provisions for the purpose of mutual legal assistance. I. Paget-Brown, 'Bank secrecy and criminal matters: Cayman Islands and U.S. co-operative development' (1988) 20 *Case Western Reserve International Law Journal* 369-391 recounts the removal of the Cayman Islands' bank secrecy provisions under US pressure. J. Knapp, 'Mutual legal assistance treaties as a way to pierce bank secrecy' (1988) 20 *Case Western Reserve International Law Journal* 405-433 charts how the US pioneered MLATs designed to remove bank secrecy as a screen for money laundering.
91   See Gilmore supra note 28 at 15.
92   In some states seizure is required for such records to become available for inspection.

The precise meaning of 'bank' as used in both sentences is ambiguous. It is possible that it is limited to registered banks. It may, however, apply to all types of financial institutions that take deposits of money in some way including building societies, insurance houses and so on. It may even extend to any person, actual or juridical, prohibited by law from disclosing information about the deposit of funds by other persons, such as lawyers who hold funds in trust. The conference records reveal little discussion by the delegates of the meaning of bank.[93] However, it is apparent that one of the objects of article 5 is to make possible the seizure and confiscation of the proceeds and profits of the drug trafficking offences set out in article 3(1). This purpose is echoed throughout the Convention as a whole. Thus, for example, the Preamble expresses the concern that the 'illicit traffic generates large financial profits and wealth enabling transnational criminal organisations to penetrate ... legitimate commercial and financial business'. In addition, the transfer or disguise of such profits and proceeds has been criminalised in their own right in terms of article 3(1) of the 1988 Convention. In practice, the laundering of profits and proceeds takes place through everything from insurance houses to post-offices. It is submitted, therefore, that in the light of the clear purpose of the 1988 Convention to eliminate money-laundering and to enable the seizure and confiscation of the profits and proceeds of the drug traffic, 'bank' should be interpreted broadly so as to include any financial institution to which deposits are made and to which domestic financial secrecy laws apply, where such secrecy laws could possibly frustrate the aforementioned clearly articulated purpose of the Convention. The extension of this interpretation to apply to any person, actual or juridical, who holds funds for another and whose custody of those funds is protected by some domestic legal privilege, is perfectly logical and in accordance with the aim of the Convention. It is conceded by some, however, that such an extensive definition must be at the election of the Party as it may be regarded as straining the ordinary meaning of 'bank'.[94]

Article 5(3)'s first sentence envisages access by law enforcement agencies to a broad range of materials beyond simply banking records. Reference to 'financial' records includes the activities of the enormous financial services industries, while 'commercial' records appears to provide for access to corporate or business records and in particular the records of sham corporations established by traffickers, as well as to records of commercial shipping lines, freight for-

93   See generally *1988 Records* vol. II at 68-69.
94   The UK's Drug Trafficking Offences Act, 1986, simply refers to a 'person', which includes all juridical and actual persons.

warders and insurers.[95] Precisely which competent authorities[96] are empowered to initiate this process, what the legal nature of this process is, and how these records are actually made available depends on the nature of the records and the laws of the Parties. There was some debate at the 1988 Conference as to whether a court's exercise of judicial discretion not to order production or seizure of records would mean that that Party had failed to implement the Convention.[97] It is apparent, however, that although the provision obliges Parties to empower their courts or authorities to order the production or seizure of records, it does not oblige Parties to produce those records, thus leaving a measure of discretion in the hands of their courts or authorities.[98]

Article 5(3) is not limited to the removal of bank secrecy for domestic purposes only. Through the wording 'in order to carry out the measures referred to in this article', it also applies to international requests for co-operation made by other Parties in terms of article 5(4).

Article 5(3) is generally viewed as a major breakthrough, especially with regard to the pursuit of laundered drug money.[99] The *1988 Commentary* notes that article 5(3) does not require Parties to abolish their bank secrecy laws, but does require them to provide for appropriate exceptions to these laws when law enforcement action is being taken against the illicit traffic.[100] The positive response of many Parties[101] has thrown into stark relief the impervious bank

---

95   *1988 Commentary* at 122.
96   These 'competent authorities' would be empowered by legislation or in some other way in exactly the same way as courts. Examples of existing authorities with the power to order the lifting of bank secrecy include investigating authorities (Italy), official commissions into drug trafficking (common law states), tax inspectors and customs authorities (India) – see generally *1988 Records* vol. II at 68-69.
97   See the questions of the Mexican delegate, *1988 Records* vol. II at 68-69.
98   See the explanation provided by the Australian delegate who noted that the grounds upon which a court might decline to order the lifting of bank secrecy included the presentation of insufficient evidence linking the commission of the proved offence with the property in question – *1988 Records* vol. II at 68. Sproule and St-Denis supra note 36 at 282 query whether this interpretation 'portends the utilisation of inventive ways to refuse access to financial records.'
99   See T.M. Catino, 'Italian and American co-operative efforts to reduce heroin trafficking: a role model for the United States and drug supplying foreign nations' (1990) 8 *Dickinson Journal of International Law* 415 at 438; Gilmore supra note 28 at 15; Sproule and St-Denis supra note 36 at 281.
100 *1988 Commentary* at 122.
101 For example, section 9 of the South African Drugs and Drug Trafficking Act 140 of 1992, entitled 'Relaxation of restrictions on the disclosure of information', allows any person prohibited by law '(a) from disclosing any information relating to the affairs

secrecy laws of other states.[102] Some Parties have made reservations to article 5(3) but other Parties have strongly objected to these reservations, placing their legality in doubt.[103]

6.2.4.5   *International co-operation on confiscation*

Prior to 1988 it was possible for a Party to the multilateral conventions to assist another Party by tracing the proceeds of drug trafficking held within its jurisdiction. However, none of the early conventions made possible the mutual enforcement of court orders to seize or confiscate that offender's criminally derived property.[104] Recognising the need for mutual legal assistance between Parties to trace and seize the proceeds of drug trafficking, article 5(4) envisages a special and novel form of mutual legal assistance unlike the general form pro-

---

or business of any other person; or (b) from permitting any person to have access to any registers, records or other documents which have a bearing on the said affairs or business' to 'disclose such information where disclosure is necessary for the prevention or combating, whether in [South Africa] or elsewhere, of a drug offence or an economic offence.' Evidence from the UK suggests that a similar provision in the Drug Trafficking Offences Act, 1986, (section 24(3)) has been very extensively used by banks and other financial institutions to disclose to police funds in their client's accounts which they suspect are drug related – see Home Affairs Committee, *Report: Drug Trafficking and Related Serious Crime* (1989) vol. II, pp. 48-49.

102 See, for example, Austria's bank secrecy law codified in the *Kreditwesengetz* (KWG) idF, November, 1986, section 23 which states that banks, their organisation members, employees, persons otherwise connected with the bank's business activity, and persons exclusively bound by a confidential business relationship with the bank's clients, are expressly forbidden to disclose or use financial information derived from their business relationship with a client. B. Zagaris, 'The emergence of an international anti-money laundering regime: implications for counselling businesses' in D. Atkins (ed.), *The Alleged Transnational Criminal* (Nijhoff, The Hague, 1995), p.127 at pp.178-182 notes Austria's increased popularity as a money laundering centre, the unwillingness of its authorities to change the law and the fact that it is not party to the 1988 Convention.

103 For example, Lebanon made a reservation (11/6/1996) to which France (7/3/1997), Germany (21/3/1997), UK (10/3/1997), Finland (24/4/1997), Italy (24/4/1997), Netherlands (11.3.1997), Sweden (7/3/1997), Austria (11/7/1997) and Greece (18/7/1997) have all objected – see *Multilateral Treaties Deposited with the Secretary General: Status as at 30 April 1999* (New York, 1999) UN Doc. St/Leg/Ser.E/17.

104 Kohler supra note 25 at 26 describes the different solutions used to overcome this lack of direct enforceability prior to the conclusion of article 5(4). States relied on legislation to allow confiscation of assets of an individual convicted in another state and bilateral MLATs expressly providing for the seizure and confiscation of assets in one state at the request of the other (e.g. article 1(2)(g) of the 1982 US-Italy MLAT, TIAS no. 8052). States could also in extradition requests ask for the return of all assets relating to the offence, or rely on coercive court orders, but the latter two methods have limitations.

vided for in article 7. It provides for a Party having jurisdiction over an article 3(1) offence to request that confiscation of proceeds or drugs/material etc. be carried out by another Party because the thing to be confiscated is within the latter's territorial jurisdiction.

Article 5(4)(a) is a flexible provision that adopts two alternative approaches to securing international co-operation with regard to confiscation, reflecting different approaches adopted in state practice.[105] By 1988 a small number of states had enacted laws that permitted the recognition of foreign penal judgments including confiscation orders against any of an offender's assets.[106] Most, however, still followed the traditional rule that did not permit the enforcement of foreign penal judgments of any sort. Certain of the latter states were prepared to enforce their own criminal confiscation orders against the assets or proceeds within their territories of someone who has committed an offence abroad. But such enforcement was conditional upon the foreign state affording them a sufficient factual basis for their authorities to find that the property was involved in or derived from drug offences committed abroad.[107]

Under the 1988 Convention, however, Parties can no longer refuse to acknowledge the existence of the proceeds of a foreign drug offence within their territory. Following a request made in terms of article 5(4) by another Party which has jurisdiction over an article 3(1) offence, the Party having territorial jurisdiction over the proceeds, property, instrumentalities or other things mentioned in article 5(1) is obliged to submit the request to its competent authorities, although it is not obliged to grant the assistance requested because there may be circumstances in which such assistance may be impossible under its domestic law.[108] In submitting the request to its competent authorities the requested Party has two choices.

Its first option is in terms of article 5(4)(a)(i) to seek a confiscation order from its competent authorities and, if granted, to give effect to that order – a system of direct execution. The Chairperson of Committee I explains that '[t]he

---

105 Kohler supra note 25 at 36.

106 By 1988, only Switzerland (article 24 of the 1951 Federal Drug Law), the UK (section 26 of the Drug Trafficking Offences Act ,1986) and the US (18 USC section 981(a)(1)(b)) had such enabling legislation.

107 See Kohler supra note 25 at 36 who gives as an example Switzerland, which in terms of LFS article 24 made it possible for such a basis to be established.

108 The *1988 Commentary* at 124 gives as examples the situation where a requesting Party has created an offence such as conspiracy in accordance with article 3(1)(c) while the requested Party has not, and the situation where the constitution of the requesting Party permits civil forfeiture while the constitution of the requested Party does not.

order in that case would be issued by the local authorities of the requested state. It was immaterial whether an order by the requesting state had been issued or not.'[109] Article 5(4)(a)(i) makes the requested Party's submission of the request to its competent authorities, usually its judicial authorities,[110] mandatory, and gives those authorities the discretion to grant or decline it, a decision dependent on the requesting Party providing sufficient information.[111] This reflects judicial practice in most states.

The second option open to a requested Party where an offence has been committed abroad but the proceeds are in its territory is in terms of article 5(4)(a)(ii) to enforce the confiscation order granted in the requesting Party – a system of indirect execution.[112] The chairperson of Committee I explains that in this case an order by the requesting state is essential.[113] Article 5(4)(a)(ii) requires that the requesting Party's order, which has to be made in terms of article 5(1), must be submitted by the requested Party to its competent authorities. The confiscation order will be issued according to the requested Party's procedural rules,[114] and the foreign order must then be given effect to the extent requested.[115] The provision in this way anticipates the kind of situation where the requesting Party's order relates to a number of items, some

---

109 *1988 Records* vol. II at 70.

110 See the statement of the US delegate, *1988 Records* vol. II at 75.

111 See article 5(4)(d)(i)) for details of the information required.

112 Kohler supra note 25 at 37 explains that article 5(4)(a)(ii) provides 'for an exequatur-type proceeding in which the requested party executes a forfeiture order which has entered into force in the country of the requesting party'. The precise legal status of the foreign order in the executing state is undefined. The *1988 Commentary* at 147 notes two possible approaches, viz. article 18(3) of the OAS Model Regulations provides that such an order 'may be recognised as evidence that the property ... may be subject to forfeiture in accordance with law', while article 14(2) of the 1990 Council of Europe Money Laundering Convention, ETS 141, provides more rigidly that a foreign order shall bind the requested party as to findings of fact. The latter does not, however, apply to the legal consequences flowing from such facts or prevent the hearing of fresh evidence.

113 *1988 Records* vol. II at 70.

114 The South African Drugs and Drug Trafficking Act 140 of 1992 has adopted the article 5(4)(a)(ii) approach. Section 56(1) provides for the registration of a foreign confiscation order in the manner to be prescribed by the Minster of Justice in terms of section 61. Section 56(2) provides for the clerk of the court to notify persons against whom the foreign confiscation order may be enforced, which person is entitled to apply for the registration of the foreign confiscation order to be set aside in terms of section 58. In terms of section 57 the foreign confiscation order becomes a civil judgment of court within a prescribed period.

115 See article 5(4)(c) and article 5(d)(ii) below.

of which may have been situated in the requesting Party's territory and some in the requested Party's territory. While the order will have been carried out with respect to the former, the requested Party's co-operation will be required with respect to the latter.[116] Article 5(4)(a)(ii)'s reference to submission to 'competent authorities' appears to mean submission to judicial authorities for the necessary legal sanction and submission to law enforcement agencies to execute the order.

The choice between the two options will depend on the Party and its domestic law. Enforcement of foreign orders is faster and more efficient and thus a better choice from a law enforcement point of view.[117] Article 5(4) does not provide many specifics with respect to the modalities for the implementation of requests, and Parties are left to work it out between themselves. The *1988 Commentary* notes that either approach may encounter significant legal difficulties when faced, for example, with a request to confiscate property not linked to a criminal conviction in the requested Party or at all, or with a request to confiscate immovable property.[118] The strength of the safeguard clause in article 5(4)(c) is testimony to these difficulties. Another problem on which article 5 gives no guidance is the ranking of requests for assistance; Parties are left to their own devices in this matter.[119]

Article 5(4)(b) obliges Parties to take preliminary restraining steps to make confiscation order requests possible,[120] again varying the traditional rule that states are not obliged to aid other states in the execution of their penal laws. It obliges a Party, in response to a request by a Party in whose jurisdiction an article 3(1) offence has occurred, to take steps to identify, trace, and freeze or seize proceeds, property, instrumentalities or any of the other things referred

---

116 See the explanation of the British delegate, *1988 Records* vol. II at 70.
117 *1988 Commentary* at 147.
118 *1988 Commentary* at 124.
119 Article 29 of the 1990 Council of Europe Money Laundering Convention, ETS 141, suggests consultation with the various parties and notes that multiple requests are no reason to refuse to take preliminary steps.
120 T. Wren, 'The enforcement of confiscation law in Great Britain' (1992) 17 *Commonwealth Law Bulletin* 1413 at 1414 recounts, for example, how documents recovered from a Colombian farm indicated the global dispersion of assets in bank accounts. The US Department of Justice, which had indicted the leader of the organisation that held these assets, Gonzales Rodriguez Gacha, transmitted a formal request to the British Home Office asking for immediate action from British authorities in terms of the Confiscation Agreement between the US and UK. The UK's National Drugs Intelligence Unit co-ordinated the work of a Customs Officer and a number of further bank accounts were identified in London. Restraining orders were issued awaiting determination of the case.

to in article 5(1) for the purpose of eventual confiscation whether by an order granted by its authorities or by the requesting Party.[121] This provision is not a replica of article 5(4)(a) simply applied to provisional measures. It makes no distinction between situations where the requesting Party's authorities have issued a court order for such measures and situations where they have not. Article 5(4)(b) obliges a requested party to respond to a request, whatever its legal origins. The measures taken are 'for the purpose of eventual confiscation'. If the requested Party, after taking provisional measures as a result of a request by another Party, chooses to confiscate the proceeds in its own right because of their connection to an offence committed in its territory, it will not be in violation of the provision.[122] If the requested Party decides to discontinue the provisional measures, article 5(4)(b) does not oblige it to give the requesting Party an opportunity to present any reasons for continuing the measures.[123] In practice, states have complied with this provision because they have realised the futility of making provision for enforcement of foreign confiscation orders without making provision for seizure – as soon as suspects become aware that they are under investigation they will remove all incriminating evidence and confiscatable property.[124] Article 5(4)(b) is also subject to the safeguard clause in article 5(4)(c).

Article 5(4)(c) makes it clear that execution of seizure and confiscation requests take place through and are thus subject to the domestic laws and particularly the procedural rules[125] of the requested Party, and to any bi- or

---

121 McClean supra note 25 at 359 notes, for example, that section 49 of the Malaysian Dangerous Drugs (Forfeiture of Property) Act of 1988 authorises searches of persons or premises at the request of a foreign government or authority, while section 50 authorises the seizure of property in cases which include those where the ground for the request by the foreign government is that the property is liable to forfeiture under the law of the foreign country.

122 *1988 Commentary* at 126.

123 Unlike article 12(2) of the Council of Europe Money Laundering Convention, ETS 141.

124 The US, for example, in 18 USC section 981(c) gives the Attorney General or the Secretary of the Treasury the power to seize and retain in their custody any property subject to forfeiture as the proceeds of a foreign drug offence pursuant to 18 USC section 981(a)(1)(b) pending final outcome of forfeiture proceedings.

125 The necessity for this term may seem confusing to states where procedural rules are part of domestic law, but its inclusion was thought necessary by the French delegate who explained that in France it means the body of judicial and administrative rules other than the laws enacted by Parliament – see *1988 Records* vol. II at 75. Some states have no legal provisions allowing for the domestic enforcement of foreign confiscation orders, but they can do so through their procedural rules.

multilateral treaty, agreement or arrangement to which the requested Party may be bound in relation to the requesting Party. Application via domestic law is necessary because it ensures respect for the requested Party's substantive and procedural law. For example, Parties may be asked either to grant an order where the basis of the confiscation does not include a criminal conviction against the owner of the property or to enforce a foreign confiscation order originally granted on such a basis. Thus a civil law state such as Austria which only provides for criminal confiscation domestically may be asked by a common law state such as the United States to enforce a civil forfeiture order. It is unlikely that in such circumstances the 1988 Convention envisages Austria complying,[126] and it would be for the requesting Party to tailor its request to the requested Party's domestic legal principles or fail in its request. A similar problem would arise when a Party like the United Kingdom which uses a value-confiscation system requests co-operation from a Party that insists that the property to be confiscated is property derived from the commission of an article 3(1) offence and is not just property held by an article 3(1) offender. Domestic law also determines the rules relating to burden of proof, notice requirements and defences to seizure and confiscation. Article 5(4)(c) does not, however, allow Parties to re-erect the veil of bank secrecy removed by article 5(3). Article 5(4)(c) does not permit a Party to block either the preliminary proceedings or confiscation proceedings because of its bank secrecy laws.[127] Alteration of a Party's domestic laws in response to article 5(3) will eliminate such problems. Article 5(4)(c)'s provision that the implementation of requests for confiscation is subject to any of the requested Party's international obligations recognises the primacy of the specifics of existing international agreements over article 5. Application via existing domestic or international law assumes such application is possible in terms of existing law. If it is not, existing law may have to give way to the provisions of article 5. The *1988 Commentary* remarks, nevertheless, that the subjection of the application of article 5 paragraphs (a) and (b), to something as informal as 'arrangements' is striking.[128]

Article 5(4)(d) is concerned mainly with procedural aspects of international co-operation in respect of confiscation. Its first sentence provides that article 7's provisions for the regulation of requests for mutual legal assistance (para-

---

126 Article 18(4)(d) of the 1990 Council of Europe Money Laundering Convention, ETS 141, makes the failure of the request to relate to a prior conviction an optional ground for the refusal of confiscation.
127 Report of the US Delegation supra note 49 at 43-44.
128 *1988 Commentary* at 127.

graphs 8 to 19), also apply in the same way to the requests for co-operation made in terms of article 5(4). Paragraphs 8 to 19 of article 7 provide for the designation of authorities to handle requests,[129] the stipulation of the language, form and content of requests,[130] the method of the execution of requests and limitation of the use of information obtained,[131] grounds for refusal of assistance or its postponement,[132] grants of immunity to persons giving evidence in a requesting Party[133] and for meeting the costs of a request.[134] Although, as the *1988 Commentary*[135] points out, article 7's procedural provisions only apply if the Parties international relations in respect of confiscation are not already governed by an existing MLAT,[136] many states are not party to such MLATs, in which case the procedural requirements in article 7 provide the necessary guidance.[137] What this means in practice is that specific procedural rules applicable to article 5(4) have simply been replaced by the flexible application of article 7's procedural safeguards.[138] Thus, for example, while co-operation in terms of article 5(4) cannot be refused in terms of article 5(3) on the grounds of bank secrecy, in terms of article 7(15)(b), it may be refused if executing the request is 'likely to prejudice the [requested Party's] sovereignty, security, *ordre public* or other essential interests'. Refusal on grounds of double jeopardy, due process and so on, that is, refusal in the interests of the owner of the property, is provided obliquely by article 7(15)(c) which allows a Party to refuse assistance if it would be prohibited by its own law from carrying out such an action itself. These grounds of refusal have been recognised in state practice.[139]

Article 5(4)(d)'s other function is to detail the information Parties are required to furnish pursuant to the different procedures established for confis-

---

129 Article 7(8).
130 Article 7, paragraphs (9) to (11). Article 7(10) is supplemented by article 5(4)(d).
131 Article 7, paragraphs (12) to (14).
132 Article 7, paragraphs (15) to (17).
133 Article 7(18).
134 Article 7(19). These costs may be met by confiscation of the property.
135 *1988 Commentary* at 128.
136 Article 7, paragraphs (6) and (7).
137 See the 'Review Group Report', *1988 Records* vol. I at 63.
138 See the statement of the Chairman of Committee I, *1988 Records* vol. II at 71.
139 For example, the UK's Drug Trafficking Offences Act, 1986, recognises in section 26 that a request for the execution of a foreign forfeiture or restraining order may be refused if the defendant is still in a position to appeal against conviction, or did not receive notice of the proceedings against him and thus could not defend his interests, or enforcement of the foreign order would be contrary to the interests of justice.

cation assistance. This provision grew out of the experience of states that had
already engaged in international co-operation in respect of confiscation, as well
as the perceived need to avoid bureaucratic delays and misunderstandings.[140]
Article 5(4)(d) accommodates the two alternative approaches taken to international confiscation. Article 5(4)(d)(i) requires that a request in terms of article
5(4)(a)(i) must contain a description of the property to be confiscated and a
statement of the facts relied upon by the requesting Party sufficient to enable
the requested Party to seek the order under its domestic law.[141] Article 5(4)(d)
(ii) requires that a request in terms of article 5(4)(a)(ii) must contain a 'legally
admissible' copy[142] of the requesting Party's[143] order of confiscation upon
which the request is based, together with a fact statement and information about
the extent to which the order is to be executed. Article 5(4)(d)(iii) requires that
a request in terms of article 5(4)(b) must contain a statement of the facts relied
upon by the requesting Party and a description of the actions required. All of
this information is in addition to that required under the provisions of article
7(10) for mutual legal assistance.

Article 5(4)(e) obliges Parties to provide the UN Secretary General with
the texts of relevant legislation and regulations and any changes to these texts.
Its purpose is to allow the Secretary General to make generally available information on the procedures to be used for domestic confiscation as well as inter-

---

140 Sproule and St-Denis supra note 36 at 283.
141 Kohler supra note 25 at 33 describes the information that is required from US authorities
for a request to be executed in Switzerland: 'To prepare a confiscation case, a Swiss
prosecutor or judge handling the investigation must receive certain types of evidence
from the United States Government: He must obtain a certified copy of a conviction
or plea bargain from a United States court, which demonstrates not only that the defendant is guilty of drug trafficking, but also that the frozen assets in Switzerland stem
directly from his unlawful activity. The Swiss magistrate must receive the exact dates,
places, and names of persons involved, and sufficient evidence of their connection with
the forfeitable assets in Switzerland. This information must be obtained through a mutual
assistance request sent to the FOPM [Swiss Federal Police Office], which will be
transmitted to the United States Attorney General.'
142 'Legally admissible' was understood by the authors of the provision to mean that the
document in question must be in accord with the laws of both Parties – see the statement
of the French delegate and the Chairman of Committee I, *1988 Records* vol. II at 71.
143 This is likely in practice to be issued by the requesting Party's court. Indeed, some
delegations to the 1988 Conference noted that it would be impossible for their countries
to give effect to a confiscation order issued by an authority other than a court of the
requesting Party – see the Netherlands delegate's statement (supported by Jamaica,
Austria and Portugal), *1988 Records* vol. II at 71.

national requests for confiscation by one Party.[144] It is mandatory to ensure the completeness of the information for which the Secretary General is to serve as a clearing-house.

Article 5(4)(f) provides that if a Party chooses to find that a treaty is 'necessary' for co-operation in terms of article 5(4) sub-paragraphs (a) and (b), the 1988 Convention is 'sufficient', that is, it shall serve as a treaty basis for such co-operation. This mandatory provision is unusual,[145] but is necessary because the novelty of the procedure means that most Parties are not legally prepared to execute other Parties' confiscation requests and require a legal basis upon which to do so. Sproule and St-Denis note:

> This formulation makes amply clear that states which become party to the Convention must be prepared to provide confiscation co-operation with other state parties. This is in spite of the fact that the states in question may have widely divergent views on the legal status of private property and what constitutes a sufficient ground to confiscate it.[146]

Finally, article 5(4)(g) encourages Parties to enter into treaties and agreements, both bilaterally and multilaterally, to enhance the operation of confiscation provisions.[147] Bilateral treaties and agreements for this purpose have been concluded,[148] and regional and other multilateral arrangements are also be-

---

144 See the statement of the German (FRG) delegate, *1988 Records* vol. II at 76.
145 Gilmore supra note 28 at 17.
146 Supra note 36 at 283.
147 The Optional Protocol Regarding Assistance in Forfeiture of the Proceeds of Crime attached to the UN Model Treaty on Mutual Assistance in Criminal Matters, GA. Res. 45/117 annex, provides a suitable model.
148 See, for example, the UK-US 1988 Agreement Concerning the Investigation of Drug Trafficking Offences and the Seizure and Forfeiture of the Proceeds and Instrumentalities of Drug Trafficking (cmnd no.755) which was concluded after alteration to domestic legislation made it possible (UK's Drug Trafficking Offences Act, 1986). Gilmore supra note 28 at 48 notes that the UK has subsequently signed a number of such bilateral agreements, and gives as an example, the Agreement with Barbados concluded in April 1991. Its article 1 reads: '(1) The Parties shall, in accordance with this Agreement, grant to each other assistance in investigations and proceedings in respect of drug trafficking, including the tracing, restraining and confiscation of the proceeds and instruments of drug trafficking. (2) This Agreement shall be without prejudice to other obligations between the Parties pursuant to other treaties or arrangements or otherwise, and shall not prevent the Parties or their law enforcement agencies from providing assistance to each other pursuant to other treaties or arrangements.'

coming popular.[149]

Article 5(4) broke new ground. Subsequently, states have been urged to respond to it and to make provision in their laws for enforcement of confiscation orders made outside their jurisdiction. Positive steps have been taken,[150] although complaints are still heard that states are not prepared to render such assistance.[151] Debate has focused on the relative merits of the article 5(4)(a)(i) and article 5(4)(a)(ii) approaches. Some Parties such as Australia have extremely sophisticated legislative schemes for the requests from other Parties in respect of restraint and confiscation, permitting the registration and enforcement of foreign restraint and confiscation orders (that is, in terms of article 5(4)(a)(i)). The Australian approach has been praised and Canada's reliance on domestic process criticised.[152] Canada makes no provision for the registration of foreign restraint or confiscation orders insisting rather upon the Canadian authorities initiating a domestic investigation with a view to charging and prosecuting the offender in Canada and then imposing its own restraint and criminal confiscation orders. Enforcement of a foreign restraint or confiscation order must be made by application to the Canadian Courts (that is, in terms of article 5(4)(a)(ii)). Execution of an existing foreign order is more effective from a law enforcement point of view as it is expeditious. It also avoids the cumbersome process of trying to apply a domestic process to a foreign request, which tends to discourage the requested Party's authorities from vigorous pursuit of investigations flowing from foreign requests. Making a request de novo does have the advantage of providing greater human rights protections to individuals because it ensures that foreigners and citizens are treated uniformly when it comes to restraint and confiscation orders. But it has been criticised for doing so at the

---

149 A major regional step was the conclusion of the 1990 Council of Europe Convention on Laundering, Search, Seizure and Confiscation of the Proceeds from Crime, ETS 141, many of the provisions of which have already been described above. This Convention is much broader in scope than article 5 of the 1988 Convention, with article 2 providing for seizure and confiscation of the proceeds of all forms of serious criminality even when the state in question does not have jurisdiction over the predicate offence.

150 See, for example, the 'Commonwealth Caribbean Conference on the International Drug Conventions and drug abuse' (1989) 15 *Commonwealth Law Bulletin* 1005 at 1006.

151 Copenhagen's Police Commissioner has complained that not all European states cooperate in the collection of money abroad adjudged to be the proceeds of crime by Danish authorities – see Garde supra note 5 at 84.

152 K. Prost, 'Breaking down the barriers: international cooperation in combating transnational crime' in *Souvenir Brochure of the International Conference on Global drugs Law* (Indian Law Institute, New Delhi, 1997), pp. 44-52 at pp. 50-51.

expense of societal interests.[153] It is questionable, however, whether the requested Party has sufficient review powers to check the abuse of individual human rights in the requesting Party in systems where only registration of foreign orders is required.

6.2.4.6   Disposition of confiscated assets

Article 5(5) deals with the final disposition of confiscated 'proceeds or property'. The general principle in article 5(5)(a) is that these matters are to be dealt with by the confiscating Party according to its 'domestic law and administrative procedures'.[154] When a Party acts in terms of article 5(1) it does so entirely on its own accord and it is only logical that the disposal decision should be its own. When a Party acts in terms of article 5(4) on behalf of another Party, then article 5(5)(a) leaves the decision in respect of disposal to it because that is where the property is found and where effective confiscation occurs.[155] Moreover, experience has shown that the domestic right to disposal is necessary to encourage Parties to co-operate internationally in the execution of seizure and confiscation.[156] The 'property' confiscated should be broadly interpreted and includes all the types of property confiscated in terms of article 5.[157] The ultimate destiny of such funds may be the national budget or, in federal states, provincial budgets. The *1988 Commentary* detects, however, a growing tendency to direct these funds to specific targets such as anti-drug and anti-money-

---

153 Supra note 152 at 51.
154 The Australian delegation understood 'domestic law' to include legal obligations arising out of international treaties, *1988 Records* vol. II at 80.
155 The *1988 Commentary* at 132 rejects the interpretation that article 5(4)(a)(ii)'s provision for execution of a foreign confiscation order means that the confiscation is made by the requesting party and that it has the right of disposal by pointing out that this was not the intention of the authors of article 5.
156 See the 'Expert Group Report', *1988 Records* vol. I at 19. L. Frei and S. Treschel 'Origins and applications of the United States – Switzerland Treaty on Mutual Assistance in Criminal Matters' (1990) 31 *Harvard International Law Journal* 77-97 at 91 note that in terms of the Swiss Federal Law (SR 812.81) implementing the 1973 US-Switzerland MLAT, 27 UST 2019, 'drug-trafficking profits situated in Swiss territory will be forfeited to the Canton where they are found, even when the offence was committed abroad.' They continue: 'Thus where the United States Department of Justice seeks evidence and a freeze of assets generated by drug trafficking, the Swiss Federal Office for Police Matters insists that the United States co-operate with Swiss authorities in securing the evidence necessary to turn those assets over to the canton. Indeed without such an understanding, a forfeiture process would be doomed to failure and a preceding freeze would be useless.'
157 *1988 Commentary* at 131.

laundering efforts.[158] Allowing a police force to benefit directly from confiscation is potentially corruptive of its motives as even at the most benign level this "market-driven" approach creates a dependency situation where confiscated drug-money becomes one of the police force's most reliable sources of income.[159] The common state practice of allocating the proceeds of confiscated assets to the funding of national therapeutic programmes[160] should be encouraged although it should not be considered a substitute for normal governmental funding allocations.

Article 5(5)(b) invites requested Parties to consider concluding bilateral or multilateral agreements to engage in two forms of asset sharing.[161] The precise timing and modality of these two forms of asset sharing have been left up to the Parties or IGO's concerned to determine.

Article 5(5)(b)(i) envisages that the value of confiscated assets or funds derived from the sale of such assets or a 'substantial part thereof' should be donated to appropriate intergovernmental organisations involved in the suppression of illicit drugs such as the UNDCP.[162] The use of such funds would be at the discretion of these IGO's, that could, for instance, use them to fund joint projects with the donating Party. But representatives at the 'Expert Group' meetings urged that because the proceeds of the illicit traffic were located mostly in the developed world, these proceeds should be distributed through the agency of the UN to assist developing states to combat the illicit traffic.[163]

---

158 *1988 Commentary* at 149 citing a recommendation of the Caribbean Financial Action Task Force.

159 See, for example, E. Blumenson and E. Nilsen, 'Policing for profit: the drugs war's hidden economic agenda' (1998) 65 *University of Chicago Law Review* 35-114 who examine in depth the effect on police motivation in the US of legislation allowing them to retain most of the assets they seize, noting that in the ten years since this permission was given, police agencies have chosen law enforcement strategies which take maximum advantage of federal forfeiture laws in order to maximise property seizures while at the same time pursuing practices which reduce fairness and ignore crime control policies, all of which leads to the aggrandisement of unaccountable police forces.

160 In Spain, for example, a fund created by Law 36 of 1995 (11/12/1995) is in terms of article 2 dedicated to addiction prevention programmes, treatment programmes, professional and social interventions, and drug prevention programmes, in addition to criminal justice measures.

161 The Moroccan, Iranian and Saudi-Arabian delegations all made reservations to this provision at the Conference on the basis that their domestic legal systems did not permit the sharing of the proceeds of property of the illicit traffic, *1988 Records* vol. II at 32.

162 The provision does not apply to non-governmental organisations working in the field of drug control.

163 See the 'Expert Group Report', *1988 Records* vol. I at 34.

It was noted at the Conference that this provision supports the UN's drug control organs because they provide assistance to states with limited resources.[164] There has been continued support for the donation of confiscated assets and isolated donations have been made.[165]

Article 5(5)(b)(ii) envisages that assets confiscated by one Party at the request of another should be shared between them on a regular or case-by-case basis. Such actions would have to conform to the Party's domestic law and administrative procedures or to any bilateral or multilateral agreements that the Party had entered into for this purpose. This provision was motivated by the consideration that the benefit of the confiscation should be shared with the requesting Party as the latter had assisted in the confiscation by furnishing information.[166] Sharing of assets is seen as one method of encouraging poorer Parties to co-operate.[167] In practice, this approach has become more popular than sharing assets with IGO's.[168] Agreements to share confiscated assets have been concluded[169] and profits shared,[170] although this appears to be the ex-

---

164 See the statement of the Ghanaian delegate, *1988 Records* vol. II at 79. This point was reiterated at the 'Commonwealth Caribbean Conference on the International Drug Conventions and Drug Abuse' (1989) 15 *Commonwealth Law Bulletin* 1005 at 1007.

165 See Paragraph 17 of the 'Recommendations of the Intergovernmental Expert Group to study the Economic and Social Consequences of Illicit Traffic in Drugs' UN Doc. E/CN.7/1991/25 in W.C. Gilmore (ed.), *International Efforts to Combat Money Laundering* (Grotius, Cambridge, 1992), p. 150 at p. 151. In 1996 Luxembourg became the first Party to donate part of such proceeds to international drug control efforts – INCB, *Report of the International Narcotics Control Board for 1996* UN Doc. E/INCB/1996/1. Luxembourg donated a further 1.7 million dollars of confiscated assets in 1998, but remained the only state to do so – UN Press Release Soc/Nar/779.

166 See the statement of the Ghanaian delegate, *1988 Records* vol. II at 79.

167 D. Stafford, *International Legal Co-operation Against Serious Crime: Inter-legal Systems Issues Impacting on International Co-operation* (unpublished conference paper, New Delhi Global Drugs Law Conference 1997), p. 7.

168 *1988 Commentary* at 150.

169 Article 7 of the OAS Model Regulations Concerning Laundering Offences Connected to Illicit Drug trafficking and related Offences anticipates inter-party transfers authorised by international agreement. Bilateral agreements have proliferated, see, for example, the Mexico-US Treaty on Mutual Legal Assistance, 9 December, 1987, (1988) 27 ILM 443. Legislative approval is a prerequisite for such transfers and the *1988 Commentary* at 151 fn.330 notes that in the US three statutory provisions authorise such transfers – 18 USC section 981(i)(1); 19 USC section 1611a(c)(2); and 21 USC section 881(e)(1)(E).

170 In August 1989, for example, the US Justice Department announced that it would give one million dollars each to Canada and Switzerland for their help in the investigation and prosecution of the Panama based Banco de Occidente – E.A. Nadelmann, 'The role

ception rather than the rule due to the obvious desire of states to keep their hands on the profits of law enforcement.[171]

6.2.4.7   The seizure and confiscation of converted assets, intermingled assets and the income from illicit assets

The transformation[172] of property from one form into another or the mixing of the asset-benefits of drug trafficking with other assets is a common practice that frequently prevents the confiscation of those assets because of problems of identification or for other reasons. The profits of illicit assets are also often immune from confiscation. More advanced domestic jurisdictions were, prior to the 1988 Convention, already adapting their law to enable the confiscation of converted proceeds and illicit profits.[173] However, making converted and intermingled property and income open to confiscation is now mandatory under article 5(6). Gilmore notes that article 5(6) provides in essence that Parties are obliged to 'render transformed, converted and intermingled property and proceeds, as well as income or other benefits derived therefrom, liable to the measures, including confiscation, provided for elsewhere in article 5.'[174] Despite resistance article 5(6) was made obligatory because the skill and speed with which large-scale traffickers are able to launder their profits would otherwise have meant that the bulk of drug profits would have been insulated from the threat of confiscation.[175] Seizure and or confiscation is not obligatory;

---

of the United States in the international enforcement of criminal law' (1990) 31 *Harvard International Law Journal* 37 at 62.

171   Zagaris and Kingma supra note 52 at 512.

172   The English case of *R v Cuthbertson* [1980] 2 All ER 401 is a good example. Following a conviction of conspiracy to provide LSD in terms of section 4 of the Misuse of Drugs Act, 1971, the trial court ordered forfeiture of assets held in French and Swiss bank accounts in terms of section 27 of the Act. An appeal was lodged inter alia on the ground that the power of forfeiture only extended to a thing shown to 'relate to' an offence. The Court of Appeal dismissed the appeal, but the House of Lords upheld it, giving as one of their reasons that in terms of section 277 of the Act, 'the power of forfeiture only applied to tangible things capable of being physically destroyed and not choses in action or other intangibles'. The conversion of the profits into credit in a bank made it impervious to forfeiture.

173   See, for example, section 4 of South Australia's Crimes (Confiscation of Profits) Act, 1986, which allows the confiscation of property acquired with the proceeds of an offence or property into which the proceeds of an offence have, in some manner, been converted.

174   Supra note 28 at 17.

175   Sproule and St-Denis supra note 36 at 284. There was resistance to this provision at the 1988 Conference on the grounds that it would violate the constitutions of certain states – see the statements of the Philippines' and Egyptian delegates, *1988 Records*

the property mentioned must simply be 'liable' to seizure and or confiscation which means that the Parties' competent authorities still retain the discretion to order these measures or not. In addition, the 1988 Conference clearly understood that article 5(6) would be construed in a manner that would not prejudice article 5(8)'s protection of bona fide third parties.[176] Article 5(6) makes provision for three different situations, differentiated according to the class of asset.

Article 5(6)(a) provides that if illicit proceeds have been 'transformed or converted' into other property, for instance by sale or exchange, Parties are obliged to apply article 5's measures to this other property instead of to the proceeds. Article 5(6)(a) applies according to the Australian delegation to the 1988 Conference to 'transfers or conversions of proceeds into property, whether it remained in the hands of the person who had first obtained the proceeds or was passed on to another person, natural or judicial.'[177] The use of the term 'measures' implies that this property is open to the provisional measures provided for in article 5(2) and to the final measures provided for in article 5(1). The *1988 Commentary* points out that the definition of proceeds in article 1(p) as including property derived 'directly or indirectly' from an offence means that article 5(6) is strictly unnecessary.[178] Nonetheless, Parties have reserved in respect of this provision.[179]

Article 5(6)(b) provides for the mandatory severance of illicit proceeds from licit property with which it has been intermingled, and then for its confiscation. Severance is necessary to prevent the confiscation of an asset of which only a fraction of the value is derived from the illicit traffic.[180] Severance is mandatory because of the rapidity of the laundering of drug profits and their blending with the licit economy. It may, however, prove difficult in reality, and in

---

vol. II at 82.

176 See *1988 Records* vol. II at 81.

177 *1988 Records*, vol. II at 82.

178 *1988 Commentary* at 133.

179 The Philippines has made a reservation to the effect that it does not consider itself bound by article 5(6)(a) – 7/6/1996, *Multilateral Treaties Deposited* (1997) at 305.

180 The delegate from the Philippines gave the example of a luxury yacht purchased in part with tainted proceeds by co-owners when one of the co-owners was acting in good faith. This is an example of both conversion and intermingling. The British delegate submitted that in such a case one method to recover the value derived from the illicit traffic and at the same time to safeguard the interests of the bona fide co-owner was to buy out his share – see generally *1988 Records* vol. II at 81. It is submitted that article 5(8) will, however, protect the innocent co-owner in such circumstances not only from loss of his half of the value of the boat but also from a forced buy-out.

practice the asset may have to be sold. In a sense what is being provided for by article 5(6)(b) is a form of value confiscation. This provision is 'without prejudice to any powers relating to seizure or freezing'. This means that in response to the practical necessity of immobilising property before identifying the nature of the interest vested in it, the article in question can be subject to the preliminary measures provided for in article 5(2). The article stipulates that the property shall be liable to confiscation 'up to the assessed value of the intermingled proceeds'. The *1988 Commentary* believes this to mean the assessed value at the point at which intermingling took place, which may in practice lead to great difficulties when the intermingling cannot be dated precisely.[181]

Article 5(6)(c) deals with income or other benefits derived from drug trafficking offences. It would include the interest accrued on a bank deposit of proceeds, a dividend on shares bought with proceeds, the value of the catch of a fishing trawler purchased with proceeds, and so forth. This provision rejects the view that these are the benefits of licit transactions and applies the principle that their illicit origin taints them.[182] It provides, in essence, that income[183] or other benefits[184] derived from either proceeds, or from property into which proceeds have been transformed or converted, or from property with which proceeds have been intermingled, shall also be liable to article 5(2)'s provisional measures and article 5(1)'s final measures, in the same manner and to the same extent as proceeds. The *1988 Commentary* notes that with regard to benefits derived from intermingled proceeds article 5(6) sub-paragraphs (b) and (c) appear to have to be read together, with the effect that 'the power to confiscate would apply to the derivative benefits in the proportion that the original proceeds bore to the property acquired from legitimate sources.'[185] Proof of derivation may be difficult, but the standards required will be a matter of

---

181 *1988 Commentary* at 134.

182 *1988 Commentary* at 135.

183 The obvious example is interest generated by capital in a bank account, which may be difficult for Islamic states to confiscate because of the injunction against usury in the Sharia.

184 This term would cover benefits such as the bonus issue of shares which some states do not regard as income.

185 *1988 Commentary* at 135. The *Commentary* also suggests that where intermingled assets have risen considerably in value, that rise can be regarded as a benefit under article 5(6)(c)open to confiscation thus avoiding the requirement in article 5(6)(b) that value of illicit proceeds be assessed at the time intermingling took place.

domestic law. Article 5(6)(c) was a novel development in 1988, and requires new legislation.[186]

Article 5(6) is useful because it provides detailed guidance for Parties on the content of the measures they are to take to recover the more elusive benefits of the illicit traffic. It delimits the vulnerable property and profits. It fails, however, to provide guidance in some difficult situations such as where the existence of proceeds or property only comes to light after a confiscation order is made. Assets of this type may be located in a non-party. The *1988 Commentary* suggests a number of measures to deal with such situations, including a legal order compelling the individual to bring the assets within the Party's jurisdiction, which provides that if he fails to do so the assets remain perpetually vulnerable to confiscation.[187]

6.2.4.8   *Reversal of the onus of proof*

Article 5(7) invites Parties to examine the possibility of reversing the onus of proof in regard to the lawful origin of the alleged proceeds of drug trafficking. The INCB notes:

> Such a reversal can take different forms; for example, there could be a rebuttable presumption that all property acquired before the beginning of the legal proceedings within a defined period of time would be treated as property derived from drug trafficking. The onus of proof in this case would shift to the offender, who must satisfy the court that the assumption is incorrect. It is expressly stated in the laws of some countries that the standard of proof applicable to confiscation proceedings is the civil standard, instead of the more onerous criminal standard of proof "beyond reasonable doubt". Some countries also provide for the possibility of proceeding

---

186 A. Dickson, 'Taking dealers to the cleaners' (1991) 141 *New Law Journal* 1120 (part two of two part article) noted, for example, that while the UK's Drug Trafficking Offences Act, 1986, and its Criminal Justice (International Co-operation) Act, 1990, catered for the situations contemplated by article 5(6)(a) and (b), they did not go as far as article 5(6)(c). She explains by example: 'Income derived from proceeds or property into which these proceeds have been converted would also include, for example, money obtained as a result of leasing a house which had been bought with the proceeds of drug trafficking or the profits from a restaurant which had been established with those proceeds. The DTOA and the 1990 Act would permit the confiscation of the house and the restaurant but not the money that had been generated by those enterprises.' Further extension of the law was required.

187 *1988 Commentary* at 143.

with confiscation independently from a conviction, in particular when the person charged with an offence has absconded or died.[188]

A national law enacted or promulgated in terms of article 5(7) would leave it to the accused trafficker to prove that his or her assets and property were acquired by licit means. It would also set the standard of proof required, an issue not covered by article 5(7). The purpose of article 5(7) is to make investigations of fraudulent conduct relating to the proceeds of drug trafficking less arduous. For that reason it is supported by the law enforcement agencies of consumer states. However, this provision is exhortatory and Parties are under no obligation to comply with it, and some Parties have made it clear that they do not feel bound to apply it.[189] Article 5(7) allows such a reversal to be tested for its consistency with a Party's domestic legal principles and the nature of its judicial and other proceedings. Parties where the presumption of innocence is constitutionally entrenched are certain to have constitutional problems with article 5(7),[190] and in jurisdictions where reverse onus provisions are in place there is evidence of reluctance to use them by prosecutors and the judiciary.[191] One of the problems with reverse onus provisions is that the reversal applies to people other than the offender, including innocent third parties.

---

188 INCB, *Report of the International Narcotics Control Board for 1996* UN Doc. E/INCB/ 1996/1, p. 5.

189 Colombia has made a reservation (10/6/1994 – *Multilateral Treaties Deposited* (1997) at 303) to this effect.

190 Article 5(7) appears to have been included in the Convention despite the misgivings of some of the delegates to the 1988 Conference because of the desire of other delegates to provide support in the shape of an international instrument for a change in domestic law to accommodate a reversal of the onus – see the statements of the Netherlands delegation, *1988 Records* vol. II at 84. The *1988 Commentary* at 136 submits, however, that providing sufficient opportunity is given to an accused person to rebut the presumption, it is likely to be regarded as compatible with international human rights provisions. It relies on the decision of the European Court of Human Rights in the *Salabiaku Case*, 7 October 1988, Series A, No.141.A, that a reverse onus provision of a similar nature in French law was in fact lawful.

191 See, for example, the report that members of the UK's Crown Prosecution Services were reluctant to use the reverse onus provision in section 24(4) of the Drug Trafficking Offences Act, 1986, and that there was considerable 'differential' in regard to its use among the judiciary – Home Affairs Committee, *Report: Drug Trafficking and Related Serious Crime* (1989) vol. II, p. 49.

6.2.4.9 *Protection of the rights of bona fide third parties*

Article 5(8) functions to protect the rights of bona fide third parties with respect to the confiscation procedure as a whole and specifically when, as is envisaged in article 5(6), licit and illicit property is mixed. While article 5(8) does not define these rights and it appears that it has been left to the Parties to do so in their domestic law, in practice they must logically include the following long established due process guarantees: the right of all interested parties to be informed of possible confiscation and of all their attendant rights; their right to be heard;[192] their right to challenge the confiscation order when already in force in cases where they had no earlier opportunity to take legal action; their right to legal assistance and to present testimony and other evidence; and their right to review of the order by a higher court. These protections must by necessary implication be available when the confiscation is purely a domestic affair or when it involves international co-operation under article 5(4).[193] The definition of bona fide has been left to the legal system of the Parties. Third parties who acquire property legally would only be protected by this provision if, in addition, their acquisition of the assets was in good faith. Article 5(8) cannot serve as a shield to protect allegedly bona fide third parties conscious that criminals are using them.[194] Examples would include situations where the proceeds of the illicit traffic are transferred in the form of gifts to relatives, payments are made to own companies, or transfers are made between entities owned by the same persons. A major problem with article 5(8) is that it only protects bona fide third parties who manage to establish in a domestic court

---

192 For example, article 28(2) of the Antiguan Drugs Act, 1973, provides that: 'The court should not order anything to be forfeited under this section, where the person claiming to be the owner of or otherwise interested in it has applied, before the making of the order, to be heard by the court, unless an opportunity has been given to him to show cause why the order should not be made.'

193 For example, where protection was not afforded in the requesting Party, and the third party wishes to exercise her rights in the requested Party.

194 The Netherlands delegate placed on record the following definition of bona fide third party: 'Any person, corporation or other legal entity, who has acquired exclusive ownership rights in, or any real or personal rights with respect to any item of property and who, at the time of the establishment of such right, did not know or should not reasonably have known that such property was, or might have become, subject to a confiscation order as referred to in [draft] article 3.' – *1988 Records* vol. II at 98. Section 5(2) of the South Australian Crimes (Confiscation of Profits) Act, 1986, provides that innocent third parties are protected from forfeiture unless they either gave no valuable consideration for the property or received it in circumstances such as to arouse a reasonable suspicion as to its origin.

that they are bona fide. In the domestic law of many Parties this may entail having to satisfy the reverse onus placed on them to prove that they did not know or that they should not reasonably have known of the illicit derivation or nature of the property.[195] In the meanwhile, their property may well already have vested in the state.[196] The dangers for the abuse of individual rights are manifold.

6.2.4.10 Seizure and confiscation under the 1988 Convention in review

Article 5 is a compromise between the need for flexibility to allow Parties to develop their own mechanisms for seizing and confiscating the proceeds and materials of drug supply offences, while still providing sufficient detail to ensure a harmonised response. An early development that had to satisfy diverse participants at the 1988 Conference,[197] it is a basic model in comparison to more sophisticated domestic provisions.[198] Yet it has attracted a great deal of praise for its innovative approach to the realising of a strategy for attacking the benefits accruing from the drug traffic,[199] and has played a significant part in precipitating the rash of asset confiscation legislation enacted since 1988.[200] A measure of its impact is that there has been more convergence of domestic practice with respect to asset forfeiture and confiscation than with regard to criminalisation of money-laundering per se.[201]

---

195 See, for example, the 'innocent ownership' standard in US law.
196 Until remedied by the Civil Asset Forfeiture Act of 2000, this was a major problem in the US because the inability to post the bond necessary to contest a civil forfeiture often meant that the government acquired the seized asset by default.
197 Zagaris supra note 102 at 130.
198 M.A. DeFeo, 'Depriving international narcotics traffickers and other organised criminals of illegal proceeds and combating money laundering' (1990) 18 *Denver Journal of International Law and Policy* 405 at 414.
199 See Gilmore supra note 28 at 18; Sproule and St-Denis supra note 36 at 281.
200 See Hernandez supra note 25 at 275-280 who records new legislation in over 24 states. A typical example, is the French *Loi No. 90-1010 du Novembre 14, 1990, portant adaptation de la legislation Francaise au dispositions de l'article 5 de la Convention des Nations Unies Contre le Traffic Illicite de Stupefiants*, which implements article 5 specifically.
201 E.U. Savona and M. De Feo, *Money trails: international money laundering trends and prevention/control policies*, report prepared for the International Conference on Preventing and Controlling Money-Laundering and the Use of the Proceeds of Crime: a Global Approach, held at Courmayeur, Italy, from 18-20 June 1994, p. 97.

It has been argued that only a global system of financial control of all illicit funds entering the legitimate economy will achieve effective control.[202] Article 5 and article 3's criminalisation of drug money laundering were the first steps towards such a system, towards what has been termed an all crimes anti-money laundering regime.[203] Development has been rapid in this area since 1988[204]

---

202 M.C. Bassiouni, 'Critical reflections on international and national control of drugs' (1990) 18 *Denver Journal of International Law and Policy* 311 at 323.

203 B. Zagaris and S.M. Castilla, 'Constructing an international financial enforcement subregime: the implementation of anti-money laundering policy' (1993) 19 *Brooklyn Journal of International Law* 871-965 at 877.

204 Space constraints make it impossible to do justice to these developments. However, the more significant developments include the following:
i) In 1985, Interpol introduced Model Legislation on Money Laundering and Forfeiture of Assets, which it promoted heavily and the UN agreed to attach as an addendum to the 1988 Convention.
ii) In 1989, The Basle Committee on Banking Regulations and Supervisory Practice issued a Statement of Principles on Money Laundering (the Basle Concordat), which encourages banks to know their customers, spot suspicious transactions and co-operate fully with law enforcement authorities. This was backed up in 1992 with the issuing of minimum standards to be applied when governments regulate international banks.
iii) The Group of Seven Industrialised Democracies (G7) in 1989 established its ad hoc Financial Action Task Force (FATF), which has also assumed considerable significance in this field, and whose membership now extends beyond the G7. The 1990 FATF report makes forty recommendations for inter alia the improvement at the national and international level of the combating of money-laundering and the enhancement of the role of the financial system in reporting and monitoring suspicious activity. The report notes that Parties agree not to let financial security policies inhibit the implementation of the recommendations. It urges each Party to the 1988 Convention to implement the Convention's money laundering provisions and confiscation provisions in national legislation. It also recommends the extension of national money laundering crimes beyond drug offences, and suggests a variety of other steps such as exchange of information etc. The 1992 FATF report sets out a process that allows members to audit each other's implementation of anti-money laundering schemes. Like the 1988 Convention, the FATF Reports seek to strengthen domestic laws and international co-operation, but unlike the 1988 Convention, which is largely silent on this issue, they also seek to draw the private sector into anti-laundering efforts. Re-evaluation of the recommendations in 1995-1996 saw emphasis on the introduction of systems of mandatory reporting of suspicious transactions, new technologies such as the internet and the mandatory criminalisation of non-drug money laundering. FATF membership has expanded to 26 OECD and financial centre jurisdictions and a permanent secretariat based in Paris has been established.
iv) In 1990, a Caribbean Financial Action Task Force (CFATF) was formed which discussed compliance with FATF's forty recommendations and produced its own 21 recommendations with regard to money laundering.

and has been the subject of extensive comment.[205] Subsequent efforts, both

---

v) The 1990 Council of Europe Convention on Laundering, Search, Seizure and Confiscation of the Proceeds of Crime, ETS 141, provides for a complete set of rules for national measures and international law enforcement and judicial co-operation with regard to laundering.

vi) The Convention Applying the Schengen Agreement of 14 June 1985 between the Governments of the States of the Benelux Economic Union, the Federal Republic of Germany and the French Republic, on the Gradual Abolition of Checks at Their Common Borders, in force 19 June 1990 provides in article 72 for an obligation on states to permit the seizure and confiscation of assets derived from illicit drug trafficking.

vii) The 1991 European Community Directive on the Prevention of the Use of the Financial System for the Purpose of Money Laundering (Council Directive 91/308, OJ 1991 L166.77) covers the same ground as the 1988 Convention's provisions criminalising money laundering, but it adopts the strictest standards globally for the control of money laundering. It requires banks and financial institutions to engage in customer identification when opening accounts, to engage in transaction reporting in respect of amounts over 15 000 ECU, to collect evidence of laundering and to co-operate with authorities. Implementation of the directive is complete in all EU member states – see Table 2 in S. White, 'European Community drug control: internal economic regulation and external conditionality' in Dorn supra note 5 at 54.

viii) The OAS's Inter-American Drug Abuse Commission (CICAD) adopted model Regulations Concerning Laundering Connected to Illicit Drug Trafficking and other Serious Offences in 1992 and these have been amended regularly since then.

ix) Other models for legislation include the 1990 UN Model Treaty on Mutual Assistance which has a Protocol concerning the Proceeds of Crime, GA Res. 45/117 (30 ILM 1434-1441) that is particularly concerned with mechanisms enabling the identification and confiscation of assets in other jurisdictions.

x) Bilateral agreements on money laundering co-operation are also beginning to be concluded, e.g. US-Venezuela Anti-Money Laundering Agreement of 1990.

xi) In 1992, the International Organisation of Securities Commissions issued a very detailed report on money laundering.

xii) The UNDCP's latest model legislation, the Model Law on Money Laundering and Confiscation in relation to Drugs, November 1995, was developed for civil law countries, while the Draft Model Drugs for Dependence Bill, 1995, part IV, Confiscation, was developed for common law systems.

xiii) In 1996, the Riga Declaration Against Money Laundering confirmed the commitment of Baltic States against money laundering.

xiv) In 1997, the Egmont Group of Financial Intelligence Units was established.

xv) In 1998, the UN General Assembly adopted a Political Declaration and Action Plan Against Money-Laundering and Resolution 20/4D Countering Money Laundering.

205 See Hernandez supra note 25 at 284-293; W.C. Gilmore, 'International efforts to combat money laundering' (1992) 18 *Commonwealth Law Bulletin* 1129 at 1136-1140; W.C. Gilmore, 'The G-7 and transnational drug trafficking: the Task Force experience' in W.C. Gilmore and P.J. Cullen (eds), *Crimes Sans Frontieres: International and European Approaches: Hume Papers on Public Policy* vol. 6 no's 1 and 2 (1998), p. 30 at pp.

recommendations and regional conventions, have used the terminology and system of the 1988 Convention's approach, unless change has been necessitated by the need to respond to the rapid evolution of the money laundering business.[206] With regard to the actual performance of this new regime, although law enforcement agencies in the United States believe that recent international money laundering legislation has been successful in curtailing money laundering,[207] and confiscation regimes have been held to work reasonably well,[208] substantial scandals suggest otherwise.[209] A 1998 UN study on money laundering concluded:

> The international narcotics trade launders a minimum of $200 billion a year. A substantial portion of that money moves through the bank secrecy, financial centre jurisdictions. Law enforcement efforts in the best of years recover in the range of $100 million to $500 million. Although some participants in laundering schemes

---

35-37. K.D. Magliveras, 'Defeating the money launderer – the international and European framework' (1992) 3 *Journal of Business* Law 161-177; H.G. Nilsson, 'The Council of Europe Laundering Convention: a recent example of a developing international criminal law' (1992) 2 *Criminal Law Forum* 419-465 (reproduces Convention); R. Parlour (ed.), *Butterworths International Guide to Money Laundering Law and Practice* (Butterworths, London, 1995); P. Solomon, 'Are money launderers all washed up in the western hemisphere? The OAS Model Regulations' (1994) 17 *Hastings International and Comparative Law Review* 433-455; Zagaris and Kingma supra note 52; B. Zagaris and S.B. MacDonald, 'Money laundering, financial fraud and technology: the perils of an instantaneous economy' (1992) 26 *George Washington Journal of International Law and Economics* 61-107; Zagaris and Castilla supra note 203; Zagaris supra note 102.

206 Supra note 203 at 877.

207 Statement by the DEA Chief of Operations, Harold D. Wankel, to the Housing and Banking Committee, Money Laundering by Drug Trafficking Organisations, 28/2/1996, cited by N. Srinivasan and R. Underwood, 'Money laundering: international efforts and recent developments in the movement of drug related money' in *Souvenir Brochure of the International Conference on Global drugs Law* (Indian Law Institute, New Delhi, 1997), p. 195 at p.198 and endnote 18.

208 The opinion of the UK's Home Office Working Group on Confiscation, *Report on the Drug Trafficking Offences Act 1986* (1991), p. 1 commenting on the effectiveness of the provisions of the Drug Trafficking Offences Act, 1986, for dealing with the proceeds of crime.

209 See Solomon supra note 205 at 434. Major banking scandals, such as that surrounding the Bank of Commerce and Credit International (BCCI), refocused attention on the need to regulate international money movement – see generally the Panel discussion, 'New frontiers in the regulation of international money movement in the wake of BCCI' (1992)

are arrested and convicted, the vast majority of professionals who assist are not. This is not a picture of success.[210]

Even the Financial Action Task Force (FATF), established in 1990 and at the heart of post-1988 Convention soft-law development of anti-laundering measures, could only claim substantive compliance with its forty recommendations by 25 of its 26 core members in 1996.[211] The international anti-money laundering regime's capacity to protect legitimate finance from the proceeds of the illicit traffic will depend on the depth of co-operation and on how quickly the regime can respond to change. There is still a lack of international co-operation, legal complications remain and technical difficulties abound especially since money launderers constantly change techniques.[212] There is also a shortage of skilled personnel who understand how money-laundering methods work.[213] Developing states require economic assistance if they are to aggres-

---

86 *American Society of International Law: Proceedings* 188-209. At p. 191 of this discussion Macdonald suggests that while the 1988 Convention's provisions in respect of money laundering indicated a trend towards international co-operation in control, the BCCI affair indicated a trend toward 'fragmentation of international banking supervision compounded by poor communication among national supervisory agencies.' However, resistance to assuming the burden of reporting suspicions is identifiable in, for example, UK financial services – see G. McFarlane, 'United Kingdom' in Dorn supra note 5 at 248. Suggestions for future control methods include a new international banking regulator such as the Bank for International Settlements (Macdonald at p. 205).

210 UN ODCCP, *Financial Havens, Banking Secrecy and Money Laundering* (Issue 8 of the UNDCP Technical Series, New York, 1998), p. 70.

211 FATF Report, July 1996.

212 On the problems of control of illicit activities presented by constantly developing technologies in international and national finance see Zagaris and Macdonald supra note 205 at 61-107. P. Jost, 'Black hawala, financial crimes and the world drug trade' in *Souvenir Brochure of the International Conference on Global drugs Law* (Indian Law Institute, New Delhi, 1997), pp. 116-128 illustrates how trust-based 'alternative remittance systems' such a 'hawala' used in India and Pakistan can also be used for the purposes of laundering drug proceeds because they enable the movement of money leaving little or no paper trail. Cybermoney on the internet and simple currency smuggling present the same problem. The use of *bureau de changes* to launder money in Europe is a growing concern.

213 One way of overcoming this shortage has been the establishment of Financial Intelligence Units (FIUs). FATF's recommendation 15 called for financial institutions to report suspicious activities to a designated authority, and states have responded by establishing FIUs to assess and process these reports. These FIUs are part of states' comprehensive anti-money laundering strategies. In 1995, a meeting of states and IGOs held at the Palls d'Egmont-Arenberg in Brussels to examine FIUs, formed the Egmont group, which seeks ways to develop more effective and practical co-operation among FIUs especially in

sively pursue anti-money laundering practice.[214] Pressure for further restriction of state sovereignty is constantly mounting.[215]

There is, however, more to the pursuit and confiscation of the proceeds of drug supply offences than law enforcement efficiency. The protection of legitimate rights from draconian legal mechanisms is also an issue. There is a danger that international society, mesmerised by the profits from confiscating the proceeds of crime, will lose sight of the penal nature of the problem and, given the implicit invitation in article 5 to use in rem proceedings, construe the confiscation process as one akin to a civil reparation for damages.[216] A further potential danger is that international society will overreact to the threat and stack the deck unfairly against the holder's of seized property. Widespread use of article 5(7)'s reversal of the onus of proof will, for example, allow a lapse in procedural safeguards.[217] The sacrifice of bank secrecy may involve unjus-

---

the area of information exchange and sharing of expertise. In 1997, there were 24 FIUs in operation and twenty more were planned or under development. A typical example, Belgium's Financial Information Processing Unit, established by Royal Decree on 11 June 1993, is an independent authority staffed by legal and financial experts. It operates under the aegis of the Ministers of Justice and Finance, and exists to monitor suspicious financial transactions. Once it is of the opinion that there is sufficient evidence that a transaction involves laundering this information is passed to prosecutors.

214 See Solomon supra note 205 at 453. L. De Koker, 'South African money laundering legislation' (1997) 22 *Journal of Juridical Science* 17 at 25 notes, for instance, that the new confiscation procedures enacted in the South African Drugs and Drug Trafficking Act 140 of 1992 had only been used once by 1995. Such a poor response is directly ascribable to poor training in both the police and procuracy in South Africa.

215 UN ODCCP, *Financial Havens, Banking Secrecy and Money Laundering* (Issue 8 of the UNDCP Technical Series, New York, 1998), p. 71.

216 See, for example, Hinton's argument that confiscation orders under the UK's Drug Trafficking Offences Act 1986 are reparative not punitive – M. Hinton, 'Are drug trafficking confiscation orders punitive?' (1992) 136 *Solicitors Journal* 1264-1265. By contrast, M.B. Stahl, 'Asset forfeiture, burdens of proof and the war on drugs' (1992) 83 *Journal of Criminal Law and Criminology* 274-337 criticises the civil forfeiture procedure under the US's Comprehensive Drug Abuse Prevention and Control Act of 1970 (21 USC section 881), arguing inter alia that it is a form of criminal punishment and thus the prosecution should be forced to prove its case beyond reasonable doubt and not on civil standards of proof. If a Party's domestic law regards the confiscation as an action in rem the danger is that due process guarantees will simply be abandoned.

217 R. Henham, 'Criminal justice and sentencing policy for drug offenders' (1994) 22 *International Journal of the Sociology of Law* 223 at 225 notes a number of erosions of due process rights discernible in the UK's Drug Trafficking Offences Act, 1986 (as amended by the Criminal Justice Act, 1993), such as section 1(7)(a)'s setting of the civil standard of proof in confiscation proceedings to determine either whether a person has benefited from drug trafficking or the amount to be recovered.

tifiable erosion of the right of privacy of many not involved in illicit drug trafficking.[218] An obvious shortcoming is that while provision for due process protection is made for bona fide third parties, no provision is made for such protection to be afforded to the subject of the confiscation order. The legal challenge of a seizure or confiscation order may well be out of the financial reach of many,[219] Parties may not provide legal aid, and the whole situation may be exacerbated when the property is in a foreign state. Complaints have been heard in states where forfeiture is common that people lose their cars and homes without due process.[220] No provision is made for liability for wrongful seizure. Perhaps, however, the most potent criticism of article 5 focuses on whether the confiscation of proceeds through confiscation legislation actually has the desired effect. Hernandez comments that in the US '[n]o evidence exists that the enactment and enforcement of ... forfeiture laws has in any way curbed the drug activity at which they are aimed.'[221] When the fact that no adequate link can be established between the deprivation of drug traffickers ill-gotten wealth and the curtailment of the drug usage driving the whole system is considered together with the fiscal interest law enforcement agencies now have in drug profits,[222] it seems that the international legal development of seizure

---

218 Hernandez supra note 25 at 235-304 trenchantly criticises the overreaching of US domestic law in this regard and questions the adoption, through the medium of international law, of similar approaches by many other states (at pp. 293-295). He outlines the predicament of the many innocent people involved in "grey economies" in the developing world. Involved in "parallel financial systems" as a hedge against political and economic instability because of the instability of their own currencies, they are going to get hurt by the operation of article 5 type laws because in terms of these laws parallel financial systems are inherently suspect.

219 In both the confiscation of proceeds of crime and the forfeiture of instrumentation, the German Criminal Code wisely grants courts the discretion to abstain from the measure in cases of social hardship (ss73-73e; 74-76a).

220 See M.A. Vance in 'Comments on Nadelmann' (1991) 5 *Notre Dame Journal of Law, Ethics and Public Policy* 809. D.R. Gordon, *The Return of the Dangerous Classes* (WW Norton, New York, 1994) notes at p. 176 that a ten month study conducted by the *Pittsburgh Press* in the US found that most property seized and confiscated was cash and cars belonging to ordinary people, many of whom were never charged, or were innocent, or were only guilty of minor offences.

221 Supra note 25 at 297. See also E.A. Nadelmann, 'Drug prohibition in the United States: costs, consequences and alternatives' (1991) 5 *Notre Dame Journal of Law, Ethics and Public Policy* 783 at 787.

222 D. Baum, 'Tunnel vision: the war on drugs, 12 years later' (1993) 79 *ABA Journal* 70 at 71 and 72 reports that $1.6 billion worth of private property is seized in the US every year and that state and local police collected $218 million in confiscated shared assets

and confiscation of the proceeds of drug offences is in danger of becoming isolated from its purpose of disempowering the illicit traffic.

6.2.5   *Seizure and confiscation in conclusion*

The 1988 Convention dramatically developed the provisions for seizure and confiscation from their foundation in the 1961 and 1971 Conventions. It broadened both the range of property open to seizure and confiscation and the range of methods used in these actions. The earlier conventions focus on seizing and confiscating drugs and material used in drug offences consequent to a conviction, while the 1988 Convention focuses on the confiscation of proceeds not necessarily linked to a conviction. This marked change in the conception of permissible targets and permissible methods against the illicit traffic has emerged because of the impact of the profits of the illicit traffic on the licit economy, and because of the perceived vulnerability of large scale drug traffickers to going after their money. Whilst the self-financing of law enforcement through confiscation is appealing to all states and many states have embraced these new methods and have applied them to all crimes, the effective application of these new tactics remains difficult because of resistance to distinguishing in the global economy between the licit and illicit derivation of property. The purported targets are drug kingpins; the impenetrability of the upper reaches of financial systems means that small fry are actually more vulnerable.

6.3   CONTROLLED DELIVERY

Article 11 of the 1988 Convention, entitled 'Controlled Delivery', endorses this investigative technique, already targeted by the 1987 United Nations Comprehensive Multidisciplinary Outline.[223] The technique is described by Cutting as follows:

> A controlled delivery occurs when a consignment of illicit drugs is detected, ... in circumstances making it possible for those goods to go forward under the control

---

in 1992.

223 Target 18, *Declaration of the International Conference on Drug Abuse and Illicit Trafficking and Comprehensive Multidisciplinary Outline of Future Activities in Drug Abuse Control*, UN Publication St/Nar/14, UN Sales No.E.88.XI.1, (New York, 1988), pp. 55-56.

and surveillance of law enforcement officers with a view to identifying and securing evidence against the persons responsible for organising the smuggling.[224]

Controlled delivery can be applied to accompanied and unaccompanied consignments, to freighted consignments, postal consignments, indeed to any form of transferral where detection and monitoring is possible. The central purpose of this technique is to bring to justice those persons or organisations involved in any way with the shipment, transportation, delivery, concealment or receipt of an illicit consignment of controlled substances that may escape detection if the intermediaries or couriers are arrested immediately upon identification of the contraband. Controlled delivery becomes significant in international drug control terms when the consignment's delivery across national boundaries is permitted. Here the co-operation of the law enforcement agencies of a number of states is essential to make sure the international drug traffickers are successfully arrested and the consignment of illicit drugs is not successfully supplied. From a legal point of view the transit-state waives its right to arrest the courier and seize the consignment of drugs and usually reserves its right to request the extradition of the courier once the consignment has reached its destination.[225]

After the UN Legal Office ruled that controlled delivery was not in contradiction to the provisions of the existing drug conventions,[226] the Customs Co-operation Council (CCC) and Interpol promoted its use.[227] The development of a controlled delivery provision in the 1988 Convention seemed the next ap-

---

224 P.D. Cutting, 'The technique of controlled delivery as a weapon in dealing with illicit traffic in narcotic drugs and psychotropic substances' (1983) 35 *Bulletin on Narcotics* 15 at 16. Cutting notes that controlled delivery does not involve "official" drug trafficking or entrapment as crimes have already been committed.

225 R. Linke, H.J. Epp and E. Kabelka, *Extradition for Drug Related Offences* (UN Publication St/Nar/5, Austria, 1985, UN Sales No. E.85.XI.6), p. 3. At p. 55, they justify controlled delivery's compliance with the general duty to enact and prosecute drug offences under the drug conventions as not being a case of the Parties abolishing or relinquishing jurisdiction and letting drugs pass, but rather of lengthening 'the scope of the administration of justice in compliance with the obligation to investigate the background of the offence and to detect the principals, organisers and financiers of the traffic.'

226 The *1988 Commentary* at 235 notes that the DND believed that controlled delivery was compatible with article 37 of the 1961 Convention because article 37 did not impose an obligation on Parties to seize drugs but rather only imposed an obligation to develop the legislative capacity to seize drugs.

227 Statement of CCC observer, *1988 Records* vol. II at 236.

propriate step. However, certain problems had to be overcome. At a practical level a mechanism had to be settled that would ensure the decision to use controlled delivery would take into account its costs and benefits in a particular situation. As the US delegation to the 1988 Conference put it, 'the decision on the costs and risks associated with the controlled delivery must be weighed against the potential benefit in identifying the traffickers involved'.[228] Legal and constitutional hurdles also existed in the domestic law of many states making the authorisation of this technique difficult. The technique was developed in common law systems that grant a large measure of discretion to law enforcement and prosecutorial authorities. Civilian systems, however, adhere to the legal duty on law enforcement and judicial authorities once they become aware of an illegal shipment to intercept it and arrest and prosecute suspects, which means the non-prosecution of suspects in a controlled delivery operation may result in the prosecutorial authorities breaching the law themselves.[229] The 1988 Conference recognised that any successful international provision on controlled delivery would have to reflect the reluctance of Parties to relax their sovereignty as well as provide a basis for the development of this technique in state practice.[230] Article 11 is the final outcome of deliberations at the 1988 Conference that tried to resolve these problems and still establish an effective provision. It attempts to provide a framework for action by the Parties, and leaves the operational details to the competent national law enforcement agencies because it recognises that the technique is essentially a covert police operation which, in order to be effective, has to be carried out with the utmost discretion.[231]

The foundation of the obligation in article 11 is the definition of controlled delivery in article 1(g). Article 1(g) confines the substances in respect of which the technique is to be used to narcotic drugs and psychotropic substances, as well as the substances in Tables I and II. The latter were included because, as the United States delegate noted, 'controlled delivery of such precursor chemicals was one of the main ways of locating illicit processing laboratories.'[232] This is also the reason why the definition makes reference to both 'illicit' consignments, meaning narcotic drugs or psychotropic substances, and 'suspect' consignments, meaning consignments of tabled substances which may not in

---

228 See Report of the US Delegation supra note 49 at 76.
229 See Gilmore supra note 28 at 36.
230 See the statement by the Mexican delegate, *1988 Records* vol. II at 231.
231 See the 'Expert Group Report', *1988 Records* vol. I at 21.
232 *1988 Records* vol. II at 243.

themselves be illicit but which may become illicit when their final destination is discovered.[233] Controlled delivery is also to be applied in respect of substances substituted for the listed drugs or tabled substances. This allows for the possibility of clean delivery, discussed below. A shortcoming of the scope of article 1(g) from the law enforcement perspective is that it does not apply to the controlled delivery of the proceeds of drug trafficking.[234] Article 1(g) refers to suspect or illicit material passing through the 'territory' of one or more Parties. This includes a Party's land, sea or air.[235] Article 1(g) makes it clear that a controlled delivery takes place with the knowledge and under the supervision of the Parties' competent authorities. Finally article 1(g) clarifies that the purpose of using the technique is to identify persons involved in the commission of article 3(1) offences and to take legal action against them.

Article 11(1) "obliges" Parties to take the necessary measures to allow for the possibility of the 'appropriate use' of controlled delivery 'at the international level'.[236] The Convention does not oblige the national use of controlled delivery, only apparently, its international use. However, the 1988 Conference recognised that some Parties would have legal difficulty in implementing article 11(1) because their systems do not recognise discretion not to prosecute, and ensured that the international use of controlled delivery was not mandatory.[237] Upon close examination, article 11(1) only requires Parties to make a bona fide attempt to use the technique internationally because the provision is subject to three conditions that in effect render it optional.

The first is that Parties are only obliged to take the necessary measures 'if permitted by' the limitations of the basic principles of their domestic legal system. The 1988 Conference recognised that 'permitted by' means that for

---

233 Explanation of the British delegate, *1988 Records* vol. II at 245-246.

234 Recommendation 36 of the 1990 FATF Recommendations encourages states to co-operate in using controlled delivery with regard to 'assets known or suspected to be the proceeds of crime.' The Interpretative Notes to this recommendation point out that certain states allow controlled delivery to be used in respect of the proceeds of crime, and the Interpretative Notes encourage states to get the necessary legal authorisation to make this possible. In France, Law 91-1264 of 19 December 1991 has a wide field of application including drugs, precursor chemicals and the proceeds and profits of drug trafficking.

235 *1988 Commentary* at 237.

236 See generally Gilmore supra note 28 at 36.

237 Sproule and St-Denis supra note 36 at 287. Colombia (10/6/1994) and Venezuela (16/7/1991) have both declared that the obligations in article 11 are conditional on respect for their constitutional principles and national legislation requiring the prosecution of offences – *Multilateral Treaties Deposited* (1997) at 303 and 306 respectively.

some Parties enabling legislation is required to make the use of controlled delivery possible, while for others controlled delivery is legally possible without such legislation.[238] Nevertheless, the *1988 Commentary* regards such legislation as advisable in order to protect those involved in handling the delivery and to prevent alleged offenders using the absence of legal authority to escape conviction.[239] Such legislation would have to allow for the authorised postponement or the waiving of the arrest of suspected persons and/or for postponement of the seizure of the contraband either for the purpose of identifying other persons involved in the smuggling or for the purposes of evidence gathering.[240]

The second condition on the provision's operation is a practical one, viz.: it operates within the practical capabilities of the Parties, recognising by the use of the phrase 'within their possibilities' the reality that some Parties do not have the law enforcement infrastructure or financial wherewithal to carry out such operations. Parties are left to decide on the appropriate use of controlled delivery.

The third condition on the provision's operation is that it does not oblige Parties to engage in controlled delivery operations when requested; it makes provision for co-operation in respect of such operations only if both Parties agree. Article 11(1) makes it clear that the consent of both Parties is necessary for the use of the technique, whether obtained through formal prior agreement if time permits, or through informal arrangement if a more expeditious response is called for by circumstances.[241] Controlled delivery in a practical sense anticipates informal links and direct communication between the different Parties' law enforcement authorities. The competent authorities of the definition in article 1(g) and article 11(1)'s loose provisions make this possible.[242] Whether the authorities that are to use the technique are the same ones that can authorise

---

238 See the statement of the Chairman of Committee II, *1988 Records* vol. II at 240.

239 *1988 Commentary* at 244.

240 France, for example, enacted Law 91-1264 of 19 December 1991 empowering law enforcement authorities, whether customs or police, to obtain, keep, transport and deliver drug related contraband under prosecutorial authorisation.

241 See the 'Expert Group Report', *1988 Records* vol. I at 22.

242 Consistent with article 9, article 11 allows for direct co-operation between individual law enforcement organs of different Parties without going through a central authority, something which may be desirable for confidentiality but undesirable when other national law enforcement agencies are not made aware of a controlled delivery and end up arresting the courier and ruining the operation. Thus for practical purposes, some national co-ordination is advisable.

its use is a question of domestic choice.[243] Agreement or arrangement between the Parties must include consensus on a number of issues. The Parties must agree that what is happening is in fact a controlled delivery.[244] They must also agree upon the modalities that are to be used and the supply of information about the particular case. They must also be satisfied about any conditions imposed by the transit Party's domestic law[245] and the recognition of the right of intervention by the transit state should its authorities perceive that the delivery is in danger of going awry.[246] It is significant that other than the limited provision in article 11(3), article 11 does not provide for the details of the operations to be undertaken, which it leaves up to the Parties to arrange or agree to. The law enforcement authorities[247] of the Parties are placed by article 1(g) in a supervisory position and they will be responsible for the actual form that the co-operation takes, and especially for the essential confidentiality required. They will, however, be guided by the definition in article 1(g) that the technique involves allowing illicit or suspect consignments of contraband or substituted substances to pass out of, through or into the territory of one or more countries with a view to identifying article 3(1) offenders. Article 11 makes it clear, as does the definition in article 1(g), that the purpose of controlled delivery is to identify persons involved in article 3(1) offences. Identification is made with a view to taking 'legal action' against such persons. Such 'legal action' is undefined, and while investigation, apprehension and

---

243 The *1988 Commentary* at 244 notes that in New Zealand (Misuse of Drugs Act, 1978) the requisite authority is bestowed on the law enforcement agency itself, while in Malta the law enforcement agency must seek the authority of a third party, the Attorney General (Section 38(1) of the Dangerous Drugs Ordinance (Amendment) Act No. 6 of 1994).

244 What one party regards as a surveillance operation could easily fall under either head and definition of the operation may be a source of conflict. However, article 9(1) provides for general co-operation in respect of the movements of drugs and tabled substances and it should in the opinion of the *1988 Commentary* at 239 cover cases on the fringes of controlled delivery.

245 The *1988 Commentary* at 244-245 notes that Cape Verde in article 33(2) of Law 78/IV/ 93 of July 1993 imposes the following conditions: detailed knowledge of the probable itinerary of carriers; guarantees of security against theft or diversion; and provision of full details of the outcome of the operation.

246 See, for example, article 61(3) of Portugal's Decree Law No.15/93, which reserves such a right.

247 Customs organisations are likely to be heavily involved in such operations.

prosecution are obviously contemplated, it is unclear whether and if so at what stage they become obligatory.[248]

Article 11(2) provides that the decisions to use controlled delivery shall be made casuistically,[249] taking into account the financial and jurisdictional problems its use may entail. Recognising controlled delivery's potential financial burden on requested Parties, article 11(2) mitigates the issue of costs to an extent by providing that 'financial arrangements' may be taken into account in the decision to use the technique. These arrangements will include the costs of the operation itself as well as consequential costs such as the costs of the disposal of confiscated drugs.[250] The use of controlled delivery may also create additional jurisdictional claims. For example, the delivery of drugs into a particular Party's territory would allow it to exercise jurisdiction although it would not have been able to if the drugs had been interdicted. Article 11(2) enables Parties to take into account the potential future exercise of jurisdiction in deciding upon the use of controlled delivery.

Article 11(3) provides that the Parties must agree on whether they will allow the delivery of narcotic drugs and psychotropic substances[251] to take place intact or whether they choose the possibility of a "clean" delivery, that is, where the drugs are removed and partially or totally substituted by some innocuous substance.[252] The advantage of clean delivery is that it does not run the risk of the criminals escaping with the contraband. This provision requires the

---

248 The 1988 Conference records do not reveal whether the authors of the provision also contemplated the situation where arrest and prosecution did not occur, for instance, where the suspect was left alone in order to allow an investigation to develop, although 'legal action' is vague enough to include such a situation.

249 This limitation is necessary given that comprehensive application of the technique overlooks the necessity of investigating its appropriateness to each case.

250 *1988 Commentary* at 241. The *Commentary* also refers to the loss of earnings by states that 'reward' their law enforcement agents for the seizure and confiscation of drugs.

251 The *1988 Commentary* at 243 suggests that clean deliveries of precursors could also be made.

252 Article 11(3) gives no guidance as to the identity of replacement substances. Gilmore supra note 28 at 36-37 believes that an 'innocuous substance' would be one not regarded as a contraband substance in article 3(1) of the 1988 Convention. In other words it would not include narcotic drugs, psychotropic substances, opium poppies, coca bushes or cannabis plants as contemplated in the 1961 (as amended) and 1971 Conventions, or the equipment, materials or substances in Tables I and II of the 1988 Convention (see article 3(1)(a)). Whether the latter list of nocuous substances would include the 'property' derived from drug trafficking offences mentioned in article 3(1)(b) and (c), is unclear, but in principle it would seem not to because it is not mentioned in article 1(g)'s definition of controlled delivery.

consent of the Parties because of the concern that the substitution of innocuous substances could give rise to legal difficulties, in particular when seeking to prove the identity and the illicit nature of the content of the seized consignment.[253] Both partial and total substitution are provided for because it may be the case, for instance, that in some Parties' domestic law the receipt of a totally innocuous substance by a trafficker is not an offence, demanding that if not all then some of the substance received must be contraband. Complete substitution, however, obviously makes surveillance a lot less risky. The United Kingdom's delegate to the 1988 Conference called article 11(3) a 'marker for the future' in the sense that while complete substitution may not have been possible in 1988, it was the desired method of controlled delivery as the technique's use grew.[254]

Article 11 is not ideal from a law enforcement perspective. Its narrow material scope could have been expanded to include the proceeds of drug offences. It is also another example in the Convention of the trade-off of practical impact to national sovereignty. The conditions in article 11(1) leave so much discretion in the hands of the Parties to decide, for instance, what their basic principles of domestic law with respect to the technique are, that the operation of controlled delivery internationally is de facto based on a case by case consensus only. But these safeguard clauses recognise that in many states accommodation of controlled delivery by revision of the principle of legality, which insists upon immediate prosecution of all offences, was going to be a slow process. However, article 11 has had an impact on strict adherence to this principle. Parties that once refused to use the technique prior to article 11's agreement, are now prepared to use it,[255] and it appears that article 11 has been very influential in this change of attitude.[256] In this sense article 11 has

---

253 The 'Review Group Report', *1988 Records* vol. I at 59.

254 See *1988 Records* vol. II at 231-232.

255 Evidence by customs officials reprinted in the UK Home Affairs Committee, *Report: Drug Trafficking and Related Serious Crime* (1989) vol. II, p. 33 indicates that Spain, which was reluctant to use the technique, now uses it. Austria amended its customs laws in 1985 to allow use of the technique – see article 121 of the 1955 Austrian Customs Law amended 10 May 1985. Article 73 of the Schengen Agreement obliges Parties to use it, subject to a domestic law chapeau – Convention Applying the Schengen Agreement of 14 June 1985 between the Governments of the States of the Benelux Economic Union, the Federal Republic of Germany and the French Republic, on the Gradual Abolition of Checks at Their Common Borders, in force 19 June 1990.

256 E.A. Nadelmann, *Cops Across Borders: The Internationalization of U.S. Criminal Law Enforcement* (The Pennsylvania State University Press, University Park, Pennsylvania, 1993), p. 236.

instigated a significant legal change globally, something accented by the fact that use of controlled delivery remains legally dubious when states have not yet implemented article 11.[257] It is worth remembering, however, that while article 11's conclusion implies a global loosening of the restrictions on entrapment of drug traffickers with regard to the particular investigative technique of controlled delivery, it does not imply acceptance of the range of other far more intrusive techniques often associated with controlled delivery.[258]

6.4   THE MONITORING AND CONTROL OF PRECURSORS AND OTHER ESSEN-
          TIAL CHEMICALS FREQUENTLY USED IN DRUG MANUFACTURE

6.4.1   Introduction

The production of drugs is chemistry, and any strategy for reducing drug supply must at some point consider the role of the chemicals used in drug production. In the following quote Interpol defines these chemical precursors, points out the difficulties in subjecting them to international legal control and suggests a strategy for their control:

> A precursor is a raw material that is specific and critical to the production of a finished chemical product. The term "immediate precursor" is usually applied to precursors which are only one reaction step away from the final product [whereas] essential chemicals are less specific or critical than precursors to the production

---

257 See, for example, the South Australian case of *R v Ridgeway* (1993) 60 SASR 207 where the prosecution, in an appeal against conviction, attempted to rely on article 11 as a justification for the inclusion of evidence gleaned by the entrapment of the appellant. Legoe J, dissenting in the minority, rejected this reliance because the statute incorporating article 11 into Australian law, the Crimes (Traffic in Narcotic Drugs and Psychotropic Substances) Act, 1990 (Cth), had not been enacted at the time of the offence. The majority of the court did not discuss the issue. But even had article 11 been in operation in Australia, it is doubtful whether it justified legally both the controlled importation of heroin from Malaysia, as well as the purchase of that heroin in Malaysia in breach of Malaysian law by a police informer in order to supply it to the accused (at p. 216 of the judgment). An appeal to the Australian High Court succeeded (*Ridgeway v Queen* (1995) 129 ALR 41) because Australian domestic law had not at that stage been altered to allow the controlled importation by law enforcement agents of drugs and the majority of the court found that the unlawful acts of the police had tainted the conviction.

258 Parties would be wise to follow the French law (article 7 of the Code of Criminal Procedure) which stipulates that authorisation for controlled delivery 'shall only be granted for acts which do not constitute an offence'.

of the final drugs, and usually have widespread legitimate industrial applications. Placing these chemicals under international control similar to drugs is not a viable solution because of the enormous quantities used in legitimate manufacturing processes. In addition, although national restrictions on chemicals may be imposed, experience shows that they can be circumvented easily when supporting measures are not imposed by other nations. The most effective strategy may be an international programme of selective monitoring and exchange of information.[259]

Strategies for the control of precursors are new in inception but not in conception. In 1934 the Opium Advisory Committee noted that control of acetic anhydride, used in producing heroin, might prove a valuable weapon against illicit manufacture of drugs.[260] Yet the international community, focused on control of drugs, waited until 1961 before it took legal steps to control these substances.

6.4.2   Supervision of precursors under the 1961 Convention

The 1961 Conference dealt directly with substances convertible into drugs. Article 3(3)(iii) of the 1961 Convention enables 'any substance convertible into a drug' to be included within the scope of the control of the 1961 Convention.[261] It enables these readily convertible substances to be placed under control by the CND incorporating them in Schedule I or II of the 1961 Convention thus subjecting them to the Convention's regime as a whole. The 1961 Conference struggled, however, with the control of substances used in the manufacture of drugs. Article 2(8) of the 1961 Convention is an optional provision that requires the Parties to use their 'best endeavours' to control the raw materials that can be used in manufacturing drugs and that are not covered elsewhere in the 1961 Convention.[262] It is concerned with substances not readily convertible into drugs. The identity of substances not readily convertible is vague. The only condition on their definition in article 2(8) is that it is possible to subject them to 'practicable' measures of supervision. Article 2(8)

---

259 ICPO General Secretariat, 'The diversion of chemicals and the clandestine manufacture of drugs' (1989) 417 *International Criminal Police Review* 18 at 21 quoted in N. Dorn, K. Murji and N. South, *Traffickers: Drug Markets and Law Enforcement* (Routledge, London, 1992), p. 164.

260 Report to the Council on the Work of the 18th Session, LN Doc. C.56.M.105.1934.XI, p. 17.

261 Schedule I lists 'convertible substances' including ecognine, its esters and derivatives which are convertible to ecognine and cocaine.

262 *1961 Records* vol. II at 77-78.

is broad and vague because the authors of the Convention found it difficult to foresee the kinds of substances that could in the future be employed in illicit drug manufacture and which could by practicable measures be made difficult to obtain.[263] Article 2(8) leaves it to each Party to identify the substances to be controlled and the measures of supervision practicable to take. In reality, the practicality of monitoring these substances depended in the 1960s and 1970s on the size of the Party's chemical industry. The central source of tension in the development of this area of law has always been the pressure from industrialised states, especially those with chemical industries, not to apply control measures to precursor substances.

6.4.3   Supervision of precursors under the 1971 Convention

While article 2(4) of the 1971 Convention allows for the scheduling of substances capable of pharmacological effects, a major lacuna in the 1971 Convention was that unlike the 1961 Convention it makes no provision for the scheduling of substances that have no pharmacological effects but which are readily convertible into psychotropic substances. Article 2(9) is the sole provision in the 1971 Convention dealing with these substances. Article 2(9) makes provision for control of substances used in the manufacture of psychotropic substances through the Parties 'best endeavours'. The 1971 Convention does not schedule precursors in any of its four schedules and does not provide for the application of any one of its four control regimes to these substances. Unlike article 2(8) of the 1961 Convention, article 2(9) of the 1971 Convention is concerned with substances that are readily convertible into psychotropic substances as well as those that are not.[264] Under article 2(9), the Parties are urged to impose supervision measures that are 'practicable'. These measures are left to the Parties' discretion, and the *1971 Commentary* suggests that the nature of these measures will 'vary from country to country and also at different times in the same country [and] ... will depend on the economic character of the country and the particular economic activities in which it is engaged.'[265] Article 2(9) is vague and weak. Its authors, like the authors of article 2(8) of the 1961 Convention, were overwhelmed by the unlimited potential scope of provisions for the control of precursors and by the difficulty of balancing the regulation of precursors against the non-regulation of materials having important legitimate economic functions.

---

263 *1961 Commentary* at 71.
264 See *1971 Commentary* at 111.
265 *1971 Commentary* at 112.

6.4.4   Control and monitoring of precursors under the 1988 Convention

6.4.4.1   Introduction

The situation under the earlier Conventions was not ideal and in 1986 the CND
called for the inclusion of measures in the new Convention to control precursors
used in the illegal processing or manufacture of illicit drugs and for provisions
to prevent the use of materials and equipment in this context.[266] These measures were to be a response to both the need for better supervision of these
substances and to the role of precursor monitoring in drug intelligence. The
UN's 1987 Comprehensive Multidisciplinary Outline targeted the 'Control of
the commercial movement of precursors, specific chemicals and equipment',
and pointed to the inadequacy of existing controls.[267] Agreement on the principle of precursor control did not, however, make for agreement on the actual
steps to be taken, because in practice those steps were bound to impact on
legitimate commerce. Recognising these problems, the Chairman of Committee
II of the 1988 Conference noted:

> Care must be taken to keep a balance between the interests of licit manufacture
> and trade and the need for the most efficient methods to monitor the compounds
> and solvents in question and to ensure law enforcement and detection of illicit
> manufacture and illicit laboratories.[268]

The UN's Comprehensive Multidisciplinary Outline states:

> While the use of some specific chemicals is in some cases limited to the manufacture
> of narcotic drugs and psychotropic substances, other chemicals, and some materials
> and equipment (for example, tableting and encapsulating machines) are traded and
> required legitimately in large volume and the shipments should therefore be
> monitored in such a way as to permit law enforcement intervention with a minimum
> of burden on legitimate commerce.[269]

---

266 See Gilmore supra note 28 at 25.
267 Target 12, *Declaration of the International Conference on Drug Abuse and Illicit
     Trafficking and Comprehensive Multidisciplinary Outline of Future Activities in Drug
     Abuse Control*, UN Publication St/Nar/14, UN Sales No.E.88.XI.1, (New York, 1988),
     pp. 40-42.
268 *1988 Records* vol. II at 246.
269 *Declaration of the International Conference on Drug Abuse and Illicit Trafficking and
     Comprehensive Multidisciplinary Outline of Future Activities in Drug Abuse Control*,
     UN Publication St/Nar/14, UN Sales No.E.88.XI.1, (New York, 1988), p. 40.

Although in 1988 developing states were the sites of illicit drug manufacture, the burden of precursor control was going to be borne mainly by industrialised states as they were largely responsible for the production of precursors.[270] There was disagreement during the preparation of the 1988 Convention as to the necessity for control of precursors,[271] but the concern of the Convention with this problem is clear from paragraph eight of the Preamble and the 1988 Conference eventually settled on articles 3 and 12 to control precursors.

Article 3 makes precursors the subject of two offences, both discussed in detail in Chapter Three. Article 3(1)(a)(iv) criminalises their 'manufacture, transport or distribution ... knowing that they are to be used in or for the illicit cultivation, production or manufacture of narcotic drugs and psychotropic substances', while article 3(1)(c)(ii) criminalises their 'possession ... knowing that they are being or are to be used in or for the illicit cultivation, production or manufacture of narcotic drugs or psychotropic substances'. The latter provision is subject to the constitutionality clause. With these offences in place, and provision made for general law enforcement co-operation in regard to the investigation of precursor offences in article 9(1)(b)(iii),[272] for confiscation of precursors in article 5(1)(b), and for international co-operation in that regard in article 5(4), the Convention directs itself to detailing the actual system of precursor monitoring. Article 12, entitled 'Substances Frequently Used in the Illicit Manufacture of Narcotic Drugs or Psychotropic Substances',[273] sets up the system for the monitoring and control of precursors. It provides for prevention of diversion of the most common precursor and essential chemicals

---

270 See generally K.L. Bland, 'The Chemical Diversion and Trafficking Act of 1988: stopping the flow of chemicals to the Andean drug cartels' (1991) 7 *American University Journal of International Law and Policy* 105-143. She notes, for example, that the US exports ninety-five percent of the chemicals used to produce cocaine.

271 See the 'Expert Group Report', *1988 Records* vol. I at 22.

272 Article 9(2)(c) provides for a qualified obligation to establish law enforcement training programmes regarding the monitoring of the international trade in precursors. Articles 14 (cultivation eradication and demand reduction), 18 (free trade zones and ports) and 19 (the use of the mails) also deal with precursor substances.

273 The INCB, *Report of the International Narcotics Control Board for 1994* UN Doc. E/INCB/1994/1, p. 7, notes that although the expression 'substances frequently used in the illicit manufacture of narcotic drugs and psychotropic substances' is used in the 1988 Convention it remains common practice to use the less technically correct term precursor.

from licit business into illicit production, and for measures to strengthen national criminal law and international co-operation in this regard.[274]

6.4.4.2   The scheduling of precursors

Article 1(t) defines 'Table I' and 'Table II' as 'the correspondingly numbered lists of substances annexed to this Convention, as amended from time to time in accordance with article 12'. Article 12, paragraphs 2 to 7, deals with the procedure to place a particular substance in either Table I or Table II. These paragraphs are discussed in Appendix A, entitled 'Substances Controlled'. It is enough to note here that agreement at the 1988 Conference on the criteria used to identify the substances to which the control and monitoring provisions of article 12 would apply, was essential for the adoption of those provisions. The flexible procedure for scheduling a substance has also permitted the obligations of article 12 to be extended over an increasing range of substances since 1988, as vulnerable substances have been identified.[275]

Table I lists immediate precursor chemicals (and their salts where the existence of salts is possible) with a narrow range of uses and which are traded in limited volume internationally.[276] Table I was required because of the failure of the 1971 Convention to provide for the scheduling of substances that had no psychotropic effect but which should be placed under control because of the possibility of their being transformed into psychotropic substances.[277]

Table II lists chemicals essential to illicit drug production that have a much wider range of uses and which are traded in much greater volumes than Table

---

274   W.C. Gilmore, 'The G-7 and transnational drug trafficking: the Task Force experience' in W.C. Gilmore and P.J. Cullen (eds), *Crimes Sans Frontieres: International and European Approaches: Hume Papers on Public Policy* Vol. 6 no's 1 and 2 (Edinburgh UP, Edinburgh, 1998), p. 30 at p. 32.

275   Gilmore supra note 274 at 33 notes that a further ten substances were added in 1992.

276   Table I consisted as at 1996 of N-acetylanthranilic acid; ephedrine; ergometrine; ergotamine; isosafrole; lysergic acid; 3.4 methylenedioyphenyl-2-propanone; 1-phenyl-2-propanone; piperonal; pseudoephedrine; safrole; and their salts where possible. Five of these substances were added in 1992 using the procedure set out in article 12 paragraphs 2 to 7- see W.C. Gilmore, 'Drug trafficking and the control of precursor and essential chemicals: the international dimension' in H.L. MacQueen and B.G. Main (eds), *Drug Trafficking and the Chemical Industry: Hume Papers on Public Policy* Vol. 4, no.1, (Edinburgh UP, Edinburgh, 1996), p. 5 and p.18.

277   The Chairman of Committee II explained that there was no way, for example, of scheduling ergotamine or other ergot alkaloids even though they were easily convertible into LSD ((+)-lysergide), *1988 Records* vol. II at 246.

I substances.[278] These organic solvents and chemical reagents cannot be monitored as closely as the substances in Table I because they are used in huge quantities by the chemical and other industries and they are not specific to the production of drugs.[279]

The enormous quantities and easy substitution of both classes of these substances had, prior to the 1988 Conference, led to different domestic approaches being taken to their control. Some states opted for full control, others for selective monitoring. The main controversy at the Conference was which option to enshrine in the Convention. The differentiation between Tables I and II allows states to compromise on what measures to apply to each kind of precursor.

6.4.4.3   The general obligation to prevent diversion

Article 12(1) appears to create a mandatory general duty on Parties to prevent the diversion of the tabled substances into the illicit traffic, coupled with an allied duty to co-operate internationally for this purpose. It obliges Parties to take 'appropriate' 'measures', but does not articulate these measures, allowing the Parties to decide what measures they 'deem appropriate'. This discretion appears to suggest that the Parties can in effect decide to do very little to prevent diversion. The principle of effectiveness demands, however, that Parties take effective measures to prevent diversion.

Diversion may occur through the use of middlemen or brokers as purchasers or the use of front companies to purchase chemicals, the use of legitimate companies to order chemicals either by misrepresentation or through coercion, the use of forged or altered documentation such as bills of lading and import permits, common smuggling techniques such as using concealed compartments in containers and mislabelling consignments, and the bribery of key officials such as customs officers.[280] Appropriate responses to these tactics include establishing a legal basis for action, then developing the administrative structures

---

278 Table II consisted as at 1996 of acetic anhydride; acetone; anthranilic acid; ethyl ether; hydrochloric acid; methyl ethyl ketone; phenylacetic acid; piperidine; potassium permangananate; sulphuric acid; toluene and their salts where possible excluding the salts of hydrochloric and sulphuric acid. Again, five of these substances were added to the list in 1992 using the procedure in article 12 – see Gilmore supra note 276.

279 The Chairman of Committee II gives as an example, ether, which because it is used by illicit laboratories to produce cocaine can lead police to these laboratories, but which can easily be substituted by dozens of other organic solvents – *1988 Records* vol. II at 246.

280 *1988 Commentary* at 255-256.

and operational procedures to respond to the particular situation within a Party and to facilitate international co-operation generally.[281]

6.4.4.4 National control and monitoring of precursors

Article 12(8) provides for the control and monitoring of precursors at the national level through, in practice, the regulation of the licit manufacture and distribution of these substances and the detection and suppression of illicit diversion. Once again, it has been left to the Parties to decide which control measures to take, and article 12(8) can be interpreted simply as a suggestion and not as an obligation. But to act in good faith, each Party must apply effective provisions for the national control and monitoring of precursors.

Article 12(8)(a) obliges Parties to 'take the measures they deem appropriate' to monitor the domestic manufacture and distribution of the tabled substances. 'Manufacture' is not defined in the 1988 Convention but must be taken to include the preparatory stages of manufacturing. The Chairman of Committee II of the 1988 Conference comments that each Party is left to decide whether to act and, revealing a perhaps unmerited trust in established industry, continues that while 'it might not be necessary to monitor large, reliable concerns, it was vital to monitor the activities of small unreliable concerns.'[282] This provision operates without prejudice to the general obligation in article 12(1) and to any obligations under the existing drug conventions.[283]

Article 12(8)(b) recommends a number of measures that the Parties may adopt to achieve article 12(8)(a)'s purpose. The choice of measures depends on the conditions within the Party. Article 12(8)(b)(i) suggests that the Parties control all persons and enterprises engaged in manufacturing and distributing precursors, but does not propose how this be done. A national register setting out those engaged in such activities would be appropriate. Article 12(8)(b)(ii)

---

281 One effective general control measure not specified in article 12 and relating to both national and international control is to centralise government control of precursors as France has done with its National Bureau for the Control of Chemical Precursors located within the Department of Industry. Governmental departments concerned with the chemical industry and with public health are likely to be able to make a significant input but to be efficient they should operate within a unified structure. International co-operation also benefits from identifiable authority, and ECOSOC has called in Resolution 1992/29 for an international directory of the responsibilities of various organs within a state in this regard, also containing a summary of each state's regulations.

282 1988 Records vol. II at 266.

283 The US delegate pointed out that this affirmation is strictly speaking unnecessary as neither the 1961 nor 1971 Conventions require the licensing of manufacturers of the substances in Tables I and II – 1988 Records vol. II at 260.

suggests that the Parties control through licensing the business and premises in which manufacturing or distribution takes place. Article 12(8)(b)(iii) suggests that the Parties oblige licensees to obtain a permit for manufacturing or distribution. The fact that this provision is optional reflects the reality that while licensing of these activities is popular today in state practice,[284] some Parties regard licensing systems as completely impractical given the volume and diversity of transactions involved.[285] Article 12(8)(b)(iv) provides that the Parties may consider taking measures to prevent the accumulation in the possession of manufacturers or suppliers of quantities of the tabled substances in excess of those required for normal trade. The decision as to what is to be regarded as an 'excess' quantity of the tabled substances remains with the Parties. Standard commercial practice such as the storage of large quantities of these substances is likely to influence the definition of excess.

6.4.4.5 Control of the international trade in precursors

Action at the national level is not the strong suit of article 12. Prevention of diversion at the international level is article 12's major emphasis. Agreement in 1988 on a suitable provision to control the international trade in precursors was difficult. Developing states into which precursors were imported argued that comprehensive control of the trade in precursors would help them in their fight against the illicit traffic. Industrialised states argued that such control would severely hamper the legitimate manufacture of precursors. The former favoured formal rigid systematic bureaucratic control; the latter, informal flexible systems for the co-operation of law enforcement agencies and industry with respect to suspicious consignments.[286] The compromise agreed upon is contained in article 12 paragraphs (9) and (10). Article 12(9) provides for the mandatory establishment of a selective system for monitoring international trade

---

284 Article 2 of the French Law of 10 December 1996 thus stipulates, for example, that the manufacture, processing, assignment without payment, or sale of the most sensitive precursor substances can only be brought about by persons holding a license obtained in accordance with the provisions set out in the law and granted by the Department of Industry.

285 See Annexure C, 'UN Convention against Illicit Trafficking in Narcotic Drugs and Psychotropic Substances: Action Required Prior to Ratification' in UK Home Affairs Committee, *Report: Drug Trafficking and Related Serious Crime* vol. II (1989), p. 164.

286 See the 'Expert Group Report', *1988 Records* vol. I at 23. The European Community was a particularly vociferous advocate of selective controls. It had competence to negotiate a provision with respect to precursors because they fall within its sphere of competence under article 113 of the EEC treaty. This was the reason why it signed and ratified the 1988 Convention.

in both Table I and Table II substances, while article 12(10) applies a more rigorous system to Table I substances only.

Article 12(9)(a) obliges Parties to establish and maintain a system to monitor the international trade in precursor substances with the purpose of facilitating the identification of suspicious transactions. The Parties are obliged to co-operate closely with the various participants in the chemical industry[287] in the application of this monitoring system. These participants in the chemical industry – 'manufacturers, importers, exporters, wholesalers and retailers' – must be obliged by domestic law to inform the competent authorities of suspicious orders and transactions. Precisely how such a suspicious order or transaction is to be identified is left undefined, but factors such as the identity of the purchase and final consignee, the final destination of the substance, the size of the consignment, and the method of payment may be useful guidelines. Article 12(9)(a) thus envisages a central role for commerce in precursor monitoring, which acknowledges that participants in the industry are best placed to detect diversion.[288] In spite of this provision's obligatory nature, European states have in practice not imposed an obligation on their private enterprises to report all suspicious transactions and rely instead on voluntary notification.[289]

Article 12(9)(b) obliges each Party to make provision in its legal and administrative system for the seizure of a consignment of precursors if there is sufficient evidence that it is intended for use in illicit drug manufacture. Article 12(9)(b) does not oblige Parties to make such seizures. The discretion to seize is left in the hands of the Parties' law enforcement agencies. The provision also insists upon the presence of sufficient evidence before seizure is permitted. It is silent on jurisdiction, but the Japanese delegation to the 1988 Conference understood that seizure was only permitted within the particular Party's territorial jurisdiction.[290] It does not oblige Parties to make provision

---

287 To assist states in the identification of manufacturers the UN maintains a list of national manufacturers of scheduled substances, published annually in the ST/NAR.4 series.

288 Gilmore supra note 274 at 32. The *1988 Commentary* at 267 points out the benefits of a two-way relationship, so that authorities can familiarise themselves with the realities of the industry and the industry with the needs of government. The *1988 Commentary* at 285 cites, as an example of co-operation, the Code of Conduct to Protect Against the Diversion of Chemicals into the Illicit Production of Drugs issued by the Plastics and Chemicals Industries Association and the Scientific Suppliers Association of Australia Inc.

289 This is, for instance, the position in Germany and Greece, but not in Italy – see L. Bollinger, 'Germany', M. Mavris, C.D. Spinellis and P. Zagoura, 'Greece', and M.L. Cesoni, 'Italy' in Dorn supra note 5 at 138, 168 and 186 respectively

290 *1988 Records* vol. II at 262.

for the confiscation of suspect shipments, as the latter process was felt to fall outside the legal competence of the administrative services responsible for implementing the envisaged monitoring system.[291] Article 5(1)(b) does, however, allow confiscation of precursors that are going to be used in an article 3(1) offence. It is worth noting that nothing in article 12(9)(b) limits its application to substances being traded internationally.[292]

Article 12(9)(c) establishes a system of pre-export notification on request. The purpose of this system is to provide information to concerned Parties so that they may investigate potential connections with illicit drug production and supply. Article 12(9)(c) obliges a Party to inform as speedily as possible the competent authorities and services of other Parties 'concerned' of any suspicions its law enforcement agencies may have that the 'import, export or transit' of a precursor is destined for illicit drug manufacture. 'Concerned' Parties may, depending on the situation, include a Party importing the substance, a transit Party, and a Party exporting the substance.[293] The competent authorities of these Parties are those contemplated in article 9.[294] Article 12(9)(c) provides that the notification should contain information about the means of payment and any other essential elements that led to the formation of the suspicion. The form of payment is singled out in the provision as a key element in the tracing of illicit transactions. A suspicion must be founded on a reasonable belief, that is, on objectively verifiable grounds. Concerned importing Parties may use article 12(10) to get even more information.

Article 12(9)(d) requires the correct labelling and documentation of imports and exports.[295] It requires 'commercial documents such as invoices, cargo manifests, customs, transport and other shipping documents' to contain the quantity and the names of the substances being imported or exported, in the manner in which these names are stated in the tables.[296] A uniform nomenclature for these substances has thus become necessary, as in practice they are

---

291 See the 'Expert Group Report', *1988 Records* vol. I at 24.
292 *1988 Commentary* at 266.
293 *1988 Commentary* at 268.
294 See the 'Expert Group Report', *1988 Records* vol. I at 24.
295 Thus, for example, section 13 of the UK's Criminal Justice (International Co-operation) Act, 1990, provides that the Secretary of State may make regulations to impose documentation requirements for transactions of scheduled substances. These regulations would require the keeping of records, they would allow the inspection of these records, and they would require the labelling of consignments (section 13(1)).
296 See, for example, article 5(1) of the Spanish Law 3 of 1996, which imposes a clear labelling requirement.

known under different names, and various lists have been drawn up.[297] Article 12(9)(d) also requires commercial documents to mention the name and address of the exporter and the importer. As the final consignee is not always known, the provision only requires that these documents should contain the name of the consignee 'when available'.

Article 12(9)(e) requires the maintenance of document records referred to in article 12(9)(d) for a minimum of two years[298] for the purpose of inspection by the competent authorities.[299]

Article 12(10) lays down an additional list of more rigorous controls which are only to be applied to Table I substances, because these substances have few legitimate and practical uses and are not shipped as frequently as the substances in Table II.[300] Article 12(10)(a), which provides for advanced warning of the arrival of Table I substances to the country of destination, is the major additional requirement. It was the main battleground between the European Community and the bulk of the delegations at the 1988 Conference.[301] Two major issues emerged.

Although it was agreed that the information provided for in article 12(10)(a) should not be isolated as in article 12(9) to selective suspicious cases, a significant bone of contention was whether information should be supplied automatically in respect of every import or only on demand. EC members rejected a blanket obligation. They argued that although comprehensive information is essential for the monitoring of the consignment by the importing Party, a

---

297 The DND's Senior Scientific Officer, *1988 Records* vol. II at 263, noted at the time of the drafting of the provision that the DND had drawn up a list using a nomenclature that set out all possible synonyms, based on the International Non-Proprietary Names for Pharmaceutical Substances. See also the Harmonised System of Nomenclature introduced by the WCO for this purpose.

298 By contrast, the European Directive (EEC) 92/109 of 14 December 1992 (OJ 1992, L370/76) stipulates three years of record holding and states have responded accordingly. See, for example, article 12 of the French Decree of 5 December 1996 which stipulates a three-year record holding period.

299 The *1988 Commentary* at 269 notes that the use of 'may be made available for inspection' implies a choice not implied in the French version of the text – *'tenus à la disposition des autorités compétentes pour examen'*.

300 See the statement of the US delegate, *1988 Records* vol. II at 257.

301 The EC favoured a selective information system. The observer for the Commission of the EC noted that more than thirty percent of all goods exported from the EC left it without the final buyer of these goods having yet been found, which led to the inevitable possibility that incorrect information as to the importer would be supplied and the goods may in fact end up in an entirely different country – *1988 Records* vol. II at 250.

compulsory system's shortcomings are an overflow of irrelevant data, lack of confidentiality, cost, and the fact that it loses sight of the provision's aim which is to provide information of real value in the following up of suspicious trans-actions.[302] As settled, article 12(10)(a) obliges Parties that export these sub-stances to ensure that prior to exportation their competent authorities supply the specified information directly to the competent authorities of the importing Party. However, this information need only be supplied on request made by the importing Party, through the Secretary-General. In the absence of a demand for information on the export made through the Secretary-General, the con-signment will enter the territory of the importing Party without notice and unmonitored. Today, there is a sense that article 12(10)(a) does not go far enough and that provision should have been made for some form of compulsory notification prior to export.[303] A related shortcoming of article 12(10)(a) is that it makes no provision for notification to transit states.[304]

The second significant dispute at the 1988 Conference in respect of article 12(10)(a) was concerned with who should this information identify other than the exporter, the first importer or all importers? EC members, exporters of large quantities of these substances, wanted to continue their practice of allowing the export of Table I substances to an undeclared importer. Their opponents regarded this as playing into the illicit traffickers' hands. They wanted the obligatory transmission of the identities of the exporter and all importers by the exporting Party in respect of every export, even where there was no reason to suspect that it was to be diverted. As settled, the information to be supplied includes, by sub-sub paragraph: (i) the name and address of the exporter and importer, and, only when available, the consignee; (ii) the name of the sub-stance; (iii) its quantity; (iv) the port of entry and date of dispatch; and (v) any other information which is mutually agreed upon by the Parties. Thus article 12(10)(a)(i) only insists on identification of the exporter and effectively the first importer, and not of the final consignee unless that information is available. Nonetheless, the United States delegate understood article 12(10)(a)(i) to mean that the exporting of Table I substances to an undeclared importer would have to be stopped by Parties,[305] while the German Democratic Republic's delegate

---

302 The EC's rationale for a selective system – see the Greek delegate's statement, *1988 Records*, vol. II at 248.
303 See *1988 Commentary* at 286 referring to ECOSOC Resolution 1995/20 requesting provision of pre-export notification without specific request.
304 *1988 Commentary* at 287.
305 *1988 Records*, vol. II at 251.

saw this practice as a violation of article 12(1)'s general obligation.[306] However, despite the questionable utility of such an approach, it seems that all that is required of Parties is that they act in good faith in providing information on the identity of the exporter, which should be easy, and the identity of an importer, even if ultimately this information is not entirely correct, because the system does not require the final importer's identity.

Article 12(10)(b) invites Parties to adopt more rigorous control measures if they feel such measures are desirable or necessary to prevent the diversion of Table I substances. It caters for the situation where more specific information is required, such as where information is required on all shipments of a particular chemical.[307] Although it was the understanding of delegates to the 1988 Conference that article 12(10)(b) allowed the measures contemplated in article 12(10)(a) to be applied to Table II substances as well, article 24, which allows the adoption of stricter measures of control by Parties, is more suited to this purpose.[308] Article 12(10)(b) may seem superfluous against the background right of every state to adopt more stringent control measures, but it does assure Parties that that right is undisturbed by the Convention and it prevents other Parties from contesting any decision they may make to apply more severe measures to precursors.[309]

6.4.4.6 General provisions in respect of precursors

Article 12(11) requires Parties requesting information under paragraphs 9 and 10 of article 12 to keep trade, business, commercial or professional secrets or trade processes confidential when asked to do so by the requested Party. The purpose of the provision of information is the detection of the illicit traffic and it must not be used for other reasons. Confidentiality is necessary to ensure the confidence of Parties in the system and, by extension, its smooth functioning.

Article 12(12) requires Parties to furnish the INCB annually with information on seizures of precursors, new precursors and methods of diversion. In terms of the provision the INCB decides the form and manner in which this information

---

306 *1988 Records*, vol. II at 253.
307 Statement of the US delegate, *1988 Records*, vol. II at 251.
308 Statements of the delegate for Kuwait and Chairman of Committee II – *1988 Records* vol. II at 256 and 257 respectively. Parties have requested pre-export notification for Table II substances – *1988 Commentary* at 271.
309 Statement of the Chairman of Committee II, *1988 Records* vol. II at 257.

is to be provided and makes available forms to this end.[310] The provision also sets out the specific information required. Article 12(12)(a) requires information on the quantities of Table I and Table II substances seized and their origin if it is known. Article 12(12)(b) requires information on any substance not tabled but which has been used in the illicit manufacture of narcotic drugs or psychotropic substances and which is, in the opinion of the Party reporting on it, significant enough to be brought to the INCB's attention. Article 12(12)(b) was included to enable the INCB to gather information and to assist it in any assessment of the possible tabling of these substances.[311] Article 12(12)(c) requires information on methods of diversion and illicit manufacture of tabled substances. The INCB has set up a database to assist governments to prevent diversion, and a communications network for this purpose has been set up linking the UNDCP, Interpol, the WCO, the EU and interested governments.[312]

Article 12(13) requires the INCB to report to the CND annually on the implementation of article 12 and requires the CND to review periodically the adequacy and appropriateness of Table I and Table II.[313] These are independent duties.

Article 12(14) excludes from the ambit of precursor monitoring two categories of substances. The first is pharmaceutical preparations of the tabled substances intended for therapeutic uses. The second is preparations of the tabled substances that have legitimate industrial uses and are compounded in such a way as to prevent their easy use or recovery by readily available means. 'Preparation' is not defined in the 1988 Convention, but it was the understanding of the delegates to the 1988 Conference that the definition in the 1961 and 1971 Conventions applied,[314] and thus it can be taken to mean any solution or mixture in whatever physical state containing one or more of the substances in Table

---

310 Form D – 'Annual information on substances frequently used in the illicit manufacture of narcotic drugs and psychotropic substances'. It requires information on stopped and suspended shipments, voluntarily cancelled shipments, clandestine laboratory seizures and any other information indicative of diversion. Voluntary supply of information on the licit trade in such substances is also requested. The 'red list', a list of alternative names including trade names of the substances in the tables is annexed to these forms.

311 See the 'Expert Group Report', *1988 Records* vol. I at 25.

312 *1988 Commentary* at 282.

313 Presently a supplement to the INCB's Annual Report.

314 Statement of the Chairman of Committee II – *1988 Records* vol. II at 267. Article 1(s) of the 1961 Convention defines 'preparation' as 'a mixture, solid or liquid, containing a drug' while article 1(f) of the 1971 Convention defines it as '(i) any solution or mixture, in whatever physical state, containing one or more psychotropic substances, or (ii) one or more psychotropic substances in dosage form.'

I or Table II. Logically, these would have to be artificially compounded mixtures or solutions and not natural products. On its face, article 12(14) does not require pharmaceutical preparations to be compounded in such a way that the substances in the tables cannot be easily extracted before they are exempt from the application of article 12. The *1988 Commentary*, however, aware that large-scale diversion of these products has occurred since 1988, suggests that they too should be subject to the qualification that they must be difficult or uneconomic to break down into the tabled substances before they are exempt.[315]

6.4.4.7   *Precursor monitoring under the 1988 Convention in review*

Article 12's major obligation is in respect of international control; its provisions for national control are only recommendations. The absence of obligatory national control weakens the structure for monitoring because international control rests to a large extent on national control. The provisions for international co-operation are unsystematic and fairly ambiguous, with many key decisions on what information to provide and when to provide it left in the hands of the Parties. Nonetheless, the INCB believes that the generality of article 12 allows sufficient flexibility to adapt precursor control to rapidly changing national situations, and to the different requirements of, for example, chemical producing and transit countries.[316]

In practice, various organs and states have suggested various methods for implementing article 12. A strong lead was taken by the Chemical Action Task Force, or CATF, which in its 1991 set of recommendations attempted to formulate appropriate control measures to a more sophisticated categorisation of substances.[317] At the regional level, the EC has been very active. In 1990,

---

315   *1988 Commentary* at 275.

316   INCB, *Effectiveness of the International Drug Control Treaties: Supplement to the Report of the International Narcotics Control Board for 1994* UN Doc. E/INCB/1994/1/Supp.1, p. 17.

317   The CATF was established, like FATF, by the G7, as a task force with the aim of ensuring that effective procedures were adopted by states to prevent the diversion of precursors and essential chemicals to the manufacture of illicit drugs. It was composed of G7 representatives and representatives of states that manufacture and trade in the substances. In its first report in 1991, it produced a list of 46 recommendations for consideration by the G7. Central to these was the recommendation that article 12 of the 1988 Convention be regarded as 'the foundation for international regulation' in this area. It thus urged states to become party to the 1988 Convention. The CATF isolated five basic regulatory control measures to prevent chemical diversion to the illicit traffic. These were:

it adopted a Regulation, focusing on regulating the international trade in precursors in response to article 12(9), with the following aims:

> Each member state shall take, in accordance with its legal system, appropriate measures to encourage operators to immediately notify the competent authorities of any circumstances, such as unusual orders for and transactions of scheduled substances [twelve are mentioned in the appendix] which indicate that such substances destined for import or export may be diverted for the illicit manufacture of narcotic drugs or psychotropic substances.[318]

a) vigilance – the duty on commercial operators to alert competent authorities about suspicious transactions;

b) administrative surveillance – the requirement that commercial operators maintain records and documents for all transactions in the subject chemicals;

c) registration/authorisation of operators – the subjection of commercial operators to a licensing or authorisation system;

d) export authorisation – the requirement of an export permit for exports the application for which must identify all consignees; and,

e) import authorisation – the obligation on importing states to exercise strict diligence when authorising imports by, for example, ascertaining the importer's competence and integrity as well as the purpose for which the chemicals are being imported.

CATF re-categorised the tabled substances in the following way: Category 1 chemicals were those used in the manufacture of synthetic drugs (7 substances in Table I); Category 2 chemicals had a wider legitimate commercial application than those in Category 1 (7 substances in Table II), and Category 3 consisted of chemicals essential for the production of cocaine and heroin (2 substances in Table II). CATF recommended that all five regulatory measures should be applied to Category 1 chemicals. It recommended that vigilance, administrative surveillance, and export and import authorisations should be applied to Category 2 chemicals 'to the extent necessary for the effective control of international transactions.' A registration procedure was recommended for acetic anhydride in heroin producing states, and it was recommended that exporters in chemical producing countries should be obliged to register. In respect of Category 3 chemicals, CATF recommended only vigilance and administrative surveillance, although it suggested the development by chemical manufacturing states of a strategy for targeting countries involved in heroin and cocaine production with the aim of determining appropriate import and export authorisation systems. The CATF continued its work in the early 1990s but it was not intended to become institutionalised, and its role has been taken over by the INCB – see Gilmore supra note 276 at 18-22.

318 Council Regulation (EEC) No.3677/90 of 13 December 1990 (OJ 1990 L357/1). See generally McClean supra note 33 at 180-183. The EC Regulation provides for an extensive response to article 12(9)'s obligations. It applies to a broadly defined category of operators and to the same list of substances tabled in the 1988 Convention. Its article 2 deals with the documentation, records and labelling as demanded by article 12(9)(d) and (e) of the 1988 Convention, while a duty of notification set out in article 3 meets the obligation in article 12(9)(c) of the 1988 Convention. Its chief obligation is a duty

While the EC fine-tuned its selective monitoring of the international trade,[319] it addressed the issue of monitoring within the Community and the requirements of article 12(8) far more comprehensively.[320] By contrast to the tentative

of pre-export notification contained in article 4. Article 4 obliges operators to supply full details of exports to the exporting state's competent authorities at least 15 working days before a customs export declaration is lodged. It gives customs officials sufficient time to decide whether to allow or forbid the export if they have reasonable grounds to suspect that the substances are to be used in the illicit manufacture of drugs. The Regulation also contains provisions for controlling the trade in precursors with non-member states. It makes special reference to the establishment of machinery for the authorisation of exports of precursors varying according to the substance involved and the destination, administrative surveillance of importation, exportation and transit, as well as an authorisation system for operators. The Regulation also sets up systems for close administrative co-operation and exchange of information between member states and the European Commission, which are designed to reinforce the effectiveness of its measures. Express provision is made for monitoring the kinds of products most frequently diverted, along with the main methods used, and for the adaptation of the Regulation to developments in the field. The Regulation allows search powers to authorities but not the seizure powers in article 12(9)(b) of the 1988 Convention. The plan has been criticised by the DEA because it does not control all the chemicals used to make cocaine – see Bland supra note 270 at 121 footnote127.

319 The 1990 Regulation was amended and supplemented to bring it into line with the more ambitious CATF recommendations through Council Regulation (EEC) No.900/92 of 31 March 1992 (OJ 1992, L96/1), Council Directive (EEC) No.92/109 of 14 December 1992, Commission Regulation (EEC) No.3769/92 of 21 December 1992 (OJ 1992, L383/17), Council Regulation (EEC) No. 2769/92 of 21 December 1992, Commission Directive (EEC) No. 93/46 of 22 June 1993, Commission Regulation (EEC) No.2959/93 of 27 October 1993 (OJ 1993, L267/8), Council Directive No. 2093/97 of 24 October 1997 – see G. Estievenart, 'The European Community and the global drugs phenomenon' in G. Estievenart (ed.), *Policies and Strategies to Combat Drugs in Europe* (Nijhoff, Dordrecht, 1995), p. 50 at p. 78. These later regulations gave expression to the category based classification scheme and application of appropriate control measures adopted by the CATF in 1991. Thus Category 3 chemicals, widely traded in the legitimate commerce, are subject by means of article 5(a)(1) of Council Regulation (EEC) No.900/92 to export authorisation only if the country of destination has been targeted. Iden-tification of a state as the source of illicit heroin or cocaine production can be unilateral but the Commission prefers to enter into a dialogue with the individual states in question – see EC Regulation No.2959/93.

320 Council Directive (EEC) 92/109 of 14 December 1992 (OJ 1992, L370/76) is concerned with the manufacture and placing on the European market of certain substances used in the illicit manufacture of narcotic drugs and psychotropic substances. The Directive requires EC members to introduce a licensing system for these substances enforced by a system of sanctions and it obliges their competent authorities to co-operate in monitoring the movement of these substances. It has been amended by Commission Directive (EEC) No.93/46 of 22 June 1993 (OJ 1993, L159/134). This Directive adopts

European approach to the international trade, the OAS adopted Model Regulations to Control Chemical Precursors that are much more rigorous.[321] At the national level the United States has led the way and considers its exacting Chemical Diversion and Drug Trafficking Act of 1988[322] to be model legislation in promoting the implementation of article 12.[323]

The INCB, which in 1993 took over the functions of the Chemical Action Task Force (CATF), has been particularly diligent in encouraging and monitoring compliance with article 12.[324] It has complained consistently about the failure

---

the licensing and authorisation recommendations in respect of the highly sensitive chemicals listed in CATF category 1. See generally Gilmore supra note 276 at 22. EC members have enacted appropriate laws – see Table 3, in S. White, 'European Community drug control: internal economic regulation and external conditionality' in Dorn supra note 5 at 55. A good example is Belgium's Royal Decree of 26 October 1993, which submits the manufacturing and distribution of certain substances to a special authorisation from the Minister of Health and requires notification of the trade and manufacture of other less sensitive substances. Records of sales have to be kept for both categories and the Decree introduces a duty to report suspicious transactions.

321 The Model Regulations to Control Chemical Precursors and Chemical Substances, Machines and Materials RM/NARCO/doc.18/90 rev.1 (1990) impose a strict regime. Licences must be issued for the handling of precursors and every transaction must be registered. Strict records must be kept. The consignee must be identified and information must be furnished regarding the transportation of the chemicals allowing easier identification of point of diversion. Provision is also made for international exchange of information and international co-operation in investigations of alleged diversions, making for a much tighter system altogether. See Bland supra note 270 at 134-139.

322 21 USC section 801 (1990).

323 Bland supra note 270 at 108 citing *U.S. Chemical Exports to Latin America: Hearing Before the Subcommittee of Foreign Commerce and Tourism of the Senate Committee on Commerce, Science and Transport* 101st Congress, 2nd Sess.1 (1990). In terms of 21 USC section 971(c)(1) manufacturers, distributors, importers and exporters of listed chemicals are obliged to notify the DEA fifteen days before any sale is completed. The DEA then investigates the prospective purchaser and if the Attorney General is satisfied that there are reasonable grounds for suspecting the shipment may be diverted, the DEA may suspend the sale. In section 830(b) 'suspicious' behaviour must also be reported to the DEA, including requests for 'extraordinary' amounts of chemicals, and 'an uncommon method of payment' or any other suspicious circumstance. In terms of section 960(d) criminal liability attaches to deliberately unreported exports suspected of being destined for the illicit traffic. The Act anticipates extraterritorial jurisdiction and investigation, with all their attendant difficulties. See Bland supra note 270 at 132-134.

324 It publishes a supplement to its annual report on the subject, for example, *Precursors and Chemicals Frequently Used in the Illicit Manufacture of Narcotic Drugs and Psychotropic Substances: Report of the International Narcotics Control Board for 1995 on the Implementation of Article 12 of the United Nations Convention Against Illicit Traffic in Narcotic Drugs and Psychotropic Substances of 1988* UN Doc. E/INCB/1995/4.

of Parties to furnish information under article 12(12) adequate enough to make
a comprehensive assessment of the situation.[325] In 1994, it directly criticised
the failure of Parties to put into operation mechanisms enabling them to obtain
information on the licit requirements for tabled substances and on the identity
of manufacturers, distributors, importers and exporters of such substances.[326]
In Resolution 20 of 1995, ECOSOC confirmed the INCB's appeal to exporting
Parties to go beyond the obligations of article 12(10) and to provide pre-export
notifications on a routine basis prior to shipment even in situations where such
notifications have not been formally requested by importing Parties.[327] Importing Parties were requested upon receipt of pre-export-notification to investigate
questionable cases and to seek the views and information of the INCB, IGO's
and other Parties as appropriate.[328]

6.4.5   Precursor monitoring in conclusion

The early drug conventions provided little in the way of mechanisms for controlling precursors, and it has been left to article 12 of the 1988 Convention to
provide the legal basis for a system of surveillance of the most sensitive of
precursor substances. That system is now largely in place in developed jurisdictions, the methods and routes of diversion are becoming more visible,[329] major
diversions are being prevented[330] and the international community has taken

---

325 INCB, *Report of the International Narcotics Control Board for 1995* UN Doc. E/INCB/
      1995/1, p. 27.
326 INCB, *Report of the International Narcotics Control Board for 1994* UN Doc. E/INCB/
      1994/1, p. 7.
327 In response to Resolution 20/1995 the INCB has developed its databank on diversion
      of precursors and a communications network has been developed linking the INCB's
      secretariat, the WCO, the European Commission, Interpol and interested states.
328 The INCB reported in 1995 that only one Party had made a special notification to the
      Secretary-General in terms of article 12(10) although such notifications are often sent
      by states to other states – INCB, *Effectiveness of the International Drug Control Treaties:
      Supplement to the Report of the International Narcotics Control Board for 1994* UN
      Doc. E/INCB/1994/1/Supp.1, p. 18.
329 INCB, *Report of the International Narcotics Control Board for 1995* UN Doc. E/INCB/
      1995/1, p. 28.
330 For example, the *Report of the International Narcotics Control Board for 1996* UN Doc.
      E/INCB/1996/1, notes at p. 30 that 16 tons of ephedrine, a meta-amphetamine precursor,
      was seized in 1996, preventing the potential production of 10 tons of the drug.

steps to ensure its implementation.[331] However, the legal and administrative framework is not yet in existence in many less-developed Parties and co-operation with these Parties takes place, if at all, at an informal level. Extension of the existing system to cover other commonly available materials, such as those used in the manufacture of synthetic drugs, is likely to be voluntary and informal and selectively targeted through links to an assessment of the risk these substances offer.[332] Precursor monitoring has not yet put a stop to the illicit drugs market. It has been suggested that precursor control should rather be used to shape the nature of the illicit market, that is, to influence which drugs are available and which are not.[333] Given the inherent limitations of international control of precursors, such an approach seems sensible, because it seeks a more effective role for precursor monitoring. It may not, however, accord with existing international obligations, because it flies in the face of the policy of blanket prohibition.

6.5   CONTROL OF MATERIALS AND EQUIPMENT USED FOR DRUG PRODUC-
         TION

In addition to trying to block the supply of precursors to illicit drug producers, the 1988 Convention also tries to obstruct the supply of: a) materials used for licit drug production such as cutting and bulking agents, non-scheduled chemical products,[334] packaging materials; and b) equipment used for the same purpose such as glassware, mixing tanks, tableting and encapsulating machines and power sources. While article 3(1)(a)(iv) criminalises the manufacture, transport or distribution of these materials and this equipment for illicit purposes, article 13, entitled 'Materials and Equipment', is a mandatory provision that requires Parties to: a) take steps nationally to prevent the trade in and diversion of materials and equipment used for illicit drug production or manufacture; and b) to co-operate internationally to achieve this purpose. The Chairman of Committee II explains the purpose of this provision as follows:

---

331 See, for example, the *Guidelines for Use by National Authorities in Preventing the Diversion of Precursor and Essential Chemicals* adopted by the UNDCP in 1993 and subsequently transmitted to all states.
332 See N. Dorn and S. White, 'Drug trafficking, nuisance and use: opportunities for a regulatory space' in Dorn supra note 5 at 265-266 on new developments in Europe.
333 Dorn et al supra note 259 at 168.
334 These would include petrol, kerosene, cement, diluents and pharmaceutical preparations available over the counter.

[I]n many countries it was known that equipment used in the pharmaceutical industry was being diverted to the illicit manufacture of drugs and ... initially it had been thought that control could be imposed over trade in such equipment. However, in view of the huge quantities involved, it was found impossible to introduce a form of control similar to that for narcotic drugs. The original purpose of [draft] article 9 had therefore been to promote co-operation between the Parties in the monitoring, follow up and regulation of trade in the equipment in question so as to prevent its use in the illicit manufacture of narcotic drugs and psychotropic substances.[335]

Article 13 requires the Parties, at the national and international levels, to monitor the licit trade in the materials and equipment used in drug production and manufacture, in the same way as they monitor drugs and precursors, in order to identify when this material and equipment is being diverted to the illicit traffic, and then to take steps to prevent diversion. Article 13 also requires the Parties to monitor the illicit trade in these materials that takes place entirely separately from the licit trade and involves no diversion from the licit trade, and to take steps to stop it.

The 'measures' to be taken by the Parties are not specified, and remain at their discretion, but they must be 'appropriate' to the purpose of preventing the trade in and diversion of materials and equipment used for illicit drug production or manufacture. The detailed control measures suggested in the draft article were considered to be too difficult to implement and potentially undesirable for the legitimate international trade in materials and equipment used by the pharmaceutical industry.[336]

With regard to the material scope of article 13, it is clear that the 'materials' to be controlled do not include precursors to the precursors listed in Tables I and II.[337] The control of some materials, like kerosene, used in drug production is impractical due to the quantities involved. However, the INCB has produced a list of non-scheduled substances likely to be diverted to the illicit traffic and some states have expanded their national monitoring systems for scheduled

---

335 *1988 Records* vol. II at 228.
336 See the 'Expert Group Report', *1988 Records* vol. I at 25. Draft article 9 went into great detail in paragraphs 2 and 3 which read: '2. The Parties shall require that the intention to export a tableting or encapsulating machine be reported in advance to an appropriate authority. If such a machine is to be exported to another Party, the authority of the Party of origin shall notify the Party of destination of the particulars of the transaction. 3. The Parties shall consider requiring: (a) The registration with the appropriate authority of tableting and encapsulating machines; (b) The notification to said authority of the domestic sale or other disposition of such machines.' – *1988 Records* vol. I at 8.
337 *1988 Records* vol. II at 224.

substances to include substances on this list.[338] The 'equipment' covered by article 13 appears to be gear used for drug production or manufacture in a narrow sense. In other words it refers to the actual means by which the substances are produced and not, for example, the aircraft and vehicles used for their transportation, weapons for the protection of laboratories, communications devices and so on.[339] The control of tableting and encapsulating machinery, laboratory equipment and the glassware used in drug manufacture and production, lighting and heating systems for horticultural purposes, and so forth, is clearly called for, and domestic legislation should penalise diversion to the illicit traffic and illicit trade in such equipment.[340] The manufacturers and suppliers of such items can play a useful role in monitoring diversion. Equipment manufactured by illicit suppliers for their own purposes is more difficult to monitor. It relies upon monitoring of component parts.[341] Drug-user paraphernalia, such as syringes etc., does not fall within the scope of this article as the article is concerned with illicit production and manufacture.[342]

The success of these measures at the national level and of international co-operation in this regard depends on the type of material or equipment involved. Much of the material and equipment used in drug production is so commonly available as to make the implementation of article 13 entirely impractical. However, more specialised material and equipment is easier to monitor and follow up. But effective monitoring and the frustration of diversion also depends upon the levels of expertise of the law enforcement agents involved, their knowledge of the licit markets for these types of material and equipment, and their willingness to share information with other national and international agencies.

6.6   MEASURES FOR SOURCE REDUCTION

6.6.1   Introduction

Source reduction methods are dealt with in this book as specific law enforcement techniques because the particular source reduction methods provided for

---

338 *1988 Commentary* at 290.
339 The Peruvian delegate suggested an extension of the article to cover these items but this was rejected by other delegations, *1988 Records* vol. II at 227 and 228.
340 As US legislation does.
341 *1988 Commentary* at 292.
342 *1988 Commentary* at 291.

by the drug conventions, such as the prohibition of cultivation and in particular the enforced eradication of drug bearing plants, usually involve suppressive action by law enforcement agencies.

The only provisions in the earlier conventions that deal directly with illicit source reduction are articles 22, 26(2) and 24(1)(b) of the 1961 Convention, and article 22(2) of the 1961 Convention as inserted by the 1972 Protocol. Following the lead of the 1987 Comprehensive Multidisciplinary Outline, which makes detailed suggestions for the identification and elimination of illicit narcotic plant cultivation and for the redevelopment of areas where such crops had been growing,[343] the authors of the 1988 Convention expanded provision for source reduction as a law enforcement tool in treaty law. The first three paragraphs of article 14 are devoted to source reduction and are discussed below. The other two paragraphs of article 14 are examined elsewhere. Paragraph 4, dealing with demand reduction, is treated under the alternatives to punishment in Chapter Five. Paragraph 5, devoted to the disposal of illicit drugs once they are in the hands of the authorities, has been examined above under seizure and confiscation in terms of the 1988 Convention, although it is relevant in the present context as it deals with a potential source of supply in the hands of corrupt officials.

---

343 Target 14 of the Comprehensive Multidisciplinary Outline relates to the 'Identification of illicit narcotic plant cultivation'. It identifies the major growing areas of opium poppies and coca bushes and the efforts made to hide illicit crops. Then it suggests a survey focusing on the precise location of illicit crops and gathering information from suitable national and international sources on growing conditions, market factors etc. with the aim of building an extensive picture of the situation. Target 15 relates to the 'Elimination of illicit plantings', which describes different techniques of manual and mechanical uprooting or flattening, and manual and aerial spraying, and the conditions suitable to their usage including safety issues. Ways of assisting farmers who have been subject to such methods are discussed, as is crop substitution and particular responses to particular crops. The emphasis is on developing and using a master plan in each state, with the assistance of international agencies, for the elimination of such plants. Target 16, discussed under crop-substitution, sees the 'Redevelopment of areas formerly under illicit drug crop cultivation' as integrally linked to eradication. See *Declaration of the International Conference on Drug Abuse and Illicit Trafficking and Comprehensive Multidisciplinary Outline of Future Activities in Drug Abuse Control*, UN Publication St/Nar/14, UN Sales No.E.88.XI.1, (New York, 1988), pp. 43-52.

6.6.2   Prohibition of cultivation and production under the 1961 Convention

The 1961 Convention sets out detailed regulatory regimes for the licit cultivation of the opium poppy, coca bush and cannabis plant. Article 22, entitled 'Special Provision Applicable to Cultivation', complements these schemes because it recognises that these plants are the sources of widely abused drugs, and that while their products are easily concealed, the cultivated plants themselves are more difficult to conceal and are thus open to greater law enforcement intervention.[344] Article 22 envisages the Party prohibiting the 'cultivation'[345] of the opium poppy,[346] the coca bush[347] or the cannabis plant.[348] The Party's decision to prohibit cultivation is based on its subjective appreciation that the objective conditions prevailing within its territory threaten the public health and welfare and allow for the divergence of drugs into the illicit traffic, and that prohibition of cultivation is the most suitable measure to stop this threat and divergence. Prohibition of cultivation will usually be easier than attempting to stop divergence from licit production. However, the provision makes it clear that divergence is not the only condition for the operation of the provision. Interpreted literally the Party must consider that there exists both divergence and a need to protect the public health and welfare before prohibition is mandatory. The *1961 Commentary* opines:

---

344 See the *1961 Commentary* at 275.

345 Article 1(i) defines 'cultivation' as 'the cultivation of the opium poppy, coca bush or cannabis plant.'

346 Article 1(q) defines 'opium poppy' as 'the plant of the species *papaver somniferum* L'. Prohibition of cultivation of the opium poppy would necessarily include prohibition of cultivation for all purposes including for poppy seeds and poppy straw as well as for opium.

347 Article 1(e) defines 'coca bush' as 'the plant of any species of the genus Erythroxylon'.

348 Article 1(c) defines 'cannabis plant' as 'any plant of the genus Cannabis'. While article 28(2) allows the cultivation of cannabis plants 'exclusively for industrial (fibre and seed) or horticultural purposes', article 22 permits prohibition of such authorised cultivation if it is a significant source of diversion to the illicit traffic, as it would no longer be cultivated 'exclusively' for the authorised purposes. However, as the leaves of cannabis plants not accompanied by the tops are not considered as drugs in the 1961 Convention, if the highly unlikely situation should arise where only the leaves and not the tops are diverted into the illicit traffic then in principle article 22 would not apply. Article 28(3) does provide, however, that Parties 'shall adopt such measures as may be necessary to prevent the misuse of, and illicit traffic in, the leaves of the cannabis plant.' Such a measure could include prohibition of cultivation in serious cases.

This additional condition appears to indicate that the authors of article 22 did not consider that any diversion whatever constitutes *ipso facto* a problem of *public* health and welfare, but only one which is sufficiently large to present such a problem. A Party is therefore not bound to prohibit cultivation if the drug in question is diverted only in relatively minor quantities.[349]

Leaving the decision in the hands of the Parties, given that they are also going to ascertain the objective grounds on which it is based, grants them an extraordinary amount of discretion. In an attempt to regain some international leverage, the *1961 Commentary* tries a number of tacks. It submits that the 'public health and welfare' to be protected by such prohibition includes the public health and welfare of the populations of other states, and any Party that considers that the conditions prevailing within its territory threaten the public health and welfare of other states must prohibit cultivation, even though its own population is not engaged in significant abuse of the drugs derived from these plants.[350] More boldly, the *1961 Commentary* submits that the decision of the Party whether to prohibit or not must be bona fide. It states:

> The decision whether the conditions of article 22 for prohibition exist is left to the *judgement*, but not entirely to the *discretion* of the Party concerned. A Government which for many years, despite its efforts, has been unable to prevent large-scale diversion of drugs from cultivation can hardly be of the opinion that the prohibition of such cultivation would not be 'the most suitable measure ... for protecting public health and welfare and preventing the diversion of drugs into the illicit traffic.'[351]

In effect, the *1961 Commentary* is suggesting that the decision must not be wholly unreasonable, especially when it contradicts the facts. Such an interpretation is perhaps more tenable when the decision contradicts the facts as agreed by the Party concerned, but it would seem that even in such a case the Party would still be free to argue that it remains of the opinion that prohibition is not necessarily the most suitable response.

Article 24(1)(b) must be read with article 22. It allows the continued cultivation of opium but obliges Parties not to permit the separation of the opium from the poppy or any increase in such production, if the Party is of the opinion that there is a risk of illicit traffic from such production. The *1961 Commentary*

---

349 *1961 Commentary* at 275.
350 *1961 Commentary* at 275-276.
351 *1961 Commentary* at 276. The *1961 Commentary* notes, however, that this opinion applies only to areas under the effective control of the government.

submits that such a risk must be significant, as experience has shown that private opium production is always accompanied by some minor diversion, and in effect minor diversion has to be tolerated or else all Parties would be obliged to prohibit opium production.[352] As with article 22, the decision is the Party's, but the *1961 Commentary* again submits that the Party must base its decision on its bona fide opinion; prohibition of production is left to the judgment of the Party but not its arbitrary discretion.[353]

Article 26 of the 1961 Convention, entitled 'The Coca Bush and Coca Leaves' is concerned with the licit cultivation of coca in paragraph 1. Article 26(2) is a special provision that obliges Parties to take further steps in respect of coca bushes than those that are applicable to poppy and cannabis plants. It confronts the problem of wild coca bushes. The provision prescribes a particular method, 'uprooting', for their destruction, and obliges the use of this method as far as is practically possible. The condition of practicality shows that the authors of the provision recognised that wild growth often occurs in remote areas in difficult terrain and is often much more difficult to uncover than cultivated growth. With respect to illicitly cultivated coca bushes, the provision simply requires their destruction without specifying how this is to be done or making it conditional on practicality. The *1961 Commentary* opines that any effective method of destruction would be satisfactory to achieve the provision's purposes.[354]

6.6.3   Prohibition of cultivation under the 1972 Protocol

While the unamended article 22 of the 1961 Convention is concerned only with prohibition of cultivation, its new paragraph 2, added by article 12 of the 1972 Protocol, obliges Parties to seize and destroy illicitly cultivated poppy and cannabis plants. Article 22(2) thus brings the position of these plants into line with the obligation to destroy illicitly cultivated coca plants under the unamended article 26(2) of the 1961 Convention. Unlike article 26(2) however, the new article 22(2) does not include a duty to seize and destroy cannabis and poppy plants that grow wild.[355]

---

352 *1961 Commentary* at 288.
353 See *1961 Commentary* at 288.
354 *1961 Commentary* at 308.
355 This idea was rejected in Committee II of the 1972 Conference inter alia because: i) there were large areas where such plants grew wild and their destruction would be too burdensome on states; ii) the delegates feared that a determined effort to destroy the

The measures used by the Parties to destroy illegally cultivated plants must be appropriate, that is, measures that are practical and can be reasonably expected of them under their special conditions.[356] Article 22(2) does not oblige Parties to destroy the products of illegally cultivated plants such as poppy straw. Nor does it oblige Parties to destroy legally cultivated opium poppies or cannabis plants, where these plants are being used for the illegal production of opium or cannabis.[357] As an alternative to destroying the plants, article 22(2) introduces the option of using the plants for scientific or research purposes, an option which accords with existing state practice.[358] The domestic law of most states allows the authorisation of the use of these plants for such purposes. The exact scope of 'scientific and research purposes' is uncertain, but it must include the use of these plants as evidence in criminal cases because such evidence would be of a scientific nature. The provision does not allow the use of seized plants to supplement licit drug production.

6.6.4   Eradication of illicit cultivation of narcotic plants under the 1988 Convention

Before 1988, the international community appeared to be moving hesitantly towards a blanket obligation to eradicate drug-containing crops as a method of source reduction. The 1961 Convention as amended provided for optional prohibition of drug bearing crops, eradication of the illicit cultivation of opium poppies, coca bushes and cannabis plants, but only the uprooting of wild coca bushes where practical. This hesitancy had much to do with the fact that crop eradication is one of the most controversial of all source reduction methods.[359] Numerous problems are associated with it. Some of the methods used, for example, burning and use of herbicides or chemicals, are environmentally destructive. The practice also hurts the poorest actors in the chain of supply, the

---

plants may bring about undesirable ecological changes; and iii) wild cannabis had a low THC content – see *1972 Records* vol. II at 219-225.

356 *1972 Commentary* at 70.

357 *1972 Commentary* at 70 notes that this would in particular be the case of opium poppies planted for seed or decorative purposes or of cannabis plants grown for industrial use or horticultural purposes.

358 See the statement of the Indian delegate, *1972 Records* vol. II at 50.

359 See generally Bland supra note 270 at 114 and 115.

peasants,[360] and undermines local economies in producer states. Finally, due to the enormous area of land under cultivation, its utility is highly questionable.

Despite these problems the inclusion of provisions on crop eradication in the draft convention was vigorously pursued by consumer states at the 1988 Conference. Producer states, especially those in Latin America, sought to extract a recognition from consumer states that the latter had a complimentary responsibility for reducing drug demand and that they should assist the producing countries in matters such as crop substitution and integrated rural development.[361] The issue of accountability was central to the debate and the eventual solution to the arguments between those who contended that production causes demand and those who believed demand causes production, was to adopt a compromise position that attacked both production and demand.[362] As a result, article 14 of the 1988 Convention is entitled 'Measures to Eradicate Illicit Cultivation of Narcotic Plants and to Eliminate Illicit Demand for Narcotic Drugs and Psychotropic Substances'. Article 14's provisions on source reduction provide for the meeting of existing international obligations in article 14(1), reduction at the national level in article 14(2) and international co-operation in respect of reduction in article 14(3).[363] While the article focuses on crop eradication, it adopts to an extent the balanced approach of the 1987 Comprehensive Multidisciplinary Outline by responding to the debilitated economic situation of illicit cultivators through the provision, for instance, of measures to tackle rural development.

---

360 The peasants are acutely aware of their interests. *The Economist*, 14 January 1995, reported that the Colombian Government's Operation Splendour, aimed at eliminating coca and poppy plants by the spraying of herbicides by 1997, came to a halt when thousands of angry peasants occupied strategic oil-pumping stations and halted pumping, demanding that spraying be halted. They had to be removed by the military with loss of life.

361 See Annexure B, 'Ratification of the UN Convention against Illicit Trafficking in Narcotic Drugs and Psychotropic Substances: Contents' in UK Home Affairs Committee, *Report: Drug Trafficking and Related Serious Crime* vol. II (1989), p. 162.

362 F. Rouchereau, 'La Convention des Nations Unies Contre le Traffic Illicite de Stupefiants et de Substances Psychotropes' (1988) 34 *Annuaire Francais de Droit Internationale* 601 at 612. She notes that during the course of the debate exaggerated tactics were employed by producer states, e.g. Bolivia and Peru argued for the legalisation of the cultivation of the coca plant for personal consumption. But the consumer states insisted that the 1988 Convention was not going to be used as a mechanism for lifting the obligations placed on producer states by the earlier conventions.

363 As noted, article 14(4) dealing with demand reduction is dealt with in Chapter Three under penalties, while article 14(5) dealing with the disposal of drugs is dealt with above in Chapter Six under seizure and confiscation.

Article 14(1) clarifies the relationship between article 14 and similar provisions of the earlier drug conventions. Article 14(1) makes it explicit that the measures taken by Parties to eradicate illicit cultivation (and eliminate illicit demand) as a result of article 14 must not be less exacting than the eradication measures taken for these purposes under the provisions of the 1961 Convention, the 1971 Convention and the 1972 Protocol.[364] The specific measure contemplated is article 22 of the 1961 Convention as amended by the 1972 Protocol.[365] Article 14(1)'s obligation is reiterated more generally by article 25 which provides that nothing in the 1988 Convention derogates from the obligations undertaken by Parties under the earlier conventions.

Article 14(2) obliges Parties to take appropriate measures to prevent the illicit cultivation of drug containing plants within their territories and to eradicate drug containing plants cultivated within their territories. The plants targeted are those containing narcotic or psychotropic substances, i.e. the opium poppy, coca bush and cannabis plant.[366] The use of the terms 'cultivation' and 'cultivated' implies that Parties are not under an obligation to eradicate or prevent the growth of wild plants. Thus article 14(2) does not provide for a blanket obligation to eradicate all non-licit plants.

Article 14(2) does not provide any specific guidance in respect of the methods to be used in the eradication of these plants. The choice of methods is thus left to the Parties. That choice is likely to be dictated by their economic position and the technical assistance they may receive from other Parties. Article 14(2) does, however, contain a safeguard clause to the effect that the prevention and eradication measures adopted must: i) respect fundamental human rights; ii) take due account of traditional licit uses, where there is historical evidence of such use; and iii) take due account of the protection of the environment.

---

364 This provision was included in the article because of concerns that subjecting the duty in article 14(2) on Parties to eradicate illicit plants to respect for the 'traditional licit uses, where there is historic evidence of such use' of these plants, was contrary to the provisions for eradication in especially the 1961 Convention as amended, and represented a step backwards – see the statements of the French and Soviet delegates, *1988 Records* vol. II at 298 and 300 respectively.

365 See the 'Expert Group Report', *1988 Records* vol. I at 25.

366 Article 1(b) defines 'cannabis plant' as 'any plant of the genus Cannabis'. Article 1(c) defines 'coca bush' as 'the plant of any species of the genus Erythroxylon'. Article 1(o) defines 'opium poppy' as 'the plant of the species *papaver somniferum* L'. Poppy straw is not included in this list because it has to be subject to a lengthy manufacturing process to yield opiates. Similar considerations excluded specific mention of coca leaf – see the statement of the Bolivian delegate, *1988 Records* vol. II at 297.

The reference to fundamental human rights is not specific about which rights it is anticipated will be endangered by illicit crop eradication, although the right to health may be directly affected by use of herbicides. Rights to work in the cultivation of drug-bearing plants and rights to property in these plants are easily limited by overriding societal interests in this context.

There is an obvious danger that the reference to traditional licit usage will present the illicit traffic with a loophole allowing continued undisturbed cultivation of drug bearing plants, especially as the 1988 Convention does not define such traditional usage other than to insist on evidence of a history of use.[367] The intention of this qualification appears to be that legitimate producers and users of coca leaves should not be discriminated against by article 14(2).[368] It is true that article 49 of the 1961 Convention made provisional arrangements for traditional medical usage of opium, coca leaf and cannabis. However, these temporary arrangements to maintain and respect coca leaf chewing and tea drinking in the 1961 Convention ended in 1988.[369] That the rationale for reference to traditional usage is questionable, is further highlighted by its selective nature. Delegates to the 1988 Conference accepted that the traditional use of opium for smoking was illegitimate while they continued to argue that the traditional use of coca leaves for chewing and so on was legitimate and needed protection.[370] It appears that both Bolivia and Peru now interpret such traditional usage as endorsement of coca leaf production for coca leaf chewing, an interpretation that other Parties oppose.[371]

The protection of the environment demands that the use of herbicides or other toxic substances with deleterious potential should be avoided. Burning

---

367 There was genuine concern in this regard at the 1988 Conference – see the statements of the Italian and Soviet delegates, *1988 Records* vol. II at 297.

368 For example, the Bolivian delegate stated that '[i]t was particularly important to ensure that the Convention did not penalise the licit cultivation of coca bushes and the licit traditional uses of coca leaf and its consumption.' – *1988 Records*, vol. II at 297. The Colombian delegate noted that 'certain ethnic groups traditionally used such plants' and there was 'a need to protect their social and cultural conditions when illicit plants were destroyed.' – *1988 Records* vol. II at 298. He later noted that 'the target of [eradication] measures should not be the peasants but the traffickers who exploited them.' – *1988 Records* vol. II at 301.

369 *1988 Records*, vol. II at 299.

370 See the Bolivian delegate's statement – *1988 Records*, vol. II at 303.

371 See for example, the UK – Annexure B, 'Ratification of the UN Convention against Illicit Trafficking in Narcotic Drugs and Psychotropic Substances: Contents' in UK Home Affairs Committee, *Report: Drug Trafficking and Related Serious Crime* vol. II (1989), p. 162.

crops and pulling them up also present risks. The Soviet delegate noted that 'the need for crop-eradication programmes should not be allowed to outweigh a legitimate concern to conserve areas vulnerable to desertification and consequent loss of habitat.'[372] In practice, externally driven eradication appears inevitably to demand environmentally destructive action, although Parties are becoming sensitive to the need to protect the environment when using herbicides.[373]

Article 14(3) obliges Parties to create the necessary foundation for international co-operation and communication on eradication. Article 14(3)(a) invites the Parties to co-operate to increase the effectiveness of their eradication efforts. The provision does not oblige Parties to use any particular method of co-operation, but notes that this co-operation may include support, when appropriate, for integrated rural development programmes leading to economically viable alternatives to illicit cultivation. Crop substitution and preferential tariffs for substitute products were mentioned in this context during the drafting process.[374] Article 14(3)(a) notes that market access,[375] resource availability and prevailing socio-economic conditions are factors that should be taken into account in the design of alternative programmes. It also invites the Parties to agree on other appropriate co-operation measures. Article 14(3)(b) obliges Parties to facilitate the exchange of scientific and technical information and the conduct of research concerning eradication. Article 14(3)(c) obliges Parties that have common frontiers to seek to co-operate in eradication programmes within their territory abutting these frontiers. This provision was included in the Convention, according to its Mexican sponsor, 'to reassure countries with common frontiers that they would have jurisdiction over activities carried out within their respective areas along those frontiers.'[376] Both obligations in subparagraphs (b) and (c) are specific applications of the general duty to co-operate in law enforcement provided for in article 9.[377]

Implicit in article 14(3) is the idea that consumer states are as responsible for the drug cultivation dependence of poor farmers in developing supply states,

---

372 *1988 Records*, vol. II at 297.
373 S.A. Gardner, 'A global initiative to deter drug trafficking: will internationalising the drug war work?' (1993) 7 *Temple International and Comparative Law Review* 287 at 301 notes that Peru has engaged in extensive testing of herbicides before use.
374 See the 'Expert Group Report', *1988 Records* vol. I at 26.
375 Market access is dictated by the level of demand for substituted crops on the open markets, and the cultivator's ease of physical access to those markets.
376 *1988 Records* vol. II at 303.
377 *1988 Commentary* at 302.

as supply states are themselves. However, the rigidly neutral text of the provision belies the imbalance in the capacity of these states to do something about changing that dependency. Article 14(3) is also vulnerable to the criticism that it is a 'best efforts" provision.

6.6.5   *Source reduction in conclusion*

In spite of article 14 of the 1988 Convention, the measures in the drug conventions for control at source of drugs remain limited and uneven. These measures are an awkward compromise between consumer and producer states. Consumer states see crop eradication in producer states as a rational method for stopping the flow of drugs to their shores. Producer states ascribe responsibility for the global drug problem to demand within producer states. They remain ambivalent about a comprehensive programme of source reduction. Their ambivalence is rooted in the dubious utility of source reduction methods, in the historical linkage of certain drug producing plants to certain areas and in the continued economic dependency on those plants in those areas.[378] In the face of their intransigent opposition to such methods, it appears that little crop eradication takes place in the most important producer states.[379]

The implementation of measures for source reduction suffers from a number of other handicaps besides the political ones. They are subject to the vagaries of physical and political accessibility to cultivation areas. At the 1998 General

---

378 Gardner supra note 373 at 301-303 notes that Bolivia in the early 1990s sought to protect its coca crop with a 'National Commission Pro-Coca' to study the licit uses of coca leaf.

379 Gardner supra note 373 at 301-303 gives Peru's coca crop eradication efforts in the early 1990s in conjunction with the UNDCP as an example of successful action by a Party in terms of article 14. This programme concentrated on crop substitution and access to foreign markets for alternative products, in addition to large-scale eradication. However, while an estimated 108 600 ha of land were under coca bush cultivation, only 74 000 square meters of coca seedbeds (not mature crops) were eradicated in the Upper Huallaga Valley in 1994. In Bolivia, where an estimated 48 100 ha were under coca cultivation, only 1 100 ha were eradicated – see the National Narcotics Intelligence Consumers Committee, *The NNICC Report 1994: The Supply of Illicit Drugs to the United States* (DEA, Washington, 1995), pp. 15-16. P. Reuter, 'The limits and consequences of U.S. foreign drug control efforts' (1992) 521 *Annals of the American Academy of Politics and Social Science* 151 at 156 reports that while throughout the 1980s the US State Department's Bureau of International Narcotic Matters (BINM) sought to induce producer states to engage in crop eradication, poor results caused it to de-emphasise this programme.

Assembly Special Session on Drugs member states agreed to develop systems to monitor drug crops and report their findings to the UNDCP. The UNDCP has since been requested by the CND to set up a high technology network including remote satellite sensing and ground surveys to produce a comprehensive global data-base on illicit cultivation to be used to pursue global eradication.[380] An equally difficult problem is getting at the plants once they have been identified; gaining access may require a military-scale operation. And once the plants are reached, there are constraints on what can be done to them. Eradication, no matter what method is adopted, is bound to have an environmental impact, and that impact is likely to be negative if it is not done with the co-operation of the people who planted the plants. The environmental impact of international provisions for enforcing eradication without co-operation deserves further study. Finally, source reduction is complicated by its multidisciplinary nature. Source reduction is not the exclusive province of law enforcement. One of the suggested methods, 'alternative development', involves the activities of agricultural economists, development experts and other non-legal experts. While these experts must establish the trust of peasant farmers even though they often work in conjunction with law enforcement agents, they do not always enjoy the full confidence of these law enforcement agents who see them as "soft" on the crime of illicit cultivation.

6.7   CONTROL OF COMMERCIAL CARRIERS

The shift of illicit trafficking into the legitimate transportation sector and particularly into commercial air-cargo and ship-borne containers parallels its penetration of the legitimate financial sector. The 1988 Convention made novel provision for control of the latter problem, and it also provides for control of the former. Article 15 of the 1988 Convention, entitled 'Commercial Carriers', recognises that traffickers exploit commercial carriers for the transhipment of drugs, and makes provision for steps to be taken to suppress this practice.[381] Article 1(d) defines a 'commercial carrier' as 'any person or any public, private

---

380 UNIS Press Release, 24 March 1999.

381 Concealment can take place within the walls of containers, in boxes intermingled with other goods and within legitimate bulk cargo. Amounts are large. For example, over 21.4 metric tons of cocaine was seized from commercial cargo vessels from January 1 to November 14, 1994. But the problem is enormous. For example, in the US, only 3% of the over four million containers entering the US in 1993 were inspected by customs. See generally the NNICC supra note 379 at 3-4.

or other entity engaged in transporting persons, goods or mails for remuneration, hire or any other benefit'. Thus article 15 applies to the activities of individuals, legal entities, public and private companies transporting persons, goods or mail[382] for any form of reward, 'whether pecuniary or not'.[383] The definition was intended to be all-inclusive and the words 'or other entity' enable the definition to apply to carriers that are neither private nor public.[384] However, the *1988 Commentary* points out that the words 'engaged in transporting' suggest that the carrier must be habitually involved in the transport of goods, rather than carrying them only on an isolated occasion.[385]

Article 15(1) obliges Parties to take 'appropriate measures' to ensure that the means of transport operated by commercial carriers within their jurisdictions are not used in the commission of article 3(1) offences. Such measures may be legislated or simply take the form of administrative guidelines.[386] Article 15(1) does not specify appropriate measures. In most instances they will involve co-operation with carriers, but they may also involve the penalisation of carriers and the seizure/confiscation of means of transport and invasive measures such as searches without consent. Searches are likely to be regarded as one of the most appropriate measures for ensuring that the illicit traffic does not use commercial carriers.[387] The procedure for such searches will depend entirely upon the Party. Article 15(1) provides only that appropriate measures include 'special arrangements' with commercial carriers thus anticipating that effective control of their means of transport is best achieved with their co-operation and consent. Growth in schemes for co-operation has been rapid since 1988.[388]

---

382 Reference to mail was included to cover private firms which carry mail outside the rules embodied in the Universal Postal Union (UPU) Conventions – see the statement of the French delegate, *1988 Records* vol. II at 220.
383 *1988 Commentary* at 29.
384 Report of the US Delegation supra note 49 at 91.
385 *1988 Commentary* at 29.
386 See the statement of the Japanese delegate and Chairman of Committee II – *1988 Records* vol. II at 218.
387 Draft article 11(1) included 'thorough searches of all means of transportation suspected of containing evidence of illicit traffic.' See the *1988 Records* vol. I at 8.
388 The WCO's 1991 Carrier Co-operation Initiative, to which there are over 200 signatories, is an attempt to develop co-operation between customs authorities and commercial carriers. More onerous "super-carrier" procedures have been assumed by a number of major carriers. These procedures, which include the submission of written standard operating procedures, are implemented when the sender, consignee or the consignment itself is considered to be "high risk". See generally the UNDCP's, *World Drug Report* (OUP, Oxford, 1998), p. 232.

Article 15(2) shifts the responsibility to the commercial carriers themselves. It obliges Parties to require commercial carriers to take 'reasonable precautions' to prevent the use of their means of transport for the commission of article 3(1) offences.[389] 'Means of transport' must be taken to include all conveyances operated by such carriers, whether owned or used, such as ships, boats, aircraft, motor vehicles, bicycles and human carriers. 'Reasonable precautions' will depend on factors such as the size of the carrier's business, its use of routes and carriage mechanisms that are known to be risky, the capacity of staff to respond appropriately and so on. The International Civil Aviation Organisation (ICAO) representative noted at the 1988 Conference that:

> The term 'reasonable precautions' ... should not impose an excessive burden on commercial carriers and should not delay the carriage of passengers and cargo. The role of the commercial air-carriers should be confined to reducing illegal access to the aircraft and associated equipment.[390]

There is no provision for the penalties attaching to a failure to take reasonable precautions. This and other matters such as legal impunity if reasonable precautions have been taken are matters of domestic law.[391]

Article 15(2) suggests two non-exclusive lists of 'reasonable precautions'. When the carrier's principal place of business is in the territory of the Party, article 15(2)(a)'s suggested precautions are: (i) training personnel to identify suspicious consignments or persons; and (ii) promoting the integrity of personnel. In other words, it recommends trying to increase the level of effectiveness of personnel and their ability to withstand corruption. Article 15(2)(b)'s more extensive list of precautions applies when the carrier operates within the Party's territory, in other words, when it actually transports goods or people, from, or

---

389 These would include article 3(1) offences not associated with the transport of drugs such as money laundering offences. Although the *1988 Commentary* at 313 points out that this may not have been intended by the authors of the Convention it is appropriate to some offences such as the large scale transportation of cash.

390 *1988 Records* vol. II at 219. One problem with assigning responsibility to the carriers is that, as the Japanese delegate pointed out, in commercial practice the carrier cannot inspect the contents of cargo carried without the authority of the consignors; he thus felt that the provision should have held the exporter responsible – *1988 Records* vol. II at 216.

391 There is thus, for example, no provision in article 15 providing that a commercial carrier must be aware of use by traffickers of its means of transport before it is subject to legal penalties. For an example of what happens when absolute liability is imposed, see the *Air Canada* case cited at note 12 supra.

to, or through the Party's territory. They are: (i) submission of cargo manifests to the competent authority in advance, whenever possible; (ii) using tamper-resistant individually verifiable seals on containers[392]; and (iii) expeditiously alerting all the appropriate authorities of suspicious circumstances that may be related to the commission of article 3(1) offences. The 'Expert Group' understood that in appropriate cases a Party was free to apply both lists of precautions to any carrier.[393]

Finally, with the goals of preventing unauthorised access to means of transport and cargo and the implementation of appropriate security measures, article 15(3) obliges each Party to 'seek to ensure' the co-operation of commercial carriers and the appropriate authorities at entry and exit points and other customs control areas. The purpose of this provision is to get the co-operation of carriers and authorities in limiting access to these choke points where vehicles, vessels, aircraft and cargo awaiting customs clearance are vulnerable to unauthorised use.

While article 15 is a novel provision that ties commercial carriers into a co-operative role in law enforcement, the draft article 11(2) went further in shifting responsibility. It obliged Parties to penalise commercial carriers that failed to prevent their use by the illicit traffic and to provide for the confiscation of the means of transport if the commercial carrier was aware of its use by the illicit traffic.[394] The present provision leaves the modality to be used and the severity of any sanctions the commercial carrier might face up to the Party. Seizure and confiscation, if the carrier acts in bad faith or simply unreasonably, is possible under article 5. Criminalisation is more difficult because secondary participation in drug trafficking offences must usually in terms of the drug conventions be intentional, although the conventions do of course urge more stringent provisions, thus allowing Parties to choose at their election to punish negligent conduct.[395] However, legislating for a positive attitude on the part

---

392 The *1988 Commentary* at 314 notes that 'container' here means the outer packaging of a consignment rather than the metal containers used in shipping.

393 See the 'Expert Group Report', *1988 Records* vol. I at 36. The US supported this interpretation in Committee and in Plenary – *1988 Records* vol. II at 218 and 34 respectively.

394 *1988 Records* vol. I at 8. These provisions were deleted in the 'Expert Group' because they were held to add nothing to the rights already enjoyed by states in international law – see the 'Expert Group Report', *1988 Records* vol. I at 27.

395 The US has chosen to both seize/confiscate and criminalise – 19 USC sections 1584 and 1594.

of carriers is difficult; encouragement is likely to be more effective. In any event, the sheer volume of container traffic must limit the impact of article 15.

6.8   MEASURES TO CONTROL THE DOCUMENTATION OF EXPORTS

Interdiction efforts are hampered by the improper, irregular and inaccurate documentation of legitimate exports. Moreover, the illicit traffic uses imprecise documentation as a cover. Article 16 of the 1988 Convention, entitled 'Commercial Documents and Labelling of Exports', focuses on ensuring the correct documentation of licit drug exports, and preventing incorrect labelling of licit drug consignments, as tactics against the illicit traffic.

Article 16(1) deals with the contents of documentation. It obliges each Party to require, either by way of legislation or through administrative arrangement, the proper documentation of lawful exports of narcotic drugs and psychotropic substances.[396] This provision operates in addition to the documentation requirements in the earlier conventions and does not alter them, but its scope is wider than these provisions as it applies to documents other than just import or export authorisations.[397] It applies to commercial documents such as invoices and cargo manifests, to administrative documents such as customs documents, to transport documents such as bills of lading and to other shipping documents. The examples of the generic types of documents given are not exclusive and other examples are contemplated.[398] Article 16(1) applies whether these documents accompany the goods or not. It insists that these commercial documents include: i) the names of the narcotic drugs and psychotropic substances being exported as set out in the respective schedules of the 1961 Convention, the 1961 Convention as amended and the 1971 Convention, i.e., their international non-

---

396 The provision does not apply to precursor substances in Tables I and II as their correct labelling is already required under article 9(d).

397 Article 31(4) sub-paragraphs (a) and (b) of the 1961 Convention require that import or export authorisations must be obtained for narcotic drugs and that these authorisations must state inter alia the name of the narcotic, the quantity and the name and address of the importer and exporter, as well as the specified period within which the import or export must take place. Article 12(1)(b) of the 1971 Convention makes similar provisions in respect of the psychotropic substances in Schedules I and II, while article 12(2)(a) requires roughly the same information for Schedule III substances.

398 The *1988 Commentary* at 321 notes that 'transport documents' may include air waybills for instance.

proprietary names; ii) the quantity being exported; and iii) the name and address of the exporter, the importer and, when available, the consignee.

Article 16(2) applies to the labelling of consignments. It does not require such consignments to be labelled as in some cases this would invite theft. The decision to require labelling or not has been left to the Parties.[399] What article 16(2) does is to oblige each Party to require that export consignments of narcotic drugs and psychotropic substances shall not be mislabelled, for example, as 'inoffensive chemicals' or 'reagents'.[400] Mislabelling, use of uncommon abbreviations and so forth presents both a health threat and an opportunity for the illicit traffic.[401]

6.9   DRUG LAW ENFORCEMENT CO-OPERATION AT SEA[402]

6.9.1   Introduction

Trafficking by sea has an enduring popularity because it enables the movement of drugs, especially of bulky drugs such as cannabis,[403] long distances in bulk without hindrance and at low cost, and it is protected by the principle of freedom of navigation. Encroachment on this freedom in the name of drug law enforcement has been gradual. None of the pre-1988 drug conventions contained provisions specifically designed to suppress trafficking by sea. However, international provisions aimed at controlling the sea-borne traffic did exist before 1988. Article 19(1)(d) of the 1958 Geneva Convention on the Territorial Sea and Contiguous Zone[404] provides:

---

399 In the spirit of article 30(4) of the 1961 Convention, many states have enacted domestic legislation stipulating that the outer wrapping of a package containing narcotic drugs or psychotropic substances shall not indicate its contents.

400 Article 16(2) impacts on the trade in substances falsely labelled as familiar medicines but which contain little or none of the active ingredients of that medicine – see the statement of the Chairman of Committee II, *1988 Records* vol. II at 223.

401 The *1988 Commentary* at 321 notes that the Expert Consultation on the Control of Brokers and Transit Operators Handling Psychotropic Substances and Precursors, organised by the INCB and the Council of Europe's Pompidou Group, 3-5 May 1995, (INCB/PS/1995/W.4), highlighted these issues.

402 See generally W.C. Gilmore, 'Drug trafficking by sea: the 1988 United Nations Convention Against Illicit Traffic in Narcotic Drugs and Psychotropic Substances' (1991) 15 *Marine Policy* 183-192.

403 See Gilmore supra note 402 at 184.

404 15 UST 1607.

1. The criminal jurisdiction of the coastal State should not be exercised on board a foreign ship passing through the territorial sea to arrest any person or to conduct any investigation in connection with any crime committed on board the ship during its passage, save only in the following cases: ...
(d) If it is necessary for the suppression of the illicit traffic in narcotic drugs.

Gilmore points out that although not evident in state practice, this exception was explicable through the inclination to apply universal jurisdiction to drug offences using the historical example of piracy.[405] Article 19(1)(d)'s effect is limited by article 19(5) of the 1958 Geneva Convention which forbids law enforcement measures in respect of offences that took place before the ship entered territorial waters. In addition, article 19(2) reserves the right of a coastal state to exercise criminal jurisdiction on board a foreign vessel that has left its internal waters but is within its territorial sea.

As traffickers took to the waves in greater numbers, driven by necessity states extended their prescriptive criminal jurisdiction over drug offences beyond territorial waters out onto the high seas. Vessels sitting just outside territorial waters acting as mother ships for inshore vessels to smuggle drugs ashore presented the most tangible threat. Although they had little treaty support, states relied on the criminal law principles of hot pursuit and constructive presence in their efforts to suppress the illicit sea-borne traffic.[406] These principles allowed strong action near the coast, but their allowable strength of action diminished progressively the further from the coast and the deeper into international waters one went.[407] States like the United States with long and vulnerable coastlines close to supply areas in the Caribbean and Central and South America began for pragmatic reasons to interdict vessels on the high seas. Interdiction and assertion of jurisdiction over their own vessels was uncontroversial, while interdiction and assertion over stateless vessels became less controversial in the 1970s and 1980s.[408] However, interdiction of foreign vessels remained

---

405 Supra note 402 at 184 citing I.A. Shearer, 'Problems of jurisdiction and law enforcement against delinquent vessels' (1986) 35 ICLQ 327. Examples of the provision in operation are *Pianka v R* [1977] 3 WLR at 870 (UK) and *R v Dakin* [1978] 15 JLR 302 (Jamaica).

406 Gilmore supra note 402 at 184. See also W.C. Gilmore, 'Hot pursuit and constructive presence in Canadian law enforcement' (1988) 12 *Marine Policy* 105-111; Shearer supra note 405 at 338.

407 See Gilmore supra note 402 at 184.

408 See S.L. Lewis, 'The Marijuana on the High Seas Act: extending U.S. jurisdiction beyond international limits' (1982) 8 *Yale Journal of World Public Order* 359-383 who explains at 361 that prior to the enactment in 1980 of the Marijuana on the High Seas Act, 21 USC section 955a(h), in order to obtain the conviction of the crew of drug

controversial.[409] The only legal option was to request the ad hoc waiver of exclusive flag jurisdiction by the state of registry. Interdicting states found it difficult to obtain timeous waiver of exclusive flag jurisdiction.[410] Despite growing concern, the 1982 United Nations Convention on the Law of the Sea[411] did not provide much relief in this area. Criminal jurisdiction over foreign vessels in lateral transit within the territorial sea was extended through article 27(1)(d) to include the illicit traffic in psychotropic substances in addition to narcotic drugs. Interdiction on the high seas was provided for in article 108. Entitled 'Illicit Traffic in Narcotic Drugs or Psychotropic Substances', it provides:

> 1. All states shall co-operate in the suppression of the illicit traffic in narcotic drugs and psychotropic substances engaged in by ships on the high seas contrary to international conventions.

---

carrying vessels seized on the high seas US authorities had to prove conspiracy or attempt to import the drugs into the US, i.e., a direct jurisdictional connection between the drugs on board a captured vessel and the US. After the enactment of the Marijuana on the High Seas Act, US authorities no longer had to prove such a nexus between the drugs and the US. The application of this extended jurisdiction to US vessels was uncontroversial, and US courts held that jurisdiction over stateless vessels could be established simply because they were stateless (*US v Marino Garcia* 679 F.2d 1373 at 1382 (11th Cir. 1982)). Eventually the US passed the Maritime Drug Enforcement Act (MDEA) 46 USC section 1902 (1988) which extended its criminal jurisdiction over 'vessels without nationality' on the high seas. See also D.B. Boggis, 'Exporting United States drug law: an example of the international legal ramifications of the "war on drugs"' (1992) 1 *Brigham Young University Law Review* 165 at 173-183; C.E. Sorenson, 'Drug trafficking on the high seas: a move towards universal jurisdiction under international law' (1990) 4 *Emory International Law Review* 207-230.

409 See Lewis supra note 408 at 379-382 who explains that US legislation in 1982 did not extend jurisdiction over foreigners aboard foreign vessels.

410 Gilmore supra note 402 at 185. See also J. Siddle, 'Anglo-American co-operation in the suppression of drug smuggling' (1982) 31 ICLQ 726-747. K. Fisher, 'Trends in extraterritorial narcotics control: slamming the stable door after the horse has bolted' (1984) 16 *New York University Journal of International Law and Policy* 353 at 381, footnote 161, notes that the US Coast Guard had to follow a Panamanian registered vessel for a day and a night while awaiting permission through diplomatic channels to board her – *US v Steifel* 507 F.Supp. 480 (SDNY 1981). Other potential problems include the onset of night or bad weather, the dumping of the contraband before permission is granted, and the suspect vessel running into a third party state's territorial waters – see statement of the US Coast Guard's Admiral Cueroni before the House of Representative's Sub-committee on Crime cited by W.C. Gilmore, 'Narcotics interdiction at sea: UK-US co-operation' (1989) 15 *Commonwealth Law Bulletin* 1480 at 1486.

411 UN Doc. A/Conf.62/122, 21 ILM 261.

2. Any state which has reasonable grounds for believing that a ship flying its flag is engaged in illicit traffic in narcotic drugs or psychotropic substances may require the co-operation of other states to suppress such traffic.

This provision does only two things, viz. it obliges Parties generally to co-operate in the suppression of the illicit traffic on the high seas and within their exclusive economic zone[412] without stipulating the nature of such co-operation, and it provides that such co-operation can be demanded by a flag state when it has an objectively based belief that a vessel flying its flag is engaged in the illicit traffic. The obvious lacuna is that it makes no specific provision for requests from non-flag states to flag states to be allowed to board and search vessels on the high seas. Continued heavy use by the illicit traffic of the high seas led to a surge in pressure for the adoption of international principles and procedures concentrating on interdiction. This pressure finally yielded article 17 of the 1988 Convention, entitled, 'Illicit Traffic by Sea'. Article 17 involves the exercise of criminal jurisdiction at sea, not its establishment, and thus must be read with article 4, which provides for the establishment of criminal jurisdiction at sea.

6.9.2   The basic obligation to co-operate

Article 17(1) provides for a basic obligation on Parties to co-operate in the suppression of the illicit transport of drugs by sea.[413] In terms of this provision the Parties' obligation to co-operate is limited by: i) their capacity – they must co-operate only 'to the fullest extent possible'; and by ii) compliance with the international law of the sea.[414] The latter limitation is of equal importance to all states, but the former admits that there is a serious disparity in the capacity of consumer states like the United States and producer states like Jamaica to carry out interdiction operations on the high seas. A more refined version of article 108(1) of the 1982 UN Convention on the Law of the Sea, article 17(1) is not particularly controversial. Other than direct co-operation in interdiction

---

412 Article 58(2).
413 The Netherlands pointed out (8/9/1993 – *Multilateral Treaties Deposited* (1997) at 303) that in this narrow context illicit traffic must in effect mean illicit transport.
414 This 'international law of the sea' is the customary law of the sea codified in the navigational articles of the 1982 UN Convention on the Law of the Sea – see 'Report of the US Delegation', supra note 49 at 95.

at sea, it may include the provision of information about the movement of shipping generally and of vessels suspected of involvement in particular.[415]

6.9.3   Interdiction of own or stateless vessels

Article 17(2) allows a Party that reasonably suspects that a vessel, which is either flying its flag or is not 'displaying a flag or marks of registry', is engaged in the illicit traffic, to request the assistance of other Parties in 'suppressing its use for that purpose'. The Party making the request must have an objectively grounded suspicion. Assistance will usually involve the boarding and searching of such vessels, but may involve other actions such as preventing them unloading or transhipping cargo and introducing the flag state's law enforcement officials to these vessels.[416] Assistance can be subject to any conditions either Party chooses to introduce. Either Party may meet costs, although it seems appropriate that the requesting Party should meet them.[417] Either Party may be held liable for damage, although it seems fairer that the requesting Party should assume liability.[418] Article 17(2) recognises differentials in the capacities of states to respond to requests for assistance by making compliance subject to the 'means available' to the requested Party. Poorer Parties may agree to co-operate only on the basis of reimbursement because co-operation is beyond their financial means. In summary then, article 17(2) develops the law in article 108(2) of the UN Convention on the Law of the Sea by, most importantly, according to the United States delegation, 'expanding the situations in which co-operation may be requested to include the interdiction of stateless vessels, thereby recognising a practice which has developed unchallenged over the years.'[419]

---

415 The *1988 Commentary* at 344. It cites Interpol, the WCO, and Mar-Info (an intelligence system on commercial shipping around Europe) as potential repositories of this information.

416 *1988 Commentary* at 342.

417 Recommendation 22 of the 1995 Report of the UN Working Group on Maritime Co-operation, UN Doc. E/CN.7/1995/13.

418 Article 26(3) of the 1995 Council of Europe Agreement on Illicit Traffic by Sea Implementing Article 17 of the United Nations Convention Against Illicit Traffic in Narcotic Drugs and Psychotropic Substances, ETS 156, adopts such an approach.

419 Report of the US Delegation supra note 49 at 95. Article 17(2) simply builds upon the provision in article 110 of the 1982 Convention on the Law of the Sea, 21 ILM 261, which allows states a right of visitation over stateless vessels, including in terms of article 92(2) vessels flying two flags.

6.9.4   Interdiction of foreign vessels

Foreign flag vessels are customarily regarded as part of the territory of the flag state over which it exercises exclusive criminal jurisdiction, yet they are frequent targets of interdiction by other states. Article 17(3) is the most controversial of the 1988 Convention's provisions for law enforcement at sea, because it involves the interdiction of these vessels by other Parties. Article 17(3) becomes operative when a Party suspects that a vessel exercising freedom of navigation and flying the flag or displaying the registry marks of another Party is engaged in illicit traffic. The requesting Party's suspicion must be grounded on facts. The words 'engaged in illicit traffic' can be interpreted broadly to include situations where the vessel has been used recently to commit offences, such as when a mother ship had just unloaded contraband for smaller vessels to take inshore. Obviously, the whole vessel need not be engaged in the illicit traffic; it will be sufficient if one or more of the crew are. Article 17(3) allows the suspicious Party to notify the flag state and to request confirmation of the vessel's registry.[420] If this is confirmed, the suspicious Party can then request the flag state to authorise it 'to take appropriate measures in regard to that vessel'.

The principle of requesting authorisation for the interdiction of a foreign vessel is not controversial. However, the maritime area in which such authorisation may be requested is controversial. Article 17(3) does not deprive any coastal state of its exclusive right to jurisdiction in its territorial waters.[421] It was the assertion by certain states at the 1988 Conference that coastal states enjoyed exclusive criminal jurisdiction in zones beyond the territorial sea, such as the exclusive economic zone (EEZ) and contiguous zone, that caused great controversy in the preparation of this provision.[422] As finally adopted, article

---

420   Article 6 of the 1958 Geneva High Seas Convention, 450 UNTS 82, requires all vessels to be registered and fly the flag of one state only; see also article 92 of the 1982 United Nations Convention on the Law of the Sea, 21 ILM 261. Recommendation 16 of the 1995 Report of the UN Working Group on Maritime Co-operation, UN Doc. E/CN.7/1995/13, suggests that all states should maintain a register containing information on vessels authorised to fly its flag and that this information should be readily available to the authority designated to deal with requests under article 17(3).

421   See the statement of the Australian delegate who introduced the final text – *1988 Records* vol. II at 308.

422   Gilmore supra note 402 at 187 recalls that the most controversial element of the draft article was its definition of the maritime area to which the provision would apply – the area 'beyond the external limits of the territorial sea'. The debate at the 1988 Conference was a repetition of attempts made at the UN Conference on the Law of the Sea by some

17(3) abandons the idea of zones and uses the concept of a vessel exercising 'freedom of navigation in accordance with international law'. This formula necessarily implies that the vessel must be sailing in a zone where freedom of navigation is possible, and thus the question of whether navigation of EEZs or contiguous zones is free of the exclusive encumbrance of coastal states' jurisdiction has been fudged. There is no consensus on the correct position under international law. Inevitably, the formula has been interpreted restrictively by the United States and other consumer states to mean navigating in any maritime area seaward of the territorial sea of a coastal state.[423] However, article 17(3) must be read with article 17(11) which ensures that actions taken in terms of article 17 do not interfere with any rights and obligations and the exercise of jurisdiction enjoyed by coastal states under the international law of the sea. These rights must include the rights of coastal states to exercise jurisdiction over drug offences in their contiguous zones and engage in hot pursuit from

---

coastal states to claim exclusive sovereignty over the exclusive economic zone (EEZ), or at the least, greater rights than the right to hot pursuit and the exercise of contiguous zone jurisdiction. Some states felt that the wording as finally adopted would encroach on the rights coastal states had in their EEZs in terms of article 56 of the Law of the Sea Convention because it would give other states the right to board, search and seize vessels in these waters – see the Brazilian view, *1988 Records* vol. II at 267-268. However, most states, interpreting article 58 of the Law of the Sea Convention as allowing all states the freedom of the high seas as set out in article 87, felt that article 17(3) of the 1988 Convention would not encroach on the coastal states' rights within the EEZ – see *1988 Records* vol. II at 268 and 269 for the Venezuelan and British views. There was greater support for the argument that article 17(3)'s wording was incompatible with the optional law enforcement rights states enjoy in their contiguous zones in terms of article 33 of the Law of the Sea Convention – see *1988 Records* vol. II at 268 and 269 for the views of the Indian, Indonesian and Algerian delegations. Some states wanted article 17(3) revised because of the need to safeguard these and other rights such as article 111 of the Law of The Sea Convention's right of hot pursuit – see *1988 Records* vol. II at 268 for the views of the French and Netherlands delegations and 270 for Argentina's view.

423 For the US view see *1988 Records* vol. II at 309. The UK has adopted a similar interpretation – see (1988) BYIL 528-529 and section 20(6) of the Criminal Justice (International Co-operation) Act, 1990, which only requires the powers of arrest of foreign vessels not to be used in the territorial waters of other states. The Netherlands made a declaration to this effect upon signature – 18/1/1989, *Multilateral Treaties Deposited* (1997) at 305. Interestingly, the 1995 Council of Europe Agreement on Illicit Traffic by Sea Implementing Article 17 of the United Nations Convention Against Illicit Traffic in Narcotic Drugs and Psychotropic Substances, ETS 156, allows action against vessels beyond the territorial sea – see W.C. Gilmore, 'Narcotics interdiction at sea: the 1995 Council of Europe Agreement' (1996) 20 *Marine Policy* 3 at 4.

territorial waters. The unresolved issue is, however, whether coastal states' jurisdiction is in any way exclusive. Article 17(11) does not clarify whether coastal states would even have to be informed of the interdiction of vessels carrying illicit drugs in their EEZs or contiguous zones by other Parties, something in which these states have both a law enforcement and commercial interest. Brazil has made a provocative reservation to the effect that article 17(11) does not prevent a coastal state from requiring prior authorisation for any action under article 17 by other states in its EEZ.[424] Other Parties, mostly consumer states, have objected, placing the legality of the Brazilian position in question.[425] More limited reservations have been made and objected to and some have been withdrawn.[426] But the controversy has not been settled and the potential for jurisdictional conflict is obvious. Given that the general object and purpose of the 1988 Convention is international co-operation to suppress the illicit traffic it would be illogical to argue that the 1988 Convention is an instrument for the extension of coastal state jurisdiction if that jurisdiction prevents the attainment of that object. Nevertheless, it is submitted that in practice it would be in the interests of all Parties to ensure that coastal states are kept informed of interdictions on the high seas adjacent to their territorial waters.

---

424 Reservation upon signature – 20/12/1988, *Multilateral Treaties Deposited* (1997) at 303.
425 Belgium, Denmark, France, Germany, Greece, Ireland, Italy, Luxembourg, Netherlands, Portugal, Spain and the UK objected to Brazil's reservation – 27/12/1989, *Multilateral Treaties Deposited* (1997) at 306.
426 Jamaica made a reservation to the effect that article 17(11) requires the consent of a coastal state for action in its EEZ 'and all other maritime areas under the sovereignty or jurisdiction of the coastal state', but it later withdrew it – 29/12/1995 and 10/121996 respectively, *Multilateral Treaties Deposited* (1997) at 304. Colombia, rather ambiguously, simply declared that it understood article 17's assistance would only be effective on the high seas and at express request and with its authorisation – 20/12/1988, *Multilateral Treaties Deposited* (1997) at 303. The US objected to the declaration 'to the extent it purports to restrict the right of other states to freedom of navigation and other internationally lawful uses of the sea related to that freedom seaward of the outer limits of any state's territorial sea' as determined under the law of the sea. Tanzania made a reservation upon signature – 20/12/1988, *Multilateral Treaties Deposited* (1997) at 306, to the effect that article 17(11) did not restrict the rights and privileges of the coastal state in its EEZ as envisaged by the Law of the Sea Convention or accord third parties greater rights than they enjoyed under that Convention in the EEZ.

Article 17(3) makes it clear that the requesting Party must receive 'authorisation' to interdict the vessel.[427] This word was deliberately used to

> stress the positive nature of the decision and of the action that the flag State in the exercise of its sovereignty was to take with regard to its vessel. Nothing in the article was intended in any way to affect the rights of the flag State with regard to its vessel and there was no obligation in the article for a flag State to provide the authorisation requested of it; it was entirely at its discretion to decide whether it would allow another State to act against its vessel or not.[428]

To function effectively it is essential for flag states to respond to requests for authorisation under article 17(3).[429] Although not specified, the logical implication of authorisation is that it will be granted only if the requested flag state is also satisfied that 'reasonable grounds' exist for the interdiction of the vessel, and thus the requesting party will in practice probably have to supply

---

427 See, for example, section 20(2) of the UK's Criminal Justice (International Co-operation) Act 1990 which provides that the Secretary of State may authorise the use of law enforcement powers against non-British ships on the high seas that are registered with Parties to the 1988 Convention only if their flag state requests the UK's assistance or it has 'authorised the United Kingdom to act'. Section 20(4) allows for the Secretary of State to give authorisation when requests are made to the UK. A. Harding, 'Criminal Justice (International Co-operation) Act 1990: Forfeiture, Money Laundering, Confiscation and Maritime Provisions' (1991) 155 *Justice of the Peace* 492 at 493 notes that authorisation may be conditional, e.g., the UK may require persons arrested on British ships to be extradited back to the UK.

428 The view of the Australian delegate – *1988 Records* vol. II at 308. Forms of authorisation other than express authorisation, such as tacit authorisation implied from a failure to respond to a request, appear not to have been contemplated by article 17(3). It may, however, be met by a blanket prior authorisation. Gilmore supra note 402 at 189, footnote 65, points out that the Canadian government's practice has been not to grant permission but to express no objection should the requesting Party demonstrate reasonable grounds for such measures – citing *1988 Records* vol. II at 315. This implied blanket permission in the presence of reasonable suspicion was also adopted by the 1981 Agreement between the US and UK (cmnd 8470). Retrospective authorisation such as the 'consensual boarding' by the US Coastguard where the Coastguard boards with only the permission of the Master of the vessel and requests authorisation from the flag state only once arrest or seizure appear warranted, is not permitted in terms of article 17(3). Thus situations such as that reported in *United States v Hernandez* 655 F. Supp. 1069 (D. Puerto Rico 1987) where consent was not obtained from the Honduran authorities by the US Coastguard until two days after the initial boarding, will be in violation of article 17(3).

429 See the 'Expert Group Report', *1988 Records* vol. I at 28.

information grounding its request. These grounds may, given the differential in maritime law enforcement capacity, only be known to the requesting Party. But the right of flag states to refuse authorisation even if such grounds exist is reserved.

Article 17(4) sets out the types of action which may be taken by the interdicting Party once permission by the flag state has been given to go ahead. The flag state's right over the vessel is safeguarded by article 17(4) because it provides that permission must be given in terms of article 17(3) or in terms of treaties between the Parties or agreements or arrangements between the Parties governing the matter, before the interdicting Party can take the authorised action. Article 17(4) then highlights the disjunctive nature of the various processes which might be taken against the vessel: boarding; search; and – only if evidence of illicit traffic were found – further appropriate action with respect to vessel, persons and cargo.[430] Such further 'appropriate action' would, according to Harding, 'include putting into port and handing any persons found to be involved in the illicit traffic over to the authorities for prosecution and, if convicted, punishment.'[431] While reference to seizure of the vessel was deliberately omitted,[432] the use of the phrase 'inter alia' emphasises the flexibility of the provision and the fact that the Parties are free to agree to forms of action other than those specified.

6.9.5   General provisions

Although article 17 is largely silent on the procedural rules governing requests for authorisation and on the precise content of such requests, paragraphs 5 to 11 provide some detail as to constraints on interdiction action and the supply of information necessary to enable speedy action.

Article 17(5) requires Parties that take action in terms of article 17 as a whole to take into account factors such as safety of life at sea, the security of the vessel and its cargo, and the commercial and legal interests of the flag state or any other interested state. The duty to take account of these interests does

---

430 Statement of the Australian delegate, *1988 Records* vol. II at 308.

431 Supra note 427 at 492. He notes that the UK had made provision for the taking of such action through section 19 of the Criminal Justice (International Co-operation) Act, 1990, which in subsection (2) makes it an offence for a person on 'a British ship, a ship registered in another state which is a Party to the Convention, or an unregistered ship to: (a) have a controlled drug in his possession; or (b) be in any way knowingly concerned in the carrying or concealing of a controlled drug on the ship.'

432 Statement of the Australian delegate, *1988 Records* vol. II at 308.

not mean that their simple existence is a bar to action. The *1988 Commentary* points out that article 17 anticipates some prejudice to legitimate commercial interests from interdiction at sea.[433]

Article 17(6) is intended to meet Parties' concerns about liability.[434] It allows the flag state to subject its granting of permission for interdiction to any conditions to be agreed with the requesting Party.[435] These conditions should be consistent with the general obligation upon the flag state to co-operate provided for in article 17(1). But in reality the requested flag state can define the terms on which it is prepared to grant authorisation.[436] Precisely what the requesting Party will be liable for is undefined. Conditions may be applied making the requesting Party liable for 'damage to the vessel or its cargo or any third party, or injury to the crew, which may be caused in the course of, or as a result of, the boarding or search of the vessel or the taking of further appropriate action.'[437] Conditions applicable to the situation subsequent to the interdiction may also be applied. The *1988 Commentary* notes that these may include arrangements as to 'costs normally borne by the intervening state, restrictions on the use of information or evidence obtained, the treatment of nationals of the flag state, the reservation of rights to object, within a specific time frame to the continued exercise of jurisdiction over the vessel or persons on board, and restrictions on taking the vessel into the jurisdiction of a third Party.'[438] Article 17(6) also meets concerns expressed at the 1988 Conference that consent was unlikely to be forthcoming without some guarantee of compensation in case the search was unjustified.[439] It is the only provision that provides indirectly for what will happen when searches prove fruitless. Compensation for delay may be necessary, especially if a ship has been forced to put into port and unload its cargo.[440] Compensation may depend on the ab-

---

433 *1988 Commentary* at 330.

434 Statement of the Australian delegate – *1988 Records* vol. II at 308.

435 The UK's Criminal Justice (International Co-operation) Act, 1990, recognises this when it provides in section 20(3) that the Secretary of State may impose such conditions on law enforcement actions on the high seas against non-British ships as are necessary 'to give effect to any conditions or limitations imposed by the [authorising] state'.

436 *1988 Commentary* at 331.

437 *1988 Commentary* at 331.

438 *1988 Commentary* at 339.

439 See the statement of the Netherlands delegate, *1988 Records* vol. II at 268.

440 The Chilean delegation, in attempting to amend the draft article to include provision for mandatory compensation in the case of a fruitless search and for no compensation in the case of a successful search, noted that searches were certain to result in delays which would cost money through increased running costs, increased insurance costs,

sence of 'reasonable grounds' for interdiction. But compensation is subject entirely to agreement. Liability for damage and injury is not governed by the Convention. If compensation is claimed, it is not clear if it can be claimed from the authorising flag state as well as from the intervening state, because it is not clear whether in legal terms the interdicting Party acts as the agent of the authorising flag state or not.

The goal of article 17(7) is to expedite replies from the Parties from whom authorisations have been requested or data in respect of the registration of a vessel is sought.[441] It also obliges a state, upon becoming party to the Convention, to designate an authority, or authorities if necessary, to receive such requests and to communicate the identity or identities of these authorities through the Secretary-General to the other Parties within one month of designation.[442] What is contemplated here is a swift exchange of information through direct contact between governmental organs familiar with the authorisation process. The UN has assembled a list of designated authorities and their contact details for this purpose.[443] Parties may in practice communicate directly or through facilitative agencies like Interpol. They should avoid using authorities other than those designated.[444]

Article 17(8) obliges the interdicting Party to promptly inform the flag state concerned of the outcome of any action taken under the article. Article 17(8)'s aim is to stress and defend the interests of the flag state.[445]

Article 17(9) exhorts Parties to consider entering bilateral or regional agreements or arrangements for the purpose of implementing or reinforcing

---

time penalties and possible rejection of the cargo – *1988 Records* vol. II at 269.

441 Gilmore supra note 423 at 8 notes that the 1995 Council of Europe Agreement provides for communication of requests by modern means including telefax (article 19(1)), answerable 24 hours a day (article 6), with a four hour wait (article 7).

442 For example, the UK in section 20 of the Criminal Justice (International Co-operation) Act, 1990, has placed such responsibility on the Secretary of State.

443 Competent National Authorities Under the International Drug Control Treaties – published in the ST/NAR.3 series. Given their law enforcement character, it may be in a Party's interests to centralise the functions of the 'appropriate agency' of article 35(a) of the 1961 Convention and article 21(a) of the 1971 Convention, and the 'competent agencies' of article 9(1)(a) and article 17(7) of the 1988 Convention, in one organ.

444 The decision by British Customs authorities to board the Maltese registered MV *Simon De Danser* on the high seas without being granted permission by the correct Maltese authorities (in Malta's case the Attorney General), resulted in the collapse of a trial for the smuggling of £14 million pounds of cannabis – *The Guardian*, 5 February 1999.

445 See the 'Expert Group Report', *1988 Records* vol. I at 29.

effectiveness of article 17's provisions. Its intention is to build upon the successes of the existing bilateral agreements saved by article 17(4).[446] These agreements can provide guidance in respect of the implementation of article 17 in a range of matters where no guidance is provided, including: choice of language for requests; form and content of requests; reasons for refusal of requests; informing masters of flag vessels of the implications of article 17 and any obligation on these masters to co-operate with the intervening state's boarding party; and appropriate training of personnel in making and responding to requests and in engaging in interdiction. Parties have responded to article 17(9) by concluding more elaborate agreements based on article 17.[447]

Article 17(10) restricts the types of vessels and aircraft that may be used in article 17(4)'s interdiction operations to warships or military aircraft, or other ships and aircraft clearly marked and distinguishable as authorised government ships and aircraft.[448]

Article 17(11) is a non-derogation provision that reserves the rights, duties and exercise of jurisdiction enjoyed by coastal states under the international

---

446 The best known of these is the 1981 agreement between the US and UK – 13 November 1981 Exchange of Notes concerning Co-operation in the Suppression of the Unlawful Importation of Narcotic Drugs into the United States (cmnd 8470, 1981). In terms of paragraph 1 of this agreement the UK gives blanket permission to the US to board private UK flag vessels if the US authorities have a reasonable belief that such vessels are carrying drugs for illicit importation into the US. By 1989, this permission had resulted in the seizure of 47 vessels, 322 arrests and confiscation of 913 233 lbs of cannabis, 29 961 lbs of hashish and 659 lbs of cocaine; see generally W.C. Gilmore, 'Narcotics interdiction at sea: UK-US co-operation' (1989) 15 *Commonwealth Law Bulletin* 1480-1497.

447 The 1995 Council of Europe Agreement, for example, is essentially an implementation agreement – see *Agreement on Illicit Traffic by Sea Implementing Article 17 of the United Nations Convention Against Illicit Traffic in Narcotic Drugs and Psychotropic Substances and Explanatory Report* (Council of Europe Publishing, Strasbourg, 1996). Gilmore supra note 423 at 4 notes that article 17(9) and other relevant provisions of the 1988 Convention acted as a frame of reference for the drafters of the 1995 Council of Europe Agreement. The 1995 Agreement's subject matter jurisdiction is explicitly confined in article 1(c) to the offences in article 3(1) of the 1988 Convention and in terms of article 27(1) only Parties to the 1988 Convention may participate in the 1995 Agreement. The substance of the 1995 Agreement provides, however, for far more detailed guidance than article 17 of the 1988 Convention. Thus, for example, articles 19, 20 and 21 detail the type of information each request should contain, while article 17(5) provides for a duty to inform owners and masters of vessels of the implications of the agreement to authorise boarding.

448 See also articles 107 and 111(5) of the 1982 Convention on the Law of the Sea which use the same language and have the same meaning.

law of the sea. It provides that any action taken under article 17 as a whole and not just paragraph 3, must respect the need not to interfere with or affect these rights, duties and privileges. Coastal states enjoy complete sovereignty over their territorial waters, and in their contiguous zones they enjoy exclusive rights in respect of matters relating to customs, taxation, health and immigration. Their rights in their EEZs are, as noted above in the discussion of article 17(3), controversial. Some delegations to the 1988 Conference stated that coastal states only have the same law enforcement rights in the EEZ as all states have on the high seas,[449] while others insisted that coastal states did not have the right to prevent other states from taking action against drug traffickers within their EEZs.[450] This issue remains controversial, but if coastal states do have a right of refusal over law enforcement operations by third party states in their EEZs as some states insist they do,[451] then they must be under a corollary duty to police this zone effectively.

6.9.6   Law enforcement co-operation at sea in conclusion

Regulation of the interdiction of drug trafficking at sea is a sensitive issue, which explains why article 17 expanded the net of international regulation of maritime drug law enforcement slowly and in a piecemeal fashion. Although the 1988 Convention sewed up some of the bigger holes in the net, holes still exist. Perhaps the biggest is the question of the exclusive criminal jurisdiction of coastal states in their contiguous zones and even more controversially in their EEZs. There was no consensus on this issue in 1988, and article 17 simply fudges it. But there are other holes. For example, article 17 says nothing about the use of force in the interdiction of foreign vessels,[452] and the 1988 Convention does not apply to vessels registered with non-parties. Moreover, the 1988 Convention makes no provision for international co-operation within the territorial sea. Consumer states, such as the United States, have lead the way in their domestic law in making provision for their own consensual law enforcement

---

449 See the statement of the Netherlands delegate, *1988 Records* vol. II at 271.
450 See the statement of the US delegate, who cited article 58(2) and its references to articles 88 to 115 and particularly articles 92, 94 and 108(1) and (2) of the 1982 Law of the Sea Convention in support of this submission – *1988 Records* vol. II at 272.
451 See the statement of the Indian delegate, *1988 Records* vol. II at 309 at 315.
452 On the problems associated with the use of force see Gilmore supra note 446 at 1495. Gilmore supra note 423 notes that the 1995 Council of Europe Agreement in article 12(1)(d) restricts the use of force to the minimum necessary.

activities in the territorial seas of other states.[453] Such innovative state practice has lead the development of international treaty law with respect to maritime drug law enforcement in the past, and seems likely to continue to do so. What inhibits the growth of the system is the fact that many Parties do not have the maritime law enforcement capacity to engage in maritime drug law enforcement. Some are cast permanently in the role of requested Party. Thus far, innovative provisions like article 17(3) of the 1988 Convention, by providing for the exercise of jurisdiction by consent,[454] continue to respect the formal sovereign equality of states. The INCB suggested in 1996, however, that the extension of the provisions relating to maritime interdiction to include precursors, and a right of visit as is provided in cases of piracy, slavery and non-authorised radio emissions, are the next steps in the development of this area of drug law

453 An example is the 1986 Maritime Drug Law Enforcement Act 46 USC section 1903 (c)(E), which requires the consent of the coastal state. Gilmore supra note 402 at 186, footnote 41, notes that the US has concluded extensive bilateral agreements for this purpose, and gives as an example the SEARIDER programme agreement with the Bahamas described by the Bahamian Ministry of National Security in *A Report on the Traffic in Cocaine and Marijuana Affecting the Bahamas in 1987 and 1988* (1989: Government of the Bahamas), p.84 as follows: 'The joint Royal Bahamas Defence Force US Coast Guard Sea Rider programme was formulated on 19 January 1986 and provides for the embarkment of a member of the RBDF aboard selected USCG Cutters operating in international waters surrounding the Bahamas. The embarked RBDF officials have the authority to authorise the US Coast Guard Cutters to enter Bahamian territorial waters to board, search and if evidence warrants, seize US, stateless or third nation vessels. Also to board, search and seize Bahamian vessels on the high seas if warranted.' The UK's Criminal Justice (International Co-operation) Act, 1990, section 20(6) authorises the exercise of law enforcement authority with the consent of the coastal state.

454 Gilmore supra note 423 at 191. Non-consensual means such as hotpursuit are thus still resorted to and expanded upon when the flag-state is not a Party to the 1988 Convention, or is unwilling to consent to interdiction, or for pragmatic reasons is simply not consulted. Principles of criminal jurisdiction at sea such as the right of hot pursuit exercised by coastal states and protected by article 17(11) may suffice. See, for example, *R v Mills* 1995 Croyden Crown Court unreported (see D.J. Harris, *Cases and Materials on International Law* London, (5th edn, Sweet and Maxwell, London, 1998), at p. 443), where hot pursuit was used to establish the constructive presence of the 'Poseidon', a vessel registered in St Vincent, in the UK's territorial waters, even though the 'Poseidon' never left international waters, and its only link was to a UK registered fishing vessel that sailed to a UK port after a cargo of cannabis worth 24 million pounds had been transferred to it from the 'Poseidon'. See generally W.C. Gilmore, 'Hot pursuit: the case of *R v Mills and others* (1995) 44 ICLQ 949. The right of hotpursuit has also been extended to 'extended constructive presence operations' in Italy (*Re Pulos* 77 ILR no.587) and Canada (*R v Sunila and Solayman* (1986) 28 DLR 4th 450).

enforcement.[455] The latter implies that a flag state's consent is going to become less important in the future, and thus, by extension, so is the sovereign equality of states. Many states will not welcome such developments.

Sensitive to the difficulties of maritime dug law enforcement, the UN has concentrated on helping Parties to perform their existing obligations. The CND has established a UN Working Group on Maritime Co-operation to promote implementation of the 1988 Convention's articles relating to law enforcement at sea.[456] The Working Group has attempted to flesh out article 17's provisions by, for example, providing for the form and content of article 17(3) requests for authorisation.[457] The UN could well, however, play a more proactive role by helping poorer Parties through technical assistance to develop their own autonomous maritime law enforcement capability. This would help to ensure that international law does not find itself adrift somewhere between the sovereignty concerns of developing states and the developing maritime law enforcement capacities of drug consumer states.

---

455 The *Report of the International Narcotics Control Board for 1996* UN Doc. E/INCB/ 1996/1, p. 10. The *1988 Commentary* at 339 notes that steps taken by states providing for advance authorisation for boarding and related measures, such as the 1991 Treaty between Italy and Spain, rely on a concept of agency within the context of the preferential jurisdiction of the flag state. The *Commentary* concedes, however, that new treaties between Parties to the 1988 Convention would be necessary to accommodate this simplification of article 17.

456 CND Res. 3(XXXXVI), UN Doc. E/CN.7/1993/L.5/Rev.1 5 April 1993; see generally Gilmore supra note 423 at 14. The Working Group met in September 1994 and February 1995 and its Report was endorsed by the CND in Res. 8(XXXVIII), Official Records of the ECOSOC, 1995, Supp. No.9 (E/1995/29), Chp. XII, Sec. A. An Expert Group met in February 1996 to develop training and technical assistance in the context of article 17 and further Expert Group meetings were held in October 1996 and January 1997 to elaborate a draft training guide for maritime law enforcement – UNDCP/HONLAC/ 1997/2, p. 7.

457 Recommendation 3 of the Working Group's Report recommends that the requesting Party provide the following information: its identity and the identity of the authority issuing the request and the agency taking the measures; a description of the vessel including name, flag and port of registration and other relevant information; known details concerning voyage and crew; sighting information and weather report; reason for request; intended action; other relevant information; action requested by the intervening state including if required confirmation of vessel registry and permission to board and search, together with time constraints.

6.10   LAW ENFORCEMENT IN FREE TRADE ZONES AND FREE PORTS

Free trade zones and free ports handle large quantities of goods and large numbers of persons. They are particularly vulnerable to the illicit traffic because although they fall within a particular Party's criminal jurisdiction, customs controls tend to be relaxed,[458] which presents opportunities for traffickers to store contraband and to smuggle it across international borders.[459] Article 18 of the 1988 Convention, entitled 'Free Trade Zones and Free Ports', attempts to ensure that they do not become a haven for traffickers. Weak provisions in the earlier conventions regulate free ports and zones, but they do not apply directly to the illicit traffic.[460] Article 18 is something of an improvement.

Article 18(1) sets up a general obligation on Parties to ensure that the measures they use against the illicit traffic[461] in free trade zones and free ports are at least as stringent as those they apply to the rest of their territory. The provision applies to traffic in narcotic drugs and psychotropic substances as well as tabled substances and the INCB has been particularly diligent in emphasising the application of these measures to precursors.[462]

Article 18(2) is a best efforts provision, obliging the Parties to endeavour to take a number of steps against the illicit traffic within free trade zones and free ports. Article 18(2)(a) places Parties under a duty to make a bona fide attempt to monitor the movement of goods and persons in these areas, and, to that end, to empower their competent authorities to perform search operations. It specifies that these authorities must be empowered to search a comprehensive list of potential hiding places including cargoes and incoming and outgoing

---

458 *1988 Commentary* at 346.

459 For example, Colon Free Zone (CFZ) in Panama (including the Free Port of Coco Solo), the largest free trade zone in the Americas, is heavily used for maritime drug transshipment and money laundering operations – see the NNICC supra note 379 at 11.

460 Article 31(2) of the 1961 Convention and article 12(3)(a) of the 1971 Convention. Annex F1 of the International Convention on the Simplification and Harmonisation of Customs Procedures, 950 UNTS 13561, sets out guidelines for the monitoring of drugs and precursors in free zones.

461 Article 1(m) defines this as 'the offences set forth in article 3, paragraphs 1 and 2.'

462 See, for example, the *Report of the International Narcotics Control Board for 1994*, UN Doc. E/INCB/1995/1, p. 30 where the INCB noted that such measures were being taken in Hong Kong and the United Arab Emirates. The ECOSOC underlined in Resolution 29 of 1992 the necessity of taking such measures in accordance with article 18 in respect of precursors and essential chemicals, and emphasised in Resolution 20 of 1995 the necessity of taking measures to control diversion of these substances when they leave or enter these areas.

vessels, pleasure craft and fishing vessels, as well as aircraft and vehicles. Searches of individuals such as crew members, passengers and personal baggage are, however, limited to appropriate situations, so as to avoid legal problems with individual rights and the practical difficulties associated with indiscriminate or blanket searches.[463] Article 18(2)(b) places Parties under a duty to make a bona fide attempt to establish and maintain a system to detect consignments suspected of containing contraband[464] passing into and out of free trade zones and free ports. Article 18(2)(c) places Parties under a duty to make a bona fide attempt to establish and maintain surveillance systems[465] in harbour and dock areas and at airports and border control points in free trade zones and free ports.

Article 18's obvious weakness is that its more detailed provisions in paragraph 2 are directive rather than mandatory. It does little to overcome the practical problem of regulating zones that are by definition unregulated. Commercial opportunities make changing the legal characters of these areas through international law unlikely.

6.11   THE PREVENTION OF THE USE OF THE MAILS

In the UN system, control of illicit use of the mail had until the conclusion of the 1988 Convention been regulated entirely by the Conventions of the Universal Postal Union (UPU),[466] a specialised UN agency. The UN's 1987 Compre-

---

463 See the 'Expert Group Report', *1988 Records* vol. I at 29. The Bolivian delegate in Committee II proposed a provision that searches 'respect human rights and be without discrimination on the basis of race, nationality, religion or similar reasons' because he believed that nationals of cocaine producing countries tended to be subject to indiscriminate and undignified searches. His amendment was rejected on the basis that the 1988 Convention would provide a blanket provision for such protections, but in fact, it does not – see generally *1988 Records* vol. II at 212 and 215.

464 Narcotic drugs, psychotropic substances and the substances in Table I and Table II.

465 These would include patrols, guard towers, electronic surveillance systems etc.

466 Thus, for example, article 13 of the 1984 Universal Postal Convention, 611 UNTS 8844, reads: 'The governments of member countries shall undertake to adopt, or to propose to the legislature of their countries, the necessary measures: ... e) for preventing and, if necessary punishing the insertion in postal items of narcotics and psychotropic substances ... where the insertion has not been expressly authorised by the Convention or the Agreements.' Article 26(5)(1) of the 1996 Convention reiterated this provision but also made provision that in no circumstances could items containing such substances be returned to sender or delivered to the addressee, thus causing problems for controlled delivery. See generally F. Malekian, *International Criminal Law: The Legal and Critical Analysis of International Crimes*, Volume II (Uppsala UP, Uppsala, 1991), pp. 376-398.

hensive Multidisciplinary Outline targets 'controls over use of the international mails for drug trafficking' because of the discovery by customs services that the mails were being used for trafficking despite the existing controls in the UPU's Conventions.[467] Postal services are a boon to smugglers of low volume high value substances like LSD, although multiple parcel-postings of bulky items like cannabis is also common. Interdiction is problematic because of high volume and legal constraints. An example of these legal constraints is that while states of origin and states of destination of the mailed item are free to open it if they suspect it contains drugs as long as they satisfy their own domestic law, transit states are unable to do so in terms of the right of freedom of transit enshrined in article 1 of the UPU Convention. Thus it was felt necessary to insert a provision in the 1988 Convention to provide for ways of overcoming such problems and for preventing the use of the post for trafficking generally.[468] Entitled 'The Use of the Mails', article 19, as with many of the other provisions in the 1988 Convention for law enforcement, moves from the general to the particular.

Article 19(1) sets out the basic obligation on the Parties to adopt measures to suppress the use of 'the mails' by the illicit traffic[469] and to co-operate to achieve this purpose. This obligation is qualified in two ways, viz.: i) it must conform to the Parties' existing obligations under the UPU's Conventions, for example freedom of transit under article 1 of the UPU Convention; and ii) it is subject to the basic principles of the Parties' domestic legal systems. The latter qualification leaves the Parties free to choose how to implement article 19(1). They may adopt or amend legislation or use some other measure to provide for article 19(1)'s implementation. The only ambiguous element of article 19(1) is its scope. The *1988 Commentary* notes that application of this provision to 'the mails' must take account of the development of delivery systems run by private commercial courier or express parcel organisations, and cannot be interpreted so as to be limited to traditionally state owned postal services.[470] It thus must include both 'public postal services and private operations which

---

467   Target 27, paragraph 321, *Declaration of the International Conference on Drug Abuse and Illicit Trafficking and Comprehensive Multidisciplinary Outline of Future Activities in Drug Abuse Control*, UN Publication St/Nar/14, UN Sales No.E.88.XI.1, (New York, 1988), p. 69.

468   The Netherlands pointed out that in this narrow context illicit traffic must in effect mean illicit transport – 8/9/1993, *Multilateral Treaties Adopted* (UN, New York, 1997), p. 305.

469   Article 1(m) defines this as 'the offences set forth in article 3, paragraphs 1 and 2.'

470   *1988 Commentary* at 353.

run comparable services'.[471] Other express delivery services may fall outside the scope of this article but will fall under article 15's provisions in respect of commercial carriers.[472]

Article 19(2) sets out specific measures to be undertaken by the Parties in amplification of article 19(1)'s obligation. These specific measures must also comply with a Party's obligations under the UPU's Conventions and its basic domestic legal principles, which may present problems for the use of certain investigative techniques like controlled delivery.[473]

The measures listed are not a numerus clausus. Article 19(2)(a) requires the Parties to co-ordinate their actions in thwarting illicit traffickers' use of the mails. Co-ordination can take place at the national level among postal services, police and customs. It may also involve international co-ordination among comparable services, which will require the rapid communication of information between authorities as provided for in article 9(1)(b)(iii).

Article 19(2)(b) requires the Parties to use 'authorised law enforcement personnel'[474] to initiate and sustain investigative and control techniques[475]

---

471 *1988 Commentary* at 353.

472 The *1988 Commentary* at 353 points out that article 1(d)'s definition of 'commercial carrier' includes 'any person … engaged in transporting …mails for remuneration.' A private aircraft contracted to transport post trans-nationally will thus be subject to both article 19 and 15.

473 The *1988 Commentary* at 356 points out that article 11(3) makes provision for clean controlled deliveries. These necessitate interference with the postal item in violation of the UPU's principle of freedom of transit.

474 The *1988 Commentary* at 355 points out that this will preclude insistence by a Party that only postal services personnel may deal with such matters.

475 According to the French delegation, investigative techniques imply searches of the mail through the use of non-invasive sensing devices, sniffer dogs, X-rays, ion-devices etc., while control techniques are those used to detect illicit substances in the mails; the techniques supplement each other – *1988 Records* vol. II at 213. The *1988 Commentary* at 358 praises the utility of 'profiling' techniques such as using risk indicators, identified on the basis of prior practical experience, in an effort to identify suspect consignments before searching them. The US in its *Manual for Compliance with the United Nations Convention against Illicit Traffic in narcotic Drugs and Psychotropic Substances* (Washington, Dept of Justice, 1992), p. 59, notes that profiling takes into account factors such as size and shape, method of sealing, manner of addressing, unusual or false names or addresses, unusual smells, destination, and any intelligence about the package. Once identified, non-invasive search techniques may be used before actual opening.

designed to detect illicit consignments of contraband[476] in the mails. Typically these will involve the detection of illicit substances in suspicious mail items, and the identification of the item, its origin and destination. If its destination is within national territory then application for a search warrant should be made and the usual procedures followed. An example of such a control technique, which also falls under the general obligation in article 19(2)(a) to co-ordinate action, occurs when mail containing contraband is discovered in transit by the authorities of a Party to the Universal Postal Convention who cannot in terms of article 1 of that Convention open the mail even if they have a search warrant. The authorities of the discovering Party would, in terms of article 19(2)(a) of the 1988 Convention, be under an obligation in these circumstances to notify the authorities of the state of destination as soon as possible and to verify the origin of the item, so that action can be taken by the authorities in the state of destination.[477]

Article 19(2)(c) requires the Parties to take legislative steps to make possible the use of suitable methods to obtain evidence required for judicial proceedings against traffickers. These steps may include the enactment of laws enabling the interception and opening of postal items, or enabling the gathering and use of evidence gleaned from investigative mechanisms such as x-ray machines.

Article 19 demands an integrated law enforcement system directed at one aspect of the illicit traffic – its use of the mail. It gives little detail as to the precise modalities of this system. Guidance may be had from the explanation and recommended courses of action in the UN's 1987 Comprehensive Multidisciplinary Outline, but further development of such systems dealing with isolated aspects of the traffic is likely to be ongoing and progressively more specialised. The UPU and WCO have taken steps towards removing legal and administrative impediments to policing the mail.[478]

---

476 It must be noted that the provision relates to 'illicit' consignments of narcotic drugs, psychotropic substances and substances in Table I and Table II, and not just any consignments of these substances, a qualification introduced to prevent Parties from having to interfere in the large scale commercial use of the mail to transmit licit consignments of these substances – see the statements of the British delegate, *1988 Records* vol. II at 213-214.

477 Chp.1, sec. A, para. 322 of the 1987 Comprehensive Multidisciplinary Outline – see *Declaration of the International Conference on Drug Abuse and Illicit Trafficking and Comprehensive Multidisciplinary Outline of Future Activities in Drug Abuse Control* UN Publication St/Nar/14, UN Sales No.E.88.XI.1, (New York, 1988).

478 *1988 Commentary* at 356-357.

6.12   SPECIFIC DRUG LAW ENFORCEMENT MEASURES IN CONCLUSION

Like the drug conventions' provisions for general co-operation on law enforcement examined in Chapter Five, the drug conventions' provisions for specific law enforcement measures examined above, perform a dual function. They exist to overcome problems with national drug law enforcement by creating domestic uniformity in policing and to overcome problems with extraterritorial law enforcement through international co-operation in policing.

Turning to the provenance of these specific law enforcement measures, it is clear that they have their roots in the successful practices of consumer states, such as the United States, concerned with suppressing drug supply at source or interdicting chains of supply. Many of these practices have been developed informally by law enforcement agents at the operational level, and legitimised in domestic legislation. However, the dissemination of these practices has been a macro-level operation. International law has been used as a mechanism for globalising these practices to increase the pressure on the illicit traffic. As with the general forms of co-operation, the crystallisation of these strategies and tactics into international legal provisions has been a political process conducted by senior government officials concerned as much with overcoming state sovereignty as overcoming the illicit traffic. Again they have been forced to try to overcome what Nadelmann calls the central paradox of international law enforcement, '[t]he need for law enforcement agents to perform outside their nation's borders a function that relies primarily on the sovereign powers of the state.'[479] A good example of this paradox in operation is the difficulty surrounding the adoption of article 17(3) of the 1988 Convention, concerned with the interdiction of suspicious foreign flag vessels on the high seas. While article 17(3) overcomes sovereignty through the provision for consensual interdiction and directs the necessary operational co-operation at the meso-level, it provides little guidance for direct police, naval or coastguard co-operation at the micro-level. Because of the political barriers they must overcome the drug conventions impose a top-down law enforcement model. The detail of legal obligation becomes less dense the lower the level of co-operation and it is thus almost unavoidable that their provisions tend to be weaker than some bilateral or domestic provisions.

Given the way the process necessary for its adoption has shaped them, it was inevitable that the specific law enforcement provisions of the drug conven-

---

479 Supra note 256 at 247.

tions would disappoint. In particular, the 1988 Convention, dedicated, unlike the earlier conventions, to law enforcement, has been criticised as not being strict enough.[480] From this perspective, a number of weaknesses reveal themselves.

First, the specific law enforcement provisions are frequently limited by domestic limitation clauses and the necessity to respect sovereignty, which dilutes their impact.

Second, the specific law enforcement provisions are cobbled together in an unsystematic way. The 1988 Convention, in particular, does not integrate its various law enforcement measures well. It takes specific aspects of the trafficking problem and deals with each in some degree of isolation from the others with the result that national legislation in many less zealous state participants in the international drug war still tends generally to be poorly integrated.[481]

Third, the drug conventions' specific law enforcement measures are not as comprehensive as they could have been. For example, although the "soft" law of the UN's 1987 Comprehensive Multidisciplinary Outline targets strategies and tactics for the disruption of major trafficking networks, admissibility of evidence in samples of bulk seizures of drugs, tightening of controls of movement through official points of entry, strengthening of external border controls and of mutual assistance machinery within economic unions of sovereign states, and surveillance of land, water and air approaches to national frontiers,[482] these targets have not been transformed into "hard" law in the drug conventions. Other areas that might have been developed include strengthening and combining immigration and border controls, profiling and monitoring recent immigrants, increasing the use of new technologies such as computerised scanner technology, consolidating and extending anti-money laundering measures, developing witness protection programmes, legalising more invasive methods of surveillance such as wire taps, legalising undercover operations and deploying greater resources both human and material.[483]

---

480 See generally Catino supra note 99 at 437-440.
481 Bassiouni supra note 202 at 331.
482 Targets 17, 21, 24, 25 and 26 respectively, *Declaration of the International Conference on Drug Abuse and Illicit Trafficking and Comprehensive Multidisciplinary Outline of Future Activities in Drug Abuse Control* (1988) UN Publication St/Nar/14, UN Sales No.E.88.XI.1, (New York, 1988), at pp. 52, 59, 64, 67, 67 respectively.
483 See generally P. Williams and E.U. Savona (eds), *The United Nations and Transnational Organized Crime* (Frank Cass, London, 1996), pp. 130-136 where these developments were regarded as essential to combat organised crime.

It may be that provisions overcoming sovereign reluctance, systematising specific law enforcement measures and expanding the scope of these measures are more easily agreed upon in a regional or sub-regional agreement such as the Schengen Convention.[484] Yet focusing on what might have been, detracts from examining the full implications of the existing law. The contrast between the earlier conventions' bland law enforcement provisions which emphasise co-operation and little else, and the 1988 Convention's law enforcement provisions which specify a varied range of law enforcement responses to the illicit traffic, indicates the coming of age of drug law enforcement in international law. The generally more hostile atmosphere in international society towards illicit drug trafficking is reflected in the substance of the law enforcement provisions of the 1988 Convention, and nowhere is the development of international law to fight a global war on drugs more obvious. States have supported the adoption of potent measures to eliminate drug production, interdict chains of supply, prise open sanctuaries for money laundering and confiscate as much as possible. In the period post-1988 the issue for drug law enforcement "hawks" has become whether states are prepared to apply these paper rules. In this period the issue for drug law enforcement "doves" has become the realisation that international drug control law provides few human rights protections to those subject to its formidable array of legal weapons.

---

[484] Convention Applying the Schengen Agreement of 14 June 1985 between the Governments of the States of the Benelux Economic Union, the Federal Republic of Germany and the French Republic, on the Gradual Abolition of Checks at Their Common Borders, in force 19 June 1990. Thus, for example, article 71(3) obliges Parties to strengthen their external border controls in order to combat drug smuggling, and provides specifically for the release of personnel and recourse to modern drug detection methods and sniffer-dogs for this purpose. Article 7(2) provides for the surveillance of places known to be used for drug trafficking.

THE SUPERVISION AND IMPLEMENTATION OF
THE PENAL ASPECTS OF THE DRUG CONVENTIONS

7.1 INTRODUCTION

Various organisations supervise and execute the international legal system suppressing illicit drugs, some from within the United Nations organisational family, and others from outside. The key organisations from within the UN system are the specialist drug control organs that derive their authority from the international drug conventions and the general UN bodies that derive their authority from the UN Charter and the decisions of ECOSOC. Important organisations from outside the UN system include Interpol and significant regional and national drug control organs. The aim of this chapter is to give the reader some idea of: (i) the nature and function of these organisations; (ii) their role in the supervision of the drug conventions; and (iii) their role in the execution of the illicit drug control system against Parties to the system and non-parties. The underlying theme of this examination is an assessment of the effectiveness of these organisations in the implementation of illicit drug control internationally.

7.2 UNITED NATIONS DRUG CONTROL ORGANS

7.2.1 General

The international drug control system is a system in which the UN is competent and the organs controlling the system fall within the UN's framework.[1] Most of these organs are forums for debate and information exchange. While some deliver services, they are not usually directly involved in law enforcement

---

1   Paragraph eleven of the Preamble of the 1988 Convention.

operations.[2] But they have played and continue to play an important role in the preparation and implementation of the legal foundations of the illicit drug control system. Ostensibly neutral, it would, however, be naive to believe that they act in an entirely neutral manner. The history of international drug control has shown that these organs are often less agents in their own right than instruments being used by competing national interests. A useful approach to examining the system is to work downwards from its upper reaches, a movement of focus from general political powers to specific technical powers.

7.2.2   ECOSOC[3]

As a non-legislative framework for discussion and recommendation to UN member states about the illicit drug problem, ECOSOC plays a nominal role in the drug control system. In terms of article 62 of the UN Charter, ECOSOC initiates studies, drafts conventions and calls conferences on the illicit drug problem. Article 68 of the UN Charter gives it the power to set up development programmes and commissions to perform its functions, one of which is to implement UN drug policy.[4] Using this power, ECOSOC functions as a rather distant supervisor of the UN drug control system. Its relationship to the CND is discussed below, but it is important to note here that the CND has more effective power in the sphere of drug control than ECOSOC itself and has assumed a functional independence.[5] ECOSOC is kept sporadically informed by the INCB's annual reports of the drug control situation and state compliance with the drug conventions.

7.2.3   The United Nations Commission on Narcotic Drugs (CND)[6]

The CND is the central policy making body within the UN dealing with drug control. Established in 1946 as a functional commission of ECOSOC, the CND

---

2   M. Anderson, *Policing the World* (Clarendon, Oxford, 1989) p. 2.
3   See generally S.K. Chatterjee, *Legal Aspects of International Drug Control* (Nijhoff, Dordrecht, 1981), pp. 228-233.
4   In terms of article 66 of the UN Charter, ECOSOC is required to carry out General Assembly recommendations with respect to drugs. ECOSOC has, in terms of article 71 of the UN Charter, a formal consultative relationship with IGOs and NGOs involved in illicit drug control.
5   Chatterjee supra note 3 at 232.
6   See generally H.L. May, 'Twenty years of narcotics control under the United Nations' (1966) 18 *Bulletin on Narcotics* 4-11; Chatterjee supra note 3 at 234-256.

formally operates under ECOSOC's authority and direction to assist ECOSOC in carrying out its UN Charter functions.[7] What gives the CND independence, however, is the explicit functional role provided for it by the drug conventions.[8] In this role it considers the changing nature and control of the illicit drug traffic, promotes international agreements for that control, plays a part in the exchange of related information and maintains links with the other international drug control organs. Its decisions remain subject to ECOSOC confirmation unless it has been given a specific function under the drug conventions.

The CND tends to be representative of the opinions of governments with a stake in international drug control because CND members are mainly government representatives whose appointment is not subject to UN approval. The CND's representational base has been broadened from 15 in 1946 to 53 in 1991 in order to keep pace with the global expansion of drug markets. Delegates have a wide variety of backgrounds and may include professional diplomats and health professionals, but significant numbers have law enforcement experience. Any UN member may be requested to participate in the CND's deliberations when an issue to be discussed concerns that state. As a functional commission of ECOSOC the CND must hold at least one session annually, and it meets once a year for three weeks in Vienna. The CND reports to ECOSOC on the work of each session and when making a recommendation does so in the form of a draft resolution of ECOSOC. The CND is heavily reliant on the UNDCP (United Nations Drug Control Programme) for administrative and technical support.

The CND's remit within the UN structure is to advise ECOSOC on all matters relating to drug control, supervision of the application of the drug conventions and the development of international drug control law.[9] It also considers any changes that may be required in the existing international drug control system. It reviews the implementation of the General Assembly's various Action Plans on Drug Abuse Control, governs the UNDCP, and approves the budget of the technical assistance programme of the Fund of UNDCP.

The CND, in addition, has a number of specific functions under the drug conventions. In terms of article 8 of the 1961 Convention (as amended) and article 17 of the 1971 Convention, the CND considers all matters affecting the

---

7   ECOSOC Resolution I (IX) amended by 199 (VIII). Article 62 of the Charter provides ECOSOC with a general authority to impose functions on the CND.

8   For example, under article 5 of the 1961 Convention the Parties entrust to the CND and INCB the functions assigned to them under the Convention.

9   ECOSOC Resolution 38 of 1991 and General Assembly Resolution 46/185 C, section XVI.

conventions' aim of suppression of the illicit traffic and the implementation of their provisions relating to the illicit traffic, and makes appropriate recommendations. The 1988 Convention makes similar provision in article 21, entitled 'Functions of the Commission'. Article 21's opening wording provides that the CND is authorised to consider all matters pertaining to the aims of the 1988 Convention. Against this broad supervisory role, article 21 then sets out matters of particular concern. Article 21(a) obliges the CND to review the operation of the 1988 Convention on the basis of the information submitted to it by Parties in accordance with article 20. Article 21(b) allows the CND to make suggestions and general recommendations based on the examination of the information it receives from the Parties. Article 21(c) allows the CND to call the attention of the INCB to any matters that may be relevant to the INCB's functions.[10] Article 21(d) obliges the CND to take appropriate action on any matter referred to it by the INCB under article 22(1)(b). Article 21(e) allows the CND to amend Table I and Table II, in conformity with the procedures laid down in article 12. Article 21(f) allows the CND to draw the attention of non-parties to decisions and recommendations that it adopts in terms of the 1988 Convention, with a view to their considering taking appropriate action.

In carrying out its functions, the CND reviews and analyses the global illicit drug control situation and monitors application of the drug conventions. The CND and the UNDCP have since 1988 taken a number of steps to facilitate the implementation of the 1988 Convention, in particular with respect to mutual legal assistance, money-laundering, control of precursors, and illicit traffic by sea. Supervision of the implementation of the 1988 Convention was considered by its authors to be politically sensitive, which explains why this function has been left in the hands of the CND, a politically representative body, and not the INCB, a technical body. The CND has also become increasingly involved in the furnishing of technical assistance to states with drug control problems either through financial assistance or training.[11]

---

10 The *Commentary on the United Nations Convention Against Illicit Traffic in Narcotic Drugs and Psychotropic Substances, 1988* (New York, 1998) UN Doc. E/CN.7/590; UN Publication Sales No.E.98.XI.5, (hereinafter the *1988 Commentary*), p. 373, notes that the INCB has, in particular, an interest in compliance with provisions of a technical nature such as articles 12, 13 and 16.

11 In terms of article 14bis of the 1961 Convention.

7.2.4   Subordinate regional bodies of the CND

In order to encourage closer regional collaboration in drug law enforcement, the CND has established a number of subordinate regional bodies. In 1974, it established the Sub-commission on Illicit Drug Traffic and Related Matters in the Near and Middle East, and the Meeting of Heads of National Drug Law Enforcement Agencies (HONLEA), Asia and the Pacific. Other HONLEA meetings followed. HONLEA, Africa, met in 1985; HONLEA, Latin America and the Caribbean, met in 1987; and HONLEA, Europe, met in 1990. International HONLEA meetings also take place. Membership in HONLEA is based on membership in ECOSOC's regional commissions; membership in the Sub-commission on Illicit Drug Traffic is recommended by the CND and approved by ECOSOC. Observers from states outside the regions and from IGOs with a mandate in drug law enforcement or related areas attend the meetings of these subordinate bodies. When they meet these bodies identify priority issues facing drug law enforcement agencies in each region. After discussion in working groups, recommendations are prepared for government action and participants report on action taken in terms of recommendations adopted at previous meetings. The recommendations adopted are then brought to the attention of the CND. Drawing senior national law enforcement personnel directly into a global network of drug control organisations serves to identify problems and disseminate solutions globally, but it also serves the important political purpose of strengthening the links between national drug control organs and the international drug control system.

7.2.5   The United Nations Drug Control Programme (UNDCP)

An amalgamation of the Division of Narcotic Drugs or DND, the Fund for Drug Abuse Control and the INCB's Secretariat, the UNDCP was established by the General Assembly in 1990[12] as the main unit of the UN Secretariat responsible for the co-ordination and direction of UN action against illicit drugs. Although since 1997 it has fallen under the management of the UN Office for Drug Control and Crime Prevention (ODCCP), it has jealously guarded its independent existence within the UN's new structures.

The enormous influence of the UNDCP in the international drug control system stems from the wide variety of functions it performs. At a formal level,

---

12   General Assembly Resolution 45/179, 21 December 1990.

it carries out most of the duties assigned to the Secretary-General under the drug conventions and UN resolutions. It also provides administrative support for the CND, for HONLEA meetings and for the INCB. In supporting the CND, for example, it prepares much of the CND's documentation, its senior officials attend CND meetings, many CND resolutions and draft conventions originate with it, and it follows up on the CND's decisions. The UNDCP has also become heavily involved in advising Parties concerning accession to and implementation of the drug conventions, and in giving them legal assistance in drafting national laws. In this role it has fostered the wave of legislative activity that took place subsequent to the conclusion of the 1988 Convention. Approximately ten percent of the UNDCP's budget is funded by the UN directly and is used for general legal responsibilities, such as treaty implementation.[13] The remaining ninety percent is supplied by the 'Fund of the UNDCP',[14] which is managed by the UNDCP as a trust fund aimed at solving drug problems. Governments make the most significant donations, but the Fund also gets money from NGOs and private sources. The Fund is used for technical co-operation to support, for example, treatment/rehabilitation and education programmes, drug research and iden-tification test development, and to help train the national law enforcement authorities of developing states and provide them with vehicles and telecom-munications equipment and other materials for the policing of drug trafficking. Finally, the UNDCP also functions as a drug control research centre. As part of this function it controls the UN Narcotics Laboratory which inter alia deter-mines the origins of confiscated drugs thus building up a geographical picture of the drug trade.[15]

To these ends the UNDCP is structured along functional lines.[16] Most sig-nificantly, from a practical point of view, it supports a global network of 'Field Offices' located in states that face complex drug-related problems. These units assist these states and monitor their application of the drug conventions. Al-though not heavily involved in the direct policing of the illicit traffic, this aspect of the UNDCP's work has grown, mostly in relation to the gathering of informa-tion as provided for by the drug conventions.

---

13 UNDCP, *World Drug Report* (OUP, Oxford, 1997), p. 169.
14 The Fund was created in 1990 and subsumed the United Nations Fund for Drug Abuse Control (UNFDAC).
15 The Laboratory periodically produces a *List of Narcotic Drugs under International Control*.
16 See the UNDCP's website – <www.undcp.org.index.html>.

7.2.6   The UN drug control information system

7.2.6.1   Introduction

The CND and UNDCP are at the centre of a sophisticated information system on illicit drug control. The information gathered provides the material for their analysis of the state of the illicit traffic and the adherence to treaty obligations by Parties, and makes it possible for the UN drug control machinery to take appropriate steps against both the illicit traffic and erring Parties. Because this system plays a significant role in their supervision of the implementation of the drug conventions and of the illicit drug problem generally it is appropriate to discuss it at this point. The system grows out of the provisions of the international drug conventions that make it obligatory for Parties to transmit important information on drug problems to the Secretary General and thus to the CND. Only some of these provisions elicit information concerned with the illicit traffic and these are discussed below.

7.2.6.2   Furnishing information under the 1961 Convention

Article 18 of the 1961 Convention, entitled 'Information to be Furnished by Parties', makes provision for the furnishing of information on narcotic drug control to the UN Secretary General by the Parties, and this provision includes within it obligations to provide information on the illicit traffic. The CND must request Parties to the 1961 Convention to provide it with the information necessary for it to carry out its functions.[17] Once made, a request is binding on the Parties, although state practice suggests that Parties are only bound to supply information at their disposal or which they can acquire with a reasonable effort.[18]

Article 18(1)(a) provides for the furnishing of an annual report by the Parties on the operation of the 1961 Convention within their territories. The annual report includes information on the annual impact of the Convention's provisions for the suppression of the illicit traffic. This information, which augments the

---

17   The *Commentary on the Single Convention on Narcotic Drugs, 1961* (New York, 1973) UN Publication Sales No. E.73.XI, (hereinafter the *1961 Commentary*), p. 209, submits, however, that the specific forms of information set out in article 18(1)'s sub-paragraphs must be furnished without the necessity of a specific request from the CND. It argues that the CND is obliged to determine the details of the illicit traffic and specific information is necessary for the performance of the CND's work.

18   *1961 Commentary* at 209-210.

specific information required by article 18(1)(c), includes statistics on drug demand (substance, source, method of consumption, user profile etc.) and supply (source, quantities, prosecutions, convictions, penalties, prices, trafficker's methods and disposal of seized drugs).[19]

Article 18(1)(b)'s requirement that the Parties submit the texts of all laws and regulations promulgated to give effect to the Convention includes the criminal laws giving effect to the Convention's penal provisions. The obligation to supply copies of these penal laws is ongoing – 'from time to time' – and thus amendments must also be supplied as they are made. This information is important for the UNDCP to build up its national drugs legislation register, a gargantuan, unfinished, task.[20] Unfortunately, article 18 does not oblige the Parties to supply information on the enforcement of these laws and on how rigorously violations have been punished, so the picture generated is incomplete.

Article 18(1)(c) provides a critical tool for the CND because it both obliges Parties to provide information on cases of the illicit traffic, and it specifies that the CND may demand the particulars of important cases. In both situations it is the CND and not the Party concerned that decides the types of cases that should be reported on and the particular information that should be provided. In the latter situation, the Parties must give the CND the particular information it wants even if the case is only considered potentially important. Cases are considered potentially important if they illuminate illicit drug sources, or because of the quantities of drugs involved, or because of the methods used by the traffickers.

The information furnished by Parties under article 18 is furnished to the UN Secretariat (now UNDCP). In terms of article 18(2), the CND determines the manner in which the Parties must supply the information, the precise dates by which it must be furnished and the form to be used.[21] The CND may require

---

19 *1961 Commentary* at 213.

20 The UNDCP issues the E/NL document series of published national laws and regulations concerning narcotic drugs and psychotropic substances on a continuing basis. The UNDCP regularly provides a summary of these laws and regulations and produces a cumulative index and tabulation of changes in the scope of control, e.g. the *Cumulative Index 1987-1990*, UN Doc. E/NL.1990.Index, UN Sales No. E.91.XI.5, New York, 1991. This system of information covers the laws issued from 1947 to 1990. In-depth analysis of specific areas of national application of international law is unavailable.

21 *1961 Commentary* at 219. The form the CND presents to Parties for reports on individual cases of drug trafficking requires them to provide a mass of detail. They are required to report on among other things the type and mass of the drug seized, the date and place of the illicit transaction or seizure, packaging, labelling and trade mark of the seized substance, type of transportation used by the trafficker including name, owner, nationality

in terms of article 18(2) that reports of the illicit traffic made in terms of article 18(1)(c) that are considered important be made 'as soon as possible', but the information is usually provided in a Party's annual report as required by article 18(1)(a). Summaries of reports are used by the CND in its annual deliberations and distributed to governments on request. These summaries are used to develop policy responses to the illicit drug problem and to monitor the effectiveness of law enforcement. Individual reports are not distributed to other Parties and are not used to aid international law enforcement co-operation on individual cases. The drafters of the 1961 Convention anticipated, as the *1961 Commentary* explains, that 'actual international police co-operation takes place on a bilateral basis through the national police services concerned, and on a multilateral basis through ... Interpol.'[22]

The 1961 Convention gives the INCB an ancillary role in the collection of information about the illicit traffic. This information forms part of the general statistical returns Parties furnish to the INCB. The purpose of this provision is to reveal the extent of the illicit traffic and the effectiveness of law enforcement action against it.[23] Thus all seizures of illicit drugs[24] must be taken into account for the purpose of calculating the figures anticipated by article 20(1)(e), and not merely those resulting from cases considered important under article 18(1)(c) and consequently reported to the UNDCP. With regard to the disposal of drugs, the INCB asks the Party to indicate separately the quantities of drugs destroyed, taken over by the Government for special purposes or utilised for licit purposes in that year even if seized previously. The INCB has complained

---

and registration of ship, aircraft or other vehicle involved, route followed by the drug, destination, place of acquisition of the drug, place of manufacture of the drug or place where the plant was cultivated from which the drug was obtained, means by which the drug was obtained (purchase, theft etc.), in cases of clandestine laboratories the apparatus seized, personal data on the trafficker (name, date and place of birth, nationality, occupation, residence, whether arrested or at large, etc.) and judicial or administrative measures taken against him – see the *1961 Commentary* at 216-217.

22 *1961 Commentary* at 216.

23 *1961 Commentary* at 243. Article 20(1)(e) obliges the INCB to supply Parties and non-parties alike with the forms to be used to furnish this information.

24 Excluding (i) cannabis leaves without tops as they are not a drug in terms of article 1(1)(b) of the Convention, and (ii) drugs contained within preparations listed in schedule III because of article 2(4).

regularly about the repeated failure of Parties to furnish the information required in terms of article 20(1)(e).[25]

7.2.6.3 Furnishing information under the 1971 Convention

The 1971 Convention requires less information from the Parties on criminal laws and activities than does the 1961 Convention. Article 16, entitled 'Reports to be Furnished by the Parties', provides for the general reporting function of the Parties. The information it obliges Parties to provide to the UN Secretariat (UNDCP)[26] includes, in terms of article 16 paragraphs (1) and (3), specific information on the illicit traffic.

Article 16(1) creates a general duty on the Parties to furnish at the CND's request the information necessary for the CND to function, including information on the illicit traffic. Concerns have been expressed about the vagueness of this obligation, which appears to give the CND a right to unlimited information.[27] However, because there is no provision in the 1971 Convention for the supply of statistical information on the illicit traffic to the INCB, the *1971 Commentary* suggests that article 16(1)'s general obligation also covers requests for statistical data on the extent of the illicit traffic and of abuse of psychotropic substances.[28] But Parties are only bound to furnish the CND with such information that they have at their disposal or are able to gather by a reasonable effort.[29]

Article 16(1) also establishes a specific duty on the Parties to provide, in addition to the information furnished under the general obligation,[30] an annual

---

25 It reminds governments of this failure. It is able to compare the seizure data presented by Parties with information made available by Interpol – INCB, *Report of the International Narcotics Control Board for 1995* UN Doc. E/INCB/1995/1, p. 11.

26 In terms of article 16(6), the Parties must provide this information in the time and manner that the CND requests, which is usually in time for use by the CND at its meetings.

27 See the statement of the Australian delegate to the 1971 Conference, *United Nations Conference for the Adoption of a Protocol on Psychotropic Substances, Official Records, Volume II* (New York, 1973) UN Doc. E/CONF.58/7/Add.1, UN Publication Sales No.E.73.XI.4 (hereinafter *1971 Records* vol. II), p.157.

28 *1971 Commentary* at 278-279.

29 *1971 Commentary* at 279.

30 The *1971 Commentary* at 280 submits, correctly I believe, that the words 'and in particular' must be taken through the practice of states in respect of the similarly worded provision in article 18(1) of the 1961 Convention to mean 'and also in particular', and thus the special obligation operates separately from the general obligation.

report[31] on the working of the Convention in their territories, which must include specific information in terms of sub-paragraphs (a) and (b). Article 16(1)(a) obliges them to report important changes in their laws and regulations concerning psychotropic substances, which must include important changes in their criminal laws and regulations.[32] Article 16(1)(b) obliges them to report significant developments in the abuse of and illicit traffic in psychotropic substances within their territories.

Article 16(3), like article 18(1)(c) of the 1961 Convention, is the pivot of the international information system on the illicit traffic in psychotropic substances. Article 16(3) obliges the Parties to report to the Secretary-General, as soon as possible after the event, important cases of the illicit traffic or significant seizures. Importance is gauged here by the incident revealing new trends, the quantities involved, assistance in the identification of sources of substances, or because of the trafficker's methods. Summaries of these reports assist the CND in its task of reviewing and responding to the illicit traffic. The information provided in the reports is, as became the practice under the 1961 Convention, not used directly for the purpose of international law enforcement co-operation in individual cases. However, this purpose may be served by the obligation in article 16(3) to communicate the report in accordance with article 21(b), which obliges the Parties to communicate copies of the report 'to the other Parties directly concerned'.[33] In addition, the *1971 Commentary* suggests that the seizure reports also be sent to Interpol. Although article 16(3) does not give the CND the authority to lay down the form such reports must take, the practice has been to use the same forms used for reports under article 18(1)(c) of the 1961 Convention.

7.2.6.4   *Furnishing information under the 1972 Protocol to the 1961 Convention*

Paragraphs (f) and (g) were added to article 35 of the 1961 Convention by article 13 of the 1972 Protocol. Article 35(f) requests Parties to furnish the UN with information on the whole range of illicit drug activity including, sig-

---

31 This report is usually combined with the annual reports required under the other drug conventions.

32 The 1971 Convention, unlike the 1961 Convention, does not provide explicitly for the furnishing of the texts of all laws and regulations promulgated to give effect to it, although the CND may request these texts under the general obligation in article 16(1).

33 *1971 Commentary* at 285.

nificantly, use.[34] This voluntary information is in addition to that required by article 18 of the unamended 1961 Convention. Although focused on the Party's domestic situation, in order to get a more complete picture of illicit supply and demand the *1972 Commentary* suggests that 'references to the foreign origin of the drugs found in the illicit traffic and to the lack of control or defective control in a foreign country causing or rendering more difficult a domestic problem, may be included in the Party's report.'[35]

The Parties themselves decide when it is appropriate to furnish information and they identify the appropriate information to be furnished.[36] These provisions were introduced in order to give the INCB greater access to information as its powers were increased by the 1972 Protocol,[37] and therefore the information is furnished to the INCB as well as to the CND. Article 35(g) gives the INCB the power to direct how and when the information is to be furnished.[38] Article 35(g) provides for the unusual situation where the INCB assists the Parties on request in the furnishing of the information to it so that the information is better organised and more useful to the INCB.[39]

7.2.6.5   *Furnishing information under the 1988 Convention*

In the 1988 Convention there are two types of obligations to furnish information.

First, there are those provisions in the 1988 Convention for the furnishing of information on specific areas of co-operation. Parties are obliged to transmit this information to the Secretary General in his clearing-house role for onward

---

34   Statement of the US delegate, *United Nations Conference to consider amendments to the Single Convention on Narcotic Drugs, Official Records, Volume II* (New York, 1973) UN Doc. E/CONF.63/10/Add.1; UN Publication Sales No. E.73.XI.8 (hereinafter *1972 Records* vol. II), p. 161.

35   See *Commentary on the 1972 Protocol Amending the Single Convention on Narcotic Drugs, 1961* (New York, 1976) UN Doc. E/CN.7/588, UN Publication Sales No.E.76.XI. 6 (hereinafter *1972 Commentary*), p. 73. See also N.G Gross and J.G. Greenwald, 'The 1972 Narcotics Protocol' (1973) 2 *Contemporary Drug Problems* 119 at 131-132.

36   Statement of the US delegate, *1972 Records* vol. II at 156.

37   Statement of the US delegate, *1972 Records* vol. II at 156. The *1972 Commentary* explains at 72-73 that the information furnished under paragraph (f) would qualify as 'information submitted by Governments to the Board under the provisions of this Convention' as defined in article 14(1)(a) and consequently could be the basis for the INCB's initiation of an article 14 embargo procedure.

38   It may specify a particular form and method for furnishing the information and specify the date by which the information is to be supplied, but its power to do so is conditional upon the Party first expressing its willingness to supply the information.

39   Comment of the US delegate, *1972 Records* vol. II at 166.

transmission to other Parties. Examples include: article 5(4)(e), which requires the furnishing of information on the texts of laws and regulations giving effect to the confiscation provisions in article 5; article 7(9), which obliges the Parties to identify the acceptable language or languages for the purposes of requests for mutual legal assistance; article 12(2), which requires provision of information on the addition to or deletion of substances in Tables I and II of the annex; and, article 17(7), which requires the notification of the designated authority or authorities to receive and respond to requests relevant to the interdiction of non-flag vessels at sea. The supply of this information is of great importance to the administration of the illicit control system, and is in addition to the information in respect of seizures and laws described below.

Second, there is provision for the furnishing of information on the application of the Convention as a whole. Under the 1988 Convention, article 21 gives the CND an oversight and supervisory role and in discharging this mandate the CND is at least partly reliant on the information that the Parties are obliged to supply in terms of article 20. Article 20, patterned on earlier provisions, is entitled, 'Information to be Furnished by the Parties'.

Article 20(1)'s opening sentence places a general obligation on the Parties to furnish the CND, via the UNDCP, with information on the functioning of the 1988 Convention as a whole within their territories. The *1988 Commentary* points out that although there is no specific provision here for furnishing information to the CND at its request, it can be argued that such information may be necessary for the CND to discharge its obligation under article 21(a) to review the operation of the Convention.[40] The sub-paragraphs of article 20(1) oblige Parties to furnish two specific types of information of particular value.

Article 20(1)(a) obliges Parties to furnish the CND with copies of the laws and regulations, whatever their source or status, that they have promulgated in order to apply the 1988 Convention. This information shows the extent to which the Party has implemented the Convention and areas where work must still be done, as well as providing model legislation for other Parties to use.[41]

---

40 *1988 Commentary* at 363. The use of 'in particular' with reference to the specific types of information to be furnished in terms of the sub-paragraphs of article 20(1), coupled with the established practice of sending annual responses to the CND's questionnaire on the working of the conventions, suggests that the CND is in a position to establish what information it needs.

41 *1988 Commentary* at 364. Parties commonly annex legislation to annual reports and the UNDCP publishes legislation in the E/NL series.

Article 20(1)(b) obliges Parties to furnish the CND with details of illicit trafficking cases that have occurred within their jurisdictions and which they consider important because of the disclosure of new trends, the quantities of drugs involved, the sources of the drugs, or the trafficking methods.

Article 20(2) makes it clear that the CND will dictate to the Parties when and how the information, general or specific, will be furnished. Unlike the earlier conventions, article 20 does not make any provision for an annual report by the Parties to the CND on the working of the Convention within its territory.[42] Nevertheless, it appears that article 20(2) implicitly allows the CND to demand information on the application of the 1988 Convention in the annual reports that Parties furnish, and the CND has adopted this approach.

7.2.6.6 The UN drug control information system in review

Through the drug conventions the international community has created an information system, a part of which is devoted to monitoring the supply of and demand for illicit drugs. Supervised by the UN's control organs, this system allows information to be shared among the Parties and these organs and plays a key role in the development of strategies for suppression of the illicit drugs. In practice, a component of the Parties' annual reports relates to the illicit traffic and serves as the basic source of information on the illicit traffic and the legal and practical steps taken against it in each reporting state for the preceding year. Other sources of information include Interpol, which from 1949 has regularly contributed a memorandum on the illicit traffic to the CND. These reports and memoranda are analysed by the UNDCP and an annual summary is drawn up. This document constitutes the review of the illicit traffic in drugs during the preceding year. It serves as the basis of the CND's main task at its annual meeting, the discussion of the illicit traffic. Bruun et al note that this information determines 'to a large extent the picture which the international community has of drug trafficking and its perception of the nature of the problem.'[43] Although it generally tries to take a friendly attitude, the CND questions states involved in unsatisfactory situations and states that do not produce annual reports, and it can demand information from Parties to the conventions and non-

---

42 A joint amendment, UN Doc. E/Conf.82/C.2/L.39 did make provision for such a report, but was rejected in favour of the present wording.

43 K. Bruun, L. Pan and I. Rexed, *The Gentlemen's Club: International Control of Drugs and Alcohol* (University of Chicago Press, Chicago, 1975), p. 226.

parties alike.[44] It commonly makes demands in the form of resolutions in which it, for example, invites a state to take measures in a given field or act to remedy a situation. It also requests the UNDCP to communicate with governments or take any action that may be necessary. Although the INCB has fewer information gathering powers in terms of the drug conventions than the CND because it is not a politically representative organ, it uses the information it gathers in monitoring the international drug trade.

In practice, although certain states, such as the United States, have made a significant input into the information system,[45] the quality of information supplied by states has been criticised,[46] and is not always reliable or complete. Bassiouni complains that the type of data report submitted by states and summarised by the UNDCP 'is almost wholly ineffective in practice, even though in theory it is useful.'[47] A significant problem and one common to many UN structures is that the Parties supply the information and because it is a commentary on their performance of their international obligations they tailor the information accordingly. Parties may not be willing to co-operate and only limited sanctions exist for Parties failing to provide reliable information or failing to respond at all to requests for information. The unreliability of information from Parties also means that the INCB may not be aware of the need to apply sanctions to the offending Party. The Parties on the other hand, have criticised the amount of information that they are asked to supply. The Jamaican delegate observed at the 1988 Conference that 'countries were being called upon to provide a growing number of increasingly voluminous reports under the provisions of the various instruments and agreements; there was a danger that the burden would become unbearable.'[48]

While this information system meets the Parties' substantive obligations under the drug conventions, its shortcomings from a law enforcement point

---

44 In terms of article 55 of the UN Charter the CND can demand all this information from non-parties to the drug conventions but who are UN members; with non-parties which are not UN members it has to rely on persuasion.

45 Bruun et al supra note 43 at 227.

46 See Bruun et al supra note 43 at 95-96.

47 M.C. Bassiouni, 'The International Narcotics Control Scheme' in M.C. Bassiouni (ed.), *1 International Criminal Law: Crimes* (Transnational, Dobbs Ferry, 1986), p. 507 at p. 522.

48 *United Nations Conference for the Adoption of a Convention against Illicit Traffic in Narcotic Drugs and Psychotropic Substances, Official Records, Volume II* (New York, 1991) UN Doc. E/CONF.82/16/Add.1, UN Publication Sales No. E.91.XI.1 (hereinafter *1988 Records* vol. II), p. 331.

of view are manifest. The system supports only the most abstract strategic decision making. Unlike national law enforcement agencies, the UN's international drug control organs do not focus on gathering information about individual offenders with the purpose of using that information to hunt those offenders down. The 1980s and 1990s saw a growth in popularity at the national level of gathering information about illicit drug related activities and processing it so that it becomes intelligence – information that can be used to guide action.[49] At the international level, because the direct communication of information between Parties is often hampered by suspicion and problems with the revelation of information about private individuals in conflict with data protection measures, the alternative of developing a multilateral applied intelligence system seems the obvious step. The UN's drug control organs have, nonetheless, been hesitant about engaging in the provision of drug intelligence because of difficulties of capacity and authority. In 1999, however, the UNDCP announced that it had, together with the World Customs Organisation (WCO) and Interpol, established a joint database on global drug seizures that already contained more than ten thousand records.[50] Again, however, the database allows the analysis and assessment of global trends in drug trafficking and the passing on of this information to governments and other decision-makers working on drug law enforcement strategies, rather than at an operational level.

7.2.7   The International Narcotics Control Board (INCB)

7.2.7.1   General
The INCB is a thirteen-member board of experts that is responsible for monitoring the international drug trade and taking measures to ensure the execution of the provisions of the drug conventions.[51] Although a creature of treaty,[52] as opposed to other UN organs which are creations of ECOSOC, and independent

---

49 See N. Dorn, K. Murji and N. South, *Traffickers: Drug Markets and Law Enforcement* (Routledge, London, 1992), pp. 149-175 generally.
50 UNDCP Press Release, 24 June 1999.
51 Articles 9 and 10 of the 1961 Convention, as amended by articles 2 and 3 of the 1972 Protocol, provide that the INCB consists of 13 members elected for 5 years by ECOSOC, three with medical or pharmacological expertise nominated by the WHO and ten with inter alia knowledge of narcotics administration and its problems nominated by Parties to the 1961 Convention with the aim of equitable geographic representation of representatives of producer, manufacturer and consumer states.
52 Articles 9-11 of the 1961 Convention.

in its technical work,[53] the General Assembly controls its budget, the UNDCP its secretariat, and in terms of the drug conventions it is accountable to ECOSOC, so it is very much a part of the UN drug control machinery.

The INCB reports annually on its supervision of the global drug trade and these reports provide a useful picture of the global drug problem. Article 23 of the 1988 Convention, entitled 'Reports of the Board', designed to mirror the INCB's reporting duty under article 15(1) of the 1961 Convention and article 18(1) of the 1971 Convention,[54] deals with the annual and periodic reporting function of the INCB under the 1988 Convention. Article 23(1) obliges the INCB to provide an annual report or reports as necessary on its work through the CND and ECOSOC. The content of these reports must contain an analysis of the information available to the INCB. It also includes, in appropriate cases, an account of the explanations, if any, given by or required by the Parties, together with any observations and recommendations which the INCB wants to make.[55] The CND is entitled to comment. Article 23(2) provides that these reports shall be communicated to the Parties and subsequently published by the Secretary-General. It also obliges the Parties to permit their unrestricted distribution. The Annual Report produced in practice is a consolidated report meeting the INCB's obligations under all the conventions and providing an overview of the implementation and effectiveness of the international drug control system as a whole, including the suppression of illicit drugs.

Although concerned mainly with monitoring the licit international production of and trade in drugs, the INCB's role in the suppression of the illicit traffic has grown steadily. Article 9(4) of the 1961 Convention, as inserted by article 2 of the 1972 Protocol, provides that the INCB must endeavour 'to prevent illicit cultivation, production and manufacture of, and illicit trafficking in and use of, drugs.' In reality, article 9(4) simply codifies the practice of the INCB under the unamended 1961 Convention.[56] Article 9(4) requires the INCB to 'endeavour' 'in co-operation with Governments' and 'subject to the terms of this Convention' to prevent illicit cultivation and so on. Co-operation is crucial here,

---

53 Article 9(2) of the 1961 Convention provides that INCB members cannot hold government posts. Article 11 provides that the INCB can elect its own President and adopt its own procedure. In practice it usually meets in private with a representative of the WHO and of the UNDCP, and, when necessary, of a particular state.

54 *1988 Records* vol. II at 323-324.

55 The *1988 Commentary* at 388 notes that the INCB may in effect report, in its annual report, on a Party's non-compliance with the Convention, a matter covered by article 22(1) but subject in terms of that article to a duty of confidentiality in article 22(5).

56 See *1972 Records* vol. II at 107.

and the INCB has tried to maintain a continuing dialogue with Parties. Operating in strict confidence, and sometimes beyond its strict competence, the INCB has frequently prevented or corrected problems on an informal basis and thus avoided the political confrontation that may have resulted had the matter been brought up in the CND.[57] The weakness in the INCB's action against the illicit traffic is that its determination as to whether the drug conventions are being implemented by the Parties is largely dependent on the statistical data on the illicit traffic provided to it by the Parties in terms of article 20(1)(e) of the 1961 Convention. The INCB is incapable of systematic and comprehensive independent analysis.[58]

7.2.7.2   The INCB and the embargo procedure in the earlier drugs conventions
Although it mainly relies in practice on informal pressure, the 1961 Convention, 1971 Convention and 1972 Protocol do give the INCB wide powers to enforce implementation by the Parties.

Article 14 of the 1961 Convention, as elaborated and reinforced by the 1972 Protocol,[59] provides the INCB with a number of measures that it can take against Parties that have failed to carry out their obligations or which constitute potentially threatening centres of illicit traffic or consumption. These measures include requests for information and explanations, public declarations that a Party has violated its obligations and both import and export embargo procedures. The embargo procedure gives the INCB a prosecutorial role, in that it collects the evidence, and a quasi-judicial role, in that it recommends the embargo and its decision cannot be overturned by a higher body. Article 14(1)(a) (and article 6(1)(a) of the 1972 Protocol amending it), provides that if, on examination of information submitted by a government or by a recognised agency, the INCB has 'objective reasons' to believe that the aims of the Convention are threatened by a Party's failure to carry out its obligations, the INCB has the right to confidentially consult with that Party or request it to supply information. After taking such action, article 14(1)(b) (and article 6(1)(b) of the 1972 Protocol) provides that the INCB may, if it finds it necessary, call upon this Party to adopt appropriate remedial measures. Article 6(1) of the 1972 Protocol has given the INCB the added power at this stage to propose to a Party that a study be carried out in its territory, and if it agrees and requests help,

---

57   *1988 Records* vol. II at 323.
58   INCB, *Report of the International Narcotics Control Board for 1994* UN Doc. E/INCB/1994/1, p. 6.
59   See generally Gross and Greenwald supra note 35 at 143-149.

to provide help and settle the details with the Party. The results of the study would be communicated to the INCB together with the remedial steps intended. If, however, none of these steps bring the desirable results and it appears that the situation is serious, in terms of article 14(1)(c) (and article 6(1)(d) of the 1972 Protocol) the INCB can call the attention of the Parties, ECOSOC and the CND to the matter. But it may only do so if one or more of the following conditions is met: (i) either the aims of the Convention are being seriously endangered and it is impossible to resolve the matter satisfactorily in any other way; (ii) or the INCB finds that there is a serious situation that needs cooperative action at the international level with a view to remedying it; (iii) or bringing such a situation to the notice of the Parties, ECOSOC, and the CND is the most appropriate method of facilitating co-operative action. If one of these conditions is met, the INCB can in terms of article 14(3) make a special report including the views of the defaulting Party to ECOSOC, and recommend in terms of article 14(2) that Parties stop the import and export of all drugs to and from that country for a designated period or until it is satisfied with the situation in that country. The Party has the right to put its case to ECOSOC. Thus the process moves from one of cautioning to punishing the Party.

The INCB has been given similar embargo powers under the 1971 Convention. It has the right to ask a Party to furnish information that it needs in connection with the Party's execution of the 1971 Convention's provisions, and article 19 allows it to recommend an embargo against a Party when it has reason to believe that the aims of the Convention are being seriously endangered by the Party's failure to carry out the Convention's provisions. As under the 1961 Convention, the procedure begins with the INCB requesting an explanation in terms of article 19(1)(a), moves to it calling upon the Party to take remedial steps in terms of article 19(1)(b), and in case of the Party failing in respect of either of these steps, calling the attention of other Parties and the CND and ECOSOC to the matter in terms of article 19(1)(c). At this stage the INCB may under article 19(2) recommend the embargo. It alone can lift the embargo when it is satisfied that the situation has returned to normal.[60]

Although these powers have never been used, they do represent potentially powerful instruments for enforcing observation of the obligations in the early drug conventions. Not surprisingly, a Party has objected to article 6 of the 1972

---

60   See Chatterjee supra note 3 at 273.

Protocol as an encroachment on sovereignty[61] and others have made reservations to article 19 of the 1971 Convention, again because they regard it as an interference in their domestic affairs.[62]

7.2.7.3   The INCB's powers under the 1988 Convention

At the 1988 Conference, certain delegations made proposals which would have granted the INCB far greater powers of supervision than it was at that stage competent to exercise, as well as greater powers to take action in cases of non-compliance.[63] But there was strong resistance to an independent technical body exercising these powers, and some delegations preferred to see these new powers being exercised by the CND, while other delegations resisted any monitoring and supervision at all.[64] In a compromise solution, the INCB was given control over the application of technical and scientific provisions, while the CND was put in charge of penal provisions, which meant than the INCB lost some of the control it exercised under the earlier conventions and the CND gained some control.[65] Article 22, entitled 'Functions of the Board', sets out the new role of the INCB.

Article 22(1) confers an investigative function on the INCB in respect of allegations that the aims of the 1988 Convention in matters relating to its competence, are not being met. The introductory sentence of article 22(1) makes it clear that the investigative powers granted to the INCB by article 22 neither limit the wide powers to deal with the illicit traffic given to the INCB by the

---

61   *1988 Records* vol. II at 35. India has made a reservation in regard to article 6 of the 1972 Protocol – 14/12/1978, *Multilateral Treaties Deposited with the Secretary General: Status as at 31 December 1996* (New York, 1997) UN Doc. St/Leg/Ser.E/15, p. 295 (hereinafter *Multilateral Treaties Deposited* (1997)).

62   See the reservations made by Iraq (17/5/1976) and Myanmar (20/6/1994) – both in *Multilateral Treaties Deposited* (1997) at 290.

63   D.W. Sproule and P. St-Denis, 'The UN Drug Trafficking Convention: An Ambitious Step' [1989] CYBIL 263 at 288 referring to the Canadian proposal in UN Doc. E/Conf.82/C.2/L.38/Rev.1, L.39/Rev.1, L.40/Rev.1 and L.41/Rev.1.

64   The Mexican delegation's proposal, UN Doc. E/Conf.82/3 at 114. Debate at the Conference concerning the role of the INCB split into four groups: those in favour of granting these powers to the INCB; those in favour of granting them to the CND; those who wanted to see authority shared; and those who called for control to stop – F. Rouchereau, 'La Convention des Nations Unies Contre le Traffic Illicite de Stupefiants et de Substances Psychotropes' (1988) 34 *Annuaire Francais de Droit Internationale* 601 at 615.

65   Rouchereau supra note 64 at 616.

earlier conventions[66] nor do they overlap with the supervisory functions of the CND under article 21.

Under article 22(1)(a) the INCB must first form a reasonable belief that the aims of the 1988 Convention in matters relating to its competence are not being met. This belief must be grounded on an examination of information available to it, the Secretary-General or the CND, or of information communicated by UN organs to it. Once this opinion is formed, the INCB is authorised to invite a Party or Parties to furnish it with information relevant to the situation. The INCB is thus granted extensive powers of scrutiny, but that is all.[67] It cannot call the attention of the Party to the matter. The scope of 'matters' in which the INCB is competent clearly includes matters falling directly under its authority in terms of provisions such as article 12 (precursor monitoring), article 13 (substances and materials used in the illicit drug manufacture) and article 16 (commercial documents and labelling of exports). Although article 22(1)(a) is not so limited explicitly, the *1988 Commentary*[68] is of the opinion that its powers of investigation in terms of article 22(1)(a) are limited to these specific articles. On the other hand, 'matters relating to its competence' has been broadly interpreted by the United States to include the INCB's oversight of any of the provisions of the 1988 Convention when a particular matter relates to its competence.[69] It believes that the INCB's competence in a wide range of areas was

---

66   See the statement of the British delegate, *1988 Records* vol. II at 35. The British delegate noted that lack of clarity with respect to the definition of the INCB's competence in matters relating to the illicit traffic 'would provide substantial scope for Parties to argue that a particular matter on which the Board had asked for relevant information was not within its competence and, therefore, that the information need not be provided.' – see *1988 Records* vol. II at 328.

67   Nevertheless, the Indian delegation, which had made a reservation to the amended 1961 Convention because it conferred excessive powers on the INCB, considered that the INCB still had too much power and contemplated making a similar reservation to article 22 of the 1988 Convention – see *1988 Records* vol. II at 328-329.

68   1988 Commentary at 379.

69   In this regard the US delegation submitted the following written statement (see *1988 Records* vol. II at 333): 'It is the view of the United States that the wording of paragraph (1)(a) of article [22] did not limit the action of the Board to any specific articles of the Convention. Document E/CONF.82/C.2/L.42 had contained limitations on the articles for which the Board would have had responsibility, but the limitation had been removed when the qualifier "in matters related to its competence" had been added. That allowed for Board oversight of implementation of all articles of the Convention in respect of matters related to its competence. That was a compromise between the proposal for full implementation responsibility without restriction, put forward by the Canadian delegation and supported by other delegations, and the Netherlands proposal in document

established under the earlier conventions, and that this allows the INCB to investigate the implementation of a provision of the 1988 Convention that falls within such an area. It may, however, be that the INCB is allowed to investigate implementation of those earlier provisions within those areas, but not necessarily the new provisions of the 1988 Convention within those areas. It is true, however, that the general concern at the Conference to restrict the powers of the INCB is to some extent contradicted by its role in realising the general purpose of the 1988 Convention, which is suppressing the illicit traffic. For that reason it is submitted that the INCB does have general scrutiny powers in respect of the 1988 Convention in areas in which it is competent in other conventions. In practice, the INCB is unlikely to deliberately provoke Parties by demanding information on sensitive issues.

Article 22(1)(b) provides that the INCB may go further than just asking for information with respect to the Parties' implementation of articles 12, 13 and 16. In terms of article 22(1)(b)(i), the INCB may, if it is satisfied that it is necessary, call upon the Party concerned to adopt such remedial measures as seem necessary for the execution of articles 12, 13 or 16. The particular remedial measures recommended will depend on the situation. If the INCB contemplates taking further action under article 22(1)(b)(iii), article 22(1)(b)(ii) provides that all communications in this regard with the Party shall be treated as confidential. In terms of article 22(1)(b)(iii), if the INCB finds that the Party concerned has not taken the remedial measures that it has been called upon to take under article 22(1)(b)(i), then the INCB may call the attention of the Parties, ECOSOC and the CND to the matter. In the event of the INCB publishing a report under article 22(1)(b)(iii), the Party concerned may insist that the report also contain its views. The problem here, as with the position under the earlier

---

E/CONF.82/C.2/L.42 to limit Board responsibility to specific articles. In the United States view, "matters related to its competence" must be interpreted as referring to the competence of the Board under the existing two Conventions as well as any functions under the new Convention. That interpretation was supported by the "chapeau", which made clear the non-derogation of functions under the existing Conventions. It was also supported by the explanatory comments made by the representative of the Netherlands during the meeting. In that context, Board responsibility and competence would extend to a broad range of actions against the illicit traffic as set out in article 35 of the Single Convention and article 21 of the Convention on Psychotropic Substances. Those articles dealt with punishable offences, alternative forms of punishment, extradition and financial aspects of drug trafficking. Article 37 of the Single Convention supported the argument for competence in such areas as seizure and confiscation.'

conventions, is that the Parties supply the information and the INCB comments. Its own investigative powers are extremely limited.

The rest of article 22 is devoted to procedural matters. Article 22(2) obliges the INCB to invite any Party to an INCB meeting at which a question of direct interest to it is to be considered under article 22. Article 22(3) provides that if the INCB takes a decision under article 22 that is not unanimous, the minority's views shall be stated. Article 22(4) provides that an article 22 decision by the INCB must be made by a two-thirds majority of the full membership of the INCB. Article 22(5) place an absolute duty of confidentiality of information on the INCB when it carries out article 22(1)(a) functions. This duty obviously ceases should the INCB publish a report in terms of article 22(1)(b)(iii). Article 22(6) limits the INCB's article 22 powers when it provides that the INCB's responsibility under article 22 shall not apply to the implementation or supervision of treaties or agreements entered into between Parties in accordance with the provisions of this Convention.[70] Article 22(7) provides that article 22 shall not be applicable to disputes between Parties falling under the settlement of disputes provision in article 32. Thus solving disputes over matters such as extradition or confiscation does not fall within the remit of the INCB.

Compared to the position under the earlier conventions, under the 1988 Convention, the INCB's oversight role has been reduced. The conspicuous lacuna in the 1988 Convention is that no provision is made for the INCB to take steps against a defaulting Party to force it to comply with the Convention's provisions. As Gianaris notes, '[i]n actuality, the Board can do nothing to reprimand a state for not co-operating with the terms of the 1988 U.N. Convention or for assisting in narcotics trafficking or related crimes.'[71] Indeed, the INCB has no power other than scrutiny in respect of all but articles 12, 13, and 16.[72] The effective weapon of adverse publicity used in the other drug conventions has also been discarded.[73] From the point of view of drug consumer states the INCB can on the basis of its record function as an appropriate and effective body to encourage compliance with penal provisions. In other fields of international regulation such as arms control, technical bodies have increased their supervision roles, and it has been argued that leaving supervision of the 1988 Convention in the

---

70 Provisions calling for such amplification of relations between the Parties include articles 5, 6, 7, 9, 11, 14 and 17.
71 W.N. Gianaris, 'The new world order and the need for an international criminal court' (1992/3) 16 *Fordham International Law Journal* 88 at 108.
72 Sproule and St-Denis supra note 63 at 289.
73 Articles 14(3) and 19(3) of the 1961 and 1971 Conventions respectively.

hands of the CND was a mistake given the politicised nature of the UN's elected bodies and the ineffectiveness of goodwill and diplomatic pressure.[74]

7.2.7.4   The INCB and implementation of the illicit drug control system in review

Information on the INCB's supervision of the illicit drug control system is scarce. All information supplied to it by governments is confidential, thus the agendas and minutes of its meetings are confidential. The INCB's reports provide little that is specific. Bruun et al complain that it is 'difficult to determine to what extent the INCB has fully used or under-used its powers, or to what extent it has kept strictly to the performance of its obligations under the treaties.'[75] We do know that the INCB has never gone as far as using the embargo powers granted it by the earlier conventions against a Party because of that Party's failure to either implement the criminal law provisions of the early drug conventions or take action against the illicit traffic.[76] While these embargo powers do serve as a latent threat to coerce compliance by Parties, they are limited to the suggestion of an embargo on the export or import of drugs and are not mandatory, and it would be politically difficult to resurrect them now. All this of course begs the question of why delegations to the 1988 Conference were so eager not to grant similar powers under the 1988 Convention.

Instead of enforcing compliance, the INCB has chosen informality. It relies on its information gathering and reporting powers to investigate and in some cases publicise situations, but uses informal pressure to get Parties to co-operate. Its methods include using constant diplomatic dialogue, such as the exchange of letters with defaulting governments, raising problems within its annual report, sending missions to the states concerned and mentioning the findings of these missions in its annual report, requesting governments to provide explanations or to take remedial measures, and drawing the attention of other Parties, the CND and ECOSOC to worrying situations.[77] It has in effect followed a policy of making "local enquiries" because nothing in the drug conventions says it cannot do so. The INCB would, however, like this policy to be concretised in

74   Sproule and St-Denis supra note 63 at 290.
75   Supra note 43 at 76.
76   INCB, *Report of the International Narcotics Control Board for 1994* UN Doc. E/INCB/ 1994/1, p. 6.
77   INCB, *Effectiveness of the International Drug Control Treaties: Supplement to the Report of the International Narcotics Control Board for 1994* UN Doc. E/INCB/1994/1/Supp.1, p. 20.

international legal provisions.[78] It is doubtful, however, whether these informal procedures or even the existing weak formal powers provided by the drug conventions are suited to the enforcement of the criminal law provisions of the conventions.[79] The general weakness of the whole drug control system's powers of enforcement has been severely criticised,[80] and that weakness is reflected in the unwillingness of states to grant a technical independent body strong enforcement powers.[81]

7.2.8   The World Health Organisation (WHO) and the WHO Expert Committee

The WHO's involvement in drug control stems from the somewhat belated realisation that the drug problem is also a medical-social problem.[82] The WHO is represented on the CND, which relies on it for advice in respect of the medical and scientific aspects of drug dependence. In turn, the WHO relies in this regard largely on the recommendations of its Expert Committee on Drug Dependence. These specialists are appointed on an ad-hoc basis for each particular session of the Committee.[83] New drugs are constantly being discovered, and the international control system is largely dependent on the findings of the Committee to bring these substances within the scope of the system. Chatterjee notes:

> This Committee recommends, inter alia, additions to the list of substances subject to control, the examination of suspected substances for possible addiction producing properties, the transfer of a substance from one schedule to another, and the deletion of a substance from a schedule of drugs, if necessary. The Director-General of the World Health Organisation decides on the question of the control of drugs on the basis of the recommendations of this Committee, and he communicates his decisions to the Secretary-General of the United Nations.[84]

---

78 INCB, *Effectiveness of the International Drug Control Treaties: Supplement to the Report of the International Narcotics Control Board for 1994* UN Doc. E/INCB/1994/1/Supp.1, p. 20.

79 See Gianaris supra note 71 at 107.

80 See for example J.A. Cabranes, 'International law and the control of the drug traffic' (1973) 7 *International Lawyer* 761 at 766.

81 Gross and Greenwald supra note 35 at 148.

82 See generally B. Rexed, K. Edmonson, I. Khan and R. Sansom, *Guidelines for the Control of Narcotic and Psychotropic Substances: In the Context of the International Treaties* (WHO, Geneva, 1984), pp. 23-28.

83 The need for continuity and 'adequate geographical distribution' is borne in mind – Chatterjee supra note 3 at 279.

84 Supra note 3 at 277.

The Committee bases each decision to place a substance under control and the particular type of control on the degree of risk the substance presents to the public health and on its medical usefulness, and not purely on pharmacological classification.[85] The merits of having the drug selection process in the hands of a Committee that meets occasionally and for short periods, can be questioned, and it is significant that under the 1988 Convention the decision to table precursor substances has been left entirely in the INCB's hands without reference to the WHO.[86] It should be noted here, however, that although the Expert Committee is vulnerable to the criticism that members of the medical profession who have little expertise in law or administration dominate it, it is one forum where these professions do have an influence on the drug control system, and this influence is a light counter-weight to the domination of the system by administrators, lawyers and policemen.

7.2.9   Other interested UN organs

The UNDCP's most direct link with other UN organs is with the management link under the ODCCP (Office for Drug Control and Crime Prevention) with the UN's Centre for International Crime Prevention (CICP) (formerly the Crime Prevention and Criminal Justice Branch).[87] They are linked because of their shared concern with internationally organised crime. A range of other UN organs can potentially involve themselves in international drug control.[88] For example,

---

85 Chatterjee supra note 3 at 280 citing (1969) 407 *WHO Technical Report Series* 6.
86 Article 12(4). This and other features of scheduling substances under UN supervision is discussed in Annexure A, Substances Controlled.
87 The principal UN organ concerned with matters relating to crime prevention and criminal justice.
88 These include the General Assembly, UNESCO (UN Educational, Scientific and Cultural Organisation) because of its educational role in drug abuse programmes; the ILO (International Labour Organisation) because of the role of drug use in the workplace; UNCTAD (the UN Conference on Trade and Development); UNIDO (UN Industrial Development Organisation); UNDP (United Nations Development Programme); UNICEF (UN Childrens Fund); Regional Economic Commissions; UNICRI (United Nations Interregional Crime and Justice Research Centre); UNAIDS (United Nations Joint Programme on AIDS); and because of human rights issues, the Centre for Human Rights, the Commission on Human Rights, and the Subcommittee on the Prevention of Discrimination and Protection of Minorities etc. These agencies are members of the ACC Subcommittee on Drug Control that meets annually to deal with co-ordination of drug control work in the UN system. The Sub-Committee is responsible for the compilation of the "System-Wide Action Plan" against drug abuse.

the CND relies on the Food and Agriculture Organisation (FAO) for technical advice on agricultural subjects and crop substitution, while the CND and the Universal Postal Union (UPU) co-operate in considering the various questions relating to the international shipment of drugs by post.

At a more senior level, the General Assembly has long had a policy role in drug control, as is evident from its supervision of ECOSOC and the frequent resolutions it has passed calling for systematic action against the illicit drug problem by states. The Security Council could technically become involved in enforcing illicit drug control by using its powers under article 94 of the UN Charter to settle problems with a defaulting state. Unlike the INCB and CND, the Security Council has in terms of article 25 of the Charter the power to impose legally binding decisions on UN member states or in terms of article 2(6) to enforce measures against non-UN members.[89] There may be some potential under the new world order dominated by a United States obsessed with drug control for the Security Council to be used as an instrument of drug control.[90]

---

89 This was pointed out by H.L. May, 'The evolution of the international control of narcotic drugs' (1950) 2 *Bulletin on Narcotics* 1 at 7.

90 S.A. Gardner, 'A global initiative to deter drug trafficking: will internationalising the drug war work?' (1993) 7 *Temple International and Comparative Law Review* 287 at 308 notes that the US, arguing that drug traffickers threatened destabilisation of Colombia and thus represented a threat to international peace and security under the UN Charter, suggested that the Security Council oversee a new international anti-drug movement. Developing states opposed the Security Council being given this role, as it was undemocratic, preferring the General Assembly take control. As a technical legal matter, in order for the Security Council to be used as a forum for international action against the illicit drug traffic, situations in drug producing states would have to be categorised either as a likely threat to the international peace and security thus meriting action under Chapter VI of the UN Charter, or as an actual threat to the international peace and security and deserving of action under Chapter VII. The US must, with respect to Colombia, have had in mind the use of Security Council Recommendations under Chapter VI, which would have carried greater weight than General Assembly Recommendations. The problem for those who would like to use the Security Council in this way is that characterisation of the destabilisation of a drug producing state by the illicit traffic as a threat, latent or patent, to international security, would be extremely difficult, particularly when such categorisation is a political decision made by a political body subject to the possibility of a political veto by one of the permanent members.

7.2.10   *The UN's structures in review*

The CND, UNDCP and INCB have the collective aim of implementing the international drug control system. They apparently combine willingly to achieve this purpose, although there have been disagreements about jurisdiction.[91] The CND has the broadest jurisdiction in respect of illicit drug control and in meeting its responsibility it relies largely on the information system created by the drug conventions to reveal and discuss illicit drug control problems in its annual meetings. The UNDCP's supervision of the illicit drug traffic flows from its supervision of global quantitative control of drug production. While it has some embargo powers that it can apply when it identifies particular problems, it performs its duties by relying instead on informal approaches to governments. The merits of political versus technical control are contentious. The CND works within the UN framework, which hampers its effectiveness but assuages sovereignty concerns. The INCB works more independently, which makes it more effective but raises sovereignty concerns. But to become obsessed with which organ has what power is to lose sight of the limits of the powers of the UN's drug control organs. To paraphrase Chatterjee, they are not guardians but monitors; they have no law-making function but initiate law-making, no judicial function but administrative and executive powers.[92] One of the functions of the system they administer is the suppression of the illicit drug traffic. Undoubtedly, however, the illicit traffic continues, and Bassiouni responds by criticising the limited authority given the drug control organs, which he states appears to be 'inadequate to halt or even slow down the illicit traffic.'[93] The problem is that the UN organs are largely subject to the self-reporting by Parties of the situations in their territories and their progress in implementing the drug conventions, and the UN organs can do little more than expose unsatisfactory situations when they do discover them. To make the existing system more effective would require the UN organs to be given far greater investigative powers and the authority to impose sanctions. Both steps are anathema to most states because of the loss of sovereignty. States may find it more acceptable to consider adopting a system in which one Party would be examined by others

---

91   Bruun et al supra note 43 at 103-110. They note that there have been disputes about the independence of the INCB from the rest of the UN and about the INCB's withholding of information from the CND.
92   Supra note 3 at 256.
93   Supra note 47 at 515.

according to an agreed protocol for examination,[94] and a college of the Parties would impose sanctions. The UN organs would lose power, but whether such a system would be effective, is speculative.

7.3   THE INTERNATIONAL CRIMINAL POLICE ORGANISATION (ICPO OR INTERPOL)[95] AND OTHER IGOS INVOLVED IN DRUG CONTROL

Interpol exists for the exchange of information on criminal matters, including drug matters, among its 175 member states.[96] Its structure is complex, with designated National Central Bureaux (NCB) at the state level serving as information and request relay stations between governments and the Interpol General Secretariat. Interpol's preventative drug control activities include the supply and analysis of information to governments about prospective crimes, law enforcement training, the unification of criminal law and the holding of conferences and so on. In this role it assists the UN drug control organs in their efforts to avert potential drug control problems. However, once an offence is committed Interpol performs curative functions not yet assumed by the UN drug control organs. Acting upon information supplied by governments through NCBs, it tries to provide sufficient information for national law enforcement officers to arrest and prosecute offenders successfully by acting as a conduit for international arrest warrants, extradition requests, and requests for evidence.[97] In order to fulfil these functions Interpol has steadily expanded its drug control activities.[98] Its Drugs Subdivision's task is to enhance co-operation and the exchange of information among national law enforcement agencies on drug

---

94   This is the position under the FATF-2 agreement of 1990.

95   See Anderson supra note 2 generally; Chatterjee supra note 3 at 499-506; R.E. Kendall, 'Drug control: policies and practices of the International Criminal Police Organisation' (1992) 44 *Bulletin on Narcotics* 3-10; W.J. Lemay, 'International co-operation through the Interpol system to counter illicit drug trafficking' (1983) 35 *Bulletin on Narcotics* 55-60. See also on the economic crime aspects of Interpol's work R.E. Kendall, 'Drug trafficking and related serious crime: the international dimension' (1991) 17 *Commonwealth Law Bulletin* 1361-1368.

96   Interpol's objectives in terms of article 2 of its 1956 Constitution are to promote mutual assistance between criminal police authorities and develop institutions likely to contribute to the efficient suppression of crime.

97   This information includes names, passport details, fingerprints and photographs.

98   See P. Marabuto, 'The International Criminal Police Commission and the illicit traffic in narcotics' (1951) 3 *Bulletin on Narcotics* 3-15 for a history of its early work against the illicit traffic.

crime, and strengthen their ability to fight drug crime.[99] Although drug control activities now form a significant part of its work,[100] Interpol is still reliant on national co-operation, and in this regard governments are often neither willing nor able to co-operate.[101]

Interpol's relationship with the UN drug control system has developed slowly. An official observer at the CND since 1949, it was granted participative status in 1972.[102] The importance of its resources were referred to specifically in resolution 3 of the 1961 Convention, and again in resolution 1 of the 1988 Conference which recommends that the widest possible use should be made by police authorities of these resources in achieving the goals of the 1988 Convention. But Interpol had no formal jurisdiction under the drug conventions until article 7(8) of the 1988 Convention was adopted allowing Parties to make requests for mutual legal assistance through Interpol in urgent circumstances. Interpol was given this role because experience had shown that its communications system and archives were extremely effective as a means of international co-operation and should be developed.[103] Although Interpol, like the UN drug control organs, monitors the international drug control system, it is much closer to national agencies in its participation in operational law enforcement. In 1986, Bassiouni suggested that Interpol be vested with the characteristics of a truly international drug police force with the right 'to participate with local authorities in arrests, searches and seizures, and other techniques of law enforcement'.[104] Article 7(8) of the 1988 Convention may have taken us closer to this position, but whether Interpol could mature into an international drugs police, is uncertain. An international drug-trafficking control agency has been proposed,[105] but police officers are generally negative about such an idea.

The World Customs Organisation (formerly the Customs Co-operation Council) is another significant IGO operating in the field of illicit drug control. It is a forum for the co-operation of the major customs authorities of more than

---

99 Kendall supra note 95 at 4-9 sets out the structure of the subdivision. Other special projects exist, including the FOPAC (*Fonds provenant d'activités criminelles*) group set up to counter money laundering.
100 Almost 60 percent of its work – *1988 Records* vol. II at 274.
101 See Chatterjee supra note 3 at 503.
102 It was transformed from NGO to IGO status, which allowed it to vote on the CND.
103 Statement of the Chinese delegate, *1988 Records* vol. II at 182.
104 Supra note 47 at 523.
105 Anderson supra note 2 at 99.

111 states.[106] Through its Enforcement Sub-Directorate, it facilitates exchange of information on topics such as smuggling methods and routes and methods of concealment. Regional Intelligence and Liaison Office projects located globally serve to gather, analyse and disseminate drugs intelligence. The WCO has emphasised the development of sophisticated anti-trafficking procedures and strong working relationships with commercial carriers in order to block the processes through which illicit drugs are trafficked.[107] It introduced the 1991 Carrier Co-operative Initiative as a vehicle for the exchange of information and intelligence between the WCO and the private commercial carrier industry.

Various other IGOs play a significant role in international drug control. Within the Secretariat of the Commonwealth of Nations, a number of divisions are actively concerned with problems related to the various aspects of drug control, and in this regard, the work of the Commonwealth Secretariat's Commercial Crime Unit has been of particular significance.[108] Finally, any list of notable drug control IGOs would be incomplete without the organisations formed by the Group of Seven major industrialised countries. In 1989, it set up the Financial Action Task Force (FATF) to study and recommend regulatory steps in respect of the threat to the global banking and financial system presented by money laundering.[109] Nineteen ninety saw the establishment

---

106 See G.D. Gotschlich, 'Action by the Customs Co-operation Council to combat illicit drug trafficking' (1983) 35 *Bulletin on Narcotics* 79-81; G.R. Dickerson, 'The Customs Co-operation Council and international customs enforcement' (1985) *The Police Chief* 16-18. Dickerson notes the importance of the drug conventions along with the 1977 Nairobi Convention (the International Convention on Mutual Administrative Assistance for the Prevention, Investigation and Repression of Customs Offences; in force 1980) as a legal basis for the WCO's activities. Annex X of the Nairobi Convention is specifically concerned with action against illicit drug smuggling and associated financial operations. The WCO is mainly involved in the pooling and supply of information, and liaises with the UN drug control organs and states in this regard.

107 UNDCP supra note 13 at 231.

108 The Commonwealth Secretariat's various agencies involved in action against the international drug traffic have been particularly active in concentrating law enforcement at the international level against the resources and property of illicit traffickers. See generally B.A.K. Rider, 'The role of the Commonwealth Secretariat in the fight against illicit drug traffic' (1983) 35 *Bulletin on Narcotics* 61-65.

109 See generally W.C. Gilmore, 'International efforts to combat money laundering' (1992) 18 *Commonwealth Law Bulletin* 1129 at 1138-1139.

of the short-lived Chemical Action Task Force (CATF), which studied and recommended regulatory steps in respect of precursors and other chemicals.[110]

7.4   REGIONAL ORGANISATIONS PARTICIPATING IN THE INTERNATIONAL DRUG CONTROL SYSTEM

The UN drug control organs encourage regional co-operation because they believe that countries within a specific geographical location or countries which share a lack of resources or particular vulnerability can best address certain drug control problems.[111] Provision was thus made in the 1988 Convention for regional organisations to participate in the international drug control system. Articles 26,[112] 27,[113] 28,[114] and 29[115] allow regional economic integration organisations that possess the necessary competence in respect of the negotiation, conclusion and application of international agreements in areas covered by the Convention to become Party to it. The Working Group that drew up these provisions felt that the word 'regional' 'should be interpreted in the widest sense to cover groupings of states, including sub-regional groups.'[116]

Illicit drug control at the regional level tends to be less sophisticated the larger and looser the organisation and more developed the smaller and more homogenous the organisation because there are fewer barriers to co-operation among smaller groups of familiar and like-minded states. Regional co-operation

---

110 See generally W.C. Gilmore, 'Drug trafficking and the control of precursor and essential chemicals: the international dimension' in H.L. MacQueen and B.G. Main (eds), *Drug Trafficking and the Chemical Industry: Hume Papers on Public Policy* Vol. 4, no.1, (Edinburgh UP, Edinburgh, 1996), pp. 18-22.

111 UNDCP supra note 13 at 176.

112 Article 26 allows 'regional economic integration organisations which have competence in respect of the negotiation, conclusion and application of the international agreements in matters covered by this Convention' to sign the 1988 Convention, and provides that 'references under the Convention to Parties, States or national services' are 'applicable to these organisations within the limits of their competence.'

113 Article 27(1) provides that the 1988 Convention is subject to 'acts of formal confirmation by regional economic integration organisations referred to in article 26(c)'. Article 27(2) provides that the regional organisation must specify the drug control matters over which it has jurisdiction, in order to protect the interests of other Parties to the 1988 Convention. Any changes to this responsibility must be communicated to the Secretary-General.

114 Article 28 is a provision identical to article 27 with respect to accession.

115 Article 29(3) sets out when the 1988 Convention comes into force for regional economic integration organisations.

116 *1988 Records* vol. II at 316.

in Europe is a good example. Fairly loose co-ordination has been undertaken under the auspices of the Council of Europe's Pompidou Group, which has been involved in various aspects of drug control such as dissemination of information about drug and precursor control methods. In 1991 it convened the first Pan-European Ministerial Conference to promote East-West co-operation on illicit drug problems, and currently forty states are members of this group. The Council of Europe's Convention on Laundering, Search, Seizure and Confiscation of the Proceeds of Crime, 1990, is a major regional initiative which now includes non-European parties such as the United States. More developed regional drug-control has been possible within stronger regional organisations like the European Union (EU).[117] The EC participated in the 1988 Conference and has ratified the 1988 Convention because of its legal competence over precursor chemicals. Drug control had been introduced onto the European agenda by the TREVI group (Terrorism, Radicalism, Extremism and International Violence) of EU justice and interior ministers in 1985. The European Committee to Combat Drugs (CELAD), set up in 1988 and representative of each member state, drafted the European Action Plan to Combat Drugs in 1990. Although CELAD has since been abolished and its responsibilities redistributed,[118] this planning process has been repeated with the latest plan covering the period 2000-2004. In their concern with strengthening anti-money laundering measures and precursor control, reinforcing existing trafficking laws and gathering statistical information, these action plans share the goals of the UN drug control system. Where these plans are an advance on the UN system is their concern with strengthening drug controls at external borders and increasing surveillance and co-operation within Europe.[119] The European Union (EU) has taken legally binding steps to implement these action plans. A 1991 Council Regulation lays down measures to prevent the diversion of precursor chemicals, a 1992 Council Directive regulates the movement of precursors within the EU, and a 1993 Council Directive is aimed at preventing the laundering of drug profits through the financial insti-

---

117 See generally G. Estievenart, 'The European Community and the global drugs phenomenon' in G. Estievenart (ed.), *Policies and Strategies to Combat Drugs in Europe* (Nijhoff, Dordrecht, 1995) pp. 50-93.

118 The Maastricht Treaty, in force in 1993, abolished CELAD and distributed responsibility for drug issues within the EU among Public Health (article 129), Common Foreign and Security Policy (Title V) and Co-operation in the fields of Justice and Home Affairs (Title VI)

119 Communication from the European Commission to the Council and the European Parliament on a European Union Action Plan to Combat Drugs, 1995-1999, cm. (94) 234 Final, Brussels.

tutions of the EU. The EU took its action plans a step further when in 1993 it set up two new drug control institutions. In Lisbon it established the European Monitoring Centre on Drugs and Drug Addiction (EMCDDA),[120] concerned with the gathering and analysis of reliable data on the full range of drug problems and the control strategies being developed in Europe. In the Hague it established the European Drugs Intelligence Centre, a non-operational agency for the exchange and analysis of information on drug trafficking among national drugs intelligence units. The latter agency's scope of operations expanded rapidly to include non-drug offences of mutual concern to European states,[121] and in July 1999 it evolved into the European Police Organisation, Europol.[122] Part of the third pillar of European Co-operation on Justice and Home Affairs, Europol has no operational powers.[123] However, in addition to operating a computer data-base for information exchange on both supply and demand, it supports and co-ordinates operations and provides technical and tactical support. The most specific and dramatic development of regional drug co-operation in Europe has been undertaken at the sub-regional level. The Schengen Agreements[124] oblige Parties to take the measures against the illicit traffic provided for in the UN drug conventions,[125] but they go further and develop direct law-enforcement co-operation methods such as cross-border police powers.[126] It is noteworthy that developments pioneered at the sub-regional level, such as the Schengen Information System (SIS), which centralises information on suspects, witnesses, persons and vehicles under surveillance and objects subject to seizure and confiscation, have been adopted in regional (EUROPOL) and international (UNDCP/Interpol) initiatives.[127]

---

120 Established in terms of Council Regulation 1302/93.

121 Terrorism, organised crime, money-laundering, illegal immigration.

122 With the coming into force of the 1995 Europol Convention – see Council Act of 26 July 1995, *Official Journal of the European Communities* No.C, p. 316.

123 There is some pressure to give Europol operational powers with cross-border capability but there is opposition within Europe to such an expansion of its functions because of the intrusion into national sovereignty – see P. Green, *Drugs, Trafficking and Criminal Policy* (Waterside Press, Winchester, 1998), p. 22.

124 Convention Applying the Schengen Agreement of 14 June 1985 between the Governments of the States of the Benelux Economic Union, the Federal Republic of Germany and the French Republic, on the Gradual Abolition of Checks at Their Common Borders, in force 19 June 1990. Article 70 provides for a working party to examine common problems and to address the technical and practical aspects of co-operation.

125 Article 71.

126 See Chapter 6 at footnote 269 and accompanying text.

127 See text accompanying footnote 50.

Regional drug control has also developed along similar lines in Asia. At a very broad level, the Colombo Plan, a plan for co-operative development in the Pacific set up in 1973, established a Drug Advisory Programme which has been heavily involved in regional drug control in concert with the UN, and helped to organise the first HONLEA meetings in 1976.[128] At a more integrated regional level, the Association of South East Asian Nations (ASEAN) established a Narcotics Desk in 1982 in order to co-ordinate anti-narcotics matters within and encourage co-operation among ASEAN states.[129] In 1986, ASEAN member states adopted a common programme to counter drug trafficking. ASEAN states made efforts to harmonise legislation on such matters as the refusal of travel documents to convicted drug offenders and the refusal of entry into member states to convicted drug offenders, and introduced the death penalty for serious drug offences. Three ASEAN training centres were established dealing with prevention in the Philippines, rehabilitation in Malaysia, and law enforcement in Thailand. In most case-related matters, however, co-operation remains a bilateral affair.[130] At a sub-regional level, the South Asian Association for Regional Co-operation (SAARC) adopted the SAARC Convention on Narcotic Drugs and Psychotropic Substances (in force in 1993) in order to regulate activities in drug control.[131]

In the Americas, the Organisation of American States (OAS) has been the most significant regional drug control organisation. After agreeing an illicit drug control programme of action in 1986, it established the thirty-four member Inter-American Drug Abuse Control Commission (CICAD) to oversee and develop its drug control policy and to work with member states to aid in formulating regional plans designed to combat illicit drug trafficking. Useful in the exchange of information on the illicit drug problem, the establishment of a drug surveillance monitoring system and other initiatives, CICAD has also supervised the ratification of the 1988 Convention by member states and their application of its provisions. One of its major efforts undertaken together with the UNDCP has been the updating and harmonising of drug legislation in Central American

---

128 See generally P.A. Abarro, 'The role of the Drug Advisory Programme of the Colombo Plan Bureau in the fight against illicit drug traffic' (1983) 35 *Bulletin on Narcotics* 67-72.

129 See generally C. Yodmani, 'The role of the Association of South East Asian Nations in fighting illicit drug traffic' (1983) 35 *Bulletin on Narcotics* 97-104.

130 See Anderson supra note 2 at 3.

131 UNDCP supra note 13 at 177.

states. In 1992, it produced Model Regulations Concerning Laundering Offences Connected to Illicit Drug Trafficking and Related Offences.[132]

While regional organisation of illicit drug control is strongest in highly integrated regions, it is more tenuous in less well-integrated regions. As a result, the UNDCP, relying on the 1988 Convention, adopts a more interventionist role in encouraging uniform application and interpretation of the drug conventions in these areas. [133]For example, the UNDCP and Organisation of African Unity (OAU) signed a Memorandum of Understanding in 1994 to increase co-operation in drug control. The UNDCP has also developed projects for co-operation with the Economic Community of Central African States (ECCAS) and the Economic Community of West African States (ECOWAS), and it encouraged the Southern African Development Community (SADC) to adopt a Protocol to the SADC Treaty addressing the drug issue. Where formal treaty relationships have been absent or difficult to establish, the UNDCP has encouraged states in a variety of sub-regions to sign memoranda of understanding on drug control.[134]

This brief overview of the illicit drug control activities of regional organisations reveals a basic pattern of involvement. These regional organisations commonly engage in long range strategic planning about the illicit drug problem, and then, against the background of the drug conventions and with the encouragement of the UN drug control organs, take steps to harmonise national laws and institutionalise research and intelligence gathering at the regional level. In many instances they are at the cutting edge of legal and institutional development. But, as with the UN organs, they remain largely supervisory in nature and operate at a strategic level. Engaging directly in drug control remains a national prerogative.

---

132 See generally B. Zagaris and C. Papavizas, 'Using the Organisation of American States to control international narcotics trafficking and money laundering' (1986) 57 *Revue Internationale de Droit Penal* 119-132.
133 UNDCP supra note 13 at 177.
134 The UNDCP supra note 13 at 176 gives the following examples: an agreement among the UNDCP, Poland, the Czech Republic, Slovenia, Hungary and the Slovak Republic in 1995; an agreement among Central Asian Republics endorsing a Sub-Regional Drug Control Co-operation Programme for Central Asia in 1996; an agreement between Mexico and Central American States in 1996; and the 1996 Barbados Plan of Action adopted by Caribbean and donor countries containing recommendations on law enforcement and maritime co-operation measures.

7.5   NATIONAL DRUG CONTROL STRUCTURES PARTICIPATING IN THE INTER-
          NATIONAL DRUG CONTROL SYSTEM

National drug control structures play a central role in the international drug
control system because the indirect implementation of the system takes place
through these national structures. But the enormous international influence of
some of these domestic structures means that they do more than just meet
domestic treaty obligations; they play a crucial role in the implementation of
the system as a whole. It is impossible to provide an exhaustive study of the
international activities of these structures here, so what follows is a brief comment on some features of their relationship with the international drug control
system.

The drug conventions encourage the development of national drug control
structures.[135] In particular, the UN has made the development of centralised
national authorities a priority because of their critical role in international co-
operation in areas requiring legal expertise, such as extradition, mutual legal
assistance and asset confiscation. However, while developed states usually have
some form of centralised authority dedicated to international legal assistance,[136] in developing states such requests are commonly handled by the general offices of justice ministries, which often lack the appropriate expertise.
As a result, the pressure for the establishment of national central authorities
is being maintained,[137] but resources are a problem. When it comes to the
establishment of national agencies for policing drugs, the position also depends
on the resources available. Developed states operate a range of law enforcement
agencies, some specialised and others not, and develop others in advance of
any international obligation to meet the changing threats offered by the illicit

---

135 See, for example, article 35(a) of the 1961 Convention and Chapter Five generally.
136 Centralisation commonly means that an umbrella body co-ordinates such activities. In
the UK, for example, international anti-drugs work is carried out by a large number
of different departments, with the Home Office playing a central co-ordinating role –
see T.J. David, 'The British Government's international anti-drugs work' (1991) 17
Commonwealth Law Bulletin 1368.
137 See, for example, D. Stafford, *International legal co-operation against serious crime:
inter-legal systems issues impacting on international co-operation* (unpublished paper,
New Delhi Global Drugs Law Conference, 1997), p. 4.

traffic.[138] In developing states drugs policing may still be performed by the ordinary police force.

What then of the impact of these national agencies on the implementation of international drug control? At a comparative level, national drug law enforcement is dramatically out of balance due to differences in capacity and political will. The heavyweights, exerting most of the power and having the most impact on international drug control, are the consumer states from the developed world, dominated by the United States.[139] The national drug strategy of the United States has obvious international implications, because the United States has extended its war against drugs internationally. The law enforcement model in other developed states has been heavily influenced by American practice. European states[140] have followed the Americans by adopting specialised drug enforcement units,[141] using American investigative techniques like controlled delivery, and granting these techniques legal sanction. The "Americanisation" of foreign drug law enforcement has its roots in the American desire for other developed states to share the burden of international drug law enforcement and other developed states have fallen into line because of significant increases in domestic drug supply.[142]

Developing drug producer and transit states are part of the problem for the United States and its allies because of the policy of these consumer states to act extraterritorially against extraterritorial drug supply. At more formal levels, consumer states have pursued the harmonisation of the drug laws of drug producer and transit states, and they have encouraged these states to co-operate in all forms of legal assistance. At operational levels, the enforcement agencies

---

138 A recent development with obvious international implications has been the establishment of Financial Intelligence Units (FIUs) dealing with money laundering intelligence and ensuring adherence to financial laws. AUSTRAC (the Australian Transaction Reports and Analysis Centre), for example, is a central body established by the Australian Parliament to receive, collate and analyse reports of transaction from cash dealers.

139 The US "drug czar", head of the Office of National Drug Control Policy (ONDCP) located in the Executive Office of the President, has a major international profile. A lot of international influence is also exerted by the State Department's Bureau of International Narcotics and Law Enforcement Affairs which uses economic aid either directly or to the UNDCP's fund to achieve its international law enforcement goals.

140 See E.A. Nadelmann, *Cops Across Borders: The Internationalization of U.S. Criminal Law Enforcement* (The Pennsylvania State University Press, University Park, 1993), p.192.

141 For example, in France, the *Office Centrale de Repression du Traffic Illicite de Stupefiants*, and in Italy, the *Servizio Centrale Antidroga*.

142 Nadelmann supra note 140 at 247.

of developing states have been enormously influential. The state with the most powerful foreign enforcement presence is, of course, the United States. Its Drug Enforcement Agency (DEA) has the largest international presence of any domestic law enforcement agency in the world,[143] while the Federal Bureau of Investigation (FBI) and US Customs also maintain permanent representatives in many countries. Large numbers of United States officials, often attached to embassies, engage in a wide variety of extraterritorial operational activities with the consent and co-operation of host countries.[144] Where the United States has lead, others have followed. Nadelmann refers to the emergence of a 'transnational police community and subculture based upon common tasks and the common objective of immobilising the criminal.'[145] Most developed states now have drug liaison officers (DLOs) posted in producer and transit states.[146] A feature of the proliferation of national drug law enforcement agencies working internationally is their lack of accountability and transparency.[147] The increasing use by the United States of its military and intelligence services in drug law enforcement falls completely outside any international agreement,[148] but

---

143 See E.A. Nadelmann, 'The role of the United States in the international enforcement of criminal law' (1990) 31 *Harvard International Law Journal* 37 at 48.

144 Among various activities they maintain communications with local police, train and undertake joint operations with local police, conduct limited unilateral activities such as surveillance and recruitment of informants, provide intelligence to local authorities and lobby for changes in local laws to facilitate drug law enforcement objectives. Although they are not permitted in terms of domestic legislation to participate directly in drug arrests abroad, they may be present at arrests and assist foreign law enforcement officials and take direct action to ensure their own safety (the 1961 Foreign Assistance Act, 22 USC section 481(c) and section 2291(c), as amended by section 504(b) of the International Security Assistance and Arms Export Control Act of 1976, 90 USC section 764, and the 1989 International Narcotics Control Act 103 USC section 1954). See generally A.B. Campbell, 'The Ker-Frisbie doctrine: a jurisdictional weapon in the war on drugs' (1990) 23 *Vanderbilt Journal of Transnational Law* 385 at 422-427; and S.R. Murphy, 'Drug diplomacy and the supply side strategy: a survey of United States practice' (1990) 43 *Vanderbilt Law Review* 1259 at 1277-1281. Nadelmann supra note 140 at 46-57 sets out the international law enforcement role of US agencies in full.

145 Supra note 140 at 188.

146 David supra note 136 at 1374 sets out the details of Britain's system of drug liaison officers which has become steadily more extensive. In 1990, it had 27 agents abroad. By 1997, that number had increased to 47.

147 J. Sheptycki, 'Law enforcement, justice and democracy in the transnational arena: reflections on the war on drugs' (1996) 24 *International Journal of the Sociology of Law* 61 at 66-71.

148 See generally Murphy supra note 144 at 1277-1289.

again other states have followed suit.[149] The extent to which these developments have been reinforced by the 1988 Convention is striking. You may recall from the discussion in Chapters Five and Six, for instance, article 9(1)(c) on joint law enforcement teams, article 9(1)(e) on drug liaison officers, article 11 on controlled delivery and article 17(10) on the role of naval vessels in maritime interdiction. On the receiving end of the co-operation offered by the agencies of developed states are the law enforcement agencies of producer and transit states. They have become heavily involved in the suppression of illicit drugs, frequently serving as vicarious police forces for the law enforcement agencies of developed states.[150] But they suffer from understaffing and inexperience[151] and find themselves in a vastly unequal relationship with the law enforcement authorities of the consumer states because of the enormous resources and capabilities of the latter. Nadelmann notes wryly that 'the fairly operational activities of US agents in foreign countries only rarely have lead to demands that foreign police agents be permitted to do likewise in the United States.'[152] Moreover, while the law enforcement agencies of the developing world may have different views as to how the international drug control system should develop, with more emphasis on demand rather than supply reduction, these views carry little weight because of their lack of political influence or professional expertise.

Assessment of the practical impact of the various organs involved in international drug control illustrates that the national organs of developed states are significantly more successful at enforcing international drug prohibition than the organs of the UN. Apart from the fact that they engage in operational policing while UN organs are non-operational, they are also subject to fewer restrictions on their actions. Nadelmann suggests that the various national drug control organs operating internationally are 'transnational organisations' rather than 'international organisations', because they perform relatively limited, specialised, and in some sense technical functions across national boundaries.[153] Unlike the UN's drug control organs, which are international or-

---

149 See Sheptycki supra note 147 at 69-71 who notes that the British Navy is now employed in drug interdiction and that British intelligence services are also entering the field.
150 Nadelmann supra note 140 at 193.
151 For example, the Indian Narcotic Control Bureau, formed in 1994, only had 160 personnel in 1997 – see D.R. Saxena, *Illicit Traffic in Narcotic Drugs and Psychotropic Substances and the Law in India* (unpublished conference paper, New Delhi Global Drugs Law Conference, 1997), p. 24.
152 Nadelmann supra note 140 at 469.
153 Nadelmann supra note 140 at 110 citing S. Huntington, 'Transnational organisations in world politics' (1973) 25 *World Politics* 333.

ganisations, they appear to be more effective because they have adopted the operating principles associated with non-governmental transnational organisations such as commercial multi-nationals – a disinterest in sovereignty – and thus do not face the problems with confronting and overcoming state sovereignty in acquitting their tasks.[154] The DEA's ostensibly non-political programme, for example, allows it in effect to submerge below politics. This is a luxury not afforded to the UN's drug control organs, which are, by contrast, forced to respect sovereignty and are thus subject to the vagaries of state politics to a much greater extent than national organs. What is significant for our purposes, however, is that the drug conventions recognise, through provision for international law enforcement co-operation and so on, the important international role of national law enforcement agencies. As Nadelmann puts it:

> As a transnational organisation, the [DEA] is a hybrid of a national police agency and an international law enforcement organisation. It represents the interests of one nation and its agents are responsible to the ambassador, yet it has a mandate and a mission effectively authorised by international conventions and the United Nations.[155]

The DEA plays the role of an international drug police by proxy, and it has a powerful influence in this role. It seems unlikely that many other states would openly agree that this is the role a national government organisation should be playing, but in the absence of an international drug police force and with a declared international war on drugs being waged, the withdrawal of national organisations such as the DEA seems unlikely. Indeed, their role is implicit within the international drug control system.

7.6   SUPERVISION AND IMPLEMENTATION OF ILLICIT DRUG CONTROL IN REVIEW

7.6.1   Introduction

The map of the institutions within the international drug control system which engage in the supervision and implementation of drug control completed, this final part of Chapter Seven is devoted to an examination of problems and weak-

---

154 See Nadelmann supra note 140 at 111 citing Huntington at 368.
155 Nadelmann supra note 140 at 129.

nesses of the system as a whole in performing these administrative and executive functions. It examines first organisational problems common to the various constituent institutional parts of the international drug control system. It then turns to specific legal weaknesses within the system, including difficulties with the settlement of disputes and the problem of reservations. Finally, it considers the execution of the system, and the innate weakness of the system as a whole.

7.6.2   Organisational problems

The international drug control system, like any other of an institutional nature, has problems, the most serious of which is funding. The UN's drug control organs often find themselves in a dire funding position. Although resolution three of the 1988 Diplomatic Conference's non-binding resolutions urged Parties to the 1988 Convention to press within the UN for approval of the necessary budgetary appropriations for drug control, a 1998 Expert Group Review of the UN's drug control machinery recognised that the fragile funding of the UNDCP had limited its operational capacity and recommended that a larger share of the regular UN budget should be allocated to it.[156] But the UN has budgetary constraints, and much of the influence of developed drug consumer states within the international drug control system is derived from the fact that a large part of the UNDCP's budget comes from their voluntary contributions.[157] IGOs such as Interpol also suffer from funding problems, in marked contrast to the funds available for illicit drug control at the national level in, for example, the United States. Despite the funding problems of international organisations, national contributions to the international drug control system as part of total drug control expenditure are very low.[158]

---

156 Recommendation A.1, *Strengthening the United Nations Machinery for Drug Control* E/CN.7/1999/5, 7 December 1998, p. 4.

157 K. Raustalia, 'Law, Liberalization and International Narcotics Trafficking', (1999) 32 *New York University Journal of International Law and Politics* 89 at 103. The UNDCP's budget for 1996-1997 was $157 million, 89.9% made up of voluntary contributions which are not always forthcoming. The annual donor's meeting is a major event in the UNDCP.

158 In 1991, for example, the US drug control budget of $11.9 billion was split as follows: 93.6% to domestic efforts, 6.3% to bilateral assistance, and 0.1% to multilateral drug control programmes such as the UNDCP – see S.E. Flynn and G.M. Grant, *The Transnational Drug Challenge and the New World Order: The Report of the CSIS Project on the Global Drug Trade in the Post-Cold War Era* (The Centre for Strategic and International Studies, Washington, 1993), p. 20.

A problem related indirectly to funding is complexity. The whole system is too complex. It reflects the proliferation of professions involved in the system. Police, social workers, politicians, bureaucrats, rural development specialists, chemists, psychologists and psychotherapists, economists, intelligence experts, lawyers and so on, can all be found within it. Complexity is exacerbated by institutional overlap. The proliferation of organisations all operating in the same field and all competing for resources both overcomplicates the system and wastes resources.[159] The size of the task undertaken, the geographical scope of the system and the system's own complexity all helps to generate an information overload. The complexity of the system also generates a large bureaucracy, which is vulnerable to criticisms of self-interest and resistance to change. The Panamanian delegate to the 1972 Conference stated provocatively that the CND and INCB 'were paralysed by bureaucracy and hence incapable of providing real assistance to countries which requested it.'[160] The formation of the UNDCP has addressed this problem to a certain extent, and recent further reorganisation of the UN's Vienna operations appears to have been carried out with the aim of reducing the bureaucracy and thus the cost of international drug control.[161] Quality assurance is an issue, but the UN drug control organs are self-regulatory. This criticism is highlighted by allegations that the UNDCP responds in a contradictory manner to the failure of its efforts to suppress illicit cultivation, and that it is inclined to public relations type reporting rather than accurate reporting of indicators.[162] Recently, further steps have been taken to address this criticism.[163]

Finally, and not unexpectedly, conflicts exist within the system. 'Turf wars' between law enforcement organisations within states can frustrate adequate inter-

---

159 For example, Anderson supra note 2 at 112-113 points out the duplication of Interpol functions by HONLEA meetings.

160 *1972 Records* vol. II at 161.

161 Placing the UNDCP and CICP under the control of the ODCCP is one such step.

162 R. Seccombe, 'Squeezing the balloon: international drugs policy' (1995) 14 *Drug and Alcohol Review* 311-316. Previously a Field Advisor with the UNDCP in Pakistan, he argues that the UNDCP's failure to control illicit cultivation has resulted in it responding contradictorily. It reports the spread of illicit cultivation in order to attract funding but also reports success in suppressing illicit cultivation. Illicit production increases are sometimes not reported to the CND or are said to be fluctuating when in fact they are increasing.

163 The UN has shown greater interest in institutional reform since the beginning of Kofi Annan's term as UN Secretary General, and an Expert Group has been convened to review the UN's international drug control work – UN Press Release GA/9423.

national co-operation.[164] Rivalry also exists between the national agencies of different states and between the UN's drug control organs. Sometimes trust relationships, crucial to international co-operation, are also absent.[165] National differences will always be a problem in a system that rests on national co-operation. Language differences, differences in legal systems and procedures, differences in appreciation of the causes and solutions of the drug problem, all present difficulties. Political considerations lead to pointless political posturing at meetings.[166]

All of these difficulties – funding, complexity, and conflict – serve to undermine the effectiveness of the system as a whole. But even more debilitating are the fundamental legal weaknesses of the system, which stem largely from its international nature.

7.6.3   Legal weaknesses within the system

Given the international drug control system's controversial nature, disputes will arise. But the drug conventions provide for ineffectual dispute resolution systems, a weakness that serves to undermine the system as a whole.

Dispute settlement under the 1961 Convention is governed by article 48. Article 48(1) requires Parties to make an attempt to settle a dispute by the peaceful means there specified, before being obliged by article 48(2) to refer it to the ICJ. However, article 50 permits Parties to make reservations to article 48, and some Parties to the 1961 Convention have made a reservation to article 48(2) to the effect that they do not accept the compulsory jurisdiction of the ICJ.[167] The very similar article 31 of the 1971 Convention provides in paragraph 1 for peaceful settlement of a dispute, and failing that, in paragraph 2 for unilateral referral to the ICJ for decision. However, article 32(2)(c) allows Parties to reserve in respect of article 31 of the 1971 Convention. Some Parties

---

164 Anderson supra note 2 at 115.
165 Anderson supra note 2 at 115.
166 Anderson supra note 2 at 114.
167 The wording of the article states that Parties 'shall' refer the dispute to the ICJ for decision, if the preliminary measures fail to resolve it. Algeria (7/4/1965), Argentina (24/10/1969), Indonesia (3/9/1976) and Romania (14/1/1974) have all made reservations to the effect that they do not recognise the compulsory jurisdiction of the ICJ in terms of article 48(2) – see *Multilateral Treaties Deposited* (1997) at 282-284.

have objected to article 31 as a whole.[168] Other Parties have objected to the granting to one Party of the unilateral right to refer the dispute to the ICJ, and have made reservations to the effect that the agreement of all Parties to the dispute is required before it can be referred to the ICJ.[169] And other Parties still have simply refused to recognise the compulsory jurisdiction of the ICJ.[170] In practical effect, the possibility of reservation means that both the provisions in the 1961 and 1971 Convention only provide for the optional jurisdiction of the ICJ. [171]

The 1988 Convention appears to provide for the compulsory jurisdiction of the ICJ but it too in reality is optional. Its dispute settlement mechanism is set out in article 32. Article 32(1) provides that should a dispute arise between Parties as to the application or interpretation of the Convention they must first try to settle it by peaceful means between themselves. If they cannot, article 32(2) provides that the dispute 'shall be referred, at the request of any one of the States Parties to the dispute, to the International Court of Justice for decision.' Article 32(3) provides for the situation where a regional economic organisation is participating in the Convention and has become party to a dispute. In terms of article 34(1) of the Statute of the International Court of Justice only states can be party to contentious cases before the ICJ, thus article 32(3) provides that such an organisation may through a UN member state request ECOSOC to request an advisory opinion of the ICJ, 'which opinion shall be regarded as decisive.' The weakness in the 1988 Convention's dispute mechanism scheme is article 32(4),[172] which allows a state or regional economic organisa-

---

168 Cuba reserved its rights in respect of article 31 on the basis that all disputes should be resolved diplomatically (26/4/1976) – *Multilateral Treaties Deposited* (1997) at 289. See also reservations by Egypt (4/6/1972), Myanmar (20/6/94), South Africa (27/1/1972), Turkey (1/4/1981) – *Multilateral Treaties Deposited* (1997) at 289-291.

169 See the reservations made by Afghanistan (21/5/1985), Belarus (15/12/1978), France (28/2/1975), Iraq (17/5/1976), Poland (3/1/1975), Russian Federation (3/11/1978), Tunisia (23/7/1979), Ukraine (20/11/1978) – *Multilateral Treaties Deposited* (1997) at 288-291.

170 Bahrain (7/2/1990), India (23/4/1975), Libyan Arab Jamahiriya (24/4/1979), Papua New Guinea (28/10/1980) – *Multilateral Treaties Deposited* (1997) at 288-290.

171 Chatterjee supra note 3 at 448 endnote 104 submits that the Parties are not obliged to accept jurisdiction and that following general principles, the common will of the parties to the dispute will determine the ICJ's jurisdiction.

172 See W.C. Gilmore, *Combating International Drugs Trafficking: The 1988 United Nations Convention Against Illicit Traffic in Narcotic Drugs and Psychotropic Substances* (Commonwealth Secretariat, London, 1991), p. 40. A number of states have taken advantage of this escape clause. Peru declared (20/12/1988) as follows: 'In accordance with the provision of article 32, paragraph 4, Peru declares, on signing the Convention

tion upon becoming a Party to the Convention to declare that it does not consider itself bound by either article 32(2) or 32(3), whichever is appropriate. Upon such a declaration article 32 is inoperative between that Party and all other Parties. Article 32(5) allows a Party to withdraw such a declaration. Commentators have been deeply critical of article 32(4). They argue that it allows Parties to avoid dispute settlement completely.[173] This weakens the 1988 Convention as a whole and furthermore, unsettled disputes can lead to a lack of co-operation among Parties and a weakening of law enforcement action against the illicit traffic.[174] As yet, a breach of the conventions' obligations has never been referred to international arbitration or judicial settlement, nor has any dispute arisen as to their interpretation. The likely explanation is that in most cases the Parties prefer to use more discreet methods of solving problems, while in the case of serious problems the Parties do not believe that the optional dispute settlement mechanism can produce concrete results.

Reservations by Parties to the drug conventions also undermine the international drug control system. Reservations in respect of the 1961 and 1971 Convention's penal provisions are not directly provided for, but are legally possible, and have been made.[175] Despite the fact that it was hoped that the 1988 Convention would prohibit reservations, it makes no provision for reservations at all and leaves the issue to general international law, which means that reservations may be made unless they are incompatible with the object

---

... that it does not consider itself bound by article 32, paragraphs 2 and 3, since, in respect of this Convention, it agrees to the referral of disputes to the International Court of Justice only if all the parties, and not just one, agree to such a procedure.' The list of objecting Parties includes: Algeria (9/5/1995) – article 32(2); Bahrain (7/2/1990) – article 32(2); Brunei (12/12/1993) – article 32(2) and (3); China (25/8/1989) – article 32(2) and (3); France (31/12/1990) article 32(2) and (3); Iran (7/12/1992) – article 32(2) and (3); Lebanon (1/3/1996) – article 32(2) and (3); Malaysia (11/5/1993) – article 32(2) and (3); Myanmar (11/6/1991) – article 32(2) and (3); Peru (16/1/1992) – article 32(2) and (3); Saudi Arabia (9/1/1992) – article 32(2) and (3); United States (20/2/1990) – article 32(2) and (3); see generally *Multilateral Treaties Deposited* (1997) at 302-307.

173   Gianaris supra note 71 at 108.

174   T.M. Catino, 'Italian and American co-operative efforts to reduce heroin trafficking: a role model for the United States and drug supplying foreign nations' (1990) 8 *Dickinson Journal of International Law* 415 at 438.

175   Article 50(1) provides for a general ban on reservations, but article 50(3) provides for a special procedure that allows reservations in the absence of objections by at least one third of the other Parties. Article 32 paragraphs (1) and (3) of the 1971 Convention are of similar effect.

and purpose of the treaty.[176] And reservations have also been made to the 1988 Convention's provisions, as should be apparent, for example, from the examination in Chapter Six of article 17(3)'s provision for consensual interdiction of foreign flag vessels at sea. Sproule and Saint-Denis comment:

> States unwilling to shoulder strong obligations will not only have available to them numerous safeguard clauses, but will also be able to reserve on provisions they deem objectionable so long as the provisions comply with the Vienna Convention's rather generous rules on reservations.[177]

Despite these misgivings, the presence of extensive safeguard clauses in the 1988 Convention appears to have limited the need for Parties to make extensive reservations.

7.6.3   The execution of the system

While substantial progress has been made towards providing a legal basis for the international drug control system in international law, the system is still seen by many as inadequate for the suppression of illicit drugs. Central to this doubt is the sense that the international measures for ensuring state compliance with the undertakings they have made are ineffective.[178] As we have seen, there are various methods of ensuring compliance, some with a stronger treaty basis than others. At the "soft" end of the scale we find publicity. While the provision of information by states to the UN drug control organs is an obligation provided by treaty, the publication of that information is not, but it has become international practice and the resulting publicity plays an important role in execution of the system because as Bassiouni states:

> Governments are extremely sensitive to any public outcry that they have failed to co-operate in such a social humanitarian activity. Such publicity is intended to be provided by published reports of the organs of international control based on information furnished by governments (annual reports, laws, statistics, estimates, seizure reports) and by discussions in various United Nations bodies and dissemination of general information.[179]

---

176 See *Genocide Convention Case* 1951 ICJ Reports at 15, and articles 19 and 20 of the 1969 Vienna Convention on the Law of Treaties, 1155 UNTS 331.
177 Supra note 63 at 290-291.
178 Bassiouni supra note 47 at 515.
179 Supra note 47 at 510.

The inherent weakness of publicity is that it relies on information furnished by states themselves, information that is not always complete or reliable. Diplomatic pressure is a next possible step if publicity fails. The UN and Parties do resort to such pressure.[180] It may be used for immediate operational goals such as forcing states to make arrests and seizures, as well as for longer-term goals such as forcing the enactment of new laws and the adoption of new policies. At the "tough" end of the scale of enforcement measures lie the INCB's unused and intrinsically weak embargo powers. Other legal options are available. It has been argued, for instance, that a failure by Parties to obey the general duty to co-operate in articles 35 and 36(2)(b) of the 1961 Convention is a breach of a contractual obligation, for which breach the Contracting Party can be taken to task.[181] Action to remedy such a breach, indeed any breach of the conventions, may include collective economic sanctions, but such action will always be ad hoc and dependent on the nature of the political support available. Raustiala sums up the UN's enforcement of the system thus:

> As a formal matter, compliance with international drug law is largely managed rather than enforced by the U.N. system. That is to say, the U.N. system provides extensive assistance to parties in implementing their international commitments and solving problems of capacity, training, or technical expertise that might result in non-compliance with their international obligations. But managerial compliance efforts are, in the case of international drug control, in practice backed up by a large, if unofficial, enforcement stick.[182]

He is referring to the unwillingness of the United States to allow the enforcement of the system to rely entirely on multilateral diplomacy. Section 490 of its Foreign Assistance Act of 1961 requires its Administration to consider the extent to which major drug producing and transit countries have met the goals and objectives of the 1988 Convention. If it decides they have not, the Act requires the Administration to de-certify the country in question, which results in the suspension of most forms of assistance by the United States together with the application of optional trade sanctions. De-certifications have occurred, and are a source of consternation to the governments of developing drug-producing states. The United States is not the only state to link aid to drug control efforts – it has been reported that the United Kingdom and European

---

180 See David supra note 136 at 1374 noting British practice.
181 Chatterjee supra note 3 at 356.
182 Supra note 157 at 111-112.

Union both use a tacit linkage of aid to co-operation in the suppression of drugs.[183] The result seems to have been equal measures of commitment to drug control by local elites in these states and efforts to block de-certification.[184] The implicit rationale for this extraordinary method of executing the system is the failure of the system to provide sufficiently "tough" measures for the enforcement of implementation. It conjures up the spectre of the potential use of even more extraordinary methods of execution. In 1935, the responsibility of a state failing to prevent the export of illicit drugs that threaten the health and welfare of the inhabitants of other states was likened to the responsibility of a state for allowing its inhabitants to fire shots across an international frontier.[185] Given the preoccupation of the United States with illicit drug production in states in Central and South America, this analogy of failing to stop the illicit traffic as constituting a form of aggression that can by extension be met by self-defence is today more pertinent than ever.[186]

Weak multilateral enforcement measures and the linchpin role of the United States point to a fundamental systemic weakness. This chapter began by examining the various organs that form part of the UN's system of drug control. The discussion focused on their supervisory roles as defined by the drug conventions, that is, their roles within international law. It then turned to international organisations and the regional economic organisations with jurisdiction over illicit drug control matters, which also have a place within this system. Finally it examined the constituent parts of the system, national drug control organs, which play a crucial role in the implementation of the system. To call it a system at all may be a misnomer, given that while mechanisms for co-operation and co-ordination are in place, the strength of these mechanisms is doubtful

---

183 Green supra note 123 at 33

184 The latest effort to pre-empt unilateral assessment by the US is the OAS' Multilateral Evaluation Mechanism which will allow OAS states to assess each other's anti-drug performance multilaterally – *International Herald Tribune*, 4 November 1999. Producer states according to Raustalia supra note 157 at 112 also labour under the impression that UN data is used by the United States in the certification process, leading to attempts to block the release of such data through fear of US bilateral action. Raustalia cites a UNDCP source as alleging that Pakistan blocked the release of a UNDCP draft report citing illicit drug production as four percent of the country's GDP for this reason.

185 See S.H. Bailey, *The Anti-Drug Campaign: An Experiment in International Control* (P.S. King, London, 1935), pp. 143-144.

186 The US has resorted to a similar argument to justify its abduction of drug traffickers from foreign states – see A. Fletcher, 'Pirates and smugglers: an analysis of the use of abductions to bring drug traffickers to trial' (1991) 32 *Virginia Journal of International Law* 233 at 259.

and organisations appear to operate largely independently of each-other and at different levels of co-operation. In effect, what begins with the small and coherent UN system of organisations expands into something much bigger and more incoherent. This larger system is of interest because it grows out of the system of international drug control created by the drug conventions. Indirect application of international law makes this system possible because it overcomes sovereignty concerns. But indirect application is also the system's greatest weakness from the point of view of the effective institutionalisation of enforcement of global prohibition because it compromises effectiveness. This inherent weakness is exemplified by the provision through the system of various fairly weak mechanisms for enforcing implementation. From the point of view of the effectiveness of enforcement of prohibition, there can be no substitute for a centralised drug control system applying prohibition directly. But that is not yet possible, hence the unilateral role of the United States.

8

CONCLUSION

[One] of the prime advantages of [the 1988] Convention which largely rep-
licates the criminal sanctions which you and your colleagues and we in the
law enforcement community have succeeded in having placed on the books
in the United States – [is that] replicating those among all the signatory
nations of the world will have a distinct advantage in not only securing a
uniformity in terms of offence, but a world-wide consensus which expresses
our abhorrence of this type of trafficking.

*(United States Attorney General Richard Thornburgh before Senate Hearing
on Ratification of the 1988 Convention)[1]*

8.1   THE INTERNATIONAL ILLICIT DRUG CONTROL SYSTEM – AN INTER-
NATIONAL LEGAL SYSTEM ENFORCING GLOBAL DRUG PROHIBITION

The statement by the United States Attorney General quoted above reflects the
two major concerns of the international drug control system. The first is a
concern born of the perception that unilateral and bilateral law enforcement
measures have failed to suppress illicit drugs. It reflects the technical concern
of the law enforcer – that international law should establish a uniform and strong
domestic drug law globally in order to institute as effective an international
illicit drug suppression system as possible, a system that provides for uniform
national responses to drug offenders and a no-hiding-place approach to transnational drug offenders and their assets. But the statement also reflects the
political concern of the policy maker – that all states should subscribe to the
policy of prohibition. Although these interests are in a dynamic relationship,

---

1   *United Nations Convention Against Illicit Traffic in Narcotic Drugs and Psychotropic
Substances* Senate Executive Report 101-15, 101st Congress, 1st Session, p.134.

it is the latter which in the main drives the former. The primary function of the international drug control system is to institutionalise drug prohibition by getting most states to agree to the need for co-operation in the suppression of illicit drugs through the criminal law irrespective of political and other differences, and to close the international debate on alternative policies.[2] The advocates of drug prohibition have institutionalised drug prohibition globally by using international law to first define licit drug production, supply and use, and then to create an international system to suppress illicit drug production, supply and use. Agreement to specific international drug conventions, setting out a range of technical measures, has provided the legislative foundation for the drug control system as a whole. This book has examined the law dealing with the penal aspects of the international control system and, to a lesser extent, the policy driving the law. Comments and conclusions about the system can usefully be grouped into these two general categories of law and policy.

8.2   AN EVALUATION OF THE INTERNATIONAL LEGAL PROVISIONS FOR THE SUPPRESSION OF ILLICIT DRUGS

8.2.1   The substantive and procedural provisions of the drug conventions

The international community has attempted to suppress illicit drugs through the progressive layering of penal provisions in the 1961 Convention, 1971 Convention, 1972 Protocol and 1988 Convention. These penal provisions apply indirectly via the agency of domestic law, and it follows that the principal barrier to realising the suppression of illicit drugs is entrenched domestic legal difference. Revisiting the examination of the substantive and procedural provisions of the drug conventions undertaken in Chapters Three to Seven demonstrates how international law attempts to harmonise domestic law and practice and reveals the kind of framework international law provides for the suppression of illicit drugs.

Chapter Three first examines the drug conventions' attempt to lay down a system of uniform drug offences in domestic law. I use the word "attempt" because although the drug conventions oblige Parties to render certain forms of drug related conduct unlawful in domestic law, a range of limitation clauses

---

2   E.A. Nadelmann, *Cops Across Borders* (The Pennsylvania State University Press, University Park, 1993) at 9. See also M. Elvins, 'Drugs and the state in a global network' (1997) 5 *The South African Journal of International Affairs* 1 at 6.

render these obligations open to domestic variation and non-application. Domestic limitation has been allowed largely because of the broad scope of these provisions; they attack almost all conduct relating to the illicit production and supply of drugs. The 1961 Convention establishes the "classical" trafficking offences that are the cornerstones of the illicit drug control system today and although the 1971 Convention adopts an open-ended approach, Parties to both conventions have enacted the same classical offences in respect of psychotropic substances. These earlier drug conventions also introduced to civilian legal systems exotic common law notions, such as conspiracy, deemed essential for the legal assault on the illicit traffic. The 1988 Convention returns to and reinforces the 1961 Convention's enumerative approach, and expands the range of conduct to include drug related financial and commercial activity, such as money laundering. However, its enumeration of offences means that its provisions are not sufficiently flexible to comfortably embrace new forms of conduct such as narco-terrorism.[3] In spite of their differences, the conventions are all concerned primarily with reducing supply rather than demand. The earlier conventions were ambiguous on the issue of using the criminal law to suppress demand, but through political pressure from drug producer states the 1988 Convention criminalises personal use. With regard to the mental element of the offences created by the conventions, the ambiguity or silence of the conventions allows Parties to vary the fault requirements of domestic drug offences widely, and problematically to apply negligent and no-fault liability. Examined as a whole, it would seem that the provisions of the drug conventions for offences are capable at most of the loose harmonisation of domestic drug offences. Perfect harmony or uniformity was never a realistic goal because of the difficulties the conventions' authors had in overcoming the barriers created by distinctive domestic grammars of criminal law, and the reluctance of some Parties to use the full range of measures to suppress the changing illicit drug economy. Chapter Three next turns to the attempt by the drug conventions to secure the uniform application by Parties of severe penalties for serious offences, such as the classical trafficking offences, and less-severe punishment for less-serious offences such as personal use offences. Because of the strong resistance by states to international intervention in their punishment regimes, the conventions do little more than construct a crude framework along these lines and leave

---

3   See F. Patel, 'Crime without frontiers: a proposal for an international narcotics court' (1990) 22 *New York University Journal of International Law and Politics* 709 at 727, who notes that the training of militia to protect drug traffickers is an offence neither anticipated nor covered by the conventions.

most of the detail to the individual Parties. The Parties in turn have in their practise applied punishments ranging from the death penalty to heavy terms of imprisonment to heavy financial penalties. The drug conventions do contain provisions for identification of drug abuse, treatment, education, after-care, rehabilitation and social reintegration, but only in the least serious cases do these provisions operate as substitutes for rather than additions to punishment. The system of control set up by the 1961 Convention is principally preventive and subordinately remedial or curative. The 1971 Convention and the 1972 Protocol attempt ineffectively to remedy the absence of curative options, while the 1988 Convention turns away from curative options and back to repression. The drug conventions reveal the international community's determination to punish drug offences harshly and the profound reluctance of the international community to pass control of the drug problem into non-law enforcement hands. Incoherence in international punishment policy – it is driven by conflicting notions of deterrence, retribution and to a much smaller extent rehabilitation – has resulted in blunt provisions that appear incapable of establishing even a loose harmonisation of the global punishment and/or treatment of drug offenders.

Chapter Four examines the provision made in the drug conventions for the global pursuit of drug offenders. Although ostensibly committed to a no-hiding place approach to drug offenders, the drug conventions, sensitive to territorial and national sovereignty, approach the issue of jurisdiction over drug offences cautiously. The earlier conventions affirm the principle of territorial jurisdiction as the primary form of jurisdiction, and then regulate extraterritorial jurisdiction through a qualified form of the principle of subsidiary universality subject to heavy domestic limitation. Considering these provisions inadequate for reaching transnational drug offenders, the authors of the 1988 Convention attempted greater extension of jurisdiction. But the 1988 Convention also reaffirms the primacy of territorial jurisdiction, and then circumscribes the reach of extraterritorial jurisdiction by subjecting its establishment to recognised links between the offender and the Party establishing jurisdiction such as nationality and the effects principle. Like the earlier conventions, the 1988 Convention relies as a fallback position on subsidiary universality, but again its provisions in this regard are heavily qualified because common law states reject universal jurisdiction over drug offences as they are committed to the extradition of extraterritorial drug offenders whatever their nationality. Unfortunately for common law states, their attempt to use the drug conventions to make extradition possible in every situation has been diluted by states concerned primarily with protecting the domestic right not to extradite drug traffickers who are their nationals. The 1961 Convention makes weak provision for extradition, the 1971 Convention's extradition provisions are slightly more effective, while the 1972 Protocol only moderately strengthens the extradition provisions of the 1961 Convention. Although the 1988 Convention's provisions on extradition echo the development of bilateral relations in extradition after 1972, they do not overcome obstacles to effective extradition such as the nationality and political offence exceptions. Indeed, the drug conventions' limited extradition provisions reflect the opposition of civilian states to the policy of universal extradition being pursued by common law states. It is patent that the international community has not reached a consensus on how to establish an effective no-hiding place approach to international drug offences.

Chapter Five turns its attention to the provision made by the drug conventions for general law enforcement co-operation. The development of these measures has been driven by the practical exigencies of policing illicit drugs nationally and internationally. The earlier conventions do little more than: i) try to centralise national control of drug law enforcement to facilitate international co-operation; ii) provide for general international co-operation; iii) provide for the furnishing of information on the illicit traffic to control organs; and iv) provide for the speedy transmission of legal papers. Limitation clauses abound. The massive increase in extraterritorial law enforcement action in the 1970s and 1980s saw the dedication of the 1988 Convention as a law enforcement instrument, designed to draw the law enforcement and legal agencies of the Parties together into much closer and more direct forms of co-operation. It makes detailed provision for mutual legal assistance in respect of the investigation, prosecution and adjudication of drug offences and neutralised bank secrecy. It also makes provision for the novel concept of transfer of proceedings, and for sophisticated forms of general law enforcement co-operation such as provision for direct communication between law enforcement agents and prosecutors, as well as international co-operation in the conduct of investigations. In addition, it obliges Parties to train their personnel in modern law enforcement methods and provides for international co-operation in this regard. Finally, hortatory provisions recognise the financial needs of transit states in respect of law enforcement co-operation. The 1988 Convention has been praised for technical legal innovation and refinement in the field of multilateral international criminal co-operation. In many areas such as direct mutual legal assistance it has been at the cutting edge of legal development. From the law enforcement point of view, however, its provisions are vulnerable to the criticism that at most they serve as frameworks for macro and meso level co-operation, providing little detailed guidance for micro level operational co-operation. Uniform application of these provisions can also be thwarted for a variety of reasons, viz.: their technical incompatibility with the criminal procedures of different states; the financial incapacity of Parties to meet extensive and expensive international commitments; and the perception that they are skewed towards the interests of drug consumer states with large external law enforcement programmes. Domestic limitation clauses bear witness to these perceived shortcomings.

Chapter Six concerns itself with the provision in the drug conventions for specific forms of law enforcement co-operation. In this area, the earlier conventions play almost no role. They only make weak provision for the seizure and confiscation of the drugs, substances and equipment used in drug offences. The 1988 Convention dramatically extends the material scope of seizure and confiscation to include the profits and proceeds of drug offences, and provides for the penetration of bank secrecy and for a discreet system of mutual legal assistance in this regard. The 1988 Convention also introduces controlled delivery, an investigative technique pioneered in consumer states, and the monitoring of the national and international trade in precursor substances. Building on the 1961 Convention's optional prohibition of the cultivation of drug bearing plants, the 1988 Convention provides for the eradication of illicit cultivation. In a sustained effort to sever supply lines the 1988 Convention also provides for the control of commercial carriers, commercial documents, free trade zones and free ports, postal drug trafficking, and for the interdiction of drug carrying vessels at sea. Considered together, the specific law enforcement provisions of the drug conventions create an impressive regime for attacking the production and transport of drugs to the consumer at various points. But aspects of this regime such as confiscation present an obvious danger to the innocent and their utility has been questioned.[4] As a whole, this regime uncomfortably straddles the conflicting interests of extraterritorial law enforcement by consumer states and the preservation of the sovereignty of producer and transit states.

Finally, Chapter Seven examines the system created for supervising the drug conventions. The CND, a body of state representatives, advises ECOSOC in respect of all drug control matters and supervises the execution of the drug conventions. In this it is assisted by the UNDCP which is concerned primarily with the administration of the system. Together, they receive information that the Parties are obliged to provide on the illicit traffic, and use this information as the basis for an annual survey of the illicit traffic. The INCB, a panel of independent

---

4   See R. Clutterbuck, *Drugs, Crime and Corruption* (MacMillan, London, 1995), p. 115.

experts, monitors the implementation of the drug conventions by the Parties. It has the competence to investigate problems and suggest embargoes against non-compliant Parties, but its enforcement powers are weak, and it relies on political embarrassment and diplomatic intervention to gain compliance. The CND, UNDCP and INCB are assisted by the WHO with respect to medical issues, and rely indirectly on Interpol with respect to direct policing and information, although the latter organisation does not act as an international drugs police force. Regional organisations amplify the scope of the system, but at operational levels national law enforcement organisations play the most significant role. The extensive extraterritorial activities of agencies such as the United States' DEA make them in effect international drugs police forces, a role recognised in the provision by the drug conventions for extraterritorial operations. The system of supervision as a whole suffers inter alia from poor mechanisms for the settlement of disputes, weak execution methods and the allowance of reservations to Parties' commitments, all of which undermine its normative capacity.

Most of the shortcomings of the drug conventions outlined above relate either to the reluctance of states to embrace an international drug control system that requires a radical revision of their domestic law or to the difficulties of agreeing on the correct technical ways to approach the problem of international drug control, particularly when the different options presented represent different views on who is responsible for the drug control problem as a whole. The establishment of the system required an awkward legal compromise accommodating opposing civil and common law approaches to substantive and procedural law, and an awkward political compromise accommodating the opposing views of consumer and producer states about responsibility for the drug problem. Because of the need for widespread consensus, specific problems were ignored or glossed over. The weaknesses of this "lowest common denominator" approach are visible in the fabric of the drug conventions through the use of ambiguous language open to conflicting interpretation, the proliferation of escape clauses, the absence of effective enforcement mechanisms, and the non-application to non-parties.[5] The ultimate consensus builder is the blanket escape clause based on sovereignty

---

5   L.R. Penna, 'Forfeiture of drug trafficking benefits: need for a viable international legal regime' (1993) 14 *Singapore Law Review* 351 at 377 suggests that the large number of Parties to the 1961 Convention has transformed it into customary international law binding upon non-parties. However, it would be difficult to establish sufficient evidence of a uniform, consistent and general state practice and opinio iuris in this regard or in respect of any of the drug conventions, given the abundant evidence of contradictory practice and opinion.

contained in article 2 of the 1988 Convention. For some states, even article 2 does not offer sufficient protection from the drug conventions.[6] In short, the fabric of the illicit drug control system is, at least from the perspective of effective global drug prohibition, full of holes. The conventions have one shortcoming, however, in which all states appear to have willingly acquiesced, because it does not threaten their interests directly.

8.2.2   The absence of human rights protections in the drug conventions

Critical of their flaws from various state-oriented perspectives, most commentators ignore the fact that the drug conventions fail to adequately protect the human rights of those individuals subject to the system, whether they are offenders, alleged offenders or innocent third parties. Rights to privacy, liberty, property, due process and so forth are all threatened by the conventions, which do little to safeguard these rights. Article 6(6) of the 1988 Convention states that Parties may refuse extradition where their authorities believe that the extradited alleged offender would be prosecuted or punished on grounds of 'race, religion, nationality or political opinions, or would cause prejudice for any of those reasons to any person affected by the request.' Article 14(2) of the 1988 Convention states that all measures designed to prevent and eradicate illicit cultivation of drug producing plants shall respect fundamental human rights, take account of traditional licit use, and protect the environment. But there is little more. Most implicit barriers, such as requirements of speciality and double criminality in extradition, are state privileges rather than individual rights, and individual offenders cannot use their violation as a defence.[7]

---

6   Colombia made the following declaration on ratification of the 1988 Convention: 'No provision of the Convention may be interpreted as obliging Colombia to adopt legislative, judicial, administrative or other legal measures that might impair or restrict its constitutional or legal system or that go beyond the terms of the treaties to which the Colombian State is a contracting party.' (10/6/1994). The US objected to the declaration as 'it purports to subordinate Colombia's obligations under the Convention to its Constitution and international treaties, as well as to that nation's domestic law generally' (23/10/95). See *Multilateral Treaties Deposited with the Secretary General: Status as at 31 December 1996* (New York, 1997) UN Doc. St/Leg/Ser.E/15, p. 303 and p. 307 respectively (hereinafter *Multilateral Treaties Deposited* (1997). The declaration does appear to go to undermine Colombia's international obligations completely and its validity is doubtful.

7   S.A. Bernholz, M.J. Bernholz and J.N. Herman, 'International extradition in drug cases' (1985) 10 *North Carolina Journal of International Law and Commercial Regulation* 353 at 355 and 369.

The drug conventions fail human rights by making provision for national laws that are heavily weighted against the alleged offender and by not restricting the application of these laws in any way when they potentially interfere only with the rights of individuals rather than states. Thus, for example, the *1988 Commentary* remarks: 'The system of confiscation constitutes a serious interference with the rights of individuals and with their economic interests. It is deliberately draconian in character.'[8] But then the Conventions leave the protection of individual human rights to national law or general international human rights law. The *1988 Commentary* continues in respect of confiscation: 'For this reason, particular care must be taken to ensure compliance with relevant constitutional protections and applicable international human rights norms.'[9]

Unfortunately, neither domestic nor international human rights norms provide the necessary safeguards. National laws are often draconian and unrestrained by the domestic protection of human rights.[10] General human rights instruments and institutions are also of no great assistance.[11] They are not directly incorporated by express reference in the drug conventions and many Parties to the drug conventions may not be party to these instruments. While international human rights law and policy and international drug control law and policy have

---

8   The *Commentary on the United Nations Convention Against Illicit Traffic in Narcotic Drugs and Psychotropic Substances,* 1988 (New York, 1998) UN Doc. E/CN.7/590; UN Publication Sales No.E.98.XI.5, (hereinafter the *1988 Commentary*), p.144.

9   *1988 Commentary* at 144.

10   For example, the Nigerian Government responded to the increasingly high profile of Nigerians in drug trafficking by issuing Decree no.33 of 1990 which places all Nigerians convicted of drug trafficking abroad in a state of double jeopardy. They face immediate re-arrest and re-prosecution if they enter Nigeria, to which country they are usually deported upon completion of their punishment abroad – see P. Green, *Drugs, Trafficking and Criminal Policy* (Waterside Press, Winchester, 1998), p. 62.

11   Only one human rights instrument, the 1950 European Convention for the Protection of Human Rights and Freedoms, ETS 46, mentions drug use. The decisions of human rights tribunals on drug offences, such as *Welch v United Kingdom* (1995) 20 ECHR 247, are rare. In this matter the European Court of Human Rights upheld a complaint that confiscation orders made under the UK's Drug Trafficking Offences Act, 1986, prior to the Act coming into force on 12 January 1987 were in contravention of article 7 of the European Convention on Human Rights which provides: 'Nor shall a heavier penalty be imposed than the one that was applicable at the time the criminal offence was committed.' Importantly, the European Court held that a confiscation order made in terms of the Act was fundamentally penal in nature and not a civil reparation, and therefore article 7 could apply primarily because such orders allowed confiscation of proceeds irrespective of whether there had been any personal enrichment and thus they went beyond the realms of reparation and prevention into that of punishment.

evolved side-by side within the United Nations, international drug control law and policy have not been subject to scrutiny for compliance with international human rights standards.[12] The UN Intergovernmental Expert Group on Extradition counters this type of criticism by stating that compliance with the drug conventions cannot result in human rights breaches and that observance of human rights makes the conventions more effective.[13] It is apparent, however, that the development of international illicit drug control has been driven by the exigencies of effective law enforcement and has avoided dealing with consequential human rights infringement. This point is well illustrated if we consider the scale and range of the discretionary powers international drug control law encourages.

At the domestic level, specialist drug legislation created in terms of the drug conventions generally allows for the expansion of expediency powers to law enforcement officials to search and seize premises, vehicles, and persons and to intercept postal communications and telephone conversations of suspected persons, as well as shift the onus of proof onto the accused.[14] The dangers of this approach are obvious to Bassiouni:

> [V]iolating the right of privacy in tracing assets; unjustified seizure of property; searches and inquisitions based on mere suspicion or insufficient evidence; arrest and detention on mere suspicion or without sufficient evidence; wiretapping and eavesdropping with less than the quantum of evidence otherwise needed in investigating other forms of criminality; unwarranted preventive detention; unjustified prolonged detention; improper limitations on the right to counsel during pre-trial or pre-accusation stages of proceedings; developing secret dossiers with prejudicial information that cannot be corrected by the person in question; and the dissemination of such information to other public agencies without the knowledge of the person in question and using harassing forms of investigation which affect a person's everyday life.[15]

---

12   N. Gilmore, 'Drug use and human rights: privacy, vulnerability, disability, and human rights infringements' (1996) 12 *The Journal of Contemporary Health Law and Policy* 355 at 401.

13   1996 Report cited by D. Stafford, 'Combating transnational crime: the role of the Commonwealth' in W.C. Gilmore and P.J. Cullen (eds), *Crimes Sans Frontieres: International and European Approaches: Hume Papers on Public Policy* Vol. 6, no's 1 and 2, (Edinburgh UP, Edinburgh, 1998), p. 41 at p. 48.

14   D. Cotic, *Drugs and Punishment* (UNSDRI, Rome, 1988), p. 115.

15   M.C. Bassiouni, 'Effective national and international action against organised crime and terrorist criminal activities' (1990) 4 *Emory International Law Review* 9 at 30.

While the drug conventions may not stipulate such measures with precision, they provide the broad framework and introduce a no-holds-barred ethos into domestic drug control law.[16] Indeed, provisions such as article 39 of the 1961 Convention, article 23 of the 1971 Convention and article 24 of the 1988 Convention encourage Parties to take more severe drug control measures without any due process guarantees being attached.[17] Bassiouni points out that dangers to lawfulness apply to an even greater extent at the level of interstate co-operation 'because of the inadequacy of procedural safeguards.'[18] Thus, for example, the drug conventions make no provision for the access of the alleged offenders to the system. Alleged offenders are not given rights to review decisions that may be detrimental to them, and Parties are not obliged to make legal assistance mechanisms available to assist in the construction of their defences. Moreover, international law enforcement co-operation is usually beyond national or international review. It has been pointed out that the drug conventions do little to ensure that the operation of the laws and administrative arrangements they propagate depend more on rules than on the discretion of the operators of these rules.[19] The counter argument is that the drug conventions were designed to operate in tandem with existing informal channels of law enforcement co-operation, because of the restrictions on the use of evidence gained through formal channels of legal assistance.[20] Denial that such collusion is 'irregular', however, ignores the fact that the whole system may be flawed in accepting informal co-operation. Finally, the fact that the international drug control organs are self-regulating means that there is no independent inter-

---

16 See, for example, the Parliamentary Debate on the provision of indefinite detention in section 12 of the South African Drugs and Drug Trafficking Act 140 of 1992. In the parliamentary debate political parties opposed to the legislation pointed out that while it was designed to incorporate the 1988 Convention's provisions into South African law, the 1988 Convention made no provision for such detention – see *South African Parliamentary Reports (Hansard)*, 18 June 1992, col.11808. Nevertheless, it was still considered an appropriate response.

17 The *1988 Commentary* at 49, aware of the potential for abuse, regards this power as being subject to international law's protection of human rights. Interestingly, Colombia has declared (10/6/1994 – *Multilateral Treaties Deposited* (1997) at 304) that it considers article 24 of the 1988 Convention as not conferring broader powers upon the Colombian government than those conferred by the Colombian Constitution, even in states of emergency.

18 Supra note 15 at 31.

19 Bassiouni supra note 15 at 32.

20 Stafford supra note 13 at 48-9.

national control of them. These organs have played a central role in the international elaboration of the war on drugs and as Kingham and Wallon note:

> The United Nations are both judge and party here, being both responsible for the application of the international anti-drug treaties, and simultaneously guarantor of respect for the Universal Declaration of Human Rights.[21]

The international drug control organs pursue prohibition regardless of the human rights records of individual governments and national agencies involved in this process.[22]

The absence of human rights provisions in the drug conventions is a function of the process of their development. They have an in-built bias to law enforcement as they are designed by enforcers to be law enforcement efficient. Their reliance on domestic protection of human rights labours under the deliberate delusion that such protection exists. Any restrictions are in the interests of states, not of individuals and particularly not of transnational drug offenders who exist outside of most national political constituencies and whose interests are bound to be neglected in the creation of any criminal law directed at them. There is, however, a growing awareness of the impact of international criminal law on human rights[23] which recognises that individuals cannot rely for protection on traditional state exercised bars such as the principle of double criminality. There is movement towards the treatment of the individual as a full participant in proceedings able to rely directly on international human rights instruments.[24] International drug control law may be forced in the future to expressly incorporate human rights protections as individuals exercise their rights under general

---

21   R.A. Kingham and A. Wallon, 'The role of the European Citizen's Associations in strategies and policies to combat drugs' in G. Estievenart (ed.), *Policies and Strategies to Combat Drugs in Europe* (Nijhoff, Dordrecht, 1995) p. 311 at p. 316.

22   See, for example, the willingness of the UNDCP to do business with the Taliban in Afghanistan despite its egregious human rights record – K. Fish, 'The United Nations and the Taliban: an unholy alliance in the name of drug control' (1998) 35 *The Drug Policy Letter* 15-16.

23   See, for example, C. Van Den Wyngaert, 'Rethinking the law of international criminal co-operation: the restrictive function of international human rights through individual-oriented bars' in A. Eser and O. Lagodny (eds), *Principles and Procedures for a New Transnational Criminal Law* (Max Planck Institute, Freiburg, 1991) pp. 489-503.

24   See Van Den Wyngaert supra note 23 at 491 referring to the application of the 1950 European Convention on Human Rights and the *Soering* Case ECHR Series A vol. 161 (1989).

human rights law,[25] thus exposing the absence of protections in the drug conventions[26] and the inadequacy of the protections provided by general international human rights instruments.[27] The UN's Model Treaties on Extradition and Mutual Legal Assistance, which have human rights protections written into them, offer good examples. Law enforcement authorities are likely to resist change to the existing system, but the recognition of individuals as subjects of international law must and will inevitably permeate the international drug control system and turn it into a system of international criminal justice.

8.2.3   The implementation of the drug conventions

Thus far we have deliberated over the content of what states agreed to when they signed up to the drug conventions. States have solidified their legal obligations by becoming party to the conventions in significant numbers.[28] Completion of the process envisaged by the architects of the conventions requires the transformation of the Parties' agreements into domestic law and the application of that domestic law; a material failure of application leads to a situation of "virtual legality". It has not been my intention to engage in a study of implementation here; however, a few tentative conclusions can be drawn from the available material on state practice.

Transformation is inevitably imperfect because the indirect incorporation of international criminal law norms into national criminal laws is an uneven and uncertain process.[29] The evidence available suggests that although the

---

25   The 1981 African Charter on Human and Peoples' Rights, 21 ILM 58; the 1969 American Convention on Human Rights, 1144 UNTS 123; the 1950 European Convention for the Protection of Human Rights and Freedoms, ETS 46; the 1966 International Covenant on Civil and Political Rights, 999 UNTS 171 etc. See generally C. Gane, 'Human rights and international cooperation in criminal matters' in W.C. Gilmore and P.J Cullen (eds), *Crimes Sans Frontieres: International and European Approaches: Hume Papers on Public Policy* Vol. 6, no's 1 and 2, (Edinburgh UP, Edinburgh, 1998) 161-172.

26   In the same way that *Soering v United Kingdom* ECHR Series A vol. 161 (1989) at 35 exposed the aridity of human rights protections in extradition treaties generally.

27   T. Blom and A. Khan, 'The Netherlands' in N. Dorn (ed.), *Regulating European Drug Problems* (Kluwer, The Hague, 1999), p. 203 at p. 225 point out that article 6 of the European Convention of Human Rights provides rules for a fair trial only in the case of a criminal charge.

28   See footnotes 3-6 of Chapter One for the numbers of parties to each instrument.

29   M.C. Bassiouni, *A Draft International Criminal Code and a Draft Statute for an International Criminal Tribunal* (Nijhoff, Dordrecht, 1987), p. 70.

transformation of the earlier conventions has been very slow,[30] the transformation of these conventions is more complete than that of the 1988 Convention.[31]
Application follows the same pattern and the reasons for this relate to
familiarity, capacity and inclination. Parties tend to adopt and apply the
provisions with which they have had time to become familiar such as the classical trafficking offences, rather than the novel provisions in the 1988 Convention dealing with, for instance, money laundering. Parties find it cheaper to
adopt and apply the limited earlier provisions than the expensive obligations
undertaken in terms of the 1988 Convention.[32] Consumer states have more
of a vested interest in these later provisions and tend to implement them; the
countervailing interests of producer states make them resist implementation.
The incentive to feign commitment is patent;[33] numerous benefits accrue from
apparent engagement with international law and with the powerful consumer
states that support the law. But pressure to conform materially comes from the
UN in its managerial role and from the United States and other major consumer
states. The development of large-scale domestic drug use in states formerly
untouched by such use also acts as an incentive for material conformity. As
a result, while the drug conventions may not have produced a universal drug
control law, they have had more than purely symbolic impact. They have resulted in a convergence of state practice with regard to illicit drugs at the
national level. The definition of drug offences in domestic legislation is strong
evidence of this. This convergence is not an even process, and it weakens
particularly in the more difficult areas of extraterritorial drug control where
sovereign sensibilities are delicate. In these latter areas, however, the model

---

30 The provisions of the 1961 Convention took decades to transform into domestic law.
    For example, many of the 1961 Convention's provisions were only transformed into
    law in Pakistan in the Prohibition (Enforcement of Hadd) Order, President's Order No.
    4 of 1979, Gazette of Pakistan, Extra, Part 1, 9 February 1979.
31 For example, the South African Drugs and Drug Trafficking Act 140 of 1992 enacted
    to give effect to the 1988 Convention only implements the provisions of the 1988
    Convention on a selective basis, making no provision for the Convention's provisions
    on extradition, controlled delivery, eradication of cultivation, prevention of trafficking
    by air, postal services or sea. Legislation implementing these provisions was only enacted
    in the late 1990s.
32 The UK Home Affairs Committee, *Report: Drug Trafficking and Related Serious Crime*
    vol. II (1989) comments at p. 76 on the expense of implementing the Drug Trafficking
    Offence Act, 1986, especially its provisions relating to money-laundering and con-
    fiscation.
33 S.K. Chatterjee, *Legal Aspects of International Drug Control* (Nijhoff, Dordrecht, 1981),
    p. 449.

of international criminal law enforcement adopted in the drug conventions provides an opportunity for extra-territorial drug enforcement by Parties with an interest in pursuing the reduction of illicit drug supply from abroad.

8.2.4   Formalised informality in the extraterritorial suppression of illicit drugs

The opportunity given to Parties to engage in extraterritorial drug law enforcement is well illustrated if we classify the drug conventions in terms of Heymann's two models of international criminal law enforcement.[34] The "prosecutorial" model, favoured by the United States, is a highly informal goal driven model, championed by policeman and prosecutors. Legal principles are immaterial, the means used are flexible, co-operation is crucial, and controls are based on levels of reasonable demand and reciprocity. A pragmatic co-operative structure is created between or among states that have great trust in each other and faith in each other's legal systems. The "international law" model, favoured by civil law states, is a highly structured model whose goals and means are rigidly specified, advocated by scholars and judges. A complete set of rules coherently applying principles such as sovereignty creates a system that can be used to control any group of states, a system that fits into a larger international criminal justice system, a world order. Thus Heymann posits a linear order – at the international law pole we find a formalised centralised system, while at the prosecutorial pole we find an informal decentralised system. International co-operation in the suppression of drugs has, it is submitted, tended toward the prosecutorial pole as a pragmatic response to the problems of and policies of individual consumer states like the United States. This tendency is indicated by a plethora of bilateral arrangements and treaties and by large-scale informal law enforcement co-operation in practice. Although the formalisation of drug control in the drug conventions and particularly in the 1988 Convention appears to indicate a shift to an international law model, the influence of the prosecutorial model is still very strong. Indeed, the drug conventions arguably facilitate the prosecutorial model to the benefit of consumer states by creating a regulatory space and by keeping that regulatory space open for unilateral action and informal co-operation. The drug conventions do not clog this space with specific obligations and specific exceptions. Think for example, of the loose provisions for action once a state has given permission

---

34   P.B. Heymann, 'Two models of national attitudes toward international co-operation in law enforcement' (1990) 31 *Harvard International Law Journal* 99-107.

for the interdiction of its vessel by a foreign state in terms of article 17(3) of the 1988 Convention. This model of the illicit drug control system serves as a specific example of Brown's suggestion that with regard to international criminal co-operation as a whole the prosecutorial system is in fact embedded in the international system and they are not two extremes on a linear scale.[35] Although this is something which requires closer examination, the reasons for the adoption of this model are, it is suggested, broadly as follows: the international framework ensures the symbolic value of drug prohibition, while the prosecutorial model embedded in that framework grants those consumer states most affected by drug use a large measure of control in applying prohibition extraterritorially. In other words, it allows consumer states to unilaterally actualise a policy that in fact, rather than symbolically, does not enjoy global support.

8.3   AN EVALUATION OF THE APPLICATION OF THE POLICY OF DRUG PRO-
         HIBITION IN INTERNATIONAL LAW

The technical provisions of the drug conventions are underpinned and informed by the policy of global drug prohibition. The de facto subjects of this policy, the citizens of the Parties to the drug conventions, appear to have had little to do with its adoption or application. Nadelmann styles its chief instigators 'transnational moral entrepreneurs', anti-drug crusaders compelled to convert everyone to their belief in prohibition, driven to create a 'global prohibition regime'.[36] He argues convincingly that the global pursuit of drug prohibition by consumer states indicates more than just a desire to cut external sources of supply[37] and he believes that the extraordinary efforts that states like the United States put into this "regime" stem from fear and moral condemnation of drug use, righteousness and the compulsion to proselytise.[38] Importantly,

---

35   Heymann's model has been criticised by A. Brown, 'Towards a prosecutorial model for mutual assistance in criminal matters' in W.C. Gilmore and P.J. Cullen (eds), *Crimes Sans Frontieres: International and European Approaches: Hume Papers on Public Policy* Vol. 6, no's 1 and 2, (Edinburgh UP, Edinburgh,1998) p. 50 at p. 51. He argues that the prosecutorial model is in reality embedded in the international law model and they are not two extremes on a linear scale.

36   See E. Nadelmann, 'Global prohibition regimes: the evolution of norms in international society' (1990) 44 *International Organisation* 479 at 481.

37   See Nadelmann supra note 36 at 505.

38   See Nadelmann supra note 36 at 508.

because this war is directed at individual transgressors within foreign states and not at those states themselves, it does not threaten powerful constituencies or vested interests in other states.[39] The regulatory schemes of the licit drug control system have met the concerns of pharmaceutical companies, while moral condemnation of drugs has been easy for the local political elites of drug producing states to support, a support indicated by signing the conventions and enacting the necessary legislation.[40] In essence then, the global drug prohibition "regime" appears to be the legal expression of a just global war on drugs. The principal target of this war is the illicit supply of drugs because policy makers in influential consumer states believe that it is easier to cut off the supply of drugs than to change the behaviour of users. Supply reduction is also less expensive in both political[41] and financial terms than harm or demand reduction, and any tampering with the system is strongly resisted by the law enforcement agents, lawyers and bureaucrats who run it and guide its development.[42] Despite the best efforts of those waging this war, the illicit traffic has shown itself to be remarkably resilient and adaptable. Drugs are widely available to users and their retail price has remained relatively stable.[43] Reaching producers through international law is difficult for a number of reasons. Significant among these is normative weakness. The symbolic consensus among local elites and foreign prohibitionists about international drug prohibition has only had a limited normative effect on the general populace of drug producing states. These people did not share in the construction of this international morality and they are subject to economic, social and psychological pressures that discourage observ-

---

39   See Nadelmann supra note 36 at 510.

40   See Nadelmann supra note 36 at 511.

41   Polls have indicated, for example, that Americans support supply reduction rather than demand reduction -see K.L. Bland, 'The Chemical Diversion and Trafficking Act of 1988: stopping the flow of chemicals to the Andean drug cartels' (1991) 7 *American University Journal of International Law and Policy* 105 at 109, footnote 27.

42   The operational arms of international drug control have a vested interest in the system's existence and develop it to suit their perceptions of the need for heavier intervention – see Elvins supra note 2 at 11. Sheptycki gives as an example the introduction of controlled delivery as an investigative technique in Europe by police who first employed it without legal sanction and who slowly persuaded first prosecutors, then judges, then legislators and finally the international community to sanction (through adopting article 11 of the 1988 Convention) – see J. Sheptycki, 'Law enforcement, justice and democracy in the transnational arena: reflections on the war on drugs' (1996) 24 *International Journal of the Sociology of Law* 61 at 67.

43   See E.A. Nadelmann in Panel discussion 'Drugs and small arms: can law stop the traffic?' (1987) 81 *American Society of International Law: Proceedings* 44 at 52.

ance of it. Many of them are, for example, economically dependent upon illicit agricultural drug production. They resent external interference and support traffickers and revolutionary groups allied to the traffickers.[44] Cultural diversity also weakens the normative power of international law. In the face of the weak internal aspect of these laws, all that is left is the application of harsher externally imposed sanctions. But the strong external sovereignty and weak internal sovereignty of producer states undermine externally imposed laws, because such states can neither be policed internationally nor police themselves.[45] Compounding deep-seated legal weakness are the strong attractions of the illicit drug supply.[46] Engaging in the traffic only requires limited readily available resources and no particular skill. Drugs are easily concealed and unlikely to be reported to the authorities. Most importantly, demand for illicit drugs is substantial and relatively inelastic. Although supply reduction efforts drive prices up, users are prepared to pay whatever it costs, and supplies find a way to meet demand.[47] The liberalisation of the global economy also confounds prohibition because it encourages trade of all kinds.[48] Efforts to impose heavier and more stringent legal regimes within producer states appear to have failed[49] and even

44   See Bland supra note 41at 116-120 and the authors cited there.

45   Nadelmann supra note 36 at 486.

46   Nadelmann supra note 36 at 512.

47   For example, P. Reuter, 'The limits and consequences of U.S. foreign drug control efforts' (1992) 521 *Annals of the American Academy of Politics and Social Science* 151-162 shows that all the supply reduction efforts to reduce cocaine production in the Andean region and imports to US (crop eradication etc.) serve to do is drive up the price of cocaine derivatives in the US; they do not actually effect the quantity of supply at all. The reason for this is that while such efforts impose a cost on the producer and supplier, it is not big enough to prevent supply, and such a cost is simply passed on to the consumer in the form of price increase. See also T.B. Fowler, 'The international narcotics trade: can it be stopped by interdiction' (1996) 18 *Journal of Policy Modelling* 233-270 whose economic models of drug supply suggest that supply interdiction cannot work.

48   K. Raustalia, 'Law, Liberalization and International Narcotics Trafficking' (1999) 32 *New York University Journal of International Law and Politics* 89 at 116-127. He notes that the global free market makes illicit supply, for example, easier by improving transport infrastructure, increasing the volume of cross-border trade, increasing the load on customs officers and increasing the opportunity for money laundering. Restructuring of the economies of drug producer states through austerity programmes may also drive their citizens into drug supply.

49   For example, D.N. Jauhar, *Rethinking Drug Legislation in India* (unpublished conference paper, New Delhi Global Drugs Law Conference, 1997) p. 8, complains that India's Narcotic Drugs and Psychotropic Substances Act, 1985 (as amended in 1988 in response to the 1988 Convention), although enacted as a deterrent to drug traffickers with harsh

if it were politically possible to adopt the kind of draconian regime necessary to suppress external sources of supply to consumer states, it seems likely that internal sources would grow to meet demand.[50]

The costs of making war on drugs internationally also undermine support for the international drug control system. These costs include creating, administering and implementing the system, the costs of media attention, the costs of public concern and so on. The social costs are also enormous and continue to increase. Large prison populations grow, as do the numbers of users particularly among young people. Drug law enforcement funding increases, and funding is diverted from other law enforcement activities, from treatment and research, and in poorer states from other pressing economic and social demands. But the primary costs of global prohibition are the costs of ignoring the social, economic, psychological and physiological reasons for drug usage because this ignorance leads to the endurance of these causes. Little solace is offered by the argument that things might have been much worse if global prohibition had not been imposed and maintained.[51]

In summary then, it appears that international law has got caught up in a drugs war model of drug control, a public order model rather than a public health model. This public order model has its origins in the United States and international drug control law has become the mechanism for the global dissemination of this model. It would be fair, following Nadelmann, to suggest that the international harmonisation of drug law though the drug conventions has in fact been an 'Americanisation' of that law.[52] International subscription to the technical necessity for this process or to the anti-drugs morality that underpins it is largely absent except among those who pedal the model and the political elites who buy it. This lack of international support is reflected in the drug conventions themselves. Take for example, the principle aut dedere aut judicare, the principle of subsidiary universality, said to rest on the civitas maxima, a social or moral order common to all humanity.[53] Although subsidiary universality could serve as a useful tool to implement a no-hiding-place

---

sentences and the possibility of capital punishment, has proved a failure. He notes that of the drugs cases that came before the special courts in New Delhi in 1994-1996, 76 (11 foreigners) resulted in convictions and 1906 in acquittals (77 foreigners).

50   E.A. Nadelmann, 'Commonsense drug policy' (1998) 77 *Foreign Affairs* 111 at 113.

51   The argument made by the UNDCP in its *World Drug Report* (OUP, Oxford, 1998), p. 237.

52   Nadelmann supra note 2 at 470.

53   M.C. Bassiouni and E.M. Wise, *Aut Dedere Aut Judicare: The Duty to Extradite or Prosecute in International Law* (Nijhoff, Dordrecht, 1995), p. 28.

approach to transnational drug traffickers, its imperfect expression in the drug conventions points to the conclusion that at least in respect of drug offences there is no deep seated consensus in the civitas maxima on the policy of international drug prohibition. The rhetoric of universality is hollow. Active prohibitionist consumer states use international law to try to get passive drug dependent producer or unaffected states to do what they think such unresponsive states should do. The latter states subscribe to the principle of prohibition but protected by their sovereignty and undermined by a lack of popular support, do little more than give consumer states some scope to act on their own. It has been argued that most states do not have the necessary will to make prohibition work either in the content of the drug conventions or in their practice, and although the global community is still interested in appearing to make an effort, it will ultimately move away from prohibition.[54] Precisely when the international focus will shift to the causes of drug usage is a matter for speculation.

8.4   FUTURE DEVELOPMENTS

8.4.1   The prognosis is for more of the same

In spite of the failure to achieve prohibition, the future emphasis of international drug control law is likely, in the short term, to remain on the enforcement of the penal provisions of the drug conventions. This is despite the fact that as Stares states:

> There is little reason to believe that the primary policy emphasis on negative controls to deter and deny the production, trafficking and consumption of illicit drugs will be any more successful in the future than it has been in the past. The standard supply-reduction tactics – eradication and interdiction – will surely achieve periodic successes in which production or trafficking is suppressed in a specific area, but given the incentive structure of the illicit business, the overall effect is likely to be marginal or short lived at best. The historical record provides overwhelming evidence of this. Increasing the penalties for illicit drug trafficking and consumption in order to deter others is also of dubious long-term value. Besides the costs that

---

54   M.C. Bassiouni, 'Critical reflections on international and national control of drugs' (1990) 18 *Denver Journal of International Law and Policy* 311 at 330.

this imposes on society in terms of law enforcement and civil liberties, it is difficult to sustain the deterrent effect.[55]

Yet a dramatic step like legalisation is an unlikely prospect. Stares continues:

Ultimately, however, the prospects for a radical departure from the prevailing prohibitionist stance look remote. Reversing or jettisoning nearly a century of effort when the putative benefits are so uncertain and the potential costs are so high would represent a Herculean leap of faith. Only an extremely severe and widespread deterioration of the situation globally is likely to produce the level of consensus that would have to be attained – domestically and internationally – to bring about such an attitudinal shift and generate the necessary political impetus.[56]

All the near term offers is an incremental extrapolation of the existing approach within the existing legal framework. Efforts to globalise hardened demand reduction tactics such as mandatory work-place blood testing[57] and low-level drug law enforcement measures aimed at separating or breaking the link between retailers and consumers[58] may require amendment[59] of the drug conventions. But it is more likely that consumer states will use the space left open to them by the drug control system to become even more heavily involved in the development and maintenance of the criminal justice systems of producer states, moving beyond training to the direct financing and running of the anti-drug elements of these systems. The development of mechanisms for direct international law enforcement such as a multinational drug police would constitute a significant step away from this model to a universal umbrella for illicit drug

---

55   P.B. Stares, *Global Habit: The Drug Problem in a Borderless World* (Brookings Institution, Washington DC, 1996), p.106.
56   Supra note 55 at 111.
57   See J.B. Jacobs and L. Zimmer, 'Drug treatment and workplace drug testing: politics, symbolism and organisational dilemmas' (1991) 9 *Behavioural Sciences and the Law* 345-360.
58   See N. Dorn and K. Murji, 'Low-level drug enforcement' (1992) 20 *International Journal of Sociology of Law* 159-171.
59   Article 31 of the 1988 Convention, entitled 'Amendments', leaves the process largely in the hands of the Parties (in a scheme similar to that in article 47 of the 1961 Convention and article 30 of the 1971 Convention which are identical). A proposed amendment is circulated and enters into force after two years (long enough for a Party to complete the necessary legislative changes) if no other Party has objected to it, and it comes into operation for each particular Party ninety days after that Party deposits an instrument of acceptance with the UN Secretary-General. If any Party rejects an amendment, a process begins which may result in ECOSOC calling a diplomatic conference.

control. But the frustration of efforts to establish the proposed International Criminal Court's jurisdiction over drug offences indicates that there is resistance to a shift to universalism. Examination of these efforts gives a clear picture of the likely development of the illicit drug control system within its present structure.

8.4.2   *The international criminal court and the "international drug offence"*

The recent development of the International Criminal Court (ICC) began with a call by Caribbean states in 1989 for an ICC with subject matter jurisdiction over illicit trafficking in drugs across national frontiers.[60] Ironically, however, by the time the new convention for the court was settled in Rome in 1998, these offences were excluded from its jurisdiction. The story of this exclusion has been told in detail elsewhere.[61] What essentially happened, however, was that in spite of the backing of the INCB,[62] as the prospect of an ICC became more real, opposition to the inclusion of treaty crimes like drug trafficking within the ICC's jurisdiction grew. Under this pressure the scope of drug crimes over which the ICC was to have jurisdiction slowly contracted to include only serious offences, [63]then only to exceptionally serious offences having an 'international dimension'[64] and finally only to large-scale transboundary offences.[65] However, these concessions were not enough. Article 5 of the Rome Statute[66] limits the ICC's jurisdiction to a set of "core" crimes that concern the international community as a whole. Exclusion of drug offences from the ICC's jurisdiction was considered a compromise, because it was linked to a future review of the

---

60   UNGAOR 6th Comm. 44th Session, UN Doc. A/C.6/44/SR.38-41 (1989).

61   See generally N. Boister, 'The exclusion of treaty crimes from the jurisdiction of the International Criminal Court: law, pragmatism, politics' (1998) 3 *Journal of Armed Conflict Law* 27-43.

62   See *Report of the International Narcotics Control Board for 1996* UN Doc. E/INCB/1996/1, p. 4.

63   Article 26(2)(b) of the 1993 Draft Statute for an ICC, 'Report of the ILC, 45th session' UNGAOR 48th Session, Supp. No.10, UN Doc. A/48/10 (1993), p. 284.

64   Article 20(e) of the 1994 Draft Statute and the annex respectively, 'Report of the ILC, 46th Session' UNGAOR 49th Session, Supp. No.10, UN Doc. A/49/10/1994 (1994).

65   *Report of the Preparatory Committee on the Establishment of an International Criminal Court*, UN Doc. A/Conf/183/2/Add.1.

66   UN Doc. A/Conf.183/C.1/L.76/Add.2.

ICC's jurisdiction for inclusion of such crimes.[67] However, a review and inclusion is not going to happen soon, and the mere fact that the ICC's statute will have to be amended to include such offences will be a formidable barrier to the ICC ever taking responsibility for them. The reasons why Caribbean states supported the inclusion of drug offences within the jurisdiction of the Court, the legal problems with this inclusion and the practical and political reasons as to why it was rejected, illuminates much of the ground covered in this book.

The advantages of including drug offences within the ICC's jurisdiction relate mainly to the inadequacies of the present system with respect to jurisdiction and extradition. In particular, inclusion would allow a requested state to delegate its authority to the ICC rather than surrender jurisdiction to a requesting state where such surrender is legally or politically difficult.[68] It would also make for more predictable prosecution of unreachable and uncontrollable drug barons than national prosecution and help to avoid the intimidation and corruption of the criminal justice systems of vulnerable states by drug traffickers.[69]

The main disadvantage is the awkward legal basis for such inclusion. The drug offences have a contractual basis and are not self-executing. Objections were made to the inclusion of drug offences under the ICC's jurisdiction because the drug conventions neither establish universal jurisdiction over drug offences even in respect of the states that are party to them nor invite the jurisdiction

---

67 Drug offences have been relegated to Resolution E annexed to the Final Act of the 1998 Conference, where the 1998 Conference recommends that a Review Conference pursuant to article 111 of the Statute should at some undisclosed future date 'consider ... drug crimes with a view to arriving at an acceptable definition and then inclusion in the list of crimes within the jurisdiction of the Court.' Article 111 of the Rome Statute allows the UN Secretary General to convene a Review Conference seven years after the entry into force of the Statute to consider amendments to it, and such amendments are specifically not restricted to those dealing with the crimes in article 5. However, this apparently unlocked door is partially obstructed by article 110 which makes it clear that in the case of adoption by the Review Conference of amendments to article 5, such amendments will only enter into force for those Parties which expressly accept the amendment. Article 110(5) specifically provides that in respect of a Party that has not accepted the amendment, the ICC 'shall not exercise its jurisdiction regarding a crime covered by the amendment when committed by that State Party's nationals or on its territory.'

68 See Patel supra note 3 at 734-736.

69 See N.R. Rampilla, 'Towards prosecuting the illicit drug traffickers before the proposed international criminal court – a challenge beyond 2000' in *Souvenir Brochure of the International Conference on Global drugs Law* (Indian Law Institute, New Delhi, 1997), p. 167 at p. 171.

of an ICC.[70] Under the present international drug control scheme either alteration of the conventions to apply subsidiary universality without qualification[71]
or provision for express consent by a Party to these conventions to the jurisdiction of the ICC would be required to give the ICC jurisdiction over drug offences.[72] But the broad definition of the offences within the drug conventions
makes the taking of these measures difficult.[73] This is why so much effort
was put into the redefinition of these offences during the development of the
Rome Statute. The problem becomes one of distinguishing serious offences
from those less serious and crimes with an international dimension from those
that do not have such a dimension. Although the drug conventions do not make
this distinction, the motivation, goal and impact of a particular offence can be
used to distinguish a serious offence from one less serious.[74] Adopting this
type of approach, the Caribbean states proposed to the Rome Conference that
drug offences should be included within the ICC's jurisdiction when committed:

(a) on a large scale (and)(or) in a transboundary context,
(b) within the framework of an organised and hierarchical structure;
(c) with the use of violence and intimidation against private persons, judicial persons
or other institutions, or members of the legislative, executive or judicial arms of
government, (thereby) creating fear or insecurity within a state or disrupting its
economic, social, political or security structures or with other consequences of a
similar nature; or
d) in a context in which corrupt influence is exerted over the public, the media and
public institutions.[75]

Restricting the ICC's jurisdiction to these high-threshold offences addresses the
chief practical objection to the ICC taking jurisdiction over drug offences – that
the high incidence of drug offences would swamp the ICC. This objection had
been put in the Preparatory Committee responsible for the final draft of the
Rome Statute where it was argued

---

70 See the *Revised Report of the Working Group on the Draft Statute for and International
    Criminal Court,* UN Doc. A/CN.4/L.490 (July 1993), p. 22.
71 The method proposed by draft article 53(2)(b) of the 1994 Draft Statute.
72 The method implied by article 110(5) of the Rome Statute.
73 'Report of the ILC, 45th session', UNGAOR 48th Session Supp. No.10, UN Doc. A/48/
    10 (1993), p. 282.
74 See Bassiouni supra note 15 at 23.
75 Proposal of Barbados, Dominica, Jamaica and Trinidad and Tobago, UN Doc. A/
    Conf.183/C.1/L.48.

that drug trafficking should not be included because these crimes were ... of such a quantity as to flood the court; the court would not have the necessary resources to conduct lengthy and complex investigations required to prosecute the crimes; the investigation of the crimes often involved highly sensitive information and confidential strategies; and the crimes could be more effectively investigated and prosecuted by national authorities under existing international co-operation arrangements.[76]

What is striking is that these arguments are similar to those raised at the 1988 Conference by the American and British delegates against the application of universal jurisdiction to drug offences. They indicate that drug consumer states are not willing to trust the ICC to prosecute drug traffickers and would rather extradite and prosecute these traffickers themselves.[77] Scharf explains the US reluctance thus:

> The Departments of Justice and Treasury are firmly opposed to any international criminal court that would have jurisdiction over narco-terrorists, reportedly out of concern that the establishment of an international criminal court would undermine the U.S. government's existing international law enforcement efforts and because, if those cases went to an international court, the departments would lose the sizeable funds they now collect through asset forfeiture.[78]

The existing indirect system of control over drug offences implies individual freedom within the system, and that freedom is most valued by the most powerful individuals within that system. Weaker states favour direct international control of drug trafficking because they have no confidence in the indirect system, which involves massive actual inroads into their sovereignty. Trinidad and Tobago and Colombia both indicated that an ICC would present an attractive third alternative to extradition or prosecution without their accompanying political problems.[79] These states would prefer a system to which all states are

---

76 Preparatory Committee on the Establishment of an International Criminal Court, *Summary of the Proceedings of the Preparatory Committee during the period 25 March – 12 April 1996* UN Doc. A/AC.249/1, 7 May 1996, paras 71-72.

77 J. Dugard, 'Obstacles in the way of an international criminal court' (1997) 56 *Cambridge Law Journal* 329 at 334. See also M.P. Scharf, 'Getting serious about an international criminal court' (1994) 6 *Pace international Law Review* 103 at 105.

78 M.P. Scharf, 'The politics of establishing an International Criminal Court' (1995) 6 *Duke Journal of International and Comparative Law* 167-173 at 171.

79 M.P. Scharf , 'The jury is still out on the need for an international criminal court' (1991) *Duke Journal of Comparative and International Law* 135 at 151-152.

equally subject. In essence, ICC jurisdiction over drug offences would mean a shift away from the informal prosecutorial model of international co-operation over drug offences where states such as the United States have an inordinate influence. It would strengthen the international law model because international drug control would find a new central locus of control in the ICC. But the Hobbesian reality of international relations meant that this shift did not take place in 1998.

It seems, however, that a change in the attitude of consumer states such as the United States is not the only barrier to the ICC expanding the core crimes to include drug offences. The international community as a whole, it is submitted, would have to exhibit a much greater conviction than presently exists that these offences seriously endanger its interests and shock its collective conscience. It is true that drug traffickers are part of the reason for major international breaches of the peace such as the invasion of Panama by the United States in 1989 to capture Noriega. Under threat of extradition traffickers also destabilise and threaten the sovereignty of states such as Colombia, and their corruptive power does undermine the security of states.[80] However, at present it is not states but individuals that sponsor drug offences and most states do not perceive these offences as either a threat to the international order or as the breach of a fundamental norm. In a recent case the majority of the Canadian Supreme Court held:

> There is no indication in international law that drug-trafficking on any scale is to be considered contrary to the purposes and principles of the United Nations.... There is simply no indication that the drug trafficking comes close to the core or even forms a part of the corpus of fundamental human rights.[81]

---

80   See Patel supra note 3 at 712-714. J.S. Krasna, 'Narcotics and the national security of producer states' *The Journal of Conflict Studies,* Spring 1996, University of New Brunswick, <utratext.hil.unb.ca/Texts/JCS>, argues that drug trafficking threatens the political, military, economic, societal and environmental security of producer states.

81   Bastarache J (with L'Hereux-Dubé, Sopinka, Gonithier, Mclachlin JJ) in *Pushpanathan v Minister of Citizenship and Immigration and others* [1998] 4 LRC 365 at 395 and 396. The case involved the issue of whether a convicted drug trafficker could rightfully claim refugee status under the 1969 UN Convention Relating to the Status Of Refugees or whether his conviction meant that he was excluded from the scope of the Convention in terms of article 1(f)(c) as someone 'guilty of acts contrary to the purposes and principles of the United Nations'.

Dissenting judges[82] relied heavily on the drug conventions to indicate the gravitas with which the international community viewed drug trafficking, but were patently hampered by the fact that the drug conventions themselves claim not that drug trafficking is an international crime but only that 'it is an international criminal activity'.[83] Yarnold concludes that drug offences 'neither present a threat to world peace nor do they "shock the conscience" of the world community'.[84] Until it does so, drug trafficking will neither be an international crime nor fall within the ICC's jurisdiction.

In a sense, the expansion proposed by Caribbean states is a proposal by the elites of developing producer and transit states who find the drug conventions' basic policy of prohibition difficult to enforce. The switch to a stronger international model of drug control would simply be a response to the policy of prohibition, not a fundamental move away from it, and for this reason, it is ultimately doomed to failure. In effect, expanding the jurisdiction of the ICC to include drug offences would simply lead us further down a blind alley. The history of international drug control suggests a more positive option.

8.4.3   The future of illicit drug control through international law

The development of international drug control law has taken place in three distinct overlapping phases addressing three distinct aspects of the drug problem.

The first phase, regulation of licit drug production, distribution and consumption was developed in the period 1913 to 1972 and is fully mature. The 1961 Convention, 1971 Convention and 1972 Protocol are mainly concerned with this aspect of drug control. The primary shortcoming of the first phase was that while it clarified licit behaviour in respect of drugs, it provided little guidance in respect of the steps to be taken against illicit behaviour.

The second phase, and the subject matter of this book, the suppression of illicit drug related activities, began abortively with the 1936 Suppression Convention failing to garner any real support from states. A small number of provisions in the 1961 and 1971 Conventions and the 1972 Protocol concerned themselves with penal law but did not take it much further. The 1988 Convention was thus developed specifically to suppress illicit drugs. Further development is possible. The major problem with the second phase of international

---

82 Cory J at 417. Major J concurred.
83 Preamble to the 1988 Convention.
84 B.M. Yarnold, 'Doctrinal basis for the international criminalisation process' (1994) 8 *Temple International and Comparative Law Review* 85 at 103.

drug control is that it has been strongly influenced by major consumer states like the United States. Through a combination of provisions relating to the definition of offences, the extraterritoriality of national jurisdiction and law enforcement assistance, it is skewed towards the interests of these consumer states. The adjustment of the system to meet the needs of all states equally is necessary. One way of achieving this realignment is to place more serious drug offences under the jurisdiction of the ICC; another is to make unqualified universal jurisdiction over these offences obligatory through a protocol to the 1988 Convention. But whether such measures can solve the global drug problem is debatable. Restricting the prosecutorial space of the system by a more centralised system of international law does not mean a movement away from drug prohibition. It is an effort to make prohibition work. Yet supply is likely to continue, inexorably, to meet demand. A more radical solution is required – a complete shift in emphasis away from a crime control model to dealing with the victims of drug abuse and the social and psychological conditions which lead to drug abuse.

International drug control law appears to be stalled on the threshold of a third phase addressing the needs and problems of users. Advocates of the definition of the drug problem as a public health and social welfare issue have been knocking on the door of the control organs and conferences since the 1970s. The small number of optional provisions in the 1961, 1971 and 1988 Conventions and 1972 Protocol are clearly insufficient. The most "concrete" steps taken thus far have been those suggested in the 1987 Comprehensive Multidisciplinary Outline. However, the drug consumption problem is now a problem shared by most states, which appears to be leading toward a grudging re-evaluation of the lack of progress made in the first two phases. Major studies have revealed the cost-effectiveness of treatment when compared to supply reduction.[85] States are beginning to centralise control over drug treatment.[86]

---

85   A study commissioned by the Rand Corporation on the merits of supply versus demand reduction in controlling cocaine revealed in 1994 that to achieve the same effect on reducing consumption of cocaine it cost $783 million in expenditure on source-country control, $366 million on interdiction, $246 million on domestic law enforcement, and $34 million on treatment. The study found that treatment ranked as the most cost-effective when the measure of effectiveness was the number of users, or societal costs of crime or lost-productivity due to cocaine use – see P.C. Rydell and S.S. Everingham, *Controlling Cocaine: Supply versus Demand Programs* (Rand Corp, Drug Policy Research Center, Santa Monica, California, 1994) pp. ix-xix.

The next appropriate step is the development of an international convention that focuses on the social and psychological realities that underpin drug use.

Under the rubric of demand reduction the proposed convention would outline and enforce a global drug use prevention programme with the goal of promoting internationally and not only in the developed world a general anti-drug use ethos. The convention would oblige states to use education, workplace, community and mass media programmes to illustrate the harmful effects of drug use. The convention would also have to address the results of use. It would have to include an international drug treatment-training programme focused primarily on raising the levels of expertise among health care professionals in countries where such expertise is lacking or absent.

The convention would, however, have to go further than education and treatment. Green identifies the existing policy trap: 'Rather than examine the root causes of poverty, urban deprivation, unemployment, homelessness and social misery, demand focused policy orients itself almost entirely around drug education and the treatment of addicts.'[87] The convention would have to address the social and economic conditions that promote use by adopting a development policy targeting vulnerable consumers, a policy integrated within the global development policy. The convention would also have to come to grips with those who continue to use drugs by adopting harm reduction policies. The UN drug control organs are presently opposed to policies of harm reduction.[88] The difficulty is that harm reduction methods such as the supply of clean hypodermic needles are technically in violation of international law because government officials have to not only permit an offence to occur but also to assist in that offence. But international law can live with this kind of contradiction, focusing not on the logical integrity of the law but on the desirable outcome, the reduction of harm from drug usage. In effect, international law does so already by allowing Parties to use the discretion in punishment left to them by the drug conventions to de-penalise possession for personal use.

A more controversial step would be for the proposed convention to guide the global decriminalisation of certain drugs such as cannabis. This would mean a movement away from absolute global prohibition on the basis that the be-

---

86   The British Government announced in June 2000 that it was to establish a National Drug Treatment Control Agency to co-ordinate treatment at a national level – *The Guardian,* 8 June 2000.

87   Supra note 10 at 12.

88   See, for example, the INCB's opposition to Switzerland's prescription of heroin to addicts – INCB, *Report of the International Narcotics Control Board for 1995* UN Doc. E/INCB/ 1995/1, p. 63.

haviour of individuals in respect of some drugs is more properly controlled through a process of socialisation than through formal legal control. The control organs of the international drug control system remain firmly opposed to decriminalisation, something evidenced by the INCB's continual criticism of Dutch drug policy.[89] Nevertheless, a substantial de facto decriminalisation has already taken place in practice,[90] and respected commentators believe that the international community will turn to decriminalisation.[91] Demand reduction, harm reduction, depenalisation, decriminalisation – all accept drug usage and abandon the pretence of the attainability of a drug free society.

The idea of adopting such a convention is not new,[92] but it has been and is likely to continue to be resisted. The United States has already shown resistance to the globalisation of harm reduction measures.[93] The INCB favours the supplementation of existing conventions by demand reduction provisions. But the INCB is

> not convinced that specific, universally binding treaty provisions on demand reduction could be agreed upon or that such a treaty would be an appropriate instrument to deal with such an issue. The Board considers that demand reduction is a national task, which in a number of countries may have to be carried out with international support, and that demand reduction programs are to be designed at the national and

89 Referring to aspects of this policy including the policy of tolerance of soft drug use and coffee shops selling cannabis products, the INCB expressed again in 1995 its 'continued concern at the persistence of certain practices, only slightly altered, which call into question the Government of the Netherlands' fidelity to its treaty obligations.' – INCB, *Report of the International Narcotics Control Board for 1995* UN Doc. ENCB/ 1995/1, p. 58.

90 The Frankfurt Resolution is a good example of official concession that prohibition has failed. Adopted by official representatives of Amsterdam, Zurich, Hamburg and Frankfurt in 1990, it advocates the legal purchase, possession and use of cannabis, and non-punishment of purchase, possession and use of small quantities of other drugs. A number of cities party to the resolution have formed themselves into the European Cities on Drug Policy (ECDP). The ECDP is opposed by the cities of the European Cities Against Drugs (ECAD) who support prohibition.

91 Bassiouni supra note 54 at 335.

92 When at the 1988 Conference Mexican pressure focused some attention on demand, it was suggested that a new convention could be elaborated in the future on the problem of demand. D.W. Sproule and P. St-Denis, 'The UN Drug Trafficking Convention: An Ambitious Step' 1989 CYBIL 263 at 266 note that both Canada and The Federal Republic of Germany made this suggestion to Mexico.

93 Nadelmann supra note 50 at 124.

local levels, based on knowledge of the real drug abuse situation and taking into consideration the cultural, political, economic and legal environment.[94]

It came as no surprise that when the 1998 UN General Assembly's special session reviewed the basic policy documents of the drug control programme, it adopted inter alia Guiding Principles on Demand Reduction containing standards to guide governments to set up effective prevention, treatment and rehabilitation programmes, while at the same time emphasising the need for states to pursue with vigour law enforcement measures.[95] It is submitted, however, that relegating demand reduction to national control is to remove from the realm of international legal obligation the confrontation of the problems of individual users and the problems of the societies from which they spring.

Looking at the problem another way, the globalisation of the law and order approach to drug usage has not done away with the problem, it has simply stabilised it in a particular form – as a problem of supply. It needs to be recast in international law as a problem of demand because international suppression of the illicit traffic and use of drugs can never achieve total eradication of the problem. It is more likely that we will have to live with this problem and attempt to stabilise drug use at reasonable levels. Whether we continue to rely on law enforcement as one environmental factor among many to determine usage is a question for the future, but we must not allow the spectre of legalisation, which comes complete with problems of its own,[96] to divert attention away from the pressing question of how to reform the international war on drugs so as to reduce drug usage more effectively as well as preserve human rights. The threat of legalisation is presently used to justify the closing of international society's mind in respect of drugs. What is needed is an expansion of the options and a concretisation of that expansion in international law in

---

94 INCB, *Report of the International Narcotics Control Board for 1994,* UN Doc. E/INCB/ 1994/1, p. 3.

95 Resolution S-20/4 8 September 1998. Precursor control, legal assistance, crop eradication etc. were major areas of emphasis, despite the UN Secretary GeneralKofi Annan's claim that the UN was 'not starting a new "war on drugs" [and that] [i]n fact there never was one.' GA Press Release 9423. Realising the political significance of the 1998 Special Session, campaigners for an open debate on international drug policy presented a letter to the UN Secretary General signed by thousands of international signatories include former heads of state, judges, policemen, parliamentarians and so forth calling for such a debate – *Guardian,* 6 June 1998.

96 See for example, the problems raised by J.B. Jacobs, 'Imagining drug legalization' (1990) 101 *The Public Interest* 28-42 who notes that the absence of fully worked out proposals for legalisation focuses concentration on the shortcomings of prohibition.

order to open international society's mind about drugs. In their present form, the drug conventions serve as an institutional barrier to such a change.

ANNEX: SUBSTANCES CONTROLLED

1   ALL DRUGS

This annex briefly examines which substances are controlled by the international drug conventions and how they are placed under control in terms of these conventions. The general principle is that all substances with recognised dependence producing properties are subject to international control. There are obvious exceptions such as alcohol and tobacco, but they fall outside the system for reasons of policy and not because of an assessment of their addictive properties. Indeed, there has never been an adequate definition of addictive drugs. The terms used, viz.: drugs, narcotics, dependence producing substances and so on have never found universal acceptance. International legislators have simply chosen to enumerate the substances to which the Conventions apply and to provide machinery for including under the scope of the Conventions other substances with the same or similar effect as those originally covered.[1]

Most of the main drug types fall under international control, viz.: the opiates, coca derivatives, cannabis, synthetics, barbiturates, amphetamines. The catalogue is being added to continually so a list of all drugs covered by a particular drug convention is attached in a schedule to that instrument. Bruun et al explain the reason for this:

> In the earlier treaties the drugs are named in the text, which means that, as a rule, to change the type of control to which a drug is subjected, the treaty must be amended. The more recent treaties arrange drugs in separate schedules, corresponding to different regimes of control. A change in the degree of control of any drug

---

1   B.A. Renborg, *International Drug Control* (Washington, Carnegie Endowment for International Peace, 1947), p. 51.

can be brought about by moving it into another schedule, without amending the treaty.[2]

National legislation usually follows the same approach. Drugs are placed in different schedules attached to drug legislation. In most states the same or similar offences are linked to the drugs in these schedules but different penalties attach. These schedules are then amended as the drug conventions' schedules are amended, unless a state has taken the lead in respect of a particular drug.

2   THE PROCEDURE FOR SCHEDULING DRUGS UNDER THE 1961 CONVENTION (AND AS AMENDED)[3]

Article 36 of the 1961 Convention, the provision requiring Parties to penalise conduct contrary to the Convention's provisions, requires Parties to do so in connection with any of the 'drugs' covered by the Convention. Without distinction as to their organic or synthetic origin, article 2 of the Convention divides narcotic drugs into four different schedules based on an assessment of their properties, and different control regimes are applied to the drugs in these schedules. In terms of article 2(1) all the general regulative control articles apply to Schedule I drugs,[4] in terms of article 2(2) less stringent provisions apply to the drugs listed in Schedule II,[5] while in terms of article 2(4) an even greater number of exceptions to the control articles are applied to the drug preparations included in Schedule III.[6] Schedule IV is a list of the drugs considered most

---

2   K. Bruun, L. Pan and I. Rexed, *The Gentlemen's Club: International Control of Drugs and Alcohol* (University of Chicago Press, Chicago, 1975), p. 47.
3   There are no relevant provisions in the 1972 Protocol.
4   Schedule I is composed of those substances which: a) have addiction-producing or addiction-sustaining properties greater than codeine and more or less comparable to those of morphine; b) are convertible into substances having addiction-producing or addiction-sustaining properties with an ease or yield such as to constitute a risk of abuse greater than codeine; or c) have a liability to abuse comparable to that of cocaine.
5   Schedule II is composed of those substances which: a) have addiction-producing or addiction-sustaining properties not greater than codeine but at least as great as dextropropoxyphene; or (b) are convertible into a substance having addiction-producing or addiction sustaining properties with an ease and yield such as to constitute a risk of abuse not greater than that of codeine.
6   Schedule III is composed of preparations a) intended for legitimate use; and which b) have a specified drug content and are compounded with one or more ingredients in such a way that the drug content cannot be recovered by readily applicable means or in yield

dangerous, to which it is recommended in terms of article 2(5) that additional, special control measures should be applied including prohibition of manufacture, traffic or use, except for medical or scientific use.[7] The opium poppy, the coca bush, the cannabis plant, poppy straw and cannabis leaves are subject to special measures of control under article 2(6) of the 1961 Convention and article 1 of the 1972 Protocol.

Article 3 of the 1961 Convention contains the procedure for making a change in the schedules.[8] In carrying out these procedures the WHO, relying upon the expertise of its ad-hoc Expert Committee, plays a crucial role. The most important procedure is the placing of new drugs under control. This procedure can only be initiated by Parties or by WHO, who must notify the Secretary-General and furnish him with information in support of the notification.[9] The Secretary-General must notify the other Parties and the WHO if necessary of the potential scheduling.[10] The WHO makes the necessary recommendation upon which the CND takes the final decision.[11] While the WHO is deliberating, however, due to the urgency of the need for control over drugs not included in Schedules I or II, Parties may at their discretion provisionally apply the standard control measures of the Convention (i.e. those applicable to Schedule I drugs),[12] and in addition, the CND may issue a mandatory direction that Parties apply these provisional controls until it makes its decision.[13]

The decision making process for placing a new drug under control is set out in article 3(3)(iii) and takes place in two stages. Stage one consists of the WHO, customarily relying on the decision of its Expert Committee, making a finding that the substance is a) liable to similar abuse and productive of similar ill effects as the drugs in Schedule I or Schedule II, or b) is convertible into such a drug.

---

which would constitute a risk to public health.

7 Schedule IV is composed of those substances which a) have strong addiction-producing properties or a liability to abuse not offset by therapeutic advantages that cannot be afforded by some other drug; and/or b) for which expunging from general medical practice is desirable because of the risk to public health.

8 See Bruun et al supra note 2 at 47-8. S.K. Chatterjee, *Legal Aspects of International Drug Control* (Nijhoff, Dordrecht, 1981), pp. 345-355 provides a more in depth study.

9 Article 3(1).

10 Article 3(2).

11 Article 3(7).

12 Article 3(3)(i).

13 Article 3(3)(ii).

Criteria a) depends on similarity in abuse and effect to scheduled substances. Thus the criteria used to schedule the drugs by the Technical Committee at the 1961 Conference remain important. The two tests it used in preparing Schedules I and II were the substance's 'degree of liability to abuse' and 'its risk to public health and social welfare'. The UN's official *Commentary on the Single Convention on Narcotic Drugs, 1961* (hereinafter the *1961 Commentary*)[14] notes that as a result of the application of these two tests 'the substances in these two Schedules, that is, the drugs under the narcotics regime have morphine like, cocaine like, or cannabis like effects or are convertible into "drugs" having such effects.' Thus in placing a new substance under control the WHO Expert Committee must determine its similarity of abuse and ill-effects to morphine, cocaine or cannabis-type drugs. The test leaves the Committee a measure of discretion, and it is guided by the risk the substance presents to 'public health and social welfare'. Criteria b), convertibility of a substance into a scheduled drug, is not dependent upon that substance belonging to a certain chemical group. The *1961 Commentary*[15] notes, however, that not every possible substance convertible into a scheduled drug was intended to be covered by the drafters of the 1961 Convention in this provision, but that the convertibility required 'must be of such a kind as to make it, by the ease of process and by the yield, practicable and profitable for a clandestine manufacturer to transform the substance in question into controlled drugs.' If the substance is found by WHO to be liable to similar abuse and productive of similar ill effects as drugs already controlled, or convertible into a controlled substance, then WHO will notify the CND of this finding. Stage two consists of the CND deciding, upon the basis of the WHO's recommendation, that the 'substance shall be added to Schedule I or Schedule II.' The WHO is obliged to make a recommendation as to which schedule the drug will go into. The CND makes the actual decision. The CND takes its votes in this case by simple majority. The CND's decision is binding immediately on the Parties upon receipt of notification thereof. The CND's decision may be reviewed by ECOSOC, which may accept or reject the original proposal by WHO or alter it by placing the drug in a schedule other than the one proposed.

Article 3(4) provides for the situation where the WHO recommends that a preparation should not be placed in Schedule I or II by the CND. The article allows the CND to 'exempt' the preparation from the controls of these two

---

14   *Commentary on the Single Convention on Narcotic Drugs, 1961* (New York, 1973) UN Publication Sales No. E.73.XI.1, pp. 86-87 (hereinafter *1961 Commentary*).
15   *1961 Commentary* at 88-89.

schedules and place it in Schedule III, intended for preparations with a recognised medical use and containing specified amounts of drugs compounded in such a way that they offer no risk of harm. In terms of the provisions, however, the CND may refuse to accept the WHO's recommendation to exempt the substance.

Schedule IV is reserved for drugs with

strong addiction producing properties or a liability to abuse not offset by therapeutical advantages which cannot be afforded by some other drug, and/or ... for which deletion from general medical practice is desirable because of the risk to public health.[16]

Article 3(5) allows the WHO to recommend that Schedule I drugs with these properties be placed in Schedule IV. Once again, however, the CND need not comply with the WHO's recommendation.

Article 3(6) allows the CND, again in accordance with the WHO's recommendation, to amend any of the schedules by transferring a drug from Schedule I to Schedule II or vice versa, or deleting any drug or preparation, as the case may be, from a schedule.

3 THE PROCEDURE FOR SCHEDULING SUBSTANCES UNDER THE 1971 CONVENTION

Barbiturates, tranquilisers and amphetamines fall outside the scope of the 1961 Convention, hence the elaboration of the 1971 Convention, which like the 1961 Convention, has four schedules of substances to which different control regimes apply.[17] From the point of view of criminal law, article 22 of the 1971 Convention, the provision that requires Parties to penalise conduct contrary to the Convention's provisions, implicitly requires Parties to do so in connection with any psychotropic substance covered by the Convention.

---

16 *United Nations Conference for the Adoption of a Single Convention on Narcotic Drugs Official Records Volume II* (New York, 1964) UN Doc. E/CONF.34/24/ Add.1; UN Publication Sales No. 63.XI.5, p. 264.

17 The substances covered include 'hallucinogenics, stimulants similar to the amphetamines, depressants similar to the barbiturates and to those tranquilisers' – *Commentary on the Convention on Psychotropic Substances, 1971* (New York, 1976) UN Doc. E/CN.7/589; UN Publication Sales No.E.76.XI.5, p.50 (hereinafter *1971 Commentary*).

As under the 1961 Convention, article 2(1) of the 1971 Convention provides that either a party or the WHO may, if it has information relating to an uncontrolled substance and believes that it should be scheduled, notify the Secretary-General to this effect, justifying its opinion and thus setting in motion the process for scheduling. This process is also used to initiate the transfer of a substance from one schedule to another or the deletion of a substance from the schedules. Under article 2(2) the Secretary-General is obliged to transmit the notification to the Parties, the CND and if the notification is made by a Party, the WHO. Article 2(3) obliges the Parties to examine the possibility of provisional application to the substance of the control measures applicable to Schedule I or II substances, as appropriate, if the notification transmits information which indicates that the substance is suitable for inclusion in either of these schedules.

Under the 1971 Convention, the WHO is required to spell out in greater detail than under the 1961 Convention, the criteria it applies in evaluating a drug for control. Under article 2(4), the WHO Expert Committee must perform a number of actions.

First, it has two options. It must assess whether the substance had the capacity to produce in terms of article 2(4)(a)(i) a 'state of dependence' and 'central nervous system stimulation or depression, resulting in hallucination or disturbances in motor function or thinking or behaviour or perception or mood.' If not, it must assess whether the substance is in terms of article 2(4)(a)(ii) open to 'similar abuse and similar effects' as a scheduled substance. Once either determination is made, then it must also determine under article 2(4)(b) that there is sufficient evidence of either existing or potential abuse of the substance 'so as to constitute a public health and social problem warranting the placing of the substance under international control.' Once it has determined this is the case, then the WHO Expert Committee is obliged to communicate an assessment of the substance to the CND. Included in the assessment must be its opinion of the extent or likelihood of abuse, the degree of seriousness of the public health and social problem and the degree of usefulness of the substance in medical therapy; together with any recommendations on appropriate control measures.

The WHO may in terms of the provision examine a substance solely on the basis of its chemical structure, but Chatterjee opines, that following its usual practice, it will take into account the effects the substance might produce.[18]

---

18   Supra note 8 at 460.

the WHO has the discretion over what abuse and ill effects 'similar' to an already scheduled substance means. Chatterjee notes that the Convention appears to have emphasised through these criteria the dependence producing characteristics of the controlled substances, but then points out that already scheduled substances like LSD may not be dependence producing, and suggests that the true criteria for classification is the capacity of the substance to cause harm.[19] While according to article 2(5) the Expert Committee's assessment is determinative as to medical and scientific matters, the CND takes the decision to schedule the substance and in doing so it has the right to seek advice elsewhere, and may alter the proposal. This innovation was apparently included because it was felt that not only medical and scientific considerations should govern such decisions, but that other factors such as social and administrative considerations should also play a role.[20] A two-thirds majority is required in the CND when voting on such a question.

Under article 2(6) the same procedure as set out above is used for the deletion of a substance from a schedule or for its transfer from one schedule to another.

Article 2(7) obliges the Secretary-General to communicate the CND's decision to all UN members, the WHO, the INCB and those Parties to the 1971 Convention who are not UN members. The CND's decision is not binding until 180 days after receipt by the Parties of notification thereof, and a Party may take exception to such a decision and make a reservation. However, it is obliged to apply a lesser category of controls to the substance, including in every case the adoption of 'measures in accordance with article 22 for the repression of acts contrary to the laws or regulations adopted pursuant to the aforegoing obligations'.[21]

Article 2(8) provides for review of the CND's decision, and article 2(9) urges Parties to 'apply such measures of supervision as practicable' to substances not falling under the scope of the Convention but which may be used in the manufacture of psychotropic substances.

Under article 3(1) of the 1971 Convention, preparations containing psychotropic substances are subject to the same measures of control as the psychotropic substances which they contain, and if there is more than one, the measures of control apply to the more strictly controlled substance. However, the escape clauses in article 3(2) and (3) exempt a Party from complying with certain re-

---

19 Supra note 8 at 460-1.
20 See Chatterjee supra note 8 at 472.
21 Article 2(7)(a)(vi), (b)(vi), (c)(v) and (d)(iii).

quirements under various articles including article 22's penal provisions, whenever that Party decides that a

> preparation containing a psychotropic substance other than a substance in Schedule I is compounded in such a way that it presents no, or negligible, risk of abuse and the substance cannot be recovered by readily applicable means in a quantity liable to abuse, so that the preparation does not give rise to a public health and social problem ... .

If a Party makes such a finding it notifies the Secretary-General of the preparation's name and composition and the measures of control from which it is exempted, and this notification is transmitted to the other Parties and drug control organs and to the WHO. Under article 3(4) if a Party or the WHO has information indicating that the exception should be terminated, it is obliged to communicate this information to the Secretary-General who is obliged to pass it on to the Parties, the CND and as the case may be, to the WHO, which shall also make a finding, which may be different, and the CND, taking into account the WHO's assessment, will finally decide if the preparation should be controlled or not. Communication of the decision and termination/non-termination follows accordingly.

4   DRUGS AND SUBSTANCES COVERED BY THE 1988 CONVENTION

4.1   The general provisions

For most purposes the material scope of the 1988 Convention is defined by the 1961 and 1971 Conventions as in effect it simply elaborates the criminal law provisions of those conventions. Thus article 1(n) provides that 'narcotic drug' means 'any of the substances, natural or synthetic, in Schedules I and II of the Single Convention on Narcotic Drugs, 1961, and that Convention as amended by the 1972 Protocol Amending the Single Convention on Narcotic Drugs' while article 1(r) defines 'psychotropic substance' as 'any substance, natural or synthetic, or/and natural material in Schedules I, II, III and IV of the Convention on Psychotropic Substances, 1971'. Only in respect of the scheduling of a precusor substance does it provide for a new procedure.

4.2 Precursors and the procedure for scheduling precursors under the 1988 Convention

Article 12 of the 1988 Convention is a novel provision providing for the control and monitoring of precursor substances at the national and international levels. Essential to its effective implementation is an efficient mechanism for bringing the specified substances under control. Article 1(t) defines 'Table I' and 'Table II' as 'the correspondingly numbered lists of substances annexed to this Convention, as amended from time to time in accordance with article 12'. The process for inclusion and amendment is set out in paragraphs (2) to (7) of article 12. This procedure was used in 1992 to add five substances to each Table.[22]

Article 12(2) makes it clear that the procedure for addition of substances to the lists in Tables I and II, deletion of substances from these Tables and transfer of substances from one Table to another is that set out in paragraphs 2 to 7 of article 12. Article 12(2) also clarifies that it is the Parties or the INCB that initiate the process for inclusion, transfer or deletion. If a Party or the INCB has information that it feels may require the inclusion of a substance in Table I or Table II, article 12(2) requires it to notify the Secretary-General and furnish him with the information in support of this notification.

Article 12(3) sets out what the Secretary-General must do with such a notification. He must transmit it, together with any other relevant information, to the Parties, the CND, and, if notification is made by a Party, to the INCB. The Parties are then required to return their comments on this notification to him, together with all additional information that may assist the INCB to make an assessment and the CND to reach a decision on this assessment. This obligation applies whether the notification is in respect of the addition, deletion or transfer of a substance. In practice the Secretary General notifies all states in order to get as broad a response as possible.[23]

Article 12(4) sets out the test to be used by the INCB in its assessment of the substance once notification has been received by the Secretary General. The INCB is obliged to take into account two important considerations in ap-

---

22 See W.C. Gilmore, 'Drug trafficking and the control of precursor and essential chemicals: the international dimension' in H.L. MacQueen and B.G. Main (eds), *Drug Trafficking and the Chemical Industry: Hume Papers on Public Policy* Vol. 4, no.1, (Edinburgh UP, Edinburgh, 1996), p. 18.

23 'Scheduling of substances under article 12 of the 1988 United Nations Convention against Illicit Traffic in Narcotic Drugs and Psychotropic Substances: the role of the INCB, and terms of reference, guidelines and rules for the INCB Advisory Expert Group' INCB/WP.1/Rev.1, para. 3.

plying this test, viz.: (i) the extent, importance and diversity of the substance's licit use; and (ii) the possibility and ease of using the alternate substances both for licit and illicit purposes. The test is set out in sub-paragraphs (a) and (b). Sub-paragraph (a) provides that the INCB must find that the substance in question 'is frequently used in the illicit manufacture of a narcotic drug or psychotropic substance'. Sub-paragraph (b) provides that the INCB must find that the volume and extent of the illicit manufacture of such drugs creates such serious public health or social problems that international action is necessary. If both legs of the test are satisfied then the INCB is obliged to transmit an assessment of the substance to the CND. Included in this assessment must be its conclusions as to the likely consequences to licit use and illicit manufacture of scheduling the substance, and its recommendations for any appropriate monitoring measures.[24] This procedure applies whether the assessment is in respect of the addition, deletion or transfer of a substance. The INCB, recognising the special knowledge required to make such assessments, has established an Advisory Expert Group to assist it in doing so[25] and has laid down guidelines for the review process.[26]

Article 12(5) then sets out how the CND decides to schedule a substance. The paragraph provides that this decision must take into account the Parties' comments, the INCB's comments and recommendations, and any other relevant factors. The INCB's assessment is, however, determinative as to scientific matters. The decision to schedule a substance in either Table I or II must be by a two-thirds majority of the CND's members. This procedure applies whether the decision is to add, delete or transfer the substance.

Article 12(6) sets out who must be informed by the CND of a decision in respect of the scheduling of a substance. It requires the CND to communicate such a decision through the Secretary-General to the INCB and to all Parties and potential parties to the 1988 Convention. This obligation applies whether the decision is to add, delete or transfer the substance. The decision becomes

---

24 The *Commentary on the United Nations Convention Against Illicit Traffic in Narcotic Drugs and Psychotropic Substances, 1988* (New York, 1998) UN Doc. E/CN.7/590; UN Publication Sales No.E.98.XI.5, p. 261(hereinafter the *1988 Commentary*) notes that factors taken into account in this assessment include the chemical function and actual use of the substances, the different types of drugs manufactured using the substance and the different manufacturing processes, seizure patterns, and the number, suitability and use of alternatives.

25 Decision 48/26.

26 These relate to the level of harm caused by the drug manufactured using this substance, the level of control over this drug, trends in supply of such a drug and current levels of abuse, and input from WHO – see note 26 supra.

effective one hundred and eighty days after the date of such communication. Unlike the position under the earlier conventions,[27] no provision is made for Parties to enter reservations in respect of newly included substances to allow them time to adjust their legal and administrative systems to comply with application of article 12's controls to the new substance.

Article 12(7) provides for review of the CND's decisions. Sub-paragraph (a) makes it clear that the CND's decisions to add, delete or transfer substances are subject to review by ECOSOC at any Party's request. The provision sets out the procedure for reviewing the CND's decision. Parties requesting review of the CND's decision must file such a request, together with all the relevant information upon which this request is based, with the Secretary General within one hundred and eighty days after the date of notification of the decision. Sub-paragraph (b) obliges the Secretary-General to transmit copies of the review request and relevant information to the CND, INCB and to all the Parties, inviting them to comment within ninety days. Comments are to be submitted to the ECOSOC for consideration. Sub-paragraph (c) gives the ECOSOC the power to confirm or reverse the CND's decision. Notification of the ECOSOC's decision must be transmitted to all Parties and to all potential parties, to the CND and to the INCB.

5   CONCLUSION

The scheduling procedures in the Conventions are very similar. The governments notify drug control organs of the need to bring a substance under control, and while the decision is taken by the CND, the real assessment is made by a small group of experts applying a fairly loose test. Since 1961 the test has become slightly more elaborate, and the organisation responsible for providing the expert opinion has changed. The key organisation under the 1961 Convention is the WHO's Expert Committee, while under the 1971 Convention its influence has been diluted a little through the CND's power to seek advice elsewhere. The unusual thing about the procedure set out in the 1988 Convention for the scheduling of precursors is that the INCB completely subsumes the role of the WHO. The INCB President informed the 1988 Conference that it would arrange the role of the WHO and would use the services of special consultants and

---

27   For example, article 2(7) of the 1971 Convention.

consult with the (then) DND's laboratory.[28] This may be explicable because precursors are substances with a commercial value, but then so are drugs themselves. It may be that the real reason for this change is because the CND did not have complete confidence in the WHO Expert Committee's technical and administrative background and its commitment to drug prohibition. The fact that the CND is the central power in the process of placing drug and precursors under international control has been attacked in the past because of the restraint it places on domestic actions in respect of controlled drugs and substances, particularly preventing Parties from choosing to decriminalise or legalise such drugs and substances unilaterally.[29] Ideally, should Parties choose to remove substances from control the whole of the international community should do so. There is no doubt that this is one of the few substantial powers the CND wields, and it is a power that serves as a barrier towards global growth of policies of decriminalisation because of the prevailing law and order ethos within the CND.

---

28   *United Nations Conference for the Adoption of a Convention against Illicit Traffic in Narcotic Drugs and Psychotropic Substances Official Records Volume II* (New York, 1991) UN Doc. E/CONF.82/16/Add.1, UN Publication Sales No.E.91.XI.1.p. 247.

29   See, for example, Comment 'The Convention on Psychotropic Substances: domestic consequences of ratification' (1978) 63 *Iowa Law Review* 950 at 953 which cites this as a reason why the US should not ratify the 1971 Convention (it finally did).

BIBLIOGRAPHY

BOOKS AND ARTICLES

Abarro P.A., 'The role of the Drug Advisory Programme of the Colombo Plan Bureau in the fight against illicit drug traffic' (1983) 35 *Bulletin on Narcotics* 67-72.

Abramovsky A., 'Extraterritorial abductions: America's "Catch and Snatch" policy run amok' (1991) 31 *Virginia Journal of International Law* 151-210.

Adams M., 'How to destroy the market for drugs?' (1993) 66 *The Police Journal* 42-46.

Akehurst M., 'Jurisdiction in international law' (1972/3) 46 BYIL 145-257.

Allsop S. and Nicholas R., 'Harm minimisation' in *Souvenir Brochure of the International Conference on Global drugs Law* (Indian Law Institute, New Delhi, 1997), pp. 22-28.

Anderson M., *Policing the World* (Clarendon, Oxford, 1989).

Anderson M., 'The Agenda for police co-operation' in M. Anderson and M. Den Boer (eds), *Policing Across National Boundaries* (Pinter, London, 1994), pp. 3-21.

Anslinger H.J., 'The implementation of treaty obligations in regulating the traffic in narcotic drugs' (1959) 8 *American University Law Review* 112-116.

Anslinger H.J. and Tompkins W.F., *The Traffic in Narcotics* (Funk and Wagnalls, New York, 1953).

Bailey S.H., *The Anti-Drug Campaign: An Experiment in International Control* (PS King, London, 1935).

Bassiouni M.C., 'Transnational control of narcotics' (1972) *Proceedings of the American Society of International Law* 227-233.

Bassiouni M.C., 'International criminal law' in S.H. Kadish (ed.), *Encyclopaedia of Crime and Justice* Volume 3 (MacMillan, New York, 1983), pp. 901-910.

Bassiouni M.C., 'Characteristics of international criminal law conventions' in M.C. Bassiouni (ed.), *1 International Criminal Law: Crimes* (Transnational, Dobbs Ferry, 1986), pp. 1-13.

Bassiouni M.C., 'The International Narcotics Control Scheme' in M.C. Bassiouni (ed.), *1 International Criminal Law: Crimes* (Transnational, Dobbs Ferry, 1986), pp. 507-524.

Bassiouni M.C., 'Extradition: the United States model' in M.C. Bassiouni (ed.), *2 International Criminal Law: Procedure* (Transnational, Dobbs Ferry, 1986), pp. 405-426.

Bassiouni M.C., *A Draft International Criminal Code and a Draft Statute for an International Criminal Tribunal* (Nijhoff, Dordrecht, 1987).

Bassiouni M.C., 'Effective national and international action against organised crime and terrorist criminal activities' (1990) 4 *Emory International Law Review* 9-42.

Bassiouni M.C., 'Critical reflections on international and national control of drugs' (1990) 18 *Denver Journal of International Law and Policy* 311-337.

Bassiouni M.C., 'The need for an international criminal court in the new international world order' (1992) 25 *Vanderbilt Journal of Transnational Law* 151-182.

Bassiouni M.C. and Wise E.M., *Aut Dedere Aut Judicare: The Duty to Extradite or Prosecute in International Law* (Nijhoff, Dordrecht, 1995).

Bassiouni M.C. and Thony J.F., 'The international drug control system' in M.C. Bassiouni (ed.), *1 International Criminal Law: Crimes* 2nd edn (Transnational, Ardsley-on-Hudson, 1999), pp. 905-947.

Barnett J.R., 'Extradition treaty improvements to combat drug trafficking' (1985) 15 *Georgia Journal of International and Comparative Law* 285-315.

Baum D., 'Tunnel vision: the war on drugs, 12 years later' (1993) 79 *American Bar Association Journal* 70-74.

Benyon J., Turnbill L., Willis A. and Woodward R., 'Understanding police co-operation in Europe: setting a framework for analysis' in M. Anderson and M. Den Boer (eds), *Policing Across National Boundaries* (Pinter, London, 1994), pp. 46-65.

Bernholz S.A., Bernholz M.J. and Herman J.N., 'International extradition in drug cases' (1985) 10 *North Carolina Journal of International Law and Commercial Regulation* 353-382.

Bin R.M., 'Drug Lords and the Colombian Judiciary: A story of threats, bribes and bullets' (1986) 5 *UCLA Pacific Basin Law Journal* 178-182.

Bland K.L., 'The Chemical Diversion and Trafficking Act of 1988: stopping the flow of chemicals to the Andean drug cartels' (1991) 7 *American University Journal of International Law and Policy* 105-143.

Blakesly C.L., 'United States jurisdiction over extraterritorial crime' (1982) *Journal of Criminal Law and Criminology* 1109-1163.

Blakesly C.L., 'Extraterritorial jurisdiction' in M.C. Bassiouni (ed.), *2 International Criminal Law: Procedure* (Transnational, Dobbs Ferry, 1986), pp. 3-53.

Blakesly C.L. and Lagodny O., 'Finding harmony amidst disagreement over extradition, jurisdiction, the role of human rights, and issues of extra-territoriality under international criminal law' (1991) 24 *Vanderbilt Journal of Transnational Law* 1-73.

Blakesly C.L., *Terrorism, Drugs, International Law and the Protection of Human Liberty* (Transnational, Ardsley-on-Hudson, 1992).

Blum Y.Z., 'Extradition: a common approach to the control of international terrorism and the traffic in narcotic drugs' (1978) 13 *Israel Law Review* 194-202.

Blumenson E. and Nilsen E., 'Policing for profit: the drugs war's hidden economic agenda' (1998) 65 *University of Chicago Law Review* 35-114.

Boggis D.B., 'Exporting United States drug law: an example of the international legal ramifications of the "war on drugs"' (1992) 1 *Brigham Young University Law Review* 165-190.

Bourne P.G., 'Drug abuse in the United States: a public policy review' (1977) 6 *Contemporary Drug Problems* 473-477.

Bowett D.W., 'Jurisdiction: changing patterns of authority over activities and resources' in R.S.J. MacDonald and D.M. Jhonston (eds), *The Structure and Process of International Law* (Nijhoff, Dordrecht, 1983), pp. 555-580.

Brown A.N., 'Drug Trafficking and the control of precursor and essential chemicals: UK domestic law and practice' in H.L. MacQueen and B.G. Main (eds), *Drug Trafficking and the Chemical Industry: Hume Papers on Public Policy* Vol. 4, no.1, (Edinburgh UP, Edinburgh, 1996), pp. 25-49.

Brown A.N., 'Towards a prosecutorial model for mutual assistance in criminal matters' in W.C. Gilmore and P.J. Cullen (eds), *Crimes Sans Frontieres: International and European Approaches: Hume Papers on Public Policy* Vol. 6, no's 1 and 2, (Edinburgh UP, Edinburgh, 1998), p. 50.

Brule C., 'The role of the Pompidou Group of the Council of Europe in combating drug abuse and illicit drug trafficking' (1983) 35 *Bulletin on Narcotics* 73.

Bruun K., Pan L. and Rexed I., *The Gentlemen's Club: International Control of Drugs and Alcohol* (University of Chicago Press, Chicago, 1975).

Bucknell P. and Ghodse H., *Misuse of Drugs* (Waterlow, London, 1991).

Cabranes J.A., 'International law and the control of the drug traffic' (1973) 7 *International Lawyer* 761-769.

Cagliotti C.N., 'The role of the South American Agreement on Narcotic Drugs and Psychotropic Substances in the fight against illicit drug trafficking' (1983) 35 *Bulletin on Narcotics* 83-95.

Campbell A.B., 'The Ker-Frisbie doctrine: a jurisdictional weapon in the war on drugs' (1990) 23 *Vanderbilt Jnl of Transnational Law* 385-433.

Catino T.M., 'Italian and American co-operative efforts to reduce heroin trafficking: a role model for the United States and drug supplying foreign nations' (1990) 8 *Dickinson Journal of International Law* 415-440.

Chatterjee S.K., *Legal Aspects of International Drug Control* (Nijhoff, Dordrecht, 1981).

Chatterjee S.K., *A Guide to the International Drugs Conventions* (Commonwealth Secretariat, London, 1988).

Chatterjee S.K., *Drug Abuse and Drug Related Crimes* (Nijhoff, Dordrecht, 1989).

Clark R.S., 'Offences of international concern: multilateral state treaty practice in the forty years since Nuremberg' (1988) 57 *Nordic Journal of International Law* 49-118.

Clutterbuck R., *Drugs, Crime and Corruption* (MacMillan, London, 1995).

Coggins P. and Roberts W.A., 'Extraterritorial jurisdiction: an untamed adolescent' (1991) 17 *Commonwealth Law Bulletin* 1391-1412.

Collison M., 'Punishing drugs: criminal justice and drug use' (1993) 33 *British Journal of Criminology* 382-399.

Comment, 'Narcotics Regulation' (1953) 62 *Yale Law Journal* 751-787.

Comment, 'The Convention on Psychotropic Substances: domestic consequences of ratification' (1978) 63 *Iowa Law Review* 950-974.

Commonwealth, 'Commonwealth Caribbean Conference on the International Drug Conventions and drug abuse' (1989) 15 *Commonwealth Law Bulletin* 1005-1011.

Cotic D., *Drugs and Punishment: An up-to-date Interregional Survey on Drug Related Offences* (UN Social Defence Research Institute, Rome, 1988, UN Sales No. E.88.III.N.I).

Currie A.J., Decker J.F. and Van Der Vaart J., 'International control of cannabis sativa' (1973) *Journal of Drug Issues* 240-255.

Cutting P.D., 'The technique of controlled delivery as a weapon in dealing with illicit traffic in narcotic drugs and psychotropic substances' (1983) 35 *Bulletin on Narcotics* 15-22.

David T.J., 'The British Government's international anti-drugs work' (1991) 17 *Commonwealth Law Bulletin* 1368-1376.

Dawkins K., 'International law and legalising cannabis' [1997] *New Zealand Law Journal* 281-284.

DeFeo M.A., 'Depriving international narcotics traffickers and other organized criminals of illegal proceeds and combating money laundering' (1990) 18 *Denver Journal of International Law and Policy* 405-415.

De Koker L., 'South African money laundering legislation' (1997) 22 *Journal of Juridical Science* 17-39.

Dickerson G.R., 'The Customs Co-operation Council and international customs enforcement' (1985) *The Police Chief* 16-18.

Dickson A., 'Taking dealers to the cleaners' (1991) 141 *New Law Journal* 1068-1069 (part one of two part article).

Dickson A., 'Taking dealers to the cleaners' (1991) 141 *New Law Journal* 1120-1122 (part two of two part article).

Division of Narcotic Drugs, 'Twenty years of narcotics control under the United Nations' (1966) 18 *Bulletin on Narcotics* 1-65.

Dorn N. (ed.), *Regulating European Drug Problems: Administrative Measures and Civil Law in the Control of Drug Trafficking, Nuisance and Use* (Kluwer , The Hague, 1999).

Dorn N. and Murji K., 'Low level drug enforcement' (1992) 20 *International Journal of the Sociology of Law* 159-171.

Dorn N., Murji K. and South N., *Traffickers: Drug Markets and Law Enforcement* (Routledge, London, 1992).

d'Oliveira J., *International Mutual Legal Assistance and Other Forms of International Legal Co-operation* (unpublished conference paper, New Delhi Global Drugs Law Conference, 1997).

Dugard J., 'Obstacles in the way of an international criminal court' (1997) 56 *Cambridge Law Journal* 329-342.

Dunant O. and Wassmer M., 'Swiss bank secrecy: its limits under Swiss and international laws' (1988) 20 *Case Western Reserve International Law Journal* 541-575.

Eisenlohr L.E.S., *International Narcotics Control* (George Allen and Unwin, London, 1934).

Eldridge W.B., *Narcotics and the Law: A Critique of the American Experiment in Narcotic Drug Control* (2nd edn, The University of Chicago Press, Chicago and London, 1967).

Ellington S.B., 'United States v. Noriega as a reason for an international criminal court' (1993) 11 *Dickinson Journal of International Law* 451-475.

Ellis A.and Pisani R., 'The United States treaties on mutual assistance in criminal matters' in M.C. Bassiouni (ed.), *2 International Criminal Law: Procedure* (Transnational, Dobbs Ferry, 1986), pp. 151-179.

Elvins M., 'Drugs and the state in a global network' (1997) 5 *The South African Journal of International Affairs* 1-26.

Estievenart G. (ed.), *Policies and Strategies to Combat Drugs in Europe* (Nijhoff, Dordrecht, 1995).

Estievenart G., 'The European Community and the global drugs phenomenon' in G. Estievenart (ed.), *Policies and Strategies to Combat Drugs in Europe* (Nijhoff, Dordrecht, 1995), pp. 50-93.

Evans K., 'The hundred per cent solution' (1993) 143 *New Law Journal* 751-752.

Fish K., 'The United Nations and the Taliban: an unholy alliance in the name of drug control' (1998) 35 *The Drug Policy Letter* 15-16.

Fisher K., 'Trends in extraterritorial narcotics control: slamming the stable door after the horse has bolted' (1984) 16 *New York University Journal of International Law and Politics* 353-413.

Fletcher A., 'Pirates and smugglers: an analysis of the use of abductions to bring drug traffickers to trial' (1991) 32 *Virginia Journal of International Law* 233-264.

Flynn S.E. and Grant G.M., *The Transnational Drug Challenge and the New World Order: The Report of the CSIS Project on the Global Drug Trade in the Post-Cold War Era* (The Centre for Strategic and International Studies, Washington, 1993).

Fraser A. and George M. 'Cautions for cannabis' (1992) 8 *Policing* 88-102.

Freestone D., 'The principle of co-operation: terrorism' in C. Warbrick and V. Lowe (eds), *The United Nations and the Principles of International Law* (Routledge, London, 1994), pp. 137-159.

Frei L. and Treschel S., 'Origins and applications of the United States - Switzerland Treaty on Mutual Assistance in Criminal Matters' (1990) 31 *Harvard International Law Journal* 77-97.

Fredericks M.A., 'Counter-narcotics law enforcement co-operation: a necessity' in *Souvenir Brochure of the International Conference on Global drugs Law* (Indian Law Institute, New Delhi, 1997), pp. 29-32.

Friman H.R., 'International pressure and domestic bargains: regulating money laundering in Japan' (1994) 21 *Criminal Law and Social Change* 253-266.

Ferencz B.B., 'An international criminal code and court: where they stand and where they're going' (1992) 30 *Columbia Journal of Transnational Law* 345-399.

Gardner S.A., 'A global initiative to deter drug trafficking: will internationalising the drug war work?' (1993) 7 *Temple International and Comparative Law Review* 287-317.

Ghodse H., *The Criminal Justice System and the Treatment of Drug Misuse* (unpublished paper, New Delhi Global Drugs Law Conference, 1997).

Gianaris W.N., 'The new world order and the need for an international criminal court' (1992/3) 16 *Fordham International Law Journal* 88-119.

Gilbert G., 'Crimes sans frontieres: jurisdictional problems in English law' (1992) 63 BYIL 415-441.

Gilmore N., 'Drug use and human rights: privacy, vulnerability, disability, and human rights infringements' (1996) 12 *The Journal of Contemporary Health Law and Policy* 355-447.

Gilmore W.C., 'Hot pursuit and constructive presence in Canadian law enforcement' (1988) 12 *Marine Policy* 105-111.

Gilmore W.C., 'Narcotics interdiction at sea: UK-US co-operation' (1989) 15 *Commonwealth Law Bulletin* 1480-1497.

Gilmore W.C., 'International action against drug trafficking: trends in United Kingdom law and practice' (1990) 24 *International Lawyer* 365-392.

Gilmore W.C., *Combating International Drug Trafficking: The 1988 United Nations Convention Against Illicit Traffic in Narcotic Drugs and Psychotropic Substances* (Commonwealth Secretariat, London, 1991).

Gilmore W.C., 'Drug trafficking by sea: the 1988 United Nations Convention Against Illicit Traffic in Narcotic Drugs and Psychotropic Substances' (1991) 15 *Marine Policy* 183-192.

Gilmore W.C., 'International action against drug trafficking: trends in United Kingdom law and practice through the 1980's' (1991) 17 *Commonwealth Law Bulletin* 287-313.

Gilmore W.C., 'International efforts to combat money laundering' (1992) 18 *Commonwealth Law Bulletin* 1129-1142.

Gilmore W.C. (ed.), *International Efforts to Combat Money Laundering* (Grotius, Cambridge, 1992).

Gilmore W.C., 'International initiatives' in R. Parlour (ed.), *Butterworths International Guide to Money Laundering Law and Practice* (Butterworths, London, 1995), pp. 15-27.

Gilmore W.C. (ed.), *Mutual Assistance in Criminal and Business Regulatory Matters* (Grotius, Cambridge, 1995).

Gilmore W.C., 'Narcotics interdiction at sea: the 1995 Council of Europe Agreement' (1996) 20 *Marine Policy* 3-14.

Gilmore W.C., 'Drug trafficking and the control of precursor and essential chemicals: the international dimension' in H.L. MacQueen and B.G. Main (eds), *Drug Trafficking and the Chemical Industry: Hume Papers on Public Policy* Vol. 4, no.1, (Edinburgh UP, Edinburgh, 1996), pp. 18-22.

Gilmore W.C., 'The G-7 and transnational drug trafficking: the Task Force experience' in W.C. Gilmore and P.J. Cullen (eds), *Crimes Sans Frontieres: International and European Approaches: Hume Papers on Public Policy* Vol. 6, no's 1 and 2, (Edinburgh UP, Edinburgh, 1998), pp. 30-38.

Goodrich L.M., 'New trends in narcotics control' (1960) 530 *International Conciliation* 181-242.

Gordon D.R., *The Return of the Dangerous Classes: Drug Prohibition and Policy Politics* (WW Norton, New York, 1994).

Gotschlich G.D., 'Action by the Customs Co-operation Council to combat illicit drug trafficking' (1983) 35 *Bulletin on Narcotics* 79-81.

Green P., *Drugs, Trafficking and Criminal Policy* (Waterside Press, Winchester, 1998).

Gregg R.W., 'The Single Convention for Narcotic Drugs' (1961) 16 *Food Drug Cosmetic Law Journal* 187-208.

Gregg R.W., 'The United Nations and the opium problem' (1964) 13 ICLQ 96-115.

Grilli A.M., 'Preventing billions from being washed offshore: a growing approach to stopping international drug trafficking' (1987) 14 *Syracruse Journal of International Law and Commerce* 65-88.

Gross N.G. and Greenwald G.J., 'The 1972 Narcotics Protocol' (1973) 2 *Contemporary Drug Problems* 119-163.

Harding A., 'Criminal Justice (International Cooperation) Act 1990: Forfeiture, Money Laundering, Confiscation and Maritime Provisions' (1991) 155 *Justice of the Peace* 492-493.

Harring S.L., 'Death, drugs and development: Malaysia's mandatory death penalty for drug traffickers and the international war on drugs' (1991) 29 *Columbia Journal of Transnational Law* 364-405.

Henham R., 'Criminal justice and sentencing policy for drug offenders' (1994) 22 *International Journal of the Sociology of Law* 223-238.

Henrichs W., 'Problems of competence in international law with regard to the punishment of narcotic drug offences and the extradition of narcotics offenders' (1960) 3 *Bulletin on Narcotics* 1-7.

Hernandez B.E., 'RIP to IRP - Money laundering and drug trafficking controls score a knockout victory over bank secrecy' (1993) 18 *North Carolina Journal of International Law and Commercial Regulation* 235-304.

Heymann P.B., 'Two models of national attitudes toward international cooperation in law enforcement' (1990) 31 *Harvard International Law Journal* 99-107.

Hinton M., 'Are drug trafficking confiscation orders punitive?' (1992) 136 *Solicitors Journal* 1264-1265.

Holt E., *The Opium Wars in China* (Putnam, London, 1964).

Inglis B., *The Forbidden Game* (Hodder and Stoughton, London, 1975).

Inglis B., *The Opium War* (Hodder and Stoughton, London, 1976).

Jauhar D.N., *Rethinking Drug Legislation in India* (unpublished conference paper, New Delhi Global Drugs Law Conference, 1997).

Jacobs J.B., 'Imagining drug legalization' (1990) 101 *The Public Interest* 28-42.

Jacobs J.B. and Zimmer L., 'Drug treatment and workplace drug testing: politics, symbolism and organizational dilemmas' (1991) 9 *Behavioural Sciences and the Law* 345-360.

Johns C.J., *Power, Ideology, and the War on Drugs* (Prager, New York, 1992).

Jost P., 'Black hawala, financial crimes and the world drug trade' in *Souvenir Brochure of the International Conference on Global drugs Law* (Indian Law Institute, New Delhi, 1997), pp. 116-128.

Kallenbach C., '*Plomo o plata*: irregular rendition as a means of gaining jurisdiction over Colombian drug kingpins' (1990) 23 *New York University Journal of International Law and Politics* 169-216.

Kaufman V., 'United Nations: International Conference on Drug Abuse and Illicit Trafficking' (1988) 29 *Harvard International Law Journal* 581-586.

Keig L.A., 'A proposal for direct use of the United States military in drug enforcement operations abroad' (1988) 23 *Texas International Law Journal* 291-316.

Kelley J.P., 'United States - Colombian extradition treaty: efforts to prosecute drug lords' (1990) 14 *Suffolk Transnational Law Journal* 162-182.

Kendall R.E., 'Drug control: policies and practices of the International Criminal Police Organisation' (1992) 44 *Bulletin on Narcotics* 3-10.

King R., 'Law and enforcement policies' (1957) 22 *Law and Contemporary Problems* 113.

King R., *The Drugs Hang Up: Americas Fifty Year Folly* (CC Thomas, Springfield, 1972).

Kingham R.A. and Wallon A., 'The role of the European Citizen's Associations in strategies and policies to combat drugs' in G. Estievenart (ed.), *Policies and Strategies to Combat Drugs in Europe* (Nijhoff, Dordrecht, 1995), pp. 311-318.

Kirby M., 'Drugs - an international prohibition' (1992) 18 *Commonwealth Law Bulletin* 312-320.

Knapp J., 'Mutual legal assistance treaties as a way to pierce bank secrecy' (1988) 20 *Case Western Reserve International Law Journal* 405-433.

Kohler N., 'The confiscation of criminal assets in the United States and Switzerland' (1990) 13 *Houston Journal of International Law* 1-38.

Krasna J.S., 'Narcotics and the national security of producer states' *The Journal of Conflict Studies*, Spring 1996, University of New Brunswick, <http://utratext.hil.unb.ca/Texts/JCS>.

Krajewski K., 'How flexible are the UN drug conventions?' in *Agenda and Delegates Materials Regulating Cannabis: Options for Control in the 21st Century: An International Symposium* (Release/Lindesmith Centre, 1998).

Lagodny O., 'Legally protected interests of the abducted alleged offender' (1993) 1&2 *Israel Law Review* 339-361.

Lande A., 'The Single Convention on Narcotic Drugs, 1961' (1962) 16 *International Organisation* 776-797.

Landis K.T., 'The seizure of Noriega: a challenge to the *Ker-Frisbie* doctrine' (1991) 6 *American University Journal of International Law and Policy* 571-607.

Leeson J., 'Refusal to extradite: an examination of Canada's indictment of the American legal system' (1996) 26 *Georgia Journal of International and Comparative Law* 641-658.

Leigh M.N., 'Contemporary practice of the United States relating to international law: territorial jurisdiction' (1990) 84 AJIL 725-729.

Leinward M.A., 'The international law of treaties and United States legalization of marijuana' (1971) 10 *Columbia Journal of Transnational Law* 413-441.

Leroy B., 'The United Nations strategy' in G. Estievenart (ed.), *Policies and Strategies to Combat Drugs in Europe* (Nijhoff, Dordrecht, 1995), pp. 27-38.

Leroy B., 'European legislative systems in relation to demand in 1993: recent developments and comparative study' in G. Estievenart (ed.), *Policies and Strategies to Combat Drugs in Europe* (Nijhoff, Dordrecht,1995), pp. 112-130.

Lewis S.L., 'The Marijuana on the High Seas Act: extending U.S. jurisdiction beyond international limits' (1982) 8 *Yale Journal of World Public Order* 359-383.

Lindesmith A.L., *The Addict and the Law* (Indiana UP, Bloomington, 1965).

Lindesmith A.L., 'The drug-control bureaucracy creates the "drug-problem"' in I. Silver (ed.), *The Crime Control Establishment* (Prentice Hall, Engelwood Cliffs, 1974), pp. 58-69.

Linke R., Epp H.J. and Kabelka E., *Extradition for Drug Related Offences* (UN Publication St/Nar/5, Austria, 1985, UN Sales No. E.85.XI.6).

Littas R., 'The SEPAT-plan and its development' (1979) *International Criminal Police Review* 101-104.

Lowenstein L.F., 'Legalising or not legalising drugs' (1993) 66 *The Police Journal* 296-301.

Lowes P.D., *The Genesis of International Narcotics Control* (Librairie Droz, Geneva, 1966).

Macdonald S.B. and Zagaris B. (eds), *International Handbook on Drug Control* (Greenwood Press, Westport, 1992).

Magliveras K.D., 'Defeating the money launderer - the international and European framework' (1992) 3 *Journal of Business Law* 161-177.

Malekian F., *International Criminal Law: The Legal and Critical Analysis of International Crimes* Volume II (Uppsala UP, Uppsala, 1991).

Mann F.A., 'The doctrine of jurisdiction in international law' (1964-I) 113 *Recueil des Cours* 9.

Mann F.A., 'The doctrine of international jurisdiction revisted after twenty years' (1984-III) 186 *Recueil des Cours* 19.

Marotta E., 'Drugs as a priority in co-operation in the fields of justice and home affairs' in G. Estievenart (ed.), *Policies and Strategies to Combat Drugs in Europe* (Nijhoff, Dordrectht, 1995), p.198.

May H.L., 'Narcotic Drug Control - Development of International Action and the Establishment of Supervision under the United Nations' (1948) 441 *International Conciliation* 303-380.

May H.L., 'The evolution of the international control of narcotic drugs' (1950) 2 *Bulletin on Narcotics* 1-12.

May H.L., 'Narcotic drug control' (1952) 485 *International Conciliation* 489-536.

McClean D., 'Mutual assistance in criminal matters: the Commonwealth initiative' (1988) 37 ICLQ 177-190.

McClean D., 'Seizing the proceeds of crime: the state of the art' (1989) 38 ICLQ 334-360.

McClean D., *International Judicial Assistance* (Clarendon, Oxford, 1992).

McCormack T. and Simpson G., 'A new international criminal law regime?' (1995) 42 *Netherlands International Law Review* 177-206.

Morrison W., 'Modernity, knowledge and the criminalisation of drug usage' in I. Loveland (ed.), *Frontiers of Criminality* (Sweet & Maxwell, London, 1995), pp. 195-218.

Mulder C. and Swart B., 'Sub-regional arrangements: the Benelux Countries' in M.C. Bassiouni (ed.), *1 International Criminal Law: Crimes* 2nd edn (Transnational, Ardsley-on-Hudson, 1999), pp.393-400.

Murji K., 'Drug enforcement strategies' (1993) 32 *Howard Law Journal* 215-230.

Murphy J.F., 'International Crimes' in C.C. Joyner (ed.), *The United Nations and International Law* (CUP/American Society of International Law; Cambridge; 1997), pp. 362-381.

Murphy J.W., 'Implementation of international narcotics control: the struggle against opium cultivation in Pakistan' (1983) 6 *Boston College International and Comparative Law Review* 199-241.

Murphy S.R., 'Drug diplomacy and the supply side strategy: a survey of United States practice' (1990) 43 *Vanderbilt Law Review* 1259-1309.

Murray C. and Harris L., *Mutual Assistance in Criminal Matters* (Sweet and Maxwell, London, 2000).

Musto D.F., *The American Disease: Origins of Narcotics Control* (expanded edition, OUP, New York, 1987).

Nadelmann E.A., 'Negotiations in criminal law assistance treaties' (1985) 33 *American Journal of Comparative Law* 467-505.

Nadelmann E.A., 'Unlaundering dirty money abroad: U.S. foreign policy and financial secrecy jurisdictions' (1986) 18 *Inter-American Law Review* 33-81.

Nadelmann E.A., 'The DEA in Latin America: dealing with institutionalized corruption' (1989) 62 *Police Journal* 31-42 (part one of two part article).

Nadelmann E.A., 'The Drug Enforcement Agency in Latin America: the ins and outs of working around corruption' (1989) 62 *Police Journal* 157-173 (part two of two part article).

Nadelmann E.A., 'Global prohibition regimes: the evolution of norms in international society' (1990) 44 *International Organisation* 479-526.

Nadelmann E.A., 'The role of the United States in the international enforcement of criminal law' (1990) 31 *Harvard International Law Journal* 37-76.

Nadelmann E.A., 'Drug prohibition in the United States: costs, consequences and alternatives' (1991) 5 *Notre Dame Journal of Law, Ethics and Public Policy* 783-808; 'Comments on Nadelmann' 809-815; 'Nadelmann's response' 817-822.

Nadelmann E.A., 'The evolution of United States involvement in the international rendition of fugitive criminals' (1993) 25 *New York University Journal of International Law and Politics* 813-885.

Nadelmann E.A., *Cops Across Borders: The Internationalization of U.S. Criminal Law Enforcement* (The Pennsylvania State University Press, University Park, Pennsylvania, 1993).

Nahas G., 'Drugs, the brain and the law' (1991) 5 *Notre Dame Journal of Law, Ethics and Public Policy* 729-746.

Nellis J.L., 'International narcotics control efforts and policies as seen in congress' (1977) 6 *Contemporary Drug Problems* 479-490.

Nilsson H.G., 'The Council of Europe Laundering Convention: a recent example of a developing international criminal law' (1992) 2 *Criminal Law Forum* 419-465 (reproduces Convention).

Noll A., 'International treaties and the control of drug use and abuse' (1977) 6 *Contemporary Drug Problems* 17-39.

Noll A., 'Drug abuse and penal provisions of the international drug control treaties' (1977) 19 *Bulletin on Narcotics* 41-57.

Oehler D., 'Criminal Law, International' in R. Bernhardt (ed.), *Encyclopaedia of Public International Law* Volume I (Elsevier, Amsterdam, 1992), pp. 877-883.

Okagbue I., *The Death Penalty as an Effective Deterrent to Drug Abuse and Drug Trafficking: Myth or Reality* (Nigerian Centre for Advanced Legal Studies, Lagos, 1991).

Okera S.Y., 'International extradition and the Medellin cocaine cartel: surgical removal of Colombian cocaine traffickers for trial in the United States' (1992) 13 *Loyola of Los Angeles International and Comparative Law Journal* 955-1008.

O'Malley P. and Mugford S., 'The demand for intoxicating commodities: implications for the war on drugs' in N. South (ed.), *Drugs, Crime, and Criminal Justice* (Dartmouth, Aldershot, 1995), pp. 441-467.

Oppenheimer T., 'Drug abuse control: mutual assistance between members of the Commonwealth' (1990) 16 *Commonwealth Law Bulletin* 979-992.

Ostrowski J., 'Answering the critics of drug legalization' (1991) 5 *Notre Dame Journal of Law, Ethics and Public Policy* 823-851.

Paget-Brown I., 'Bank secrecy and criminal matters: Cayman Islands and U.S. cooperative development' (1988) 20 *Case Western Reserve International Law Journal* 369-391.

Panel discussion, 'Drugs and small arms: can law stop the traffic?' (1987) 81 *American Society of International Law: Proceedings* 44-59.

Panel discussion, 'International drug trafficking and money laundering' (1988) 82 *American Society of International Law: Proceedings* 444-455.

Panel discussion, 'International drug traffic' (1990) 84 *American Society of International Law: Proceedings* 1-12.

Panel discussion, 'New frontiers in the regulation of international money movement in the wake of BCCI' (1992) 86 *American Society of International Law: Proceedings* 188-209.

Parlour R. (ed.), *Butterworths International Guide to Money Laundering Law and Practice* (Butterworths, London, 1995).

Patel F., 'Crime without frontiers: a proposal for an international narcotics court' (1990) 22 *New York University Journal of International Law and Politics* 709-747.

Penna L.R., 'Forfeiture of drug trafficking benefits: need for a viable international legal regime' (1993) 14 *Singapore Law Review* 351-381.

Prost K., 'Breaking down the barriers: international co-operation in combating transnational crime' in *Souvenir Brochure of the International Conference on Global drugs Law* (Indian Law Institute, New Delhi, 1997), pp. 44-52.

Puttler A., 'Extraterritorial application of criminal law: jurisdiction to prosecute drug traffic conducted by aliens abroad' in K.M. Meesen (ed.), *Extraterritorial Jurisdiction in Theory and Practice* (Kluwer, London, 1996), pp. 103-121.

Rampilla N.R., 'Towards prosecuting the illicit drug traffickers before the proposed international criminal court - a challenge beyond 2000' in *Souvenir Brochure of the International Conference on Global drugs Law* (Indian Law Institute, New Delhi, 1997), pp. 167-171.

Raustalia K., 'Law, Liberalization and International Narcotics Trafficking' (1999) 32 *New York University Journal of International Law and Politics* 89-145.

Renborg B.A., *International Drug Control: A Study of International Administration by and Through the League of Nations* (Washington, Carnegie Endowment for International Peace, 1947 - reprinted by Kraus Reprint Co. New York, 1972).

Renborg B.A., 'International drug control' (1957) 22 *Law and Contemporary Problems* 86.

Reuter P., 'The limits and consequences of U.S. foreign drug control efforts' (1992) 521 *Annals of the American Academy of Politics and Social Science* 151-162.

Reuter P. and MacCoun R., 'Assessing the legalisation debate' in G. Estievenart (ed.), *Policies and Strategies to Combat Drugs in Europe* (Nijhoff, Dordrecht, 1995) pp. 39-49.

Rexed B., Edmonson K., Khan I. and Sansom R., *Guidelines for the Control of Narcotic and Psychotropic Substances: In the Context of the International Treaties* (WHO, Geneva, 1984).

Rider B.A.K., 'The role of the Commonwealth Secretariat in the fight against illicit drug traffic' (1983) 35 *Bulletin on Narcotics* 61-65.

Rouchereau F., 'La Convention des Nations Unies Contre le Traffic Illicite de Stupefiants et de Substances Psychotropes' (1988) 34 *Annuaire Francais de Droit Internationale* 601-617.

Rodd R., 'The politics of failure: a perspective on the war on drugs' in *Souvenir Brochure of the International Conference on Global drugs Law* (Indian Law Institute, New Delhi, 1997), pp. 52-65.

Roecks C.R., 'Extradition, human rights, and the death penalty: when nations must refuse to extradite a person charged with a capital crime' (1994) 25 *California Western International Law Journal* 189-234.

Rolley R., 'United Nations activities in international drug control' in S.B. Macdonald and B. Zagaris (eds), *International Handbook on Drug Control* (Greenwood Press, Westport, 1992), pp. 415-433.

Ryan K.F., 'Globalizing the problem: The United States and international drug control' in E.L. Jensen and J. Gerber (eds), *The New War on Drugs: Symbolic Politics and Criminal Justice Policy* (ACJS and Anderson Publishing Co., Cincinatti, 1998), pp. 141-156.

Rydell P.C. and Everingham S.S., *Controlling Cocaine: Supply versus Demand Programs* (Rand Corp, Drug Policy Research Center, Santa Monica, California, 1994).

Salbu S.R., 'Extraterritorial restriction of bribery: a premature evocation of the normative global village' (1999) 24 *Yale International Law Journal* 223 at 226-255.

Sallon C. and Beddingfield D., 'Drugs, money and the law' (1993) *Criminal Law Review* 165-173.

Savona E.U. and De Feo M., *Money trails: international money laundering trends and prevention/control policies*, report prepared for the International Conference on Preventing and Controlling Money-Laundering and the Use of the Proceeds of Crime: a Global Approach, held at Courmayeur, Italy, from 18-20 June 1994.

Saxena D.R., *Illicit Traffic in Narcotic Drugs and Psychotropic Substances and the Law in India* (unpublished conference paper, New Delhi Global Drugs Law Conference, 1997).

Scharf M.P., 'Getting serious about an international criminal court' (1994) 6 *Pace International Law Review* 103-118.

Scharf M.P., 'The politics of establishing an International Criminal Court' (1995) 6 *Duke Journal of International and Comparative Law* 167-173.

Schutte J.J.E., 'Transfer of criminal proceedings: the European system' in M.C. Bassiouni (ed.), *2 International Criminal Law: Procedure* (Transnational, Dobbs Ferry, 1986), pp. 319-336.

Schutte J.J.E., 'Extradition for drug offences: new developments under the 1988 UN Convention Against Illicit Traffic in Narcotic Drugs and Psychotropic Substances' (1991) 62 *Revue Internationale de Droit Penal* 135-157.

Seccombe R., 'Squeezing the balloon: international drugs policy' (1995) 14 *Drug and Alcohol Review* 311-316.

Shearer I.A., 'Problems of jurisdiction and law enforcement against delinquent vessels' (1986) 35 ICLQ 320-343.

Sheptycki J., 'Law enforcement, justice and democracy in the transnational arena: reflections on the war on drugs' (1996) 24 *International Journal of the Sociology of Law* 61-75.

Solomon P., 'Are money launderers all washed up in the western hemisphere? The OAS Model Regulations' (1994) 17 *Hastings International and Comparative Law Review* 433-455.

Sorenson C.E., 'Drug trafficking on the high seas: a move towards universal jurisdiction under international law' (1990) 4 *Emory International Law Review* 207-230.

Spencer D.E., 'Bank liability under the UN Drug Trafficking Convention' (1990) 9 *International Financial Law Review* 16-19.

Sproule D.W. and St-Denis P., 'The UN Drug Trafficking Convention: An Ambitious Step' [1989] CYBIL 263-293.

Srinivasan N. and Underwood R., 'Money laundering: international efforts and recent developments in the movement of drug related money' in *Souvenir Brochure of the*

International Conference on Global drugs Law (Indian Law Institute, New Delhi, 1997), pp. 198-204.

Stahl M.B., 'Asset forfeiture, burdens of proof and the war on drugs' (1992) 83 *Journal of Criminal Law and Criminology* 274-337.

Stafford D., *International Legal Co-operation Against Serious Crime: Inter-legal Systems Issues Impacting on International Co-operation* (unpublished paper, New Delhi Global Drugs Law Conference, 1997).

Stafford D., 'Combating transnational crime: the role of the Commonwealth' in W.C. Gilmore and P.J. Cullen (eds), *Crimes Sans Frontieres: International and European Approaches: Hume Papers on Public Policy* Vol. 6, no's 1 and 2, (Edinburgh UP, Edinburgh, 1998), pp. 44-49.

Stares P.B., *Gobal Habit: The Drug Problem in a Borderless World* (Brookings Institution, Washington DC, 1996).

Starke J.G., 'The Convention of 1936 for the Suppression of the Illicit Traffic in Dangerous Drugs' (1937) 31 AJIL 31-43.

Stewart D.P., 'Internationalizing the war on drugs: the UN Convention Against Illicit Traffic in Narcotic Drugs and Psychotropic Substances' (1990) 18 *Denver Journal of International Law and Policy* 387-404.

Sunga L.S., 'Illicit traffic in narcotic drugs' in *The Emerging System of International Criminal Law: Developments in Codification and Implementation* (Kluwer, Hague, 1997), pp. 207-219.

Taisch F., 'Swiss statutes concerning money laundering' (1992) 26 *The International Lawyer* 695-714.

Tauber J., 'A systems participants glossary of a drug court' in *Souvenir Brochure of the International Conference on Global drugs Law* (Indian Law Institute, New Delhi, 1997), pp.159-166.

Taylor A.H., *American Diplomacy and the Narcotics Traffic, 1900-1939: A Study in International Humanitarian Reform* (Duke UP, Durham, 1969).

Terry C.E. and Pellins M., *The Opium Problem* (Bureau of Social Hygiene, New York, 1928 - reprint Patterson-Smith, Montclair NJ, 1970).

Torr D. (ed.), *Marx on China, 1853-1860* (Lawrence and Wishart, London, 1968).

Van Atta D.M., 'Effects of the single convention on narcotic drugs upon the regulation of marijuana' (1968) 19 *Hastings Law Journal* 848-861.

Van Den Wyngaert C., 'Rethinking the law of international criminal co-operation: the restrictive function of international human rights through individual-oriented bars' in A. Eser and O. Lagodny (eds), *Principles and Procedures for a New Transnational Criminal Law* (Max Planck Institute, Freiburg im Breisgau, 1991), pp. 489-503.

Waddel J.G., 'International Narcotics Control' (1970) 64 AJIL 310-321.

Wadler D.G., 'Operation Blast Furnace: The United States involvement in Bolivia to put the heat on drug traffickers' (1987) 2 *Journal of International Dispute Resolution* 175-203.

Wells A., *International Drug Control: Recent Developments, Patterns and Trends* (unpublished conference paper, New Delhi Global Drugs Law Conference, 1997).

Wells A., *International Legal and Policy Framework* (unpublished conference paper, New Delhi Global Drugs Law Conference, 1997).

White S., 'European Community drug control: internal economic regulation and external conditionality' in N. Dorn (ed.), *Regulating European Drug Problems* (Kluwer, Hague, 1999), pp. 31-55.

Williams P. and Savona E.U. (eds), *The United Nations and Transnational Crime* (Frank Cass; London, 1996).

Wise E.M., 'The obligation to extradite or prosecute' (1993) 1&2 *Israel Law Review* 268-287.

Woltring H.F. and Greig J., 'State-sponsored kidnapping of fugitives: an alternative to extradition?' in D. Atkins (ed.), *The Alleged Transnational Criminal* (Nijhoff, The Hague, 1995), pp. 115-125.

Wren T., 'The enforcement of confiscation law in Great Britain' (1991) 17 *Commonwealth Law Bulletin* 1412-1416.

Wright H., 'The International Opium Commission' Part 1 (1909) 3 AJIL 648-673; Part 2 (1909) 3 AJIL 827-868; 'Treaties and Documents Concerning Opium' (1909) 3 AJIL Supplement 253.

Wright H., 'The International Opium Convention' Part 1 (1912) 6 AJIL 865-889; Part 2 (1913) 7 AJIL 109-139.

Wright Q., 'The Opium Question' (1924) 18 AJIL 281-295.

Wright Q., 'The American Withdrawal From the Opium Conference' (1925) 19 AJIL 348-355.

Wright Q., 'The Opium Conference' (1925) 19 AJIL 559-569.

Wright Q., 'The Narcotics Convention of 1931' (1934) 28 AJIL 475-486.

Yarnold B.M., 'Doctrinal basis for the international criminalization process' (1994) 8 *Temple International and Comparative Law Review* 85-115.

Yodmani C., 'The role of the Association of South East Asian Nations in fighting illicit drug traffic' (1983) 35 *Bulletin on Narcotics* 97-104.

Zagaris B., 'Developments in international judicial assistance and related matters' (1990) 18 *Denver Journal of International Law and Policy* 339-386.

Zagaris B. and Kingma E., 'Asset forfeiture international and foreign law: an emerging regime' (1991) 5 *Emory International Law Review* 445-513.

Zagaris B. and MacDonald S.B., 'Money laundering, financial fraud and technology: the perils of an instantaneous economy' (1992) 26 *George Washington Journal of International Law and Economics* 61-107.

Zagaris B. and Castilla S.M., 'Constructing an international financial enforcement subregime: the implementation of anti-money laundering policy' (1993) 19 *Brooklyn Journal of International Law* 871-965.

Zagaris B., 'The emergence of an international anti-money laundering regime: implications for counselling businesses' in D. Atkins (ed.), *The Alleged Transnational Criminal* (Nijhoff, The Hague, 1995), pp. 127-217.

GENERAL INDEX

INDEX OF CONVENTION PROVISIONS